S0-AKG-450

Contents

The Plain Language Guide to the World Summit on Sustainable Development

Janet R Strachan
Georgina Ayre
Jan McHarry
and
Rosalie Callway

COMMONWEALTH
SECRETARIAT

London • Sterling, VA

First published by Earthscan in the UK and USA in 2005

ISBN: 1-85383-928-0 paperback

Typesetting by MapSet Ltd, Gateshead, UK
Printed and bound in the UK by Cromwell Press Ltd, Trowbridge
Cover design by Susanne Harris
Cover illustration: Mandala of the Elements © Lucy Hawkes 2004. The design is based
on the mandala – the Buddhist symbol of balance and integration. The animals in the
circles (from the right, clockwise) are influenced by Native American Indian art, and
represent earth, water, fire, and air, and the sun at the centre is energy or space. The
design represents balancing and harmony between the elements – the raw materials of
life – necessary for a healthy and sustainable planet and its peoples.

For a full list of publications please contact:

Earthscan
8–12 Camden High Street
London, NW1 0JH, UK
Tel: +44 (0)20 7387 8558
Fax: +44 (0)20 7387 8998
Email: earthinfo@earthscan.co.uk
Web: **www.earthscan.co.uk**

22883 Quicksilver Drive, Sterling, VA 20166-2012, USA

Earthscan is an imprint of James and James (Science Publishers) Ltd and publishes in
association with the International Institute for Environment and Development

A catalogue record for this book is available from the British Library

Library of Congress Cataloging-in-Publication Data
The plain language guide to the world summit on sustainable development /
Jan McHarry ... [et al].
        p. cm.
   Includes bibliographical references and index.
   ISBN 1-85383-928-0 (pbk.)
   1. Sustainable development. 2. World Summit on Sustainable Development (2002 :
Johannesburg, South Africa) I. McHarry, Jan.
   HC79.E5W6723 2005
   338.9'27–dc22

                                                                                2004019979

Printed on elemental chlorine-free paper

Part II: Implementing the Johannesburg Plan of Implementation

Annexes
(Source texts)

Foreword by the Commonwealth Secretary-General

The Commonwealth is a unique association, whose strength lies in the diversity of its membership and its ability to network and exchange best practices based on similar political, legal, administrative and education systems, and a shared language. The countries that make up its membership account for almost one third of the world's population and encompass many faiths, races, languages and cultures. Commonwealth countries are spread over every continent. They range from some of the largest in the world to small and micro-states; from the poorest to some of the wealthiest; and from natural resource-based economies to highly industrialized and knowledge-based ones. The Commonwealth's principles and the equal participation and voice of its member states have much to offer the international community as it works towards implementing the World Summit on Sustainable Development's (WSSD's) outcomes.

We all want the WSSD to be a landmark in the way we implement sustainable development policies, not a footnote in the history of false hopes that the last decades have seen. Its success will be measured by the real change it generates in the lives of people throughout the world. For this to happen, sustainable development must become a day-to-day reality for everyone – one of clean air and water; affordable shelter; access to health services; thriving ecosystems; peace and stability; the opportunity to develop fully as individuals and communities; equitable and democratic participation; the rule of law; and, most of all, freedom from the terrible shadow of disease, famine and poverty.

The poorest people in the world may know very little about the outcomes of the WSSD. What they know is that their lives will only be improved by decisive action. This is why all stakeholders – governments, civil society and the business sector – have a responsibility to live up to the commitments made at the summit.

One of the great assets of the Commonwealth in the pursuit of sustainable development is this diversity, and the equal participation, of its member states within the framework of shared fundamental principles. The Commonwealth is also a network of local governments, businesses, and professional and civil society organizations that will be an asset in implementing the outcomes from the WSSD. A deep commitment is needed to long-term partnerships, based on equity and collaboration that shows a spirit of generosity in their approach.

The Commonwealth has played an active role in three key international negotiations that have set the development agenda for the next decade by addressing critical concerns on trade, finance and sustainable development: the World Trade Organization (WTO) Doha Ministerial Meeting (December 2001); the Financing for Development Summit in Monterrey (March 2002); and the World Summit on Sustainable Development (September 2002). Together with the Millennium Development Goals (MDGs) – which have mobilized governments, international institutions and civil society to reduce poverty with renewed vigour and commitment – these processes must be brought more closely together to ensure that practical steps are taken, in a true spirit of international collaboration, to create prosperity and equity for all, and to reverse the continuing loss of environmental resources and quality that underpin the social, cultural, spiritual and economic foundations of our societies.

In February 2003, Commonwealth environment ministers considered the key challenges that they, as policy-makers, face in implementing the Johannesburg agreements. They sought greater dialogue on, and engagement with, partnerships for sustainable development that were announced in conjunction with the WSSD. In particular, they saw the need for ongoing efforts to promote awareness and understanding of the outcomes from WSSD amongst groups in society, business and government, in order to promote their full engagement in such partnerships. Commonwealth Heads of Government, at their meeting in Abuja in December 2003, welcomed the outcomes of the WSSD and pledged to work towards the full and effective implementation of Agenda 21 and the Johannesburg Plan of Implementation (JPOI).

This guide is a Commonwealth contribution towards these objectives. I am particularly pleased that the Commonwealth has developed it in close collaboration with Stakeholder Forum, and hope that the guide will be widely used in the Commonwealth and beyond to promote understanding and engagement in the WSSD process at all levels.

Don McKinnon
October 2004

Preface

The Plain Language Guide was inspired by a publication, in 1993, by the Centre for Our Common Future called *The Earth Summit's Agenda for Change*. Here, we have reprinted the original Preface by Warren (Chip) Lindner, which expressed the vision that sprang from Rio and was embedded in the Johannesburg summit. Chip was the then director of the Centre for Our Common Future and had been the secretary to the Brundtland Commission. He went on to be the political adviser to the chair of the 1998 World AIDS Conference and successfully campaigned for the conference to have its next conference, its first in a developing country, in South Africa. Chip died of an AIDS-related illness in November 2000. He felt that we had all, particularly developed countries, failed to live up to our commitments made at Rio. It was his hope that the legacy of Johannesburg would be different.

Felix Dodds
Executive Director
Stakeholder Forum for Our Common Future
October 2004

The Lindner Preface

The Earth Summit was an unprecedented event. It brought together more heads of government than any meeting in history. It effectively focused the world's attention on the most critical issues we face as a global community. And it adopted a global plan of action, Agenda 21, to address those issues. For all of these achievements history will, no doubt, accord it an honoured place.

In retrospect, however, history may, and I believe should, recognize that its most significant contribution was the process that it adopted to achieve its objectives. By attempting, at times more successfully than at others, to bring all sectors of society into its deliberative and decision-making functions, it became the first international experiment in democratizing intergovernmental decision-making.

Given the nature of the problems that confront us as a community of nations and peoples, we are now more than ever bound together by a common destiny. And solutions to those problems will have to be found both nationally and internationally. That means that international institutions and national governments must become increasingly more accountable and responsive to the views and expectations of the world's people as a whole. Indeed, it means that as we approach the next century we must move even further in the direction of a global democracy.

In preparing for the Earth Summit, the first tentative steps in this direction were taken. Never before have so many representatives of peoples' organizations from so many countries directly participated in the formulation of national and international policies. Never before have so many senior representatives of governments met in open debate with citizens from countries other than their own, as they did in the ECO 1992 public forums held throughout the world in preparation for the summit. Never before have so many representatives of civil society gathered together to address their own responsibilities in respect of environment and development issues as they did at the 1992 Global Forum in Rio.

These epoch-making first attempts at global democracy must be repeated, and they must be strengthened.

But to play a meaningful role in governance, people in all societies need the information necessary to prepare them for responsible participation. By making Agenda 21 and other Rio agreements accessible to people in an easy and understandable format, this book will help to provide some of that information.

In publishing *The Earth Summit's Agenda for Change*, we would like it to be a testament, and a tribute, to the thousands of individuals throughout the world – women, youth, journalists, citizen activists, teachers, business people, religious leaders, local authorities, trade unionists, representatives of indigenous people, scientists and researchers – who participated in framing the thinking of governments at the Earth Summit and contributed to the evolution of Agenda 21. The global momentum to achieve sustainable development and to implement the principles of Agenda 21 will only succeed with their continued participation in decisions that affect their lives, both nationally and internationally.

Establishing the precedent of broad public participation was the real hallmark of the Earth Summit. The Centre for Our Common Future is pleased to have played a part in helping to make that happen and remains committed to working with all groups and sectors of society in building the 'global partnership' called for in Rio.

W H Lindner
Executive Director
Centre for our Common Future
1993

Acknowledgements

We would like to give special thanks to the following individuals for peer reviewing specific chapters of the book: Dorothy Gordon; Jeffery Barber; Ruth Mubiru; Nora Ourbah; Berbalk Dagamara; Joanna Phillips; Harold Goodwin; Janet Stephenson; Claudia Strauss; Russell Howorth; Richard Ballhorn; Michael Massey; Thais Corral; Lars Goran Engfeldt; Pieter van der Gaag; Fanny Calder; Alice Palmer; Maria Onestini; Irene Dankelman; Jack Jeffery; Peter Warren; Maria Luiza; Mirian Vilela; Sian Pullen; and Yasmin von Schirndingy. Their expertise, pithy comments, time and knowledge greatly enhanced the guide. Any shortcomings that remain lie entirely at the door of the authors of the guide.

Thanks also go to colleagues in the Economic Affairs Division of the Commonwealth Secretariat for their advice and support: Indrajit Coomaraswamy; Eliawony Kisanga; Linda Chu; Ivan Mbirimi; Bridget Chilala; Bishaka Mukerjee; and Andreas Antoniou. Thanks go to Felix Dodds for being – Felix Dodds, and to Stakeholder Forum for their vision and drive in encouraging the hosting of the World Summit. Our personal thanks go to Simon Webb, Charles and Anne, Chris Church and Faith Ayre for all their support.

List of Acronyms and Abbreviations

ACC	United Nations Administrative Committee on Coordination
ACP	Africa, Caribbean and Pacific group of countries
AIDS	Acquired Immunodeficiency Syndrome
ANPED	Northern Alliance for Sustainability
AOSIS	Alliance of Small Island States
APEC	Asian Pacific Economic Cooperation
BOD	biological oxygen demand
BPoA	Barbados Programme of Action on the Sustainable Development of Small Island Developing States
Caricad	Caribbean Centre for Development Administration
Caricom	Caribbean Community Secretariat
CBD	United Nations Convention on Biological Diversity
CBTF	Capacity-Building Task Force on Trade, Environment and Development
CCCCC	Caribbean Community Climate Change Centre
CCD	United Nations Convention to Combat Desertification
CDB	Caribbean Development Bank
CDERA	Caribbean Disaster Emergency Response Agency
CEHI	Caribbean Environmental Health Institute
CFC	chlorofluorocarbon
CIS	Commonwealth of Independent States
CITES	United Nations Convention on International Trade in Endangered Species of Wild Fauna and Flora
COP	Convention of the Parties
CPF	Collaborative Partnership on Forests
CROP	Council of Regional Organizations in the Pacific
CSD	United Nations Commission on Sustainable Development
DAC	Development Assistance Committee (OECD)
DDAGTF	Doha Development Agenda Global Trust Fund
DESA	United Nations Department of Economic and Social Affairs
DFID	UK Department for International Development
DMD	Doha Ministerial Declaration
DOALOS	United Nations Division for Ocean Affairs and the Law of the Sea
DTIE	Division of Technology, Industry and Economics (UNEP)
EC	European Commission
EC	European Community
ECCB	Eastern Caribbean Central Bank

ECE	United Nations Economic Commission for Europe
ECLAC	United Nations Economic Commission for Latin America and the Caribbean
ECOSOC	United Nations Economic and Social Council
EEA	European Environment Agency
EEZ	Exclusive Economic Zone
ESCAP	United Nations Economic and Social Commission for Asia and the Pacific
ESCWA	United Nations Economic and Social Commission for Western Asia
EST	environmentally sound technology
EU	European Union
FAO	United Nations Food and Agriculture Organization
FDI	foreign direct investment
FFA	South Pacific Forum Fisheries Agency
FSM	Fiji School of Medicine
G8	Group of 8 industrialized nations: Canada, France, Germany, Italy, Japan, Russia, the UK and the US
GATS	General Agreement on Trade in Services
GATT	General Agreement on Tariffs and Trade
GDP	gross domestic product
GEENET	Global Environmental Epidemiology Network
GEF	Global Environment Facility
GEO	Global Environment Outlook (UNEP)
GESAMP	Joint Group of Experts on the Scientific Aspects of Marine Environmental Protection (United Nations agencies)
GIS	Geographical Information Systems
GMO	genetically modified organism
GNESD	Global Network on Energy for Sustainable Development
GNI	gross national income
GNP	gross national product
GPA	Global Programme of Action for the Protection of the Marine Environment from Land-based Activities
GRI	Global Reporting Initiative
GTI	Global Taxonomy Initiative
HECA	Healthy Environments for Children Alliance
HIPC	Heavily Indebted Poor Countries
HIV	Human Immunodeficiency Virus
HLSOC	High-level Summit Organizing Committee for the WSIS
IAEA	International Atomic Energy Agency
IATF	United Nations Inter-agency Task Force on Disaster Reduction
ICAO	International Civil Aviation Organization
ICLEI	International Council for Local Environment Initiatives
ICPD	International Conference on Population and Development
ICRI	International Coral Reef Initiative
ICSPAC	International Coalition on Sustainable Consumption and Production
ICT	information and communication technology
IEA	International Energy Agency

IFAD	International Fund for Agricultural Development
IFAP	International Federation of Agricultural Producers
IFC	International Finance Corporation
IFCS	Intergovernmental Forum on Chemical Safety
IFF	Intergovernmental Forum on Forests
IFI	International Financial Institution
IIED	International Institute for Environment and Development
IIF	Institute of International Finance
ILO	International Labour Organization
IMO	International Maritime Organization
IOC	Indian Ocean Commission Secretariat
IOC	Intergovernmental Oceanographic Commission of UNESCO
IMF	International Monetary Fund
INFORSE	International Network for Sustainable Energy
IPCC	Intergovernmental Panel on Climate Change
IPEC	International Programme on the Elimination of Child Labour
IPF	Intergovernmental Panel on Forests
IRPTC	International Register of Potentially Toxic Chemicals
ISDR	International Strategy for Disaster Reduction
ISO	International Organization for Standardization
ITC	International Trade Centre
ITPGR	International Treaty on Plant Genetic Resources for Food and Agriculture
ITU	International Telecommunication Union
IUCN	World Conservation Union
JPOI	Johannesburg Plan of Implementation
LA21	Local Agenda 21
LDCs	least developed countries
LMO	living modified organism
MARPOL	International Convention for the Prevention of Pollution from Ships
MDG	Millennium Development Goal
MEA	Multilateral Environmental Agreement
mm	millimetres
MMSD	Mining, Minerals and Sustainable Development
NAAEC	North American Agreement on Environmental Cooperation
NCSD	National Councils for Sustainable Development
NEPAD	New Partnership for African Development
NGO	non-governmental organization
ODA	Official Development Assistance
ODP	ozone depleting potential
ODS	ozone-depleting substance
OECD	Organisation for Economic Co-operation and Development
OECS	Organization of Eastern Caribbean States
OHRLLS	United Nations Office of the High Representative for the Least Developed Countries, Landlocked Developing Countries and Small Island Developing States
PIDP	Pacific Islands Development Programme

PIFS	Pacific Islands Forum Secretariat
POP	persistent organic pollutant
PP10	Partnership for Principle 10
PRTR	Pollutant Release and Transfer Register
R&D	research and development
RONA	United Nations Environment Programme Regional Office for North America
ROWA	United Nations Environment Programme Regional Office for West Asia
SADC	Southern African Development Community
SARD	Sustainable Agriculture and Rural Development
SEI	Singapore Environment Institute
SIDS	Small Island Developing States
SISEI	Système de Circulation d'Information et de Suivi de l'Environnement sur Internet en Afrique
SME	small- and medium-sized enterprises
SOCA	Sub-committee on Oceans and Coastal Areas (ACC)
SOPAC	South Pacific Applied Geoscience Commission
SPAC	sustainable production and consumption
SPBEA	South Pacific Board for Educational Assessment
SPC	Secretariat for the Pacific Community
SPREP	South Pacific Regional Environment Programme
SPTO	South Pacific Tourism Organization
TB	tuberculosis
TICAD	Tokyo International Conference on African Development
TNC	transnational corporation
TRIPS	Trade-Related Aspects of Intellectual Property Rights
UK	United Kingdom
UN	United Nations
UNAIDS	Joint United Nations Programme on HIV/AIDS
UNCED	United Nations Conference on Environment and Development
UNCHR	United Nations Commission on Human Rights
UNCHS	United Nations Centre for Human Settlements (now UN-Habitat)
UNCLOS	United Nations Convention on the Law of the Sea
UNCTAD	United Nations Conference on Trade and Development
UNDP	United Nations Development Programme
UNDPI	United Nations Department of Public Information
UNECE	United Nations Economic Commission for Europe
UNECLAC	United Nations Economic Commission for Latin America and the Caribbean
UNEP	United Nations Environment Programme
UNEP-ROLAC	United Nations Environment Programme – Regional Office for Latin America and Caribbean
UNESCO	United Nations Educational, Scientific and Cultural Organization
UNFCCC	United Nations Framework Convention on Climate Change
UNFF	United Nations Forum on Forests
UNFPA	United Nations Population Fund
UNGA	United Nations General Assembly

UNGASS	United Nations General Assembly Special Session
UN-Habitat	United Nations Human Settlements Programme
UNHCHR	United Nations High Commissioner on Human Rights
UNHCR	United Nations High Commissioner for Refugees
UNICEF	United Nations Children's Fund
UNIFEM	United Nations Development Fund for Women
UNIDO	United Nations Industrial Development Organization
UNITAR	United Nations Institute for Training and Research
UNPD	United Nations Population Division
UNRISD	United Nations Research Institute for Social Development
UPU	Universal Postal Union
US	United States
USP	University of the South Pacific
UWI	University of the West Indies
WBCSD	World Business Council on Sustainable Development
WEHAB	water and sanitation, energy, health, agriculture and biological diversity
WFP	World Food Programme
WHO	World Health Organization
WIPO	World Intellectual Property Organization
WMO	World Meteorological Organization
WRI	World Resources Institute
WSIS	World Summit on the Information Society
WSSCC	Water Supply and Sanitation Collaborative Council
WSSD	World Summit on Sustainable Development
WTO	World Trade Organization
WTO	World Tourism Organization
WTTC	World Travel and Tourism Council
WWF	World Wide Fund for Nature

Background

 ## The World Summit on Sustainable Development (WSSD)

The World Summit on Sustainable Development (WSSD) took place in Johannesburg from 26 August to 4 September 2002. It involved over 21,000 participants, including representatives of 191 governments and 104 heads of state or government. The aim of the summit was to complete a ten-year review of implementation of the 1992 United Nations Conference on Environment and Development (UNCED) – or the Rio Earth Summit – and to 'reinvigorate' global commitment to sustainable development. The three overarching objectives of the summit were 'eradicating poverty', 'protecting the natural resource base of economic and social development' and 'changing unsustainable patterns of production and consumption'.

In the run-up to the summit, there were calls for the negotiations to focus on just a few multidisciplinary areas. This proved difficult to achieve in practice; but, informally, some focus was achieved through the 'WEHAB agenda', proposed by the UN Secretary-General. This stands for 'water and sanitation, energy, health, agriculture and biodiversity' and formed the basis for thematic sessions in Johannesburg.

One negotiated outcome of the summit was a 54-page plan of implementation that builds on the achievements in sustainable development made since 1992. WSSD also adopted a political statement, the Johannesburg Declaration on Sustainable Development, in which world leaders committed themselves 'to expedite the achievement of the time-bound, socio-economic and environmental targets' contained in the Johannesburg Plan of Implementation (JPOI). The summit also provided a unique forum where new multi-stakeholder partnerships or initiatives could be announced. These partnerships aimed to strengthen the implementation of Agenda 21 (the 40-chapter blueprint for action that was adopted at UNCED).

By the final preparatory session in Bali (in May 2002), 70 to 80 per cent of the draft JPOI had been agreed. Negotiators convened two days in advance of the summit to start work on the outstanding issues. These included application of the Rio principles (such as the 'precautionary approach' and the 'common but differentiated responsibility' of states), as well as deliberations over good governance and the establishment of a World Solidarity Fund to address poverty. Other difficult issues included targets on sanitation, energy and climate change, along with proposals on establishing ten-year programmes on sustainable consumption and production patterns, health and human rights, globalization and natural resource issues, including targets on reversing trends in the loss of natural resources and biodiversity, the negotiation of a mechanism on benefit-sharing from the use of biological resources, and issues related to the sustainable use and conservation of fish and ocean resources. Lying at the heart of some of the toughest talks were the financial and technical resources needed to support sustainable development actions and concerns related to trade, especially issues addressed in the World Trade

Organization's (WTO's) Doha 'Development Round' work programme and improved market access for developing countries' agricultural products.

The Johannesburg Declaration and the JPOI represent an important international commitment to continued and increased efforts at bringing about sustainable development. The summit also provided an impetus for the launch of new multi-stakeholder partnerships to address sustainable development problems. Together with the UN Millennium Summit and the Monterrey Summit on Finance for Development, WSSD sets the framework for sustainable development over the first decades of the 21st century.

The Johannesburg Plan of Implementation (JPOI)

The Johannesburg Plan of Implementation is grounded in the outcomes of the 1992 UNCED. It includes well over 20 new targets and draws together significant outcomes from recent international meetings into a sustainable development framework. These include the Millennium Development Goals (MDGs); the Monterrey Consensus on Financing for Development; the WTO Doha Agenda; the Dakar Framework for Action on Education for All; the World Summit on Social Development; the Third United Nations Conference on the Least Developed Countries; and numerous multilateral environmental agreements and regional sustainable development initiatives and strategies.

The Rio Summit focused on environment and development and helped to elaborate both the concept of, and practical approaches to, sustainable development through the integration of the three components of sustainable development (economic development; social development and environmental protection). WSSD recognized that much more had to be done to bring about this integration, strengthening the focus on poverty, social concerns and implementation of Agenda 21.

The JPOI is arranged in 11 chapters, which address the following:

I *Introduction*. Principles for sustainable development, including Rio principles; implementation of Agenda 21 and internationally agreed development goals; good governance within each country and at the international level; peace, security, stability and respect for human rights and fundamental freedoms, including the right to development; the importance of ethics.

II *Poverty eradication*. National programmes and strategies; women's participation in decision-making; indigenous people and their communities; agriculture; rural infrastructure; desertification; sanitation; energy and industrial development for the poor; slum dwellers; child labour.

III *Changing unsustainable patterns of consumption and production*. Policies, programmes, strategies, planning and decision-making; measures and tools to promote sustainable patterns of consumption and production; investment in cleaner production; corporate environmental and social accountability; energy; transport; waste; management of chemicals and hazardous waste; heavy metals.

IV *Protecting and managing the natural resource base of economic and social development*. Water and sanitation; oceans and marine resources; vulnerability; disaster management; climate change; agriculture; desertification; biodiversity; mountains; tourism; forests; mining.

V *Sustainable development in a globalizing world*. Characteristics; opportunities and challenges of globalization.

VI *Health and sustainable development.* HIV/AIDS, tuberculosis (TB), malaria and other epidemics; health services; environmental health.

VII *Sustainable development in small island developing states.* Barbados Programme of Action on the Sustainable Development of Small Island Developing States (BPoA); ocean and coastal resources; freshwater; pollution and waste; tourism; extreme weather events; vulnerability indices; climate change; energy; health; poverty eradication.

VIII *Sustainable development for Africa.* New Partnership for African Development (NEPAD); desertification; health; natural disasters and conflict; water resources; agriculture; management of chemicals; digital divide; tourism; UN-Habitat Agenda.

IX *Other regional initiatives.* Concerns and priorities in the following UN regions: Latin America and the Caribbean; Asia and the Pacific; West Asia; Economic Commission for Europe.

X *Means of implementation.* Trade; finance; debt; technology transfer; role of the scientific community; education; capacity-building; information for decision-making.

XI *Institutional framework for sustainable development.* Role of the United Nations General Assembly (UNGA), the United Nations Economic and Social Council (ECOSOC), the United Nations Commission on Sustainable Development (CSD) and international institutions; strengthening the institutional framework at regional, national and local levels; participation of major groups.

The WSSD's commitments encompassed international targets in the areas of chemicals management, water and sanitation, including:

- a deadline of 2020 to achieve the use and production of chemicals in ways that lead to the minimization of significant adverse effects on human health and the environment;
- a target of 2015 for halving the proportion of people who do not have access to basic sanitation;
- fisheries stocks to be maintained or restored on an urgent basis and, where possible, by 2015; and
- achievement of a significant reduction in the current rate of loss of biological diversity by 2010.

Additionally, governments agreed to negotiate an international instrument, under the auspices of the Convention on Biological Diversity (CBD), on sharing the benefits arising from the use of biological resources. They also established a World Solidarity Fund to help eradicate poverty. Negotiations on trade closely reflected language agreed by trade ministers at the Doha ministerial meeting in 2002; but the agreement promotes 'mutual supportiveness' between the multilateral trading system and multilateral environmental agreements, while recognizing the importance of maintaining the integrity of both sets of instruments. No concrete, time-bound targets could be agreed on renewable energy, though the section on small island developing states (SIDS) has a commitment to the availability of adequate, affordable and environmentally sound energy services by strengthening ongoing, and supporting new, efforts on energy supply and services by 2004. Delegates agreed to take action to phase out energy subsidies that inhibit sustainable development. The way in which partnerships should interact with, or link to, the WSSD process and its follow-up was also debated at length. These partnership initiatives will be free-standing, but the CSD was mandated to act 'as a focal point for the discussion of partnerships that promote sustainable development'.

Origins of the World Summit on Sustainable Development

The first UN environment conference (the United Nations Conference on the Human Environment) took place in Stockholm in June 1972. It was a pioneering event that agreed a declaration and action plan on the human environment and established the United Nations Environment Programme (UNEP), which continues to take forward the environmental agenda set in 1972.

In 1987, the Brundtland Report (*Our Common Future*) was published by Gro Harlem Brundtland, the then prime minister of Norway. It gave the most definitive and well-used explanation of sustainable development as 'development that meets the needs of the present without compromising the ability of future generations to meet their own needs'.[1]

The report was unique in addressing the need for economic development without depleting natural resources or harming the environment, and was central in framing discussions at the United Nations Conference on Environment and Development (UNCED), or the Earth Summit. Convened in June 1992 in Rio de Janeiro, UNCED was attended by over 100 heads of state and government (more than had ever attended an international conference before) and was unique in its size and participation. Though UNCED was seen by some at the time as somewhat disappointing, its outcomes were, nevertheless, significant. They consisted of a political declaration of principles on environment and development (the Rio Declaration), a 40-chapter 'blueprint' for implementing sustainable development (Agenda 21 – so called as it forms an agenda for the 21st century), a declaration of Forest Principles, and two new multilateral environmental conventions on climate change (the United Nations Framework Convention on Climate Change, or UNFCCC) and on biodiversity (the United Nations Convention on Biological Diversity, or CBD). The summit led to new approaches to including different groups of society in policy debate and action and it established a new mechanism within the United Nations (the CSD) to monitor and promote implementation of the outcomes from Rio.

Agenda 21

Agenda 21 is a comprehensive 40-chapter action plan for sustainable development. It addresses both social and economic dimensions of sustainable development, as well as the conservation and management of specific natural resources and ecosystems. Agenda 21 promotes a strongly bottom-up, participatory approach involving a wide range of different civil society groups. Local government has played a particularly constructive role in developing and implementing Agenda 21 at the community level through the Local Agenda 21 process (see 'Major groups' below).

Rio Declaration

The *Rio Declaration on Environment and Development* is a statement of 27 principles to guide action on environment and development. Similar in style to the Stockholm principles of 1972, it was the subject of long and intense negotiations. The Rio Declaration includes the concepts of sustainable development, the precautionary approach and the 'polluter pays' principle and as such has brought these formally to the international arena. It also recognizes that in 'view of the different contributions to global environmental degradation, states have common but differentiated responsibilities'. Here, developed countries acknowledge the responsibility they bear in the international pursuit of sustainable development and the technologies and financial resources they command.

Climate change and biodiversity conventions

Two new conventions were opened for signature at Rio and rapidly came into force. These were the *United Nations Framework Convention on Climate Change* (UNFCCC) and the *Convention on Biological Diversity* (CBD). Both of these conventions have been further elaborated – through the Kyoto Protocol under the UNFCCC and the Cartagena Protocol on Biosafety under the CBD. At the WSSD, the debate on climate concerns remained as vigorous as ever with states that had ratified the Kyoto Protocol urging states that had not yet done so to ratify the protocol in a timely manner. On biodiversity, key issues included the protection of traditional knowledge and agreement to negotiate an international instrument on the fair and equitable sharing of benefits arising out of the utilization of genetic resources.

Forests, desertification and small island developing states

Negotiations at UNCED on forest issues were particularly difficult and could only be concluded through agreement on a non-binding set of *Forest Principles*. Multilateral discussions on forest issues continued after Rio through an Intergovernmental Panel on Forests and subsequently through an Intergovernmental Forum on Forests, and then the United Nations Forum on Forests and Collaborative Partnership on Forests. These processes have deepened the analysis on forest issues; but it has not been possible to secure more concrete or binding international action.

Rio also initiated negotiations on *desertification*, leading to the 1994 United Nations Convention to Combat Desertification (CCD). The CCD has experienced a lack of financing, which was reflected in the discussions at the WSSD on the inclusion of desertification as a focal area for funding by the Global Environment Facility (GEF).

Agenda 21 (Chapter 17) also initiated the 1994 UN Global Conference on the Sustainable Development of Small Island Developing States (SIDS) which adopted the Barbados Programme of Action on the Sustainable Development of *Small Island Developing States* (BPoA), a comprehensive agenda for sustainable development in small island states. These concerns are reflected in Chapter VIII of the Johannesburg Plan of Implementation, which agrees to a review and international meeting, which will take place in Mauritius in January 2005.

Finance

The most difficult and protracted issue for discussion at Rio was the question of *finance* and it remained centre stage at the WSSD, too. Consistently, developing countries have sought new and additional funding for sustainable development actions. However, there is a widespread perception that the continued lack of such funding has been a major constraint in implementing the Rio agreements. Key mechanisms for financing sustainable development include the Global Environment Facility (GEF), established in 1990 to address global environmental problems (ozone depletion, climate change, biodiversity loss and international water pollution). The fund is administered by the World Bank, UNEP and the United Nations Development Programme (UNDP), and finances the incremental costs of those domestic actions which produce global environmental benefits. This stipulation places constraints on the availability of GEF funds to finance actions under Agenda 21. The other important development since Rio was the International Conference on Financing for Development, held in March 2002 at Monterrey in Mexico. Through this, governments committed themselves to a range of actions that would promote a supportive environment for investment, addressing debt concerns and increasing the flow of funding to better support development.

United Nations Commission on Sustainable Development (CSD)

Rio resulted in the creation of a new body in the United Nations, the *Commission on Sustainable Development*, to follow up the outcomes of the Earth Summit. Housed within the UN's Department of Economic and Social Affairs (DESA), CSD's principle role has been to facilitate broad-based policy dialogues on sustainable development, to support the negotiation of texts related to UNCED follow-up and to pioneer stakeholder participation in UN decision-making. While many saw the multidisciplinary dialogues as useful, it was also felt that the CSD was not as effective as it could be. Concerns included the time-consuming nature of the annual negotiations, which it was felt provided little added value to other processes. The low status of the commission within the UN system was another concern, making it difficult for the body to be strategic in its promotion of sustainable development. Reform of the CSD became a focus for negotiation in the run-up to WSSD and after the summit when the CSD considered ways in which to promote the review and implementation of the outcomes (Johannesburg Plan of Implementation, Chapter XI).

Major groups

The 1992 Rio Earth Summit experienced a new level of engagement by civil society in United Nations' negotiations, swept along by a wave of public activism on environment and development issues. Non-governmental organisations (NGOs) had organized a parallel event in Stockholm in 1972, the first of its kind, and their engagement throughout the run-up to Rio – particularly during the work of the Brundtland Commission, which examined issues related to environment and development and the emerging concept of sustainable development – brought a deeper understanding of the need for public engagement in formulating and implementing sustainable development policies and actions. As a result, Agenda 21 calls for new forms of participation at all levels in making sustainable development happen. It devotes individual chapters to the roles and responsibilities of nine 'major groups' of civil society: women; children and youth; indigenous people; NGOs; local authorities; workers and trade unions; business and industry; scientific and technological communities; and farmers. Subsequently, the CSD has engaged the nine major groups through multi-stakeholder dialogues and the key role of major groups in partnerships for sustainable development is well recognized. The 11th session of the CSD (April 2003) highlighted scientists and educators amongst the major groups who should be involved in follow-up work to the WSSD undertaken by the CSD.

 ## Purpose of this book

The aim of this book is to provide a quick way in to the Johannesburg Plan of Implementation to help promote an understanding of the agreement and practical action on the commitments. Throughout the plan there is a call for 'action at all levels' based on the active participation of all groups in society working in fields as diverse as health care; social welfare; education and training; economic planning; natural resources management; environmental protection; trade; investment; and business development. We hope the guide will be particularly useful to those who were not centrally involved in the negotiations, but wish to take forward action on sustainable development in their own areas and in partnership with other groups. This guide does not provide a political analysis of the negotiations or the JPOI: such material is available elsewhere. Rather, it is a resource book for those working in community groups, business, local government, central government departments, regional institutions and the international community.

We recognize that the JPOI is a finely balanced text whose every word has been considered and intensely negotiated. We have tried to be neutral in our summaries of the agreement; but any attempt to simplify the JPOI for the reader runs the risk of upsetting the fine balance of the original. Despite the challenges, we feel this risk is worth taking to bring the JPOI to as wide an audience possible. *However, we urge all readers to refer to the original JPOI text (provided as Annex A in this guide) to consider the precise meaning or intention of the JPOI in any given area.* To help, we have included clear references to the original JPOI paragraph numbers.

Resources in this book

Context

Background and context to the decisions taken at the WSSD.

At a glance

Some statistics related to the issues covered in the JPOI chapter.

Key words

A checklist of the key issues addressed in the JPOI chapter.

Chapter in summary

Each chapter of the JPOI is presented in the form of a summary. Bold type has been used by the authors to highlight key words and guide the eye of the reader: these are not intended to give interpretation or emphasis to the text. Actions are almost always signalled in the JPOI as being intended 'at all levels', from local to international.

As far as possible, we have tried to keep the spirit of the original; but a negotiated text can be, by its very nature, ambiguous. *We strongly urge readers to refer to the original text when considering the precise meaning of the JPOI* (see Annex A in this guide). References to each and every paragraph of the JPOI are included within the narrative summaries for each chapter in square brackets – for example, [*7m*]. A reference to II.8a, indicates paragraph 8a in Chapter II.

Targets and commitments

New and pre-existing targets included in the chapter, drawn from a list prepared by the United Nations CSD.

Themes of the chapter across the JPOI

A narrative review of how key themes within the chapter are dealt with elsewhere in the JPOI. Further cross-referencing is available through the Index.

Key United Nations bodies and Bretton Woods institutions

Key United Nations bodies and Bretton Woods institutions involved in work related to the issues addressed in the chapter and likely to play a role in implementing WSSD outcomes. In Agenda 21, certain UN bodies were identified as the lead agency or 'task manager' for the 40 issues outlined in the agreement. For example, the UN Department of Economic and Social Affairs (DESA) Division for Sustainable Development is the task manager for sustainable consumption and production issues.

Conferences, agreements and processes

International processes and agreements that are related to the themes of the JPOI chapter or directly referred within the text. This is not an exhaustive listing, but provides a rough time-line of key source agreements and events.

Indicators for measuring progress in implementation

Examples of established and accepted indicators, which could be used to assess whether JPOI goals are being met.

Partnership examples

An illustration of the kinds of partnerships that were accepted and announced in connection with the WSSD. All examples given are detailed on the CSD's partnership website and further information is available from the contact points provided.

Other resources

Each chapter has some specific reference material giving short explanations of the processes, institutions, subjects or multilateral agreements that are referred to in the JPOI.

 Note

1   Brundtland, G (ed) (1987) *Our Common Future: World Commission on Environment and Development*, Oxford University Press, Oxford

Part I

The Johannesburg Plan of Implementation

Introduction

 ## Chapter I in summary

The 1992 United Nations Conference on Environment and Development (*UNCED*) in Rio de Janeiro provided the fundamental principles and programme of action for achieving sustainable development. The Johannesburg Plan of Implementation (JPOI) strongly reaffirms:

- The **Rio principles**;
- Full implementation of **Agenda** 21;
- The 1997 Programme for the Further Implementation of Agenda 21; and
- Achievement of **internationally agreed development goals** (for example, the United Nations Millennium Declaration and outcomes of major UN conferences/agreements since 1992) *[1]*.

The JPOI builds on achievements since UNCED and helps to realize the remaining goals. To do this, governments commit themselves to strengthening **international cooperation** and undertaking **concrete actions and measures at all levels**:

- Taking into account the Rio principles, including principle 7 on the **common but differentiated responsibilities** of states in the pursuit of sustainable development; and
- Promoting the **integration of the three pillars** of sustainable development – economic development, social development and environmental protection – as interdependent and mutually reinforcing pillars *[2]*.

AT A GLANCE

Three cross-cutting objectives of, and essential requirements for, sustainable development are:

1. poverty eradication;
2. changing unsustainable patterns of production and consumption; and
3. protecting and managing the natural resource base of economic and social development.

KEY WORDS

- **integrating the three pillars of sustainable development**
- **action at all levels**
- **common but differentiated responsibilities**
- **poverty eradication**
- **consumption and production**
- **natural resource base**
- **implementation to benefit all**
- **partnerships**
- **good governance**
- **peace, security and stability**
- **human rights and fundamental freedoms**
- **right to development**
- **cultural diversity**
- **ethics**

Poverty eradication, changing unsustainable patterns of production and consumption, and protecting and managing the natural resource base of economic and social development are overarching objectives of, and essential requirements for, sustainable development *[2]*. The outcomes of the World Summit on Sustainable Development (WSSD) should be **implemented to the benefit of all**, and implementation should involve all relevant actors through **partnerships** *[3]*.

Good governance, within each country and at the international level, is essential for sustainable development. At the national level, the following elements are the basis for sustainable development:

- Sound environmental, social and economic policies;
- Democratic institutions that are responsive to the needs of the people;
- The rule of law;
- Anti-corruption measures;
- Gender equality; and
- An enabling environment for investment.

As a result of **globalization**, external factors have become critical in determining the success or failure of developing countries in their national efforts. The gap between developed and developing countries shows the continued need for a **dynamic and enabling international economic environment**, particularly on finance, technology transfer, debt and trade. The importance of the following for sustainable development is recognized:

- Full and effective participation of developing countries in global decision-making *[4]*;
- **Peace, security, stability and respect for human rights and fundamental freedoms**, including the **right to development**;
- Respect for **cultural diversity** *[5]*; and
- **Ethics** *[6]*.

 # Rio principles elsewhere in the JPOI

The Rio principles, stated in the 1992 Rio Declaration on Environment and Development, are woven in throughout the JPOI. The principles will be built on in strengthening the institutional framework for sustainable development and taken into account in promoting sustainable consumption and production patterns; cooperation to reduce air pollution; corporate responsibility and accountability; and increased efforts to implement Agenda 21 and internationally agreed development goals. In all but one of these specific areas (corporate responsibility), the principle of common but differentiated responsibilities (principle 7) is referenced, and is quoted in full in Chapter X on the need for increased efforts at implementation. The precautionary approach (principle 15) is evoked with respect to the use and production of chemicals and in science-based decision-making. In its focus on policies and measures to promote sustainable patterns of consumption and production, the application of principle 16 is requested, which states that the polluter should, in principle, bear the cost of pollution caused by their activities. This principle should also be taken into account in promoting the internalization of environmental costs and the use of economic instruments. Industry is encouraged to improve social and environmental performance, bearing in mind principle 11, which addresses the use of environmental legislation and standards, while further efforts should be made to ensure access at the national level to environmental information and public participation in decision-making, in further implementation of principle 10. A number of the Rio principles are addressed in a more general way – for example, principles 5 (poverty eradication) and 8 (production and consumption patterns) are the subject of specific chapters; principle 9 (cooperation to strengthen capacity-building) is addressed all the way through the agreement; or principle 13 (liability and compensation), which has only one related reference addressing the marine transport of radioactive material.

TARGETS AND COMMITMENTS

- Full implementation of Agenda 21 and Millennium Development Goals (MDGs).
- Integration of the three pillars of sustainable development.
- Full involvement of developing countries in decision-making processes.
- Action on poverty, consumption and production patterns, the natural resource base, good governance, peace, security, respect for human rights and fundamental freedoms, the right to development, and cultural diversity.

 # Resources

Agenda 21

www.un.org/esa/sustdev/documents/UNCED_Docs.htm
This 40-chapter action plan, agreed at the United Nations Conference on Environment and Development (UNCED), covers natural resources; the role of different groups; social and economic development; and institutional issues.

Millennium Declaration (2000)

www.un.org/millennium
Adopted by the United Nations General Assembly (UNGA) in September 2000, the

Millennium Declaration contains commitments on human rights, good governance and democracy, as well as measurable goals and targets for combating poverty, hunger, disease, illiteracy, environmental degradation and discrimination against women. It is the basis of the Millennium Development Goals.

Millennium Development Goals (MDGs)

www.un.org/millenniumgoals/index.shtml (UN)
www.undp.org/mdg (UNDP)
www.developmentgoals.org (World Bank)
The United Nations Secretary-General's 'Road Map' (September 2001) set out concrete targets for goals and commitments in the Millennium Declaration. These were further developed into the Millennium Development Goals (MDGs).

Monterrey Consensus

www.un.org/esa/ffd
The Monterrey Consensus was agreed at the International Conference on Financing for Development (March 2002). Its commitments are to increase financial resources for development (domestic and international); promote trade; strengthen cooperation for development; address debt; and improve the international monetary, financial and trading systems.

Programme for the Further Implementation of Agenda 21

www.un.org/esa/earthsummit (on Rio+5)
This programme was adopted by United Nations General Assembly (UNGA) in 1997 following a review of progress on UNCED implementation.

Rio Declaration on Environment and Development

www.un.org/esa/sustdev/documents/UNCED_Docs.htm
The Rio Declaration is a statement of 27 principles on environment and development, adopted at UNCED. They include the following referred to in the background chapter: principle 7 '*In view of the different contributions to global environmental degradation, States have common but differentiated responsibilities*'; principle 15 '*to protect the environment, the precautionary approach shall be widely applied by States according to their capabilities. Where there are threats of serious or irreversible damage, lack of full scientific certainty shall not be used as a reason for postponing cost-effective measures to prevent environmental degradation*'; and principle 16 '*National authorities should endeavour to promote the internalization of environmental costs and the use of economic instruments, taking into account the approach that the polluter should, in principle, bear the cost of pollution*'.

United Nations Commission on Sustainable Development (CSD)

www.un.org/esa/sustdev/csd/about_csd.htm
The CSD reviews UNCED and World Summit on Sustainable Development (WSSD)

implementation. It develops policy recommendations, supports multi-stakeholder dialogues and promotes partnerships.

United Nations Conference on Environment and Development (UNCED)

www.un.org/esa/sustdev/documents/UNCED_Docs.htm
This is the Earth Summit, held in Rio de Janeiro in 1992. Outcomes were the Rio Declaration; Agenda 21; the Forest Principles; the United Nations Framework Convention on Climate Change (UNFCCC) and the Convention on Biological Diversity (CBD), the United Nations CSD.

Key United Nations bodies and Bretton Woods institutions

- United Nations Commission on Sustainable Development (CSD)
- United Nations Department of Economic and Social Affairs (DESA)
- United Nations Development Programme (UNDP)
- United Nations Economic and Social Council (ECOSOC)
- United Nations Environment Programme (UNEP)
- United Nations General Assembly (UNGA)
- United Nations Regional Commissions
- World Bank

CONFERENCES, AGREEMENTS AND PROCESSES

- United Nations Conference on Environment and Development (UNCED), Rio Declaration on Environment and Development, Agenda 21 (1992)
- Programme for the Further Implementation of Agenda 21 (1997)
- Millennium Declaration and Millennium Development Goals (MDGs) (2000)
- United Nations Conference on Financing for Development, Monterrey, Mexico (2002)

2 Poverty Eradication

 ## Context

Poverty eradication was one of three overarching objectives of the World Summit on Sustainable Development (WSSD). Poverty is not simply an issue of income: when asked, the poor highlight a range of other important issues, including health, safety, education, food and basic services. People's experience of poverty can vary widely, but they all speak about their vulnerability and exclusion by the state and society (DFID, 2002). The inter-linkages between poverty and the environment remain an issue of discussion and contention. The livelihoods and well-being of poorer people often depend upon sound environmental management. The poor also suffer disproportionately from the ill effects of environmental decline and poorly planned human activities. Better environmental management is essential to lasting poverty reduction (UNDP, 2002), along with measures promoting social and environmental justice.

KEY WORDS

- **Millennium Development Goals (MDGs)**
- **World Solidarity Fund**
- **gender mainstreaming**
- **indigenous people**
- **health**
- **land and sustainable agriculture**
- **food security**
- **water and sanitation**
- **energy**
- **industrial development**
- **slum dwellers**
- **child labour**

Access to clean water for both urban and rural poor was a priority at the WSSD. In November 2002, the United Nations Committee of Economic, Social and Cultural Rights declared water as a human right, placing an obligation on governments to progressively extend access to sufficient, affordable, accessible and safe water supplies and safe sanitation services to all citizens without discrimination. A right to water will not result in universal access instantly; but the adoption of the right is an encouraging sign that member governments of the UN are placing higher priority on these services (Water Aid, 2003).

Agenda 21 includes chapters on 'combating poverty' and 'promoting human settlement development'. The Johannesburg processes took a further step forward in heightening the profile of links between poverty eradication and sustainable development.

 ## Chapter II in summary

Eradicating poverty

Poverty eradication is the greatest challenge facing the world today and is essential for sustainable development. Each country has responsibility for its own sustainable development and poverty eradication, with national policies

AT A GLANCE

⚙ One in five people on the planet, two-thirds of them women, live in abject poverty (UNDP, 2000).

⚙ Of the world's 6 billion people, 2.8 billion live on less than US$2 a day, and 1.2 billion on less than US$1 a day (International Energy Agency, 2002; UNEP, 2002).

⚙ Water-related diseases such as diarrhoea and cholera kill an estimated 3 million people a year in developing countries, the majority children under the age of five (Water Aid website, 2003).

⚙ 1.2 billion people are without access to clean drinking water (UNEP, 2002).

⚙ 2.4 billion people lack access to adequate sanitation (UNEP, 2002).

⚙ 1.6 billion people – one quarter of the world's population – have no access to electricity (International Energy Agency, 2002).

⚙ 2.4 billion people rely on traditional biomass – wood, agricultural residues, dung – for cooking and heating (International Energy Agency, 2002).

'Improving sanitation and providing clean water are critical if the lives of the urban poor are to be improved. Access to such life saving basic needs is an important first step in the process of slum upgrading' (Anna Tibaijuka, under secretary-general of the UN and executive director of UN-Habitat at the launch of a Water and Sanitation Trust Fund, 7 October 2002).

and development strategies playing an important role. Action is needed at all levels to help developing countries meet **internationally agreed poverty-related goals** *[7]*, including to:

- Halve, by 2015, the proportion of people who have an **income** of less than US$1 a day, suffer from **hunger** and lack access to **safe drinking water** *[7a]*;
- Establish a **World Solidarity Fund** to eradicate poverty and promote social and human development *[7b]*;
- Develop **national programmes for sustainable development and local and community development** to empower poor people and their organizations *[7c]*;
- Promote **women**'s participation in decision-making at all levels; 'mainstream' gender perspectives; eliminate violence and discrimination; and improve women's health and economic status *[7d]*;
- Improve access by **indigenous peoples** and their communities to economic activities and employment *[7e]*;
- Deliver **basic health services** for all and reduce **environmental health threats** *[7f]*;
- Ensure that boys and girls are able to complete a full course of primary schooling and have equal access to all levels of **education** *[7g]*;
- Provide access to **agricultural resources** to people living in poverty, especially women and indigenous communities. This may include land

tenure arrangements that support indigenous and common property resource management systems *[7h]*;

- Build **rural infrastructure**: diversify the economy and improve access to markets, market information and credit for the rural poor *[7i]*;
- Transfer **basic sustainable agricultural techniques and knowledge** to small-scale and medium-scale farmers, fishers and the rural poor *[7j]*;
- Increase **food availability and affordability**, through community-based partnerships linking rural and urban people and enterprises *[7k]*; and
- **Combat desertification** and reduce the impacts of drought and floods through better use of weather information and forecasts, early warning systems and conservation practices *[7l]*.

Water and sanitation

The Millennium Development Goal (MDG) of halving the proportion of people who are unable to reach or afford **safe drinking water** by 2015 is complemented by a new target of halving, by the same year, the proportion of people who do not have access to **basic sanitation** *[8]*. Action is required at all levels to strengthen:

'Poverty is pain; it feels like a disease. It attacks a person not only materially but also morally. It eats away one's dignity and drives one into total despair' (a poor woman, Moldova, 1997, cited in Narayan et al, 2000).

- Household sanitation systems *[8a]*;
- Sanitation in **public institutions**, especially schools *[8b]*;
- Safe **hygiene practices** *[8c]*; **education/outreach** for children *[8d]*; and affordable and socially and culturally acceptable **technologies** and practices *[8e]*;
- Innovative financing and partnerships *[8f]*; and
- Integration of water and sanitation in **national sustainable development and poverty reduction strategies** *[7m]*, and sanitation in **water resources management strategies** *[8g]*.

Energy

To help achieve the MDGs and generate services that alleviate poverty, better collaboration is needed to improve access to reliable and affordable energy services for sustainable development *[9]*. The emphasis is on *'reliable, affordable, economically viable, socially acceptable and environmentally sound energy services and resources'*, with action taken at all levels on:

- Better access, including rural electrification, decentralized energy systems, increased use of renewable energy sources, cleaner liquid and gaseous fuels, and enhanced energy efficiency *[9a]*;
- Modern **biomass** technologies and fuelwood sources; commercialized biomass operations *[9b]*; sustainable use of **biomass** and other renewable energies *[9c]*;
- Cleaner use of **liquid and gaseous fossil fuels**, when these are considered more environmentally sound, socially acceptable or cost effective *[9d]*;

- National energy policies and regulatory frameworks creating energy sector conditions that improve access by the poor to services in rural, peri-urban and urban areas *[9e]*;
- International and regional cooperation on energy services, especially in rural and isolated areas *[9f]*; and
- Accelerated access by the poor to services, facilitated through financial and technical assistance, public–private partnerships and national policies on energy for sustainable development *[9g]*.

Industrial development

To strengthen the contribution of industrial development to poverty eradication and sustainable natural resource management *[10]*, action at all levels is required to:

- Improve industrial productivity, competitiveness and industrial development in developing countries *[10a]*;
- Increase income-generating employment, taking into account the International Labour Organization (ILO) Declaration on Fundamental Principles and Rights at Work *[10b]*;
- Promote micro-, small- and medium-sized enterprises, especially agro-industry, through training *[10c]*;
- Help rural communities in developing countries to benefit from small-scale mining *[10d]*;
- Develop safe low-cost technologies to conserve fuel for cooking and heating water *[10e]*; and
- Support natural resource management that creates sustainable livelihoods for the poor *[10f]*.

'Poverty has so many causes that no one solution will solve all the problems in every country' (Agenda 21, 1992).

Slum dwellers

To secure the MDG of achieving a significant improvement in the lives of at least 100 million slum dwellers by 2020 *[11]*, actions at all levels addressing the poor is required to:

- Improve access to land and property, adequate shelter and basic services especially for female heads of households [11a];
- Use low-cost and sustainable materials and appropriate technology for housing *[11b]*;
- Increase decent employment, credit and income *[11c]*;
- Remove unnecessary regulatory and other obstacles for micro-enterprises and the informal sector *[11d]*; and
- Support local authorities with slum upgrade programmes and facilitate access to information on housing legislation *[11e]*.

Child labour

- Immediate measures will be taken to eliminate the worst forms of **child labour** as defined by ILO convention 182 and to put strategies in place to eliminate child labour that is contrary to accepted international standards *[12]*; and
- International cooperation will be offered to developing countries on request to address child labour and its root causes *[13]*.

 Poverty eradication elsewhere in the JPOI

'We welcome the Johannesburg Summit focus on the indivisibility of human dignity and are resolved through decisions and targets, timetables and partnerships to speedily increase access to basic requirements such as clean water, sanitation, adequate shelter, energy, healthcare, food security and the protection of biodiversity'
(Johannesburg Declaration on Sustainable Development, paragraph 18).

The Johannesburg Plan of Implementation (JPOI) recognizes poverty eradication as one of three overarching objectives of, and essential requirements for, sustainable development. It includes MDGs on poverty, safe drinking water, food security and hunger, and supports frameworks that embody poverty reduction strategies. Action is agreed to integrate health concerns within poverty strategies. The JPOI notes that the risks of climate change mean that poverty and other issues remain central concerns. It also addresses the links between poverty and agriculture, sustainable mountain development, sustainable forest management, and secure equitable access to land tenure. Small island developing states (SIDS) and regional chapters all include poverty eradication objectives. The JPOI acknowledges the benefits of globalization as well as the challenges, including poverty, exclusion and inequality, and the need for resources to achieve internationally agreed goals on poverty. Sound economic policies, solid democratic institutions and improved infrastructure are seen as the basis for sustained economic growth, poverty eradication and employment creation.

TARGETS AND COMMITMENTS

- **Poverty**. Halve, by 2015, proportion of people whose income is less than US$1 a day *[7a]* (MDG).

- **Poverty fund**. Establish World Solidarity Fund to eradicate poverty and promote social and human development *[7b]* (new target).

- **Water and sanitation**. Halve, by 2015, proportion of people unable to reach or afford safe drinking water, and proportion of people without access to basic sanitation *[8]* and *[7a]* (MDG and new target).

- **Hunger**. Halve, by 2015, proportion of people suffering from hunger *[40a]* and *[7a]* (MDG).

- **Slums**. By 2020, achieve significant improvement in the lives of at least 100 million slum dwellers *[11]* (MDG).

EXAMPLES OF INDICATORS FOR MEASURING PROGRESS IN IMPLEMENTATION

- Proportion of population below US$1 per day (Millennium Development Goal, or MDG)

- Poverty gap ration (incidence x depth of poverty) (MDG)

- Proportion of population below minimum level of dietary energy consumption (MDG)

- Literacy rate of 15- to 24-year olds (MDG)

- Proportion of population with sustainable access to an improved water source, urban and rural (MDG)

- Proportion of urban population with access to improved sanitation (MDG)

- Percentage of population living below the poverty line (Commission on Sustainable Development, or CSD)

- Gini Index of income inequality (CSD)

- Unemployment rate (CSD)

Other relevant CSD indicators are found under health, education and housing.

Partnership example

UNDP Capacity 2015

Leading partner: United Nations Development Programme (UNDP)

Dates: January 2003–January 2015

Objective: Building capacity to benefit from globalization and to realize the MDGs while achieving sustainable development.

Capacity 2015 will build on experience gained since the United Nations Conference on Environment and Development (UNCED) to help countries move from strategic planning for sustainable development to effective implementation. The main objectives include helping countries to reap the benefits of globalization; ensuring that sustainable development processes put in place during the 1990s face the challenges of the 21st century; and strengthening capacities to achieve the MDGs.

- Communities, local government and the private sector will have strengthened capacities to sustain vibrant local economies in order to improve livelihoods and to eliminate poverty.

Partnership example (contd)

- Legislation will have been reviewed and reformed, governance processes improved and institutional bottlenecks to achieving local sustainable development eliminated.

- There will be increased participation in the global market and increased inward investment.

- National and local development strategies will be under implementation and oriented towards achieving the MDGs.

- National and local development strategies will be in place that support civic engagement and responsible leadership.

- Networks will be in place that engage communities and authorities in monitoring the achievement of the MDGs.

- New national and local strategies, including poverty reduction strategies, will have been developed, reviewed and revised utilizing the principles of sustainable development, ensuring full convergence between Agenda 21 and later developments.

- The principles of the Multilateral Environmental Agreements (MEAs) will have been combined and integrated within activities at the local level and funding will have been mobilized from global sources.

- Programmes will be in place to meet the specific challenges of sustainability and global market access of the small island developing states (SIDS).

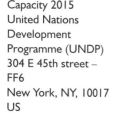

Contact information:
Capacity 2015
United Nations
Development
Programme (UNDP)
304 E 45th street –
FF6
New York, NY, 10017
US
www.undp.org/
capacity2015

 Resources

Child labour

www.ilo.org/public/english/standards/ipec/index.htm

www.ilo.org/public/english/standards/ipec/ratification/convention/
text.htm (text)

The International Programme on the Elimination of Child Labour (IPEC) is a United Nations/International Labour Organization (ILO) initiative that promotes the ILO Worst Forms of Child Labour Convention, 1999 (No 182).

Cities without Slums Initiative

www.citiesalliance.org/citiesalliancehomepage.nsf

This initiative was developed in 1999 by Cities Alliance, a major alliance of cities and development partners (United Nations, World Bank, regional development banks, NGOs, business leaders, and national and local partners).

International Labour Organization (ILO) Declaration on Fundamental Principles and Rights at Work

www.ilo.org/public/english/standards/decl/index.htm
Agreed on June 1998, this declaration covers freedom of association and the right to collective bargaining; elimination of forced and compulsory labour; abolition of child labour; and elimination of discrimination in the workplace.

Millennium Development Goals (MDGs)

www.un.org/millenniumgoals/index.shtml (UN)
www.undp.org/mdg (UNDP)
www.developmentgoals.org (World Bank)
The United Nations Secretary-General's 'Road Map' (September 2001) set out concrete targets for goals and commitments in the Millennium Declaration. These were further developed into the MDGs.

United Nations Children's Fund (UNICEF)

www.unicef.org
UNICEF champions children's rights, education, HIV/AIDS and child labour, as well as the United Nations Convention on the Rights of the Child.

United Nations Convention to Combat Desertification in Those Countries Experiencing Serious Drought and/or Desertification, Particularly in Africa (CCD)

www.unccd.int/main.php
The Convention to Combat Desertification was completed in 1996. Countries must develop national action programmes in conjunction with local stakeholders; detailed annexes address desertification in specific regions.

United Nations Development Programme (UNDP)

www.undp.org
The UNDP helps to build national capacity for sustainable development, especially the MDGs. It works through country offices and a global network, and publishes the *Human Development Report*.

Universal Declaration of Human Rights (1948)

www.un.org/Overview/rights.html
On 10 December 1998, the UN General Assembly adopted the Universal Declaration of Human Rights. The declaration contains 30 articles which member states have pledged to achieve with the aim of promoting universal respect for and observance of human rights and fundamental freedoms.

United Nations Human Settlements Programme (UN-Habitat)

www.unhabitat.org
This is the lead United Nations agency on human settlements. The Habitat Agenda was adopted at the Habitat II Summit (Istanbul, 1996) and promotes equitable human settlements, poverty eradication and sustainable development.

World Summit for Social Development

www.un.org/esa/socdev/wssd/
Held in Copenhagen in 1995, this summit addressed poverty, unemployment and social integration. It adopted the Copenhagen Declaration on Social Development, as well as a programme of action. Its five-year review was held in Geneva in June 2000.

CONFERENCES, AGREEMENTS AND PROCESSES

- Agenda 21, Chapters 3 and 7 (1992)

- World Conference on Human Rights, Vienna (1993)

- International Conference on Population and Development (ICPD), Cairo (1994)

- World Summit on Social Development (Commitment 2) Copenhagen (1995)

- United Nations Commission on Sustainable Development-3 (CSD-3) Decision 3.6 (1995)

- Fourth World Conference on Women, Beijing (1995)

- Habitat II Conference, Istanbul (1996)

- CSD-4 Decision 4.2 (1996)

- United Nations General Assembly Special Session (UNGASS) Resolution on Eradicating Poverty, paragraph 27 (1997)

- United Nations Decade on Eradication of Poverty (1997– 2006)

- CSD-6 (1998)

- United Nations Millennium Declaration (2000)

- Beijing+5 (Women), New York (2000)

- Millennium Development Goals (MDG) on poverty, hunger and drinking water (2000–2015)

- Istanbul+5 (Habitat), New York (2001)

- CSD (2004–2015) to consider poverty eradication as cross-cutting theme

CONFERENCES, AGREEMENTS AND PROCESSES (CONTD)

⧗ World Summit on Sustainable Development (WSSD) target on sanitation (2015)

⧗ MDG target on slum dwellers (2020)

Key United Nations bodies and Bretton Woods institutions

◌ Combating poverty (overall)

International Labour Organization (ILO)

United Nations Children's Fund (UNICEF)

United Nations Conference on Trade and Development (UNCTAD)

United Nations Development Programme (UNDP)

United Nations Food and Agriculture Organization (FAO)

United Nations Human Settlements Programme (UN-Habitat)

World Bank

◌ Millennium Development Goals (MDGs)

United Nations Development Programme (UNDP)

World Bank

◌ Human settlements

United Nations Development Programme (UNDP)

United Nations High Commissioner for Refugees (UNHCR)

United Nations High Commissioner on Human Rights (UNHCHR)

United Nations Human Settlements Programme (UN-Habitat)

World Bank

 ## References

DFID (UK Department for International Development) (2002) *Poverty and the Environment*, DFID, London

DFID, EC, UNDP and the World Bank (UK Department for International Development, European Commission, United Nations Development Programme and the World Bank) (2002) *Linking Poverty Reduction and Environmental Management: Policy Challenges and Opportunities*, July 2002, www.undp.org/wssd/docs/LPREM.pdf

International Energy Agency (2002) *World Energy Outlook 2002 – Highlights*, www.worldenergyoutlook.org

Narayan, D, Patel, R, Rademadier, A and Koch-Sholte, S (2000) *Can Anyone Hear Us?* Voices of the Poor Series, World Bank and Oxford University Press, Oxford

UN (United Nations) (2002a) *We the Peoples: The Role of the United Nations in the 21st Century*, UN, New York, paragraphs 70, 73, www.un.org/millennium/sg/report/key.htm

UN (2002b) *Johannesburg Plan of Implementation*, Johannesburg Declaration on Sustainable Development and Plan of Implementation of the World Summit on Sustainable Development, www.un.org/esa/sustdev

UNCED (United Nations Conference on Environment and Development) (1992) *Agenda 21*, Chapter 3, 'Combating poverty', www.un.org/esa/sustdev/documents/agenda21/english/agenda21toc.htm

UNDP (United Nations Development Programme) (2000) *Overcoming Human Poverty: Poverty Report 2000*, UNDP, New York

UNDP (2003) *Human Development Report: Millennium Development Goals – A Compact among Nations to End Human Poverty*, UNDP, New York

UNEP (United Nations Environment Programme) (2002) *Global Environmental Outlook 3*, www.unep.org/geo, Earthscan, London

Water Aid (2003) www.wateraid.org.uk

Water Aid and Tear Fund (2000) *Human Waste Report*, www.wateraid.org

World Bank poverty website, www.worldbank.org/poverty/data/trends/index.htm

World Bank (2001) *World Development Report 2000/2001: Attacking Poverty*, Oxford University Press, Oxford

World Bank (2004) *World Development Report: Making Services Work for Poor People*, World Bank, Washington, DC

Changing Unsustainable Patterns of Consumption and Production

3 _____

 ## Context

Twenty per cent of the world's population use an estimated 80 per cent of the world's resources. Such inequality can not continue. Current patterns of resource use *'would push the world beyond what is sustainable; so either the developing world has to be held back or the developed world has to find ways to sustain current standards of living using far fewer resources'* (UK House of Commons Select Committee on Environment, Transport and Regional Affairs, 1998). A working definition of sustainable consumption is *'the use of services and related products which respond to basic needs and bring a better quality of life while minimizing the use of natural resources and toxic materials, as well as the emissions of waste and pollutants over the life cycle so as not to jeopardize the needs of future generations'* (Ministry of the Environment, Norway, 1994).

Environmental pressures are starting to influence the way in which products are designed, manufactured and discarded. Optimizing resource efficiency is the underlying idea behind the *'Factor 4/Factor 10'* concept, initially developed by the Wuppertal Institute in Germany (von Weizacker et al, 1997). This recognizes that developed countries need to reduce the intensity of their material and energy use by at least a factor of four over the next 20 to 30 years and up to a factor of ten in the long term to create 'environmental space' for developing countries to grow. The Johannesburg Plan of Implementation (JPOI) makes several references to the need for clean production centres to act as entrepreneurial drivers for new materials policy and to promote a cyclical, rather than a linear, flow of natural resources. This idea was originally developed by the Organisation for Economic Co-operation and Development (OECD) and has been implemented in several countries, including Germany and Japan (UNEP, www.uneptie.org, 2002).

Moving towards a low pollution, low carbon economy offers a host of opportunities for stakeholders to work collaboratively to address knowledge gaps and numerous technical and economic challenges that include design for low-waste production; product design for longevity, repair, disassembly and reuse; applications for recycled products; and vital changes in consumer awareness and behaviour.

KEY WORDS

- **sustainable consumption and production patterns**
- **ten-year framework of programmes**
- **eco-efficiency**
- **cleaner production**
- **corporate responsibility and accountability**
- **energy for sustainable development**
- **transport**
- **waste**
- **chemicals**

AT A GLANCE

⊠ Current estimates suggest that we have overshot our global 'carrying capacity' by over 30 per cent (WWF International, 2000).

⊠ Almost 1 billion people in 70 countries consume less today than 25 years ago, while the richest 20 per cent of the world's population now accounts for 86 per cent of private consumption (UNDP, 1999).

⊠ The global chemistry industry has grown almost ninefold since 1972, and a 3 per cent annual growth is expected to continue over the next three decades, with a considerable increase in trade (OECD, 2001).

 # Chapter III in summary

Global sustainable development depends upon fundamental changes in the way that societies produce and consume. Acknowledging the principle of 'common but differentiated responsibility', the JPOI requests all countries to **promote sustainable consumption and production patterns**, with developing countries taking the lead. Governments, international organizations, the private sector and all major groups have an active role to play *[14]*.

'The Earth has enough for everyone's need, but not for everyone's greed'
(Mahatma Gandhi).

Ten-year framework of programmes

A **ten-year framework of programmes** will support regional and national initiatives to accelerate the shift towards sustainable consumption and production. This will promote social and economic development within the **carrying capacity** of ecosystems by addressing the **delinking of economic growth and environmental degradation** and mobilizing resources to help build capacity in developing countries *[15]*. Actions needed at all levels include:

* Identifying specific tools, policies and measures, including **life cycle analysis** and **national indicators** for measuring progress *[15a]*;
* Adopting relevant policies and measures that follow the 'polluter pays' principle (principle 16, Rio Declaration) *[15b]*;
* Developing **policies** to improve products and services while reducing environmental and health impacts *[15c]*;
* **Raising awareness** on the importance of sustainable production and consumption, particularly among young people *[15d]*;
* Employing voluntary, 'effective, transparent, verifiable, non-misleading and non-discriminatory' **consumer information tools** *[15e]*; and
* Developing **financial resources** to increase eco-efficiency through capacity-building, technology transfer and the exchange of technology *[15f]*.

Cleaner production and eco-efficiency

Increasing **investment in cleaner production and eco-efficiency** requires incentives, support schemes and policies that establish necessary regulatory, financial and legal frameworks *[16]*. Actions include:

* Establishing **cleaner production programs and centres**, and particularly assisting small and medium-sized enterprises (SMEs) to improve productivity *[16a]*;
* Creating **incentives** for investment in cleaner production and eco-efficiency *[16b]*;
* Providing **information** on cost-effective examples and best practice *[16c]*; and
* Providing **training** programmes to SMEs about the use of information and communication technologies *[16d]*.

Decision-making processes and corporate responsibility

The issue of production and consumption patterns will be integrated within sustainable development policies and programmes, and poverty eradication strategies *[17]*.

Corporate environmental and social responsibility and accountability will be improved *[18]*, with actions to encourage:

* Industry to improve social and environmental performance through voluntary initiatives, such as environmental management systems, codes of conduct, certification and public reporting *[18a]*;
* Dialogue between enterprises and communities *[18b]*;
* Financial institutions to incorporate sustainability within their decision-making processes *[18c]*; and
* Development of workplace partnerships, including training and education *[18d]*.

Relevant authorities are encouraged to take sustainable development into account in **decision-making processes**, such as planning, infrastructure investment, business development and public procurement *[19]*, with action to:

* Support the development of sustainable development strategies, including decision-making in **investment** *[19a]*;
* Promote the **internalization of environmental costs** and the use of economic instruments *[19b]*;
* Promote **public procurement** policies that encourage environmentally sound goods and services *[19c]*;
* Provide **capacity-building and training** on implementing these measures *[19d]*; and
* Use **environmental impact assessments** *[19e]*.

'Energy is essential for development. Yet 2 billion people currently go without, condemning them to remain in the poverty trap' (UN Secretary-General Kofi Annan, 2002).

Energy

The JPOI calls on governments and stakeholders to implement the recommendations of the ninth session of the United Nations Commission on Sustainable Development (CSD) on energy *[20]*, including actions to:

'The public sector, civil society, individuals acting as parents and consumers and voters all have crucial parts to play in the struggle for sustainability. Industry, however, may have the most vital role of all' (Frankel, 1998).

- Mobilize financial resources, transfer technology, build capacity and help to spread environmentally sound technologies *[20a]*;
- Integrate energy considerations – energy efficiency, affordability and accessibility – within socio-economic programmes, the policies of **major energy-consuming sectors**, and the planning, operation and maintenance of **long-lived energy consuming infrastructures** *[20b]*;
- Develop **alternative energy technologies** to give a greater share of the energy mix to renewable energy, improve energy efficiency and improve reliance on advanced energy technologies, including cleaner fossil-fuel technologies *[20c]*;
- **Combine** the increased use of renewable energy, efficiency and advanced/cleaner fuel technologies with the sustainable use of traditional energy resources to help meet the growing need for energy services in achieving sustainable development *[20d]*;
- **Diversify** energy supply by developing cleaner, more efficient, affordable and cost-effective technologies and their transfer to developing countries. Substantially increase the global share of **renewable energy sources** *[20e]*;
- Reduce **flaring and venting of gas** associated with crude oil production *[20f]*;
- Use **indigenous energy sources** and infrastructures for local uses, promoting participation by rural communities and Agenda 21 groups, and the use of renewable energy to meet daily needs *[20g]*;
- Establish **domestic programmes for energy efficiency** *[20h]*;
- Accelerate development and use of affordable and cleaner **energy efficiency and energy conservation technologies** *[20h]*;
- Transfer technology to developing countries on concessional/favourable terms *[20i]*;
- Recommend that **international financial institutions** and others help to establish policy and regulatory frameworks to create a **level playing field** between renewable energy, energy efficiency, advanced energy technologies and centralized, distributed and decentralized energy systems *[20j]*;
- Promote increased **research and development** (R&D) in energy technology, focusing on strengthening national and regional R&D institutions *[20k]*;
- Network **centres of excellence** on energy for sustainable development *[20l]*;
- Promote **education** about available energy sources and technologies *[20m]*;
- Use **financial instruments and mechanisms**, particularly the Global Environment Facility (GEF), to help developing countries, particularly least

developed countries and small island developing states, meet their needs for training, know-how and institution-building [20n];

- Improve the functioning, transparency and information flows about **energy markets** [20o];
- Use policies to **reduce market distortions** that would promote energy systems compatible with sustainable development [20p];
- Phase out subsidies in this area that hinder sustainable development [20q];
- Improve the **functioning of national energy markets** to support sustainable development, overcome market barriers and improve accessibility [20r];
- Strengthen **national/regional energy institutions/arrangements** for better regional/international cooperation on energy for sustainable development and to assist developing countries in their domestic efforts to provide energy services to all [20s];
- Implement actions within the framework of **CSD-9** relating to access to energy [20t];
- Promote **cooperation** between international and regional institutions dealing with energy for sustainable development [20u];
- Promote **cross-border energy trade**, including interconnection of electricity grids, and oil and natural gas pipelines [20v]; and
- Strengthen dialogue amongst regional, national and international producers and energy consumers [20w].

Transport

The JPOI calls for **integrated approaches to policy-making for transport services and systems**. This includes policies and planning for land use, infrastructure, public transport systems and goods delivery networks to help ensure safe, affordable and energy efficient transportation with less pollution, congestion, negative health impacts and urban sprawl [21]. Actions at all levels will:

- Implement **transport strategies** for sustainable development [21a]; and
- Promote **investment and partnerships** towards sustainable transportation systems [21b].

Waste

Negative environmental effects of **waste** will be minimized, and resource efficiency improved, by preventing and minimizing waste, and by maximizing reuse, recycling and the use of environmentally sound materials [22]. Action is needed to:

- Develop **waste management systems** with a priority on waste prevention, reduction, reuse and recycling. Encourage small-scale waste recycling initiatives that provide opportunities for income generation [22a]; and
- Encourage the production of **reusable consumer goods** and **biodegradable products** [22b].

'Efficiency can safely be called a no-regrets strategy. If it is made a high priority in many countries and by business worldwide, it will buy a lot of time' (von Weizsacker et al, 1997).

Chemicals management

The JPOI calls for a renewed commitment towards the **sound management of chemicals** throughout their life cycle and the tackling of hazardous wastes. By 2020, chemicals should be used and produced in ways that minimize significant adverse impacts upon human health and the environment. All processes should be transparent, using science-based risk assessment and management, and based on the precautionary principle. Developing countries will require assistance to strengthen their capacities to meet these objectives *[23]*. Action is needed to:

- Ratify and implement **international instruments on chemicals and hazardous waste**, including the Rotterdam Convention on Prior Informed Consent Procedures for Certain Hazardous Chemicals and Pesticides in International Trade, and the Stockholm Convention on Persistent Organic Pollutants *[23a]*;
- Further develop a **strategic approach to international chemicals management** by 2005, based on the Bahia Declaration and priorities for Action beyond 2000 *[23b]*;
- Implement the globally harmonized system for the **classification and labelling of chemicals** with a view to having the system fully operational by 2008 *[23c]*;
- Encourage **partnerships** to promote environmentally sound management of chemicals and hazardous wastes *[23d]*;
- Prevent **international illegal trafficking** of hazardous chemicals and wastes and damage from **transboundary movement and disposal of wastes** *[23e]*;
- Develop **coherent and integrated information on chemicals** *[23f]*; and
- Reduce risks posed by **heavy metals**, including through a review of relevant studies and assessments *[23g]*.

Consumption and production elsewhere in the JPOI

Changing unsustainable patterns of production and consumption is an overarching goal of the World Summit on Sustainable Development (WSSD). Actions are agreed on increasing access to energy services, increasing the use of renewable energy resources and increasing energy efficiency to assist with poverty alleviation, combat desertification and ensure sustainable development of small island developing states (SIDS), as well as to assist with reaching targets within the New Partnership for African Development (NEPAD). Additionally, effective management and efficient use of resources is fundamental to protecting the natural resource base, and the sound management of chemicals has particular implications for the protection of oceans and coasts. Tools such as corporate accountability are recommended.

TARGETS AND COMMITMENTS

- **Consumption and production**. Ten-year framework of programmes to accelerate the shift towards sustainable consumption and production [15] (new target).

- **International agreements**. Ratify and implement relevant international instruments on chemicals and hazardous waste, including the Rotterdam Convention so that it can enter into force by 2003 and the Stockholm Convention so that it can enter into force by 2004 [23a].

- **Chemicals management**. Further develop a strategic approach to international chemicals management, based on the Bahia Declaration and Priorities for Action beyond 2000, by 2005 [23b].

- **Classification**. Implement the new globally harmonized system for the classification and labelling of chemicals as soon as possible, with a view to having it fully operational by 2008 [23c].

- **Health**. By 2020, use and produce chemicals in ways that do not lead to significant adverse effects on human health and the environment [23] (new target).

- **Energy supply**. Diversify energy supply and substantially increase the global share of renewable energy in order to increase the renewable contribution to total energy supply [20e].

- **Energy efficiency**. Establish domestic programmes for energy efficiency with the support of the international community. Accelerate the development and dissemination of energy efficiency and energy conservation technologies, including the promotion of research and development [20b, 20c, 20h, 20i, 20k, 21].

EXAMPLES OF INDICATORS FOR MEASURING PROGRESS TO IMPLEMENTATION

- Intensity of material use (United Nations Commission on Sustainable Development, or CSD)

- Intensity of energy use (CSD)

- Annual energy consumption per capita (CSD)

- Generation of industrial and municipal waste (CSD)

- Generation of hazardous waste (CSD)

- Waste recycling and reuse (CSD)

- Distance traveled per capita by mode of transport (CSD)

Partnership example

Awareness-raising and training on sustainable consumption and production

Leading partner: United Nations Environment Programme (UNEP) Division of Technology, Industry and Economics (DTIE)

Dates: January 2003–December 2005

This US$2 million capacity-building effort aims to improve decision-makers' ability to implement sustainable consumption and production policies. It relies upon practical training materials, training courses and advisory services. The programme's substantive content is derived from the section on sustainable consumption in the *United Nations Guidelines on Consumer Protection*, and includes segments on how to implement national policy frameworks and how to better market cleaner products and services. The primary target groups are developing and transition countries and small- and medium-sized enterprises (SMEs).

At the project's end, the goal is increased awareness and skills of 300 to 500 staff in governments and heads of SMEs in about 30 countries (in Africa, Asia, Latin America and the Caribbean, and Eastern Europe), as well as increased awareness and improved implementation of the *United Nations Guidelines for Consumer Protection*.

Partners involved include The Netherlands, Sweden and the Czech Republic (as of March 2003); intergovernmental organizations, including inputs from the United Nations Industrial Development Organization (UNIDO) and the United Nations Educational, Scientific and Cultural Organization (UNESCO); and major groups, including Consumers International, in cooperation with partners from the business and industry and scientific community, as well as National Cleaner Production Centres and National Civil Society Groups.

Contact information:
United Nations
Environment
Programme (UNEP)
Division of
Technology, Industry
and Economics
39–43, quai André
Citroën 75739 Paris
Cedex 15, France
www.uneptie.org/
pc/sustain

Resources

ANPED (Northern Alliance for Sustainability)

www.anped.ord

Bahia Declaration and Priorities for Action beyond 2000, Intergovernmental Forum on Chemical Safety (IFCS)

www.who.int/ifcs
IFCS is an international forum on the environmentally sound management of chemicals, as described in Chapter 19, Agenda 21. The Bahia Declaration (2000) called for global cooperation to tackle priority actions.

Basel Convention on the Control of Transboundary Movements of Hazardous Wastes and their Disposal.

www.basel.int
This convention aims to minimize the generation of hazardous waste in terms of quantity and toxicity; to dispose of it as close to source as possible; and to reduce movement of hazardous materials.

Cleaner Production

www.uneptie.org/pc/home.htm
The United Nations Environment Programme's (UNEP's) Production and Consumption Unit promotes more sustainable forms of industrial development through cleaner production; sustainable consumption; risk reduction; environmental management tools; and waste management.

Global Environment Facility (GEF)

www.gefweb.org
The GEF helps developing countries to fund projects/programmes that protect the global environment. It designated a financial mechanism for conventions on biodiversity, climate change and persistent organic pollutants. It also supports work on desertification, international waters and the ozone layer.

Global Reporting Initiative (GRI)

www.globalreporting.org
The GRI is a multi-stakeholder process and independent institution that is developing and disseminating globally applicable sustainability reporting guidelines for voluntary use by organizations reporting economic, environmental and social dimensions of their activities/products/services. The official UNEP collaborating centre, the GRI works in cooperation with UN Secretary-General Kofi Annan's Global Compact (www.unglobalcompact.org).

3

International Coalition on Sustainable Consumption and Production (ICSPAC)

www.icspac.net

The ICSPAC is an information exchange and policy advocacy vehicle for non-governmental organizations (NGOs) and citizen organizations in promoting sustainable production and consumption (SPAC) policies and practices.

International Organization for Standardization (ISO)

www.iso.ch

The ISO is a worldwide federation of national standards bodies that promotes standardization to facilitate the international exchange of goods and services. It develops cooperation in all the spheres of intellectual, scientific, technological and economic activity.

Pollutant Release and Transfer Registers (PRTRs)

www.chem.unep.ch/prtr/default.htm

The International Register of Potentially Toxic Chemicals (IRPTC), hosted by UNEP, is an international clearinghouse for PRTRs.

Rotterdam Convention – Agreement on Prior Informed Consents on Hazardous Chemicals (1998)

www.pic.int

This agreement enables countries to monitor and control trade in harmful pesticides and industrial chemicals. It uses a legally binding 'prior informed consent' approach for imports; promotes safe use of chemicals through labelling standards; and provides technical assistance and other support.

Stockholm Convention on Persistent Organic Pollutants (POPs)

www.pops.int

This is a global treaty (2001) to protect human health/environment from POPs by eliminating them or reducing their release in the environment. POPS are chemicals that remain intact for long periods, become widely distributed geographically, persist in the food chain, accumulate in the fatty tissue of living organisms, and are toxic to humans and wildlife.

Sustainable Consumption

www.uneptie.org/pc/sustain

Sustainable consumption is an umbrella term that brings together resource efficiency; renewable energy; waste minimization; life-cycle approaches; meeting needs; quality of life; and equity. It aims to provide the same or better services in a sustainable way to meet basic requirements and aspirations for improvement of current/future generations (UNEP, 1994).

United Nations Environment Programme (UNEP) Global Mercury Assessment

www.chem.unep.ch/mercury/default.htm
This is a process that is developing a global assessment of mercury and its compounds and an outline of options for addressing significant global adverse impacts.

UNEP

Sustainable Consumption, www.uneptie.org/pc/sustain

United Nations Guidelines on Consumer Protection

www.uneptie.org/pc/sustain/guidelines/guidelines.htm
Adopted by the UN in 1999, these guidelines are based on the work of the Commission on Sustainable Development (CSD). It provides a comprehensive framework to promote sustainable consumption and protection. UNEP/Consumers International have surveyed implementation in various countries: recycling and energy and water conservation were the most common activities. The consumer protection approach helps to integrate sustainability issues with safety, quality, functionality and other aspects of product performance (CSD, 2003).

CONFERENCES, AGREEMENTS AND PROCESSES

Consumption and production

- ⧗ Agenda 21, Chapter 4, 'Changing consumption patterns' (1992)

- ⧗ United Nations Commission on Sustainable Development (CSD) 2, 3, 4, 7, Decision 2/5, 3/4, 4/13, 7/2, 'Consumption and production patterns' (1994, 1995, 1996, 1999)

- ⧗ Oslo Symposium on Sustainable Consumption (1994)

- ⧗ United Nations General Assembly Special Session (UNGASS), Paragraph 28, 'Changing consumption and production patterns' (1997)

- ⧗ CSD-6 Decision 6/1, 'Consumer protection guidelines for sustainable consumption' (1998)

- ⧗ United Nations Guidelines for Consumer Protection (1986 and 1999 revision)

- ⧗ International Expert Meeting on the Ten-Year Framework of Programmes for Sustainable Consumption and Production Patterns, Marrakech (June 2003)

- ⧗ CSD to address linkages on sustainable consumption and production patterns in each of its annual work cycles (2004–2017)

- ⧗ CSD to consider progress on the Ten-Year Framework of Programmes on Sustainable Consumption and Production Patterns (2010–2011)

CONFERENCES, AGREEMENTS AND PROCESSES (CONTD)

Chemicals

- Agenda 21, Chapter 19, 'Toxic chemicals' (1992)

- United Nations Commission on Sustainable Development (CSD) 2, 5, Decision 2/1, 5/57, 'Toxic chemicals' (1994, 1997)

- Code of Ethics on the International Trade in Chemicals (1994)

- CSD-3, Decision 3/8/101 (1995)

- International Register of Potentially Toxic Chemicals (IRPTC)

- Prior informed consent (for certain hazardous chemicals) (Rotterdam, 1998)

- Persistent Organic Pollutants Convention (Stockholm, 2001)

- International Register on Biosafety

- CSD to consider chemicals (2010–2011)

Transport

- Agenda 21, Chapter 9, 'Atmosphere', and Chapter 7, 'Human settlements' (1992)

- United Nations Commission on Sustainable Development (CSD) 9, Decision 9/47, 'Transport' (2001)

- CSD to consider transport issues (2010–2011)

Energy

- Agenda 21, Chapter 9, 'Atmosphere', and Chapter 7, 'Human settlements' (1992)

- United Nations General Assembly Special Session (UNGASS), Decision 42, 'Energy' (1997)

- United Nations Commission on Sustainable Development (CSD) 9, Decision 9/1, 'Energy for sustainable development' (2001)

- CSD to consider energy for sustainable development (2006–2007)

Waste

- Agenda 21, Chapter 19, 'Environmentally sound management of hazardous wastes', Chapter 21, 'Environmentally sound management of solid wastes and sewage-related issues' and Chapter 22, 'Safe and environmentally sound management of radioactive wastes' (1992)

CONFERENCES, AGREEMENTS AND PROCESSES (CONTD)

⧗ United Nations General Assembly Special Session (UNGASS) 'Hazardous wastes' and paragraph 59 – 'Radioactive wastes' (1997)

⧗ United Nations Commission on Sustainable Development (CSD) is to include waste management within its work programme for 2010–2011

See the 'Resources' section for other relevant organizations and web links.

Key United Nations bodies and Bretton Woods institutions

Consumption and production

⚙ International Energy Agency (IEA)

⚙ United Nations Conference on Trade and Development (UNCTAD)

⚙ United Nations Department of Economic and Social Affairs (DESA), Division for Sustainable Development (Agenda 21 Task Master)

⚙ United Nations Development Programme's (UNDP's) *Human Development Report*

⚙ United Nations Environment Programme's (UNEP's) Industry and Environment, Sustainable Consumption, Cleaner Production Programme

⚙ United Nations Food and Agriculture Organization (FAO)

⚙ United Nations Industrial Development Organization (UNIDO)

⚙ World Meteorological Organization (WMO)

Chemicals

⚙ United Nations Environment Programme's (UNEP's) International Register of Potentially Toxic Chemicals (IRPTC) (Agenda 21 Task Master)

⚙ World Health Organization (WHO) Global Environmental Epidemiology Network (GEENET)

Transport

⚙ Global Initiative on Transport Emissions

⚙ United Nations Conference on Trade and Development (UNCTAD) transport technical services

3

Key United Nations bodies and Bretton Woods institutions (*contd*)

Energy

- Ad Hoc Inter-Agency Task Force on Energy
- United Nations Atomic Energy Agency
- United Nations Development Programme's (UNDP's) Sustainable Energy Programme
- United Nations Educational, Scientific and Cultural Organization's (UNESCO's) Solar Programme
- United Nations Environment Programme's (UNEP's) Cleaner Production Programme
- United Nations Framework Convention on Climate Change (UNFCCC)
- United Nations Industrial Development Organization (UNIDO)

Wastes (hazardous, solid, radioactive)

- International Atomic Energy Agency (IAEA) (Agenda 21 Task Master – radioactive wastes)
- United Nations Environment Programme (UNEP) (Agenda 21 Task Master – hazardous wastes)
- United Nations Human Settlements Programme (UN-Habitat) (Agenda 21 Task Master – solid wastes)

 # References

CSD (United Nations Commission on Sustainable Development) (2003) Paper for International Expert Meeting on a Ten-Year Framework of Programmes for Sustainable Consumption and Production, June (Chapter III of the Johannesburg Plan of Implementation), Discussion Paper, prepared for the United Nations Division for Sustainable Development, June 2003

Frankel, C (1998) *In Earth's Company: Business, Environment and the Challenge of Sustainability*, New Society Publishers, Canada, p13

IIED (International Institute for Environment and Development) (1998) *Consumption in a Sustainable World*, Report of the workshop held in Norway, 2–4 June 1998, IIED, London

Internation Symposium on Sustainable Consumption (1994) Ministry for the Environment, Norway

OECD (Organisation for Economic Co-operation and Development) (2001) *Environmental Outlook for the Chemical Industry*, OECD, Paris

Oleson, G B (2002) 'WSSD and Sustainable Energy', *Sustainable Energy News*, INFORSE Europe, no 38, October, pp14–15

UK House of Commons Select Committee on Environment, Transport and Regional Affairs (1998) *Sustainable Waste Management*, HMSO, London

United Nations Secretary-General Kofi Annan (2002) 'cited in Connor, H, Watch the Indicators, Sustainable Energy Watch Global Report for Rio', *Sustainable Energy News*, INFORSE Europe, no 38, October, p12

UNCED (United Nations Conference on Environment and Development) (1992) Rio Declaration on Environment and Development, www.unep.org/Documents/Default.asp?DocumentID=78&ArticleID=1163

UNDP (United Nations Development Programme) (1999) *Human Development Report 1999*, UNDP, New York

UNEP (United Nations Environment Programme) (1994) *Report of the Oslo Symposium on Sustainable Consumption*, Ministry of Environment, Norway

UNEP (2002a) *Industry as a Partner for Sustainable Development: 10 Years after Rio – The UNEP Assessment*, UNEP, Paris

UNEP (2002b) *Global Environmental Outlook 3*, Earthscan, London.

von Weizacker, E, Lovins, A B and Lovins, L H (1997) *Factor Four: Doubling Wealth, Halving Resource Use – The New Report to the Club of Rome*, Earthscan, London

WWF International (World Wide Fund for Nature) (2000) *Living Planet Report 2000*, WWF, Gland, Switzerland

Protecting and Managing the Natural Resource Base of Economic and Social Development

4

 Context

The well-being of humanity depends upon the wealth of goods and services that natural resources provide. Yet, as the Johannesburg Plan of Implementation (JPOI) acknowledges, 'human activities are having an increasing impact on the integrity of ecosystems' [24]. We continue to overuse the natural resource base rather than work in balance with it. The United Nations Environment Programme's (UNEP's) well-respected *Global Environment Outlook 3* (UNEP, 2002), published in the run-up to the World Summit on Sustainable Development (WSSD), noted that '*[p]overty and excessive consumption ... continue to put enormous pressure on the environment. The unfortunate result is that sustainable development remains largely theoretical for the majority of the world's population*' (UNEP, 2002).

Agenda 21 (Chapters 9–18) outlines strategies to conserve and manage natural resources for development, highlighting the impact of human activities on fragile ecosystems such as deserts and mountains, and offers mechanisms to link key environment and development issues. It calls for a collective global responsibility on the part of governments and all sectors of society to take concrete action. Despite the gains made since the Earth Summit in Rio, many areas of Agenda 21 remain a matter for serious concern – in particular, oceans, energy, water resources and sustainable food production. While the WSSD process made commitments to reverse the current trends in natural resource degradation as soon as possible, the question is, how soon is 'soon'? Forestry experts warn that the '*natural forest resource as an asset of the planet is not yet being cared for sustainably*' (Evans, 2002). The Convention on Biological Diversity (CBD) was a major agreement at the 1992 Earth Summit and the WSSD process was seen by non-governmental organizations (NGOs) and many others as a valuable opportunity for this to be taken forward and developed into a more binding agreement (ANPED, 2002). However, the WSSD actually saw a step backwards from Rio's promise to stop the loss of biodiversity by 2010; this time world leaders merely committed to slow it down (Crace, 2003).

Tackling poverty is imperative as degrading natural environments hit the poor hardest of all through greater food insecurity, increased vulnerability to

AT A GLANCE

- 47 per cent of the main fish stocks or species groups are fully exploited and are producing catches that have reached, or are very close to, their maximum sustainable limits (FAO, 2002).

- 800 million people are chronically malnourished and approximately one third of the world's population lack food security (FAO, 2001a).

- An estimated 97 per cent of natural disaster-related deaths each year occur in developing countries with huge economic impact (ISDR, 2002).

- More than US$1.1 billion has been given to help 114 developing countries phase out ozone depleting substances. By the year 2000, the total consumption of such chemicals had been reduced by 85 per cent. The ozone layer is expected to recover to pre-1980 levels by the middle of the 21st century (UNEP, 2002).

- An estimated 250 million people have been directly affected by desertification, and nearly 1 billion are at risk (FAO, 2001b).

- 75 per cent of the genetic diversity of agricultural crops has been lost since 1900 (FAO, 2001a).

- Ten of the world's 25 top-selling drugs in 1997 were derived from natural sources (UNEP, 2002).

- 13 million people are directly involved in small-scale mining and the livelihoods of a further 80 million to 100 million are affected (IIED and WBCSD, 2002).

'When we try to pick out anything by itself, we find it hitched to everything else in the universe' (John Muir, naturalist, 1869).

natural disasters, inadequate access to the basics of life, poor health and unsuitable settlement location. For sustainable development, poverty alleviation and protection of the natural resource base must go hand in hand.

 ## Chapter IV in summary

Managing the natural resources base in a sustainable and integrated manner is essential for sustainable development. The current trend towards resource degradation must be reversed as soon as possible. To do so will require strategies that should include targets adopted at the national, and possibly regional, levels to protect ecosystems and achieve integrated management of land, water and living resources. The strengthening of capacity to facilitate this management will be essential at all levels [24].

Water and sanitation

The JPOI includes the Millennium Development Goal (MDG) of halving, by 2015, the proportion of people who are unable to reach or to afford **safe drinking water** and agrees a new target to cut by 2015 the number of people without access to **basic sanitation**. These targets will be achieved through action to *[25]*:

- Mobilize financial resources, transfer technology, promote best practice and support capacity-building for **water and sanitation infrastructure and services** in a way that meets the **needs of the poor** and is **gender sensitive** *[25a]*;

'We express our deep concern that at the beginning of the 21st century 1.2 billion people live a life of poverty without access to safe drinking water, and that almost 2.5 billion have no access to proper sanitation. Safe and sufficient water and sanitation are basic human needs. The worldwide struggle to alleviate poverty must bring safe and decent living conditions to those who are deprived of these basic requirements' (Ministerial Declaration, signed by over 60 ministers who attended the Bonn Conference, 2001).

- Improve access to **public information and participation** (including by women) to support decision-making on water resources management *[25b]*;
- Promote priority action by governments on **water management** and capacity-building. Provide finance and technologies to implement Chapter 18 of Agenda 21 *[25c]*;
- Intensify **water pollution** prevention through affordable sanitation technologies, wastewater treatment, lessening the effects of groundwater contamination, and monitoring systems and legal frameworks *[25d]*; and
- Adopt prevention and protection measures to promote **sustainable water use** and address water shortages *[25e]*.

Integrated water resources management

The JPOI agrees a new target to develop **integrated water resources management and water efficiency plans by 2005**, with support to developing countries *[26]* through actions to:

- Develop national/regional strategies and programmes on **integrated river basin, watershed and groundwater management** and introduce measures to improve **efficiency** in water infrastructure, reducing losses and increasing **water recycling** *[26a]*;
- Employ the **full range of policy instruments**, without cost recovery becoming a barrier to poor people accessing safe water, and adopt an integrated water basin approach *[26b]*;
- Improve the **efficient use** of water resources. Allocate them among **competing uses**, giving priority to basic human needs, and balancing needs to preserve and restore ecosystems with human domestic, industrial and agricultural needs *[26c]*;
- Reduce the effects of **extreme water-related events** *[26d]*;
- Support the spread of technology and capacity-building for **non-conventional water resources** and conservation to developing countries and regions facing water scarcity *[26e]*;

- Support energy-efficient and cost-effective **desalination** of seawater, **water recycling** and **water harvesting from coastal fogs** in developing countries *[26f]*; and
- Use public/private and other forms of partnership that are transparent, accountable and give priority to people living in poverty *[26g]*.

The JPOI supports countries in their efforts to **monitor and assess the quantity and quality of water resources** *[27]* and calls for action to improve:

- Water resources management and scientific understanding of the **water cycle**, through joint observation and research, knowledge-sharing, capacity-building and technology transfer, including **remote sensing and satellite** technologies *[28]*; and
- Coordination among international and intergovernmental bodies/processes working on water issues through the International Year of Freshwater 2003 and beyond *[29]*.

Sustainable development of oceans, seas, islands and coastal areas

Oceans, seas, islands and coastal areas are an essential component of the Earth's ecosystem and are critical for global food security and for sustaining nations' economic development and well-being, particularly in developing countries. To secure the sustainable development of the oceans *[30]*, actions at all levels will:

- Invite states to ratify and implement the **United Nations Convention on the Law of the Sea** *[30a]*;
- Promote implementation of Chapter 17 of Agenda 21, which provides the programme of action for achieving the sustainable development of oceans, coastal areas and seas *[30b]*;
- Establish an **inter-agency coordination mechanism** on ocean and coastal issues within the UN system *[30c]*;
- Apply the **ecosystems approach** by 2010 *[30d]*;
- Promote **integrated coastal and ocean management** at the national level, assisting coastal states to developing ocean policies and measures in this area *[30e]*;
- Strengthen **regional cooperation** between organizations and programmes *[30f]*;
- Assist developing countries in coordinating policies/programmes at regional and sub-regional levels, aimed at **conservation and sustainable management of fishery resources**. Implement **integrated coastal area management plans** *[30g]*; and
- Note the work and review of the UN's open-ended informal consultative process to facilitate an annual review of developments in ocean affairs *[30h]*.

'Sanitation is a dirty word in most societies. Many people, including politicians, seem to prefer other more savoury topics. Often sanitation programmes are tacked on to water projects as an afterthought. This must stop. Sanitation is now a crucial issue in its own right' (cited in Water Aid and Tearfund, 2002).

Sustainable fisheries

To achieve **sustainable fisheries** *[31]*, action will be taken to:

- Maintain or restore fish stocks to levels that can produce the **maximum sustainable yield**, achieving this goal urgently for depleted stocks, if possible by 2015 *[31a]*;
- Ratify/accede to relevant UN and associated regional fisheries agreements and arrangements, including those on **straddling and highly migratory fish stocks**, and conservation and management **measures by fishing vessels on the high seas** *[31b]*;
- Implement the 1995 Code of Conduct for Responsible Fisheries *[31c]*;
- Urgently develop national and regional plans of action to put into effect the **Food and Agriculture Organization (FAO) international action plans** on management of fishing capacity (by 2005) and on illegal, unreported and unregulated fishing (by 2004). Use effective monitoring, reporting and enforcement systems, and **control of fishing vessels**, to achieve the international plan of action to prevent and eliminate **illegal, unreported and unregulated fishing** *[31d]*;
- Encourage fisheries management organizations to give due consideration to the **rights, duties and interests of coastal states**, and the special requirements of developing states, when addressing the issue of the allocations of the share of fishery resources for straddling stocks and highly migratory fish stocks *[31e]*;
- Remove **subsidies** that contribute to illegal, unreported and unregulated fishing, and overcapacity, while completing efforts at the World Trade Organization (WTO) to clarify and improve its disciplines on fisheries subsidies *[31f]*;
- Strengthen **donor coordination and partnerships** between international financial institutions, bilateral agencies and others to help countries to build their capacities in the sustainable management and use of fisheries *[31g]*; and
- Support the sustainable development of **aquaculture**, including small-scale aquaculture *[31h]*.

Conservation and management of oceans

The JPOI promotes conservation and management of the oceans *[32]* through actions at all levels to:

- Maintain the productivity and biodiversity of important and vulnerable marine and coastal areas *[32a]*;
- Implement work under the **Jakarta Mandate** of the Convention on Biological Diversity (CBD) on the conservation and sustainable use of marine and coastal biological diversity *[32b]*;

'More effective prevention strategies would save not only tens of billions of dollars, but save tens of thousands of lives. Funds currently spent on intervention and relief could be devoted to enhancing equitable and sustainable development instead, which would further reduce the risk for war and disaster. Building a culture of prevention is not easy. While the costs of prevention have to be paid in the present, its benefits lie in a distant future. Moreover, the benefits are not tangible; they are the disasters that did NOT happen' (UN Secretary-General Kofi Annan, 1999).

- Adopt diverse approaches, including the ecosystem approach; elimination of destructive fishing practices; **establishment of marine protected areas**, including representative networks by 2012 and **time/area closures** for the protection of nursery grounds/periods; and **integrated planning and management**, including watersheds [32c];
- Develop programmes to halt the loss of **marine biodiversity**, including coral reefs and wetlands [32d]; and
- Implement the **Ramsar Convention**, its joint work programme with the CBD and the **International Coral Reef Initiative** to strengthen activities covering wetland ecosystems in coastal zones, such as **coral reefs, mangroves, seaweed beds and tidal mud flats** [32e].

The JPOI also advances implementation of the **Global Programme of Action** (GPA) for the Protection of the Marine Environment from Land-based Activities and the Montreal Declaration on the Protection of the Marine Environment from Land-based Activities, with an emphasis between 2002 and 2006 on **municipal wastewater**, the physical alteration and destruction of **habitats** and **nutrients** [33]. Actions will:

- Facilitate partnerships, resources, scientific research, capacity-building and the diffusion of technical knowledge [33a];
- Strengthen capacities to **mainstream the GPA** in national plans [33b];
- Elaborate **regional action** and improve links with strategic plans that cover the sustainable development of coastal and marine resources [33c]; and
- Make every effort to achieve **substantial progress** by the GPA conference in 2006 [33d].

Maritime safety and pollution

To improve **maritime safety** and protection of the marine environment from **pollution** [34], action will be taken to:

- Invite states to ratify/implement relevant instruments of the International Maritime Organization (IMO), including those on **environmental damage caused by ships** and the use of **toxic anti-fouling paints**. Urge the IMO to consider stronger mechanisms to secure implementation [34a]; and
- Accelerate measures to address **alien species in ballast water** [34b].

The JPOI calls for efforts to examine/improve measures and internationally agreed regulations related to safety that are relevant to the international maritime transportation and other transboundary movement of **radioactive materials**, radioactive waste and spent fuel, recognizing the importance of having effective **liability mechanisms** in place [35].

To improve the **scientific understanding and assessment of marine and coastal ecosystems** in support of decision-making [36], action will be taken to:

'Hunger, which afflicts one in five of the developing world's people, is a profound impediment to the advancement of individuals and societies. Without proper intervention, undernutrition and the death and disease it causes are repeated with each generation. The hungry suffer in silence and are often invisible: to the casual observer, many of them show no outward sign of the severity of their hunger' (FAO, undated).

4

- Increase **scientific/technical collaboration** including integrated assessments, transfer of marine science, technology and techniques for conservation and management, and expanded ocean-observing capacities *[36a]*;
- Establish,by 2004, a **regular UN process** for global reporting on the state of the marine environment, including the socio-economic aspects *[36b]*;
- Build capacity in **marine science, information and management**, promoting environmental impact assessments and environmental evaluation and reporting techniques for projects/activities that could harm marine/coastal ecosystems *[36c]*; and
- Strengthen the ability of the United Nations Educational, Scientific and Cultural Organization's (UNESCO's) Intergovernmental Oceanographic Commission, the FAO and others to build capacity in marine science and the sustainable management of oceans *[36d]*.

Vulnerability, risk assessment and disaster management

'Rapid urban growth, particularly when it is accompanied by a large influx of poor migrants from rural areas, is one of the main factors contributing to increased vulnerability to natural hazards in many parts of the world'
(ISDR, 2002).

An integrated and multi-hazard approach to addressing **vulnerability, risk assessment and disaster management** is an essential element of a safer world. This encompasses all aspects from prevention, mitigation and preparedness, to response and recovery *[37]*. Actions are required to:

- Strengthen the **role of the International Strategy for Disaster Reduction (ISDR)** *[37a]*;
- Establish effective **regional and national strategies** and scientific/technical institutional support for disaster management *[37b]*;
- Strengthen **institutional capacities** and promote joint international **observation/research**, including surface-based monitoring and satellite data *[37c]*;
- Reduce risks of **flooding and drought** in vulnerable countries. Promote **wetland and watershed** protection and restoration and better land-use planning. Widely apply techniques to assess potentially negative effects of climate change on wetlands *[37d]*;
- Improve techniques for assessing effects of climate change. Encourage the Intergovernmental Panel on Climate Change (IPCC) to continue to assess those adverse effects *[37e]*;
- Encourage the use of **traditional and indigenous knowledge** to lessen the impact of disasters. Promote **community-based disaster management planning** by local authorities *[37f]*;
- Support the voluntary contribution of NGOs, the scientific community and others to managing natural disasters *[37g]*;
- Strengthen **early warning systems** and information networks, consistent with the ISDR *[37h]*;

- Develop capacities to collect and disseminate scientific/technical information, including improved early warning systems for extreme weather events such as **El Niño/La Niña** *[37i]*; and
- Cooperate to prevent and address major **technological disasters** and other disasters that affect the environment *[37j]*.

Climate

Changes in the Earth's **climate** and its adverse effects are a common concern of humankind. All countries face increased risks from climate change and, as a result of this, poverty, land degradation, human health, and access to water and food remain at the centre of global attention. The United Nations Framework Convention on Climate Change (UNFCCC) is the key instrument for addressing climate change. In the UN Millennium Declaration, heads of state and government agreed to make every effort to ensure that the **Kyoto Protocol** to the UNFCCC came into force, preferably by the Rio anniversary in 2002, and to embark on the required cuts in greenhouse gas emissions. States that have ratified the Kyoto Protocol strongly urge states that have not done so to ratify the Kyoto Protocol in a timely way *[38]*. Actions are required at all levels to:

- Meet all UNFCCC commitments and obligations *[38a]*;
- Work cooperatively to achieve its objectives *[38b]*;
- Assist developing countries and countries with economies in transition in accordance with the UNFCCC and Marrakech accords *[38c]*;
- Build **scientific and technical capabilities** with continuing support to the IPCC in exchanging data and information *[38d]*;
- Develop and transfer **technological solutions** *[38e]*;
- Develop and transfer **innovative technology** in key sectors of development such as energy *[38f]*;
- Promote systematic **observation and monitoring** of the Earth's atmosphere, land and oceans by improving monitoring stations, increasing satellite use and producing high-quality data for all countries to use *[38g]*;
- Improve implementation of strategies to monitor the Earth's atmosphere, land and oceans, including integrated global observations *[38h]*; and
- Support initiatives, such as the Arctic Council initiative, that assess the consequences of climate change and impacts on **local and indigenous communities** *[38i]*.

Air pollution and atmosphere

In order to effectively reduce **air pollution** (including transboundary pollution, acid deposition and ozone depletion), better cooperation and action at all levels is required, bearing in mind the Rio principles, including the recognition that states have different but common responsibilities in view of their different

'The physical characteristics of mountains have made them important strongholds of biological and cultural diversity. Their remoteness, difficulty of access and rugged terrain have combined to make them among the last places on Earth to be exploited and developed … the reverence that mountains tend to awaken in cultures around the world provides a powerful source of motivation for preserving biodiversity' (Bernbaum, 1999).

contributions to global environmental degradation *[39]*. Action at all levels will help to:

- Strengthen the ability of developing countries and countries with economies in transition to measure, reduce and assess the impacts of air pollution, including **health impacts** *[39a]*;
- Implement the **Montreal Protocol** on Substances that Deplete the Ozone Layer by ensuring an adequate replenishment of its fund by 2003/2005 *[39b]*;
- Support the regime for protection of the ozone layer established in the Vienna Convention and the Montreal Protocol *[39c]*;
- Improve access by developing countries to suitable alternatives to **ozone-depleting substances** by 2010 and help them to comply with the Montreal Protocol's phase-out schedule *[39d]*; and
- Take measures to address illegal traffic in ozone-depleting substances *[39e]*.

'Our planet's essential goods and services depend upon the variety and variability of genes, species, populations and ecosystems. Biological resources feed and clothe us and provide housing, medicines and spiritual nourishment ... the current decline in biodiversity is largely the result of human activity and represents a serious threat to human development' (Agenda 21, 1992, Chapter 15).

Agriculture

Agriculture helps to address the needs of a growing global population and is inextricably linked to poverty eradication. A greater role for **women** is imperative in all aspects of rural development, agriculture, nutrition and food security. **Sustainable agriculture and rural development** are essential to an integrated and environmentally sustainable approach that both increases food production and improves **food security** *[40]*, and require actions to:

- Halve, by the year 2015, the proportion of people who suffer from **hunger** and realize the right to a standard of living, including food, that is adequate for health and well-being. Promote **food security** and fight hunger in combination with anti-poverty measures that are consistent with the World Food Summit outcomes and obligations under the International Covenant on Economic, Social and Cultural Rights *[40a]*;
- Implement **integrated land management and water-use plans**, strengthening the ability of governments, local authorities and communities to monitor and manage those plans *[40b]*;
- Increase understanding of the sustainable use, protection and management of **water resources** *[40c]*;
- Enhance the **sustainable productivity of land and efficient use of water** in agriculture, forestry, wetlands, artisanal fisheries and aquaculture, paying attention to indigenous and local community-based approaches *[40d]*;
- Help developing countries to protect **oases** from silt, land degradation and increasing salinity *[40e]*;
- Improve the participation of **women** in sustainable agriculture and food security *[40f]*;
- Strengthen national research and extension services and farmer organizations to spread **good practice and integrate existing information systems on land-use practices** *[40g]*;

- Protect **indigenous resource management systems** and support the contribution of all stakeholders to rural planning and development *[40h]*;
- Guarantee well-defined and enforceable **land and water rights**, and **security of land tenure**, recognizing that there are different laws and systems of land access and tenure, and providing assistance with land reform *[40i]*;
- Reverse the decline of public-sector **finance** for sustainable agriculture and promote private-sector investment in agricultural research and natural resource management *[40j]*;
- Employ **market-based incentives** to encourage agricultural enterprises and farmers to manage water wisely, using methods such as **small-scale irrigation and wastewater recycling and reuse** *[40k]*;
- Improve access to existing **markets** and develop new markets for value-added agricultural products *[40l]*;
- Increase **brown-field redevelopment** *[40m]*;
- Enhance international cooperation to combat the illicit cultivation of narcotic plants *[40n]*;
- Promote environmentally sound, effective and efficient techniques for **soil fertility** and agricultural **pest control** *[40o]*;
- Coordinate existing initiatives on sustainable agriculture and food security *[40p]*;
- Invite countries that have not done so to ratify the **International Treaty on Plant Genetic Resources for Food and Agriculture** *[40q]*; and
- Promote the conservation, sustainable use and management of traditional and **indigenous agricultural systems**. Strengthen indigenous models of agriculture production *[40r]*.

Desertification and drought

To address the causes of **desertification and land degradation**, restore land and address poverty resulting from desertification, the JPOI outlines requirements for **strengthening implementation** of the **United Nations Convention to Combat Desertification** (CCD) *[41]*. They include actions to:

- Mobilize **finance, transfer technologies and building capacity** *[41a]*;
- Formulate **national action programmes**, backed by decentralized local projects *[41b]*;
- Encourage the CCD, the CBD and the UNFCCC to continue to exploring potential **areas of mutual benefit** *[41c]*;
- Integrate measures addressing **desertification** and the effects of **drought** in sectors such as land, water, forests, agriculture, rural development, early warning systems, environment, energy, natural resources, health and education, poverty and sustainable development *[41d]*;
- Provide affordable local access to information to improve monitoring and **early warning** *[41e]*;

'The term 'biodiversity' does not exist in my people's understanding or language. If I were to translate the term in our language, I would say it is everything in this world, down in the sea and things that we can touch. At the same time, it is more than this – more than just things that can be touched or things that are alive. The air, the water and the sun must also be included. If one being or part of biodiversity is disturbed or not kept in the perfect manner, an imbalance is created which will affect all other things' (Segundad, 2001).

- Call on the **Global Environment Facility** (GEF) Assembly to designate land degradation (desertification and deforestation) as a focal area and consider making GEF the financial mechanism of the CCD *[41f]*; and
- Improve the sustainability of **grassland** resources through better management, law enforcement and support *[41g]*.

Mountains

Mountain ecosystems support particular livelihoods, and include significant watershed resources, biological diversity and a unique flora and fauna. Many of these ecosystems are fragile and vulnerable to the effects of climate change *[42]*. Action is needed to:

- Integrate **environmental, economic and social components of sustainable mountain development** at policy and programme levels and strengthen international cooperation to improve **poverty eradication** initiatives *[42a]*;
- Address deforestation, erosion, land degradation, loss of biodiversity, disruption of water flows and the retreat of glaciers *[42b]*;
- Implement **gender-sensitive** policies aimed at eliminating the inequities facing mountain communities *[42c]*;
- **Promote diversification and traditional mountain economies**, sustainable livelihoods and small-scale production systems *[42d]*;
- Promote the full participation and involvement of mountain communities in decisions that affect them and **integrate indigenous** knowledge, heritage and values in all development initiatives *[42e]*; and
- Mobilize support for applied research and capacity-building, provide assistance for the sustainable development of mountain ecosystems, and reduce poverty among people living in mountain areas, taking into account the spirit of the International Year of Mountains in 2002 *[42f]*.

'By degrading forests, engineering rivers, filling in wetlands and destabilizing the climate, we are unravelling the strands of a complex ecological safety net... We have altered so many natural systems so dramatically, their ability to protect us from disturbances is greatly diminished' (Abramovitz, 2001).

Sustainable tourism

The JPOI promotes **sustainable tourism** (including non-consumptive and ecotourism) to increase the benefits flowing from tourism resources to local populations, while maintaining cultural and environmental integrity, protecting ecologically sensitive areas and natural heritages, and strengthening rural and local communities *[43]*. Actions will be taken to:

- Improve international cooperation, foreign direct investment and partnerships *[43a]*;
- Develop programmes, including education/training, that encourage people to participate in ecotourism and enable indigenous local communities to benefit *[43b]*;
- Provide technical assistance to support **sustainable tourism business** development, investment and **tourism awareness** programmes *[43c]*;

- Assist host communities in **managing visits** to maximize the benefits while ensuring the least impact on, or risk to, traditions, culture and the environment *[43d]*; and
- Promote **diversification of economic activities**, including access to markets and commercial information, and participation of emerging local enterprises, especially small- and medium-sized enterprises (SMEs) *[43e]*.

Biodiversity

Biodiversity plays a critical role in sustainable development and poverty eradication. It is essential to the functioning and systems of the planet, human well-being, livelihoods and the cultural integrity of people. However, biodiversity is being lost at an unprecedented rate due to human activities: this trend can only be reversed through enabling local people to benefit from conservation and sustainable use of biological diversity, particularly in countries of origin of genetic resources, as noted in Article 15 of the **Convention on Biological Diversity** (CBD). This convention is the key agreement for the **conservation and sustainable use of biological diversity**, and the **fair and equitable sharing of benefits** arising from the use of genetic resources. Achieving a **significant reduction** in the current rate of loss of biological diversity by 2010, and a more coherent implementation of the three objectives of the CBD, requires new and additional resources for developing countries *[44]* and actions to:

'It is imperative we do more to ensure that mining's [environmental] fallout is mitigated and that local communities – in particular, the millions of artisanal miners – share in the benefits' (UN Secretary-General Kofi Annan, 2002).

- Integrate **CBD objectives** within programmes and policies, especially in economic sectors and international financial institutions *[44a]*;
- Promote ongoing **work under the CBD** on the sustainable use of biological diversity (including sustainable tourism) as a cross-cutting issue *[44b]*;
- Encourage effective links between the CBD and other **multilateral environmental agreements** *[44c]*;
- Implement the CBD through national, regional and global action programmes, particularly **national biodiversity strategies and action plans**. Strengthen their integration into relevant cross-sectoral strategies for sustainable development and poverty eradication, including **community-based use of biological diversity** *[44d]*;
- Promote use of the **ecosystem approach** elaborated through the CBD *[44e]*;
- Promote **international support and partnerships** for the conservation and sustainable use of biodiversity in ecosystems at **World Heritage sites** and to protect **endangered species** *[44f]*;
- Support initiatives for biodiversity **hot spot areas** and the development of national and regional **ecological networks and corridors** *[44g]*;
- Enhance indigenous and community-based biodiversity conservation in developing countries *[44h]*;
- Strengthen control of **invasive alien species** *[44i]*;

- Recognize the rights of local and indigenous communities who are **holders of traditional knowledge**, innovations and practices. With their involvement and approval, develop **benefit-sharing** mechanisms for the use of such knowledge *[44j]*;
- Encourage **all stakeholders** to contribute to CBD implementation, recognizing the role of youth, women and indigenous and local communities in conserving and using biodiversity in a sustainable way *[44k]*;
- Promote effective participation of **indigenous and local communities** in decisions and policy-making concerning the use of their traditional knowledge *[44l]*;
- Support efforts to develop and implement national **sui generis systems** and **traditional systems** *[44m]*;
- Promote implementation of, and work on, the Bonn Guidelines on Access to Genetic Resources and Fair and Equitable Sharing of Benefits Arising out of Their Utilization *[44n]*;
- Negotiate under the CBD an international **regime to promote and safeguard fair and equitable sharing of benefits** arising out of the use of genetic resources *[44o]*;
- Encourage successful conclusion of processes under the World Intellectual Property Organization Intergovernmental Committee on **Intellectual Property and Genetic Resources, Traditional Knowledge and Folklore**, and work on **Article 8(j)** of the CBD *[44p]*;
- Promote measures for access to the results and benefits arising from **biotechnologies** based on genetic resources *[44q]*;
- Promote discussions on relationships between the **CBD** and agreements related to international **trade and intellectual property rights**, as outlined in the Doha Ministerial Declaration, to enhance synergy and mutual supportiveness, but without prejudging the outcomes *[44r]*;
- Promote implementation of the work programme of the **Global Taxonomy Initiative** *[44s]*; and
- Invite all states that have not ratified the **CBD, the Cartagena Protocol on Biosafety** and other biodiversity-related agreements to do so, encouraging signatories to promote effective implementation *[44t]*.

Forests

Sustainable forest management of both natural and planted forests, and for timber and non-timber forest products, is essential to sustainable development. It is a way of eradicating poverty, reducing deforestation, halting the loss of biodiversity, cutting land and resource degradation, improving food security, and providing access to safe drinking water and affordable energy. Achieving sustainable forest management is an essential goal of sustainable development *[45]* and requires actions to:

- Increase political commitment to sustainable forest management, setting it as a priority on the international political agenda *[45a]*;
- Support the United Nations Forum on Forests (with the assistance of the Collaborative Partnership on Forests) to act as the key intergovernmental mechanism for sustainable forest management *[45b]*;
- Take immediate action to enforce **domestic forest law** and tackle **illegal international trade in forest products** (including forest biological resources) *[45c]*;
- Take immediate action to achieve **sustainable timber harvesting** *[45d]*;
- Address the needs of areas currently suffering from **poverty** and the highest rates of deforestation, where international cooperation would be welcomed by affected governments *[45e]*;
- Strengthen **partnerships and international cooperation** to facilitate increased finance, transfer of environmentally sound technologies, trade, capacity-building, forest law and governance, and integrated land and resource management *[45f]*;
- Accelerate implementation of proposals made by the **United Nations Intergovernmental Panel on Forests/Intergovernmental Forum on Forests**, and intensify reporting to the United Nations Forum on Forests to contribute to an assessment of progress in 2005 *[45g]*;
- Recognize/support **indigenous and community-based forest management systems** to ensure their full participation in sustainable forest management *[45h]*; and
- Implement the CBD's work programme on all types of forest biodiversity *[45i]*.

Mining, minerals and metals

Mining, minerals and metals make an important contribution to the economic and social development of many countries *[46]*. Enhancing this contribution to sustainable development requires action at all levels to:

- Address **environmental, economic, health** and **social impacts** and benefits of mining, minerals and metals throughout their life cycle, including work on **workers' health and safety** and partnerships to **promote accountability** for sustainable mining and minerals development *[46a]*;
- Improve the **participation of stakeholders** (including local and indigenous communities and women) to help them play an active role in minerals, metals and mining development, throughout the life cycle of mining operations and taking into account national regulations and significant transboundary impacts *[46b]*; and
- Foster **sustainable mining practices** through support for mining and processing of minerals, including small-scale activities. Where appropriate, this includes better value-added processing, upgrading of scientific and technical information, and efforts to reclaim and rehabilitate degraded sites *[46c]*.

Managing the natural resources base elsewhere in the JPOI

Managing the natural resources base for development is one of the three overarching objectives of, and essential requirements for, sustainable development in the JPOI (Chapter I), and references to natural resources are a continuous thread through all chapters. Many targets, including those on safe drinking water, sanitation, integrated water resource management and chemicals, are closely related to a reversal of trends in environmental degradation, as is the need to maintain the natural resource base to ensure sustainable livelihoods for the poor. Approaches to changing unsustainable patterns of resources use are outlined in Chapter III, while measures to ensure that globalization is managed in a framework that enables rather than inhibits effective natural resources management are addressed in Chapters V and XI.

TARGETS AND COMMITMENTS

Drinking water. Halve, by the year 2015, the proportion of people without access to safe drinking water *[25]* (MDG).

Sanitation. Halve, by the year 2015, the proportion of people who do not have access to basic sanitation *[25]* (new target).

Integrated water management. Develop integrated water resources management and water efficiency plans by 2005 *[26]* (new target).

Ecosystem approach for oceans. Encourage the application, by 2010, of the ecosystem approach for the sustainable development of the oceans *[30d]* (new target).

Fish stocks. On an urgent basis, and where possible by 2015, maintain or restore depleted fish stocks to levels that can produce the maximum sustainable yield *[31a]* (new target).

Marine environment. Use of diverse approaches and tools, including ecosystem approach, elimination of destructive fishing practices and establishment of marine protected areas, including representative networks by 2012 *[32c]* (new target).

Global oceans reporting. Establish, by 2004, a regular process under the UN for global reporting and assessment of the state of the marine environment *[36b]* (new target).

FAO action plans. Put into effect FAO international plans of action by agreed dates: for the management of fishing capacity, by 2005; and to prevent, deter and eliminate illegal, unreported and unregulated fishing, by 2004 *[31d]*.

TARGETS AND COMMITMENTS (CONTD)

- **Fishing.** Eliminate subsidies that contribute to illegal, unreported and unregulated fishing and to overcapacity [31f].

- **Inter-agency coordination on marine issues.** Establish an effective, transparent and regular inter-agency coordination mechanism on ocean and coastal issues within the UN system [30c].

- **Ozone fund.** Ensure adequate replenishment of the Montreal Protocol fund by 2003/2005 [39b].

- **Access to ozone-depleting alternatives.** Improve access by developing countries to alternatives to ozone-depleting substances by 2010; assist them with the Montreal Protocol phase-out schedule [39d] (new target).

- **Biodiversity loss.** Achieve, by 2010, a significant reduction in the current rate of loss of biological diversity [44].

- **Forest reporting.** Intensify efforts on reporting to the United Nations Forum on Forests to contribute to an assessment of progress in 2005 [45g] (new target).

- **Implementation of Intergovernmental Panel on Forests/Intergovernmental Forum on Forests (IPF/IFF) proposals.** Accelerate implementation of the IPF/IFF proposals for action by countries and by the Collaborative Partnership on Forests [45g].

EXAMPLES OF INDICATORS FOR MEASURING PROGRESS IN IMPLEMENTATION

- Proportion of population with sustainable access to an improved water source, urban and rural (Millennium Development Goal, or MDG)

- Proportion of urban population with access to improved sanitation (MDG)

- Percentage of population with adequate sewage disposal facilities (Commission on Sustainable Development, or CSD)

- Population with access to safe drinking water (CSD)

- Water consumption, price of water (United Nations Human Settlements Programme, or UN-Habitat)

- Concentration of faecal coliform in freshwater (CSD)

- Biological oxygen demand (BOD) in water bodies (CSD)

EXAMPLES OF INDICATORS FOR MEASURING PROGRESS IN IMPLEMENTATION (CONTD)

- Percentage of total population living in coastal areas (CSD)

- Algae concentration in coastal waters (CSD)

- Annual catch by major species (CSD)

- Economic and human loss due to natural disasters (CSD)

- Disaster prevention and mitigation instruments (UN-Habitat)

- Carbon dioxide emissions (per capita) and consumption of ozone-depleting chlorofluorocarbons (CFCs) (ozone depleting potential (ODP) tonnes) (MDG)

- Proportion of population using solid fuels (MDG)

- Emissions of greenhouse gases (CSD)

- Consumption of ozone-depleting substances (CSD)

- Ambient concentration of air pollutants in urban areas (CSD)

- Prevalence of underweight children under five years of age (MDG)

- Proportion of population below minimum level of dietary energy consumption (MDG)

- Agricultural support estimate for Organisation for Economic Co-operation and Development (OECD) countries as percentage of their gross domestic product (GDP) (MDG)

- Arable and permanent crop land area (CSD)

- Use of fertilizers (CSD)

- Use of agricultural pesticides (CSD)

- Water availability and quality (UN Food and Agriculture Organization (FAO) Food Security Indicator)

- Soil quality (FAO Food Security Indicator)

- Crop diversity (FAO Food Security Indicator)

- Land tenure, access and control (FAO Food Security Indicator)

- Land affected by desertification (CSD)'

- Ratio of area protected to maintain biological diversity to surface area (MDG)

- Area of selected key ecosystems (CSD)

- Protected area as a percentage of total area (CSD)

EXAMPLES OF INDICATORS FOR MEASURING PROGRESS IN IMPLEMENTATION (CONTD)

- Abundance of selected key species (CSD)
- Proportion of land area covered by forest (MDG)
- Forest area as a percentage of land area (CSD)
- Wood harvesting intensity (CSD)
- Forest resource access (FAO Food Security Indicator)

Partnership example

International Partnership for Sustainable Development in Mountain Regions

Leading partners: United Nations Food and Agriculture Organization (FAO) – International Year of Mountains Coordination Unit and United Nations Environment Programme (UNEP) Mountain Programme.

Dates: 2002–2012

- Improve, strengthen and promote greater cooperation between major groups, all mountain stakeholders, such as donors, implementing agencies, non-governmental organizations (NGOs), the private sector, mountain communities, academia and other field practitioners.

- Focus on the effective implementation of prioritized actions to manage mountain ecosystems through sustainable development and to address chronic poverty in mountain regions through concrete programmes and support from all stakeholders.

- Provide an instrument to implement the Johannesburg Plan of Implementation (JPOI) commitments on mountains (paragraph 42), intended as a way to further implement Chapter 13 of Agenda 21.

- Allow all partners to enter into specific sub-partnerships that could be organized around thematic areas of action – for example, biodiversity conservation, food security and poverty alleviation – or geographic regions or institutional concerns (for example, mountain policy and law).

- Enhance linkages with existing multilateral instruments, such as the United Nations Convention on Biological Diversity (CBD), the United Nations Convention to Combat Desertification (CCD), the United Nations Framework Convention on Climate Change (UNFCCC), the International Strategy for Disaster Reduction (ISDR) and others.

Partnership example (*contd*)

Partners involved include governments (Austria, Bhutan, Ghana, Indonesia, Italy, Jordan, Kyrgyz Republic, Lao Republic, Monaco, Peru, Sri Lanka, Switzerland, US, Venezuela – as of August 2002); intergovernmental organizations, including FAO, UNEP, the United Nations Educational, Scientific and Cultural Organization (UNESCO), the United Nations Development Programme (UNDP), the United Nations Population Fund (UNFPA) and CBD; development banks and research centres; and major groups, including the Mountain Forum, the World Conservation Union (IUCN), the Banff Centre for Mountain Coordination, the World Mountain People Association, the World Wide Fund for Nature (WWF-International) and the European Observatory of Mountain Forests.

Resources

Water and sanitation

International Year of Freshwater (2003)

www.wateryear2003.org

The International Year of Freshwater focused the attention of individuals, communities, countries and the global family of concerned citizens on protecting and respecting our water resources.

Oceans, seas and marine resources

Agreement on the Conservation and Management of Straddling Fish Stocks and Highly Migratory Fish Stocks (1995)

www.un.org/Depts/los/fish_stocks_conference/fish_stocks_conference.htm

This agreement ensures long-term conservation and sustainable use of straddling fish stocks and highly migratory fish stocks. It covers fish stocks occurring within the exclusive economic zones (EEZs) of two or more coastal states, or both within and beyond the EEZ.

United Nations Food and Agriculture Organization (FAO)

www.fao.org

The FAO is mandated to raise levels of nutrition and standards of living in order to improve agricultural and marine productivity. Fishery concerns include the 1995 Code of Conduct for Responsible Fisheries.

Global Programme of Action for Protection of the Marine Environment from Land-based Activities (GPA), Montreal Declaration

www.gpa.unep.org

The GPA prevents degradation of the marine environment from land-based activities by facilitating the duty of states to preserve and protect the marine environment. It supports an integrated management approach, and mobilizes support for developing countries' activities. Its review in 2001 resulted in the Montreal Declaration.

Intergovernmental Oceanographic Commission (IOC)

www.ioc.unesco.org

The IOC supports oceanic research programmes to increase knowledge about marine resources and their relationship to sustainable development.

International Atomic Energy Agency (IAEA)

www.iaea.org

The IAEA is an intergovernmental forum for scientific and technical cooperation that promotes nuclear safety and non-proliferation.

International Coral Reef Initiative (ICRI)

www.icriforum.org

The ICRI was established in 1994 to stop and reverse the global degradation of coral reefs and ecosystems, including seagrass beds and mangrove forests. The partnership exists to implement Agenda 21 and other agreements related to coral reefs.

International Maritime Organization (IMO)

www.imo.org

The IMO is a UN body concerned with maritime legislation that addresses marine pollution, including through the International Convention for the Prevention of Pollution from Ships, 1973 (MARPOL regime) and related protocols, as well as the movement of hazardous materials, dumping at sea, illegal fishing and invasive species.

International Plan of Action to Prevent, Deter and Eliminate Illegal, Unreported and Unregulated Fishing (2001)

www.fao.org

Addressing the crisis in world fisheries, this non-binding international plan includes activities both on the high seas and within EEZs.

Jakarta Mandate on the Conservation and Sustainable Use of Marine and Coastal Biological Diversity

www.biodiv.org/programmes/areas/marine

Agreed under the United Nations Convention on Biological Diversity (CBD), this mandate focuses on integrated marine and coastal area management, sustainable use of living resources, protected areas, mariculture and alien species.

Ramsar Convention (1971)

www.ramsar.org

The Ramsar Convention is a framework for national action and international cooperation on the conservation and wise use of wetlands (including mangroves/coral reefs) and their resources.

Reykjavik Declaration on Responsible Fisheries (1995)

www.fao.org

This is a voluntary FAO code of conduct that provides principles and standards on the conservation, management and development of fisheries. It also covers the capture, processing and trade of fish and fishery products, fishing operations, aquaculture, research and integrating fisheries within coastal area management.

United Nations Convention on the Law of the Sea (1982)

*www.un.org/Depts/los/convention_agreements/convention_overview_
convention.htm*

This is a globally recognized comprehensive regime that deals with all matters relating to the law of the sea.

United Nations Environment Programme (UNEP) Regional Seas Programme

www.gpa.unep.org/seas/seas.htm

Initiated in 1974, this programme adopts a regional approach to controlling marine pollution and managing marine and coastal resources. It is a means of implementing the GPA.

Vulnerability, risk assessment, disaster management

International Strategy for Disaster Reduction (ISDR)

www.unisdr.org

This is a UN coordinating mechanism on disaster reduction. It supports policy integration, serves as an international information clearinghouse, develops awareness campaigns, and produces articles, journals and other materials related to disaster reduction.

Climate and atmosphere

Arctic Council

www.arctic-council.org
The Arctic Council is a high-level intergovernmental forum that addresses challenges faced by Arctic governments and peoples. Its members are Canada, Denmark, Finland, Iceland, Norway, Russian Federation, Sweden and the US.

Intergovernmental Panel on Climate Change (IPCC)

www.ipcc.ch/index.html
Established by the World Meteorological Organization (WMO) and UNEP, the IPCC assesses published scientific, technical and socio-economic information relevant to understanding the risk of human-induced climate change, its potential impacts and the options for adaptation and mitigation.

Marrakesh Accords

Agreed at the 7th Convention of the Parties to the UNFCCC in 2001, the Marrakesh Accords, among other things, detail the rules, modalities and guidelines for the implementation of the Kyoto Protocol Flexible Mechanism

United Nations Framework Convention on Climate Change (UNFCCC) (1992), Kyoto Protocol

www.unfccc.int
The objective of the UNFCCC is to stabilize greenhouse gas concentrations in the atmosphere at a level that would prevent dangerous anthropogenic interference with the climate system. It should occur within a time frame that is sufficient to allow ecosystems to adapt naturally to climate change, to ensure that food production is not threatened, and to enable economic development to occur in a sustainable manner. The Kyoto Protocol (1997) sets legally binding targets to cut greenhouse gas emissions.

Vienna Convention for the Protection of the Ozone Layer and the Montreal Protocol on Substances that Deplete the Ozone Layer

www.unep.org/ozone
This convention aims to protect human health and the environment from the effects of ozone depletion by controlling the production and consumption of ozone-depleting substances (ODS) and by phasing them out to an agreed schedule. It takes the circumstances of developing countries into account in implementing measures.

4

Agriculture

International Treaty on Plant Genetic Resources for Food and Agriculture (2001)

www.fao.org/ag/cgrfa/itpgr.htm

This is a legally binding FAO treaty on the conservation and use of plant genetic resources, covering all plant genetic resources relevant for food and agriculture. It balances the rights of different groups and encourages national and international collections of seeds and plants. It will work alongside the Bonn Guidelines on Access to Genetic Resources (2002).

United Nations Food and Agriculture Organization (FAO)

www.fao.org

The FAO is mandated to raise levels of nutrition and standards of living, to improve agricultural productivity, and to improve conditions of rural populations. The FAO helped launch a Sustainable Agriculture and Rural Development (SARD) initiative at the World Summit on Sustainable Development (WSSD) in order to accelerate action to reduce world hunger.

World Food Programme (WFP)

www.wfp.org

The WFP is a frontline UN organization fighting to eradicate world hunger. WFP's vision is a world where every person has access at all times to the food needed for an active and healthy life.

World Food Summit (1996)

www.fao.org

The World Food Summit reaffirmed 'the right of everyone to have access to safe and nutritious food, consistent with the right to adequate food and the fundamental right of everyone to freedom from hunger'. It called for equitable development strategies to reduce poverty, putting an emphasis on social justice and the achievement of better nutrition for all, especially vulnerable and marginalized groups. The 2002 review looked at ways of accelerating progress against a background of persistent food insecurity.

Desertification and drought

Global Environment Facility (GEF)

www.gefweb.org

The GEF helps developing countries fund projects/programmes that protect the global environment. It designates financial mechanisms for conventions on biodiversity, climate change and persistent organic pollutants. It also supports work on desertification, international waters and the ozone layer.

United Nations Convention to Combat Desertification in Those Countries Experiencing Serious Drought and/or Desertification, Particularly in Africa (CCD)

www.unccd.int/main.php
Agreement to negotiate the CCD came out of UNCED in 1996. Detailed annexes address desertification in specific regions; countries must develop national action programmes in conjunction with local stakeholders (UNEP, 2002).

Mountains

International Year of Mountains (2002)

www.mountains2002.org
The International Year of Mountains was coordinated by the FAO to create heightened international awareness of the dangers facing mountain ecosystems/communities; an action plan was developed to tackle the problems and a Global Mountain Summit was held.

Sustainable tourism

World Tourism Organization (WTO)/Global Code of Ethics

www.world-tourism.org
The WTO is an intergovernmental body working with UNEP and the United Nations Educational, Scientific and Cultural Organization (UNESCO) to promote sustainable tourism through guidelines, handbooks, the exchange of good practice and demonstration projects. It adopted a Global Code of Ethics for Tourism.

Biodiversity and biotechnology

Bonn Guidelines on Access to Genetic Resources and Fair and Equitable Sharing of Benefits Arising out of Their Utilization (2002)

www.biodiv.org/programmes/socio-eco/benefit/bonn.asp
These are voluntary guidelines under the Convention on Biological Diversity (CBD) to assist governments to structure national/regional legislation/mechanisms to ensure fair access to genetic resources and the sharing of benefits. It calls for transparency in policy and suggests prior informed consent procedures.

Cartagena Protocol on Biosafety (2002)

www.biodiv.org/biosafety/protocol.asp
This protocol was developed under the CBD to address potential risks to biodiversity posed by living modified organisms (LMOs) resulting from modern biotechnology (also known as genetically modified organisms – GMOs). It seeks the safe transfer, handling and use of LMOs, and takes into account risks to human health.

United Nations Convention on Biological Diversity (CBD)

www.biodiv.org
The CBD was agreed at UNCED (1992) with three main goals: the conservation of biological diversity; the sustainable use of its components; and the fair and equitable sharing of benefits arising from the use of genetic resources. Under the CBD, the Cartagena Biosafety Protocol (2000) focuses on living modified organisms resulting from modern biotechnology and the Jakarta Mandate (1995) addresses marine and coastal biological diversity.

Global Taxonomy Initiative (GTI)

www.biodiv.org/programmes/cross-cutting/taxonomy
The GTI was formed under the CBD to address the lack of taxonomic information and expertise in many parts of the world. Taxonomy is the science of identifying and naming the species of plants, animals and micro-organisms.

World Heritage Sites (UNESCO)

whc.unesco.org/nwhc/pages/home/pages/homepage.htm
Sites designated under the World Heritage Convention are considered to be of outstanding value to humanity. Once listed, their protection becomes a responsibility shared by the international community as a whole.

Forests

Collaborative Partnership on Forests (CPF)

www.un.org/esa/forests
The CPF was formed by 11 international forest-related organizations, within and outside the UN, to support the United Nations Forum on Forests and to enhance coordination/international cooperation.

Forest Principles (1992)

www.un.org/documents/ga/conf151/acon15126-3annex3.htm
This is a non-binding statement of principles on the management, conservation and sustainable development of all types of forests and is an outcome of UNCED.

Intergovernmental Panel on Forests (IPF) (1995–1997)/Intergovernmental Forum on Forests (IFF) (1997–2000)

www.un.org/esa/forests
Following UNCED, the IPF and IFF processes formulated a common vision for the management, conservation and sustainable development of all types of forests. This work is now taken forward by a permanent intergovernmental body: the United Nations Forum on Forests (UNFF).

United Nations Forum on Forests (UNFF)

www.un.org/esa/forests

The UNFF is an intergovernmental policy forum to promote the management, conservation and sustainable development of all types of forests and to strengthen long-term political commitment to this end. It was established in 2000 as part of a new international arrangement on forests to carry on the work of the IPF and IFF. It has expressed concern on the 'continuing high rate of worldwide deforestation, as well as forest and land degradation'.

CONFERENCES, AGREEMENTS AND PROCESSES

Drinking water and sanitation

- Agenda 21, Chapter 18 (1992)
- United Nations General Assembly Special Session (UNGASS) (1997)
- United Nations Commission on Sustainable Development (CSD) 6, Decision 1 (1998)
- International Conference on Freshwater, Bonn (2001)
- Third World Water Forum, Kyoto (March 2003)
- International Year on Freshwater (2003)
- CSD to consider water and sanitation (2003–2005)
- Millennium Development Goal (MDG) on drinking water and World Summit on Sustainable Development (WSSD) sanitation target (2015)

Oceans, seas and coasts

- Agenda 21, Chapter 17 (1992)
- Convention on Biological Diversity (CBD) Convention of the Parties (COP) Decision 5/6
- United Nations Convention on the Law of the Sea (UNCLOS) (1982)
- Global Programme of Action for the Protection of the Marine Environment from Land-based Activities (GPA) and the Washington Declaration (1995)
- Reykjavik Declaration on Responsible Fisheries in the Marine Ecosystem (2001)
- The United Nations Conference on Straddling and Highly Migratory Fish Stocks (1995)
- Food and Agriculture Organization (FAO) Code of Conduct of Responsible Fisheries (1995)
- United Nations Commission on Sustainable Development (CSD) 4 (1996)

CONFERENCES, AGREEMENTS AND PROCESSES (CONTD)

- United Nations General Assembly Special Session (UNGASS), paragraph 36 (1997)
- CSD-7, Decision 1 (1999)
- CSD to consider oceans and seas, and marine resources (2013–2015)
- International Convention for the Prevention of Pollution from Ships (MARPOL) (73/78)
- Antifouling Systems Convention (2002)
- International Maritime Organization (IMO) International Convention for the Control and Management of Ships' Ballast Water and Sediments (2004)

Vulnerability, disaster reduction and management

- United Nations International Decade for Natural Disaster Reduction (1990–1999)
- Yokohama Strategy (1994)
- United Nations General Assembly Special Session (UNGASS) 54/219 (2000)
- United Nations Commission on Sustainable Development (CSD) to consider disaster management and vulnerability (2014–2015)

Climate change

- Vienna Convention for the Protection of the Ozone Layer (1985) and Montreal Protocol (1987)
- Agenda 21, Chapter 9 (incorporates energy and transport) (1992)
- United Nations General Assembly Special Session (UNGASS), paragraphs 42, 47, 48 (1997)
- United Nations Framework Convention on Climate Change (UNFCCC, 1992) and the associated Kyoto Protocol (1998)
- United Nations Commission on Sustainable Development (CSD) 9, Decision 1 (2001)
- CSD to consider climate change, air pollution and atmosphere (2005–2007)

Agriculture

- Agenda 21, Chapter 14 (1992)
- United Nations Commission on Sustainable Development (CSD) 3, Decision 6 (1995)

CONFERENCES, AGREEMENTS AND PROCESSES (CONTD)

- United Nations General Assembly Special Session (UNGASS), paragraph 62 (1997)
- World Food Summit (1996) CSD-8, Decision 4 (2000)
- World Food Summit +5 (2002)
- CSD to consider agriculture, rural development and land (2007–2009)
- Millennium Development Goal (MDG) on hunger (2015)

Desertification

- Agenda 21, Chapter 12 (1992)
- United Nations Convention to Combat Desertification (CCD) (1994)
- United Nations Commission on Sustainable Development (CSD) 3, Decision 3 (1995)
- United Nations General Assembly Special Session (UNGASS), paragraph 64 (1997)
- CSD to consider desertification and drought (2007–2009)

Mountains

- Agenda 21, Chapter 13 (1992)
- United Nations Commission on Sustainable Development (CSD) 3, Decision 4 (1995)
- United Nations General Assembly Special Session (UNGASS) Designation of International Year of Mountains (2002)
- CSD to consider mountains (2011–2013)

Tourism

- United Nations Commission on Sustainable Development (CSD) 7, Decision 3 (1999)
- International Year of Ecotourism (2002)
- Responsible Tourism Partnership Cape Town Declaration (2002)
- World Tourism Eco Summit (Quebec Declaration) (2002)
- CSD to consider tourism (2011–2013)

Biodiversity and biotechnology

- United Nations Convention on Wetlands of International Importance Especially as Waterfowl Habitat (Ramsar Convention) (1971)

CONFERENCES, AGREEMENTS AND PROCESSES (CONTD)

- United Nations Educational, Scientific and Cultural Organization (UNESCO) Convention Concerning the Protection of the World Cultural and Natural Heritage (1972)

- United Nations Convention on International Trade in Endangered Species of Wild Fauna and Flora (CITES) (1973)

- United Nations Convention on the Conservation of Migratory Species of Wild Animals and Further Agreements (1979)

- Agenda 21, Chapters 15, 16 (1992)

- United Nations Convention on Biological Diversity (CBD) (1992)

- United Nations General Assembly Special Session (UNGASS), paragraph 66 (1997)

- United Nations Commission on Sustainable Development (CSD) 3, Decisions 3, 7 (1995) and CSD-6 (1998)

- CSD to consider biodiversity and biotechnology (2011–2013)

Forests

- Forest Principles and Agenda 21, Chapter 11 (1992)

- United Nations Commission on Sustainable Development (CSD) 3 (1995)

- United Nations Economic and Social Council (ECOSOC) Resolution 2000/35

- CSD-8 (2000)

- CSD to consider forests (2011–2013)

Mining

- United Nations Commission on Sustainable Development (CSD) to consider mining (2009–2011)

See the 'Resources' section for other relevant organizations and web links.

Key United Nations bodies and Bretton Woods institutions

Drinking water and sanitation

- Administrative Committee on Coordination Sub-committee on Water Resources (Agenda 21 Task Master)
- United Nations Commission on Sustainable Development (CSD)
- United Nations Department of Economic and Social Affairs (DESA)
- United Nations Development Programme (UNDP)
- United Nations Educational, Scientific and Cultural Organization (UNESCO)
- United Nations Environment Programme (UNEP)
- United Nations Food and Agriculture Organization (FAO)
- United Nations Human Settlements Programme (UN-Habitat)
- Water Supply and Sanitation Collaborative Council (WSSCC)
- World Health Organization (WHO)

Oceans, seas and coasts

- International Atomic Energy Agency (IAEA)
- International Labour Organization (ILO)
- International Maritime Organization (IMO)
- Sub-committee on Oceans and Coastal Areas (SOCA) of the United Nations Administrative Committee on Coordination (ACC)
- UNEP/Global Programme of Action for Protection of the Marine Environment from Land-based Activities (GPA)
- United Nations Convention on Biological Diversity (CBD) (Agenda 21 Task Master)
- United Nations Department of Economic and Social Affairs (DESA)
- United Nations Development Programme (UNDP)
- United Nations Division for Ocean Affairs and the Law of the Sea (DOALOS)
- United Nations Educational, Scientific and Cultural Organization/Intergovernmental Oceanographic Commission (UNESCO/IOC)
- United Nations Environment Programme (UNEP)
- United Nations Food and Agriculture Organization (FAO)

Key United Nations bodies and Bretton Woods institutions (*contd*)

- United Nations Industrial Development Organization (UNIDO)
- World Bank

Vulnerability and disaster management

- United Nations Development Programme (UNDP)
- United Nations Environment Programme (UNEP)
- United Nations Human Settlements Programme (UN-Habitat)
- United Nations Inter-agency Task Force (IATF) on Disaster Reduction
- United Nations International Strategy for Disaster Reduction (ISDR)
- World Health Organization (WHO)

Climate change

- Global Environment Facility (GEF)
- Intergovernmental Panel on Climate Change (IPCC)
- International Atomic Energy Agency (IAEA)
- International Energy Agency (IEA)
- United Nations Environment Programme and World Meteorological Organization (UNEP/WMO) (Agenda 21 Task Master)
- United Nations Framework Convention on Climate Change (UNFCCC)

Agriculture

- International Federation of Agricultural Producers (IFAP)
- International Fund for Agricultural Development (IFAD)
- United Nations Food and Agriculture Organization (FAO) (Agenda 21 Task Manager)
- United Nations Population Fund (UNFPA)
- World Bank
- World Food Programme (WFP)

Desertification

- United Nations Convention on Biological Diversity (CBD)
- United Nations Development Programme (UNDP)

Key United Nations bodies and Bretton Woods institutions (*contd*)

- ⚙ United Nations Environment Programme (UNEP) (Agenda 21 Task Master)
- ⚙ United Nations Food and Agriculture Organization (FAO)

Mountains

- ⚙ United Nations Educational, Scientific and Cultural Organization (UNESCO)
- ⚙ United Nations Food and Agriculture Organization (FAO) (Agenda 21 Task Master)

Tourism

- ⚙ International Civil Aviation Organization (ICAO)
- ⚙ United Nations Convention on Biological Diversity (CBD)
- ⚙ United Nations Educational, Scientific and Cultural Organization (UNESCO)
- ⚙ United Nations Environment Programme (UNEP) (Agenda 21 Task Master)
- ⚙ World Tourism Organisation (WTO) (Agenda 21 Task Master)
- ⚙ World Travel and Tourism Council (WTTC)

Biodiversity and Biotechnology

- ⚙ UNEP World Conservation Monitoring Centre
- ⚙ United Nations Environment Programme (UNEP) (Agenda 21 Task Master – biodiversity)
- ⚙ United Nations Industrial Development Organization (UNIDO) (Agenda 21 Task Master – biotechnology)
- ⚙ World Bank
- ⚙ World Conservation Union (IUCN)
- ⚙ World Intellectual Property Organization (WIPO)

Forests

- ⚙ United Nations Convention on Biological Diversity (CBD)
- ⚙ United Nations Department of Economic and Social Affairs (DESA)
- ⚙ United Nations Development Programme (UNDP)
- ⚙ United Nations Educational, Scientific and Cultural Organization (UNESCO)

> **Key United Nations bodies and Bretton Woods institutions (contd)**
>
> ⚙ United Nations Environment Programme (UNEP)
>
> ⚙ United Nations Forum on Forests (UNFF)
>
> ⚙ United Nations Framework Convention on Climate Change (UNFCCC)
>
> ⚙ World Bank
>
> **Mining**
>
> ⚙ International Labour Organization (ILO)
>
> ⚙ United Nations Conference on Trade and Development (UNCTAD)
>
> ⚙ United Nations Department of Economic and Social Affairs (DESA)
>
> ⚙ United Nations Environment Programme (UNEP)
>
> ⚙ United Nations Industrial Development Organization (UNIDO)
>
> ⚙ World Bank
>
> See the 'Resources' section for web links.

 # References

Abramowitz, J (2001) 'Human actions worsen natural disasters', Worldwatch Institute press release, Washington, DC, 18 October, www.worldwatch.org/press/news2001/10/18

Annan, K (1999) 'Introduction', in *United Nations Secretary-General's Annual Report on the Work of the Organisation of the United Nations*, UN, New York

Annan, K (2002) 'Executive summary', in *Breaking New Ground: Mining, Minerals and Sustainable Development – the Report of the MMSD Project*, IIED/World Business Council on Sustainable Development, Earthscan, London

ANPED (Northern Alliance for Sustainability) (2000) *World Summit on Sustainable Development*, www.anped.org

Bernbaum, E (1999) Cultural and Spiritual Values of Biodiversity, UNEP, Nairobi

Crace, J (2003) 'Costing the earth', *Guardian*, 10 September 2003, p68

DFID (UK Department for International Development) (2002) *Poverty and the Environment*, DFID, London

DFID, EC, UNDP, World Bank (UK Department for International Development, European Commission, United Nations Development Programme and the World Bank) (2002) *Linking Poverty Reduction and Environmental Management: Policy Challenges and Opportunities*, www.undp.org/wssd/docs/LPREM.pdf, July 2002

Evans, J (2002) 'Sustainable forest management – What has really happened since Rio?' *Sustainable Development International*, spring 2002, pp149–151

FAO (United Nations Food and Agriculture Organization) (undated) 'The spectrum of malnutrition', Briefing sheet, FAO, Italy

FAO (2001a) *The State of Food Insecurity in the World*, www.fao.org

FAO (2001b) *Food Security and the Environment*, Briefing Sheet, www.fao.org

FAO (2002) *The State of World Fisheries and Aquaculture*, FAO, Sofia

IIED and WBCSD (International Institute for Environment and Development and the World Business Council on Sustainable Development) (2002) *Breaking New Ground: Mining, Minerals and Sustainable Development*, Report of the MMSD Project, Earthscan, London

ISDR (International Strategy for Disaster Reduction) (2002) *Natural Disasters and Sustainable Development: Understanding the Links between Development, Environment and Natural Disasters*, Background Paper No 5, ISDR, www.unisdr.org

Price, M (2002) *Ten Years after Rio: The International Year of Mountains*, Sustainable Development International, www.mountains2002.org, pp145–147

Segundad, P (2001) 'Cultural and spiritual values of biodiversity: Excerpted from statements by representatives of indigenous and traditional communities in response to a request from UNEP for information on how they value biodiversity, collected by the Environment Liaison Centre International', in Addison Posey, D (ed) *Cultural and Spiritual Values of Biodiversity*, UNEP and Intermediate Technology Publications, Nairobi, Kenya

UNCHS (United Nations Centre for Human Settlements, UN-Habitat) (2001) *State of the World's Cities 2001*, United Nations Publications, New York

UNDP (United Nations Development Programme) Regional Bureau for Europe and the Commonwealth of Independent States (2003) *Environmental Governance Sourcebook*, UNDP, Bratislava

UNEP (United Nations Environment Programme) (2002) *Global Environment Outlook 3*, Earthscan, London, www.unep.org

United Nations Commission on Sustainable Development (CSD) website, www.un.org/esa/sustdev

United Nations Food and Agriculture Organization (2001a) *The State of Food Insecurity in the World*, www.fao.org

Water Aid and Tearfund (2002) *The Human Waste Report*, Water Aid and Tearfund, London

Worldwatch (2001) 'Human actions worsen natural disasters', Press Release, 18 October 2001

WRI (World Resources Institute) in collaboration with UNEP (United Nations Environment Programme), UNDP (United Nations Development Programme) and the World Bank (2002) *World Resources 2000–2001: People and Ecosystems – The Fraying Web of Life*, WRI, Washington, DC

WRI in collaboration with UNEP, UNDP and the World Bank (2003) *World Resources 2002–2004: Decisions for the Earth – Balance, Voice, and Power*, WRI, Washington, DC

Globalization

 ## Context

Globalization is characterized by a 'growing access to goods and services from all over the world, large flows of capital between countries, and technological advances that can make vast distances a negligible factor in business decisions' (UNDP, UNEP, World Bank and WRI, 2003). It is also a growing interdependence of the world's people through a 'shrinking space, shrinking time and disappearing borders' (UNDP, 1999). While this offers great opportunities for enriching people's lives, the benefits and opportunities have not been shared equitably (UNEP, 2002). Some see globalization as the way forward towards a better standard of living for all or as an inevitable process that requires careful management, if the benefits are to be captured for all. Others are questioning, challenging and even resisting the forces of globalization, and pointing out the manifestation of growing income gaps, increasing environmental damage and increased cultural uniformity. While many international bodies are starting to adjust their policies to include the active participation of civil society and its demands for implementation and enforcement of acceptable trade, labour and environmental standards worldwide (UNEP, 2002), developing countries are also concerned that trade policy measures for labour and environmental purposes should not be a justification for, or a disguised restriction to, international trade. The commitment towards active promotion of corporate responsibility and accountability was welcomed as a step forward, and the pairing of the two concepts – 'responsibility' and 'accountability' – has been seen as an achievement of the World Summit on Sustainable Development (WSSD) in taking forward the Rio agreements.

 ## Chapter V in summary

Globalization offers both opportunities and challenges for sustainable development. There are new **opportunities** in areas such as trade, investment and capital flows, technology (including information technology), growth in the world economy and improved living standards. The challenges include serious financial crises, insecurity, poverty, exclusion and inequality within and among

AT A GLANCE

- Trade accounts for some 58 per cent of the global economy – up from 27 per cent in 1970 (UNDP, UNEP, World Bank, WRI, 2003).

- One fifth of the world's population living in the highest income countries have 86 per cent of world gross domestic product (GDP), 82 per cent of world export markets, 68 per cent of foreign direct investment and 74 per cent of telephone lines. The one fifth of poorest countries have about 1 per cent in each category (UNDP, 1999).

- In 1991, private finance and official development aid (grants, loans and other assistance) to developing countries were approximately equal at about US$60 billion each. By 2000, private finance had multiplied by a factor of four, to US$226 billion, while development aid had decreased by half to US$35 billion (UNDP, UNEP, World Bank, WRI, 2003).

'The world is rushing headlong into greater integration, driven mostly by a philosophy of market profitability and economic efficiency. We must bring human development and social protection into the equation... Globalization needs a human face' (Richard Jolly, co-ordinator of the 1999 Human Development Report, cited in UNDP, 1999a).

societies. Developing countries and countries with economies in transition face special difficulties in responding to these challenges. Globalization should be fully **inclusive and equitable**, with **policies and measures** to help these countries respond effectively to the challenges and opportunities *[47]*, including action at all levels on:

- Promoting 'open, equitable, rules-based, predictable and non-discriminatory' **multilateral trading and financial systems** that benefit all countries in pursuit of sustainable development *[47a]*;
- Open and transparent decision-making processes and structures in **international financial and trade institutions** *[47b]*;
- Capacity of developing countries to **benefit from liberalized trade** through national productivity and competitiveness, commodity diversification, and stronger community-based entrepreneurial capacity, transportation and communication infrastructure *[47c]*;
- International Labour Organization (ILO) work on the social dimension of globalization *[47d]*; and
- **Trade-related technical assistance and capacity-building programmes** to, amongst other things, take advantage of market access opportunities and examine the relationship between trade, environment and development *[47e]*.

Further actions relate to:

- **The World Trade Organization's (WTO's) work programme**: implementing the outcomes of the Doha Ministerial Conference; strengthening trade-related capacity-building; and meaningful participation of developing countries in multilateral trade negotiations *[48]*;

- Promoting corporate responsibility and accountability through intergovernmental agreements and measures, international initiatives, public–private partnerships and appropriate national regulations [49];
- Building capacities of developing countries to improve ease of access, accuracy, timeliness and coverage of information on countries and financial markets [50];
- Strengthening regional trade and cooperation agreements to help achieve sustainable development [51]; and
- Narrowing the digital divide by providing support and transferring technology [52].

 # Globalization elsewhere in the JPOI

'As long as globalization is dominated by economic aspects and by the spread of markets, it will put a squeeze on human development... We need a new approach to governance, one that preserves the advantages offered by global markets and competition while allowing for human, community and environmental resources that will ensure that globalization works for people and not just for profits'
(Sakiko Fakuda-Parr, Director of the Human Development Report Office, 1999).

The Johannesburg Plan of Implementation (JPOI) recognizes the continuing need for a dynamic and enabling international economic environment to support improved opportunities in the areas of finance, technology transfer, debt and trade (JPOI, Chapter X). It calls for the full and effective participation of developing countries in global decision-making and identifies the need for WSSD outcomes to be implemented through partnerships, which were acknowledged in the Monterrey Consensus as being crucial in pursuing sustainable development in a globalizing world. In Africa, poverty remains a major challenge and the majority of African countries have not benefited fully from the opportunities of globalization.

TARGETS AND COMMITMENTS

Actively promote **corporate responsibility and accountability**, including through the full development and effective implementation of intergovernmental agreements and measures, international initiatives and public–private partnerships, and appropriate national regulations [49] (new target).

EXAMPLES OF INDICATORS FOR MEASURING PROGRESS IN IMPLEMENTATION

- Percentage of population living below the poverty line (United Nations Commission on Sustainable Development, or CSD)
- Gross domestic product (GDP) per capita (CSD)
- Investment share in GDP (CSD)
- Balance of trade in goods and services (CSD)
- Main telephone lines per 1000 inhabitants (CSD)
- Number of internet subscribers per 1000 inhabitants (CSD)
- Global monitoring of policies for achieving Millennium Development Goals (MDGs) and Monterrey commitments (World Bank)

Partnership example

Capacity-Building Task Force on Trade, Environment and Development, Phase II (CBTF II)

Leading partners: United Nations Environment Programme (UNEP) and United Nations Conference on Trade and Development (UNCTAD)

Dates: 2002–2005 (Phase I initiated in 2000)

The partnership seeks to enhance the human and institutional capacity of developing countries in order to deal with issues arising at the intersection of trade liberalization, environmental protection and economic development. The aims include:

- Assisting beneficiary countries in developing mutually supportive policies that would maximize the net benefits of trade for sustainable development.
- Seeking a close correlation with the Doha Work Programme and the related technical assistance programme administered by the World Trade Organization (WTO) Secretariat.

CBTF II is the main vehicle for capacity-building activities by UNCTAD and UNEP in trade, environment and development in support of the decisions to be taken by the World Summit on Sustainable Development (WSSD). It has a regional emphasis, which accords with the expected outcomes of WSSD with regard to implementation of its work programme. The partnership will undertake thematic research, country projects, training sessions, policy dialogues and networking based on a participatory, 'learning-by-doing' approach and involving national institutions with core competencies in trade and the environment in their design and implementation.

Contact information:
Chief, Economics and Trade Branch
United Nations Environment Programme (UNEP)
15 Chemin des Anémones
1219 Chatelaine
Geneva
www.unep.org

 # Resources

Capacity-building Task Force on Trade, Environment and Development (CBTF)

www.unep-unctad.org/cbtf/cbtf2/F1.htm

The CBTF is a United Nations Environment Programme (UNEP)/United Nations Conference on Trade and Development (UNCTAD) partnership to strengthen the capacity of developing countries and transition economies in addressing trade, environment and development issues.

Digital divide

The term 'digital divide' refers to the gap between those who have access to, and effectively use, new information and communication technologies (ICTs), and those who do not have this capacity. See World Summit on the Information Society (WSIS).

Doha Ministerial Declaration

wto.org/english/tratop_e/dda_e/dohaexplained_e.htm
The outcome of the Fourth World Trade Organization (WTO) Ministerial (November 2001) includes a work programme and negotiating agenda for a WTO Development Round. Elements of the declaration include agriculture; services; market access for non-agricultural products; trade-related aspects of intellectual property rights; trade and competition policy; transparency in government procurement; trade facilitation; WTO rules; trade and the environment; electronic commerce; small economies; trade, debt and finance; trade and transfer of technology; technical cooperation and capacity-building; least developed countries; and special and differential treatment.

Global Compact

www.unglobalcompact.org
Proposed by UN Secretary-General Kofi Annan at the World Economic Forum (January 1999), the Global Compact was launched at the UN in July 2000. It is a voluntary international initiative that brings together companies with UN agencies, and labour and civil society, in order to advance responsible corporate citizenship focused on nine principles in the areas of human rights, labour and the environment.

International financial and trade institutions

Principally, these include the Bretton Woods institutions (the World Bank and the International Monetary Fund (IMF) – also referred to as the International Financial Institutions, or IFIs) and the WTO.

Monterrey Consensus

www.un.org/esa/ffd/ffdconf
The Monterrey Consensus is the outcome of the International Conference on Financing for Development (March 2002). Governments committed themselves to increasing resources for development through means to mobilize domestic and international finance; promote trade; strengthen cooperation for development; address debt issues; and improve the international monetary, financial and trading systems.

Multilateral trading and financial systems

This category covers multilateral, plurilateral (between just some members of an institution/agreement), regional and bilateral trade and financial rules, regulations and mechanisms. Principally, it involves those systems developed through the General Agreement on Tariffs and Trade (GATT), which evolved in 2000 into the WTO, and other

'Growing globalization calls for mechanisms to redress unsustainable imbalances caused by unhealthy trade practices. Not all countries have the competitive edge provided by access to modern information and communication technologies... Moreover, countries and donors will have to fulfil the promises they make in Johannesburg. In the past, many promises of financial support for Agenda 21 have not been kept... The same applies to the slow ratification of agreements. Many treaties and protocols are not yet operational because ratification falls short of what might have been possible. Implementation and action are the key words for Johannesburg. Too much is at stake for new disappointments, which can easily be avoided if we all keep our promises' (Jan Pronk, Special Envoy of the UN Secretary-General for the WSSD, cited in UNDP, 2002)

multilateral arrangements such as the Africa, Caribbean and Pacific group of countries (ACP)/European Union (EU) agreements and regional trade agreements; and multilateral finance mechanisms used by governments that are accessed through the World Bank and the IMF.

International Finance Corporation (IFC)

www.ifc.org
The IFC promotes sustainable private-sector investment in developing countries as a way of reducing poverty and improving people's lives. It is a member of the World Bank Group.

International Telecommunication Union (ITU)

www.itu.int
The ITU is a UN body through which governments and the private sector coordinate global telecom networks and services.

International Trade Centre (ITC)

www.intracen.org/menus/itc.htm
The ITC is a technical cooperation agency of the United Nations Conference on Trade and Development (UNCTAD) and the WTO. It supports developing and transition economies with product and market development; development of trade support services; trade information; human resource development; international purchasing and supply management; and trade promotion.

United Nations Research Institute for Social Development (UNRISD)

www.unrisd.org/
The Business Responsibility for Sustainable Development project (2000–2005) of the UNRISD promotes research and policy dialogue on corporate social and environmental responsibility. It examines whether transnational corporations (TNCs) and others are taking meaningful steps to improve their social and environmental record, particularly in developing countries.

World Summit on the Information Society (WSIS)

www.itu.int/wsis
The WSIS was held in two phases – in Geneva (December 2003) and in Tunis (November 2005) – to develop and foster a clear statement of political will and a concrete plan of action for achieving the goals of the Information Society, while fully reflecting all the different interests at stake.

'We need to build a system, a set of rules, or a framework that will help make globalization a more positive force for improving all people's lives. This new environment must promote equity and involve greater international cooperation, particularly in the areas of finance, capacity-building, technology transfer, debt relief and trade' (Nitin Desai, UN Under Secretary-General for Economic and Social Affairs, cited in United Nations Department of Public Information, October 2001)

CONFERENCES, AGREEMENTS AND PROCESSES

Monterrey Consensus

- International Conference on Financing for Development, Monterrey (March 2002)

Trade

- World Trade Organization (WTO) Doha Ministerial Declaration (November 2001)

- WTO Ministerial Meeting, Cancun (September 2003)

- Africa, Caribbean and Pacific group of countries (ACP)/European Union (EU) Phase II negotiations on Economic Partnership Agreements (from September 2003)

- Regional processes, such as the Free Trade Area of the Americas process and Asian Pacific Economic Cooperation (APEC) (ongoing)

Corporate responsibility

- United Nations Commission on Sustainable Development (CSD) 6: industry and sustainable development (1998)

- Organisation for Economic Co-operation and Development (OECD) Guidelines for Multinational Enterprises: Corporate Governance Principles (1999)

- United Nations Global Compact (July 2000)

- European Community (EC) Green Paper on Corporate Social Responsibility (July 2001)

- EC Communication on Corporate Social Responsibility (2002)

- Guidelines for Good Corporate Governance in the Commonwealth (2002)

- Commonwealth Guidelines for Corporate Citizenship (2003)

- Group of 8 industrialized nations (G8) Declaration on Fostering Growth and Promoting a Responsible Market Economy, Evian (June 2003)

- European Parliament Report on Corporate Social Responsibility (2003)

Digital divide

- Plenipotentiary Conference of the International Telecommunication Union (ITU) (1998)

- World Summit on the Information Society (WSIS): Phase I, Geneva (December 2003); Phase II, Tunis (November 2004)

Key United Nations bodies and Bretton Woods institutions

Monterrey Consensus

- International Monetary Fund (IMF)
- United Nations Development Programme (UNDP)
- United Nations Economic and Social Council (ECOSOC)
- World Bank

Trade

- International Trade Centre (ITC)
- United Nations Conference on Trade and Development (UNCTAD)
- World Trade Organization (WTO)

Corporate Responsibility

- Global Corporate Governance Forum (World Bank, Organisation for Economic Co-operation and Development (OECD) and bilateral partners)
- International Finance Corporation (IFC)
- United Nations Global Compact: Office of the High Commissioner for Human Rights; United Nations Environment Programme (UNEP); International Labour Organization (ILO); United Nations Development Programme (UNDP); United Nations Industrial Development Organization (UNIDO)

Social Dimensions

- International Labour Organization (ILO)
- United Nations Development Programme (UNDP)
- United Nations Research Institute for Sustainable Development

Digital Divide

- International Telecommunication Union (ITU)
- High-Level Summit Organizing Committee (HLSOC) for the World Summit on the Information Society (WSIS): includes Food and Agriculture Organization (FAO); International Atomic Energy Agency (IAEA); International Civil Aviation Organization (ICAO); International Labour Organization (ILO); International Maritime Organization (IMO); ITU; United Nations Conference on Trade and

5

Key United Nations bodies and Bretton Woods institutions (*contd*)

Development (UNCTAD); United Nations Development Programme (UNDP); United Nations Environment Programme (UNEP); United Nations Educational, Scientific and Cultural Organization (UNESCO); United Nations High Commissioner for Refugees (UNHCR); United Nations Industrial Development Organization (UNIDO); United Nations Institute for Training and Research (UNITAR); Universal Postal Union (UPU); United Nations Regional Economic Commissions; World Health Organization (WHO); World Intellectual Property Organization (WIPO); World Meteorological Organization (WMO); World Trade Organization (WTO); and the World Bank.

 # References

Annan, K (2003) 'Opening session – ECOSOC', Geneva, July, 2003

UNDP (United Nations Development Programme) (1999) *Human Development Report 1999*, Oxford University Press, New York

UNDP, UNEP (United Nations Environment Programme), the World Bank and WRI (World Resources Institute) (2003) *World Resources 2002–2004: Decisions for the Earth; Balance, Voice and Power*, WRI: Washington, DC

UNEP (United Nations Environment Programme) (2002) *Global Environment Outlook 3*, Earthscan, London, www.unep.org

United Nations Department of Public Information (2001) *Johannesburg Summit 2002. World Summit on Sustainable Development, 2–11 September*, p9

Health and Sustainable Development

6

 ## Context

The Rio principles state that human beings are entitled to a healthy and productive life in harmony with nature. However, the reality for many people is very different. While there is a complex interplay of factors that determine health, the major diseases of poverty and adverse environmental conditions are currently considered an impediment to economic progress, and ill health has the potential to reverse decades of progress, especially in developing countries. Evidence suggests that poor environmental quality is associated with approximately one quarter of all preventable illness in the world, with diarrhoeal diseases and acute respiratory infections the most common. Two-thirds of all preventable ill health due to environmental conditions occurs amongst children (WHO, 2002). A few measures could go a long way towards improving the health of billions of people in the developing world. These include providing greater access to safe drinking water, expanding basic sanitation and waste disposal technologies and improving air quality in urban areas (UNDPI, 2001). Another important measure is the improvement of indoor air quality through increased access to cleaner sources of household energy for cooking and heating. However, problems related to health and the environment cannot be solved if poverty is not addressed. Three diseases – HIV/AIDS, tuberculosis (TB) and malaria – dominate the global burden of disease, causing more than 5.5 million deaths every year. Addressing major causes of ill health and strengthening health services for all, including the most disadvantaged groups such as women and the poor, are major priorities in sustainable development.

KEY WORDS

- **healthcare systems and services**
- **infant and maternal mortality**
- **traditional medicine and knowledge**
- **food**
- **work and health**
- **HIV/AIDS, TB and malaria**
- **public health research**
- **environmental health**
- **water and sanitation**
- **waste and pollution control**
- **respiratory diseases**
- **cleaner fuels**
- **lead in paint and gasoline**

 ## Chapter VI in summary

Sustainable development can only be achieved by securing the necessary health gains for the whole population through poverty eradication and by bringing debilitating diseases under control. There is an urgent need to address the root causes of ill health and their impact on development. Particular attention has to be paid to women, children and other vulnerable groups, including the elderly, those with disabilities and indigenous people [53].

AT A GLANCE

- Some 35 people an hour die as a result of armed conflict (WHO, 2002).

- Malaria kills 3000 African children a day (Smith, 2002).

- Every year, environmental hazards kill 3 million children under the age of five (WHO 2002).

- Bathing in polluted seas is estimated to cause 250 million cases of gastroenteritis (GESAMP, 2001).

- In 2001, 3 million people died from AIDS, with the vast majority of these deaths occurring in developing countries (UNAIDS, 2002).

- More than 200 million people live in countries where the average life expectancy is less than 45 years (WHO, 2002).

- Over 250 million work-related incidents per year (WHO, 2002).

- 1.5 million people a year die of tuberculosis (WHO, 2002).

- A woman living in sub-Saharan Africa has a 1 in 16 chance of dying in pregnancy or childbirth. This compares with a 1 in 2800 risk for women in developed regions (WHO, 2003b).

'... an integral approach towards environment, health and sustainable development will only benefit the poor if access to resources necessary for survival and life itself is accepted as a human right for all'

(Jan Pronk, Special Envoy of the UN Secretary-General for the WSSD and chair of IIED, 2003).

Healthcare systems and services

Healthcare systems will be strengthened to deliver basic healthcare services to all in an 'efficient, accessible and affordable manner' and in a way that conforms with human rights and fundamental freedoms, and is consistent with national laws and cultural and religious values [54]. Action is needed at all levels to:

- Integrate health concerns within poverty eradication and sustainable development programmes and strategies [54a];
- Promote equitable and improved access to healthcare services [54b];
- Implement the World Health Organization's (WHO's) Health for All Strategy, including information systems [54c];
- Improve human resources management and development in healthcare services including affordable and safe medicines and vaccines [54d];
- Promote partnerships to increase health literacy by 2010 [54e];
- Reduce by 2015 the mortality rates for infants and children under five years of age by two-thirds and maternal mortality rates by three-quarters, compared to 2000 [54f];
- Target research on priority public health issues [54g];
- Promote and use traditional medicine, knowledge and practices with modern medicine, where appropriate [54h];

- Ensure **equal access of women** to healthcare services, focusing on maternal and emergency obstetric care *[54i]*;
- Promote **healthy lifestyles**, including reproductive and sexual health, in line with recent UN conferences *[54j]*;
- Assess **health and environment linkages** and use the knowledge to develop policy responses *[54k]*;
- Transfer and disseminate **technologies for safe water, sanitation and waste management** *[54l]*;
- Strengthen ILO and WHO programmes to reduce **occupational deaths, injuries and illness** *[54m]*;
- Improve access to, and availability of, **safe, culturally acceptable and nutritionally adequate food** *[54n]*; and
- Address **non-communicable diseases and conditions**, including cardiovascular disease, cancer, diabetes, chronic respiratory conditions, mental health and violence, and associated risk factors, such as alcohol, tobacco, unhealthy diets and lack of exercise *[54o]*.

HIV/AIDS, malaria, tuberculosis

To implement all commitments made at the 2001 United Nations General Assembly Special Session on HIV/AIDS, including the **Millennium Development Goal (MDG) target** to reduce HIV amongst young men and women aged 15 to 24 by 25 per cent in the most affected countries by 2005 and globally by 2010, and to **combat malaria, tuberculosis** and other diseases *[55]*, action is required at all levels to:

- Provide special assistance to **children orphaned by HIV/AIDS** through national strategies, regional cooperation and international initiatives *[55a]*;
- Ensure the **Global Fund to Fight AIDS, Tuberculosis and Malaria** has sufficient resources, and that countries in most need have access to this fund *[55b]*;
- Protect **workers' health** and promote occupational safety, including through the voluntary International Labour Organization (ILO) Code of Practice on HIV/AIDS and the World of Work *[55c]*; and
- Mobilize funding for research and development into diseases of the poor, such as HIV/AIDS, malaria and tuberculosis. This funding will be both public and private and directed at developing **new vaccines and drugs** *[55d]*.

'The most devastating social and economic impacts of AIDS are still to come. Widespread treatment access would substantially mitigate the devastating impact of HIV/AIDS, which affects everything from agriculture to national defence. Effective HIV prevention programmes must be scaled up dramatically if we want a realistic chance at reducing the number of new infections'
(Peter Piot, Executive Director of UNAIDS).

Respiratory disease and air pollution

To address the impact of **respiratory diseases**, particularly on women and children *[56]*, action will be taken to:

- Strengthen regional and national programmes with assistance to developing countries *[56a]*;
- Phase out **lead in gasoline** *[56b]*;

- Reduce emissions through use of **cleaner fuels and pollution control techniques** *[56c]*; and
- Provide affordable energy to rural populations, reducing their dependence on **traditional fuel for cooking and heating** *[56d]*.

Lead poisoning

To protect children's health, action will be taken to phase out **lead in lead-based paints** (and other sources of exposure) and step up efforts to monitor and treat lead poisoning *[57]*.

 Health elsewhere in the JPOI

'It has been estimated that roughly 60 per cent of the global burden of disease from acute respiratory infections, 90 per cent from diarrhoeal disease, 50 per cent from chronic respiratory conditions and 90 per cent from malaria could be avoided by simple environmental interventions' (Christine K Durbak, 2002).

The Johannesburg Plan of Implementation (JPOI) includes MDGs on access to clean drinking water, food security, mortality rates and action to combat HIV/AIDS, TB and malaria. Health concerns related to poverty are addressed in Chapter II of the JPOI. Detrimental impacts from exposure to chemicals, pesticides, solid waste and other pollution are addressed through commitments on the sound management of chemicals by 2020; the ratification/ implementation of relevant international agreements on chemicals; chemical safety and hazardous waste; and the development of sustainable consumption and production programmes and policies that will reduce health impacts (JPOI, Chapter III). A range of health concerns associated with water and sanitation, climate change, air pollution, biosafety and natural disasters are addressed in Chapter IV, while the matter of medicines for all and of the Trade-related Aspects of Intellectual Property Rights (TRIPS) Agreement are addressed in Chapter X. Regional chapters call for action to integrate health concerns within poverty eradication strategies, and to tackle specific health concerns in each region, including HIV/AIDS, TB, malaria, diabetes, dengue fever and the Ebola virus.

TARGETS AND COMMITMENTS

⚙ HIV/AIDS, malaria, tuberculosis. Reduce HIV prevalence among young men and women aged 15 to 24 by 25 per cent in the most affected countries by 2005 and globally by 2010, as well as combat malaria, tuberculosis and other diseases [55] (MDG).

⚙ Health literacy. Enhance health education to improve health literacy on a global basis by 2010 [54e] (new target).

⚙ Mortality rates. Develop programmes and initiatives to reduce, by 2015, mortality rates for infants and children under the age of five by two-thirds, and maternal mortality rates by three-quarters, of the prevailing rate in 2000 [54f] (Millennium Development Goal, or MDG).

EXAMPLES OF INDICATORS FOR MEASURING PROGRESS IN IMPLEMENTATION

- Prevalence of underweight children (under the age of five) (Millennium Development Goal, or MDG)

- Proportion of population below minimum level of dietary energy consumption (MDG)

- Reduction of under five mortality rate by two-thirds between 1990 and 2015 (MDG)

- Infant mortality rate (MDG)

- Proportion of one-year-old children immunized against measles (MDG)

- Maternal mortality ratio (MDG)

- Proportion of births attended by skilled health professional (MDG)

- HIV prevalence among 15- to 24-year-old pregnant women (MDG)

- Number of children orphaned by HIV/AIDS (MDG)

- Prevalence and death rates associated with malaria; proportion of population in malaria risk areas using effective malaria prevention and treatment measures (MDG)

- Prevalence and death rates associated with TB (MDG)

- Life expectancy at birth, by sex (World Health Organization, or WHO)

- Number of hospital beds per 100,000 individuals (WHO)

- Decreased number of people living in areas that fail to meet air quality standards (WHO)

- Decreased number of people whose drinking water fails to meet national safe drinking water standards (WHO)

Other relevant indicators are the WHO Healthy Cities (Health and Sustainability) indicators, and the CSD indicators.

> **Partnership example**
>
> **The Healthy Environments for Children Alliance (HECA)**
>
> **Leading organization:** World Health Organization (WHO)
>
> **Dates:** 2002 – ongoing
>
> The aim of HECA is to build a global alliance to tackle key environment and poverty-related risks to children's health that are responsible for the loss of millions of healthy years of life each year. The alliance will focus on, and catalyse action within, environments where children live, learn, play and sometimes work. Particular attention will be given to improving the home environment – traditionally neglected – but where children spend a major part of their lives, and where the most significant health threats converge. The alliance will focus on health risks associated with lack of access to clean water, to sanitation and to clean indoor and outdoor air. It will act to reduce risks associated with disease vectors, hazardous chemicals and non-intentional injuries. The HECA held its first meeting of stakeholders in December 2002 – attended by over 80 representatives of non-governmental organizations (NGOs), UN and intergovernmental organizations, governments, academia and the private sector.

Contact information:
Agenda 21 and
Manager Healthy
Environments for
Children Alliance
(HECA) Secretariat
World Health
Organization (WHO)
20 Avenue Appia
CH-1211 Geneva 27
Switzerland.
www.who.int/heca

 # Resources

Millennium Development Goals (MDGs)

www.un.org/millenniumgoals/index.shtml (UN)
www.undp.org/mdg (UNDP)
www.developmentgoals.org (World Bank)
The United Nations Secretary-General's 'Road Map' (September 2001) set out concrete targets for goals and commitments in the Millennium Declaration. These were further developed into the MDGs.

Fourth World Conference on Women, Beijing, (1995)

www.un.org/womenwatch/daw/followup/beijing+5.htm
This conference adopted the Beijing Platform for Action to strengthen women's rights to civic and economic participation, and to education and reproductive health. It was reviewed in 2000.

Global Fund to Fight Aids, Tuberculosis and Malaria

www.theglobalfund.org/en/
This fund was created to finance a dramatic turnaround in the fight against AIDS, tuberculosis and malaria. It will address new and existing programmes to stop the spread of disease.

International Conference on Population and Development (ICPD), Cairo (1994)

www.unfpa.org/icpd/10/index
The ICPD shifted the emphasis from population 'control' towards people-centred development, including human and reproductive rights for women. It called for priority measures to 'improve quality of life and health by ensuring a safe and sanitary living environment' for all, aimed at 'avoiding overcrowded housing conditions, reducing air pollution, ensuring access to clean water and sanitation, improving water management, and increasing the safety of the workplace'. The ICPD set an ambitious 20-year plan of action and was reviewed in 1999.

International Labour Organization (ILO) Code of Practice on HIV/AIDS

www.ilo.org/public/english/protection/trav/aids/code/codemain.htm
The ILO's code of practice comprises fundamental principles that cover prevention; management and mitigation of impacts on the world of work; care and support of workers infected and affected by HIV/AIDS; and elimination of stigma and discrimination.

Joint United Nations Programme on HIV/AIDS (UNAIDS)

www.unaids.org
The goals of UNAIDS are to catalyse, strengthen and support an expanded response to prevent the spread of HIV; provide care and support for those afflicted; reduce vulnerability of individuals and communities; and alleviate socio-economic and human impacts of the epidemic.

Roll Back Malaria Initiative (World Health Organization – WHO)

www.rbm.who.int
This initiative was founded by WHO, the World Bank, the United Nations Children's Fund (UNICEF) and the United Nations Development Programme (UNDP) in 1998. It is a global partnership of governments, the UN, non-governmental organizations (NGOs), researchers, manufacturers and control workers, and is committed to halving the malaria burden by 2010 by building and sustaining partnerships at global and country levels; providing technical and operational support to affected countries; stimulating research and development; and monitoring progress and outcomes.

United Nations General Assembly Special Session (UNGASS) on HIV/AIDS, June 2001

www.unaids.org/en/events/un+special+session+on+hiv_aids.asp
This session agreed a United Nations Declaration of Commitment on HIV/AIDS.

World Health Organization (WHO)

www.who.int
The WHO is a specialized UN agency working on global health strategies to obtain a level of health for all citizens, enabling them to lead socially and economically productive lives.

WHO definition of health (1948)

'[Health] is a state of complete physical, social and mental well-being and not merely the absence of disease or infirmity. The enjoyment of the highest attainable standard of health is one of the fundamental rights of every human being, without distinction of race, religion, political beliefs, or economic or social conditions.'

WHO Health for All Strategy

www.who.int/archives/hfa
Launched in 1977, this strategy was revised in 1998 to include 21 targets in a framework for action for the 21st century (Health 21). Its underlying principle is to reduce inequalities in health through multi-sectoral strategies involving communities and to find sustainable solutions for health improvement.

WHO Healthy Cities Project

www.healthycities.org
This project puts health and sustainable development on the agenda of decision-makers in cities and builds a lobby for public health at local level. A global initiative, it was developed as part of the WHO European Region's response to the Health for All Strategy. It includes health and sustainability indicators.

World Summit for Children (1990)

www.unicef.org/specialsession
This summit agreed action to improve living conditions for children and their chances for survival by increasing access to healthcare services for women and children; to create more opportunities for education; to provide better sanitation and greater food supply; and to protect children in danger. UNGASS (2001) reviewed progress on implementation and agreed a plan of action to fulfil outstanding commitments.

World Summit for Social Development, Copenhagen (1996) and Five-year Review, 2000

www.un.org/esa/socdev/wssd/index.htm
Key themes of this summit were poverty, meeting basic human needs, reducing economic and social inequalities and providing sustainable livelihoods. Equitable access to primary healthcare was one of ten commitments agreed.

CONFERENCES, AGREEMENTS AND PROCESSES

- World Health Organization (WHO) Health for All Strategy (1977, revised 1998)

- WHO Global Aids Strategy for the Prevention and Control of Aids (1987)

- United Nations General Assembly Special Session (UNGASS) endorses Global HIV/AIDS Strategy (1987)

- Agenda 21, Chapter 6 (1992)

- United Nations Convention on Biological Diversity (CBD) (1992)

- Declaration on the Elimination of Violence against Women (1993)

- United Nations International Conference on Population and Development, Cairo (1994)

- United Nations Commission on Sustainable Development (CSD) 2 (1994) and CSD-3 (1995)

- Fourth World Conference on Women, Beijing (1995)

- United Nations World Summit on Human Settlements, Habitat II, Istanbul (1996)

- United Nations World Summit for Social Development (1996)

- World Food Summit, Rome (1996)

- Renewed Health for All in the 21st Century Strategy adopted at WHO Assembly (1998)

- International Conference on Population and Development (ICPD) +5 review, New York (1999)

- Third Ministerial Conference on Environment and Health (Europe), London (1999)

- United Nations Millennium Declaration, Millennium Development Goals (MDGs) (2000)

- Beijing+5, New York (2000)

- World Food Summit review, Rome (2000)

- Istanbul+5, New York (2001)

- Stockholm Convention on Persistent Organic Pollutants (2001)

- United Nations General Assembly (UNGA) 26th Special Session on HIV/AIDS (2001)

- United Nations Global Fund to fight AIDS, TB and Malaria (2001)

- UNGASS Special Session on Children (2002)

- CSD considers health and sustainable development as a cross-cutting issue each year (2004–2017).

See the 'Resources' section at the end of this chapter for other relevant organizations and web links.

Key United Nations bodies and Bretton Woods Institutions

Health (overall)

- United Nations Children's Fund (UNICEF)
- United Nations Development Programme (UNDP)
- United Nations Environment Programme (UNEP)
- United Nations Food and Agriculture Organization (FAO)
- United Nations Human Settlements Programme (UN-Habitat)
- United Nations Population Fund (UNFPA)
- World Bank
- World Health Organization (WHO) (Agenda 21 Task Manager)

HIV/AIDS, TB and Malaria

- International Labour Organization (ILO)
- Joint United Nations Programme on HIV/AIDS (UNAIDS)
- United Nations Children's Fund (UNICEF)
- United Nations Development Fund for Women (UNIFEM)
- United Nations Development Programme (UNDP)
- United Nations Drug Control Programme
- United Nations Educational, Scientific and Cultural Organization (UNESCO)
- United Nations Environment Programme (UNEP)
- United Nations Population Fund (UNFPA)
- World Bank
- World Health Organization (WHO)

 References

Durbak, C (2002) 'Childhood antecedents to adult illness', Statement to the World Information Transfer's 11th International Conference on Health and Environment: Global Partners for Global Solutions, New York

GESAMP (2001) *Protecting the Oceans from Land-based Activities: Land-based Sources and Activities Affecting the Quality and Uses of the Marine, Coastal and Associated Freshwater Environment*, GESAMP Reports and Studies No71, Nairobi, United Nations Environment Programme (UNEP), www.gesamp.imo.org./no71/index.htm

Pronk, J (2003) 'Water: Problems and solutions', Speech delivered to World Information Transfer's 12th International Conference on Health and Environment: Global Partners for Global Solutions, New York

Smith, P (2002) 'Roll back malaria – making a sustainable difference', *Sustainable Development International*, spring 2002, pp163–166

UNAIDS (Joint United Nations Programme on HIV/AIDS) (2003) www.unaids.org

UNDPI (United Nations Department of Public Information) (2001) *Johannesburg Summit 2002*, DPI2233, October 2001

UNEP (United Nations Environment Programme) (2002) *Global Environment Outlook 3*, Earthscan, London

UNFPA (United Nations Population Fund) (2002) *State of the World Population Report: People, Poverty and Possibilities*, www.unfpa.org

WHO (World Health Organization) (2002) *Health and Sustainable Development – Key Health Trends*, WHO WSSD Briefing Pack with various WHO publications and summaries prepared by Dr Yasmin von Schindling

WHO (2003a) 'Health provides a model for more effective development aid', Press Release, 20 March 2002, www.who.int/inf/en/pr-2002-20.html

WHO (2003b) 'Maternal deaths disproportunately high in developing countries', WHO Press Release on new findings from WHO, UNICEF and UNFPA, 20 October 2003

Small Island Developing States

7

 ## Context

Small island developing states (SIDS) are amongst the most vulnerable in the world. Because of their size, SIDS are unable to capture economies of scale in their domestic markets and political, managerial and technical capacities. They are characterized by open economies in which international trade is more significant than it is in larger states, and they tend to rely on just a few external markets and less diverse production. Remoteness brings with it higher costs in energy, transportation and communications, while extreme weather events can also eradicate a country's gross domestic product (GDP) overnight. Ocean and coastal zones are the backbone of well-being and development in SIDS, so the health of these environments is critical. Coastal areas tend to be densely populated areas and may be low lying, making these countries especially vulnerable to the impacts of sea-level rise, climate change and climate variability (Commonwealth Secretariat, 1997; UNGASS, 1999).

Globalization has great potential benefits for SIDS, especially through developments in information and communications technologies; but it can also lead to greater marginalization where least developed SIDS are unable to make the changes needed to take advantage of the new opportunities. The Rio Earth Summit in 1992 recognized SIDS as a special case for sustainable development. This led to the 1994 Global Conference on the Sustainable Development of Small Island Developing States and the Barbados Programme of Action (BPoA), which is the principle international framework for addressing the sustainable development concerns of SIDS.

Chapter VII in summary

SIDS are a special case for environment and development [58]. Action is needed at all levels to:

- Accelerate the national and regional implementation of the 1994 **Barbados Programme of Action** (BPoA), with adequate resources [58a];

KEY WORDS

- **Barbados Programme of Action on the Sustainable Development of Small Island Developing States (BPoA)**

- **coastal areas and exclusive economic zones (EEZs)**

- **fisheries**

- **freshwater**

- **pollution and waste**

- **trade**

- **tourism**

- **vulnerability**

- **climate**

- **energy**

- **health**

- **poverty eradication**

AT A GLANCE

- In half of all small island developing states (SIDS), tourism represents 20 to 50 per cent of export earnings (FAO, 1999).

- Small states' relative importance in global export trade declined by 38 per cent during the last 20 years, suggesting they have not benefited from gains made in world trade (Commonwealth Secretariat, 2002).

- About 58 per cent of the world's coral reefs and 34 per cent of all fish species are at risk from human activities (World Bank, 2003).

- Unemployment among young people in the Caribbean ranges from 25 to 50 per cent (UNEP, 1999a).

- According to the Intergovernmental Panel on Climate Change's (IPCC's) *Third Assessment Report* of 1999, sea levels in SIDS' regions are expected to rise by as much as 5mm per year for the next 100 years as a result of global warming (Nurse, 2002).

- Implement **sustainable fisheries management** and improve financial returns from fisheries by strengthening relevant regional fisheries management organizations *[58b]*;
- Delimit and sustainably manage **coastal areas, exclusive economic zones and continental shelves** *[58c]*;
- Support **SIDS-specific work** relating to marine and coastal biological diversity and freshwater *[58d]*;
- Effectively address **waste and pollution** and health-related impacts by undertaking initiatives by 2004 to implement in SIDS the **Global Programme of Action** for the Protection of the Marine Environment from Land-based Activities (GPA) *[58e]*;
- Ensure that ongoing negotiations and elaboration of the World Trade Organization (WTO) work programme on **trade in small economies** takes due account of SIDS *[58f]*;
- Develop community-based initiatives on **sustainable tourism** by 2004 and capacities to diversify tourism products, while protecting culture and traditions and managing natural resources *[58g]*;
- Assist SIDS in support of local communities and appropriate SIDS' organizations for comprehensive **hazard and risk management**, prevention, mitigation, preparedness and relief related to disasters, extreme weather events and other emergencies *[58h]*;
- Support finalization and early operationalization of economic, social and environmental **vulnerability indices** *[58i]*;
- Assist SIDS in mobilizing resources and partnerships for adapting to the adverse effects of **climate change, sea level rise and climate variability** *[58j]*; and
- Support SIDS' capacity-building efforts to implement **intellectual property regimes** *[58k]*.

'Biodiversity is culture itself' (Kotosata To'o, director of O le Siosiomaga Society Inc, Samoa, cited in Senanayake, 1999).

Energy

Adequate, affordable and environmentally sound **energy services** for the sustainable development of SIDS will be supported through, among other things *[59]*:

- Efforts on energy supply and services by 2004 *[59a]*;
- Efficient use of different energy sources (including indigenous and renewable sources) *[59b]*; and
- Building capacity in energy management *[59b]*.

Health

On **health** issues, action will support SIDS to develop capacity and strengthen *[60]*:

- Healthcare services for promoting equitable access to healthcare *[60a]*;
- Healthcare systems for making drugs and technology available to fight major diseases, such as HIV/AIDS, tuberculosis, diabetes, malaria and dengue fever *[60b]*;
- Efforts to reduce and manage waste and pollution *[60c]*; and
- Efforts to implement initiatives aimed at **poverty eradication** *[60d]*.

'The islands of the Caribbean, the Indian and Pacific Oceans face the largest increase in flood risk, with the number of people at risk being some 200 times higher than most other parts of the world' (Hay, 2000).

Barbados Programme of Action on the Sustainable Development of Small Island Developing States Review

A full and comprehensive review of BPoA implementation will be undertaken in 2004, possibly with an international meeting, to discuss the programme *[61]*.

 ## Small island developing states elsewhere in the JPOI

Elements in the Johannesburg Plan of Implementation (JPOI) that are of particular concern to SIDS are those on energy; waste management; sustainable fisheries; oceans, seas, islands and coastal areas; climate change; health; poverty eradication; sustainable tourism; and disaster management. The WTO work programme on small, vulnerable economies is further highlighted in Chapter X of the JPOI, while Chapter IV includes actions to support implementation of the BPoA and Agenda 21's programme of action on the sustainable development of oceans, coastal areas and seas, and efforts to assist coastal states in the area of integrated coastal management. Improved access to, and availability of, safe, reliable and affordable energy supplies are essential for enabling SIDS to capitalize on the potential benefits offered by globalization (JPOI, Chapter II). The commitment of reducing by half the number of people without access to sanitation by 2015 will be critical to the development of SIDS through improved living standards and health of the population (JPOI, Chapter IV).

TARGETS AND COMMITMENTS

☼ **Barbados Programme of Action.** Undertake a full and comprehensive review of the implementation of the BPoA in 2004 (new target).

☼ **Global Programme of Action.** Undertake initiatives by 2004 to implement the Global Programme of Action for the Protection of the Marine Environment from Land-based Activities (GPA) (new target).

☼ **Tourism.** Develop community-based initiatives on sustainable tourism by 2004 (new target).

☼ **Energy.** Support the availability of adequate, affordable and environmentally sound energy services by strengthening ongoing, and supporting new, efforts on energy supply and services by 2004 (new target).

EXAMPLES OF INDICATORS FOR MEASURING PROGRESS IN IMPLEMENTATION

☼ Date of ratification/signature of United Nations Framework Convention on Climate Change (UNFCCC) and/or the Kyoto Protocol

☼ Date of ratification/signature of the United Nations Convention on the Law of the Sea (UNCLOS) (and other related agreements), the Convention on Biological Diversity (CBD) and/or the Cartagena Protocol on Biosafety

☼ Annual catch by major species (United Nations Commission on Sustainable Development, or CSD)

☼ Disaster prevention and mitigation instruments (United Nations Human Settlements Programme , or UN-Habitat)

☼ Abundance of selected key species (CSD)

☼ Proportion of population using solid fuels (Millennium Development Goal, or MDG)

☼ Waste recycling and reuse (CSD)

☼ Annual energy consumption per capita (CSD)

☼ Life expectancy at birth, by sex (World Health Organization, or WHO)

☼ *National Assessment Report* for Barbados Plan of Action (BPoA)

'The 1990 UN Disaster Relief Organization's review of the economic impact of disasters over the past 20 years found that of the 25 most disaster prone countries, 13 are SIDS [small island developing states]. With few exceptions, SIDS are prone to extremely damaging cyclones, storm surges, volcanic eruptions, earthquakes, forest fires, extended drought and extensive floods' (FAO 1999).

Partnership example

Pacific Island Initiative: Capacity-building through Education and Training for the Sustainable Use and Management of Natural Resources and the Environment in the Pacific

Leading partners: South Pacific Regional Environment Programme (SPREP) and the University of the South Pacific (USP)

Dates: 2002–2012

The initiative was launched by countries of the Pacific sub-region during the World Summit on Sustainable Development (WSSD) and will include, as key players, Pacific Island countries and several South Pacific organizations – the South Pacific Regional Environment Programme (SPREP), the University of the South Pacific (USP) and the Pacific Islands Development Programme (PIDP); the Secretariat of the Pacific Community; the South Pacific Applied Geoscience Commission (SOPAC); the South Pacific Board of Education and Assessment; the Pacific Islands Forum Secretariat; international agencies and non-governmental organizations (NGOs); and national NGOs and civil society. Its aim is to establish a regional training and education framework aimed at developing and strengthening mechanisms, processes and tools to support training and education for environmental management, protection and sustainable development in the region. The overall vision is of achieving 'increased and strengthened capacity for Pacific Islands' governments and people to manage their island environment and achieve sustainable development, poverty reduction and sustainable livelihoods'.

 # Resources

Barbados Programme of Action on the Sustainable Development of Small Island Developing States (BPoA)

www.unep.ch/islands/dsidspoa.htm
Adopted in 1994 by the UN, the BPoA addresses climate change/sea-level rise; disasters; wastes; coastal/marine resources; freshwater; land; energy; tourism; biodiversity; institutions; technical cooperation; transport/communications; science/technology; human resources; implementation; and monitoring and review.

Global Environment Facility (GEF)

www.gefweb.org/
The GEF was established 1991 and helps developing countries to fund projects that protect the global environment. It is a financial mechanism for conventions on biodiversity,

climate change, persistent organic pollutants, desertification, protecting international waters and the ozone layer.

United Nations Convention on the Law of the Sea (UNCLOS)

www.un.org/Depts/los/index.htm
Adopted in 1982, UNCLOS covers all aspects of sea/ocean use and resources, such as agreed limits (between national and international waters and zonal delimitation); navigation; exclusive economic zones (EEZs); continental shelves; high seas; the seabed; protection of the marine environment; marine scientific research; and settlement of disputes.

Caribbean Regional Fisheries Mechanism

www.caricom-fisheries.com/
This mechanism promotes the sustainable use of fisheries/aquaculture resources. A network of stakeholders, it is comprised of a ministerial body, the Caribbean Fisheries Forum for Technical/Scientific Decisions and the Caribbean Fisheries Technical Unit.

Convention on the Conservation and Management of Highly Migratory Fish Stocks in the Western and Central Pacific Ocean

www.ocean-affairs.com/convention.html
Agreed in 2000, this seeks to ensure long-term conservation and sustainable use of highly migratory fish stocks in the western and central Pacific Ocean.

Global Programme of Action for the Protection of the Marine Environment from Land-based Activities (GPA)

www.gpa.unep.org/
Adopted in 1995, the GPA is a source of guidance on sustained action to prevent, reduce, control and/or eliminate marine degradation from land-based activities. Its secretariat is the United Nations Environment Programme (UNEP).

Agreement on the Conservation and Management of Straddling Fish Stocks and Highly Migratory Fish Stocks

*www.un.org/Depts/los/convention_agreements/convention_overview_fish_*
*   stock.htm*
www.unep.ch/seas/main/legal/lstrad.html
Opened for signature in 1995, this agreement seeks to ensure long-term conservation/sustainable use of straddling fish stocks and highly migratory fish stocks through effective implementation of UNCLOS (see above). It covers stocks in EEZs of two or more coastal states, or both within and beyond the EEZ.

7

Vulnerability indices

*   www.un.org/esa/sustdev/sids/sidsvind.htm: UN review of vulnerability indices in 1999;
*   www.cobalt.sopac.org.fj/Projects/Evi/Index.htm: South Pacific Applied Geoscience Commission (SOPAC) environmental vulnerability index;
*   www.commonwealthsmallstates.org: Commonwealth vulnerability index;
*   www.home.um.edu.mt/islands/research.html: work since 1990 by Professor Lino Briguglio, Islands and Small States Institute, University of Malta, on an economic vulnerability index (Briguglio, 1995, 2003);
*   United Nations Conference on Trade and Development (UNCTAD) statistical profiles of least developed countries and use of an economic vulnerability index; and
*   United Nations Economic Commission for Latin America and the Caribbean (UNECLAC): Sub-regional Headquarters for the Caribbean work on a social vulnerability index.

Small Island Developing States (SIDS)

The UN identifies 53 small islands and coastal states as SIDS: they are members and observers of the Alliance of Small Island States (AOSIS) and members/associate members of the UN Regional Economic Commissions.

Alliance of Small Island States (AOSIS)

www.sidsnet.org/aosis/
AOSIS is a coalition of small island and low-lying coastal countries that share similar development challenges and vulnerability. It is the principle lobby and negotiating voice for small states in the UN system.

United Nations Office of the High Representative for the Least Developed Countries, Landlocked Developing Countries and Small Island Developing States (OHRLLS)

www.un.org/special-rep/ohrlls/ohrlls/default.htm
Established in 2001, OHRLLS provides support and advocacy on focus countries.

Regional Organizations of Small Island Developing States (SIDS)

In addition to the institutions listed, some key regional institutions supporting implementation of the Barbados Programme of Action (BPoA) are the following:

Pacific

The Council of Regional Organizations in the Pacific (CROP) brings together ten main regional organizations in the Pacific: the Pacific Islands Forum Secretariat (PIFS); the South Pacific Applied Geoscience Commission (SOPAC); the Secretariat for the Pacific Community (SPC); the South Pacific Regional Environment Programme (SREP); the University of the South Pacific (USP); the Pacific Islands Development Programme (PIDP); the South Pacific

Forum Fisheries Agency (FFA); the South Pacific Board for Educational Assessment (SPBEA); the South Pacific Tourism Organization (SPTO); and the Fiji School of Medicine (FSM).

Caribbean

Key institutions in the Caribbean include the Caribbean Community Secretariat (Caricom); the Organization of Eastern Caribbean States (OECS); the Caribbean Environmental Health Institute (CEHI); the Caribbean Disaster Emergency Response Agency (CDERA); the Caribbean Centre for Development Administration (Caricad); the Caribbean Community Climate Change Centre (CCCCC); the Caribbean Development Bank (CDB); the University of the West Indies (UWI); and the Eastern Caribbean Central Bank (ECCB).

AIMS Region (Atlantic, Indian Ocean, Mediterranean, South China Seas)

Key institutions include the Indian Ocean Commission Secretariat (IOC) and the Singapore Environment Institute (SEI).

CONFERENCES, AGREEMENTS AND PROCESSES

- Agenda 21, Chapter 17 (1992)

- Barbados Programme of Action on the Sustainable Development of Small Island Developing States (BPoA) (1994)

- United Nations General Assembly (UNGA) Resolution 50/116 of 20 December beginning work on a vulnerability index (1995)

- United Nations Commission on Sustainable Development (CSD) 7 on the five-year review of implementing the BPoA (1999)

- United Nations General Assembly Special Session (UNGASS) on implementing the BPoA (1999)

- Fourth World Trade Organization (WTO) Ministerial Conference, Doha, Qatar, Doha Ministerial Declaration, paragraph 35 on small economies (2001)

- International meeting on implementation of BPoA (Mauritius, 2004/5)

7

Key United Nations bodies and Bretton Woods institutions

- Alliance of Small Island States (AOSIS)
- United Nations Conference on Trade and Development (UNCTAD)
- United Nations Department of Economic and Social Affairs (DESA)
- United Nations Development Programme (UNDP)
- United Nations Educational, Scientific and Cultural Organization (UNESCO)
- United Nations Environment Programme (UNEP)
- United Nations International Strategy for Disaster Reduction (ISDR)
- United Nations Office of the High Representative for the Least Developed Countries, Landlocked Developing Countries and Small Island Developing States (OHRLLS)
- United Nations Regional Commissions

 # References

Briguglio, L (1995) 'The economic vulnerability of small island developing states', *World Development*, vol 23, pp1615–1632

Briguglio, L (2003) 'The economic vulnerability index – some conceptual and methodological issues', *Occasional Papers on Islands and Small States,* no 5, Islands and Small States Institute, Malta

Commonwealth Secretariat (1997) *A Future for Small States: Overcoming Vulnerability*, Report by a Commonwealth Advisory Group, Commonwealth Secretariat, London

Commonwealth Secretariat (2002) 'Small States: Economic Review and Basic Statistics', Annual Series, vol 7, autumn 2002, Commonwealth Secretariat, London

FAO (United Nations Food and Agriculture Organization) (1999) *State of the World's Forests*, FAO, Rome

Hay, J E (2000) 'Climate change and small island states: A popular summary of science-based findings and perspectives and their links with policy', Paper presented at the Second Alliance of Small Island States, Workshop on Climate Change Negotiations, Management and Strategy, 26 July–4 August 2000, Samoa

Hughes, A and Brewster, H (2002) *Lowering the Threshold*, Commonwealth Secretariat, London

Nurse, L (2002) 'Climate change and coastal vulnerability in small island states', Presentation at the Alliance of Small Island States' Inter-regional Preparatory Meeting for the World Summit on Sustainable Development, Singapore, 7–11 January 2002, www.sidsnet.org/workshop/singapore_agenda.html

Senanayake, R (1999) *Voices of the Earth, Cultural and Spiritual Values of Biodiversity: A Complementary Contribution to the Global Biodiversity Assessment*, Intermediate Technology Publications, on behalf of UNEP, Kenya, p165

Turner, R K, Subak, S and Adger, N (1996) 'Pressures, trends and impacts in coastal zones: Interactions between socioeconomic and natural systems', *Environmental Management*, vol 20, no 2, pp159–173

UNEP (United Nations Environment Programme) (1999a) *Caribbean Environment Outlook*, UNEP, Regional Office for Latin America and the Caribbean, Mexico

UNEP (1999b) *Western Indian Ocean Environment Outlook*, UNEP, Regional Office for Latin America and the Caribbean, Mexico

UNGASS (United Nations General Assembly Special Session) (1999) *Report of the Ad Hoc Committee of the Whole of the Twenty-second Special Session of the General Assembly*, United Nations, New York, UN General Assembly Official Records, Twenty-second Special Session, Supplement No 3 (A/S-22/9/Rev.1)

World Bank (2001) *Atlas 2001*, World Bank, Washington, DC

World Bank (2003) *World Bank Development Report 2003: Sustaining Development in a Dynamic World, Transforming Institutions, Growth and Quality of Life*, World Bank/Oxford University Press, Washington, DC, New York

WTO (World Trade Organization) (2001) *Doha WTO Ministerial Declaration*, WTO, Geneva, 20 November 2001, WT/Min(01)/Dec/1

Sustainable Development for Africa

8

 ## Context

Africa's wealth of resources offers myriad opportunities for sustainable development; yet the region has not been able to realize the full potential of these opportunities and entered the 21st century with enormous challenges. The demand for energy in Africa is set to grow exponentially; but the continuing lack of access to affordable and appropriate technologies is seriously constraining Africa's sustainable development options. Increasing numbers of African countries face water stress and scarcity, as well as critical levels of land degradation (UNEP, 2002), and the region is likely to be hit hardest by climate change (UNEP, 2001). The rising costs of water treatment, food imports, medical treatment and soil conservation measures are increasing human vulnerability and health insecurity and draining African countries of their economic resources (UNEP, 2002). The HIV/AIDS pandemic is affecting all aspects of human, social and economic development and weakening 'the ability of today's generation to pass on its skills and knowledge to the next' (Devarajan, 2003). In the face of these challenges, Africa's commitment to implementing multilateral environmental agreements is impressive (UNEP, 2002), and there are many regional and local sustainable development initiatives underway that address the concerns of the poor. The New Partnership for African Development (NEPAD) is key amongst these and was identified at the World Summit on Sustainable Development (WSSD) for special attention and support to direct international efforts towards Africa's development needs.

 ## Chapter VIII in summary

Sustainable development remains elusive for many African countries. Poverty is a major challenge and most African countries have not benefited fully from the opportunities of globalization, exacerbating the continent's marginalization. Efforts to achieve sustainable development have been hindered by conflicts, insufficient investment, limited market access opportunities and supply-side constraints, unsustainable debt burdens, declining levels of official

KEY WORDS

- **New Partnership for African Development (NEPAD)**
- **technology transfer**
- **education**
- **HIV/AIDS**
- **energy**
- **land degradation**
- **desertification**
- **disasters and conflicts**
- **water and sanitation**
- **land**
- **agriculture and food security**
- **chemicals**
- **digital divide**
- **tourism**
- **human settlements**

AT A GLANCE

- In 2000, there were 3.6 million refugees in Africa, 56 per cent of whom were under 18 years of age (UNHCR, 2001).

- In Africa, 340 million people or half the population live on less than US$1 per day (UNEP, 2002).

- The mortality rate of children under five years of age is 140 per 1000 (UNEP, 2002).

- Life expectancy at birth is only 54 years of age (UNEP, 2002).

- Only 58 per cent of the population have access to safe water (UNEP, 2002).

- The rate of illiteracy for people over 15 is 41 per cent (UNEP, 2002).

- Two-thirds of Africa's mountain area has been affected by 'high intensity conflict' (UNEP, 2002).

- There are only 18 mainline telephones per 1000 people in Africa, compared with 146 for the world as a whole and 567 for high-income countries (UNEP, 2002).

development assistance, and the impact of HIV/AIDS. The international community welcomes the **New Partnership for Africa's Development** (NEPAD) and pledges support towards the implementation of this vision and other development frameworks that are owned and driven by African countries and which embody poverty reduction strategies *[62]*. Action is required at all levels to:

- Create an **enabling environment** to achieve economic growth and sustainable development, and support African efforts for peace, stability and security, conflict resolution and prevention, democracy, good governance, and respect for human rights and fundamental freedoms, including the right to development and gender equality *[62a]*;
- Implement the vision of NEPAD and other efforts, including through **financing, technical and institutional cooperation** and **capacity-building** *[62b]*;
- Promote **technology** development, transfer and diffusion to Africa, and develop African centres of excellence *[62c]*;
- Develop **effective science and technology institutions** and research activities capable of developing and adapting world class technologies *[62d]*;
- Support national programmes and strategies on **education**, helping to ensure all children are able to complete a full course of primary schooling by 2015, with boys and girls having equal access to all levels of education *[62e]*;

8

- Enhance **industrial productivity, diversity and competitiveness** [62f] and the contribution of industry to Africa's sustainable development, especially **mining, minerals and metals** *[62g]*;
- Strengthen capacities in **environmental impact assessment, environmental legislative and institutional reform** for sustainable development, and in negotiating and implementing **multilateral environmental agreements** *[62h]*;
- Implement the **African Process for the Protection and Development of the Marine and Coastal Environment** *[62i]*;
- Deal with **energy** problems in Africa, including through support for NEPAD, which seeks to secure access for at least 35 per cent of the African population, especially people in rural areas, within 20 years *[62j(i)]*;
- Promote cleaner, more efficient use of natural gas, increased use of renewable energy, improved energy efficiency and access to advanced energy technologies *[62j(ii)]*;
- Mobilize resources for adaptation to the negative effects of **climate change, extreme weather events, sea level rise and climate variability**, and assist national climate change strategies and mitigation programmes *[62k]*;
- Develop affordable **transport systems and infrastructure** *[62l]*;
- Address the poverty affecting **mountain communities** *[63m]*; and
- Support afforestation, reforestation and **sustainable forest management**, including by combating deforestation, providing finance and technical support, and improving the policy and legal framework of the forest sector *[62n]*.

'Johannesburg must deliver a concrete programme of action if it is to have real impact on the lives of the millions of people around the world who still live in poverty'
(Mohammed Valli Moosa, Minister of Environmental Affairs and Tourism, Republic of South Africa, 2002).

The Johannesburg Plan of Implementation (JPOI) calls for financial and technical support for national implementation of the **Convention to Combat Desertification** (CCD) and to **integrate indigenous knowledge systems** within land and natural resources management practices. Measures are needed to improve **extension services** to rural communities, and to promote better **land, watershed management and agricultural practices** to overcome land degradation *[63]*.

Health

To strengthen healthcare systems in Africa *[64]*, finance and other support will be mobilized to:

- Promote **equitable access to healthcare** *[64a]*;
- Make available drugs and technology to fight and control **communicable diseases**, including HIV/AIDS, malaria, tuberculosis, and trypanosomiasis and **non-communicable diseases**, including those caused by poverty *[64b]*;
- Build the capacity of **medical and paramedical personnel** *[64c]*;
- Promote **indigenous knowledge**, including traditional medicine *[64d]*; and
- Research and control **Ebola** disease *[64e]*.

Disasters and vulnerability

The JPOI calls for action to deal effectively with **natural disasters and conflicts**, recognizing that conflicts in Africa have hindered, and in many cases obliterated, the gains and efforts made towards sustainable development. The most vulnerable members of society, including women and children, have borne the brunt of the impact *[65]*. Efforts at all levels will include support for:

- **Disaster management** capacities, including early warning and observation systems, assessments, prevention, preparedness, response and recovery *[65a]*;
- **Rapid response mechanisms** to enable Africa to deal more effectively with displaced people *[65b]*;
- Prevention, resolution, management and mitigation of **conflicts** and an early response to help avert tragic humanitarian consequences *[65c]*; and
- **Refugee host countries** in rehabilitating infrastructure and environments damaged in the process of receiving and settling refugees *[65d]*.

Water and sanitation

To promote **integrated water resources development**, measures will be taken to develop and effectively manage water resources while protecting water quality and aquatic ecosystems *[66]*. This includes action at all levels to:

- Provide access to **drinkable domestic water**, **hygiene education** and **improved household sanitation** and **waste management** through encouraging investment prioritizing the poor *[66a]*;
- Develop **integrated river basin and watershed management** strategies and plans for all major water bodies *[66b]*;
- Strengthen capacities for **data collection and processing** for planning, monitoring and enforcement purposes and water resource management arrangements *[66c]*; and
- Protect water resources and combat **water pollution**, and develop non-conventional water resources, including **desalination, rainwater harvesting** and **water recycling** *[66d]*.

Agriculture and food security

To achieve significantly **improved agricultural productivity and food security** and to achieve the Millennium Development Goals (MDGs), including halving by 2015 the proportion of people who suffer from hunger *[67]*, initiatives will be taken at all levels to:

- Support **national programmes and investment** in infrastructure, technology and extension services to regenerate the African agricultural sector and develop sustainable fisheries. African countries should be in the process of developing and implementing **food security strategies** by 2005 *[67a]*;

- Secure **equitable access to land tenure** and clarify **resource rights and responsibilities** through reform processes that respect the law, provide access to credit, enable poverty eradication and promote efficient and ecologically sound use of land. Enable women producers to become decision-makers and landowners, including the right to inherit land [67b];
- **Improve market access for goods particularly from least developed countries** [67c];
- Invest in **regional trade, market infrastructure and economic integration** [67d]; and
- Support **livestock development programmes** aimed at controlling animal diseases [67e].

Management of chemicals

Measures will be taken to achieve the sound management of chemicals, focusing on hazardous chemicals and wastes, through assistance with:

- National chemical profiles;
- Regional and national frameworks for chemicals management; and
- Establishing chemical focal points [68].

Digital divide

To bridge the digital divide and create digital opportunities, action will help to:

- Create an enabling environment for investment;
- Accelerate programmes to connect essential institutions; and
- Stimulate the adoption of information and communication technologies in government, commerce and elsewhere [69].

Tourism and biodiversity

Sustainable tourism that contributes to Africa's social, economic and infrastructure development will be supported [70] through action at all levels on:

- Implementing local, national and sub-regional projects, with an emphasis on **marketing African products** such as adventure tourism, ecotourism and cultural tourism [70a];
- National and cross-border conservation areas to promote ecosystem conservation and sustainable tourism [70b];
- Promoting the use of indigenous knowledge in natural resource management and ecotourism [70c];
- Assisting host communities to manage tourism projects to maximize benefits while limiting negative impacts on their traditions, culture and environment [70d]; and

'Every one of us can make a contribution. And quite often we are looking for the big things and forget that, wherever we are, we can make a contribution... Sometimes I tell myself, I may only be planting a tree here; but just imagine what's happening if there are billions of people out there doing something. Just imagine the power of what we can do' (Wangari Maathai, founder of Kenya's Green Belt Movement; now Deputy Prime Minister of Environment, Natural Resources and Wildlife, Kenya, 1977).

- Conservation of Africa's **biological diversity**, sustainable use of its components and the fair and equitable sharing of benefits arising from the use of genetic resources *[70e]*.

Habitat agenda

African countries will be supported in their efforts to implement the Habitat Agenda and the Istanbul Declaration by initiatives to:

- Strengthen capacities on sustainable urbanization and human settlements;
- Provide support for adequate shelter and basic services, and development of effective governance systems in cities and settlements; and
- Strengthen the United Nations Human Settlements Programme (UN-Habitat)/United Nations Environment Programme (UNEP) on managing water for African cities *[71]*.

 # Africa elsewhere in the JPOI

Commitments throughout the Johannesburg Plan of Implementation (JPOI) are pertinent to Africa. They include those on poverty eradication, water, sanitation and energy. The JPOI supports integrated land and water management, based upon the ecosystem approach, to help manage limited resources more effectively and to help combat the growing impact of climate change. Commitments to strengthen implementation of the United Nations Convention to Combat Desertification (CCD) are highlighted, along with actions to improve sustainable agricultural productivity and food security in line with the MDGs. Land reform issues identified in Chapter IV are critical to Africa's progress and efforts towards stemming the HIV/AIDS epidemic, including a new WSSD target on health literacy, are highly relevant to the NEPAD vision and all African countries. Other relevant commitments include those on access to energy and the use of financial instruments and mechanisms to increase capacity-building, training and strengthened technical knowledge.

TARGETS AND COMMITMENTS

- **Food security.** Support African countries in developing and implementing food security strategies by 2005 *[67a]* (new target).

- **Agriculture.** Improve sustainable agricultural productivity and food security in accordance with the Millennium Development Goals (MDGs), in particular to halve, by 2015, the proportion of people who suffer from hunger *[67]* (new target).

- **Energy.** Support Africa's efforts to implement New Partnership for African Development (NEPAD) objectives on energy, which seek to secure access for at least 35 per cent of the African population within 20 years, especially in rural areas *[62j(i)]* (new target).

EXAMPLES OF INDICATORS FOR MEASURING PROGRESS IN IMPLEMENTATION

- Proportion of the population living on below US$1 per day (Millennium Development Goal, or MDG)
- Prevalence of underweight children under five years of age (MDG)
- Proportion of the population below minimum level of dietary energy consumption (MDG)
- Net enrolment ratio in primary education (MDG)
- Literacy rate of 15- to 24-year olds (MDG)
- Under five mortality rate (MDG)
- Number of children orphaned by HIV/AIDS (MDG)
- Prevalence and death rates associated with malaria (MDG)
- Prevalence and death rates associated with tuberculosis (MDG)
- Proportion of population with sustainable access to an improved water source, urban and rural (MDG)
- Proportion of households with access to secure tenure (MDG)
- Economic and human loss due to natural disasters (United Nations Commission on Sustainable Development, or CSD)
- Proportion of urban population with access to improved sanitation (MDG)
- Proportion of population with sustainable access to an improved water source, urban and rural (MDG)
- Proportion of population with access to affordable essential drugs on a sustainable basis (MDG)
- Telephone lines and cellular subscribers per 100 population (MDG)
- Personal computers in use per 100 population and internet users per 100 population (MDG)

 # Resources

United Nations Environment Programme (UNEP)

www.unep.org

UNEP was the outcome of the 1972 Stockholm Conference on the Human Environment. It provides leadership and encourages partnership in caring for the environment by inspiring, informing and enabling nations/peoples to improve their quality of life without compromising that of future generations.

Partnership example

Global Network on Energy for Sustainable Development (GNESD)

Leading partner: United Nations Environment Programme (UNEP)

Dates: January 2003–December 2006

The objective of the Global Network on Energy for Sustainable Development (GNESD) is to make it easier for partners to contribute to the provision of environmentally sound energy services that underpin sustainable development. It will do so by supporting (amongst its partners) information exchange, learning, analysis and study, policy support, and capacity-building. It will work with a number of 'centres of excellence' in, amongst other places, Dakar, Nairobi, Cape Town, New Delhi, Beijing, Bangkok and Rio de Janeiro, as well as with partnerships established by governments, industry, international institutions and non-governmental organizations (NGOs). This North–South network of energy, development and environment institutions will allow members to cooperate on a range of energy for sustainable development topics; improve their ability to acquire and apply knowledge and experience; access quality advisory services; and improve their understanding of the links between sustainable energy and other environment/development priorities, as well as technology and policy options. It will ideally result in changes in government policies and programmes to favour energy for sustainable development approaches.

Contact information:
Interim Secretariat
Global Network on
Energy for Sustainable
Development
(GNESD)
Risoe National
Laboratory, Bldg 142
Frederiksborgvej 399
PO Box 49
DK 4000 Roskilde
Denmark
www.gnesd.org

United Nations Human Settlements Programme (UN-Habitat)

www.unhabitat.org
UN-Habitat is the lead UN agency for human settlements, including the Habitat Agenda (a practical road map to an urbanizing world, adopted by 171 governments at Habitat II, Istanbul, 1996).

United Nations Convention to Combat Desertification in Those Countries Experiencing Serious Drought and/or Desertification, Particularly in Africa (CCD)

www.unccd.ch
The CCD came into force in 1996 following the United Nations Conference on Environment and Development (UNCED) mandate to negotiate. In March 2003, 186 countries were parties. Activities to control/alleviate desertification are closely linked to needs/participation of local land users. UNEP has adopted a regional focus and requires national action programmes developed with local stakeholders (UNEP, 2002).

United Nations Convention on Biological Diversity (CBD)

www.biodiv.org

The CBD was also an outcome of UNCED. Three main goals of the CBD are the conservation of biological diversity; the sustainable use of its components; and the fair/equitable sharing of benefits arising from the use of genetic resources. The CBD includes the Cartagena Biosafety Protocol (living/genetically modified organisms) and the Jakarta Mandate (marine and coastal biodiversity).

Convention on International Trade in Endangered Species of Wild Fauna and Flora (CITES)

www.cites.org

CITES came into force in 1975 and ensures that the international trade in species of wild animals and plants does not threaten their survival.

New Partnership for African Development (NEPAD)

www.nepad.org

Adopted in July 2001 at the Summit of Organization of African Unity, NEPAD is a commitment by leaders to the people of Africa, addressing current challenges (Moosa, 2002). Objectives include to eradicate poverty; place African countries on the path of sustainable growth and development; halt marginalization of Africa in globalization; and accelerate empowerment of women. NEPAD recognizes the value of partnerships between African countries and with the international community.

Tokyo International Conference on African Development (TICAD)

Launched in 1993 by governments, the private sector and other stakeholders, the TICAD promotes high-level dialogue between African leaders and their partners, and mobilizes support for Africa's own development efforts.

 References

Devarajan, S (2003) 'Economic cost of AIDS', World Bank Press Release, 23 July 2003, www.worldbank.org

Moosa, M V (2002) 'African Renaissance', *Our Planet*, UNEP, vol 13, no 2, pp13–14

UNCHS (United Nations Centre for Human Settlements) (2000) *Habitat*, vol 6, no 1, p36

UNEP (United Nations Environment Programme) (2001) *Annual Report, 2001*, UNEP, Nairobi

UNEP (2002) *Global Environment Outlook 3*, Earthscan, London, www.unep.org/geo

UNHCR (United Nations High Commissioner for Refugees) (2001) *Refugee Children in Africa. Trends and Patterns in the Refugee Population in Africa Below the Age of 18 Years, 2000*, UNHCR, Geneva

World Bank (2000) *World Development Report, 2000/2001*, World Bank and Oxford University Press, Oxford, www.worldbank.org/wdr

CONFERENCES, AGREEMENTS AND PROCESSES

⧗ African Convention on the Conservation of Nature and Natural Resources (1968)

⧗ United Nations Convention to Combat Desertification (CCD) (1994)

⧗ World Summit on Social Development (Commitment 7) Copenhagen (1995)

⧗ South African Development Community (SADC) Policy and Strategy for Environment and Sustainable Development (1996)

⧗ United Nations Millennium Declaration (2000)

⧗ United Nations Decade to Roll Back Malaria, Particularly in Africa (2001–2010)

⧗ African Union launched; New Partnership for African Development (NEPAD) adopted (June 2001)

⧗ Pan-African Conference on Water in Africa (2003)

See the 'Resources' section at the end of this chapter for other relevant processes, organizations and web links.

Key United Nations bodies and Bretton Woods institutions

⧉ International Fund for Agricultural Development (IFAD)

⧉ International Monetary Fund (IMF)

⧉ Joint United Nations Programme on HIV/AIDS (UNAIDS)

⧉ United Nations Children's Fund (UNICEF)

⧉ United Nations Conference on Trade and Development (UNCTAD)

⧉ United Nations Development Programme (UNDP)

⧉ United Nations Economic Commission for Africa

⧉ United Nations Environment Programme (UNEP)

⧉ United Nations Food and Agriculture Organization (FAO)

⧉ United Nations High Commissioner for Refugees (UNHCR)

⧉ United Nations Human Settlements Programme (UN-Habitat)

⧉ World Health Organization (WHO)

⧉ World Bank

9 Other Regions

 ## Context

With Small Island Developing States (SIDS) and African countries given their own chapters within the Johannesburg Plan of Implementation (JPOI), Chapter IX addresses the priorities of the following UN regions: Latin America and the Caribbean; Asia and the Pacific; West Asia; and the Economic Commission for Europe, which includes North America. Of course, these regions exhibit startling differences in all three pillars of sustainable development. Chapters VII to IX are a recognition of this diversity and reflect a growing concern to strengthen regional and sub-regional responses to sustainable development. The JPOI reflects a number of regionally agreed strategies and priorities. Experience gained through the World Summit on Sustainable Development (WSSD) preparatory process, and the preparation of participatory national strategies for sustainable development, should further support the policy cohesion and coordination that is called for in the JPOI.

 ## Chapter IX in summary

KEY WORDS

* **Latin America and the Caribbean**

* **Asia and the Pacific**

* **West Asia**

* **Economic Commission for Europe**

* **regional action and cooperation**

* **capacity-building**

* **partnerships**

* **institutional frameworks**

Important sustainable development initiatives have been developed within the UN regions. The Johannesburg Plan of Implementation (JPOI) recognizes the value of these efforts and calls for further action, and coordination at all levels, to take these initiatives further *[72]*.

Latin America and the Caribbean

Initiative of Latin America and the Caribbean on Sustainable Development:

* Recognizes the importance of **regional action** towards sustainable development;
* Builds on the **Platform for Action on the Road to Johannesburg 2002**; and
* Seeks **concrete actions** in areas such as biodiversity; water resources; vulnerabilities and sustainable cities; social aspects; and economic aspects

AT A GLANCE

◻ Latin America and the Caribbean is the most urbanized region in the developing world. 75 per cent of the population live in urban areas, with 40 to 60 per cent of urban residents living in informal settlements (UNEP, 2002; UN Population Division, 2001).

◻ The Asia and Pacific region contains 12 megacities – Beijing, Calcutta, Delhi, Dhaka, Jakarta, Karachi, Metro Manila, Mumbai, Osaka, Seoul, Shanghai and Tokyo – with 12 per cent of the world's urban population (UN Population Division, 2001).

◻ In many countries of West Asia, water rationing is used to limit domestic demand. Jordan restricts water supplies in Amman to only three days a week. In Damascus, water can be used for less than 12 hours a day (UNEP, 2002).

◻ The pollution of surface and groundwater by excess nutrients from agricultural sources is a major cause for concern in Europe (EEA, 2002).

'... the significance of the Aarhus Convention is global. It is by far the most impressive elaboration of principle 10 of the Rio Declaration, which stresses the need for citizen's participation in environmental issues and for access to information on the environment held by public authorities ... it is the most ambitious venture in the area of 'environmental democracy' so far undertaken under the auspices of the United Nations'
(UN Secretary-General Kofi Annan, 2002).

and institutional arrangements, taking into account ethics for sustainable development [73].

The initiative envisages **actions among countries** in the region, fostering South–South cooperation and **attracting support** from groups of countries and multilateral and regional organizations. It is a framework for cooperation open to **partnerships** [74].

Asia and the Pacific

The **Phnom Penh Regional Platform on Sustainable Development for Asia and the Pacific**:

• Recognizes that the region contains over half of the world's population and the largest number of people living in poverty; sustainable development in Asia and the Pacific is critical to achieving sustainable development globally [75];

• Identifies **seven initiatives for action**: capacity-building for sustainable development; poverty reduction; cleaner production and sustainable energy; land management and biodiversity conservation; protection and management of freshwater resources; oceans, coastal and marine resources and sustainable development in small island developing states (SIDs); and action on atmosphere and climate change; and

• Identifies follow-up action of these initiatives through national strategies and relevant regional and sub-regional initiatives, including the **Regional**

Action Programme for Environmentally Sound and Sustainable Development and the Kitakyushu Initiative for a Clean Environment *[76]*.

West Asia

The West Asia Region is known for **scarce water** and **limited fertile land**. Progress has been made towards a more knowledge-based production of higher value-added commodities *[77]*. **Priorities** include: poverty alleviation; relief of debt burden and sustainable management of natural resources; integrated management of water resources and coastal zones; control of land and water pollution; and programmes to combat desertification *[78]*.

Economic Commission for Europe region

The Economic Commission for Europe (ECE) Regional Ministerial Meeting for the WSSD recognized the major role and responsibilities of the region in global efforts to achieve sustainable development. Priority actions, identified in the Ministerial Statement to the WSSD and **different approaches and mechanisms** to implement Agenda 21, may be needed in each country *[79]*:

'We learned with the elders that we are a tiny part of this immense universe with all the animals, the plants and the waters. Together we have to take care of the vessel in which we are all journeying' (Ailton Krenak, indigenous leader, Brazil, 2002).

- **Ongoing efforts** include: the **Environment for Europe process**; the fifth ECE Ministerial Conference (Kiev, May 2003); development of an environmental strategy for the 12 countries of Eastern Europe; the Caucasus and Central Asia; the Central Asian Agenda 21; Organisation for Economic Co-operation and Development (OECD) work on sustainable development; and the European Union (EU) sustainable development strategy.
- Relevant **conventions and processes** include: the Convention on Access to Information, Public Participation in Decision-Making and Access to Justice in Environmental Matters (Aarhus Convention); the Alpine Convention; the North American Commission for Environmental Cooperation; the International Boundary Waters Treaty Act; the Iqaluit Declaration of the Arctic Council; and processes to implement Agenda 21 in the Baltic and Mediterranean *[80]*.

 ## Other regional initiatives elsewhere in the JPOI

Regional frameworks and structures figure prominently throughout the Johannesburg Plan of Implementation (JPOI). Specific issues highlighted as requiring inter- and intra-regional cooperation and coordination include: oceans; coastal and marine resources; desertification; biodiversity; human settlements (JPOI, Chapter IV); and poverty reduction programmes (JPOI, Chapter II). Chapter X of the JPOI makes reference to the need for regional coordination in sharing information, making the best use of existing resources and for all forms of capacity-building. Concerns of Latin America/Caribbean and Asia/Pacific regions with respect to their small island developing states are discussed in Chapter VII. Recognizing that environmental impacts transcend state boundaries, Chapter XI urges the strengthening of institutional arrangements for protecting ecosystems and their individual components. It is noted that people's vulnerability to natural disasters can be lessened through effective regional strategies, including monitoring and early warning systems. Regional cooperation is called for to provide assistance to children orphaned by HIV/AIDS, and for more effective regional responses to environmental threats to health (JPOI, Chapter VI).

The UN's Regional Commissions are tasked with assisting in mobilizing technical and financial assistance from regional development banks for the implementation of regionally and sub-regionally agreed sustainable development programmes for education, technology transfer and capacity-building (JPOI, Chapter X). In its refocused remit, the United Nations Commission on Sustainable Development (CSD) is urged to make more effective use of existing regional structures and, in particular, to use regional reports more fully in planning and decision-making. Multi-stakeholder participation and partnerships are promoted in this context. Overall, it is recognized that strengthened regional capacities are essential for sustainable development (JPOI, Chapter XI).

TARGETS AND COMMITMENTS

Commitments in Chapter IX of the JPOI relate to the implementation of previously agreed regional initiatives and priorities, including the:

- Initiative of Latin America and the Caribbean on Sustainable Development;

- Phnom Penh Regional Platform on Sustainable Development for Asia and the Pacific;

- Regional Action Programme for Environmentally Sound and Sustainable Development (Asia and the Pacific Region);

- Kitakyushu Initiative for a Clean Environment;

- Arab Declaration to the World Summit on Sustainable Development (WSSD);

- Ministerial Statement to the WSSD adopted by the Economic Commission for Europe (ECE) Regional Ministerial Meeting for the WSSD;

- Environment for Europe Process.

EXAMPLES OF INDICATORS FOR MEASURING PROGRESS IN IMPLEMENTATION

- Proportion of population below US$1 a day (Millennium Development Goal, or MDG)

- Proportion of urban population with access to improved sanitation (MDG)

- Proportion of population with sustainable access to an improved water source, urban and rural (MDG)

- Proportion of population below minimum level of dietary energy consumption (MDG)

- Literacy rate of 15- to 24-year olds (MDG)

- Under five mortality rate (MDG)

- Proportion of births attended by skilled health professional (MDG)

- Prevalence and death rates associated with malaria (MDG)

- HIV Prevalence among 15- to 24-year-old pregnant women (MDG)

- Proportion of population with access to affordable essential drugs on a sustainable basis (MDG)

Partnership example

HIV/AIDS in the World of Work: A Tripartite Response in the Caribbean

Leading partner: International Labour Organization (ILO)

Dates: 2004–2007 (expected time frame)

This project aims to prevent HIV/AIDS among workers, enhancing workplace protection and reducing the adverse consequences of the epidemic on Caribbean development. More specifically, it will focus on:

- reducing the spread of HIV;

- a comprehensive strategic response to HIV/AIDS on work;

- implications of HIV/AIDS on work;

- capacity of governments, organizations of employers and workers, and people living with HIV/AIDS in education, awareness-raising and implementation;

- reducing stigma and discrimination; and

- improving capacity to determine financial costs of the epidemic and its impact on the social security system.

Contact information:
Technical Cooperation
and Advisory Services
International Labour
Organization (ILO)
International Labour
Office
4, Route des Morillons
CH-1211 Geneva 22
Switzerland
www.mirror/public/
english/protection/
trav/aids/

Resources

Other regional initiatives

www.un.org/jsummit/html/documents/prep2reg_outcomes.html
See this website for outcomes of regional preparatory processes for the World Summit on Sustainable Development (WSSD).

Initiative of Latin America and the Caribbean on Sustainable Development

This initiative was endorsed at the First Special Meeting of the Forum of Ministers of the Environment of Latin America and the Caribbean in Johannesburg on 31 August 2002.

Platform for Action on the Road to Johannesburg 2002

This platform was adopted by the governments of Latin America and the Caribbean in Rio de Janeiro (23–24 October 2001), meeting as the regional preparatory conference for the WSSD.

Phnom Penh Regional Platform on Sustainable Development for Asia and the Pacific

The Phnom Penh platform was adopted by members of the United Nations Economic and Social Commission for Asia and the Pacific (ESCAP) at the high-level regional meeting for the WSSD (Phnom Penh, 27–29 November 2001).

Fourth Ministerial Conference on Environment and Development in Asia and the Pacific

www.unescap.org/mced2000/outcom.htm
Occurring in Kitakyushu, Japan (31 August–5 September 2000), this conference adopted the *Regional Action Programme for Environmentally Sound and Sustainable Development 2001–2005*, as well as the Kitakyushu Initiative for a Clean Environment.

West Asia Regional Preparatory Committee Meeting for the WSSD

Attended by 10 North African and 12 Middle Eastern countries (Cairo, 24 October 2001), this meeting adopted the Arab Declaration to the WSSD.

Economic Commission for Europe (ECE) Regional Ministerial Meeting for the WSSD

Attended by members of the United Nations Economic Commission for Europe (ECE) region (includes Europe, North America, Nordic countries and Israel) (Geneva, 24–25 September 2001), this meeting adopted the Ministerial Statement to the WSSD.

Environment for Europe Process

www.unece.org/env/europe/welcome.html
United Nations ECE ministers have met since 1991. The Third Ministerial (1995) adopted an Environmental Programme for Europe. The Fourth Ministerial (1998) adopted the Aarhus Convention (see below).

Fifth ECE Ministerial Conference (Kiev, 21–23 May 2003)

www.kyiv-2003.info/main/index.php
The Fifth ECE Conference considered 'Environment for Europe: Progress and priorities for future years'. A number of regional environmental agreements were also signed.

Organisation for Economic Co-operation and Development (OECD)

www.oecd.org/home/
The OECD is based in Paris with a membership of 30 industrialized nations. It fosters good governance in the public sphere and private sector, and develops internationally agreed instruments, decisions and recommendations to promote rules where multilateral agreement is necessary for individual countries to make progress in a globalized economy. Work covers macro-economics, trade, education, development and science and innovation.

European Union (EU) Sustainable Development Strategy

www.europa.eu.int/comm/sustainable/pages/strategy_en.htm
Proposed by the European Commission (EC) and discussed by the EU (Göteborg, June 2001), this strategy outlines measures to address important threats to well-being, including climate change, poverty and emerging health risks.

Aarhus Convention

www.unece.org/env/pp/treatytext.htm
The Aarhus Convention on Access to Information, Public Participation in Decision-Making and Access to Justice in Environmental Matters was adopted in 1998 at the Fourth ECE Ministerial Conference. It entered into force on 30 October 2001.

Convention on the Protection of the Alps (Alpine Convention)

www.convenzionedellealpi.org/
The Alpine Convention was adopted in Salzburg on 7 November 1991. Parties pursue a comprehensive policy for the preservation/protection of the Alps by applying the principles of prevention, payment by the polluter and cooperation. Measures cover population and culture; regional planning; prevention of air pollution; soil conservation; water management; conservation of nature and the countryside; mountain farming; mountain forests; tourism and recreation; transport; energy; and waste management.

North American Commission on Environmental Cooperation

www.cec.org/home/index.cfm?varlan=english
Created by Canada, Mexico and the US under the North American Agreement on Environmental Cooperation (NAAEC) to address regional environment concerns, this commission helps to prevent potential trade and environment conflicts and promotes effective enforcement of environmental law.

Boundary Waters Treaty

www.ijc.org/rel/agree/water.html
Adopted on 1 November 1909, the Boundary Waters Treaty entered into force on 5 May 1910 to prevent uses, obstructions or diversions that materially affect the level or flow of boundary waters between the US and Canada (unless permitted by special agreement or approved by the International Joint Commission established under the treaty). The two parties also agree not to cause cross-border pollution of boundary waters.

Iqaluit Declaration of the Arctic Council

www.eppr.arctic-council.org/reports/980917.html
The Iqualuit Declaration was adopted at the First Ministerial Meeting of the Arctic Council (Iqaluit, Canada, 17–18 September, 1998) to promote cooperation/consultation among Arctic states with involvement of Arctic indigenous communities and other inhabitants, especially on sustainable development and environmental protection.

Baltic Agenda 21

www.ee/baltic21/
The Baltic Agenda was adopted at the Seventh Ministerial Session of the Council of the Baltic Sea States (Nyborg, Denmark, 22–23 June 1998). It was a joint, long-term effort by 11 countries of the Council of the Baltic Sea States to attain sustainable development in the region.

CONFERENCES, AGREEMENTS AND PROCESSES

Latic America and the Caribbean

- Global Conference on the Sustainable Development of Small Island Developing States (SIDS) adopts the Barbados Programme of Action (BPoA) (1994)
- Platform for Action on the Road to Johannesburg, Rio de Janeiro (E/CN.17/2002/PC.2/5/Add.2) (October 2001)
- Initiative of Latin America and the Caribbean on Sustainable Development (2002)
- International Meeting on the Barbados Programme of Action (BPoA) (2004)

CONFERENCES, AGREEMENTS AND PROCESSES (CONTD)

Asia and Pacific

- Global Conference on the Sustainable Development of Small Island Developing States (SIDS) adopts the Barbados Programme of Action (BPoA) (1994)

- Fourth Ministerial Conference on Environment and Development in Asia and the Pacific adopted the Kitayushu Initiative for a Clean Environment; and the Regional Action Programme for Environmentally Sound and Sustainable Development (2001–2005) (2000)

- Regional Platform on Sustainable Development for Asia and the Pacific, Phnom Penh (2001)

- Regional Action Programme for Environmentally Sound and Sustainable Development (2002)

- International Meeting on the Barbados Programme of Action (BPoA) (2004)

- Likely review of the Regional Action Programme for Environmentally Sound and Sustainable Development (2001–2005) by the Fifth Ministerial Conference on Environment and Development in Asia and the Pacific (2005)

West Asia

- Fourth Ministerial Conference on Environment and Development in Asia and the Pacific (Economic and Social Commission for Asia and the Pacific (2000)

- Jeddah Declaration on the Islamic Perspective on the Environment (2000)

- Tehran Declaration on Religions, Cultures and the Environment (2000)

- Abu Dhabi Declaration on the Future of the Arab Environment Programme (2001)

- West Asia Regional Preparatory Committee meeting for World Summit on Sustainable Development (WSSD) adopts the Arab Declaration to WSSD (2001)

Europe

- International Boundary Waters Treaty Act (1909)

- Environment for Europe process (initiated 1991 – ongoing)

- Towards Sustainability: European Community (EC) programme of policy and action in relation to the environment and sustainable development (better known as the Fifth EC Environmental Action Programme) (1993)

CONFERENCES, AGREEMENTS AND PROCESSES (CONTD)

- Mediterranean Agenda 21 (1994)

- Alpine Convention (1995)

- Nordic Strategy on Sustainable Development (1998)

- The Iqaluit Declaration of the Arctic Council (1998)

- The Baltic Agenda 21 (1998)

- Convention on Access to Information, Public Participation in Decision-Making and Access to Justice in Environmental Matters (Aarhus Convention) (1998)

- European Union (EU) Sixth Environmental Action Plan 'Environment 2010: Our Future, Our Choice' (2001)

- Ministerial statement to World Summit on Sustainable Development (WSSD) adopted by the United Nations Economic Commission for Europe (ECE) Regional Ministerial Meeting for WSSD (2001)

- Central Asian Agenda 21 – type II partnership (2003–2012)

- Fifth ECE Ministerial Conference – Environment for Europe, Kiev (May 2003)

- Review of progress in the implementation of priority actions for the ECE region as set out in the 2001 Ministerial Statement (2011)

Key United Nations bodies and Bretton Woods institutions

Latin America and the Caribbean

- United Nations Children's Fund (UNICEF) Americas and the Caribbean

- United Nations Development Programme (UNDP) country offices

- United Nations Economic Commission for Latin America and the Caribbean (ECLAC) – Santiago, Chile and Port-of-Spain, Trinidad

- United Nations Environment Programme (UNEP) Regional Office – Mexico City, Mexico

- United Nations Human Settlements Programme (UN-Habitat) Regional Office for Latin America and the Caribbean, Rio de Janeiro, Brazil

Key United Nations bodies and Bretton Woods institutions (*contd*)

Asia and the Pacific

- United Nations Children's Fund (UNICEF) East Asia and Pacific

- United Nations Development Programme (UNDP) country offices

- United Nations Economic and Social Commission for Asia and the Pacific (ESCAP) – Bangkok, Thailand

- United Nations Environment Programme (UNEP) Regional Office – Bangkok, Thailand

- United Nations Human Settlements Programme (UN-Habitat) Regional Office for Asia and the Pacific, Fukuoka, Japan

West Asia

- United Nations Development Programme (UNDP) country offices

- United Nations Economic and Social Commission for Western Asia (ESCWA) – Beirut, Lebanon

- United Nations Environment Programme (UNEP) Regional Office for West Asia (ROWA) – Manama, State of Bahrain

Economic Commission for Europe Region

- North American Commission for Environmental Cooperation

- Organisation for Economic Co-operation and Development (OECD)

- UNEP Regional Office for North America (RONA) – Washington, DC, US

- United Nations Children's Fund (UNICEF) Central and Eastern Europe and Baltic States

- United Nations Development Programme (UNDP) Regional Bureau for Europe and the Commonwealth of Independent States (CIS)

- United Nations Economic Commission for Europe (UNECE) – Geneva, Switzerland

- United Nations Environment Programme (UNEP) Regional Office – Geneva, Switzerland

 # References

Annan, K, Secretary-General of the UN (2002) In: Stakeholder Forum Network 2015 Bulletin Issue No 1, 2003

Arab Declaration to the World Summit on Sustainable Development (WSSD) (2001) United Nations Economic and Social Council, Commission on Sustainable Development acting as the Preparatory Committee for the WSSD, second preparatory session (28 January–8 February 2002), 1 December 2001, New York (E/CN.17/2002/PC.2/)

Commission of the European Communities (2001) *A Sustainable Europe for a Better World: A European Union Strategy for Sustainable Development*, Commission of the European Communities, Brussels, 15 May 2001, Communication from the Commission, COM(2001)264 final

CSD (United Nations Commission on Sustainable Development) (2001) *Rio de Janeiro Platform for Action on the Road to Johannesburg 2002*, United Nations Economic and Social Council, Commission on Sustainable Development acting as the Preparatory Committee for the WSSD, second preparatory session (28 January–8 February 2002), 1 December 2001, Brussels (E/CN.17/2002/PC.2/5/Add.2)

ECOSOC (United Nations Economic and Social Council) (2002) Ministerial Statement to the World Summit on Sustainable Development (WSSD) (adopted by the Economic Commission for Europe Regional Ministerial Meeting for the Summit on 25 September 2001), United Nations Economic and Social Council, Commission on Sustainable Development acting as the Preparatory Committee for the WSSD, second preparatory session (28 January–8 February 2002), 7 December 2001, New York (E/CN.17/2002/PC.2/5/Add.1)

EEA (European Environment Agency) (2002) *European Environment Agency, Europe's Environment: The Third Assessment*, EEA, Environmental Assessment Report No 10, 2003

ESCAP (United Nations Economic and Social Commission for Asia and the Pacific) (2000a) *Kitakyushu Initiative for a Clean Environment*, ESCAP, Bangkok

ESCAP (2000b) *Regional Action Programme for Environmentally Sound and Sustainable Development, 2001–2005*, ESCAP, Bangkok, 2000

ESCAP (2001) *Phnom Penh Regional Platform on Sustainable Development for Asia and the Pacific*, Task Force for the Preparation of WSSD in Asia and the Pacific (ESCAP, Asian Development Bank, UNDP, UNEP), Bangkok, 29 November 2001 (ENR/HRM/WWS/1/Rev.1) (also available as: E/CN.17/2002/PC.2/8)

Groombridge, B and Jenkins, M D (2000) *Global Biodiversity: Earth's Living Resources in the 21st Century*, The World Conservation Press, Cambridge

Krenak, A (2002) cited in Liz Hosken, 'Earth Democracy', *Resurgence Magazine*, no 214, September/October, p12

UNDP (United Nations Development Programme) (2003) *Human Development Report 2003, Millennium Development Goals: A Compact among Nations to End Human Poverty*, hdr.undp.org/reports/global/2003

UNEP (United Nations Environment Programme) (2002) *Global Environment Outlook – 2 (GEO-2)*, Earthprint, www.unep.org/geo/geo2000

UNEP–ROLAC (Regional Office for Latin America and Caribbean) (2002) *Latin America and Caribbean Initiative for Sustainable Development*, UNEP, Regional Office for Latin America and the Caribbean, Mexico, 30 August 2002, UNEP/LAC-SMIG.I/2

UN-Habitat (United Nations Human Settlements Programme) (2001) General Assembly, Special Session for an Overall Review and Appraisal of the Implementation of the Habitat Agenda, New York, 6–8 June 2001

UNPD (United Nations Population Division) (2001) *World Urbanisation Prospects Revision 2001*, UNPD, Istanbul

Means of Implementation

10

 ## Context

Agenda 21 agreed that official development assistance (ODA) would be a main source of financing for implementation in developing countries and that substantial new and additional funding was required for funding sustainable development. At the World Summit on Sustainable Development (WSSD), the perception that developed countries had fallen short of their 1992 commitments on financing formed the backdrop of what became some of the toughest negotiations of the summit. In the end, the WSSD reiterated existing commitments on financing, and placed a stronger emphasis on mobilizing resources and creating an enabling environment for investment, private international financial flows, public–private partnerships and the effective use of ODA. The other means of implementation outlined in Agenda 21 (transfer of environmentally sound technologies; science for sustainable development; promoting education; public awareness and training; capacity-building; and information for decision-making) all remain within the Johannesburg Plan of Implementation (JPOI) under Chapter X. National mechanisms and international institutional arrangements are addressed in Chapter XI.

Implementation was a central theme at WSSD and remains the litmus test of commitment to the JPOI. Klaus Töpfer of the United Nations Environment Programme (UNEP) called for the summit to be one of:

> '... implementation of existing declarations. We have very important and very good declarations, first and foremost the Earth Summit's Agenda 21. Now it is high time to implement them, with a targeted, benchmarked timetable-orientated action programme... It must be a summit of concrete actions, reliable and accountable, with the aim of overcoming poverty ... and changing unsustainable consumption patterns in the developed countries' (UNEP, 2002).

KEY WORDS

- **enabling environment**
- **foreign direct investment (FDI)**
- **official development assistance (ODA)**
- **debt**
- **trade**
- **human rights**
- **right to self-determination**
- **environmentally sound technologies**
- **science and technology**
- **issues of global public interest**
- **terrorism**
- **education**
- **capacity-building (human, institutional, infrastructure)**
- **information**

AT A GLANCE

☼ In 2001, net private flows of external financing to emerging market economies was US$133.2 billion compared to US$11.1 billion in official flows (IIF, 2003).

☼ Monterrey commitments would raise the official development assistance (ODA) gross national income (GNI) ratio to 0.26 per cent by 2006, still well below the ratio of 0.33 per cent consistently achieved until 1992. The amount promised also falls considerably short of the US$50 billion annual additional resources that have been projected as needed to meet the Millennium Development Goals (MDGs) (Commonwealth Secretariat, 2003).

☼ The banks involved in the Equator Initiative (a partnership which addresses poverty through the conservation and sustainable use of biodiversity in the equatorial belt by fostering community partnerships) provided over US$9 billion in loans for infrastructure projects in 2002 (WRI, 2003).

☼ In 2002, net transfers on foreign investment (after taking account of profit remittances), though positive for all regions except the Middle East and North Africa, were insufficient to offset the net transfer on debt for all developing countries (Commonwealth Secretariat, 2003).

'A lot of people believe that there must be a global deal, with contributions from both developed and developing countries. Economic cooperation is not a matter of charity, but of investment, and investment with a very high return' (Klaus Töpfer, executive director of UNEP, 2002).

 ## Chapter X in summary

Implementation of Agenda 21, the JPOI and internationally agreed development goals requires:

- A **substantially increased effort** by countries and the international community, based on the recognition that each country has primary responsibility for its own development and that the role of national policies and development strategies cannot be overemphasized;
- Rio principles to be taken into account, including the **common but differentiated responsibility** of states;
- A significant increase in financial resources, as set out in the Monterrey Consensus, including **new and additional financial resources**, particularly for developing countries;
- Implementation of the commitments of relevant **major UN conferences**, such as the Third United Nations Conference on the Least Developed Countries and the Global Conference on the Sustainable Development of Small Island Developing States; and
- Implementation of relevant **international agreements** made since 1992, particularly the International Conference on Financing for Development and

the Fourth World Trade Organization (WTO) Ministerial Conference that was held in Doha in 2001, including building on them as part of a process of achieving sustainable development [81].

Enabling financial environment

Governments' first step towards ensuring that the 21st century becomes the century of sustainable development for all will be action to **mobilize and increase the effectiveness of financial resources** and to achieve the national and international economic conditions needed to fulfil the internationally agreed development goals [82]. In the common pursuit of growth, poverty eradication and sustainable development, critical challenges are:

- Ensuring necessary **internal conditions**;
- Improved efficacy, coherence and consistency of **macro-economic policies**; and
- An **enabling domestic environment** for mobilizing domestic resources, increasing productivity, reducing capital flight, encouraging the private sector and attracting and making effective use of international investment and assistance.

The international community should support efforts to create such an environment [83].

Foreign direct investment

Greater flows of **foreign direct investment** (FDI) will be facilitated to support sustainable development activities in developing countries, including infrastructure development [84], including through:

- Domestic and international conditions that will increase the flow of FDI to developing countries [84a]; and
- Use of **export credits** to encourage sustainable development and FDI [84b].

Official development assistance

Substantial increases in **official development assistance** (ODA) and other resources are needed if developing countries are to achieve the internationally agreed development goals. To build support for ODA and **improve aid effectiveness**, governments will cooperate to improve policies and development strategies at both the national and international levels [85]. Actions include:

- Making available increased ODA commitments announced at the International Conference on Financing for Development in Monterrey. Developed countries that have not done so are urged to make concrete efforts to fulfil the **target of 0.7 per cent of gross national product (GNP) as ODA**, and to implement their commitments on ODA in the Programme of Action for the Least Developed Countries for the Decade 2001–2010. Developing countries are encouraged to build on the progress achieved in ensuring that ODA is used effectively *[85a]*; and

- Targeting ODA more effectively towards poverty eradication, sustained economic growth and sustainable development. Institutions should intensify efforts to **harmonize operational procedures** *[85b]*.

Financial mechanisms and institutions

Full and effective use will be made of **existing financial mechanisms and institutions** *[86]* by actions to:

- Strengthen ongoing efforts to reform the existing **international financial architecture** to foster a transparent, equitable and inclusive system *[86a]*;
- Improve **transparency and information about financial flows** to contribute to stability in the international financial environment. Measures that lessen the impact of **excessive volatility** in short-term capital flows must be considered *[86b]*;
- Ensure that funds are **made available on a timely and predictable basis to international organizations** and agencies for their sustainable development activities *[86c]*;
- Encourage the **private sector, private foundations and civil society** to provide financial and technical assistance to developing countries *[86d]*; and
- Support new and existing **public–private financing mechanisms** to improve infrastructure and benefit small entrepreneurs, small- and medium-sized enterprises (SMEs) and community-based enterprises *[86e]*.

Governments welcomed the third replenishment of the **Global Environment Facility (GEF)**, which was encouraged to leverage additional funds from public and private organizations and to streamline procedures and its project cycle *[87]*. Governments will also explore new public and private **innovative sources of finance** for development, noting the possibility of using **special drawing rights** allocations *[88]*.

Debt

Debt relief and, where appropriate, debt cancellation will be used to reduce unsustainable **debt burdens** and address the debt problems of developing countries, especially the poorest and most heavily indebted ones. There should be an increase in the use of **grants** for the poorest debt-vulnerable countries. Countries are encouraged to develop **national comprehensive strategies** to monitor and manage external liabilities *[89]*. Action is required to:

- Implement the enhanced **heavily indebted poor countries (HIPC) initiative** *[89a]*;
- Encourage the participation of all creditors in the HIPC initiative *[89b]*;
- Bring together international **debtors and creditors** in relevant international forums to restructure unsustainable debt *[89c]*;
- Acknowledge the problems of debt sustainability in some **non-HIPC low-income countries** *[89d]*;
- Encourage exploration of **innovative mechanisms** to address debt problems, including **'debt for sustainable development'** swaps *[89e]*; and
- Ensure that resources provided for debt relief do not detract from ODA *[89f]*.

Doha development round

Trade plays a major role in achieving sustainable development and eradicating poverty. The JPOI encourages WTO members to pursue the work programme agreed at the **Fourth WTO Ministerial Conference in Doha** in 2001 *[90]*, and urges them to:

- Facilitate the accession of developing countries that apply for **WTO membership** *[90a]*;
- Support the **Doha work programme** as a commitment by countries to mainstream appropriate trade policies in their development programmes and policies *[90b]*;
- Implement substantial **trade-related technical assistance and capacity-building**, supporting the Doha Development Agenda Global Trust Fund *[90c]* and implementing the New Strategy for World Trade Organization Technical Cooperation for Capacity-building, Growth and Integration *[90d]*; and
- Support implementation of the Integrated Framework for Trade-related Technical Assistance to Least Developed Countries *[90e]*.

Exports of developing countries

In accordance with the **Doha Ministerial Declaration** (DMD), governments are determined to take concrete action to address the concerns raised by developing countries on implementing WTO agreements and decisions *[91]*. They call on WTO members to:

- Fulfil the commitments of the DMD on **market access**, particularly for products of export interest to developing countries *[92]*;
- Review all **special and differential treatment** provisions with a view to strengthening them and making them more precise *[92a]*;
- Reduce or eliminate **tariffs on non-agricultural products**, especially on products of export interest to developing countries *[92b]*;

- Fulfil, without prejudging the outcome of negotiations, the commitment for comprehensive negotiations initiated under article 20 of the **Agreement on Agriculture**, take note of the **non-trade concerns** reflected in negotiating proposals submitted by WTO members and confirm that these will be taken into account in the negotiations *[92c]*; and
- Work towards the objective of **duty-free and quota-free access for all** least developed countries' exports *[93]*.

Small and vulnerable economies and commodity-dependent countries

Actions include to:

- Actively pursue the WTO work programme related to **small, vulnerable economies** in a way that supports their efforts towards sustainable development *[94]*; and
- Build the capacity of **commodity-dependent countries** to diversify their exports and address the instability of commodity prices and declining terms of trade. Strengthen activities covered by the Second Account of the Common Fund for Commodities to support sustainable development *[95]*.

To enhance the benefits for developing countries and economies in transition from trade liberalization *[96]*, action will be taken to:

- Improve **trade infrastructure and institutions** *[96a]*;
- Increase the capacity of developing countries to **diversify and increase exports** to cope with commodity price instability *[96b]*; and
- Increase the **value added** of developing country exports *[96c]*.

Mutual supportiveness of trade, environment and development

To continue to enhance the **mutual supportiveness of trade, environment and development** *[97]*, action at all levels will:

- Encourage the **WTO committees** on trade and environment and on trade and development to act as a forum for identifying and debating developmental and environmental aspects of the negotiations *[97a]*;
- Support the completion of the Doha Declaration's work programme on subsidies in order to promote sustainable development and encourage the **reform of subsidies that have considerable negative effects on the** environment *[97b]*;
- Encourage cooperation on trade, environment and development between the secretariats of the WTO, the United Nations Committee on Trade and Development (UNCTAD), the United Nations Development Programme

'A strategy for sustainable development involves people who understand what is needed, have the necessary information at their fingertips, are part of an integrated national drive towards a sustainable future, and have participated in the vital decisions that affect them' (Philip Dobie of UNDP, undated).

(UNDP) and the United Nations Environment Programme (UNEP), and other relevant international and regional organizations *[97c]*; and

- Encourage the voluntary use of **environmental impact assessments** as a national-level tool to help identify trade, environment and development linkages *[97d]*.

Mutual supportiveness between the multilateral trading system and multilateral environmental agreements will be promoted in a way that is consistent with sustainable development goals, supportive of the WTO's work programme, and recognizes the importance of maintaining the integrity of both sets of instruments *[98]*.

To complement and support the Doha Declaration and Monterrey Consensus, further action is agreed to **enhance the benefits of trade liberalization**, especially for developing countries and countries with economies in transition *[99]*, by:

'The ability of a country to follow a path of sustainable development is determined by the capabilities of its peoples and institutions. Capacity-building is the sum of efforts needed to nurture, enhance and utilize the skills of people and institutions to progress towards sustainable development' (Capacity 21, UNDP, www.undp.org).

- Establishing and strengthening existing **trade and cooperation agreements** aimed achieving sustainable development *[99a]*;
- Supporting voluntary WTO compatible, market-based initiatives to create and expand markets for **environmentally friendly goods and services**, including **organic products** *[99b]*; and
- Introducing measures to simplify, and make more transparent, **domestic regulations and procedures** that affect trade *[99c]*.

Health and the Agreement on Trade-Related Aspects of Intellectual Property Rights

To address the **public health problems** that affect many developing countries, especially in relation to HIV/AIDS, tuberculosis, malaria and other epidemics, the JPOI reiterates its commitment to the Doha Declaration on the **Trade-Related Aspects of Intellectual Property Rights (TRIPS) Agreement and public health**, and reaffirms that the agreement can and should be interpreted in a manner that is supportive of WTO members' right to protect health and to promote access to **medicines for all** *[100]*.

Trade policy for environmental purposes/ environmental measures

States should cooperate in promoting a **supportive and open international economic system** that leads to economic growth and sustainable development in all countries in order to better address the problems of environmental degradation:

- **Trade policy measures for environmental** purposes should not constitute a means of arbitrary or unjustifiable trade discrimination or a disguised restriction on international trade.

- Unilateral actions to deal with environmental challenges outside the importing country should be avoided.
- As far as possible, environmental measures to address **transboundary or global environmental problems** should be based on international consensus *[101]*.

Human rights

Steps will be taken to avoid **unilateral measures** that are not in accordance with international law and the Charter of the United Nations, and which impede the full achievement of economic and social development by the population of affected countries, particularly women and children, and that creates obstacles that hinder their well-being or full enjoyment of their human rights. This includes the right of everyone to have a standard of living that is adequate for their heath as well as their right to food, medical care and necessary social services. Governments will ensure that food and medicine are not used as tools for political pressure *[102]*.

Right to self-determination

Effective measures will be taken to remove obstacles to the realization of the right of peoples to **self-determination**, particularly peoples living under colonial and foreign occupation *[103]*. This will not be construed as supporting any action that would dismember or impair the territorial integrity or political unity of sovereign and independent states that conduct themselves in compliance with the principle of equal rights and self-determination of peoples, and therefore have a government that represents the whole people of the territory *[104]*.

Environmentally sound technologies/technology transfer

With respect to **environmentally sound technologies** (ESTs), the JPOI focuses on addressing the needs of developing countries and countries with economies in transition, including through the use of **favourable trade terms** such as concessional and preferential terms on a mutually agreed basis *[105]*. Commitments are made to:

- Provide **information** more effectively *[105a]*;
- Improve existing **national institutional capacities** in developing countries on ESTs *[105b]*;
- Facilitate country-driven **technology needs assessments** *[105c]*;
- Establish **legal and regulatory frameworks** in supplier and recipient countries to assist EST transfer *[105d]*; and
- Promote access to, and transfer of, technology related to **early warning systems** and programmes to help reduce the impacts of natural disasters to developing countries *[105e]*.

In order to improve the transfer of technologies to developing countries, especially from country to country and at a regional level *[106]*, urgent action at all levels will:

- Improve the **collaboration among universities, research institutions, government agencies and the private sector** *[106a]*;
- Develop networks of technology and productivity centres, research, training and development institutions and **centres for cleaner production** *[106b]*;
- Create **partnerships** that bring about investment and technology transfer, development and diffusion, sharing of best practices, and collaboration between corporations and research institutes to improve industrial efficiency, agricultural productivity, environmental management and competitiveness *[106c]*;
- Assist with accessing knowledge and ESTs that are publicly owned or in the public domain *[106d]*; and
- Support mechanisms for the **development, transfer and diffusion of ESTs** *[106e]*.

Science and technology

Assistance will be provided to developing countries in building **centres for sustainable development**, enabling them to access a larger share of multilateral and global research and development programmes *[107]*. Their capacity will also be built in **science and technology for sustainable development** through collaboration, partnerships and networking between **centres of scientific excellence** *[108]*.

To improve policy and decision-making at all levels based on better **collaboration between natural and social scientists, and between scientists and policy-makers** *[109]*, urgent action will be taken to:

- Increase the use of scientific knowledge and technology, and the beneficial use of local and indigenous knowledge *[109a]*;
- Make greater use of **integrated scientific assessments, risk assessments and interdisciplinary and inter-sectoral approaches** *[109b]*;
- Support international scientific assessments that help inform decision-making (such as the Intergovernmental Panel on Climate Change – IPCC) with the broad participation of developing country experts *[109c]*;
- Assist developing countries in **implementing science and technology policies** *[109d]*;
- Establish **partnerships** between scientific, public and private institutions, and integrate **scientists' advice** within decision-making bodies *[109e]*; and
- Improve **science-based decision-making**, reaffirming the **precautionary approach** as set out in principle 15 of the Rio Declaration on Environment and Development *[109f]*.

Developing countries' capacities in **environmental protection and management** will be increased *[110]* through urgent actions to:

* Improve the use of science and technology for environmental monitoring and modelling *[110a]*;
* Promote the use of satellite technologies for data collections and better aerial and ground-based observations *[110b]*; and
* Set up or develop **national statistical services** to provide sound data on science education and research and development activities *[110c]*.

Regular channels will be established between policy-makers and the scientific community to deliver science and technology advice in implementing Agenda 21. **Networks on science and education** for sustainable development will help countries to share their knowledge and experiences *[111]*, while **information and communication technologies (ICTs)** will be used to increase the frequency of communication and knowledge-sharing and access to ICTs. This work will build on the efforts of the United Nations Information and Communication Technology Task Force, amongst others *[112]*.

The JPOI calls for support of publicly funded research and development entities in building strategic alliances to create **cleaner production and product technologies** *[113]*, and for the better integration of publicly funded research and development with development programmes *[119]*.

Issues of global public interest

Commitments include to examine **issues of global interest** through open, transparent and inclusive workshops *[114]* and to take concerted action against **international terrorism** *[115]*.

Education

Education is critical for promoting sustainable development and, as such, it is essential to mobilize resources at all levels to complement the efforts of national governments *[116]* towards the following goals and actions:

* The **Millennium Development Goal (MDG)** of ensuring that, by 2015, children everywhere, boys and girls alike, will be able to complete a full course of primary schooling *[116a]*; and
* Providing all children, particularly those living in rural areas and those living in poverty, and especially girls, with the chance to complete a full course of primary education *[116b]*.

Support will be provided to **education, research, public awareness programmes and development institutions** in developing countries and countries with economies in transition *[117]* to:

- Sustain educational infrastructures and programmes *[117a]*; and
- Avoid the frequent and serious financial constraints faced by many institutions of higher learning *[117b]*.

The JPOI calls for the **impact of HIV/AIDS on the educational system** to be addressed *[118]* and for resources to be used to improve the integration of sustainable development in education development programmes. Resources need to be allocated for **basic education** *[119]* and **gender disparity** must be eliminated in primary and secondary education by 2005, as well as at all levels of education no later than 2015 to meet the MDGs. These objectives will be achieved with '**gender mainstreaming**' and by creating a gender-sensitive education system *[120]*.

Sustainable development will be integrated within education systems at all levels to promote education as a key agent for change *[121]*. Education for sustainable development will be part of **education action plans** that are relevant to local conditions and lead to community development *[122]*. The JPOI calls for community members to be provided with a wide range of **continuing education** opportunities to end illiteracy and promote life-long learning and sustainable development *[123]*. To support the use of education to promote sustainable development *[124]*, urgent actions will:

- Integrate information and communication technologies (**ICTs**) within school curriculum development, ensuring access by communities and establishing an enabling environment for ICTs *[124a]*;
- Promote greater access by students, researchers and engineers from developing countries to the **universities** and research institutions of developed countries *[124b]*;
- Further implement **United Nations Commission on Sustainable Development (CSD)** work on education for sustainable development [124c]; and
- Recommend that the United Nations General Assembly (UNGA) adopts a **decade of education for sustainable development starting in 2005** *[124d]*.

Capacity-building

Capacity-building initiatives and partnerships will be stepped up, with the focus on human, institutional and infrastructure capacity *[125]*. The JPOI supports initiatives from local to regional levels within **centres of excellence** for education, research and training *[126]*. It also supports stronger capacity-building for developing countries, including the **UNDP's Capacity 21 programme** *[127]* to:

- Assess their own capacity development needs and opportunities at different levels *[127a]*;

- Design capacity-building programmes that will focus on meeting the challenges of globalization and attaining internationally agreed development goals *[127b]*;
- Develop the capacity of civil society and youth to participate in the design and implementation of sustainable development policies and strategies *[127c]*; and
- Build national capacities for effective implementation of Agenda 21 *[127d]*.

Information

Governments will ensure access at the national level to **environmental information, judicial and administrative proceedings and public participation in decision-making**. This relates to principle 10 of the Rio Declaration on Environment and Development (on access to environmental information and public participation): principles 5 (poverty eradication), 7 (common but differentiated responsibilities) and 11 (on the use of environmental legislation and standards) will also be taken into account *[128]*. Actions include:

- Strengthening national and regional **information and statistical services** that are relevant to sustainable development, using disaggregated data *[129]*;
- Working at the national level on **indicators for sustainable development**, including its gender aspects *[130]*; and
- Working in accordance with paragraph 3 of Decision 9/4 of the CSD (on information for decision-making and participation) *[131]*.

The JPOI promotes the development and wider use of **Earth observation technologies**, including satellite remote sensing, global mapping and geographic information systems (GIS). These will help to provide data on environmental impacts, land use and land-use changes *[132]*. Urgent actions will:

- Coordinate **global observing systems** and research programmes, and build capacity to provide integrated global observations *[132a]*;
- Develop information systems that make possible the sharing of valuable data such as **Earth observation data** *[132b]*; *and*
- Encourage initiatives and partnerships for **global mapping** *[132c]*.

Developing countries, in particular, will be supported in their efforts to *[133]*:

- Collect data that are accurate, long term, consistent and reliable *[133a]*;
- Use **satellite and remote sensing** technologies to improve ground-based observations *[133b]*; and
- Access, explore and use geographic information by using satellite remote sensing, satellite global positioning, mapping and GIS *[133c]*.

Efforts to prevent and lessen the impacts of natural disasters will be supported *[134]* by the provision of affordable **disaster-related information for early-warning** purposes *[134a]* and the translation of data from global meteorological observation systems into timely and useful products *[134b]*.

With respect to **support for decision-making**, the JPOI calls for wider application of **environmental impact assessments** *[135]* and the promotion of methodologies to be used in policies, strategies and projects in sustainable development decision-making at the local and national levels. The choice of methodology should be adequate to country-specific conditions and voluntary *[136]*.

 ## Means of implementation elsewhere in the JPOI

Elements that make up the means of implementation are deeply cross-cutting in nature and occur throughout the Johannesburg Plan of Implementation (JPOI). There are links, in particular, with issues in Chapter V (on globalization) and Chapter XI (on the institutional framework for sustainable development). These relate to the need to create internal national conditions conducive to investment and efforts to promote an open, equitable, rules-based, predictable and non-discriminatory multilateral trading and financial system. Actions that support commitments on finance, capacity-building and information are addressed at different levels (international, regional and national) in Chapter XI. Trade issues are addressed in Chapter V, but also with respect to energy, chemicals, fisheries, biodiversity and forests in Chapter IV. The JPOI includes commitments to provide 'financial and technical assistance' in a wide range of areas. It acknowledges the need to maximize the use of existing resources, including ODA, and to find new and innovative sources of finance. Funding issues related to multilateral agreements and mechanisms occur throughout the JPOI, focusing on areas such as desertification, disaster management, climate change, capacity-building and the sustainable development of small island developing states (SIDS).

TARGETS AND COMMITMENTS

▣ **Education.** By 2015 ensure that children everywhere, boys and girls alike, will be able to complete a full course of primary schooling (Millennium Development Goal, or MDG).

▣ **Education.** Eliminate gender disparity in primary and secondary education by 2005 (Dakar Framework for Action on Education for All) and at all levels of education no later than 2015 (MDG).

▣ **Education.** Recommend a United Nations Decade of Education for Sustainable Development, starting in 2005 (new target).

TARGETS AND COMMITMENTS (CONTD)

Further commitments in Chapter X of the JPOI relate to the MDG on developing a global partnership for development. Broadly, they include efforts to:

- **Finance.** Mobilize and increase the effectiveness of financial resources and achieve the national and international conditions to fulfil internationally agreed development goals; create the necessary conditions to increase foreign direct investment (FDI) in developing countries; build support for official development assistance (ODA); make full and effective use of existing financial mechanisms and institutions; foster a transparent, equitable and inclusive (financial) system; and ensure timely provision of funds to international organizations for their sustainable development activities.

- **Debt.** Reduce unsustainable debt burdens and address the debt problems of developing countries.

- **Trade.** Support the Doha work programme (including its aspects on market access and small, vulnerable economies); enhance the mutual supportiveness of trade, environment and development; address public health problems that affect many developing countries; develop the capacity of commodity-dependent countries; and enhance the benefits of trade liberalization for developing countries and countries with economies in transition.

- **Environmentally sound technologies** (ESTs). Support existing, or establish new, mechanisms for development, transfer and diffusion of ESTs.

- **Science and technology.** Strengthen centres for sustainable development and networking of centres of excellence in developing countries; make greater use of scientific advice and integrated scientific assessments, risk assessments and interdisciplinary and inter-sectoral approaches; and improve use of environmental monitoring and modelling.

- **Education.** Integrate sustainable development within education systems; use education to promote sustainable development; and address the impact of HIV/AIDS on the education system.

- **Capacity-building.** Enhance capacity-building and partnerships with the focus on human, institutional and infrastructure capacity, and on meeting the challenges of globalization and attaining internationally agreed development goals.

10

TARGETS AND COMMITMENTS (CONTD)

▢ **Information.** Ensure access at the national level to environmental information and public participation in decision-making (Rio principle 10); undertake further work at the national level on indicators for sustainable development, including gender aspects; strengthen national statistical services; promote wider use of Earth observation technologies and coordination of global observing systems for integrated global observations; make available affordable disaster-related information for early warning; and apply environmental impact assessments and other tools for sustainable development decision-making and policy-making more widely.

EXAMPLES OF INDICATORS FOR MEASURING PROGRESS IN IMPLEMENTATION

▢ Total official development assistance (ODA) given or received as a percentage of gross national product (GNP) (United Nations Commission on Sustainable Development , or CSD)

▢ Donor countries reaching their UN target of 0.7 per cent of GNP as ODA (Monterrey Consensus)

▢ Global monitoring of policies for achieving Millennium Development Goals (MDGs) and Monterrey commitments (World Bank)

▢ Debt to GNP ratio (CSD)

▢ Progress reports on implementation of the heavily indebted poor countries (HIPC) initiative (International Monetary Fund, or IMF)

▢ Number of countries that have eliminated tariffs on goods originating from least developed countries (World Trade Organization, or WTO)

▢ Expenditure on research and development as a percent of GDP (CSD)

Partnership example

Capacity-building on the applications of information and communication technology (ICT) for the establishment of environmental information systems for sustainable development in Africa – SISEI

Leading partner: United Nations Institute for Training and Research (UNITAR)

Dates: September 2002–December 2005

Significant efforts are underway in Africa to manage natural resources and the environment, involving scientific and technical research, implementation of appropriate programmes, projects in the field and the harnessing of local know-how. The results (products, information, data) represent a unique scientific, technical and cultural heritage for sustainable development and the fight against poverty in Africa. An identified problem is the uneven dispersal of this information through inadequate systems and compartmentalization. This loss of 'institutional memory' is recognized as a major obstacle to sustainable development in Africa.

The SISEI (Système de Circulation d'Information et de Suivi de l'Environnement sur Internet en Afrique) initiative responds to calls in Agenda 21 and other international instruments (the United Nations Framework Convention on Climate Change – UNFCCC – and the Convention on Biological Diversity – CBD) to strengthen the collection and exchange of information. It builds upon several International Telecommunication Union (ITU) conferences where the role of telecommunication and information technologies for environmental protection and sustainable development has been highlighted. SISEI will provide countries and regional organizations with systems for the validation, circulation and harnessing of relevant environmental information with a view to strengthening the participative approach at the different decision-making and operational levels, thereby promoting more informed decision-making. It also encourages the environmental community to share experiences and information. This approach aims to create synergy between human and financial resources, establishing environmental information systems within national programmes, such as development plans, national environmental action plans and poverty eradication plans.

Contact information: United Nations Institute for Training and Research (UNITAR) UNITAR Palais des Nations CH-1211 Genève 10 Suisse www.sisei.net

Resources

Programme of Action for the Least Developed Countries for the Decade 2001–2010

www.un.org/special-rep/ohrlls/ldc/reports.htm

This programme was adopted at the Third United Nations Conference on the Least Developed Countries (LDCs) (Brussels, May 2001) to accelerate development in LDCs. Paragraph 83 relates to implementation of donor commitments on official development assistance (ODA) and support to LDCs with information systems and indicators on aid effectiveness (UN, 2001).

Global Environment Facility (GEF)

www.gefweb.org/

Established 1991, the GEF helps developing countries fund projects that protect the global environment. It is a financial mechanism for international agreements on biodiversity, climate change, persistent organic pollutants, desertification, international waters and the ozone layer. The third replenishment of the GEF Trust Fund (Washington, DC, 6–7 August 2002) completed with about US$2.92 billion.

Heavily Indebted Poor Countries (HIPC) Initiative

www.worldbank.org/hipc/

The HIPC initiative was established in 1996 to reduce the external debt of the poorest countries facing an unsustainable debt situation that can not be resolved through traditional mechanisms. Creditors provide assistance beyond current mechanisms and a trust fund supports activities under HIPC.

Monterrey Consensus

www.un.org/esa/ffd/ffdconf

The Monterrey Consensus was the outcome of the International Conference on Financing for Development (March 2002). Governments committed to increase resources for development. Elements of the consensus include domestic and international finance; trade; debt; development assistance; and reform of international financial and trading systems.

Paris and London Clubs for Debt Restructuring

www.clubdeparis.org/

The Paris Club is an informal body where debt restructuring is negotiated with bilateral official creditors. Its secretariat is the French Ministry of Finance. The London Club is a process for restructuring sovereign debt owed to commercial banks. Each club is formed by the debtor country and has an advisory committee chaired by a leading financial firm. Clubs are dissolved when restructuring is completed.

Doha Ministerial Declaration

wto.org/english/tratop_e/dda_e/dohaexplained_e.htm
The outcome of the Fourth World Trade Organization (WTO) Ministerial (November 2001), the Doha Declaration includes a work programme and negotiating agenda for a WTO Development Round. Elements of the declaration include agriculture; services; market access for non-agricultural products; trade-related aspects of intellectual property rights (TRIPS); trade and competition policy; transparency in government procurement; trade facilitation; WTO rules; trade and environment; electronic commerce; small economies; trade, debt and finance; trade and transfer of technology; technical cooperation and capacity-building; least developed countries (LDCs); and special and differential treatment.

Article 20 of the Agreement on Agriculture

Process adopted under the Agreement on Agriculture (negotiated as part of the Uruguay Round of trade negotiations) to bring agricultural trade issues into the General Agreement on Tariffs and Trade (GATT), now the WTO. Article 20 provides that negotiations for further liberalization of trade, and improvements in rules and preferential treatment for developing countries, would be launched before the end of 1999.

Agreement on Trade-Related Aspects of Intellectual Property Rights (TRIPS)

www.wto.org/
The TRIPS Agreement was negotiated in the Uruguay Round of trade negotiations and sets out minimum standards for the protection of intellectual property rights and procedures for their enforcement. Provisions relate to patents, copyright, trademarks, industrial designs, layout designs for integrated circuits, undisclosed information and geographical indications.

Declaration on the TRIPS Agreement and Public Health

www.wto.org/
Agreed at the Doha Ministerial Meeting on 14 November 2001 (WTO, 2001b), this declaration agrees that the Trade-Related Aspects of Intellectual Property Rights (TRIPS) Agreement should be implemented in a manner supportive of WTO members' right to protect public health and to promote access to medicines for all.

Doha Development Agenda Global Trust Fund (DDAGTF)

www.wto.org/
The DDAGTF was created following the Doha WTO Ministerial Conference in November 2001 to support technical assistance and help developing countries build capacity and participate fully in the Doha Development Agenda. A pledging meeting in March 2002 raised 30 million Swiss francs for the fund.

New Strategy for WTO Technical Cooperation for Capacity-building, Growth and Integration

www.wto.org/
Prepared through the WTO Committee on Trade and Development, this strategy endorses paragraph 38 of the Doha Declaration on technical cooperation and capacity-building, and provides definition, objectives and core elements of a WTO technical assistance comprehensive strategy (WTO, 2001c).

Integrated Framework for Trade-related Technical Assistance to Least Developed Countries

www.wto.org/
This framework was undertaken by six core agencies (International Trade Centre – ITC; International Monetary Fund – IMF; United Nations Conference on Trade and Development – UNCTAD; United Nations Development Programme – UNDP; the World Bank; and WTO) to support developing and least-developed countries in the new round of trade negotiations and the negotiations of the Doha Development Agenda on the basis of complementary expertise of the agencies.

Common Fund for Commodities

www.common-fund.org/
This is an intergovernmental UN financial institution to improve socio-economic development of commodity producers, concentrating on commodity development projects. It is financed through voluntary contributions; capital subscriptions that are transferred to the 'Second Account'; and interest. Voluntary funds are used for either grants or loans. Capital of the Second Account is used for loan-financing of projects. Capital of the First Account is an endowment fund and cannot be used directly.

Dakar Framework for Action on Education for All

www.unesco.org/education/efa/ed_for_all/framework.shtml
Adopted at the World Education Forum in April 2000, the Dakar framework reaffirms the goals set at the World Conference on Education for All agreed at Jomtien, Thailand, in 1990 (UNESCO, 2000).

Decision 9/4 of the United Nations Commission on Sustainable Development (CSD) on Information for Decision-making and Participation, New York, April 2001

www.un.org/esa/sustdev/csd/ecn172001-19e.htm#Decision%209/4
Decision 9/4 offers recommendations for action at different levels to enhance information for decision-making in support of sustainable development.

United Nations Charter

www.un.org/aboutun/charter/
This is a founding UN document, agreed and signed on 26 June 1945, in San Francisco at the United Nations Conference on International Organization. When the charter came into force on 24 October 1945, the UN officially came into being.

Intergovernmental Panel on Climate Change (IPCC)

www.ipcc.ch/
The IPCC assesses the scientific, technical and socio-economic information relevant to understanding the scientific basis of the risk of human-induced climate change, its potential impacts and options for adaptation and mitigation. Reports are based on published and peer-reviewed research. It supports the United Nations Framework Convention on Climate Change (UNFCCC) on methodologies for national greenhouse gas inventories.

United Nations Information and Communication Technology Task Force

www.unicttaskforce.org/
Established 2001, this task force provides overall leadership in the UN on strategies for developing information and communication technologies to bridge the digital divide.

United Nations Development Programme's (UNDP's) Capacity 21

www.undp.org/capacity21/
The UNDP's Capacity 21 Trust Fund has its origins in the 1992 United Nations Conference on Environment and Development (UNCED) and works with countries to build national capacities for implementing Agenda 21.

CONFERENCES, AGREEMENTS AND PROCESSES

General

⌛ United Nations Commission on Sustainable Development (CSD) discussions on 'means of implementation' elements as cross-cutting themes (1993–1999)

⌛ Barbados Programme of Action on the Sustainable Development of Small Island Developing States (BPoA) (1994)

⌛ Programme of Action for the Least Developed Countries for the Decade (2001–2010)

⌛ Third United Nations Conference on the Least Developed Countries, Brussels (2001)

⌛ World Trade Organization (WTO) Ministerial Meeting, Doha (2001)

CONFERENCES, AGREEMENTS AND PROCESSES (CONTD)

- WTO Ministerial Meeting, Cancun (2003)
- International Meeting on the Barbados Programme of Action, Mauritius (2004)
- WTO Ministerial Meeting (2005)

Finance

- Heavily indebted poor countries (HIPC) initiative established (1996)
- Adoption of the Monterrey Consensus at the International Conference on Financing for Development, Monterrey (2002)
- Third replenishment of the Global Environment Facility (GEF) Trust Fund completed (2002)
- International conference to review implementation of the Monterrey Consensus (details to be decided not later than 2005)

Trade

- World Trade Organization (WTO) Ministerial Meeting, Doha (2001)
- Pledging conference held for the Doha Development Agenda Global Trust Fund (DDAGTF) (2002)
- WTO Ministerial Meeting, Cancun (2003)
- Africa, Caribbean and Pacific group of countries (ACP)/European Union (EU) Phase II negotiations on economic partnership agreements commence (2003)
- WTO Ministerial Meeting (2005)

Education

- Dakar Framework for Action on Education for All adopted by the World Education Forum in Thailand (2000)
- Decade of Education for Sustainable Development commences (2005)

Information

- Plenipotentiary Conference of the International Telecommunication Union (ITU) (1998)
- Decision 9/4 of the United Nations Commission on Sustainable Development (CSD) on information for decision-making and participation (2001)
- World Summit on the Information Society (WSIS): Phase I, Geneva (December 2003); Phase II, Tunis (November 2005)

Key United Nations bodies and Bretton Woods institutions

Finance

- Global Environment Facility (GEF)
- International Monetary Fund (IMF)
- United Nations Development Programme (UNDP)
- United Nations Economic and Social Council (ECOSOC)
- World Bank

Trade

- United Nations Conference on Trade and Development (UNCTAD)
- United Nations Development Programme (UNDP)
- United Nations Environment Programme (UNEP) Economics and Trade Unit
- World Trade Organization (WTO)

Education

- Joint United Nations Programme on HIV/AIDS (UNAIDS)
- United Nations Educational, Scientific and Cultural Organization (UNESCO)

Capacity-building

- United Nations Commission on Sustainable Development (CSD)
- United Nations Conference on Trade and Development (UNCTAD)
- United Nations Development Programme (UNDP) Capacity 21 (and successor initiative, Capacity 2015)
- United Nations Environment Programme (UNEP)
- United Nations Human Settlements Programme (UN-Habitat)

Information

- High-level Summit Organizing Committee (HLSOC) coordinating efforts in the UN system for the World Summit on the Information Society (WSIS) (includes FAO, IAEA, ICAO, ILO, IMO, ITU, UNCTAD, UNDP, UNEP, UNESCO, UNHCR, UNIDO, UPU, WHO, WIPO, WMO, WTO, UNITAR, UN Regional Economic Commissions, World Bank)
- International Strategy for Disaster Reduction (ISDR)
- International Telecommunication Union (ITU)
- United Nations Educational, Scientific and Cultural Organization (UNESCO)
- United Nations Environment Programme (UNEP)

References

Commonwealth Secretariat (2001) 'Rio+10 – Key issues and concerns related to implementation of the Rio Agreements: Technology transfer, finance, capacity-building and global governance for sustainable development', Paper for the Commonwealth Consultative Group on Environment, London, CCGE(01)1, www.thecommonwealth.org/

Commonwealth Secretariat (2003) *World Economic Situation and Prospects (with particular reference to the Commonwealth)*, London, Commonwealth Finance Ministers Meeting, FMM(03)3, p2

Dobie, P (undated) 'Models for national strategies: Building capacity for sustainable development', *Capacity 21 (UNDP) Series, Approaches to Sustainability*, UNDP, New York

IIF (Institute of International Finance, Inc) (2003). *Capital Flows to Emerging Market Economies*, 21 September 2003, www.iif.com

Töpfer, K (2002) 'Towards Johannesburg', *Our Planet*, UNEP, vol 13, no 1, p20

UN (United Nations) (2001) *Programme of Action for the Least Developed Countries for the Decade 2001–2010*, Adopted by the Third United Nations Conference on the Least Developed Countries in Brussels on 20 May 2001, UN, New York, 8 June 2001, p51 (A/CONF.191/11)

UN (2002) *Report of the International Conference on Financing for Development, Monterrey, Mexico, 18–22 March 2002*, UN, New York (A/CONF.198/11)

UNEP (2002) *Global Environment Outlook 3*, Earthscan, London

UNESCO (United Nations Educational, Scientific and Cultural Organization) (2000) *The Dakar Framework for Action, Education for All: Meeting our Collective Commitments*, Adopted by the World Education Forum, Dakar, Senegal, 26–28 April 2000, UNESCO, Paris (ED-2000/WS/27)

WRI, in collaboration with UNEP, World Bank and UNDP (2003) *World Resources 2002–2004: Decisions for the Earth – Balance, Voice and Power*, WRI, Washington, DC, p165

WTO (World Trade Organization) (1999) *The Legal Texts: The Results of the Uruguay Round of Multilateral Trade Negotiations*, Cambridge University Press, Cambridge

WTO (2001a) *Ministerial Declaration*, Adopted 14 November 2001, WTO Ministerial Conference Fourth Session, Doha, 9–14 November 2001, WTO, Geneva, 20 November 2001 (WT/MIN(01)/DEC/1)

WTO (2001b) *Declaration on the TRIPS Agreement and Public Health*, Adopted on 14 November 2001, Ministerial Conference Fourth Session, Doha, 9–14 November 2001, WTO, Geneva. (WT/MIN(01)/DEC/2)

WTO (2001c) *A New Strategy for WTO Technical Cooperation: Technical Cooperation for Capacity-building, Growth and Integration*, WTO, Geneva, Committee on Trade and Development, 21 September 2001 (WT/COMTD/W/90)

Institutional Framework for Sustainable Development

 Context

A reform and strengthening of institutions, and the wider framework within which they work, is needed to support sustainable development. The integration of economic, social and environmental policies continues to challenge institutions at all levels (UNEP, 2002). Wider participation by all stakeholders and good governance are also needed, and these are based on greater accountability, transparency, access to information, equity and social justice. Such issues have been well recognized. In 2002, the **Human Development Report** called for more democratic principles in global institutions and reiterated not only the need for new frameworks to be efficient and effective, but also to be just, equitable and conducive to human development (UNDP, 2002). Similarly, the 2002–2004 World Resources Institute (WRI) report **Decisions for the Earth: Balance, Voice and Power** makes it clear that 'poor environmental governance – decisions taken without transparency, participation of all stakeholders, and full accountability – is a failure we can no longer live with in an era when human decisions, not natural processes, dominate the global environment' (WRI, 2003). Others have noted that voluntary processes and non-governmental organizations (NGOs) could also benefit from improved governance and processes.

Discussions on institutional reform in the run-up to the World Summit on Sustainable Development (WSSD) looked for greater consistency within and between different sectors and at all levels of policy and decision-making. Strengthening the institutional framework for sustainable development at the regional level was a major focus of discussions. With respect to the UN, the emphasis was on coordination mechanisms and closer integration of the three pillars of sustainable development, as well as reform of the United Nations Commission on Sustainable Development (CSD) to maximize its effectiveness. There were inputs to the process from the United Nations Environment Programme (UNEP), which undertook an extensive process to examine 'international environmental governance', including the structure, role and financing of UNEP; coordination of multilateral environmental agreements; capacity-building and technology transfer; and UN coordination. The

KEY WORDS

- **United Nations General Assembly (UNGA)**
- **United Nations Economic and Social Council (ECOSOC)**
- **United Nations Commission on Sustainable Development (CSD)**
- **international institutions**
- **United Nations Regional Economic Commissions**
- **regional development strategies**
- **national institutional frameworks**
- **national strategies for sustainable development**
- **sustainable development councils**
- **public participation**
- **local authorities**
- **participation of major groups**
- **environment and human rights**

AT A GLANCE

☒ Good governance at all levels is essential for sustainable development.

☒ It requires a stronger institutional framework at every level: international, regional, national and local.

☒ There should be full participation of all stakeholders through transparent and accountable processes.

Johannesburg Plan of Implementation (JPOI) recognizes these processes and provides recommendations to strengthen and reform governance at every level.

 Chapter XI in summary

An **effective institutional framework** for sustainable development is essential to full implementation of Agenda 21 and the WSSD, and to meet emerging challenges. Measures to strengthen the framework must build on Agenda 21, the Programme for the Further Implementation of Agenda 21 (1997) and the Rio Declaration. Actions should promote **internationally agreed development goals**, including the Millennium Development Goals (MDGs), taking into account the Monterrey Consensus and outcomes of major UN conferences/international agreements since 1992. The framework should respond to the needs of all countries, especially developing countries, and include the means for implementation. It should lead to stronger international, regional, national and local institutions and organizations *[137]*.

'We are made wise not by the recollections of our past, but by the responsibility for our future'
(George Bernard Shaw, from A Treatise on Parents and Children).

Good governance is essential for sustainable development. Sustained economic growth, poverty eradication and employment opportunities depend upon sound economic policies, democratic institutions and improved infrastructure. Other essential elements are **freedom**; **peace and security**; **domestic stability**; respect for **human rights**, including the **right to development**; the **rule of law**; **gender equality**; **market-orientated policies**; and an overall commitment to **just and democratic societies** *[138]*.

Objectives

Measures are required to strengthen **institutional arrangements** at all levels, using the framework of Agenda 21 *[139]* to:

- Strengthen **commitments** towards sustainable development *[139a]*;
- Balance the **integration** of economic, social and environmental dimensions *[139b]*;
- Strengthen **implementation** of Agenda 21 by mobilizing resources and capacity-building programmes, particularly for developing countries *[139c]*;

- Improve **coherence, coordination and monitoring** *[139d]*;
- Promote the **rule of law** and **strengthen governmental institutions** *[139e]*;
- Increase **effectiveness and efficiency** by limiting duplication/overlap of activities by international organizations within and outside the UN *[139f]*;
- Improve involvement of **civil society** and other **stakeholders** in implementing Agenda 21, promoting transparency and broad **public participation** *[139g]*;
- Strengthen capacities at all levels, particularly at the local level and in developing countries *[139h]*; and
- Strengthen **international cooperation** towards implementation of Agenda 21 and the WSSD *[139i]*.

International level

The **international community** *[140]* should:

- **Integrate** sustainable development goals in the work of relevant UN bodies, the Global Environment Facility (GEF) and international financial and trade institutions, taking into account national sustainable development approaches *[140a]*;
- Strengthen **collaboration**, within and between organizations in the UN system, international financial institutions, the GEF and the World Trade Organization (WTO), using the United Nations Chief Executives Board for Coordination, the United Nations Development Group, the Environment Management Group and other coordinating bodies. Step up inter-agency collaboration, especially at operational level and through partnerships *[140b]*;
- Better integrate the **three dimensions of sustainable development** policies and programmes. Promote sustainable development in the work of organizations that focus primarily on social issues. Strengthen the **social dimension** of sustainable development by emphasizing follow-up to the WSSD and by supporting social protection systems *[140c]*;
- Fully implement UNEP's decision on **international environmental governance** and invite the 57th United Nations General Assembly (UNGA) to consider the issue of universal membership for UNEP *[140d]*;
- Complete negotiations on a comprehensive **UN convention against corruption**, including on repatriating funds illicitly acquired back to countries of origin *[140e]*;
- Promote **corporate responsibility, accountability** and **exchange of best practices** through multistakeholder dialogues and other initiatives *[140f]*; and
- Act at all levels to implement the **Monterrey Consensus** *[140g]*.

'Real generosity towards the future lies in giving all to the present' (Albert Camus, French novelist, 1913–1960).

The JPOI recognizes the importance of **good governance** at the international level, emphasizing the need to promote **global economic governance** by addressing international finance, trade, technology and investment patterns that affect the prospects of developing countries. The international community should support structural and macro-economic reform, a comprehensive solution to the external debt problem and increasing market access for developing countries. Efforts to reform the international financial 'architecture' need to be sustained with greater transparency and the participation of developing countries in decision-making. A universal, rules-based, open, non-discriminatory and equitable multilateral trading system, and meaningful trade liberalization, can substantially stimulate worldwide development, benefiting all countries *[141]*.

A vibrant and effective UN system is fundamental to international cooperation on sustainable development. This requires a firm commitment to the ideal of the United Nations, principles of international law, and the United Nations Charter, and to strengthening the UN system and other multilateral institutions and their operations. States should fulfill their commitment to negotiate and finalize a **UN convention against all forms of corruption**, including the repatriation of illicitly acquired funds, and promote cooperation to **eliminate money laundering** *[142]*.

'The United Nations once dealt only with governments. By now we know that peace and prosperity cannot be achieved without partnerships involving governments, international organizations, the business community and civil society. In today's world, we depend on each other' (UN Secretary-General Kofi Annan, cited in WRI, 2003).

United Nations General Assembly (UNGA)

UNGA should adopt sustainable development as a key element of the overarching framework for UN activities, particularly to help achieve the MDGs and give overall political direction to implementing Agenda 21 *[143]*.

United Nations Economic and Social Council (ECOSOC)

Implementing its role as the central coordinating mechanism of the UN system, and to promote the implementation of Agenda 21 by strengthening system-wide coordination *[144]*, ECOSOC should:

- Increase its **role in overseeing system-wide coordination** and the balanced integration of the economic, social and environmental aspects of UN approaches to promote sustainable development *[144a]*;
- Organize **consultations** on themes related to Agenda 21 implementation *[144b]*;
- Make full use of its high-level coordination, operational activities and the general segments to take into account all aspects of the UN work on sustainable development. Encourage active participation of all major groups in high-level segments and the work of functional commissions *[144c]*;
- Promote greater coordination and effectiveness in the work of the **functional commissions** and other bodies responsible for implementing Agenda 21 *[144d]*;
- Transfer the work of the **Committee on Energy and Natural Resources for Development** to the CSD *[144e]*;

- Ensure a **close link** between the roles of ECOSOC in following up **WSSD** and the **Monterrey Consensus**. Explore arrangements for meetings with Bretton Woods institutions and the WTO, as set out in the Monterrey Consensus *[144f]*; and
- Intensify efforts to ensure that **gender mainstreaming** is integral to its work on Agenda 21 *[144g]*.

United Nations Commission on Sustainable Development (CSD)

The CSD should continue as the UN's high-level commission on sustainable development and serve as a forum on integrating its three aspects (economic, social and environmental). The CSD needs to be strengthened, including with an enhanced role in **reviewing and monitoring progress** on Agenda 21 and fostering **coherence** in implementation, initiatives and partnerships *[145]*.

The CSD should give greater emphasis to actions enabling implementation at all levels, including **partnerships** involving governments, international organizations and relevant stakeholders *[146]*. The CSD should:

- Review and evaluate progress and promote Agenda 21's implementation *[147a]*;
- Focus on **cross-sectoral aspects of sectoral issues**, and provide a forum on integrating policies, facilitating interactions among ministers who deal with the different dimensions of sustainable development *[147b]*;
- Address new **challenges and opportunities** on Agenda 21's implementation *[147c]*;
- Limit **negotiating sessions** to every two years *[147d]*; and
- Address a **limited number of themes** each session *[147e]*.

In facilitating implementation *[148]*, the CSD should:

- Review progress and promote further implementation of Agenda 21, identifying **constraints and making recommendations** for dealing with these *[148a]*;
- Act as a focal point for discussing partnerships, sharing lessons learned, progress and best practices *[148b]*;
- Review financial assistance, technology transfer and capacity-building, making full use of existing information and considering more effective use of **national reports and regional experience** *[148c]*;
- Provide a forum for exchanging experiences on **sustainable development planning, decision-making** and implementation of **sustainable development strategies** *[148d]*; and
- Take into account significant legal developments in sustainable development and the role of intergovernmental bodies in promoting implementation *[148e]*.

'While many viewed the official outcomes of the WSSD as modest, at best, their limitations probably reflect the difficulty of reconciling apparent conflicts between the environmental, social and economic aspects of sustainable development as nations perceive them today'
(Speth, 2003).

The CSD was requested to consider and take decisions on its future work programme during its 12th session in May 2003 *[149]*. Such issues included:

- Balanced implementation of mandates of CSD contained in the General Assembly resolution 47/191 *[149a]*;
- More direct and substantial involvement of **international organizations** and **major groups** *[149b]*;
- Greater consideration of **scientific contributions** and involvement of scientific networks *[149c]*;
- Furthering the contribution of **educators** *[149d]*; and
- The scheduling and length of future meetings *[149e]*.

The CSD should take further measures to promote best practices, lessons learned and use of contemporary methods of data collection and dissemination *[150]*.

International institutions

International institutions, including the financial institutions, the WTO and the GEF, acting within their mandates, should work to *[151]*:

- Promote effective and collective support to implement Agenda 21 *[151a]*; and
- Enhance effectiveness/coordination to implement Agenda 21, the WSSD, relevant parts of the Millennium Declaration, the Monterrey Consensus and the Doha WTO Ministerial Conference *[151b]*.

The JPOI requests the United Nations Secretary-General to promote system-wide cooperation/coordination and information exchange, using the United Nations System Chief Executives Board for Coordination, and to keep ECOSOC and the CSD informed of actions being taken to implement Agenda 21 *[152]*.
The JPOI also calls for action to:

- Significantly strengthen support for United Nations Development Programme (UNDP) capacity-building, drawing on the Capacity 21 programme *[153]*;
- Strengthen cooperation between UNEP and other UN agencies/bodies, the Bretton Woods institutions and the WTO *[154]*; and
- Strengthen the contribution of UNEP, the United Nations Human Settlements Programme (UN-Habitat), UNDP and the United Nations Conference on Trade and Development (UNCTAD) to sustainable development and Agenda 21, especially in capacity-building *[155]*.

To promote effective implementation of Agenda 21 at the international level *[156]*:

'People are no longer satisfied with declarations. They demand firm action and concrete results. They expect that the nations of the world, having identified a problem, will have the vitality to act' (the late Olaf Palme, former Swedish prime minister, whose country hosted the Stockholm Conference in 1971, cited in UNEP, 2002).

148

- Reduce the number and length of international meetings, and allow more time for discussion of practical matters related to implementation *[156a]*;
- Encourage partnership initiatives to implement the WSSD, taking note of preparatory work for the summit *[156b]*; and
- Make full use of information and communication technologies *[156c]*.

Strengthening the international institutional framework is an evolutionary process. It is necessary to keep institutional arrangements under review, identify gaps, eliminate duplication of function and continue to strive to greater integration, efficiency and coordination *[157]*.

Regional level

Implementation of Agenda 21 and the WSSD at **regional and sub-regional** levels should be pursued through UN Regional Commissions and other regional/sub-regional bodies *[158]*, with **improved cooperation** between the regional commissions, UN funds, programmes and agencies, regional development banks and other institutions, and increased support for the development and implementation of regionally agreed sustainable development strategies and action plans *[159]*.

UN Regional Commissions *[160]* are encouraged to:

- Promote the three pillars of sustainable development in a balanced way and enhance their **own capacity**, with external support where appropriate *[160a]*;
- Facilitate integration of sustainable development within the work of regional, sub-regional and other bodies – for example, by strengthening the exchange of information, national experience, best practice, case studies and partnerships *[160b]*;
- **Mobilize** technical assistance and funding, including for regionally and sub-regionally agreed sustainable development programmes *[160c]*; and
- Continue to promote multi-stakeholder participation and partnerships to implement Agenda 21 at regional/sub-regional levels *[160d]*.

'Action cannot be delivered by governments alone. It will require partnerships between all the relevant stakeholders, including governments, local communities, the private sector, non-governmental organizations and international agencies' (Mohammed Valli Moosa, Minister of Environmental Affairs and Tourism, Republic of South Africa, 2002).

Regionally/sub-regionally agreed sustainable development initiatives, such as the **New Partnership for African Development (NEPAD)** and the **Barbados Programme of Action on the Sustainable Development of Small Island Developing States (BPoA)** should be supported *[161]*.

National level

To strengthen implementation at the national level, **states** *[162]* should:

- Promote coherent/coordinated approaches to **institutional frameworks** for sustainable development at all national levels, including establishing or strengthening mechanisms or authorities *[162a]*; and

- Take immediate steps to progress **national strategies for sustainable development** and begin their implementation by 2005. Support strategies through international cooperation. Where applicable, these could be formulated as poverty reduction strategies, incorporating the three dimensions of sustainable development *[162b]*.

'Improved environmental governance will help us to deliver results – not simply for their obvious and important environmental ends, but because they have other beneficial impacts on economies, on societies and on the health of people... On this small planet, the fate of all people is bound together. Improving the well-being of any improves it for all... Sustainable development is therefore ultimately about our relationships with each other and with the planet on which we live. Future progress will not come from expressions of intent but from changes to the underlying structures that govern those relationships' (David Andersen, Canadian Minister of the Environment and President of UNEP's Governing Council, 2002).

Each country has the primary responsibility for its own sustainable development and the role of national policies and development strategies cannot be overemphasized. Countries should promote sustainable development at the **national level** by:

- Enacting clear and effective **laws** and strengthening **governmental institutions**, including infrastructure and fair, transparent and accountable administrative and judicial institutions *[163]*; and
- Promoting **public participation** – for example, through access to information regarding legislation, regulations, activities, policies and programmes. Also, foster full public participation in sustainable development policy formulation and implementation, enabling women to participate fully and equally *[164]*.

The JPOI promotes **sustainable development councils** or other national/local coordinating structures to provide a high-level focus on sustainable development policies, furthered by multi-stakeholder participation *[165]*. It also calls for the **support** of country efforts to improve national/local institutional arrangements for sustainable development. This could include cross-sectoral approaches in formulating strategies for sustainable development (for example, poverty reduction strategies; aid coordination; participatory approaches and enhancing policy analysis, management and implementation capacity) and mainstreaming gender perspectives in these activities *[166]*.

The role and capacity of **local authorities** and other **stakeholders** in implementing Agenda 21 and the WSSD, and in supporting local Agenda 21, should be enhanced. In this, the JPOI encourages partnerships between local authorities, and other levels of government and stakeholders – for example, as called for in the Habitat Agenda *[167]*.

Major groups

- Enhance partnerships between governmental and **non-governmental actors**, including all **major groups** and **voluntary groups** *[168]*.
- Acknowledge the consideration being given to the possible relationship between **environment and human rights**, including the right to development, with full and transparent participation of member states of the UN and observer states *[169]*.
- Promote and support **youth participation** in sustainable development activities – for example, by supporting local **youth councils** or their equivalents *[170]*.

Institutional framework issues elsewhere in the JPOI

The Johannesburg Plan of Implementation (JPOI) is interwoven with references to issues and challenges that fall under the heading of governance: institutions, institutional structures, accountability and transparency, legal issues, partnerships, participation, stakeholders and major groups (including indigenous people, children and women). The need for good governance is stated early on (JPOI, Chapter I) and appears throughout the text. The JPOI states that efforts to strengthen the institutional framework for sustainable development should based upon the Rio principles. Chapters V and X include references to governance, with recommendations related to finance and trade, and the role of science, technology, information and education. The regional chapters, particularly Chapter VIII (Africa) refers to institutional changes required to lever current systems towards sustainable development. References to partnerships are found in every chapter of the JPOI.

Other cross-cutting themes

Other themes include:

- Governance;
- Participation;
- Finance (on international finance institutions);
- Trade (on international trade institutions);
- Stakeholders;
- Major groups;
- Youth and children;
- Indigenous people, communities and knowledge;
- Women and gender equality;
- Local authorities;
- Scientific and technological community;
- Farmers/fishers;
- Business and industry; and
- NGOs.

'Here in Johannesburg you have failed us! Signatures do not feed people. Words on paper do not stop deforestation. Where are the mechanisms? Where are the time frames? Where are the commitments?' (Youth spokeswoman Catherine Kampling in a statement during the Youth Caucus, which presented the concerns of young people to the final session of the WSSD, 2003).

11

TARGETS AND COMMITMENTS

- **National strategies.** Take immediate steps to make progress in the formulation and elaboration of national strategies for sustainable development and begin their implementation by 2005 *[162]*.

- **Governance.** Adopt new measures to strengthen institutional arrangements for sustainable development at international, regional, national and local levels *[139]*.

- **United Nations Commission on Sustainable Development (CSD).** Enhance the role of the CSD, including in reviewing/monitoring implementation of Agenda 21 and fostering coherence of implementation, initiatives and partnerships *[145]*.

- **Integrated approach.** Facilitate the integration of environmental, social and economic dimensions of sustainable development within the work programmes of the United Nations Regional Commissions *[160, 160a, 160d]*.

EXAMPLES OF INDICATORS FOR MEASURING PROGRESS IN IMPLEMENTATION

- Does a country have a national sustainable development strategy (United Nations Commission on Sustainable Development, or CSD)?

- Is the national sustainable development strategy being implemented? What is its degree of effectiveness (CSD)?

- Is there implementation of multilateral environmental agreements? What is the ratio between agreements legislated for and agreements ratified (CSD)?

- Do local authorities have Local Agenda 21 plans? More than 6400 local governments in 113 countries have adopted or are in the process of formulating Local Agenda 21 plans (ICLEI, 2002).

Partnership example

Partnership for principle 10 (PP10)

Leading partner: World Resources Institute (WRI)

Dates: 2002–2012

Principle 10 of the Rio Declaration (1992) commits national governments to an inclusive process of public participation in environmental decisions. It aims to improve conditions for good environmental governance at the national level and increase citizen access to environmental information, participation and justice in environmental decision-making by translating these principles into action. It also:

- Promotes transparent, inclusive and accountable decision-making at the national level.

- Provides a common forum for governments, civil society organizations, donors and other groups to work together to implement practical solutions that provide the public with access to information, participation and justice for environmentally sustainable decisions.

- Strengthens the implementation of Agenda 21 goals for inclusive and informed decision-making for sustainable development.

- Addresses the main implementation gaps in national systems for public participation identified through independent assessments, in partnership with the Access Initiative.

Common gaps include:

- Poor and insufficient access to information about water quality.

- Lack of access to information about the risks and pollution from industrial facilities.

- Poor participation in policy development in 'real' industrial sectors.

- poor participation in project-level decisions.

- Poor enabling conditions for access to justice, including high costs and limited standing.

PP10 seeks to address these gaps by:

- Addressing deficits in the framework for public participation.

- Building capacity of the government to support public participation.

- Building capacity of the public to monitor progress and use the system.

Early partners included the United Nations Development Programme (UNDP); the World Bank; the European Union (EU); European governments, including UK, Italy and Hungary, as well as Uganda and Tanzania; and a diverse range of civil society organizations.

Contact information:
World Resources
Institute (WRI)
10 G Street, NE (Suite 800)
Washington, DC
20002 US
www.pp10.org

Resources

The United Nations World Summit for Social Development, 1995, and Five-year Review, June 2000

www.un.org/esa/socdev/wssd/index.htm
This summit addressed the three core themes: poverty, unemployment and social integration. Governments agreed on the need to put people at the centre of the development process. 186 countries adopted the Copenhagen Declaration on Social Development and the Programme of Action and ten commitments covering the core themes.

United Nations Environment Programme (UNEP) Decision on International Environmental Governance (7th Session)

www.unep.org/governingbodies/gc/specialsessions/gcss_vii/Documents/ k0200009.pdf
This was a two-year review addressing the strengths and weaknesses of international environmental governance, providing recommendations for reform.

Global Ministerial Environment Forum

www.unep.org/malmo/malmo_minsterial.htm
At this meeting of environment ministers, in Sweden in May 2000, the Malmö Ministerial Declaration expressing deep concern about the increasing rate of deterioration of the environment and the natural resource base was adopted.

United Nations Economic and Social Council (ECOSOC)

Under overall authority of the United Nations General Assembly (UNGA), ECOSOC coordinates the economic and social work of the UN and the broader UN system; is the central forum for discussing international economic and social issues; plays a key role in fostering international cooperation for development; and consults with non-governmental organizations (NGOs), forming a link between the UN and civil society.

United Nations Commission on Sustainable Development (CSD)

Created in 1992 as a follow-up to UNCED, the CSD is also known as the Earth Summit. See the chapter on implementing the WSSD: The role of the United Nations Commission on sustainable development, for detailed information.

United Nations Development Programme (UNDP) and Capacity-building

www.undp.org
The UN global development network helps countries to build their own national capacity to achieve sustainable development by developing and sharing knowledge and best practices, building partnerships and mobilizing resources towards the Millennium Development Goals (MDGs).

United Nations Regional Commissions

Five commissions (for Europe, Africa, Latin America and the Caribbean, Asia and the Pacific, and Western Asia) promote economic development and strengthened economic relations in their respective regions.

New Partnership for African Development (NEPAD) (see Chapter 8, Resources)

Adopted at the 37th session of the Organization of African Unity in 2001, the New Partnership for African Development is a vision and strategic framework for Africa's renewal. NEPAD arises out of a mandate given by the Organization of African Unity to five initiating Heads of State (Algeria, Egypt, Nigeria, Senegal, South Africa) to develop an integrated socio-economic framework document for Africa.

Barbados Programme of Action on the Sustainable Development of Small Island Developing States (BPoA) (see Chapter 7, Resources)

Agreed in Barbados in 1994, the BPoA is a 14 point action plan which addresses the special development needs of Small Island developing States.

National Strategies for Sustainable Development

Defined by the Organisation for Economic Co-operation and Development (OECD)/Development Assistance Committee (DAC) as a 'strategic and participatory process of analysis, debate, capacity strengthening, planning and action towards sustainable development'. A target for implementing these plans (agreed at the 1997 Earth Summit review) is 2005.

Sustainable development councils

www.ncsdnetwork.org
National Councils for Sustainable Development (NCSD) seek to strengthen civic society participation in local and multi-stakeholder decision-making mechanisms and activities related to the implementation of the United Nations Conference on Environment and Development (UNCED) agreements. The Earth Council (an independent, international body) has, since 1992, been instrumental in promoting the creation and strengthening of NCSD.

Local Agenda 21 (LA21)

The original aim, as set by Agenda 21, was to develop a local plan for sustainable development, focusing on key issues, including poverty, health and livelihoods, as well as resource and environmental issues, by 1996, later revised to 2000. LA21 is also about the process of building partnerships at the local level between different sectors to implement the LA21 plans. It is a continuing process rather than a single activity, event or document.

UN-Habitat (United Nations Human Settlements Programme)

www.unhabitat.org/governance

Major groups (see Background to this publication, pxviii)

In recognizing the contribution that civil society makes to the achievement of sustainable development, Agenda 21 clearly defines nine major groups. These are:

- NGOs
- Business and industry
- Trade unions and their workers
- Farmers
- Indigenous people
- Local authorities
- Children and young persons
- Women
- Scientific and technical community

The WSSD went one stage further to formally recognize the role and responsibility of major groups in implementing Agenda 21 and the Johannesburg Plan of Implementation and encouraged their full participation in the follow-up to the World Summit on Sustainable Development.

CONFERENCES, AGREEMENTS AND PROCESSES

- Charter of the United Nations (1945)
- Universal Declaration of Human Rights (1948)
- International Covenant on Economic, Social and Cultural Rights (1976)
- Declaration on the Right to Development (1986)
- Agenda 21, Rio Declaration, United Nations Conference on Environment and Development (UNCED) (1992)
- Barbados Programme of Action on the Sustainable Development of Small Island Developing States (BPoA) (1994)
- World Summit for Social Development, Copenhagen (1995)
- General Assembly resolutions 47/191 (1992), 48/162 (1994) and 50/227 (1996)
- Programme for the Further Implementation of Agenda 21 (1997)
- World Summit for Social Development's five-year review, Geneva (2000)
- Millennium Declaration (2000)

CONFERENCES, AGREEMENTS AND PROCESSES (CONTD)

⧗ Fourth World Trade Organization (WTO) Ministerial Meeting, Doha (2001)

⧗ New Partnership for African Development (NEPAD) (2001)

⧗ Monterrey Consensus, Finance for Development International Conference (2002)

⧗ Draft United Nations Convention against Corruption (2003, ongoing)

Key United Nations bodies and Bretton Woods institutions

International

⊡ Global Environment Facility (GEF)

⊡ International Monetary Fund (IMF)

⊡ United Nations Commission on Sustainable Development (CSD)

⊡ United Nations Development Group

⊡ United Nations Development Programme (UNDP)

⊡ United Nations Economic and Social Council (ECOSOC)

⊡ United Nations Environment Management Group

⊡ United Nations Environment Programme (UNEP) Governing Council/Global Ministerial Environment Forum

⊡ United Nations General Assembly (UNGA)

⊡ United Nations System Chief Executives Board for Coordination

⊡ World Bank

⊡ World Trade Organization (WTO)

Regional

⊡ Regional development banks

⊡ United Nations funds

⊡ United Nations programmes and agencies

⊡ United Nations Regional Economic Commissions

National

⊡ Local authorities

⊡ National governments

Key United Nations bodies and Bretton Woods institutions (*contd*)

 United Nations Development Programme (UNDP) (Capacity 2015)

United Nations Human Settlements Programme (UN-Habitat)

Major groups

United Nations Commission on Human Rights (UNCHR)

United Nations Commission on Sustainable Development (CSD)

United Nations Committee on Economic, Social and Cultural Rights

United Nations Economic and Social Council (ECOSOC)

United Nations High Commissioner for Human Rights

United Nations Human Settlements Programme (UN-Habitat)

References

Anderson, D (2002) 'Beyond Brackets', *Our Planet*, UNEP, vol 13, no 2, pp11–12

DESA (United Nations Department of Economic and Social Affairs) (2002) *Johannesburg Summit 2002: Key Outcomes of the Summit*, DESA, New York, www.johannesburg summit.org/html/documents/summit_docs/2009_keyoutcomes_commitments.pdf.

Hemmati, M (2001) *Multi-Stakeholder Processes for Governance and Sustainability – Beyond Deadlock and Conflict*, Earthscan, London

ICLEI (2002) *Local Strategies for Sustainability. Presentation by the International Council for Local Environmental Initiatives (ICLEI), Special Report on Selected Side-events at WSSD PC IV*, Bali, Indonesia, 27 May–7 July 2002, International Institute for Sustainable Development and UNDP, www.iisd.ca/2002/pc4/enbots/jun04.html

Kampling, C (2003) Statement of the concerns of young people to the final session of the World Summit on Sustainable Development, reprinted in *Earthlines*, Youth and Environment Network, CEE, no 38, spring 2003

Moosa, M V (2002) 'African Renaissance', *Our Planet*, UNEP, vol 13, no 2, p13

Renner, M (2002) *The Anatomy of Resource Wars*, Worldwatch Paper 162, Worldwatch, Washington, DC

Speth, J (2003) 'Perspectives on the Johannesburg Summit', *Environment*, vol 45, no 1, pp24–29

UNDP (United Nations Development Programme) (2002) *Human Development Report 2002: Deepening Democracy in a Fragmented World*, Oxford University Press, New York

UNDP, Regional Bureau for Europe and the Commonwealth of Independent States (2003) *Environmental Governance Sourcebook*, UNDP, Bratislava

UNEP (United Nations Environment Programme) (2002) *Global Environment Outlook 3*, Earthscan, London

WRI (World Resources Institute) in collaboration with UNEP (United Nations Environment Programme), UNDP (United Nations Development Programme) and the World Bank (2003) *World Resources 2002–2004: Decisions for the Earth: Balance, Voice, and Power*, WRI, Washington, DC

Part II

Implementing The Johannesburg Plan of Implementation

WSSD Partnerships for Sustainable Development

12

 Introduction

The World Summit on Sustainable Development (WSSD) had two kinds of outcomes: negotiated texts – the Johannesburg Declaration and the Johannesburg Plan of Implementation (JPOI) – and partnerships for sustainable development. The proposal that the WSSD would act as a forum for announcing new partnerships that focused on implementation was, in part, a recognition that a great deal of work had been done in the areas of policy-making, coordination mechanisms, legal frameworks and strategies; but there was still a long way to go with practical action on the ground. Furthermore, it was recognized that governments alone can not deliver sustainable development and that a wide range of groups in society needed to be galvanized and actively brought into the process, both for their perspectives and skills, and the additional resources that they could bring. It was agreed that WSSD Partnerships for Sustainable Development, sometimes referred to as Type II Partnerships (in recognition that these were a second type of outcome from the summit), would be international in scope and aimed at contributing to implementation of intergovernmental agreements related to sustainable development, particularly the JPOI, the Millennium Development Goals (MDGs) and Agenda 21.

 Criteria for WSSD partnerships

The broad principles guiding WSSD partnerships – elaborated during preparations for the summit – were captured by the United Nations Commission on Sustainable Development (CSD) in its **Guiding Principles for Partnerships for Sustainable Development** (CSD, 2002), sometimes referred to as the Bali Guidelines.

Around half of the 500 partnerships that applied for registration at WSSD met the guidelines. These partnerships were included in the UN's website and were given the opportunity to take part in the launch and other events at the WSSD. The most common shortcomings of those that were rejected were that they were either not international in their scope or they were not new.

Partnerships: A test of trust

The matter of partnerships was intensely debated in the run up to the WSSD and in the United Nations Commission on Sustainable Development (CSD) in 2003. NGOs and a number of developing countries expressed concerns that partnerships could take some of the focus off the obligations of governments. This issue was directly addressed by the United Nations Secretary-General in his report on **Follow-up to Johannesburg and the Future Role of the CSD** (CSD, 2003a), which stated that partnerships would not be a substitute for **'government responsibilities and commitments to action'**. Other issues included:

- Concerns that the objectives and focus of partnerships should be directly relevant to regional-, national- or community-level sustainable development strategies and priorities.
- There should be transparency and accountability in how partnerships are set up and operated. Some were particularly concerned about corporate responsibility and accounting when partnerships involved private-sector partners. Others were keen to ensure that arrangements did not stifle innovation or create undue reporting burdens.
- Whether there would be access to adequate and predictable funding.
- Arrangements for review and evaluation. This included concerns to identify where there were gaps in the provision of partnerships and a debate around the role of the CSD in monitoring partnerships.

 Advantages of partnerships

Partnerships have a number of important advantages (Calder, 2003):

- They can bring together all necessary actors to ensure that truly integrated and holistic approaches to development can be identified and implemented.
- The involvement of stakeholders can result in a more comprehensive analysis of challenges and better strategies for addressing them.
- Stakeholders bring with them different skills and perspectives. This can encourage innovation and may bring innovative sources of funding to the table.
- There is a potential for deeper and more lasting systemic change when all affected groups are involved in the design of solutions: if these encompass policy change, they can be more far reaching than project-type interventions.
- Partnerships can help coordinate resources and action with a framework of sustainable development priorities of governments and communities.
- Partnerships have the potential to go further in practical terms than can be agreed formally.

Implementing the JPOI

The Johannesburg Plan of Implementation (JPOI) identifies the CSD as the focal point within the UN for developing, monitoring and reporting on partnerships for sustainable development. At its 11th session (2003), the CSD formally agreed criteria and guidelines for partnerships that draw on the Bali Guiding Principles, as follows.

Partnerships should:

- Be developed and implemented in accordance with criteria and principles, taking into account the Bali Guidelines;
- Be voluntary, multi-stakeholder initiatives, which contribute to the implementation of Agenda 21 and the WSSD;
- Complement, not substitute, commitments to implementing the above international commitments;
- Be new, based on predictable and sustained resources, and balance the three dimensions of sustainable development in their design and implementation;
- Have sectoral geographical balance, and be transparent and accountable, exchanging relevant information with governments and stakeholders;
- Result in technology transfer and capacity-building in developing countries partnership; and
- Mobilize new resources where relevant to support these partnerships.

Additionally:

- Partnerships should be publicly announced, detailing their contribution to implementation, and be consistent with national laws and national strategies;
- Lead partners should inform national focal points for sustainable development in all relevant countries, and bear in mind guidance from governments;
- UN funds, programmes and agencies should conform to their intergovernmentally agreed mandates and not divert funds from mandated programmes to partnerships;
- Registered partnerships should take into account that registration is voluntary and is based on reporting;
- Reporting should preferably happen every two years, be transparent, participatory and credible, and should focus on the contribution to implementation; and
- The CSD secretariat should make information on partnerships widely available and produce a summary report on partnerships.

Under the work programme of the CSD, partnership fairs will be hosted every two years during the 'Review Session' (see p171). This will allow the sharing of experience and good practice, and provide a mechanism by which the contribution of partnerships to the implementation of the outcomes of Rio and the WSSD can be showcased. The fairs will also provide a platform for launching new partnerships and for networking by potential partners and funders, while 'how-to' sessions will provide practical advice and information on partnership issues, both in terms of implementation and the way in which they are dealt with within the CSD.

All interested groups have the option of developing their own partnerships in response to the WSSD. The potential for South–South partnerships needs to be further explored and successful regional partnerships expanded outwards, or transferred to, other regions. A wide range of information on CSD partnerships is available on the CSD website, including registration forms, case studies, and details and analysis of the partnerships that have been agreed.

New partnerships need to be carefully designed, with thought given to appropriate facilitation (Calder, 2003) in order to provide a clear structure for the partnership and ensure that all stakeholders feel fully engaged in the decision-making process. Most importantly, the facilitator needs to be neutral and able to act as an 'honest broker' between different elements of the partnership. Further guidance about effective stakeholder engagement has been developed by Stakeholder Forum in the book **Multi-stakeholder Processes for Governance and Sustainability: Beyond Deadlock and Conflict** (Hemmati, 2002).

Bali Guiding Principles for World Summit on Sustainable Development (WSSD) Partnerships

The following is a summary of the Bali Guiding Principles for WSSD Partnerships (CSD, 2002).

Objective of partnerships

- To contribute to and reinforce the implementation of the outcomes of the WSSD and help to achieve further implementation of Agenda 21 and the Millennium Development Goals (MDGs).

General principles and values

- Voluntary and 'self-organizing'; based on mutual respect and shared responsibility of the partners involved.

- Take into account the Rio Declaration's principles and values expressed in the Millennium Declaration.

Bali Guiding Principles for World Summit on Sustainable Development (WSSD) Partnerships (*contd*)

Deliver globally agreed commitments

- Commitments complement, and are anchored in, the intergovernmentally agreed outcomes of the WSSD.

- Not intended to substitute commitments made by governments.

- Deliver globally agreed commitments by mobilizing capacity for producing action on the ground.

- Help to achieve implementation of Agenda 21 and the MDGs.

Integrated approach to sustainable development

- Integrate economic, social and environmental dimensions of sustainable development.

- Approach is consistent with sustainable development strategies and poverty reduction strategies of the countries, regions and communities where their implementation takes place.

Multi-stakeholder approach

- Have a multi-stakeholder approach, preferably involving a range of significant players.

- Approach is arranged among any combination of partners, including governments, regional groups, local authorities, non-governmental organizations (NGOs), international institutions and the private sector.

- All partners are involved from an early stage, with additional partners able to join on an equal basis.

Transparency and accountability

- Developed and implemented in an open and transparent manner and in good faith.

- Ownership of the partnership and its outcomes is shared among all partners. All partners are equally accountable.

- Performance is monitored and reviewed against objectives and targets and is reported in regular intervals (self-reporting). Reports are accessible to the public.

Tangible results

- Intended outcome and benefits are defined.

- Clear objectives are set with specific measurable targets and time frames.

Bali Guiding Principles for World Summit on Sustainable Development (WSSD) Partnerships (*contd*)

All partners are explicitly committed to their role in achieving the aims and objectives.

Funding arrangements

Available and/or expected sources of funding are identified.

At least the initial funding is assured at the time of the summit, if announced there.

New partnerships

Partnerships should be *new* – that is, developed within the framework of the WSSD process.

Or partnerships should provide significant added value in the context of the WSSD (for example, with more partners taken on board, replicating existing initiatives, extending these to other geographical regions, or increasing financial resources, etc).

Local involvement/international impact

The Bali Guiding Principles are international in impact but seek to involve local communities in design and implementation.

Follow-up

The United Nations Commission on Sustainable Development (CSD) is kept informed about activities and progress in achieving targets.

The CSD should serve as a focal point for discussion of partnerships that promote sustainable development, including sharing lessons learned, progress made and best practices.

Submission of partnerships after the summit will be considered in the follow-up process.

Source: CSD, 2002

 # Resources

United Nations Commission on Sustainable Development (CSD) Partnerships website

www.un.org/esa/sustdev/partnerships/partnerships.htm
This is the official CSD website, providing comprehensive information on all elements of the CSD, including past, present and future processes, events and documents.

References

Calder, F (2003) *WSSD Partnerships for Sustainable Development*, Commonwealth Secretariat, London

CSD (United Nations Commission on Sustainable Development) (2002) *Guiding Principles for Partnerships for Sustainable Development ('Type II Outcomes') to be Elaborated by Interested Parties in the Context of the World Summit on Sustainable Development: Explanatory Note by the Vice-Chairs Jan Kara and Diane Quarless*, CSD, New York, 7 June 2002

CSD (2003a) *Follow-up to Johannesburg and the Future Role of the CSD – The Implementation Track: Report of the Secretary-General*, CSD, New York, 11th Session, 28 April–9 May 2003, United Nations Economic and Social Council, E/CN.17/2003/2

CSD (2003b) *United Nations Commission on Sustainable Development Report on the 11th Session* (27 January 2003 and 28 April–9 May 2003), United Nations, New York, Economic and Social Council Official Records, Supplement No 9, E/2003/29, E/CN.17/2003/6

Hemmati, M (2002) *Multi-stakeholder Processes for Governance and Sustainability: Beyond Deadlock and Conflict*, Earthscan, London

The Role of the United Nations Commission on Sustainable Development (CSD)

13

Introduction

The United Nations Commission on Sustainable Development (CSD) was born in 1993 out of the United Nations Conference on Environment and Development (UNCED) in Rio de Janeiro in 1992 – the Rio Earth Summit. The CSD exists for three principle reasons. To:

*   Monitor and assess implementation of Agenda 21 and to ensure effective follow-up to the Rio Earth Summit;
*   Provide review and policy guidance to help implement the outcomes of the WSSD; and
*   Act as a high-level forum within the UN to coordinate discussions on sustainable development and facilitate stakeholder dialogues.

Structure

The CSD is a functional commission of the United Nations Economic and Social Council (ECOSOC). It has:

*   53 member countries, elected through ECOSOC;
*   A rolling membership with three-year terms of office;
*   One third of members elected each year;
*   A chair, which is held for one year and is rotated amongst each of the five UN regions; and
*   A bureau and a secretariat provided by the United Nations Department of Economic and Social Affairs (DESA).

Major groups

Broad public participation is a fundamental prerequisite of sustainable development. Agenda 21 recognizes the specific roles and responsibilities of nine major groups of civil society: women; children and youth; indigenous people and their communities; non-governmental organizations (NGOs); local authorities; workers and their trade unions; business and industry; the scientific and technological community; and farmers. The WSSD also recognizes scientists and educators.

The CSD has been heralded as one of the most progressive models of multi-stakeholder engagement in intergovernmental processes in recent times. It organizes **multi-stakeholder dialogues** to ensure the direct participation of civil society and to enable major groups to substantively and formally contribute to decision-making within the CSD. As a result of the WSSD, efforts are being made to improve this process with:

- Major groups represented in interactive dialogues during high-level segments;
- Balanced gender and regional representation;
- Active involvement of stakeholders in partnerships and capacity-building activities; and
- More action-orientated multi-stakeholder dialogues.

First ten years: Follow-up to Rio

The CSD attempted an 'inclusive agenda' to review progress on issues related to all 47 chapters of Agenda 21 through annual sessions at which stakeholder dialogues were held and resolutions negotiated. Each year the CSD considered a seleect number of issues (for example, the themes for 1997 were tourism, oceans and seas, consumption and production patterns, and small island developing states – SIDS), as well as cross-cutting issues (such as finance), which were addressed each year. In reality, it was an overburdened agenda with unwieldy discussions and sometimes a superficial review of progress.

In June 1997, heads of government and senior representatives from over 130 countries met in New York to consider what progress had been made since Rio. This Special Session of the United Nations General Assembly (UNGA), dubbed Rio+5, failed to generate much political attention or momentum, or any real new spirit of international cooperation – though it did agree a Programme for the Further Implementation of Agenda 21. The assessment of progress since Rio recognized some positive developments – particularly at local and community levels – but pointed to growing problems of poverty, inequality and environmental degradation.

World Summit on Sustainable Development

At the WSSD, it was widely recognized that the CSD had not been functioning as effectively as it could, and that some changes were required if it was to fulfil its mandate to better support the international implementation of sustainable development agreements.

Reforms of the CSD called for in Chapter XI of the Johannesburg Plan of Implementation (JPOI) are:

- Integration of the three mutually supportive dimensions of sustainable development in a balanced manner (to an extent, this means a stronger review of social concerns than had been achieved to date);
- Monitoring and review through the exchange of experience, knowledge and views, lessons learned and best practice;
- Improved linkages between endeavours at all levels – global, regional, national and local;
- Coherence between implementation of Agenda 21 and associated initiatives;
- Greater involvement at the regional level;
- Addressing opportunities and challenges to implementation;
- Innovative ways of working to ensure effective progress;
- Broader participation of all stakeholders, particularly UN agencies/international financial institutions and major groups;
- Involvement and recognition of educators and scientists;
- A focused work programme on a limited number of issues; and
- Negotiations limited to every two years.

Follow-up to Johannesburg

The CSD met in full for the first time, after the WSSD, in April 2003 to take decisions on its organizational reform and future work programme. It adopted guidelines for Type II partnerships (see p161–164) and a future work programme (see below) that will take the CSD up to 2017.

With respect to the structure of its work programme, this is arranged in a biennial 'implementation cycle', divided into:

- Year 1 – review session.
- Year 2 – policy session.
- Each cycle will address a **thematic cluster** of issues and **cross-cutting issues** [see below].
- The CSD will address constraints and obstacles to implementation and seek opportunities and solutions to these.
- The thematic cluster of issues will be reviewed periodically and recommendations will be made on new themes and system-wide coordination.
- High-level segments, involving ministers from all relevant portfolios, will be organized each year to give guidance and political oversight of decision-making.

The review session

The **review session** will be informed by a 'state of implementation' report by the United Nations Secretary-General, enabling the CSD to:

* Exchange regional experiences, best practice and lessons learned and facilitate dialogues between experts, with capacity-building as a critical element; and
* Identify priority challenges, obstacles, opportunities, recommendations and lessons learned.

United Nations Regional Commissions are invited to organize Regional Implementation Meetings with the CSD secretariat to make inputs to the Secretary-General's **State of Implementation** report.

The policy session

The **policy session** will be informed by discussions during the review sessions, as well as during intergovernmental preparatory meetings. Decisions will be negotiated on practical measures to promote implementation.

UNITED NATIONS COMMISSION ON SUSTAINABLE DEVELOPMENT'S (CSD'S) MULTI-YEAR WORK PROGRAMME

Cross-cutting issues (considered each year):

⚙ Poverty eradication

⚙ Changing unsustainable patterns of consumption and production

⚙ Protecting and managing the natural resource base of economic and social development

⚙ Sustainable development in a globalizing world

⚙ Health and sustainable development

⚙ Sustainable development of Small Island Developing States (SIDS)

⚙ Sustainable development for Africa

⚙ Other regional initiatives

⚙ Means of implementation

⚙ Institutional framework for sustainable development

⚙ Gender equality

⚙ Education

13

UNITED NATIONS COMMISSION ON SUSTAINABLE DEVELOPMENT'S (CSD'S) MULTI-YEAR WORK PROGRAMME (CONTD)

Thematic clusters

2004/2005:

- Water
- Sanitation
- Human settlements

2006/2007:

- Energy for sustainable development
- Industrial development
- Air pollution/atmosphere
- Climate change

2008/2009:

- Agriculture
- Rural development
- Land
- Drought
- Desertification
- Africa

2010/2011:

- Transport
- Chemicals
- Waste management
- Mining
- Ten-year framework of programmes on sustainable consumption and production patterns

2012/2013:

- Forests
- Biodiversity

UNITED NATIONS COMMISSION ON SUSTAINABLE DEVELOPMENT'S (CSD'S) MULTI-YEAR WORK PROGRAMME (CONTD)

- Biotechnology
- Tourism
- Mountains

2014/2015:

- Oceans
- Marine resources
- Small island developing states (SIDS)
- Disaster management and vulnerability

2016/2017:

- Overall appraisal of implementation of Agenda 21, the programme for the further implementation of Agenda 21 and the Johannesburg Plan of Implementation (JPOI)

CONFERENCES, AGREEMENTS AND PROCESSES

- United Nations Conference on Environment and Development (UNCED), Rio de Janeiro (1992)
- 47th United Nations General Assembly (UNGA) (1992)
- 19th United Nations General Assembly Special Session (UNGASS) (1997)
- 55th UNGA (2000)
- United Nations Commission on Sustainable Development (CSD) 10 (2001–2002)
- World Summit on Sustainable Development (WSSD) (2002)
- 57th UNGA (2002)
- CSD-11 (2003)

> ## Key United Nations bodies and Bretton Woods institutions
>
> Global Environment Facility (GEF)
>
> International Monetary Fund (IMF)
>
> United Nations Department of Economic and Social Affairs (DESA)
>
> United Nations Development Programme (UNDP)
>
> United Nations Economic and Social Council (ECOSOC)
>
> United Nations Environment Programme (UNEP)
>
> United Nations General Assembly (UNGA)
>
> World Bank
>
> World Trade Organization (WTO)

Resources

United Nations Commission on Sustainable Development (CSD)

www.un.org/esa/sustdev/
This is the official website on all elements of the CSD: past, present and future sessions, events and documents.

19th Special Session of the United Nations General Assembly (UNGA)

www.un.org/documents/ga/res/spec/aress19-2.htm
This session adopted the programme for the Further Implementation of Agenda 21, in September 1997, with the purpose of re-energizing commitments to achieving the goals and targets made during the Rio Earth Summit in 1992.

 # References

CSD (United Nations Commission on Sustainable Development) (2003a) *Follow-up to Johannesburg and the Future Role of the CSD – The Implementation Track: Report of the Secretary-General*, CSD, New York, 11th Session, 28 April–9 May 2003, United Nations Economic and Social Council, E/CN.17/2003/2

CSD (2003b) *United Nations Commission on Sustainable Development Report on the 11th Session* (27 January 2003 and 28 April–9 May 2003), United Nations, New York, Economic and Social Council Official Records, Supplement No 9, E/2003/29, E/CN.17/2003/6

A/RES/47/191 (1992) *Institutional Arrangements to Follow Up the United Nations Conference on Environment and Development*, www.un.org/documents/ga/hcs/47/a47r191.htm

A/RES/S-19/2 (1997) *Programme for the Further Implementation of Agenda 21*, www.un.org/documents/ga/hcs/spec/arkss19-2.htm

A/RES/55/199 (2000) *Ten-year Review of Progress Achieved in the Implementation of the Outcome of the United Nations Conference on Environment and Development*, www.nyo.unep.org/pdfs/55199.pdf

A/RES/57/235 (2003) *World Summit on Sustainable Development*

Plan of Implementation of the World Summit on Sustainable Development[*]

Annex A

I Introduction

1. The United Nations Conference on Environment and Development, held in Rio de Janeiro in 1992,[1] provided the fundamental principles and the programme of action for achieving sustainable development. We strongly reaffirm our commitment to the Rio principles,[2] the full implementation of Agenda 21[2] and the Programme for the Further Implementation of Agenda 21.[3] We also commit ourselves to achieving the internationally agreed development goals, including those contained in the United Nations Millennium Declaration[4] and in the outcomes of the major United Nations conferences and international agreements since 1992.

2. The present plan of implementation will further build on the achievements made since the United Nations Conference on Environment and Development and expedite the realization of the remaining goals. To this end, we commit ourselves to undertaking concrete actions and measures at all levels and to enhancing international cooperation, taking into account the Rio principles, including, inter alia, the principle of common but differentiated responsibilities as set out in principle 7 of the Rio Declaration on Environment and Development.[5] These efforts will also promote the integration of the three components of sustainable development – economic development, social development and environmental protection – as interdependent and mutually reinforcing pillars. Poverty eradication, changing unsustainable patterns of production and consumption and protecting and managing the natural resource base of economic and social development are overarching objectives of, and essential requirements for, sustainable development.

3. We recognize that the implementation of the outcomes of the Summit should benefit all, particularly women, youth, children and vulnerable groups. Furthermore, the implementation should involve all relevant actors through partnerships, especially between Governments of the North and South, on the one hand, and between Governments and major groups, on the other, to achieve the widely shared goals of sustainable development. As reflected in the Monterrey Consensus,[6] such partnerships are key to pursuing sustainable development in a globalizing world.

4. Good governance within each country and at the international level is essential for sustainable development. At the domestic level, sound environmental, social and economic policies, democratic institutions responsive to the needs of the people, the rule of law, anti-corruption measures, gender equality and an enabling environment for investment are the basis for sustainable development. As a result of globalization, external factors have become critical in determining the success

or failure of developing countries in their national efforts. The gap between developed and developing countries points to the continued need for a dynamic and enabling international economic environment supportive of international cooperation, particularly in the areas of finance, technology transfer, debt and trade and full and effective participation of developing countries in global decision-making, if the momentum for global progress towards sustainable development is to be maintained and increased.

5. Peace, security, stability and respect for human rights and fundamental freedoms, including the right to development, as well as respect for cultural diversity, are essential for achieving sustainable development and ensuring that sustainable development benefits all.

6. We acknowledge the importance of ethics for sustainable development and, therefore, emphasize the need to consider ethics in the implementation of Agenda 21.

II Poverty eradication

7. Eradicating poverty is the greatest global challenge facing the world today and an indispensable requirement for sustainable development, particularly for developing countries. Although each country has the primary responsibility for its own sustainable development and poverty eradication and the role of national policies and development strategies cannot be overemphasized, concerted and concrete measures are required at all levels to enable developing countries to achieve their sustainable development goals as related to the internationally agreed poverty-related targets and goals, including those contained in Agenda 21, the relevant outcomes of other United Nations conferences and the United Nations Millennium Declaration. This would include actions at all levels to:

(a) Halve, by the year 2015, the proportion of the world's people whose income is less than 1 dollar a day and the proportion of people who suffer from hunger and, by the same date, to halve the proportion of people without access to safe drinking water;

(b) Establish a world solidarity fund to eradicate poverty and to promote social and human development in the developing countries pursuant to modalities to be determined by the General Assembly, while stressing the voluntary nature of the contributions and the need to avoid duplication of existing United Nations funds, and encouraging the role of the private sector and individual citizens relative to Governments in funding the endeavours;

(c) Develop national programmes for sustainable development and local and community development, where appropriate within country-owned poverty reduction strategies, to promote the empowerment of people living in poverty and their organizations. These programmes should reflect their priorities and enable them to increase access to productive resources, public services and institutions – in particular, land, water, employment opportunities, credit, education and health;

(d) Promote women's equal access to and full participation in, on the basis of equality with men, decision-making at all levels, mainstreaming gender perspectives in all policies and strategies, eliminating all forms of violence and discrimination against women and improving the status, health and economic welfare of women and girls through full and equal access to economic opportunity, land, credit, education and healthcare services;

(e) Develop policies and ways and means to improve access by indigenous people and their communities to economic activities and increase their employment through, where appropriate, measures such as training, technical assistance and credit facilities. Recognize that traditional and direct dependence on renewable resources and ecosystems, including sustainable harvesting, continues to be essential to the cultural, economic and physical well-being of indigenous people and their communities;

(f) Deliver basic health services for all and reduce environmental health threats, taking into account the special needs of children and the linkages between poverty, health and environment, with provision of financial resources, technical assistance and knowledge transfer to developing countries and countries with economies in transition;

(g) Ensure that children everywhere, boys and girls alike, will be able to complete a full course of primary schooling and will have equal access to all levels of education;

(h) Provide access to agricultural resources for people living in poverty, especially women and indigenous communities, and promote, as appropriate, land tenure arrangements that recognize and protect indigenous and common property resource management systems;

(i) Build basic rural infrastructure, diversify the economy and improve transportation and access to markets, market information and credit for the rural poor to support sustainable agriculture and rural development;

(j) Transfer basic sustainable agricultural techniques and knowledge, including natural resource management, to small- and medium-scale farmers, fishers and the rural poor, especially in developing countries, including through multi-stakeholder approaches and public–private partnerships aimed at increasing agriculture production and food security;

(k) Increase food availability and affordability, including through harvest and food technology and management, as well as equitable and efficient distribution systems, by promoting, for example, community-based partnerships linking urban and rural people and enterprises;

(l) Combat desertification and mitigate the effects of drought and floods through measures such as improved use of climate and weather information and forecasts, early warning systems, land and natural resource management, agricultural practices and ecosystem conservation in order to reverse current trends and minimize degradation of land and water resources, including through the provision of adequate and predictable financial resources to implement the United Nations Convention to Combat Desertification in Those Countries Experiencing Serious Drought and/or Desertification, particularly in Africa,[7] as one of the tools for poverty eradication;

(m) Increase access to sanitation to improve human health and reduce infant and child mortality, prioritizing water and sanitation in national sustainable development strategies and poverty reduction strategies where they exist.

8. The provision of clean drinking water and adequate sanitation is necessary to protect human health and the environment. In this respect, we agree to halve, by the year 2015, the proportion of people who are unable to reach or to afford safe drinking water (as outlined in the Millennium Declaration) and the proportion of

people who do not have access to basic sanitation, which would include actions at all levels to:

(a) Develop and implement efficient household sanitation systems;

(b) Improve sanitation in public institutions, especially schools;

(c) Promote safe hygiene practices;

(d) Promote education and outreach focused on children, as agents of behavioural change;

(e) Promote affordable and socially and culturally acceptable technologies and practices;

(f) Develop innovative financing and partnership mechanisms;

(g) Integrate sanitation into water resources management strategies.

9. Take joint actions and improve efforts to work together at all levels to improve access to reliable and affordable energy services for sustainable development sufficient to facilitate the achievement of the Millennium development goals, including the goal of halving the proportion of people in poverty by 2015, and as a means to generate other important services that mitigate poverty, bearing in mind that access to energy facilitates the eradication of poverty. This would include actions at all levels to:

(a) Improve access to reliable, affordable, economically viable, socially acceptable and environmentally sound energy services and resources, taking into account national specificities and circumstances, through various means, such as enhanced rural electrification and decentralized energy systems, increased use of renewables, cleaner liquid and gaseous fuels and enhanced energy efficiency, by intensifying regional and international cooperation in support of national efforts, including through capacity-building, financial and technological assistance and innovative financing mechanisms, including at the micro and meso levels, recognizing the specific factors for providing access to the poor;

(b) Improve access to modern biomass technologies and fuelwood sources and supplies and commercialize biomass operations, including the use of agricultural residues, in rural areas and where such practices are sustainable;

(c) Promote a sustainable use of biomass and, as appropriate, other renewable energies through improvement of current patterns of use, such as management of resources, more efficient use of fuelwood and new or improved products and technologies;

(d) Support the transition to the cleaner use of liquid and gaseous fossil fuels, where considered more environmentally sound, socially acceptable and cost-effective;

(e) Develop national energy policies and regulatory frameworks that will help to create the necessary economic, social and institutional conditions in the energy sector to improve access to reliable, affordable, economically viable, socially acceptable and environmentally sound energy services for sustainable development and poverty eradication in rural, peri-urban and urban areas;

(f) Enhance international and regional cooperation to improve access to reliable, affordable, economically viable, socially acceptable and environmentally sound energy services, as an integral part of poverty reduction programmes, by facilitating the creation of enabling environments and addressing capacity-building needs, with special attention to rural and isolated areas, as appropriate;

(g) Assist and facilitate on an accelerated basis, with the financial and technical assistance of developed countries, including through public–private partnerships, the access of the poor to reliable, affordable, economically viable, socially acceptable and environmentally sound energy services, taking into account the instrumental role of developing national policies on energy for sustainable development, bearing in mind that in developing countries sharp increases in energy services are required to improve the standards of living of their populations and that energy services have positive impacts on poverty eradication and improve standards of living.

10. Strengthen the contribution of industrial development to poverty eradication and sustainable natural resource management. This would include actions at all levels to:

(a) Provide assistance and mobilize resources to enhance industrial productivity and competitiveness, as well as industrial development, in developing countries, including the transfer of environmentally sound technologies on preferential terms, as mutually agreed;

(b) Provide assistance to increase income-generating employment opportunities, taking into account the Declaration on Fundamental Principles and Rights at Work of the International Labour Organization;[8]

(c) Promote the development of micro-, small- and medium-sized enterprises, including by means of training, education and skill enhancement, with a special focus on agro-industry as a provider of livelihoods for rural communities;

(d) Provide financial and technological support, as appropriate, to rural communities of developing countries to enable them to benefit from safe and sustainable livelihood opportunities in small-scale mining ventures;

(e) Provide support to developing countries for the development of safe low-cost technologies that provide or conserve fuel for cooking and water heating;

(f) Provide support for natural resource management for creating sustainable livelihoods for the poor.

11. By 2020, achieve a significant improvement in the lives of at least 100 million slum dwellers, as proposed in the Cities without slums initiative. This would include actions at all levels to:

(a) Improve access to land and property, to adequate shelter and to basic services for the urban and rural poor, with special attention to female heads of household;

(b) Use low-cost and sustainable materials and appropriate technologies for the construction of adequate and secure housing for the poor, with financial and technological assistance to developing countries, taking into account their culture, climate, specific social conditions and vulnerability to natural disasters;

(c) Increase decent employment, credit and income for the urban poor, through appropriate national policies, promoting equal opportunities for women and men;

(d) Remove unnecessary regulatory and other obstacles for microenterprises and the informal sector;

(e) Support local authorities in elaborating slum upgrading programmes within the framework of urban development plans and facilitate access, particularly for the poor, to information on housing legislation.

12. Take immediate and effective measures to eliminate the worst forms of child labour as defined in International Labour Organization Convention 182, and elaborate

and implement strategies for the elimination of child labour that is contrary to accepted international standards.

13. Promote international cooperation to assist developing countries, upon request, in addressing child labour and its root causes, inter alia, through social and economic policies aimed at poverty conditions, while stressing that labour standards should not be used for protectionist trade purposes.

III Changing unsustainable patterns of consumption and production

14. Fundamental changes in the way societies produce and consume are indispensable for achieving global sustainable development. All countries should promote sustainable consumption and production patterns, with the developed countries taking the lead and with all countries benefiting from the process, taking into account the Rio principles, including, inter alia, the principle of common but differentiated responsibilities as set out in principle 7 of the Rio Declaration on Environment and Development. Governments, relevant international organizations, the private sector and all major groups should play an active role in changing unsustainable consumption and production patterns. This would include the actions at all levels set out below.

15. Encourage and promote the development of a 10-year framework of programmes in support of regional and national initiatives to accelerate the shift towards sustainable consumption and production to promote social and economic development within the carrying capacity of ecosystems by addressing and, where appropriate, delinking economic growth and environmental degradation through improving efficiency and sustainability in the use of resources and production processes and reducing resource degradation, pollution and waste. All countries should take action, with developed countries taking the lead, taking into account the development needs and capabilities of developing countries, through mobilization, from all sources, of financial and technical assistance and capacity-building for developing countries. This would require actions at all levels to:

(a) Identify specific activities, tools, policies, measures and monitoring and assessment mechanisms, including, where appropriate, life-cycle analysis and national indicators for measuring progress, bearing in mind that standards applied by some countries may be inappropriate and of unwarranted economic and social cost to other countries, in particular developing countries;

(b) Adopt and implement policies and measures aimed at promoting sustainable patterns of production and consumption, applying, inter alia, the polluter-pays principle described in principle 16 of the Rio Declaration on Environment and Development;

(c) Develop production and consumption policies to improve the products and services provided, while reducing environmental and health impacts, using, where appropriate, science-based approaches, such as life-cycle analysis;

(d) Develop awareness-raising programmes on the importance of sustainable production and consumption patterns, particularly among youth and the relevant segments in all countries, especially in developed countries, through, inter alia, education, public and consumer information, advertising and other media, taking into account local, national and regional cultural values;

(e) Develop and adopt, where appropriate, on a voluntary basis, effective, transparent, verifiable, non-misleading and non-discriminatory consumer information tools to provide information relating to sustainable consumption and production, including human health and safety aspects. These tools should not be used as disguised trade barriers;

(f) Increase eco-efficiency, with financial support from all sources, where mutually agreed, for capacity-building, technology transfer and exchange of technology with developing countries and countries with economies in transition, in cooperation with relevant international organizations.

16. Increase investment in cleaner production and eco-efficiency in all countries through, inter alia, incentives and support schemes and policies directed at establishing appropriate regulatory, financial and legal frameworks. This would include actions at all levels to:

(a) Establish and support cleaner production programmes and centres and more efficient production methods by providing, inter alia, incentives and capacity-building to assist enterprises, especially small- and medium-sized enterprises, particularly in developing countries, in improving productivity and sustainable development;

(b) Provide incentives for investment in cleaner production and eco-efficiency in all countries, such as state-financed loans, venture capital, technical assistance and training programmes for small- and medium-sized companies, while avoiding trade-distorting measures inconsistent with the rules of the World Trade Organization;

(c) Collect and disseminate information on cost-effective examples in cleaner production, eco-efficiency and environmental management and promote the exchange of best practices and know-how on environmentally sound technologies between public and private institutions;

(d) Provide training programmes to small- and medium-sized enterprises on the use of information and communication technologies.

17. Integrate the issue of production and consumption patterns into sustainable development policies, programmes and strategies, including, where applicable, into poverty reduction strategies.

18. Enhance corporate environmental and social responsibility and accountability. This would include actions at all levels to:

(a) Encourage industry to improve social and environmental performance through voluntary initiatives, including environmental management systems, codes of conduct, certification and public reporting on environmental and social issues, taking into account such initiatives as the International Organization for Standardization standards and Global Reporting Initiative guidelines on sustainability reporting, bearing in mind principle 11 of the Rio Declaration on Environment and Development;

(b) Encourage dialogue between enterprises and the communities in which they operate and other stakeholders;

(c) Encourage financial institutions to incorporate sustainable development considerations into their decision-making processes;

(d) Develop workplace-based partnerships and programmes, including training and education programmes.

19. Encourage relevant authorities at all levels to take sustainable development considerations into account in decision-making, including on national and local

development planning, investment in infrastructure, business development and public procurement. This would include actions at all levels to:

(a) Provide support for the development of sustainable development strategies and programmes, including in decision-making on investment in infrastructure and business development;

(b) Continue to promote the internalization of environmental costs and the use of economic instruments, taking into account the approach that the polluter should, in principle, bear the costs of pollution, with due regard to the public interest and without distorting international trade and investment;

(c) Promote public procurement policies that encourage development and diffusion of environmentally sound goods and services;

(d) Provide capacity-building and training to assist relevant authorities with regard to the implementation of the initiatives listed in the present paragraph;

(e) Use environmental impact assessment procedures.

* * *

20. Call upon Governments as well as relevant regional and international organizations and other relevant stakeholders to implement, taking into account national and regional specificities and circumstances, the recommendations and conclusions adopted by the Commission on Sustainable Development concerning energy for sustainable development at its ninth session, including the issues and options set out below, bearing in mind that in view of the different contributions to global environmental degradation, States have common but differentiated responsibilities. This would include actions at all levels to:

(a) Take further action to mobilize the provision of financial resources, technology transfer, capacity-building and the diffusion of environmentally sound technologies according to the recommendations and conclusions of the Commission on Sustainable Development, as contained in section A, paragraph 3, and Section D, paragraph 30, of its decision 9/1[9] on energy for sustainable development;

(b) Integrate energy considerations, including energy efficiency, affordability and accessibility, into socio-economic programmes, especially into policies of major energy-consuming sectors, and into the planning, operation and maintenance of long-lived energy consuming infrastructures, such as the public sector, transport, industry, agriculture, urban land use, tourism and construction sectors;

(c) Develop and disseminate alternative energy technologies with the aim of giving a greater share of the energy mix to renewable energies, improving energy efficiency and greater reliance on advanced energy technologies, including cleaner fossil fuel technologies;

(d) Combine, as appropriate, the increased use of renewable energy resources, more efficient use of energy, greater reliance on advanced energy technologies, including advanced and cleaner fossil fuel technologies, and the sustainable use of traditional energy resources, which could meet the growing need for energy services in the longer term to achieve sustainable development;

(e) Diversify energy supply by developing advanced, cleaner, more efficient, affordable and cost-effective energy technologies, including fossil fuel technologies and renewable energy technologies, hydro included, and their transfer to developing countries on concessional terms as mutually agreed. With a sense of urgency, substantially increase the global share of renewable energy sources with the objective of increasing its contribution to total energy supply, recognizing the role of national and voluntary regional targets as well as initiatives, where they exist, and ensuring that energy policies are supportive to developing countries' efforts to eradicate poverty, and regularly evaluate available data to review progress to this end;

(f) Support efforts, including through provision of financial and technical assistance to developing countries, with the involvement of the private sector, to reduce flaring and venting of gas associated with crude oil production;

(g) Develop and utilize indigenous energy sources and infrastructures for various local uses and promote rural community participation, including local Agenda 21 groups, with the support of the international community, in developing and utilizing renewable energy technologies to meet their daily energy needs to find simple and local solutions;

(h) Establish domestic programmes for energy efficiency, including, as appropriate, by accelerating the deployment of energy efficiency technologies, with the necessary support of the international community;

(i) Accelerate the development, dissemination and deployment of affordable and cleaner energy efficiency and energy conservation technologies, as well as the transfer of such technologies, in particular to developing countries, on favourable terms, including on concessional and preferential terms, as mutually agreed;

(j) Recommend that international financial institutions and other agencies' policies support developing countries, as well as countries with economies in transition, in their own efforts to establish policy and regulatory frameworks which create a level playing field between the following: renewable energy, energy efficiency, advanced energy technologies, including advanced and cleaner fossil fuel technologies, and centralized, distributed and decentralized energy systems;

(k) Promote increased research and development in the field of various energy technologies, including renewable energy, energy efficiency and advanced energy technologies, including advanced and cleaner fossil fuel technologies, both nationally and through international collaboration; strengthen national and regional research and development institutions/centres on reliable, affordable, economically viable, socially acceptable and environmentally sound energy for sustainable development;

(l) Promote networking between centres of excellence on energy for sustainable development, including regional networks, by linking competent centres on energy technologies for sustainable development that could support and promote efforts at capacity-building and technology transfer activities, particularly of developing countries, as well as serve as information clearing houses;

(m) Promote education to provide information for both men and women about available energy sources and technologies;

(n) Utilize financial instruments and mechanisms, in particular the Global Environment Facility, within its mandate, to provide financial resources to developing countries, in particular least developed countries and small island developing States, to meet their capacity needs for training, technical know-how and strengthening national institutions in reliable, affordable, economically viable, socially acceptable and environmentally sound energy, including promoting energy efficiency and conservation, renewable energy and advanced energy technologies, including advanced and cleaner fossil fuel technologies;

(o) Support efforts to improve the functioning, transparency and information about energy markets with respect to both supply and demand, with the aim of achieving greater stability and predictability, and to ensure consumer access to reliable, affordable, economically viable, socially acceptable and environmentally sound energy services;

(p) Policies to reduce market distortions would promote energy systems compatible with sustainable development through the use of improved market signals and by removing market distortions, including restructuring taxation and phasing out harmful subsidies, where they exist, to reflect their environmental impacts, with such policies taking fully into account the specific needs and conditions of developing countries, with the aim of minimizing the possible adverse impacts on their development;

(q) Take action, where appropriate, to phase out subsidies in this area that inhibit sustainable development, taking fully into account the specific conditions and different levels of development of individual countries and considering their adverse effect, particularly on developing countries;

(r) Governments are encouraged to improve the functioning of national energy markets in such a way that they support sustainable development, overcome market barriers and improve accessibility, taking fully into account that such policies should be decided by each country, and that its own characteristics and capabilities and level of development should be considered, especially as reflected in national sustainable development strategies, where they exist;

(s) Strengthen national and regional energy institutions or arrangements for enhancing regional and international cooperation on energy for sustainable development, in particular to assist developing countries in their domestic efforts to provide reliable, affordable, economically viable, socially acceptable and environmentally sound energy services to all sections of their populations;

(t) Countries are urged to develop and implement actions within the framework of the ninth session of the Commission on Sustainable Development, including through public–private partnerships, taking into account the different circumstances of countries, based on lessons learned by Governments, international institutions and stakeholders, including business and industry, in the field of access to energy, including renewable energy and energy-efficiency and advanced energy technologies, including advanced and cleaner fossil fuel technologies;

(u) Promote cooperation between international and regional institutions and bodies dealing with different aspects of energy for sustainable development within their existing mandate, bearing in mind paragraph 46(h) of the Programme of Action for the Further Implementation of Agenda 21, strengthening, as appropriate, regional and national activities for the promotion of education and capacity-building regarding energy for sustainable development;

(v) Strengthen and facilitate, as appropriate, regional cooperation arrangements for promoting cross-border energy trade, including the interconnection of electricity grids and oil and natural gas pipelines;

(w) Strengthen and, where appropriate, facilitate dialogue forums among regional, national and international producers and consumers of energy.

* * *

21. Promote an integrated approach to policy-making at the national, regional and local levels for transport services and systems to promote sustainable development, including policies and planning for land use, infrastructure, public transport systems and goods delivery networks, with a view to providing safe, affordable and efficient transportation, increasing energy efficiency, reducing pollution, congestion and adverse health effects and limiting urban sprawl, taking into account national priorities and circumstances. This would include actions at all levels to:

(a) Implement transport strategies for sustainable development, reflecting specific regional, national and local conditions, to improve the affordability, efficiency and convenience of transportation, as well as urban air quality and health and reduce greenhouse gas emissions, including through the development of better vehicle technologies that are more environmentally sound, affordable and socially acceptable;

(b) Promote investment and partnerships for the development of sustainable, energy efficient multi-modal transportation systems, including public mass transportation systems and better transportation systems in rural areas, with technical and financial assistance for developing countries and countries with economies in transition.

* * *

22. Prevent and minimize waste and maximize reuse, recycling and use of environmentally friendly alternative materials, with the participation of government authorities and all stakeholders, in order to minimize adverse effects on the environment and improve resource efficiency, with financial, technical and other assistance for developing countries. This would include actions at all levels to:

(a) Develop waste management systems, with the highest priority placed on waste prevention and minimization, reuse and recycling, and environmentally sound disposal facilities, including technology to recapture the energy contained in waste, and encourage small-scale waste-recycling initiatives that support urban and rural waste management and provide income-generating opportunities, with international support for developing countries;

(b) Promote waste prevention and minimization by encouraging production of reusable consumer goods and biodegradable products and developing the infrastructure required.

* * *

23. Renew the commitment, as advanced in Agenda 21, to sound management of chemicals throughout their life cycle and of hazardous wastes for sustainable development, as well as for the protection of human health and the environment, inter alia, aiming to achieve, by 2020, that chemicals are used and produced in ways that lead to the minimization of significant adverse effects on human health and the environment, using transparent science-based risk assessment procedures and science-based risk management procedures, taking into account the precautionary approach, as set out in principle 15 of the Rio Declaration on Environment and Development, and support developing countries in strengthening

their capacity for the sound management of chemicals and hazardous wastes by providing technical and financial assistance. This would include actions at all levels to:

(a) Promote the ratification and implementation of relevant international instruments on chemicals and hazardous waste, including the Rotterdam Convention on Prior Informed Consent Procedures for Certain Hazardous Chemicals and Pesticides in International Trade[10] so that it can enter into force by 2003 and the Stockholm Convention on Persistent Organic Pollutants[11] so that it can enter into force by 2004, and encourage and improve coordination, as well as supporting developing countries in their implementation;

(b) Further develop a strategic approach to international chemicals management based on the Bahia Declaration and Priorities for Action beyond 2000 of the Intergovernmental Forum on Chemical Safety[12] by 2005, and urge that the United Nations Environment Programme, the Intergovernmental Forum, other international organizations dealing with chemical management and other relevant international organizations and actors closely cooperate in this regard, as appropriate;

(c) Encourage countries to implement the new globally harmonized system for the classification and labelling of chemicals as soon as possible with a view to having the system fully operational by 2008;

(d) Encourage partnerships to promote activities aimed at enhancing environmentally sound management of chemicals and hazardous wastes, implementing multilateral environmental agreements, raising awareness of issues relating to chemicals and hazardous waste, and encouraging the collection and use of additional scientific data;

(e) Promote efforts to prevent international illegal trafficking of hazardous chemicals and hazardous wastes and to prevent damage resulting from the transboundary movement and disposal of hazardous wastes in a manner consistent with obligations under relevant international instruments, such as the Basel Convention on the Control of Transboundary Movements of Hazardous Wastes and Their Disposal;[13]

(f) Encourage development of coherent and integrated information on chemicals, such as through national pollutant release and transfer registers;

(g) Promote reduction of the risks posed by heavy metals that are harmful to human health and the environment, including through a review of relevant studies, such as the United Nations Environment Programme global assessment of mercury and its compounds.

IV Protecting and managing the natural resource base of economic and social development

24. Human activities are having an increasing impact on the integrity of ecosystems that provide essential resources and services for human well-being and economic activities. Managing the natural resources base in a sustainable and integrated manner is essential for sustainable development. In this regard, to reverse the current trend in natural resource degradation as soon as possible, it is necessary to implement strategies which should include targets adopted at the national and,

where appropriate, regional levels to protect ecosystems and to achieve integrated management of land, water and living resources, while strengthening regional, national and local capacities. This would include actions at all levels as set out below.

25. Launch a programme of actions, with financial and technical assistance, to achieve the Millennium development goal on safe drinking water. In this respect, we agree to halve, by the year 2015, the proportion of people who are unable to reach or to afford safe drinking water, as outlined in the Millennium Declaration, and the proportion of people without access to basic sanitation, which would include actions at all levels to:

    (a) Mobilize international and domestic financial resources at all levels, transfer technology, promote best practice and support capacity-building for water and sanitation infrastructure and services development, ensuring that such infrastructure and services meet the needs of the poor and are gender sensitive;

    (b) Facilitate access to public information and participation, including by women, at all levels in support of policy and decision-making related to water resources management and project implementation;

    (c) Promote priority action by Governments, with the support of all stakeholders, in water management and capacity-building at the national level and, where appropriate, at the regional level, and promote and provide new and additional financial resources and innovative technologies to implement Chapter 18 of Agenda 21;

    (d) Intensify water pollution prevention to reduce health hazards and protect ecosystems by introducing technologies for affordable sanitation and industrial and domestic wastewater treatment by mitigating the effects of groundwater contamination and by establishing, at the national level, monitoring systems and effective legal frameworks;

    (e) Adopt prevention and protection measures to promote sustainable water use and to address water shortages.

26. Develop integrated water resources management and water efficiency plans by 2005, with support to developing countries, through actions at all levels to:

    (a) Develop and implement national/regional strategies, plans and programmes with regard to integrated river basin, watershed and groundwater management and introduce measures to improve the efficiency of water infrastructure to reduce losses and increase recycling of water;

    (b) Employ the full range of policy instruments, including regulation, monitoring, voluntary measures, market and information-based tools, land-use management and cost recovery of water services, without cost recovery objectives becoming a barrier to access to safe water by poor people, and adopt an integrated water basin approach;

    (c) Improve the efficient use of water resources and promote their allocation among competing uses in a way that gives priority to the satisfaction of basic human needs and balances the requirement of preserving or restoring ecosystems and their functions, in particular in fragile environments, with human domestic, industrial and agriculture needs, including safeguarding drinking water quality;

    (d) Develop programmes for mitigating the effects of extreme water-related events.

(e) Support the diffusion of technology and capacity-building for non-conventional water resources and conservation technologies to developing countries and regions facing water scarcity conditions or subject to drought and desertification, through technical and financial support and capacity-building;

(f) Support, where appropriate, efforts and programmes for energy-efficient, sustainable and cost-effective desalination of seawater, water recycling and water harvesting from coastal fogs in developing countries through such measures as technological, technical and financial assistance and other modalities;

(g) Facilitate the establishment of public–private partnerships and other forms of partnership that give priority to the needs of the poor within stable and transparent national regulatory frameworks provided by Governments, while respecting local conditions, involving all concerned stakeholders, and monitoring the performance and improving accountability of public institutions and private companies.

27. Support developing countries and countries with economies in transition in their efforts to monitor and assess the quantity and quality of water resources, including through the establishment and/or further development of national monitoring networks and water resources databases and the development of relevant national indicators.

28. Improve water resource management and scientific understanding of the water cycle through cooperation in joint observation and research, and for this purpose encourage and promote knowledge-sharing and provide capacity-building and the transfer of technology, as mutually agreed, including remote-sensing and satellite technologies, particularly to developing countries and countries with economies in transition.

29. Promote effective coordination among the various international and intergovernmental bodies and processes working on water-related issues, both within the United Nations system and between the United Nations and international financial institutions, drawing on the contributions of other international institutions and civil society to inform intergovernmental decision-making; closer coordination should also be promoted to elaborate and support proposals and undertake activities related to the International Year of Freshwater 2003, and beyond.

* * *

30. Oceans, seas, islands and coastal areas form an integrated and essential component of the Earth's ecosystem and are critical for global food security and for sustaining economic prosperity and the well-being of many national economies, particularly in developing countries. Ensuring the sustainable development of the oceans requires effective coordination and cooperation, including at the global and regional levels, between relevant bodies, and actions at all levels to:

(a) Invite States to ratify or accede to and implement the United Nations Convention on the Law of the Sea of 1982,[14] which provides the overall legal framework for ocean activities;

(b) Promote the implementation of Chapter 17 of Agenda 21, which provides the programme of action for achieving the sustainable development of oceans, coastal areas and seas through its programme areas of integrated management and sustainable development of coastal areas, including exclusive economic zones; marine environmental protection; sustainable use and conservation of marine living resources; addressing critical uncertainties for the management of the marine environment and climate change; strengthening international, including regional, cooperation and coordination; and sustainable development of small islands;

(c) Establish an effective, transparent and regular inter-agency coordination mechanism on ocean and coastal issues within the United Nations system;

(d) Encourage the application by 2010 of the ecosystem approach, noting the Reykjavik Declaration on Responsible Fisheries in the Marine Ecosystem[15] and decision V/6 of the Conference of Parties to the Convention on Biological Diversity (CBD);[16]

(e) Promote integrated, multidisciplinary and multi-sectoral coastal and ocean management at the national level and encourage and assist coastal States in developing ocean policies and mechanisms on integrated coastal management;

(f) Strengthen regional cooperation and coordination between the relevant regional organizations and programmes, the regional seas programmes of the United Nations Environment Programme, regional fisheries management organizations and other regional science, health and development organizations;

(g) Assist developing countries in coordinating policies and programmes at the regional and sub-regional levels aimed at the conservation and sustainable management of fishery resources and implement integrated coastal area management plans, including through the promotion of sustainable coastal and small-scale fishing activities and, where appropriate, the development of related infrastructure;

(h) Take note of the work of the open-ended informal consultative process established by the United Nations General Assembly in its resolution 54/33 in order to facilitate the annual review by the Assembly of developments in ocean affairs and the upcoming review of its effectiveness and utility to be held at its 57th session under the terms of the above-mentioned resolution.

31. To achieve sustainable fisheries, the following actions are required at all levels:

(a) Maintain or restore stocks to levels that can produce the maximum sustainable yield with the aim of achieving these goals for depleted stocks on an urgent basis and, where possible, not later than 2015;

(b) Ratify or accede to and effectively implement the relevant United Nations and, where appropriate, associated regional fisheries agreements or arrangements, noting in particular the Agreement for the Implementation of the Provisions of the United Nations Convention on the Law of the Sea of 10 December 1982 relating to the Conservation and Management of Straddling Fish Stocks and Highly Migratory Fish Stocks[17] and the 1993 Agreement to Promote Compliance with International Conservation and Management Measures by Fishing Vessels on the High Seas;[18]

(c) Implement the 1995 Code of Conduct for Responsible Fisheries,[19] taking note of the special requirements of developing countries as noted in its article 5, and the relevant international plans of action and technical guidelines of the Food and Agriculture Organization of the United Nations;

(d) Urgently develop and implement national and, where appropriate, regional plans of action, to put into effect the international plans of action of the Food and Agriculture Organization of the United Nations, in particular the International Plan of Action for the Management of Fishing Capacity[20] by

2005 and the International Plan of Action to Prevent, Deter and Eliminate Illegal, Unreported and Unregulated Fishing[21] by 2004. Establish effective monitoring, reporting and enforcement, and control of fishing vessels, including by flag States, to further the International Plan of Action to Prevent, Deter and Eliminate Illegal, Unreported and Unregulated Fishing;

(e) Encourage relevant regional fisheries management organizations and arrangements to give due consideration to the rights, duties and interests of coastal States and the special requirements of developing States when addressing the issue of the allocation of share of fishery resources for straddling stocks and highly migratory fish stocks, mindful of the provisions of the United Nations Convention on the Law of the Sea and the Agreement for the Implementation of the Provisions of the United Nations Convention on the Law of the Sea of 10 December 1982 relating to the Conservation and Management of Straddling Fish Stocks and Highly Migratory Fish Stocks, on the high seas and within exclusive economic zones;

(f) Eliminate subsidies that contribute to illegal, unreported and unregulated fishing and to over-capacity, while completing the efforts undertaken at the World Trade Organization to clarify and improve its disciplines on fisheries subsidies, taking into account the importance of this sector to developing countries;

(g) Strengthen donor coordination and partnerships between international financial institutions, bilateral agencies and other relevant stakeholders to enable developing countries, in particular the least developed countries and small island developing States and countries with economies in transition, to develop their national, regional and sub-regional capacities for infrastructure and integrated management and the sustainable use of fisheries;

(h) Support the sustainable development of aquaculture, including small-scale aquaculture, given its growing importance for food security and economic development.

32. In accordance with Chapter 17 of Agenda 21, promote the conservation and management of the oceans through actions at all levels, giving due regard to the relevant international instruments to:

(a) Maintain the productivity and biodiversity of important and vulnerable marine and coastal areas, including in areas within and beyond national jurisdiction;

(b) Implement the work programme arising from the Jakarta Mandate on the Conservation and Sustainable Use of Marine and Coastal Biological Diversity of the Convention on Biological Diversity,[22] including through the urgent mobilization of financial resources and technological assistance and the development of human and institutional capacity, particularly in developing countries;

(c) Develop and facilitate the use of diverse approaches and tools, including the ecosystem approach, the elimination of destructive fishing practices, the establishment of marine protected areas consistent with international law and based on scientific information, including representative networks by 2012 and time/area closures for the protection of nursery grounds and periods, proper coastal land-use and watershed planning, and the integration of marine and coastal areas management into key sectors;

(d) Develop national, regional and international programmes for halting the loss of marine biodiversity, including in coral reefs and wetlands;

(e) Implement the Ramsar Convention,[23] including its joint work programme, with the Convention on Biological Diversity[24] and the programme of action called for by the International Coral Reef Initiative to strengthen joint management plans and international networking for wetland ecosystems in coastal zones, including coral reefs, mangroves, seaweed beds and tidal mud flats.

33. Advance implementation of the Global Programme of Action for the Protection of the Marine Environment from Land-based Activities[25] and the Montreal Declaration on the Protection of the Marine Environment from Land-based Activities,[26] with particular emphasis during the period from 2002 to 2006 on municipal wastewater, the physical alteration and destruction of habitats and nutrients by actions at all levels to:

(a) Facilitate partnerships, scientific research and diffusion of technical knowledge; mobilize domestic, regional and international resources; and promote human and institutional capacity-building, paying particular attention to the needs of developing countries;

(b) Strengthen the capacity of developing countries in the development of their national and regional programmes and mechanisms to mainstream the objectives of the Global Programme of Action and to manage the risks and impacts of ocean pollution;

(c) Elaborate regional programmes of action and improve the links with strategic plans for the sustainable development of coastal and marine resources, noting, in particular, areas that are subject to accelerated environmental changes and development pressures;

(d) Make every effort to achieve substantial progress by the next Global Programme of Action conference in 2006 to protect the marine environment from land-based activities.

34. Enhance maritime safety and protection of the marine environment from pollution by actions at all levels to:

(a) Invite States to ratify or accede to and implement the conventions and protocols and other relevant instruments of the International Maritime Organization relating to the enhancement of maritime safety and protection of the marine environment from marine pollution and environmental damage caused by ships, including the use of toxic anti-fouling paints, and urge the International Maritime Organization (IMO) to consider stronger mechanisms to secure the implementation of IMO instruments by flag States;

(b) Accelerate the development of measures to address invasive alien species in ballast water. Urge the International Maritime Organization to finalize its draft International Convention on the Control and Management of Ships' Ballast Water and Sediments.

35. Governments, taking into account their national circumstances, are encouraged, recalling paragraph 8 of resolution GC (44)/RES/17 of the General Conference of the International Atomic Energy Agency, and taking into account the very serious potential for environment and human health impacts of radioactive wastes, to make efforts to examine and further improve measures and internationally agreed regulations regarding safety, while stressing the importance of having effective liability mechanisms in place relevant to international maritime transportation and other transboundary movement of radioactive material, radioactive waste and spent fuel, including, inter alia, arrangements for prior notification and consultations done in accordance with relevant international instruments.

36. Improve the scientific understanding and assessment of marine and coastal ecosystems as a fundamental basis for sound decision-making through actions at all levels to:

(a) Increase scientific and technical collaboration, including integrated assessment at the global and regional levels, including the appropriate transfer of marine science and marine technologies and techniques for the conservation and management of living and non-living marine resources and expanding ocean-observing capabilities for the timely prediction and assessment of the state of marine environment;

(b) Establish by 2004 a regular process under the United Nations for global reporting and assessment of the state of the marine environment, including socio-economic aspects, both current and foreseeable, building on existing regional assessments;

(c) Build capacity in marine science, information and management, through, inter alia, promoting the use of environmental impact assessments and environmental evaluation and reporting techniques for projects or activities that are potentially harmful to the coastal and marine environments and their living and non-living resources;

(d) Strengthen the ability of the Intergovernmental Oceanographic Commission of the United Nations Educational, Scientific and Cultural Organization, the Food and Agriculture Organization of the United Nations and other relevant international and regional and sub-regional organizations to build national and local capacity in marine science and the sustainable management of oceans and their resources.

* * *

37. An integrated, multi-hazard, inclusive approach to address vulnerability, risk assessment and disaster management, including prevention, mitigation, preparedness, response and recovery, is an essential element of a safer world in the 21st century. Actions are required at all levels to:

(a) Strengthen the role of the International Strategy for Disaster Reduction and encourage the international community to provide the necessary financial resources to its Trust Fund;

(b) Support the establishment of effective regional, sub-regional and national strategies and scientific and technical institutional support for disaster management;

(c) Strengthen the institutional capacities of countries and promote international joint observation and research through improved surface-based monitoring and increased use of satellite data, dissemination of technical and scientific knowledge, and the provision of assistance to vulnerable countries;

(d) Reduce the risks of flooding and drought in vulnerable countries by, inter alia, promoting wetland and watershed protection and restoration, improved land-use planning, improving and applying more widely techniques and methodologies for assessing the potential adverse effects of climate change on wetlands and, as appropriate, assisting countries that are particularly vulnerable to those effects;

(e) Improve techniques and methodologies for assessing the effects of climate change, and encourage the continuing assessment of those adverse effects by the Intergovernmental Panel on Climate Change;

(f)   Encourage the dissemination and use of traditional and indigenous knowledge to mitigate the impact of disasters and promote community-based disaster management planning by local authorities, including through training activities and raising public awareness;

(g)   Support the ongoing voluntary contribution of, as appropriate, non-governmental organizations, the scientific community and other partners in the management of natural disasters according to agreed, relevant guidelines;

(h)   Develop and strengthen early warning systems and information networks in disaster management, consistent with the International Strategy for Disaster Reduction;

(i)   Develop and strengthen capacity at áll levels to collect and disseminate scientific and technical information, including the improvement of early warning systems for predicting extreme weather events, especially El Niño/La Niña, through the provision of assistance to institutions devoted to addressing such events, including the International Centre for the Study of the El Niño phenomenon;

(j)   Promote cooperation for the prevention and mitigation of, preparedness for, response to and recovery from major technological and other disasters with an adverse impact on the environment in order to enhance the capabilities of affected countries to cope with such situations.

* * *

38.   Change in the Earth's climate and its adverse effects are a common concern of humankind. We remain deeply concerned that all countries, particularly developing countries, including the least developed countries and small island developing States, face increased risks of negative impacts of climate change and recognize that, in this context, the problems of poverty, land degradation, access to water and food and human health remain at the centre of global attention. The United Nations Framework Convention on Climate Change[27] is the key instrument for addressing climate change, a global concern, and we reaffirm our commitment to achieving its ultimate objective stabilization of greenhouse gas concentrations in the atmosphere at a level that would prevent dangerous anthropogenic interference with the climate system, within a time frame sufficient to allow ecosystems to adapt naturally to climate change, to ensure that food production is not threatened and to enable economic development to proceed in a sustainable manner, in accordance with our common but differentiated responsibilities and respective capabilities. Recalling the United Nations Millennium Declaration, in which heads of State and Government resolved to make every effort to ensure the entry into force of the Kyoto Protocol to the United Nations Framework Convention on Climate Change,[28] preferably by the tenth anniversary of the United Nations Conference on Environment and Development in 2002, and to embark on the required reduction of emissions of greenhouse gases, States that have ratified the Kyoto Protocol strongly urge States that have not already done so to ratify it in a timely manner. Actions at all levels are required to:

(a)   Meet all the commitments and obligations under the United Nations Framework Convention on Climate Change;

(b)   Work cooperatively towards achieving the objectives of the Convention;

(c)   Provide technical and financial assistance and capacity-building to developing countries and countries with economies in transition in accordance with commitments under the Convention, including the Marrakesh Accords;[29]

(d) Build and enhance scientific and technological capabilities, inter alia, through continuing support to the Intergovernmental Panel on Climate Change for the exchange of scientific data and information, especially in developing countries;

(e) Develop and transfer technological solutions;

(f) Develop and disseminate innovative technologies with regard to key sectors of development, particularly energy, and of investment in this regard, including through private-sector involvement, market-oriented approaches and supportive public policies and international cooperation;

(g) Promote the systematic observation of the Earth's atmosphere, land and oceans by improving monitoring stations, increasing the use of satellites and appropriate integration of these observations to produce high-quality data that could be disseminated for the use of all countries, in particular developing countries;

(h) Enhance the implementation of national, regional and international strategies to monitor the Earth's atmosphere, land and oceans, including, as appropriate, strategies for integrated global observations, inter alia, with the cooperation of relevant international organizations, especially the specialized agencies, in cooperation with the Convention;

(i) Support initiatives to assess the consequences of climate change, such as the Arctic Council initiative, including the environmental, economic and social impacts on local and indigenous communities.

39. Enhance cooperation at the international, regional and national levels to reduce air pollution, including transboundary air pollution, acid deposition and ozone depletion, bearing in mind the Rio principles, including, inter alia, the principle that, in view of the different contributions to global environmental degradation, States have common but differentiated responsibilities, with actions at all levels to:

(a) Strengthen capacities of developing countries and countries with economies in transition to measure, reduce and assess the impacts of air pollution, including health impacts, and provide financial and technical support for these activities;

(b) Facilitate implementation of the Montreal Protocol on Substances that Deplete the Ozone Layer by ensuring adequate replenishment of its fund by 2003/2005;

(c) Further support the effective regime for the protection of the ozone layer established in the Vienna Convention for the Protection of the Ozone Layer and the Montreal Protocol, including its compliance mechanism;

(d) Improve access by developing countries to affordable, accessible, cost-effective, safe and environmentally sound alternatives to ozone-depleting substances by 2010, and assist them in complying with the phase-out schedule under the Montreal Protocol, bearing in mind that ozone depletion and climate change are scientifically and technically interrelated;

(e) Take measures to address illegal traffic in ozone-depleting substances.

* * *

40. Agriculture plays a crucial role in addressing the needs of a growing global population and is inextricably linked to poverty eradication, especially in developing countries. Enhancing the role of women at all levels and in all aspects of rural development, agriculture, nutrition and food security is imperative. Sustainable

agriculture and rural development are essential to the implementation of an integrated approach to increasing food production and enhancing food security and food safety in an environmentally sustainable way. This would include actions at all levels to:

(a) Achieve the Millennium Declaration target to halve by the year 2015 the proportion of the world's people who suffer from hunger and realize the right to a standard of living adequate for the health and well-being of themselves and their families, including food, including by promoting food security and fighting hunger in combination with measures which address poverty, consistent with the outcome of the World Food Summit and, for States' Parties, with their obligations under Article 11 of the International Covenant on Economic, Social and Cultural Rights;[30]

(b) Develop and implement integrated land management and water-use plans that are based on sustainable use of renewable resources and on integrated assessments of socio-economic and environmental potentials and strengthen the capacity of Governments, local authorities and communities to monitor and manage the quantity and quality of land and water resources;

(c) Increase understanding of the sustainable use, protection and management of water resources to advance long-term sustainability of freshwater, coastal and marine environments;

(d) Promote programmes to enhance in a sustainable manner the productivity of land and the efficient use of water resources in agriculture, forestry, wetlands, artisanal fisheries and aquaculture, especially through indigenous and local community-based approaches;

(e) Support the efforts of developing countries to protect oases from silt, land degradation and increasing salinity by providing appropriate technical and financial assistance;

(f) Enhance the participation of women in all aspects and at all levels relating to sustainable agriculture and food security;

(g) Integrate existing information systems on land-use practices by strengthening national research and extension services and farmer organizations to trigger farmer-to-farmer exchange on good practices, such as those related to environmentally sound, low-cost technologies, with the assistance of relevant international organizations;

(h) Enact, as appropriate, measures that protect indigenous resource management systems and support the contribution of all appropriate stakeholders, men and women alike, in rural planning and development;

(i) Adopt policies and implement laws that guarantee well-defined and enforceable land- and water-use rights and promote legal security of tenure, recognizing the existence of different national laws and/or systems of land access and tenure, and provide technical and financial assistance to developing countries as well as countries with economies in transition that are undertaking land tenure reform in order to enhance sustainable livelihoods;

(j) Reverse the declining trend in public-sector finance for sustainable agriculture, provide appropriate technical and financial assistance, and promote private-sector investment and support efforts in developing countries and countries with economies in transition to strengthen agricultural research and natural resource management capacity and dissemination of research results to the farming communities;

(k) Employ market-based incentives for agricultural enterprises and farmers to monitor and manage water use and quality, inter alia, by applying such methods as small-scale irrigation and wastewater recycling and reuse;

(l) Enhance access to existing markets and develop new markets for value-added agricultural products;

(m) Increase brown-field redevelopment in developed countries and countries with economies in transition, with appropriate technical assistance where contamination is a serious problem;

(n) Enhance international cooperation to combat the illicit cultivation of narcotic plants, taking into account their negative social, economic and environmental impacts;

(o) Promote programmes for the environmentally sound, effective and efficient use of soil fertility improvement practices and agricultural pest control;

(p) Strengthen and improve coordination of existing initiatives to enhance sustainable agricultural production and food security;

(q) Invite countries that have not done so to ratify the International Treaty on Plant Genetic Resources for Food and Agriculture;[31]

(r) Promote the conservation and sustainable use and management of traditional and indigenous agricultural systems, and strengthen indigenous models of agricultural production.

* * *

41. Strengthen the implementation of the United Nations Convention to Combat Desertification in Those Countries Experiencing Serious Drought and/or Desertification, particularly in Africa,[7] to address causes of desertification and land degradation in order to maintain and restore land, and to address poverty resulting from land degradation. This would include actions at all levels to:

(a) Mobilize adequate and predictable financial resources, transfer of technologies and capacity-building at all levels;

(b) Formulate national action programmes to ensure timely and effective implementation of the Convention and its related projects, with the support of the international community, including through decentralized projects at the local level;

(c) Encourage the United Nations Framework Convention on Climate Change, the Convention on Biological Diversity and the Convention to Combat Desertification to continue exploring and enhancing synergies, with due regard to their respective mandates, in the elaboration and implementation of plans and strategies under the respective Conventions;

(d) Integrate measures to prevent and combat desertification, as well as to mitigate the effects of drought through relevant policies and programmes, such as land, water and forest management, agriculture, rural development, early warning systems, environment, energy, natural resources, health and education, and poverty eradication and sustainable development strategies;

(e) Provide affordable local access to information to improve monitoring and early warning related to desertification and drought;

(f) Call on the Second Assembly of the Global Environment Facility (GEF) to take action on the recommendations of the GEF Council concerning the designation of land degradation (desertification and deforestation) as a focal area of GEF as a means of GEF support for the successful implementation of the

Convention to Combat Desertification; and consequently, consider making GEF a financial mechanism of the Convention, taking into account the prerogatives and decisions of the Conference of the Parties to the Convention, while recognizing the complementary roles of GEF and the Global Mechanism of the convention in providing and mobilizing resources for the elaboration and implementation of action programmes;

(g) Improve the sustainability of grassland resources through strengthening management and law enforcement and providing financial and technical support by the international community to developing countries.

* * *

42. Mountain ecosystems support particular livelihoods and include significant watershed resources, biological diversity and unique flora and fauna. Many are particularly fragile and vulnerable to the adverse effects of climate change and need specific protection. Actions at all levels are required to:

(a) Develop and promote programmes, policies and approaches that integrate environmental, economic and social components of sustainable mountain development and strengthen international cooperation for its positive impacts on poverty eradication programmes, especially in developing countries;

(b) Implement programmes to address, where appropriate, deforestation, erosion, land degradation, loss of biodiversity, disruption of water flows and retreat of glaciers;

(c) Develop and implement, where appropriate, gender-sensitive policies and programmes, including public and private investments that help eliminate inequities facing mountain communities;

(d) Implement programmes to promote diversification and traditional mountain economies, sustainable livelihoods and small-scale production systems, including specific training programmes and better access to national and international markets, communications and transport planning, taking into account the particular sensitivity of mountains;

(e) Promote full participation and involvement of mountain communities in decisions that affect them and integrate indigenous knowledge, heritage and values in all development initiatives;

(f) Mobilize national and international support for applied research and capacity-building, provide financial and technical assistance for the effective implementation of the sustainable development of mountain ecosystems in developing countries and countries with economies in transition, and address the poverty among people living in mountains through concrete plans, projects and programmes, with sufficient support from all stakeholders, taking into account the spirit of the International Year of Mountains 2002.

* * *

43. Promote sustainable tourism development, including non-consumptive and ecotourism, taking into account the spirit of the International Year of Ecotourism 2002, the United Nations Year for Cultural Heritage in 2002, the World Ecotourism Summit 2002 and its Quebec Declaration, and the Global Code of Ethics for Tourism as adopted by the World Tourism Organization in order to increase the benefits from tourism resources for the population in host communities while maintaining the cultural and environmental integrity of the host communities and

enhancing the protection of ecologically sensitive areas and natural heritages. Promote sustainable tourism development and capacity-building in order to contribute to the strengthening of rural and local communities. This would include actions at all levels to:

(a) Enhance international cooperation, foreign direct investment and partnerships with both private and public sectors, at all levels;

(b) Develop programmes, including education and training programmes, that encourage people to participate in ecotourism, enable indigenous and local communities to develop and benefit from ecotourism, and enhance stakeholder cooperation in tourism development and heritage preservation in order to improve the protection of the environment, natural resources and cultural heritage;

(c) Provide technical assistance to developing countries and countries with economies in transition to support sustainable tourism business development and investment and tourism awareness programmes, to improve domestic tourism and to stimulate entrepreneurial development;

(d) Assist host communities in managing visits to their tourism attractions for their maximum benefit, while ensuring the least negative impacts on and risks for their traditions, culture and environment, with the support of the World Tourism Organization and other relevant organizations;

(e) Promote the diversification of economic activities, including through the facilitation of access to markets and commercial information, and participation of emerging local enterprises, especially small- and medium-sized enterprises.

* * *

44. Biodiversity, which plays a critical role in overall sustainable development and poverty eradication, is essential to our planet, human well-being and to the livelihood and cultural integrity of people. However, biodiversity is currently being lost at unprecedented rates due to human activities; this trend can only be reversed if the local people benefit from the conservation and sustainable use of biological diversity, in particular in countries of origin of genetic resources, in accordance with article 15 of the Convention on Biological Diversity. The Convention is the key instrument for the conservation and sustainable use of biological diversity and the fair and equitable sharing of benefits arising from use of genetic resources. A more efficient and coherent implementation of the three objectives of the Convention and the achievement, by 2010, of a significant reduction in the current rate of loss of biological diversity will require the provision of new and additional financial and technical resources to developing countries, and includes actions at all levels to:

(a) Integrate the objectives of the Convention into global, regional and national sectoral and cross-sectoral programmes and policies, in particular in the programmes and policies of the economic sectors of countries and international financial institutions;

(b) Promote the ongoing work under the Convention on the sustainable use on biological diversity, including on sustainable tourism, as a cross-cutting issue relevant to different ecosystems, sectors and thematic areas;

(c) Encourage effective synergies between the Convention and other multilateral environmental agreements, inter alia, through the development of joint plans and programmes, with due regard to their respective mandates, regarding common responsibilities and concerns;

(d) Implement the Convention and its provisions, including active follow-up of its work programmes and decisions through national, regional and global action programmes, in particular the national biodiversity strategies and action plans, and strengthen their integration into relevant cross-sectoral strategies, programmes and policies, including those related to sustainable development and poverty eradication, including initiatives which promote community-based sustainable use of biological diversity;

(e) Promote the wide implementation and further development of the ecosystem approach, as being elaborated in the ongoing work of the Convention;

(f) Promote concrete international support and partnership for the conservation and sustainable use of biodiversity, including in ecosystems, at World Heritage sites and for the protection of endangered species, in particular through the appropriate channelling of financial resources and technology to developing countries and countries with economies in transition;

(g) To effectively conserve and sustainably use biodiversity, promote and support initiatives for hot spot areas and other areas essential for biodiversity and promote the development of national and regional ecological networks and corridors;

(h) Provide financial and technical support to developing countries, including capacity-building, in order to enhance indigenous and community-based biodiversity conservation efforts;

(i) Strengthen national, regional and international efforts to control invasive alien species, which are one of the main causes of biodiversity loss, and encourage the development of effective work programme on invasive alien species at all levels;

(j) Subject to national legislation, recognize the rights of local and indigenous communities who are holders of traditional knowledge, innovations and practices, and, with the approval and involvement of the holders of such knowledge, innovations and practices, develop and implement benefit-sharing mechanisms on mutually agreed terms for the use of such knowledge, innovations and practices;

(k) Encourage and enable all stakeholders to contribute to the implementation of the objectives of the Convention and, in particular, recognize the specific role of youth, women and indigenous and local communities in conserving and using biodiversity in a sustainable way;

(l) Promote the effective participation of indigenous and local communities in decision- and policy-making concerning the use of their traditional knowledge;

(m) Encourage technical and financial support to developing countries and countries with economies in transition in their efforts to develop and implement, as appropriate, inter alia, national sui generis systems and traditional systems according to national priorities and legislation, with a view to conserving and the sustainable use of biodiversity;

(n) Promote the wide implementation of and continued work on the Bonn Guidelines on Access to Genetic Resources and Fair and Equitable Sharing of Benefits arising out of their Utilization as an input to assist the Parties when developing and drafting legislative, administrative or policy measures on access and benefit-sharing, as well as contract and other arrangements under mutually agreed terms for access and benefit-sharing;

(o) Negotiate within the framework of the Convention on Biological Diversity, bearing in mind the Bonn Guidelines, an international regime to promote and safeguard the fair and equitable sharing of benefits arising out of the utilization of genetic resources;

(p) Encourage successful conclusion of existing processes under the auspices of the Intergovernmental Committee on Intellectual Property and Genetic Resources, Traditional Knowledge and Folklore of the World Intellectual Property Organization, and in the ad hoc open-ended working group on article 8(j) and related provisions of the Convention;

(q) Promote practicable measures for access to the results and benefits arising from biotechnologies based upon genetic resources, in accordance with articles 15 and 19 of the Convention, including through enhanced scientific and technical cooperation on biotechnology and biosafety, including the exchange of experts, training human resources and developing research-oriented institutional capacities;

(r) With a view to enhancing synergy and mutual supportiveness, taking into account the decisions under the relevant agreements, promote the discussions, without prejudging their outcome, with regard to the relationships between the Convention and agreements related to international trade and intellectual property rights, as outlined in the Doha Ministerial Declaration;[32]

(s) Promote the implementation of the programme of work of the Global Taxonomy Initiative;

(t) Invite all States that have not already done so to ratify the Convention, the Cartagena Protocol on Biosafety to the Convention[33] and other biodiversity-related agreements, and invite those that have done so to promote their effective implementation at the national, regional and international levels and to support developing countries and countries with economies in transition technically and financially in this regard.

* * *

45. Forests and trees cover nearly one third of the Earth's surface. Sustainable forest management of both natural and planted forests and for timber and non-timber products is essential to achieving sustainable development, as well as a critical means to eradicate poverty, significantly reduce deforestation, halt the loss of forest biodiversity and land and resource degradation, and improve food security and access to safe drinking water and affordable energy; in addition, it highlights the multiple benefits of both natural and planted forests and trees and contributes to the well-being of the planet and humanity. The achievement of sustainable forest management, nationally and globally, including through partnerships among interested Governments and stakeholders, including the private sector, indigenous and local communities and non-governmental organizations, is an essential goal of sustainable development. This would include actions at all levels to:

(a) Enhance political commitment to achieve sustainable forest management by endorsing it as a priority on the international political agenda, taking full account of the linkages between the forest sector and other sectors through integrated approaches;

(b) Support the United Nations Forum on Forests, with the assistance of the Collaborative Partnership on Forests, as key intergovernmental mechanisms to facilitate and coordinate the implementation of sustainable forest management at the national, regional and global levels, thus contributing, inter alia, to the conservation and sustainable use of forest biodiversity;

(c) Take immediate action on domestic forest law enforcement and illegal international trade in forest products, including in forest biological resources, with the support of the international community, and provide human and institutional capacity-building related to the enforcement of national legislation in those areas;

(d) Take immediate action at the national and international levels to promote and facilitate the means to achieve sustainable timber harvesting and to facilitate the provision of financial resources and the transfer and development of environmentally sound technologies, and thereby address unsustainable timber-harvesting practices;

(e) Develop and implement initiatives to address the needs of those parts of the world that currently suffer from poverty and the highest rates of deforestation and where international cooperation would be welcomed by affected Governments;

(f) Create and strengthen partnerships and international cooperation to facilitate the provision of increased financial resources, the transfer of environmentally sound technologies, trade, capacity-building, forest law enforcement and governance at all levels and integrated land and resource management to implement sustainable forest management, including the proposals for action of the Intergovernmental Panel on Forests/Intergovernmental Forum on Forests;

(g) Accelerate implementation of the proposals for action of the Intergovernmental Panel on Forests/Intergovernmental Forum on Forests by countries and by the Collaborative Partnership on Forests and intensify efforts on reporting to the United Nations Forum on Forests to contribute to an assessment of progress in 2005;

(h) Recognize and support indigenous and community-based forest management systems to ensure their full and effective participation in sustainable forest management;

(i) Implement the expanded action-oriented work programme of the Convention on Biological Diversity on all types of forest biological diversity, in close cooperation with the Forum, Partnership members and other forest-related processes and conventions, with the involvement of all relevant stakeholders.

* * *

46. Mining, minerals and metals are important to the economic and social development of many countries. Minerals are essential for modern living. Enhancing the contribution of mining, minerals and metals to sustainable development includes actions at all levels to:

(a) Support efforts to address the environmental, economic, health and social impacts and benefits of mining, minerals and metals throughout their life cycle, including workers' health and safety, and use a range of partnerships, furthering existing activities at the national and international levels among interested Governments, intergovernmental organizations, mining companies and workers and other stakeholders to promote transparency and accountability for sustainable mining and minerals development;

(b) Enhance the participation of stakeholders, including local and indigenous communities and women, to play an active role in minerals, metals and mining development throughout the life cycles of mining operations, including after closure for rehabilitation purposes, in accordance with national regulations and taking into account significant transboundary impacts;

(c) Foster sustainable mining practices through the provision of financial, technical and capacity-building support to developing countries and countries with economies in transition for the mining and processing of minerals, including small-scale mining, and, where possible and appropriate, improve value-added processing, upgrade scientific and technological information and reclaim and rehabilitate degraded sites.

V Sustainable development in a globalizing world

47. Globalization offers opportunities and challenges for sustainable development. We recognize that globalization and interdependence are offering new opportunities for trade, investment and capital flows and advances in technology, including information technology, for the growth of the world economy, development and the improvement of living standards around the world. At the same time, there remain serious challenges, including serious financial crises, insecurity, poverty, exclusion and inequality within and among societies. The developing countries and countries with economies in transition face special difficulties in responding to those challenges and opportunities. Globalization should be fully inclusive and equitable, and there is a strong need for policies and measures at the national and international levels, formulated and implemented with the full and effective participation of developing countries and countries with economies in transition, to help them to respond effectively to those challenges and opportunities. This will require urgent action at all levels to:

(a) Continue to promote open, equitable, rules-based, predictable and non-discriminatory multilateral trading and financial systems that benefit all countries in the pursuit of sustainable development. Support the successful completion of the work programme contained in the Doha Ministerial Declaration and the implementation of the Monterrey Consensus. Welcome the decision contained in the Doha Ministerial Declaration to place the needs and interests of developing countries at the heart of the work programme of the Declaration, including through enhanced market access for products of interest to developing countries;

(b) Encourage ongoing efforts by international financial and trade institutions to ensure that decision-making processes and institutional structures are open and transparent;

(c) Enhance the capacities of developing countries, including the least developed countries, landlocked developing countries and small island developing States, to benefit from liberalized trade opportunities through international cooperation and measures aimed at improving productivity, commodity diversification and competitiveness, community-based entrepreneurial capacity and transportation and communication infrastructure development;

(d) Support the International Labour Organization and encourage its ongoing work on the social dimension of globalization, as stated in paragraph 64 of the Monterrey Consensus;

(e) Enhance the delivery of coordinated, effective and targeted trade-related technical assistance and capacity-building programmes, including taking advantage of existing and future market access opportunities, and examining the relationship between trade, environment and development.

48. Implement the outcomes of the Doha Ministerial Conference by the members of the World Trade Organization, further strengthen trade-related technical assistance and capacity-building and ensure the meaningful, effective and full participation of developing countries in multilateral trade negotiations by placing their needs and interests at the heart of the work programme of the World Trade Organization.

49. Actively promote corporate responsibility and accountability, based on the Rio principles, including through the full development and effective implementation of intergovernmental agreements and measures, international initiatives and public–private partnerships and appropriate national regulations, and support continuous improvement in corporate practices in all countries.

50. Strengthen the capacities of developing countries to encourage public/private initiatives that enhance the ease of access, accuracy, timeliness and coverage of information on countries and financial markets. Multilateral and regional financial institutions could provide further assistance for these purposes.

51. Strengthen regional trade and cooperation agreements, consistent with the multilateral trading system, among developed and developing countries and countries with economies in transition, as well as among developing countries, with the support of international finance institutions and regional development banks, as appropriate, with a view to achieving the objectives of sustainable development.

52. Assist developing countries and countries with economies in transition in narrowing the digital divide, creating digital opportunities and harnessing the potential of information and communication technologies for development through technology transfer on mutually agreed terms and the provision of financial and technical support and, in this context, support the World Summit on the Information Society.

VI Health and sustainable development

53. The Rio Declaration on Environment and Development states that human beings are at the centre of concerns for sustainable development, and that they are entitled to a healthy and productive life, in harmony with nature. The goals of sustainable development can only be achieved in the absence of a high prevalence of debilitating diseases, while obtaining health gains for the whole population requires poverty eradication. There is an urgent need to address the causes of ill health, including environmental causes, and their impact on development, with particular emphasis on women and children, as well as vulnerable groups of society, such as people with disabilities, elderly persons and indigenous people.

54. Strengthen the capacity of healthcare systems to deliver basic health services to all in an efficient, accessible and affordable manner aimed at preventing, controlling and treating diseases, and to reduce environmental health threats, in conformity with human rights and fundamental freedoms and consistent with national laws and cultural and religious values, and taking into account the reports of relevant

United Nations conferences and summits and of special sessions of the General Assembly. This would include actions at all levels to:

(a) Integrate the health concerns, including those of the most vulnerable populations, into strategies, policies and programmes for poverty eradication and sustainable development;

(b) Promote equitable and improved access to affordable and efficient healthcare services, including prevention, at all levels of the health system, essential and safe drugs at affordable prices, immunization services and safe vaccines and medical technology;

(c) Provide technical and financial assistance to developing countries and countries with economies in transition to implement the Health for All Strategy, including health information systems and integrated databases on development hazards;

(d) Improve the development and management of human resources in healthcare services;

(e) Promote and develop partnerships to enhance health education with the objective of achieving improved health literacy on a global basis by 2010, with the involvement of United Nations agencies, as appropriate;

(f) Develop programmes and initiatives to reduce, by the year 2015, mortality rates for infants and children under five by two-thirds, and maternal mortality rates by three-quarters, of the prevailing rate in 2000, and reduce disparities between and within developed and developing countries as quickly as possible, with particular attention to eliminating the pattern of disproportionate and preventable mortality among girl infants and children;

(g) Target research efforts and apply research results to priority public health issues, in particular those affecting susceptible and vulnerable populations, through the development of new vaccines, reducing exposures to health risks, building on equal access to healthcare services, education, training and medical treatment and technology, and addressing the secondary effects of poor health;

(h) Promote the preservation, development and use of effective traditional medicine knowledge and practices, where appropriate, in combination with modern medicine, recognizing indigenous and local communities as custodians of traditional knowledge and practices, while promoting effective protection of traditional knowledge, as appropriate, consistent with international law;

(i) Ensure equal access of women to healthcare services, giving particular attention to maternal and emergency obstetric care;

(j) Address effectively, for all individuals of appropriate age, the promotion of healthy living, including their reproductive and sexual health, consistent with the commitments and outcomes of recent United Nations conferences and summits, including the World Summit for Children, the United Nations Conference on Environment and Development, the International Conference on Population and Development, the World Summit for Social Development and the Fourth World Conference on Women, and their respective reviews and reports;

(k) Launch international capacity-building initiatives, as appropriate, that assess health and environment linkages and use the knowledge gained to create more effective national and regional policy responses to environmental threats to human health;

(l) Transfer and disseminate, on mutually agreed terms, including through public–private multi-sector partnerships, with international financial support, technologies for safe water, sanitation and waste management for rural and urban areas in developing countries and countries with economies in transition, taking into account country-specific conditions and gender equality, including specific technology needs of women;

(m) Strengthen and promote programmes of the International Labour Organization and World Health Organization to reduce occupational deaths, injuries and illnesses, and link occupational health with public health promotion as a means of promoting public health and education;

(n) Improve availability and access for all to sufficient, safe, culturally acceptable and nutritionally adequate food, increase consumer health protection, address issues of micro-nutrient deficiency and implement existing internationally agreed commitments and relevant standards and guidelines;

(o) Develop or strengthen, where applicable, preventive, promotive and curative programmes to address non-communicable diseases and conditions, such as cardiovascular diseases, cancer, diabetes, chronic respiratory diseases, injuries, violence and mental health disorders and associated risk factors, including alcohol, tobacco, unhealthy diets and lack of physical activity.

55. Implement, within the agreed time frames, all commitments agreed in the Declaration of Commitment on HIV/AIDS[34] adopted by the General Assembly at its 26th Special Session, emphasizing, in particular, the reduction of HIV prevalence among young men and women aged 15 to 24 by 25 per cent in the most affected countries by 2005, and globally by 2010, as well as combat malaria, tuberculosis and other diseases by, inter alia:

(a) Implementing national preventive and treatment strategies, regional and international cooperation measures and the development of international initiatives to provide special assistance to children orphaned by HIV/AIDS;

(b) Fulfilling commitments for the provision of sufficient resources to support the Global Fund to Fight AIDS, Tuberculosis and Malaria, while promoting access to the fund by countries most in need;

(c) Protecting the health of workers and promoting occupational safety, by, inter alia, taking into account, as appropriate, the voluntary Code of Practice on HIV/AIDS and the World of Work of the International Labour Organization to improve conditions of the workplace;

(d) Mobilizing adequate public, and encouraging private, financial resources for research and development on diseases of the poor, such as HIV/AIDS, malaria and tuberculosis, directed at biomedical and health research, as well as new vaccine and drug development.

56. Reduce respiratory diseases and other health impacts resulting from air pollution, with particular attention to women and children, by:

(a) Strengthening regional and national programmes, including through public–private partnerships, with technical and financial assistance to developing countries;

(b) Supporting the phasing-out of lead in gasoline;

(c) Strengthening and supporting efforts for the reduction of emissions through the use of cleaner fuels and modern pollution control techniques;

(d) Assisting developing countries in providing affordable energy to rural communities, particularly to reduce dependence on traditional fuel sources for cooking and heating, which affect the health of women and children.

57. Phase out lead in lead-based paints and in other sources of human exposure, work to prevent, in particular, children's exposure to lead and strengthen monitoring and surveillance efforts and the treatment of lead poisoning.

VII Sustainable development of small island developing States

58. Small island developing States are a special case both for environment and development. Although they continue to take the lead in the path towards sustainable development in their countries, they are increasingly constrained by the interplay of adverse factors clearly underlined in Agenda 21, the Programme of Action for the Sustainable Development of Small Island Developing States[35] and the decisions adopted at the 22nd Special Session of the General Assembly. This would include actions at all levels to:

(a) Accelerate national and regional implementation of the Programme of Action, with adequate financial resources, including through Global Environment Facility focal areas, transfer of environmentally sound technologies and assistance for capacity-building from the international community;

(b) Implement further sustainable fisheries management and improve financial returns from fisheries by supporting and strengthening relevant regional fisheries management organizations, as appropriate, such as the recently established Caribbean Regional Fisheries Mechanism and such agreements as the Convention on the Conservation and Management of Highly Migratory Fish Stocks in the Western and Central Pacific Ocean;

(c) Assist small island developing States, including through the elaboration of specific initiatives, in delimiting and managing in a sustainable manner their coastal areas and exclusive economic zones and the continental shelf, including, where appropriate, the continental shelf areas beyond 200 miles from coastal baselines, as well as relevant regional management initiatives within the context of the United Nations Convention on the Law of the Sea and the regional seas programmes of the United Nations Environment Programme;

(d) Provide support, including for capacity-building, for the development and further implementation of:

(i) small island developing States-specific components within programmes of work on marine and coastal biological diversity;

(ii) freshwater programmes for small island developing states, including through the Global Environment Facility focal areas.

(e) Effectively reduce, prevent and control waste and pollution and their health-related impacts by undertaking initiatives by 2004 aimed at implementing the Global Programme of Action for the Protection of the Marine Environment from Land-based Activities in small island developing States;

(f) Work to ensure that, in the ongoing negotiations and elaboration of the World Trade Organization work programme on trade in small economies, due account is taken of small island developing States, which have severe structural handicaps in integrating into the global economy, within the context of the Doha development agenda;

(g) Develop community-based initiatives on sustainable tourism by 2004 and build the capacities necessary to diversify tourism products, while protecting culture and traditions and effectively conserving and managing natural resources;

(h) Extend assistance to small island developing States in support of local communities and appropriate national and regional organizations of small island developing States for comprehensive hazard and risk management, disaster prevention, mitigation and preparedness, and help relieve the consequences of disasters, extreme weather events and other emergencies;

(i) Support the finalization and subsequent early operationalization, on agreed terms, of economic, social and environmental vulnerability indices and related indicators as tools for the achievement of the sustainable development of the small island developing States;

(j) Assist small island developing States in mobilizing adequate resources and partnerships for their adaptation needs relating to the adverse effects of climate change, sea level rise and climate variability, consistent with commitments under the United Nations Framework Convention on Climate Change, where applicable;

(k) Support efforts by small island developing States to build capacities and institutional arrangements to implement intellectual property regimes.

59. Support the availability of adequate, affordable and environmentally sound energy services for the sustainable development of small island developing States by, inter alia:

(a) Strengthening ongoing and supporting new efforts on energy supply and services, by 2004, including through the United Nations system and partnership initiatives;

(b) Developing and promoting efficient use of sources of energy, including indigenous sources and renewable energy, and building the capacities of small island developing States for training, technical know-how and strengthening national institutions in the area of energy management.

60. Provide support to small island developing States to develop capacity and strengthen:

(a) healthcare services for promoting equitable access to healthcare;

(b) health systems for making available necessary drugs and technology in a sustainable and affordable manner to fight and control communicable and non-communicable diseases, in particular HIV/AIDS, tuberculosis, diabetes, malaria and dengue fever;

(c) efforts to reduce and manage waste and pollution and building capacity for maintaining and managing systems to deliver water and sanitation services, in both rural and urban areas;

(d) efforts to implement initiatives aimed at poverty eradication, which have been outlined in section 2, 'Poverty eradication'.

61. Undertake a full and comprehensive review of the implementation of the Barbados Programme of Action on the Sustainable Development of Small Island Developing States in 2004, in accordance with the provisions set forth in General Assembly

resolution S-22/2, and in this context requests the General Assembly at its 57th session to consider convening an international meeting for the sustainable development of small island developing States.

VIII Sustainable development for Africa

62. Since the United Nations Conference on Environment and Development, sustainable development has remained elusive for many African countries. Poverty remains a major challenge and most countries on the continent have not benefited fully from the opportunities of globalization, further exacerbating the continent's marginalization. Africa's efforts to achieve sustainable development have been hindered by conflicts, insufficient investment, limited market access opportunities and supply-side constraints, unsustainable debt burdens, historically declining levels of official development assistance and the impact of HIV/AIDS. The World Summit on Sustainable Development should reinvigorate the commitment of the international community to address these special challenges and give effect to a new vision based on concrete actions for the implementation of Agenda 21 in Africa. The New Partnership for African Development (NEPAD) is a commitment by African leaders to the people of Africa. It recognizes that partnerships among African countries themselves and between them and with the international community are key elements of a shared and common vision to eradicate poverty; and furthermore, it aims to place their countries, both individually and collectively, on a path of sustained economic growth and sustainable development, while participating actively in the world economy and body politic. It provides a framework for sustainable development on the continent to be shared by all Africa's people. The international community welcomes NEPAD and pledges its support to the implementation of this vision, including through utilization of the benefits of South–South cooperation supported, inter alia, by the Tokyo International Conference on African Development. It also pledges support for other existing development frameworks that are owned and driven nationally by African countries and that embody poverty reduction strategies, including poverty reduction strategy papers. Achieving sustainable development includes actions at all levels to:

(a) Create an enabling environment at the regional, sub-regional, national and local levels in order to achieve sustained economic growth and sustainable development and support African efforts for peace, stability and security, the resolution and prevention of conflicts, democracy, good governance, respect for human rights and fundamental freedoms, including the right to development and gender equality;

(b) Support the implementation of the vision of NEPAD and other established regional and sub-regional efforts, including through financing, technical cooperation and institutional cooperation and human and institutional capacity-building at the regional, sub-regional and national levels, consistent with national policies, programmes and nationally owned and led strategies for poverty reduction and sustainable development, such as, where applicable, poverty reduction strategy papers;

(c) Promote technology development, transfer and diffusion to Africa and further develop technology and knowledge available in African centres of excellence;

(d) Support African countries in developing effective science and technology institutions and research activities capable of developing and adapting to world class technologies;

(e) Support the development of national programmes and strategies to promote education within the context of nationally owned and led strategies for poverty reduction and strengthen research institutions in education in order to increase the capacity to fully support the achievement of internationally agreed development goals related to education, including those contained in the Millennium Declaration on ensuring that, by 2015, children everywhere, boys and girls alike, will be able to complete a full course of primary schooling and that girls and boys will have equal access to all levels of education relevant to national needs;

(f) Enhance the industrial productivity, diversity and competitiveness of African countries through a combination of financial and technological support for the development of key infrastructure, access to technology, networking of research centres, adding value to export products, skills development and enhancing market access in support of sustainable development;

(g) Enhance the contribution of the industrial sector, in particular mining, minerals and metals, to the sustainable development of Africa by supporting the development of effective and transparent regulatory and management frameworks and value addition, broad-based participation, social and environmental responsibility and increased market access in order to create an attractive and conducive environment for investment;

(h) Provide financial and technical support to strengthen the capacity of African countries to undertake environmental legislative policy and institutional reform for sustainable development and to undertake environmental impact assessments and, as appropriate, to negotiate and implement multilateral environment agreements;

(i) Develop projects, programmes and partnerships with relevant stakeholders and mobilize resources for the effective implementation of the outcome of the African Process for the Protection and Development of the Marine and Coastal Environment;

(j) Deal effectively with energy problems in Africa, including through initiatives to:

    (i) Establish and promote programmes, partnerships and initiatives to support Africa's efforts to implement NEPAD objectives on energy, which seek to secure access for at least 35 per cent of the African population within 20 years, especially in rural areas;

    (ii) Provide support to implement other initiatives on energy, including the promotion of cleaner and more efficient use of natural gas and increased use of renewable energy, and to improve energy efficiency and access to advanced energy technologies, including cleaner fossil fuel technologies, particularly in rural and peri-urban areas;

(k) Assist African countries in mobilizing adequate resources for their adaptation needs relating to the adverse effects of climate change, extreme weather events, sea level rise and climate variability, and assist in developing national climate change strategies and mitigation programmes, and continue to take actions to mitigate the adverse effects on climate change in Africa consistent with the United Nations Framework Convention on Climate Change;

(l) Support African efforts to develop affordable transport systems and infrastructure that promote sustainable development and connectivity in Africa;

(m) Further to paragraph 42 above, address the poverty affecting mountain communities in Africa;

(n) Provide financial and technical support for afforestation and reforestation in Africa and to build capacity for sustainable forest management, including combating deforestation and measures to improve the policy and legal framework of the forest sector.

63. Provide financial and technical support for Africa's efforts to implement the Convention to Combat Desertification at the national level and to integrate indigenous knowledge systems into land and natural resources management practices, as appropriate, and improve extension services to rural communities and promote better land and watershed management practices, including through improved agricultural practices that address land degradation, in order to develop capacity for the implementation of national programmes.

64. Mobilize financial and other support to develop and strengthen health systems that aim to:

(a) Promote equitable access to healthcare services;

(b) Make available necessary drugs and technology in a sustainable and affordable manner to fight and control communicable diseases, including HIV/AIDS, malaria and tuberculosis, and trypanosomiasis, as well as non-communicable diseases, including those caused by poverty;

(c) Build capacity of medical and paramedical personnel;

(d) Promote indigenous medical knowledge, as appropriate, including traditional medicine;

(e) Research and control Ebola disease.

65. Deal effectively with natural disasters and conflicts, including their humanitarian and environmental impacts, recognizing that conflicts in Africa have hindered, and in many cases obliterated, both the gains and efforts aimed at sustainable development, with the most vulnerable members of society, particularly women and children, being the most impacted victims, through efforts and initiatives, at all levels, to:

(a) Provide financial and technical assistance to strengthen the capacities of African countries, including institutional and human capacity, including at the local level, for effective disaster management, including observation and early warning systems, assessments, prevention, preparedness, response and recovery;

(b) Provide support to African countries to enable them to better deal with the displacement of people as a result of natural disasters and conflicts and put in place rapid response mechanisms;

(c) Support Africa's efforts for the prevention and resolution, management and mitigation of conflicts and its early response to emerging conflict situations to avert tragic humanitarian consequences;

(d) Provide support to refugee host countries in rehabilitating infrastructure and environment, including ecosystems and habitats, that were damaged in the process of receiving and settling refugees.

66. Promote integrated water resources development and optimize the upstream and downstream benefits therefrom, the development and effective management of

water resources across all uses and the protection of water quality and aquatic ecosystems, including through initiatives at all levels, to:

(a) Provide access to potable domestic water, hygiene education and improved sanitation and waste management at the household level through initiatives to encourage public and private investment in water supply and sanitation that give priority to the needs of the poor within stable and transparent national regulatory frameworks provided by Governments, while respecting local conditions involving all concerned stakeholders and monitoring the performance and improving the accountability of public institutions and private companies; and develop critical water supply, reticulation and treatment infrastructure, and build capacity to maintain and manage systems to deliver water and sanitation services in both rural and urban areas;

(b) Develop and implement integrated river basin and watershed management strategies and plans for all major water bodies, consistent with paragraph 25 above;

(c) Strengthen regional, sub-regional and national capacities for data collection and processing and for planning, research, monitoring, assessment and enforcement, as well as arrangements for water resource management;

(d) Protect water resources, including groundwater and wetland ecosystems, against pollution, and, in cases of the most acute water scarcity, support efforts for developing non-conventional water resources, including the energy-efficient, cost-effective and sustainable desalination of seawater, rainwater harvesting and recycling of water.

67. Achieve significantly improved sustainable agricultural productivity and food security in furtherance of the agreed Millennium development goals, including those contained in the Millennium Declaration, in particular to halve by 2015 the proportion of people who suffer from hunger, including through initiatives at all levels to:

(a) Support the development and implementation of national policies and programmes, including research programmes and development plans of African countries to regenerate their agricultural sector and sustainably develop their fisheries, and increase investment in infrastructure, technology and extension services, according to country needs. African countries should be in the process of developing and implementing food security strategies, within the context of national poverty eradication programmes, by 2005;

(b) Promote and support efforts and initiatives to secure equitable access to land tenure and clarify resource rights and responsibilities through land and tenure reform processes that respect the rule of law and are enshrined in national law, and provide access to credit for all, especially women, and that enable economic and social empowerment and poverty eradication, as well as efficient and ecologically sound utilization of land, and that enable women producers to become decision-makers and owners in the sector, including the right to inherit land;

(c) Improve market access for goods, including goods originating from African countries, in particular least developed countries, within the framework of the Doha Ministerial Declaration, without prejudging the outcome of the World Trade Organization negotiations, as well as within the framework of preferential agreements;

(d) Provide support for African countries to improve regional trade and economic integration between African countries. Attract and increase investment in regional market infrastructure;

(e) Support livestock development programmes aimed at progressive and effective control of animal diseases.

68. Achieve sound management of chemicals, with particular focus on hazardous chemicals and wastes, inter alia, through initiatives to assist African countries in elaborating national chemical profiles and regional and national frameworks and strategies for chemical management and establishing chemical focal points.

69. Bridge the digital divide and create digital opportunity in terms of access infrastructure and technology transfer and application through integrated initiatives for Africa. Create an enabling environment to attract investment, accelerate existing and new programmes and projects to connect essential institutions and stimulate the adoption of information communication technologies in government and commerce programmes and other aspects of national economic and social life.

70. Support Africa's efforts to attain sustainable tourism that contributes to social, economic and infrastructure development through the following measures:

(a) Implementing projects at the local, national and sub-regional levels, with specific emphasis on marketing African tourism products, such as adventure tourism, ecotourism and cultural tourism;

(b) Establishing and supporting national and cross-border conservation areas to promote ecosystem conservation according to the ecosystem approach, and to promote sustainable tourism;

(c) Respecting local traditions and cultures and promoting the use of indigenous knowledge in natural resource management and ecotourism;

(d) Assisting host communities in managing their tourism projects for maximum benefit, while limiting negative impact on their traditions, culture and environment;

(e) Support the conservation of Africa's biological diversity, the sustainable use of its components and the fair and equitable sharing of the benefits arising out of the utilization of genetic resources, in accordance with commitments that countries have under biodiversity-related agreements to which they are parties, including such agreements as the Convention on Biological Diversity and the Convention on International Trade in Endangered Species of Wild Fauna and Flora, as well as regional biodiversity agreements.

71. Support African countries in their efforts to implement the Habitat Agenda and the Istanbul Declaration through initiatives to strengthen national and local institutional capacities in the areas of sustainable urbanization and human settlements, provide support for adequate shelter and basic services and the development of efficient and effective governance systems in cities and other human settlements and strengthen, inter alia, the joint programme on managing water for African cities of the United Nations Human Settlements Programme and the United Nations Environment Programme.

IX Other regional initiatives

72. Important initiatives have been developed within other United Nations regions and regional, sub-regional and transregional forums to promote sustainable development. The international community welcomes these efforts and the results already achieved, calls for actions at all levels for their further development, while encouraging inter-regional, intra-regional and international cooperation in this respect, and expresses its support for their further development and implementation by the countries of the regions.

A. Sustainable development in Latin America and the Caribbean

73. The Initiative of Latin America and the Caribbean on Sustainable Development is an undertaking by the leaders of that region that, building on the Platform for Action on the Road to Johannesburg, 2002,[36] which was approved in Rio de Janeiro in October 2001, recognizes the importance of regional actions towards sustainable development and takes into account the region's singularities, shared visions and cultural diversity. It is targeted towards the adoption of concrete actions in different areas of sustainable development, such as biodiversity, water resources, vulnerabilities and sustainable cities, social aspects, including health and poverty, economic aspects, including energy, and institutional arrangements, including capacity-building, indicators and participation of civil society, taking into account ethics for sustainable development.

74. The Initiative envisages the development of actions among countries in the region that may foster South–South cooperation and may count with the support of groups of countries, as well as multilateral and regional organizations, including financial institutions. As a framework for cooperation, the Initiative is open to partnerships with governments and all major groups.

B. Sustainable development in Asia and the Pacific

75. Bearing in mind the target of halving the number of people who live in poverty by the year 2015, as provided in the Millennium Declaration, the Phnom Penh Regional Platform on Sustainable Development for Asia and the Pacific[37] recognized that the region contains over half of the world's population and the largest number of the world's people living in poverty. Hence, sustainable development in the region is critical to achieving sustainable development at the global level.

76. The Regional Platform identified seven initiatives for follow-up action: capacity-building for sustainable development; poverty reduction for sustainable development; cleaner production and sustainable energy; land management and biodiversity conservation; protection and management of and access to freshwater resources; oceans, coastal and marine resources and sustainable development of small island developing States; and action on atmosphere and climate change. Follow-up actions of these initiatives will be taken through national strategies and relevant regional and sub-regional initiatives, such as the Regional Action Programme for Environmentally Sound and Sustainable Development and the Kitakyushu Initiative for a Clean Environment, adopted at the Fourth Ministerial

Conference on Environment and Development in Asia and the Pacific organized by the Economic and Social Commission for Asia and the Pacific.

C. Sustainable development in the West Asia region

77. The West Asia region is known for its scarce water and limited fertile land resources. The region has made progress to a more knowledge-based production of higher value-added commodities.

78. The regional preparatory meeting endorsed the following priorities: poverty alleviation; relief of debt burden; and sustainable management of natural resources, including, inter alia, integrated water resources management, implementation of programmes to combat desertification, integrated coastal zone management and land and water pollution control.

D. Sustainable development in the Economic Commission for Europe region

79. The Economic Commission for Europe regional ministerial meeting for the World Summit on Sustainable Development recognized that the region has a major role to play and responsibilities in global efforts to achieve sustainable development by concrete actions. The region recognized that different levels of economic development in countries of the region may require the application of different approaches and mechanisms to implement Agenda 21. In order to address the three pillars of sustainable development in a mutually reinforcing way, the region identified its priority actions for sustainable development for the Economic Commission for Europe region in its Ministerial Statement to the Summit.[38]

80. In furtherance of the region's commitment to sustainable development, there are ongoing efforts at the regional, sub-regional and transregional levels, including, inter alia, the Environment for Europe process; the fifth Economic Commission for Europe ministerial conference, to be held in Kiev in May 2003; the development of an environmental strategy for the 12 countries of Eastern Europe; the Caucasus and Central Asia; the Central Asian Agenda 21; work of the Organisation for Economic Co-operation and Development on sustainable development; the European Union sustainable development strategy; and regional and sub-regional conventions and processes relevant to sustainable development, including, inter alia, the Convention on Access to Information, Public Participation in Decision-Making and Access to Justice in Environmental Matters (Aarhus Convention), the Alpine Convention, the North American Commission for Environmental Cooperation, the International Boundary Waters Treaty Act, the Iqaluit Declaration of the Arctic Council, the Baltic Agenda 21 and the Mediterranean Agenda 21.

X Means of implementation

81. The implementation of Agenda 21 and the achievement of the internationally agreed development goals, including those contained in the Millennium Declaration as well as in the present plan of action, require a substantially increased effort, both by countries themselves and by the rest of the international community, based on the recognition that each country has primary responsibility for its own

development and that the role of national policies and development strategies cannot be overemphasized, taking fully into account the Rio principles, including, in particular, the principle of common but differentiated responsibilities, which states:

> *"States shall cooperate in a spirit of global partnership to conserve, protect and restore the health and integrity of the Earth's ecosystem. In view of the different contributions to global environmental degradation, States have common but differentiated responsibilities. The developed countries acknowledge the responsibility that they bear in the international pursuit of sustainable development in view of the pressures their societies place on the global environment and of the technologies and financial resources they command."*

The internationally agreed development goals, including those contained in the Millennium Declaration and Agenda 21, as well as in the present plan of action, will require significant increases in the flow of financial resources as elaborated in the Monterrey Consensus, including through new and additional financial resources, in particular to developing countries, to support the implementation of national policies and programmes developed by them, improved trade opportunities, access to and transfer of environmentally sound technologies on a concessional or preferential basis, as mutually agreed, education and awareness-raising, capacity-building and information for decision-making and scientific capabilities within the agreed time frame required to meet these goals and initiatives. Progress to this end will require that the international community implement the outcomes of major United Nations conferences, such as the programmes of action adopted at the Third United Nations Conference on the Least Developed Countries[39] and the Global Conference on the Sustainable Development of Small Island Developing States, and relevant international agreements since 1992, particularly those of the International Conference on Financing for Development and the Fourth Ministerial Conference of the World Trade Organization, including building on them as part of a process of achieving sustainable development.

82. Mobilizing and increasing the effective use of financial resources and achieving the national and international economic conditions needed to fulfil internationally agreed development goals, including those contained in the Millennium Declaration, to eliminate poverty, improve social conditions and raise living standards and protect our environment, will be our first step to ensuring that the 21st century becomes the century of sustainable development for all.

83. In our common pursuit of growth, poverty eradication and sustainable development, a critical challenge is to ensure the necessary internal conditions for mobilizing domestic savings, both public and private, sustaining adequate levels of productive investment and increasing human capacity. A crucial task is to enhance the efficacy, coherence and consistency of macro-economic policies. An enabling domestic environment is vital for mobilizing domestic resources, increasing productivity, reducing capital flight, encouraging the private sector and attracting and making effective use of international investment and assistance. Efforts to create such an environment should be supported by the international community.

84. Facilitate greater flows of foreign direct investment so as to support the sustainable development activities, including the development of infrastructure, of developing countries, and enhance the benefits that developing countries can draw from foreign direct investment, with particular actions to:

(a) Create the necessary domestic and international conditions to facilitate significant increases in the flow of foreign direct investment to developing countries, in particular the least developed countries, which is critical to sustainable development, particularly foreign direct investment flows for infrastructure development and other priority areas in developing countries to supplement the domestic resources mobilized by them;

(b) Encourage foreign direct investment in developing countries and countries with economies in transition through export credits that could be instrumental to sustainable development.

85. Recognize that a substantial increase in official development assistance and other resources will be required if developing countries are to achieve the internationally agreed development goals and objectives, including those contained in the Millennium Declaration. To build support for official development assistance, we will cooperate to further improve policies and development strategies, both nationally and internationally, to enhance aid effectiveness, with actions to:

(a) Make available the increased commitments in official development assistance announced by several developed countries at the International Conference on Financing for Development. Urge the developed countries that have not done so to make concrete efforts towards the target of 0.7 per cent of gross national product as official development assistance to developing countries and effectively implement their commitment on such assistance to the least developed countries as contained in paragraph 83 of the Programme of Action for the Least Developed Countries for the Decade 2001–2010,[40] which was adopted in Brussels on 20 May 2001. We also encourage developing countries to build on progress achieved in ensuring that official development assistance is used effectively to help achieve development goals and targets in accordance with the outcome of the International Conference on Financing for Development. We acknowledge the efforts of all donors, commend those donors whose contributions exceed, reach or are increasing towards the targets, and underline the importance of undertaking to examine the means and time frames for achieving the targets and goals;

(b) Encourage recipient and donor countries, as well as international institutions, to make official development assistance more efficient and effective for poverty eradication, sustained economic growth and sustainable development. In this regard, intensify efforts by the multilateral and bilateral financial and development institutions, in accordance with paragraph 43 of the Monterrey Consensus, in particular to harmonize their operational procedures at the highest standards so as to reduce transaction costs and make disbursement and delivery of official development assistance more flexible and more responsive to the needs of developing countries, taking into account national development needs and objectives under the ownership of recipient countries, and to use development frameworks that are owned and driven by developing countries and that embody poverty reduction strategies, including poverty reduction strategy papers, as vehicles for aid delivery, upon request.

86. Make full and effective use of existing financial mechanisms and institutions, including through actions at all levels to:

(a) Strengthen ongoing efforts to reform the existing international financial architecture to foster a transparent, equitable and inclusive system that is able to provide for the effective participation of developing countries in the international economic decision-making processes and institutions, as well as for their effective and equitable participation in the formulation of financial standards and codes;

(b) Promote, inter alia, measures in source and destination countries to improve transparency and information about financial flows to contribute to stability in the international financial environment. Measures that mitigate the impact of excessive volatility of short-term capital flows are important and must be considered;

(c) Work to ensure that the funds are made available on a timely, more assured and predictable basis to international organizations and agencies, where appropriate, for their sustainable development activities, programmes and projects;

(d) Encourage the private sector, including transnational corporations, private foundations and civil society institutions, to provide financial and technical assistance to developing countries;

(e) Support new and existing public/private-sector financing mechanisms for developing countries and countries with economies in transition to benefit, in particular, small entrepreneurs and small, medium-sized and community-based enterprises and to improve their infrastructure, while ensuring the transparency and accountability of such mechanisms.

87. Welcome the successful and substantial third replenishment of the Global Environment Facility, which will enable it to address the funding requirements of new focal areas and existing ones and continue to be responsive to the needs and concerns of its recipient countries, in particular developing countries, and further encourage the Global Environment Facility to leverage additional funds from key public and private organizations, improve the management of funds through more speedy and streamlined procedures and simplify its project cycle.

88. Explore ways of generating new public and private innovative sources of finance for development purposes, provided that those sources do not unduly burden developing countries, noting the proposal to use special drawing rights allocations for development purposes, as set forth in paragraph 44 of the Monterrey Consensus.

89. Reduce unsustainable debt burden through such actions as debt relief and, as appropriate, debt cancellation and other innovative mechanisms geared to comprehensively address the debt problems of developing countries, in particular the poorest and most heavily indebted ones. Therefore, debt relief measures should, where appropriate, be pursued vigorously and expeditiously, including within the Paris and London Clubs and other relevant forums, in order to contribute to debt sustainability and facilitate sustainable development, while recognizing that debtors and creditors must share responsibility for preventing and resolving unsustainable debt situations, and that external debt relief can play a key role in liberating resources that can then be directed towards activities consistent with attaining sustainable growth and development. Therefore, we support paragraphs 47 to 51 of the Monterrey Consensus dealing with external debt. Debt relief arrangements should seek to avoid imposing any unfair burdens on other developing countries. There should be an increase in the use of grants for the poorest, debt-vulnerable countries. Countries are encouraged to develop national comprehensive strategies to monitor and manage external liabilities as a key element in reducing national vulnerabilities. In this regard, actions are required to:

(a) Implement speedily, effectively and fully the enhanced heavily lindebted poor countries (HIPC) initiative, which should be fully financed through additional resources, taking into consideration, as appropriate, measures to address any fundamental changes in the economic circumstances of those developing countries with unsustainable debt burden caused by natural catastrophes, severe terms-of-trade shocks or affected by conflict, taking into account initiatives which have been undertaken to reduce outstanding indebtedness;

(b) Encourage participation in the HIPC initiative of all creditors that have not yet done so;

(c) Bring international debtors and creditors together in relevant international forums to restructure unsustainable debt in a timely and efficient manner, taking into account the need to involve the private sector in the resolution of crises due to indebtedness, where appropriate;

(d) Acknowledge the problems of the debt sustainability of some non-HIPC low-income countries, in particular those facing exceptional circumstances;

(e) Encourage exploring innovative mechanisms to comprehensively address the debt problems of developing countries, including middle-income countries and countries with economies in transition. Such mechanisms may include debt-for-sustainable-development swaps;

(f) Encourage donor countries to take steps to ensure that resources provided for debt relief do not detract from official development assistance resources intended for developing countries.

90. Recognizing the major role that trade can play in achieving sustainable development and in eradicating poverty, we encourage members of the World Trade Organization (WTO) to pursue the work programme agreed at their Fourth Ministerial Conference. In order for developing countries, especially the least developed among them, to secure their share in the growth of world trade commensurate with the needs of their economic development, we urge WTO members to take the following actions:

(a) Facilitate the accession of all developing countries, particularly the least developed countries, as well as countries with economies in transition, that apply for membership in WTO, in accordance with the Monterrey Consensus;

(b) Support the work programme adopted at the Doha Ministerial Conference as an important commitment on the part of developed and developing countries to mainstream appropriate trade policies in their respective development policies and programmes;

(c) Implement substantial trade-related technical assistance and capacity-building measures and support the Doha Development Agenda Global Trust Fund, established after the Doha Ministerial Conference, as an important step forward in ensuring a sound and predictable basis for WTO-related technical assistance and capacity-building;

(d) Implement the New Strategy for Technical Cooperation for Capacity-Building, Growth and Integration endorsed in the Doha Declaration;

(e) Fully support the implementation of the Integrated Framework for Trade-Related Technical Assistance to Least Developed Countries and urge development partners to significantly increase contributions to the Trust Fund for the framework, in accordance with the Doha Ministerial Declaration.

91. In accordance with the Doha Declaration, as well as with relevant decisions taken at Doha, we are determined to take concrete action to address issues and concerns

raised by developing countries regarding the implementation of some WTO agreements and decisions, including the difficulties and resource constraints faced by them in fulfilling those agreements.

92. Call upon members of the World Trade Organization to fulfil the commitments made in the Doha Ministerial Declaration, notably in terms of market access, in particular for products of export interest to developing countries, especially least developed countries, by implementing the following actions, taking into account paragraph 45 of the Doha Ministerial Declaration:

   (a) Review all special and differential treatment provisions with a view to strengthening them and making them more precise, effective and operational in accordance with paragraph 44 of the Doha Ministerial Declaration;

   (b) Aim to reduce or, as appropriate, eliminate tariffs on non-agricultural products, including the reduction or elimination of tariff peaks, high tariffs and tariff escalation, as well as non-tariff barriers, in particular on products of export interest to developing countries. Product coverage should be comprehensive and without a priori exclusions. The negotiations shall take fully into account the special needs and interests of developing and least developed countries, including through less than full reciprocity in reduction commitments, in accordance with the Doha Ministerial Declaration;

   (c) Fulfil, without prejudging the outcome of the negotiations, the commitment for comprehensive negotiations initiated under article 20 of the Agreement on Agriculture, as referred to in the Doha Ministerial Declaration,[41] aiming at substantial improvements in market access, reductions of with a view to phasing out all forms of export subsidies, and substantial reductions in trade-distorting domestic support, while agreeing that the provisions for special and differential treatment for developing countries shall be an integral part of all elements of the negotiations and shall be embodied in the schedules of concession and commitments and, as appropriate, in the rules and disciplines to be negotiated so as to be operationally effective and to enable developing countries to effectively take account of their development needs, including food security and rural development. Take note of the non-trade concerns reflected in the negotiating proposals submitted by members of the World Trade Organization and confirm that non-trade concerns will be taken into account in the negotiations as provided for in the Agreement on Agriculture, in accordance with the Doha Ministerial Declaration.

93. Call on developed countries that have not already done so to work towards the objective of duty-free and quota-free access for all least developed countries' exports, as envisaged in the Programme of Action for the Least Developed Countries for the Decade 2001–2010.

94. Commit to actively pursue the work programme of the World Trade Organization to address the trade-related issues and concerns affecting the fuller integration of small, vulnerable economies into the multilateral trading system in a manner commensurate with their special circumstances and in support of their efforts towards sustainable development, in accordance with paragraph 35 of the Doha Declaration.

95. Build the capacity of commodity-dependent countries to diversify exports through, inter alia, financial and technical assistance, international assistance for economic diversification and sustainable resource management, and address the instability of commodity prices and declining terms of trade, as well as strengthen the

activities covered by the second account of the Common Fund for Commodities to support sustainable development.

96. Enhance the benefits for developing countries, as well as countries with economies in transition, from trade liberalization, including through public–private partnerships, through, inter alia, action at all levels, including through financial support for technical assistance, the development of technology and capacity-building to developing countries to:

    (a) Enhance trade infrastructure and strengthen institutions;

    (b) Increase developing country capacity to diversify and increase exports to cope with the instability of commodity prices and declining terms of trade;

    (c) Increase the value added of developing country exports.

97. Continue to enhance the mutual supportiveness of trade, environment and development with a view to achieving sustainable development through actions at all levels to:

    (a) Encourage the WTO Committee on Trade and Environment and the WTO Committee on Trade and Development, within their respective mandates, to each act as a forum to identify and debate developmental and environmental aspects of the negotiations in order to help achieve an outcome which benefits sustainable development in accordance with the commitments made under the Doha Ministerial Declaration;

    (b) Support the completion of the work programme of the Doha Ministerial Declaration on subsidies so as to promote sustainable development and enhance the environment, and encourage reform of subsidies that have considerable negative effects on the environment and are incompatible with sustainable development;

    (c) Encourage efforts to promote cooperation on trade, environment and development, including in the field of providing technical assistance to developing countries, between the secretariats of WTO, UNCTAD, UNDP, UNEP, and other relevant international environmental and development and regional organizations;

    (d) Encourage the voluntary use of environmental impact assessments as an important national-level tool to better identify trade, environment and development interlinkages. Further encourage countries and international organizations with experience in this field to provide technical assistance to developing countries for these purposes.

98. Promote mutual supportiveness between the multilateral trading system and the multilateral environmental agreements, consistent with sustainable development goals, in support of the work programme agreed through WTO, while recognizing the importance of maintaining the integrity of both sets of instruments.

99. Complement and support the Doha Ministerial Declaration and the Monterrey Consensus by undertaking further action at the national, regional and international levels, including through public/private partnerships, to enhance the benefits, in particular for developing countries as well as for countries with economies in transition, of trade liberalization, through, inter alia, actions at all levels to:

    (a) Establish and strengthen existing trade and cooperation agreements, consistent with the multilateral trading system, with a view to achieving sustainable development;

    (b) Support voluntary WTO-compatible market-based initiatives for the creation and expansion of domestic and international markets for environmentally friendly goods and services, including organic products, which maximize environmental and developmental benefits through, inter alia, capacity-building and technical assistance to developing countries;

(c) Support measures to simplify and make more transparent domestic regulations and procedures that affect trade so as to assist exporters, particularly those from developing countries.

100. Address the public health problems affecting many developing and least developed countries, especially those resulting from HIV/AIDS, tuberculosis, malaria and other epidemics, while noting the importance of the Doha Declaration on the Agreement on Trade-Related Aspects of Intellectual Property Rights (TRIPS Agreement) and public health,[42] in which it was agreed that the TRIPS Agreement does not and should not prevent WTO members from taking measures to protect public health. Accordingly, while reiterating our commitment to the TRIPS Agreement, we reaffirm that the Agreement can and should be interpreted and implemented in a manner supportive of WTO members' right to protect public health and, in particular, to promote access to medicines for all.

101. States should cooperate to promote a supportive and open international economic system that would lead to economic growth and sustainable development in all countries to better address the problems of environmental degradation. Trade policy measures for environmental purposes should not constitute a means of arbitrary or unjustifiable discrimination or a disguised restriction on international trade. Unilateral actions to deal with environmental challenges outside the jurisdiction of the importing country should be avoided. Environmental measures addressing transboundary or global environmental problems should, as far as possible, be based on an international consensus.

102. Take steps with a view to the avoidance of, and refrain from, any unilateral measure not in accordance with international law and the Charter of the United Nations that impedes the full achievement of economic and social development by the population of the affected countries, in particular women and children, that hinders their well-being or that creates obstacles to the full enjoyment of their human rights, including the right of everyone to a standard of living adequate for their health and well-being and their right to food, medical care and the necessary social services. Ensure that food and medicine are not used as tools for political pressure.

103. Take further effective measures to remove obstacles to the realization of the right of peoples to self-determination, in particular peoples living under colonial and foreign occupation, which continue to adversely affect their economic and social development and are incompatible with the dignity and worth of the human person and must be combated and eliminated. People under foreign occupation must be protected in accordance with the provisions of international humanitarian law.

104. In accordance with the Declaration on Principles of International Law concerning Friendly Relations and Cooperation among States in accordance with the Charter of the United Nations,[43] this shall not be construed as authorizing or encouraging any action which would dismember or impair, totally or in part, the territorial integrity or political unity of sovereign and independent States conducting themselves in compliance with the principle of equal rights and self-determination

of peoples and thus possessed of a Government representing the whole people belonging to the territory without distinction of any kind.

* * *

105. Promote, facilitate and finance, as appropriate, access to and the development, transfer and diffusion of environmentally sound technologies and corresponding know-how, in particular to developing countries and countries with economies in transition on favourable terms, including on concessional and preferential terms, as mutually agreed, as set out in Chapter 34 of Agenda 21, including through urgent actions at all levels to:
   (a) Provide information more effectively;
   (b) Enhance existing national institutional capacity in developing countries to improve access to and the development, transfer and diffusion of environmentally sound technologies and corresponding know-how;
   (c) Facilitate country-driven technology needs assessments;
   (d) Establish legal and regulatory frameworks in both supplier and recipient countries that expedite the transfer of environmentally sound technologies in a cost-effective manner by both public and private sectors and support their implementation;
   (e) Promote the access and transfer of technology related to early warning systems and to mitigation programmes to developing countries affected by natural disasters.

106. Improve the transfer of technologies to developing countries, in particular at the bilateral and regional levels, including through urgent actions at all levels to:
   (a) Improve interaction and collaboration, stakeholder relationships and networks between and among universities, research institutions, government agencies and the private sector;
   (b) Develop and strengthen networking of related institutional support structures, such as technology and productivity centres, research, training and development institutions, and national and regional cleaner production centres;
   (c) Create partnerships conducive to investment and technology transfer, development and diffusion to assist developing countries, as well as countries with economies in transition, in sharing best practices and promoting programmes of assistance, and encourage collaboration between corporations and research institutes to enhance industrial efficiency, agricultural productivity, environmental management and competitiveness;
   (d) Provide assistance to developing countries, as well as to countries with economies in transition, in accessing environmentally sound technologies that are publicly owned or in the public domain, as well as available knowledge in the public domain on science and technology, and in accessing the know-how and expertise required in order for them to make independent use of this knowledge in pursuing their development goals;
   (e) Support existing mechanisms and, where appropriate, establish new mechanisms for the development, transfer and diffusion of environmentally sound technologies to developing countries and economies in transition.

* * *

107. Assist developing countries in building capacity to access a larger share of multilateral and global research and development programmes. In this regard, strengthen and, where appropriate, create centres for sustainable development in developing countries.

108. Build greater capacity in science and technology for sustainable development, with action to improve collaboration and partnerships on research and development and their widespread application among research institutions, universities, the private sector, governments, non-governmental organizations and networks, as well as between and among scientists and academics of developing and developed countries, and in this regard encourage networking with and between centres of scientific excellence in developing countries.

109. Improve policy- and decision-making at all levels through, inter alia, improved collaboration between natural and social scientists, and between scientists and policy-makers, including through urgent actions at all levels to:

    (a) Increase the use of scientific knowledge and technology and increase the beneficial use of local and indigenous knowledge in a manner respectful of the holders of that knowledge and consistent with national law;

    (b) Make greater use of integrated scientific assessments, risk assessments and interdisciplinary and intersectoral approaches;

    (c) Continue to support and collaborate with international scientific assessments supporting decision-making, including the Intergovernmental Panel on Climate Change, with the broad participation of developing country experts;

    (d) Assist developing countries in developing and implementing science and technology policies;

    (e) Establish partnerships between scientific, public and private institutions, including by integrating the advice of scientists into decision-making bodies to ensure a greater role for science, technology development and engineering sectors;

    (f) Promote and improve science-based decision-making and reaffirm the precautionary approach as set out in principle 15 of the Rio Declaration on Environment and Development, which states:

    "In order to protect the environment, the precautionary approach shall be widely applied by States according to their capabilities. Where there are threats of serious or irreversible damage, lack of full scientific certainty shall not be used as a reason for postponing cost-effective measures to prevent environmental degradation."

110. Assist developing countries, through international cooperation, in enhancing their capacity in their efforts to address issues pertaining to environmental protection, including in their formulation and implementation of policies for environmental management and protection, including through urgent actions at all levels to:

    (a) Improve their use of science and technology for environmental monitoring, assessment models, accurate databases and integrated information systems;

    (b) Promote and, where appropriate, improve their use of satellite technologies for quality data collection, verification and updating, and further improve aerial and ground-based observations in support of their efforts to collect quality, accurate, long-term, consistent and reliable data;

    (c) Set up and, where appropriate, further develop national statistical services capable of providing sound data on science education and research and development activities that are necessary for effective science and technology policy-making.

111. Establish regular channels between policy-makers and the scientific community to request and receive science and technology advice for the implementation of Agenda 21 and create and strengthen networks for science and education for sustainable development, at all levels, with the aim of sharing knowledge, experience and best practices and building scientific capacities, particularly in developing countries.

112. Use information and communication technologies, where appropriate, as tools to increase the frequency of communication and the sharing of experience and knowledge and to improve the quality of and access to information and communications technology in all countries, building on the work facilitated by the United Nations Information and Communications Technology Task Force and the efforts of other relevant international and regional forums.

113. Support publicly funded research and development entities to engage in strategic alliances for the purpose of enhancing research and development to achieve cleaner production and product technologies through, inter alia, the mobilization from all sources of adequate financial and technical resources, including new and additional resources, and encourage the transfer and diffusion of those technologies, in particular to developing countries.

114. Examine issues of global public interest through open, transparent and inclusive workshops to promote a better public understanding of such questions.

115. Further resolve to take concerted action against international terrorism, which causes serious obstacles to sustainable development.

* * *

116. Education is critical for promoting sustainable development. It is therefore essential to mobilize necessary resources, including financial resources at all levels, by bilateral and multilateral donors, including the World Bank and the regional development banks, by civil society and by foundations to complement the efforts by national governments to pursue the following goals and actions:

    (a) Meet the Millennium development goal of achieving universal primary education, ensuring that, by 2015, children everywhere, boys and girls alike, will be able to complete a full course of primary schooling;

    (b) Provide all children, particularly those living in rural areas and those living in poverty, especially girls, with the access and opportunity to complete a full course of primary education.

117. Provide financial assistance and support to education, research, public awareness programmes and developmental institutions in developing countries and countries with economies in transition in order to:

    (a) Sustain their educational infrastructures and programmes, including those related to environment and public health education;

    (b) Consider means of avoiding the frequent, serious financial constraints faced by many institutions of higher learning, including universities around the world, particularly in developing countries and countries in transition.

118. Address the impact of HIV/AIDS on the educational system in those countries seriously affected by the pandemic.

119. Allocate national and international resources for basic education as proposed by the Dakar Framework for Action on Education for All and for improved integration

of sustainable development into education and in bilateral and multilateral development programmes, and improve integration between publicly funded research and development and development programmes.

120. Eliminate gender disparity in primary and secondary education by 2005, as provided in the Dakar Framework for Action on Education for All, and at all levels of education no later than 2015, to meet the development goals contained in the Millennium Declaration, with action to ensure, inter alia, equal access to all levels and forms of education, training and capacity-building by gender mainstreaming, and by creating a gender-sensitive educational system.

121. Integrate sustainable development into education systems at all levels of education in order to promote education as a key agent for change.

122. Develop, implement, monitor and review education action plans and programmes at the national, sub-national and local levels, as appropriate, that reflect the Dakar Framework for Action on Education for All and that are relevant to local conditions and needs leading to the achievement of community development and make education for sustainable development a part of those plans.

123. Provide all community members with a wide range of formal and non-formal continuing educational opportunities, including volunteer community service programmes, in order to end illiteracy and emphasize the importance of lifelong learning and promote sustainable development.

124. Support the use of education to promote sustainable development, including through urgent actions at all levels to:

    (a) Integrate information and communications technology in school curriculum development to ensure its access by both rural and urban communities and provide assistance, particularly to developing countries, inter alia, for the establishment of an appropriate enabling environment required for such technology;

    (b) Promote, as appropriate, affordable and increased access to programmes for students, researchers and engineers from developing countries in the universities and research institutions of developed countries in order to promote the exchange of experience and capacity that will benefit all partners;

    (c) Continue to implement the work programme of the Commission on Sustainable Development on education for sustainable development;

    (d) Recommend to the United Nations General Assembly that it consider adopting a decade of education for sustainable development, starting in 2005.

* * *

125. Enhance and accelerate human, institutional and infrastructure capacity-building initiatives and promote partnerships in that regard that respond to the specific needs of developing countries in the context of sustainable development.

126. Support local, national, sub-regional and regional initiatives with action to develop, use and adapt knowledge and techniques and to enhance local, national, sub-regional and regional centres of excellence for education, research and training in order to strengthen the knowledge capacity of developing countries and countries with economies in transition through, inter alia, the mobilization from all sources of adequate financial and other resources, including new and additional resources.

127. Provide technical and financial assistance to developing countries, including through the strengthening of capacity-building efforts, such as the United Nations Development Programme Capacity 21 programme, to:

(a) Assess their own capacity development needs and opportunities at the individual, institutional and societal levels;

(b) Design programmes for capacity-building and support for local, national and community-level programmes that focus on meeting the challenges of globalization more effectively and attaining the internationally agreed development goals, including those contained in the Millennium Declaration;

(c) Develop the capacity of civil society, including youth, to participate, as appropriate, in designing, implementing and reviewing sustainable development policies and strategies at all levels;

(d) Build and, where appropriate, strengthen national capacities for carrying out effective implementation of Agenda 21.

* * *

128. Ensure access, at the national level, to environmental information and judicial and administrative proceedings in environmental matters, as well as public participation in decision-making, so as to further principle 10 of the Rio Declaration on Environment and Development, taking into full account principles 5, 7 and 11 of the Declaration.

129. Strengthen national and regional information and statistical and analytical services relevant to sustainable development policies and programmes, including data disaggregated by sex, age and other factors, and encourage donors to provide financial and technical support to developing countries to enhance their capacity to formulate policies and implement programmes for sustainable development.

130. Encourage further work on indicators for sustainable development by countries at the national level, including integration of gender aspects, on a voluntary basis, in line with national conditions and priorities.

131. Promote further work on indicators, in conformity with paragraph 3 of decision 9/4 of the Commission on Sustainable Development.[44]

132. Promote the development and wider use of earth observation technologies, including satellite remote sensing, global mapping and geographic information systems, to collect quality data on environmental impacts, land use and land-use changes, including through urgent actions at all levels to:

(a) Strengthen cooperation and coordination among global observing systems and research programmes for integrated global observations, taking into account the need for building capacity and sharing of data from ground-based observations, satellite remote sensing and other sources among all countries;

(b) Develop information systems that make the sharing of valuable data possible, including the active exchange of Earth observation data;

(c) Encourage initiatives and partnerships for global mapping.

133. Support countries, particularly developing countries, in their national efforts to:

(a) Collect data that are accurate, long-term, consistent and reliable;

(b) Use satellite and remote-sensing technologies for data collection and further improvement of ground-based observations;

(c) Access, explore and use geographic information by utilizing the technologies of satellite remote sensing, satellite global positioning, mapping and geographic information systems.

134. Support efforts to prevent and mitigate the impacts of natural disasters, including through urgent actions at all levels to:

(a) Provide affordable access to disaster-related information for early warning purposes;

(b) Translate available data, particularly from global meteorological observation systems, into timely and useful products.

135. Develop and promote the wider application of environmental impact assessments, inter alia, as a national instrument, as appropriate, to provide essential decision-support information on projects that could cause significant adverse effects to the environment.

136. Promote and further develop methodologies at policy, strategy and project levels for sustainable development decision-making at the local and national levels, and where relevant at the regional level. In this regard, emphasize that the choice of the appropriate methodology to be used in countries should be adequate to their country-specific conditions and circumstances, should be on a voluntary basis and should conform to their development priority needs.

XI Institutional framework for sustainable development

137. An effective institutional framework for sustainable development at all levels is key to the full implementation of Agenda 21, the follow-up to the outcomes of the World Summit on Sustainable Development and meeting emerging sustainable development challenges. Measures aimed at strengthening such a framework should build on the provisions of Agenda 21, as well as the Programme for the Further Implementation of Agenda 21 of 1997 and the principles of the Rio Declaration on Environment and Development, and should promote the achievement of the internationally agreed development goals, including those contained in the Millennium Declaration, taking into account the Monterrey Consensus and relevant outcomes of other major United Nations conferences and international agreements since 1992. It should be responsive to the needs of all countries, taking into account the specific needs of developing countries, including the means of implementation. It should lead to the strengthening of international bodies and organizations dealing with sustainable development, while respecting their existing mandates, as well as to the strengthening of relevant regional, national and local institutions.

138. Good governance is essential for sustainable development. Sound economic policies, solid democratic institutions responsive to the needs of the people and improved infrastructure are the basis for sustained economic growth, poverty eradication and employment creation. Freedom, peace and security, domestic stability, respect for human rights, including the right to development, and the rule of law, gender equality, market-oriented policies, and an overall commitment to just and democratic societies are also essential and mutually reinforcing.

A. Objectives

139. Measures to strengthen institutional arrangements on sustainable development, at all levels, should be taken within the framework of Agenda 21,[45] build on developments since the United Nations Conference on Environment and Development and lead to the achievement of, inter alia, the following objectives:

(a) Strengthening commitments to sustainable development;

(b) Integration of the economic, social and environmental dimensions of sustainable development in a balanced manner;

(c) Strengthening of the implementation of Agenda 21, including through the mobilization of financial and technological resources, as well as capacity-building programmes, particularly for developing countries;

(d) Strengthening coherence, coordination and monitoring;

(e) Promoting the rule of law and strengthening of governmental institutions;

(f) Increasing effectiveness and efficiency through limiting overlap and duplication of activities of international organizations, within and outside the United Nations system, based on their mandates and comparative advantages;

(g) Enhancing participation and effective involvement of civil society and other relevant stakeholders in the implementation of Agenda 21, as well as promoting transparency and broad public participation;

(h) Strengthening capacities for sustainable development at all levels, including the local level, in particular those of developing countries;

(i) Strengthening international cooperation aimed at reinforcing the implementation of Agenda 21 and the outcomes of the Summit.

B. Strengthening the institutional framework for sustainable development at the international level

140. The international community should:

(a) Enhance the integration of sustainable development goals as reflected in Agenda 21 and support for implementation of Agenda 21 and the outcomes of the Summit into the policies, work programmes and operational guidelines of relevant United Nations agencies, programmes and funds, the Global Environment Facility and international financial and trade institutions, within their mandates, while stressing that their activities should take full account of national programmes and priorities, particularly those of developing countries, as well as, where appropriate, countries with economies in transition, to achieve sustainable development;

(b) Strengthen collaboration within and between the United Nations system, international financial institutions, the Global Environment Facility and the World Trade Organization, utilizing the United Nations System Chief Executives Board for Coordination, the United Nations Development Group, the Environment Management Group and other inter-agency coordinating bodies. Strengthened inter-agency collaboration should be pursued in all relevant contexts, with special emphasis on the operational level and involving partnership arrangements on specific issues, to support, in particular, the efforts of developing countries in implementing Agenda 21;

(c) Strengthen and better integrate the three dimensions of sustainable development policies and programmes and promote the full integration of sustainable development objectives into programmes and policies of bodies that have a primary focus on social issues. In particular, the social dimension of sustainable development should be strengthened, inter alia, by emphasizing follow-up to the outcomes of the World Summit for Social Development and its five-year review, and taking into account their reports, and by support to social protection systems;

(d) Fully implement the outcomes of the decision on international environmental governance adopted by the Governing Council of the United Nations Environment Programme at its seventh Special Session[46] and invite the General Assembly at its 57th session to consider the important but complex issue of establishing universal membership for the Governing Council/Global Ministerial Environment Forum;

(e) Engage actively and constructively in ensuring the timely completion of the negotiations on a comprehensive United Nations convention against corruption, including the question of repatriation of funds illicitly acquired to countries of origin;

(f) Promote corporate responsibility and accountability and the exchange of best practices in the context of sustainable development, including, as appropriate, through multi-stakeholder dialogue, such as through the Commission on Sustainable Development, and other initiatives;

(g) Take concrete action to implement the Monterrey Consensus at all levels.

141. Good governance at the international level is fundamental for achieving sustainable development. In order to ensure a dynamic and enabling international economic environment, it is important to promote global economic governance through addressing the international finance, trade, technology and investment patterns that have an impact on the development prospects of developing countries. To this effect, the international community should take all necessary and appropriate measures, including ensuring support for structural and macro-economic reform, a comprehensive solution to the external debt problem and increasing market access for developing countries. Efforts to reform the international financial architecture need to be sustained with greater transparency and the effective participation of developing countries in decision-making processes. A universal, rules-based, open, non-discriminatory and equitable multilateral trading system, as well as meaningful trade liberalization, can substantially stimulate development worldwide, benefiting countries at all stages of development.

142. A vibrant and effective United Nations system is fundamental to the promotion of international cooperation for sustainable development and to a global economic system that works for all. To this effect, a firm commitment to the ideals of the United Nations, the principles of international law and those enshrined in the Charter of the United Nations, as well as to strengthening the United Nations system and other multilateral institutions and promoting the improvement of their operations, is essential. States should also fulfil their commitment to negotiate and finalize as soon as possible a United Nations convention against corruption in all its aspects, including the question of repatriation of funds illicitly acquired to countries of origin and also to promoting stronger cooperation to eliminate money laundering.

C. Role of the General Assembly

143. The General Assembly of the United Nations should adopt sustainable development as a key element of the overarching framework for United Nations activities, particularly for achieving the internationally agreed development goals, including those contained in the Millennium Declaration, and should give overall political direction to the implementation of Agenda 21 and its review.

D. Role of the Economic and Social Council

144. Pursuant to the relevant provisions of the Charter of the United Nations, the provisions of Agenda 21 regarding the Economic and Social Council and General Assembly resolutions 48/162 and 50/227, which reaffirmed the Council as the central mechanism for the coordination of the United Nations system and its specialized agencies and supervision of subsidiary bodies, in particular its functional commissions, and to promote the implementation of Agenda 21 by strengthening system-wide coordination, the Council should:

    (a) Increase its role in overseeing system-wide coordination and the balanced integration of economic, social and environmental aspects of United Nations policies and programmes aimed at promoting sustainable development;

    (b) Organize periodic consideration of sustainable development themes in regard to the implementation of Agenda 21, including the means of implementation. Recommendations in regard to such themes could be made by the Commission on Sustainable Development;

    (c) Make full use of its high-level, coordination, operational activities and the general segments to effectively take into account all relevant aspects of the work of the United Nations on sustainable development. In this context, the Council should encourage the active participation of major groups in its high-level segment and the work of its relevant functional commissions, in accordance with the respective rules of procedure;

    (d) Promote greater coordination, complementarity, effectiveness and efficiency of activities of its functional commissions and other subsidiary bodies that are relevant to the implementation of Agenda 21;

    (e) Terminate the work of the Committee on Energy and Natural Resources for Development and transfer its work to the Commission on Sustainable Development;

    (f) Ensure that there is a close link between the role of the Council in the follow-up to the Summit and its role in the follow-up to the Monterrey Consensus, in a sustained and coordinated manner. To that end, the Council should explore ways to develop arrangements relating to its meetings with the Bretton Woods institutions and the World Trade Organization, as set out in the Monterrey Consensus;

    (g) Intensify its efforts to ensure that gender mainstreaming is an integral part of its activities concerning the coordinated implementation of Agenda 21.

E. Role and function of the Commission on Sustainable Development

145. The Commission on Sustainable Development should continue to be the high-level commission on sustainable development within the United Nations system and serve as a forum for consideration of issues related to integration of the three dimensions of sustainable development. Although the role, functions and mandate of the Commission as set out in relevant parts of Agenda 21 and adopted in General Assembly resolution 47/191 continue to be relevant, the Commission needs to be strengthened, taking into account the role of relevant institutions and organizations. An enhanced role of the Commission should include reviewing and

monitoring progress in the implementation of Agenda 21 and fostering coherence of implementation, initiatives and partnerships.

146. Within that context, the Commission should place more emphasis on actions that enable implementation at all levels, including promoting and facilitating partnerships involving Governments, international organizations and relevant stakeholders for the implementation of Agenda 21.

147. The Commission should:

    (a) Review and evaluate progress and promote further implementation of Agenda 21;

    (b) Focus on the cross-sectoral aspects of specific sectoral issues and provide a forum for better integration of policies, including through interaction among Ministers dealing with the various dimensions and sectors of sustainable development through the high-level segments;

    (c) Address new challenges and opportunities related to the implementation of Agenda 21;

    (d) Focus on actions related to implementation of Agenda 21, limiting negotiations in the sessions of the Commission to every two years;

    (e) Limit the number of themes addressed in each session.

148. In relation to its role in facilitating implementation, the CSD should emphasize the following:

    (a) Review progress and promote the further implementation of Agenda 21. In this context, the Commission should identify constraints on implementation and make recommendations to overcome those constraints;

    (b) Serve as a focal point for the discussion of partnerships that promote sustainable development, including sharing lessons learned, progress made and best practices;

    (c) Review issues related to financial assistance and transfer of technology for sustainable development, as well as capacity-building, while making full use of existing information. In this regard, the Commission on Sustainable Development could give consideration to more effective use of national reports and regional experience and to this end make appropriate recommendations;

    (d) Provide a forum for analysis and exchange of experience on measures that assist sustainable development planning, decision-making and the implementation of sustainable development strategies. In this regard, the Commission could give consideration to more effective use of national and regional reports;

    (e) Take into account significant legal developments in the field of sustainable development, with due regard to the role of relevant intergovernmental bodies in promoting the implementation of Agenda 21 relating to international legal instruments and mechanisms.

149. With regard to the practical modalities and programme of work of the Commission, specific decisions on those issues should be taken by the Commission at its next session, when the Commission's thematic work programme will be elaborated. In particular, the following issues should be considered:

    (a) Giving a balanced consideration to implementation of all of the mandates of the Commission contained in General Assembly resolution 47/191;

    (b) Continuing to provide for more direct and substantive involvement of international organizations and major groups in the work of the Commission;

(c) Give greater consideration to the scientific contributions to sustainable development through, for example, drawing on the scientific community and encouraging national, regional and international scientific networks to be involved in the Commission;

(d) Further the contribution of educators to sustainable development, including, where appropriate, in the activities of the Commission;

(e) Take into account the scheduling and duration of intersessional meetings.

150. Undertake further measures to promote best practices and lessons learned in sustainable development, and, in addition, promote the use of contemporary methods of data collection and dissemination, including broader use of information technologies.

F. Role of international institutions

151. Stress the need for international institutions both within and outside the United Nations system, including international financial institutions, the World Trade Organization and the Global Environment Facility, to enhance, within their mandates, their cooperative efforts to:

(a) Promote effective and collective support to the implementation of Agenda 21 at all levels;

(b) Enhance the effectiveness and coordination of international institutions to implement Agenda 21, the outcomes of the World Summit on Sustainable Development, relevant sustainable development aspects of the Millennium Declaration, the Monterrey Consensus and the outcome of the Fourth Ministerial Meeting of the World Trade Organization, held in Doha in November 2001.

152. Request the Secretary-General of the United Nations, utilizing the United Nations System Chief Executives Board for Coordination, including through informal collaborative efforts, to further promote system-wide interagency cooperation and coordination on sustainable development, to take appropriate measures to facilitate exchange of information, and to continue to keep the Economic and Social Council and the Commission informed of actions being taken to implement Agenda 21.

153. Significantly strengthen support for the capacity-building programmes of the United Nations Development Programme for sustainable development, building on the experience gained from the Capacity 21 programme, as important mechanisms for supporting local and national development capacity-building efforts, in particular in developing countries.

154. Strengthen cooperation between the United Nations Environment Programme and other United Nations bodies and specialized agencies, the Bretton Woods institutions and the World Trade Organization, within their mandates.

155. The United Nations Environment Programme, the United Nations Centre for Human Settlements, the United Nations Development Programme and the United Nations Conference on Trade and Development, within their mandates, should strengthen their contribution to sustainable development programmes and the implementation of Agenda 21 at all levels, particularly in the area of promoting capacity-building.

156. To promote effective implementation of Agenda 21 at the international level, the following should also be undertaken:

(a) Streamline the international sustainable development meeting calendar and, as appropriate, reduce the number of meetings, the length of meetings and the amount of time spent on negotiated outcomes in favour of more time spent on practical matters related to implementation;

(b) Encourage partnership initiatives for implementation by all relevant actors to support the outcome of the World Summit on Sustainable Development. In this context, further development of partnerships and partnership follow-up should take note of the preparatory work for the Summit;

(c) Make full use of developments in the field of information and communication technologies.

157. Strengthening of the international institutional framework for sustainable development is an evolutionary process. It is necessary to keep relevant arrangements under review; identify gaps; eliminate duplication of functions; and continue to strive for greater integration, efficiency and coordination of the economic, social and environmental dimensions of sustainable development aiming at the implementation of Agenda 21.

G. Strengthening institutional arrangements for sustainable development at the regional level

158. Implementation of Agenda 21 and the outcomes of the Summit should be effectively pursued at the regional and sub-regional levels, through the regional commissions and other regional and sub-regional institutions and bodies.

159. Intra-regional coordination and cooperation on sustainable development should be improved among the regional commissions, United Nations Funds, programmes and agencies, regional development banks and other regional and sub-regional institutions and bodies. This should include, as appropriate, support for development, enhancement and implementation of agreed regional sustainable development strategies and action plans, reflecting national and regional priorities.

160. In particular, taking into account relevant provisions of Agenda 21, the regional commissions, in collaboration with other regional and subregional bodies, should:

(a) Promote the integration of the three dimensions of sustainable development into their work in a balanced way, including through implementation of Agenda 21. To this end, the regional commissions should enhance their capacity through internal action and be provided, as appropriate, with external support;

(b) Facilitate and promote a balanced integration of the economic, social and environmental dimensions of sustainable development into the work of regional, sub-regional and other bodies – for example, by facilitating and strengthening the exchange of experiences, including national experience, best practices, case studies and partnership experience related to the implementation of Agenda 21;

(c) Assist in the mobilization of technical and financial assistance, and facilitate the provision of adequate financing for the implementation of regionally and sub-regionally agreed sustainable development programmes and projects, including addressing the objective of poverty eradication;

(d) Continue to promote multi-stakeholder participation and encourage partnerships to support the implementation of Agenda 21 at the regional and sub-regional levels.

161. Regionally and sub-regionally agreed sustainable development initiatives and programmes, such as the New Partnership for African Development (NEPAD) and

the interregional aspects of the globally agreed Programme of Action on the Sustainable Development of Small Island Developing States, should be supported.

H. Strengthening institutional frameworks for sustainable development at the national level

162. States should:
    (a) Continue to promote coherent and coordinated approaches to institutional frameworks for sustainable development at all national levels, including through, as appropriate, the establishment or strengthening of existing authorities and mechanisms necessary for policy-making, coordination and implementation and enforcement of laws;
    (b) Take immediate steps to make progress in the formulation and elaboration of national strategies for sustainable development and begin their implementation by 2005. To this end, as appropriate, strategies should be supported through international cooperation, taking into account the special needs of developing countries, in particular the least developed countries. Such strategies, which, where applicable, could be formulated as poverty reduction strategies that integrate economic, social and environmental aspects of sustainable development, should be pursued in accordance with each country's national priorities.

163. Each country has the primary responsibility for its own sustainable development, and the role of national policies and development strategies cannot be overemphasized. All countries should promote sustainable development at the national level by, inter alia, enacting and enforcing clear and effective laws that support sustainable development. All countries should strengthen governmental institutions, including by providing necessary infrastructure and by promoting transparency, accountability and fair administrative and judicial institutions.

164. All countries should also promote public participation, including through measures that provide access to information regarding legislation, regulations, activities, policies and programmes. They should also foster full public participation in sustainable development policy formulation and implementation. Women should be able to participate fully and equally in policy formulation and decision-making.

165. Further promote the establishment or enhancement of sustainable development councils and/or coordination structures at the national level, including at the local level, in order to provide a high-level focus on sustainable development policies. In that context, multi-stakeholder participation should be promoted.

166. Support efforts by all countries, particularly developing countries, as well as countries with economies in transition, to enhance national institutional arrangements for sustainable development, including at the local level. This could include promoting cross-sectoral approaches in the formulation of strategies and plans for sustainable development, such as, where applicable, poverty reduction strategies, aid coordination, encouraging participatory approaches and enhancing policy analysis, management capacity and implementation capacity, including mainstreaming a gender perspective in all those activities.

167. Enhance the role and capacity of local authorities as well as stakeholders in implementing Agenda 21 and the outcomes of the Summit and in strengthening the continuing support for local Agenda 21 programmes and associated initiatives

and partnerships and encourage, in particular, partnerships among and between local authorities and other levels of government and stakeholders to advance sustainable development as called for in, inter alia, the Habitat Agenda.[47]

I. Participation of major groups

168. Enhance partnerships between governmental and non-governmental actors, including all major groups, as well as volunteer groups, on programmes and activities for the achievement of sustainable development at all levels.

169. Acknowledge the consideration being given to the possible relationship between environment and human rights, including the right to development, with full and transparent participation of Member States of the United Nations and observer States.

170. Promote and support youth participation in programmes and activities relating to sustainable development through, for example, supporting local youth councils or their equivalent, and by encouraging their establishment where they do not exist.

Notes

* The text has been reproduced fully from the original UN document, A/CONF.199/20. Please refer to http://www.un.org/esa/sustdev/ for full details of references cited.

1   *Report of the United Nations Conference on Environment and Development, Rio de Janeiro, 3–14 June 1992* (United Nations publication, Sales No E.93.I.8 and corrigenda)

2   Ibid, vol I: *Resolutions Adopted by the Conference*, resolution 1, annexes I and II

3   General Assembly resolution S-19/2, annex

4   General Assembly resolution 55/2

5   Report of the *United Nations Conference on Environment and Development, Rio de Janeiro, 3–14 June 1992* (United Nations publication, Sales No E.93.I.8 and corrigenda), vol I: *Resolutions Adopted by the Conference*, resolution 1, annex I

6   *Report of the International Conference on Financing for Development, Monterrey, Mexico, 18–22 March 2002* (United Nations, publication, Sales No E.02.II.A.7), Chapter 1, resolution 1, annex

7   United Nations, Treaty Series, vol 1954, no 33480

8   See *ILO Declaration on Fundamental Principles and Rights at Work and its Follow-up Adopted by the International Labour Conference at its Eighty-sixth Session, Geneva, 16 June 1998,* (Geneva, International Labour Office)

9   *Official Records of the Economic and Social Council, 2001, Supplement No 9* (E/2001/29), chap I.B

10 UNEP/FAO/PIC/CONF.5, annex III

11 www.chem.unep.ch/sc

12 Intergovernmental Forum on Chemical Safety (IFCS), Third Session, *Forum III Final Report* (IFCS/Forum III/23w) annex 6

13 United Nations *Treaty Series,* vol 1673, no 28911

14 *Official Records of the Third United Nations Conference on the Law of the Sea,* vol XVII, United Nations, publication, Sales No E.84.V.3, Document A/CONF.62/122

15 See Food and Agriculture Organization of the United Nations document C200/INF/25, appendix I

16 See UNEP/CBD/COP/5/23, annex III

17 See *International Fisheries Instruments* (United Nations, publication, Sales No E.98.V.11) sect I; see also A/CONF.164/37

18 Ibid

19 Ibid, sect III

20 Rome, Food and Agriculture Organization of the United Nations, 1999,

21 Ibid, 2001

22 See A/51/312, annex II, decision II/10

23 *Ramsar Convention on Wetlands of International Importance Especially as Waterfowl Habitat* (United Nations, Treaty Series, vol 996, no 14583)

24 See United Nations Environment Programme, *Convention on Biological Diversity* (Environmental Law and Institution Programme Activity Centre) June 1992

25 A/51/116, annex II

26 See E/CN.17/2002/PC.2/15

27 A/AC.237/18 (Part II)/Add.1 and Corr.1, annex I

28 FCCC/CP/1997/7/Add.1, decision 1/CP.3, annex

29 FCCC/CP/2001/13 and Add.1-4

30 See General Assembly resolution 2200 A (XXI), annex

31 *Report of the Conference of the Food and Agriculture Organization of the United Nations, Thirty-first Session, Rome, 2–13 November 2001* (C2001/REP) Appendix D

32 See A/C.2/56/7, annex

33 http://www.biodiv.org/biosafety/protocol.asp

34 General Assembly resolution S-26/2, annex

35 *Report of the Global Conference on the Sustainable Development of Small Island Developing States, Bridgetown, Barbados, 25 April–6 May 1994* (United Nations, publication, Sales No E.94.I.18 and corrigenda) chap I, resolution 1, annex II

36 E/CN.17/2002/PC.2/5/Add.2

37 E/CN.17/2002/PC.2/8

38 ECE/ACC.22/2001/2, annex I

39 A/CONF.192/13

40 A/CONF.191/11

41 A/C.2/56/2, annex, paras 13 and 14

42 Ibid, paras 17–19

43 General Assembly resolution 2625 (XXV), annex

44 See *Official Records of the Economic and Social Council (2001) Supplement No 9* (E/2001/29), chap I.B

45 References in the present chapter to Agenda 21 are deemed to include Agenda 21, the Programme for the Further Implementation of Agenda 21 and the outcomes of the Summit

46 UNEP/GCSS.VII/6, annex I

47 A/CONF.165/14, chap 1, resolution 1, annex II

Johannesburg Declaration on Sustainable Development[*]

Annex B

From our origins to the future

1. We, the representatives of the peoples of the world, assembled at the World Summit on Sustainable Development in Johannesburg, South Africa, from 2 to 4 September 2002, reaffirm our commitment to sustainable development.

2. We commit ourselves to building a humane, equitable and caring global society, cognizant of the need for human dignity for all.

3. At the beginning of this Summit, the children of the world spoke to us in a simple yet clear voice that the future belongs to them, and accordingly challenged all of us to ensure that through our actions they will inherit a world free of the indignity and indecency occasioned by poverty, environmental degradation and patterns of unsustainable development.

4. As part of our response to these children, who represent our collective future, all of us, coming from every corner of the world, informed by different life experiences, are united and moved by a deeply felt sense that we urgently need to create a new and brighter world of hope.

5. Accordingly, we assume a collective responsibility to advance and strengthen the interdependent and mutually reinforcing pillars of sustainable development – economic development, social development and environmental protection – at the local, national, regional and global levels.

6. From this continent, the cradle of humanity, we declare, through the Plan of Implementation of the World Summit on Sustainable Development and the present Declaration, our responsibility to one another, to the greater community of life and to our children.

7. Recognizing that humankind is at a crossroads, we have united in a common resolve to make a determined effort to respond positively to the need to produce a practical and visible plan to bring about poverty eradication and human development.

From Stockholm to Rio de Janeiro to Johannesburg

8. Thirty years ago, in Stockholm, we agreed on the urgent need to respond to the problem of environmental deterioration.[1] Ten years ago, at the United Nations Conference on Environment and Development, held in Rio de Janeiro,[2] we agreed that the protection of the environment and social and economic development are fundamental to sustainable development, based on the Rio Principles. To achieve such development, we adopted the global programme entitled Agenda 21[3] and the Rio Declaration on Environment and Development,[3] to which we reaffirm our

commitment. The Rio Conference was a significant milestone that set a new agenda for sustainable development.

9. Between Rio and Johannesburg, the world's nations have met in several major conferences under the auspices of the United Nations, including the International Conference on Financing for Development,[4] as well as the Doha Ministerial Conference.[5] These conferences defined for the world a comprehensive vision for the future of humanity.

10. At the Johannesburg Summit, we have achieved much in bringing together a rich tapestry of peoples and views in a constructive search for a common path towards a world that respects and implements the vision of sustainable development. The Johannesburg Summit has also confirmed that significant progress has been made towards achieving a global consensus and partnership among all the people of our planet.

The challenges we face

11. We recognize that poverty eradication, changing consumption and production patterns and protecting and managing the natural resource base for economic and social development are overarching objectives of, and essential requirements for, sustainable development.

12. The deep fault line that divides human society between the rich and the poor and the ever-increasing gap between the developed and developing worlds pose a major threat to global prosperity, security and stability.

13. The global environment continues to suffer. Loss of biodiversity continues, fish stocks continue to be depleted, desertification claims more and more fertile land, the adverse effects of climate change are already evident, natural disasters are more frequent and more devastating, and developing countries more vulnerable, and air, water and marine pollution continue to rob millions of a decent life.

14. Globalization has added a new dimension to these challenges. The rapid integration of markets, mobility of capital and significant increases in investment flows around the world have opened new challenges and opportunities for the pursuit of sustainable development. But the benefits and costs of globalization are unevenly distributed, with developing countries facing special difficulties in meeting this challenge.

15. We risk the entrenchment of these global disparities, and unless we act in a manner that fundamentally changes their lives the poor of the world may lose confidence in their representatives and the democratic systems to which we remain committed, seeing their representatives as nothing more than sounding brass or tinkling cymbals.

Our commitment to sustainable development

16. We are determined to ensure that our rich diversity, which is our collective strength, will be used for constructive partnership for change and for the achievement of the common goal of sustainable development.

17. Recognizing the importance of building human solidarity, we urge the promotion of dialogue and cooperation among the world's civilizations and peoples, irrespective of race, disabilities, religion, language, culture or tradition.

18. We welcome the focus of the Johannesburg Summit on the indivisibility of human dignity and are resolved, through decisions on targets, timetables and partnerships, to speedily increase access to such basic requirements as clean water, sanitation, adequate shelter, energy, healthcare, food security and the protection of biodiversity. At the same time, we will work together to help one another gain access to financial resources, benefit from the opening of markets, ensure capacity-building, use modern technology to bring about development and make sure that there is technology transfer, human resource development, education and training to banish underdevelopment forever.

19. We reaffirm our pledge to place particular focus on, and give priority attention to, the fight against the worldwide conditions that pose severe threats to the sustainable development of our people, which include chronic hunger; malnutrition; foreign occupation; armed conflict; illicit drug problems; organized crime; corruption; natural disasters; illicit arms trafficking; trafficking in persons; terrorism; intolerance and incitement to racial, ethnic, religious and other hatreds; xenophobia; and endemic, communicable and chronic diseases, in particular HIV/AIDS, malaria and tuberculosis.

20. We are committed to ensuring that women's empowerment, emancipation and gender equality are integrated in all the activities encompassed within Agenda 21, the Millennium development goals[6] and the Plan of Implementation of the Summit.

21. We recognize the reality that global society has the means and is endowed with the resources to address the challenges of poverty eradication and sustainable development confronting all humanity. Together, we will take extra steps to ensure that these available resources are used to the benefit of humanity.

22. In this regard, to contribute to the achievement of our development goals and targets, we urge developed countries that have not done so to make concrete efforts to reach the internationally agreed levels of official development assistance.

23. We welcome and support the emergence of stronger regional groupings and alliances, such as the New Partnership for Africa's Development, to promote regional cooperation, improved international cooperation and sustainable development.

24. We shall continue to pay special attention to the developmental needs of small island developing States and the least developed countries.

25. We reaffirm the vital role of the indigenous peoples in sustainable development.

26. We recognize that sustainable development requires a long-term perspective and broad-based participation in policy formulation, decision-making and implementation at all levels. As social partners, we will continue to work for stable partnerships with all major groups, respecting the independent, important roles of each of them.

27. We agree that in pursuit of its legitimate activities the private sector, including both large and small companies, has a duty to contribute to the evolution of equitable and sustainable communities and societies.

28. We also agree to provide assistance to increase income-generating employment opportunities, taking into account the Declaration on Fundamental Principles and Rights at Work of the International Labour Organization.[7]

29. We agree that there is a need for private-sector corporations to enforce corporate accountability, which should take place within a transparent and stable regulatory environment.

30. We undertake to strengthen and improve governance at all levels for the effective implementation of Agenda 21, the Millennium development goals and the Plan of Implementation of the Summit.

Multilateralism is the future

31. To achieve our goals of sustainable development, we need more effective, democratic and accountable international and multilateral institutions.
32. We reaffirm our commitment to the principles and purposes of the Charter of the United Nations and international law, as well as to the strengthening of multilateralism. We support the leadership role of the United Nations as the most universal and representative organization in the world, which is best placed to promote sustainable development.
33. We further commit ourselves to monitor progress at regular intervals towards the achievement of our sustainable development goals and objectives.

Making it happen!

34. We are in agreement that this must be an inclusive process, involving all the major groups and Governments that participated in the historic Johannesburg Summit.
35. We commit ourselves to act together, united by a common determination to save our planet, promote human development and achieve universal prosperity and peace.
36. We commit ourselves to the Plan of Implementation of the World Summit on Sustainable Development and to expediting the achievement of the time-bound, socio-economic and environmental targets contained therein.
37. From the African continent, the cradle of humankind, we solemnly pledge to the peoples of the world and the generations that will surely inherit this Earth that we are determined to ensure that our collective hope for sustainable development is realized.

Notes

* The text has been reproduced fully from the original UN document A/CONF.199/20. Please refer to http://www.un.org/esa/sustdev/ for full details of references cited.

1 *Report of the United Nations Conference on the Human Environment, Stockholm, 5–16 June 1972* (United Nations, publication, Sales No E.73.II.A.14 and corrigendum) chap 1

2 *Report of the United Nations Conference on Environment and Development, Rio de Janeiro, 3–14 June 1992* (United Nations, publication, Sales No E.93.I.8 and corrigenda) vol I–III

3 Ibid, vol I: *Resolutions adopted by the Conference*, resolution 1, annexes I and II

4 *Report of the International Conference on Financing for Development, Monterrey, Mexico, 18–22 March 2002* (United Nations, publication, Sales No E.02.II.A.7) chap I, resolution 1, annex

5 See A/C.2/56/7, annex

6   See General Assembly resolution 55/2

7   See *ILO Declaration on Fundamental Principles and Rights at Work and Its Follow-up Adopted by the International Labour Conference at its Eighty-sixth Session, Geneva, 18 June 1998*, ILO (Geneva International Labour Office, 1998)

Index

Note: Upper case roman numerals refer to chapters in the Plan of Implementation of the World Summit on Sustainable Development located in Annex A of this volume (pp176–237)

Construction Innovation and Process Improvement

Edited by

Akintola Akintoye
Professor and Head of School, Construction
Economics & Management
University of Central Lancashire

Jack S. Goulding
Professor, Construction Project Management and
Director, Centre for Sustainable Development
University of Central Lancashire

and

Girma Zawdie
Senior Lecturer, Science, Technology and Sustainability
University of Strathclyde

WILEY-BLACKWELL
A John Wiley & Sons, Ltd., Publication

Registered Office
John Wiley & Sons Ltd, The Atrium, Southern Gate, Chichester, West Sussex, PO19 8SQ, United Kingdom

Editorial Offices
9600 Garsington Road, Oxford, OX4 2DQ, United Kingdom
2121 State Avenue, Ames, Iowa 50014-8300, USA

For details of our global editorial offices, for customer services and for information about how to apply for permission to reuse the copyright material in this book please see our website at www.wiley.com/wiley-blackwell.

The right of the author to be identified as the author of this work has been asserted in accordance with the UK Copyright, Designs and Patents Act 1988.

Library of Congress Cataloging-in-Publication Data

Akintoye, Akintola.
Construction innovation and process improvement / Akintola Akintoye, Jack S. Goulding, Girma Zawdie.
    p. cm.
  Includes bibliographical references and index.
  ISBN 978-1-4051-5648-6 (hardback)
1. Construction industry–Technological innovations. 2. Civil engineering–Technological innovations. 3. Competition. I. Goulding, Jack S. II. Zawdie, Girma, 1946– III. Title.
  HD9715.A2A435 2012
  624.068–dc23
                                                          2011045230

A catalogue record for this book is available from the British Library.

Wiley also publishes its books in a variety of electronic formats. Some content that appears in print may not be available in electronic books.

Set in 10/12pt Sabon by SPi Publisher Services, Pondicherry, India
Printed and bound in Malaysia by Vivar Printing Sdn Bhd

1   2012

Contents

Contributors

Akintola Akintoye
School of Built and Natural Environment
University of Central Lancashire
UK

Mustafa Alshawi
University of Salford
UK

Chimay J. Anumba
The Pennsylvania State University
USA

Oluwaseyi Awodele
Heriot Watt University
Edinburgh
UK

Graeme Bowles
Heriot Watt University
Edinburgh
UK

Charles Egbu
University of Salford
UK

Richard Fellows
Loughborough University
Loughborough
UK

Jack S. Goulding
University of Central Lancashire
UK

Umit Isikdag
Beykent University
Turkey

John M. Kamara
Newcastle University
Newcastle
UK

Murat Kuruoglu
Istanbul Technical University
Istanbul
Turkey

Anita Liu
University of Hong Kong
Hong Kong

Eric Lou
University of Salford
UK

Shu-Ling Lu
University of Reading
Reading
UK

Jamie Main
Capita Symonds Limited
UK

Wafaa Nadim
British University in Egypt
Egypt

Stephen Ogunlana
Heriot Watt University
Edinburgh
UK

Farzad Pour Rahimian
University of Central Lancashire
UK

Martin G. Sexton
University of Reading
Reading
UK

Mark D. Sharp
The Association of International Property
Professionals
London
UK

Joseph H.M. Tah
Oxford Brookes University
Oxford
UK

Jason Underwood
University of Salford
UK

Emilia Van Egmond
Eindhoven University of Technology
The Netherlands

Derek H.T. Walker
RMIT
Melbourne
Australia

Girma Zawdie
Strathclyde University
Glasgow
UK

Part I

Theory and Practice

Construction Innovation and Process Improvement

Akintola Akintoye, Jack S. Goulding and Girma Zawdie

1.1   Introduction

In order to promote and retain competitiveness, industry needs to focus on innovation and the improvement of their processes. Panuwatwanich *et al.* (2008) noted that innovation is necessary as a source of competitive advantage for firms operating in the construction industry, and consequently, that many firms are expending a significant amount of resources in an effort to acquire various forms of innovation in order to maintain and/or increase their competitiveness. Similarly, Aouad *et al.* (2010) highlighted that the competitiveness of firms inevitably depends on national and regional systems of innovation, which in turn depends on government policy. Therefore, given the constant changes and dynamism of the business environment, securing competitiveness is therefore high on the agenda of most firms. In this respect, securing innovation and process improvement is an influential lever for delivering this. On this theme, the increased complexity and sophistication of the Architectural Engineering and Construction (AEC) sector is now placing unparalleled demands on stakeholders to keep projects on time and within budget, with a new emergent theme of developing and maintaining robust and defendable innovation policies and procedures. Although it is not easy to sustain radical improvement in an industry that has historically been categorised as diverse and fragmented (Banwell, 1964; Latham, 1994; Fairclough, 2002), it has been recognised that there is a need for continuous and sustained improvement, using focused efforts to deliver the value needed by customers, along with addressing the industry challenge concerning waste and poor quality arising from existing structures and working practices (Egan, 1998). In this respect, Professor Watson (CSaP, 2011) reviewed the key concepts of innovation, noting that innovation was more than

Construction Innovation and Process Improvement, First Edition.
Edited by Akintola Akintoye, Jack S. Goulding and Girma Zawdie.
© 2012 Blackwell Publishing Ltd. Published 2012 by Blackwell Publishing Ltd.

invention or creativity, as it enveloped commercialisation, implementation and entrepreneurship as part of the innovation process – which required a change in culture to proactively promote and support innovation.

This book raises a number of wide ranging issues relating to construction innovation and process improvement, especially in the light of experience derived from construction practice in different countries with different contexts. The chapters therefore provide a rich collection of literature embracing theoretical and practice-empirical appeal, which gives credence to the pervasive and transformative effect that innovation can bring. Moreover, even in mature markets such as the AEC sector, where business behaviour is generally considered as risk averse, it highlights the increased importance and significance of embedding innovation initiatives into mainstream business practices. In this respect, construction practice is still evolving, with complex aspects underpinned by organisational and management responsibilities that seek to draw alignment across a wide range of players, not least contractors, subcontractors, suppliers and clients. This network of players in the industry is important, as they have a significant bearing on the manner in which innovative activities occur in the industry. It is also important to note that the nature of construction innovation is closely examined in terms of its impact on technological progress of the industry to date, and emergent technological trajectories.

The chapters in this book are divided into three broad themes of construction innovation relating to: Theory and Practice; Process Drivers; and Future Technologies. These three categories tease out the main salient issues on construction innovation and process improvement, and highlight the implications for future competitiveness and sustainability of the industry. These themes pose several questions for reflection, including 'What is particularly unique about construction innovation in theory and practice?', 'What are the major drivers of construction innovation?' and 'What factors are needed to support and deliver future construction technologies?'

In attempting to respond to these questions, this book sheds new light on these challenges, and provides readers with a number of ways forward, especially cognisant of the increased role of globalisation, the enhanced impact of knowledge and importance of innovation, as all these can have a significant impact on strategic decision making, competitive advantage, and sustainable policies and practices.

1.2   Innovation in Construction

Several definitions have been proffered for innovation. For example, Van de Ven (1986) regards innovation as any ideas, practices and technologies perceived to be new by the organisation involved. Slaughter (1998) defined innovation as the actual use of a nontrivial change and improvement in a process, product or system that is novel to the institution developing the change; whereas, Stewart and Fenn (2006) described innovation as the profitable exploitation of ideas, which have an important role to play in seeking competitive advantage. Innovation in construction can therefore be considered as the successful development and/or implementation of new ideas, products, process or practices, in order to increase organisational efficiency and performance (Egbu et al., 1998; DTI, 2003; Ling, 2003; Sexton and Barrett, 2005; Panuwatwanich et al., 2008). On the other hand, some proponents advocate that because the construction industry is largely project-based and fragmented, the patterns of innovation differ in many ways from those of other industries, and therefore, industry innovation remains hidden when co-developed at the project level (Aouad et al., 2010). However, Stewart and Fenn (2006) noted that innovation in the construction industry has been recognised in three domains: product, process and organisation. Process innovation is oriented towards production methods, and organisational innovation to approaches to managing the firm and implementation of new corporate strategic orientations. They contest that in construction, innovation is mostly seen in terms of physical process and product, particularly improvements in materials. However, Blayse and Manley (2004) identified six main factors that could influence innovation in construction as:

1. clients and manufacturers;
2. the structure of production;
3. relationships between individuals and firms within the industry;
4. relations between the industry and external parties;
5. procurement systems regulations/standards; and
6. the nature and quality of organisational resources.

They noted that these influences are the key factors that drive (or in fact hinder) business innovation.

From a process perspective, the term 'processes' are 'the fundamental building blocks' of all organisations, and both process understanding and process improvement form the lifeblood of total quality organisations. Processes transform inputs, which can include actions, methods and operations, into outputs. They are the steps by which we add value, and it should be the aim of customer focused, total quality organisations, for these outputs to satisfy or exceed the needs and expectations of their customers' (DTI, 2011). On this theme, Sarshar et al. (2004) developed a Structure Process Improvement for Construction Enterprises maturity framework to assess organisational performance. More fundamentally, the industry acknowledged that there was a need for new process configurations and innovation through life-cycle decision analysis (which had been championed in many countries and supported by industry stakeholder groups and government bodies). Moreover, both the Latham (1994) and Egan (1998) reports identified that the construction industry needed to embrace innovation and process improvement. Similarly, in Hong Kong, the government established a Construction Industry Review Committee (CIRC) that published its report, 'Construct for Excellence', in 2001. This report, amongst other recommendations, charged the industry to collectively develop a culture of innovation which deliberately concentrated and fostered innovation, both from a technology and fostered perspective.

In Australia, Sidwell *et al.* (2004) reported on the importance of reengineering the construction delivery process, noting that the fragmented and differentiated structure of the construction industry was a major characteristic that militates against improvement. The core challenge for the construction industry was therefore to develop radical project delivery processes that concentrated on front-end issues of procurement strategies, interfaces in the process, information flows, and the elimination of non-value-adding activities.

The need for construction innovation and process improvement was further emphasised by the Egan (1998) report through the Construction Task Force, which identified as one of its terms of reference to 'examine current practice and the scope for improving the industry by innovation in products and processes'; some notable areas of which included:

- lack of research and development (R&D) investment (damaging the industry's ability to keep abreast of innovation in processes and technology);
- client dissatisfaction with consultants' performance in coordinating teams, in design and innovation (to provide a speedy and reliable service and deliver value for money);
- wasted talent (failure to recognise the significant contribution that suppliers can make to innovation);
- repeated selection of new teams (inhibits learning, innovation and the development of skilled and experienced teams, preventing the industry from developing products and an identity/brand that can be understood by its clients);
- product development requires continuity from a dedicated product team (needing product design skills, with close links to the supply chain through which the skills of suppliers and their innovations can be assessed, and with access to relevant market research);
- supply chain is critical for driving innovation (and sustaining incremental and sustained performance improvement);
- project implementation requires 'organisation and management of the supply chain to maximise innovation, learning and efficiency';
- project implementation requires 'capturing suppliers' innovations in components and systems';
- component production also includes the sustained commitment to innovation in the design of components (including the development of a range of standardised components);
- continuous learning ('upgrading, retraining and continuous learning are not part of construction's current vocabulary. There is already frustration amongst component suppliers that their innovations are blocked because construction workers cannot cope with the new technologies that they are making available. This has to change');
- improvements in innovation (more can be achieved by co-operation between clients, constructors and suppliers than through competition);
- need to encourage long-term partnering arrangements between clients and providers (to secure consistency, continuity, innovation and value for money);

- need to develop knowledge centres (through which the whole industry and its clients can gain access to knowledge about good practices, innovations and the performance of companies and projects;
- need for training (new technical and managerial skills required in order to get full value from new techniques and technologies);
- learning from other industries ('...in both manufacturing and service industries there have been increases in efficiency and transformations of companies, which a decade or more ago nobody would have believed possible);
- change in culture (changing this is fundamental to increasing efficiency and quality in construction);
- improving project processes ('...construction has two choices: ignore all this in the belief that construction is so unique that there are no lessons to be learned; or seek improvement through reengineering construction, learning as much as possible from those who have done it elsewhere');
- product development ('innovating with suppliers to improve the product without loss of reliability');
- Enabling improvement ('Substantial changes in the culture and structure of UK construction are required to enable the improvements in the project process that will deliver our ambition of a modem construction industry. These include changes in working conditions, skills and training, approaches to design, use of technology and relationships between companies);
- technology as a tool ('One area in which we know new technology to be a useful tool is in the design of buildings and their components, and in the exchange of design information throughout the construction team. There are enormous benefits to be gained, in terms of eliminating waste and rework for example, from using modern CAD technology to prototype buildings and by rapidly exchanging information on design changes. Redesign should take place on computer, not on the construction site).

The above points, whilst not exhaustive, offer a number of critical areas for reflection, all of which are covered in this book through the three core themes of: Theory and Practice, Process Drivers, and Future Technologies.

1.3   Construction Innovation: Theory and Practice

Panuwatwanich *et al.* (2008) noted that innovation diffusion in design firms could be enhanced by creating a culture for innovation using innovative leaders. Moreover, Barlow and Jashpara (1998) highlighted the importance of collaborative links between firms for stimulating organisational learning. Similarly, Gann and Salter (2010) opined how clients can act as a catalyst in the construction value chain to help foster innovation by exerting pressure on supply chain partners to improve overall performance, and also by helping them to devise strategies to cope with unforeseen changes. This is particularly important, as Vennstrom and Eriksson (2010) identified that client perceived barriers to change could be divided into three types: attitudinal, industrial and institutional; noting that 'Clients wishing to act as change agents need to be aware that their use of internal versus external project management affects their chances to influence the other construction actors and implement change and innovation'. Furthermore, Aouad *et al.* (2010) noted 'Our understanding of innovation and how it occurs in the sector is far from complete but can be enriched further by detailed work that brings together different theoretical perspectives on innovation that will enable the development of context sensitive ways of recognising and measuring innovation at different levels of resolution.'

Part I of this book therefore explores the above issues, dealing with matters relating to change management, technology, sustainable construction (SuCo), and supply chain management (SCM).

Chapter 2 highlights the occurrence of innovation through organisational learning; knowledge accumulation and knowledge sharing; conflict management and coalition building, with the aim to minimise resistance to change. The overarching factor impinging upon the process of construction innovation is the cultural context within which construction activities are pursued, so that the occurrence of innovation would be expected to be highly likely where there is 'cultural readiness' arising from exposure to new ideas and practices. Cultural readiness exists where proactive management and flexible and change-responsive organisational arrangement are evident, and where management supports coalition building through the process of providing the conditions for relationship balancing and conflict resolution. Emphasis is therefore placed on removing fragmentation, embracing change, and leveraging innovation drivers to meet and deliver business goals and new market opportunities.

Chapter 3 explores the theory and practice of construction innovation in terms of the synthesis of resource-based and market-based perspectives of innovation. The market-based view of innovation is a variation of 'demand pull' innovation, which utilises the role of institutional and market factors to stimulate innovation at the firm level. Market conditions influencing innovation possibilities include both the general business environment, and the interaction or industry-specific environment. Market conditions shape the resources that firms exploit to respond to opportunities and threats. The resource-based view of innovation is based on the understanding of firms identifying and developing resources that enable them to shape market conditions. The knowledge base of the firm, which is bolstered by the firm's relationship capital, structure capital and human capital, is crucial for interfacing organisational resources with external agencies in market relations to produce the dynamic capabilities that provide the basis for innovation and sustainable competitive advantage. It concludes by highlighting the importance of exploiting existing capabilities to produce innovation in order to enhance performance; but equally, the need to invest in explorative innovation for the future.

Chapter 4 highlights the importance and impact of culture on innovation. Innovation has a cultural context that determines the nature of the prevailing demand and supply conditions, as well as the organisation and management bases of innovation. This is especially important, as it impinges and influences the ways in which knowledge infrastructures evolve. Cultural change is therefore crucial for technological progress, as any model of innovation would be incomplete without the inclusion of cultural parameters. The role of culture in construction is discussed, noting the importance and development of co-operation structures (or social systems), and the need to include learning as one of the dimensions of innovation culture. Learning culture is therefore explored, noting the importance of the prevailing cultural climate in order to determine what changes may be needed to facilitate learning and the transfer of creative problem solving. The importance of learning (and learning from other sectors) is acknowledged as being crucial for developing an innovation culture, the mandate of which requires leaders with vision and foresight to 'plan ahead' in order to fully benefit from this.

Chapter 5 examines how innovation and international technology and knowledge transfer (TKT) relates to SuCo performance. The systemic interactions between these are investigated, particularly concerning new design concepts and their integration with building elements and processes. The efficiency and effectiveness in TKT practices are evaluated within the construction firm and across different projects, at regional, national and international levels. In this respect, knowledge accumulation and learning can be seen as a pivotal driver for innovation and TKT processes, as successful production and trade performance strongly depend on capability and motivation to innovate and quickly adopt new technologies. This can help form the building blocks for either subsequent incremental innovation or new knowledge sets for future innovation in other related areas. The construction innovation system is explored, with emphasis on collaboration and technical regime. A case study from The Netherlands is used to discuss the management of innovation and SuCo using a network-based approach. Findings highlight the importance of integration, where innovative solutions in construction go beyond the traditional ways in order to match environmental gains with economic gains.

Chapter 6 raises the importance of securing construction innovation from the vantage point of 'organisational sustainability' and the organisation's role of delivering value to its core stakeholders. It therefore provides readers with an insight into the concepts of SCM, and how this can be applied innovatively to derive value-added processes and organisational sustainability. Organisational value is discussed, highlighting the importance this can have on securing competitive advantage, especially using knowledge chains, value chains and human capital chains. Thus, an important factor here is understanding the pivotal links and dependencies that SCM can have on leveraging construction innovation from several settings, not least efficiency, value delivery, social support aspects and through sustainability issues. A case study is used to present the transformational impact of SCM, and how this led to sustainable competitive advantage. Research findings highlight the importance of supply chains, and how the industry as a whole could learn from other industries, in order to garner additional value and sustainability benefits.

1.4   Construction Innovation: Process Drivers

The drivers of construction innovation leading to process improvement were categorised by Bossink (2004) as being environmental pressure, technological capability, knowledge exchange, and boundary spanning. Whilst these innovation drivers in these categories can be considered to be active at trans-firm, intra-firm and inter-firm levels, it is equally important to acknowledge the importance that external pressures place on firms to achieve innovation. Technological capability can enable organisations to experiment with and use innovative applications and methods in their construction projects; whereas, knowledge exchange represents the development and sharing of knowledge and expertise in and between organisations, and boundary spanning represents the capability of institutions and organisations to co-innovate with other institutions and organisations. These are all essential ingredients of innovation. Given this, Widén (2010) identified two approaches for driving innovation: client-driven innovation through required innovative solutions, processes, etc, and innovation secured through procurement forms applied. On a similar theme, Stewart and Fenn (2006) noted that construction innovation tended to focus on product innovations, which did not take into account strategic innovation, nor the kind of innovation required for value-adding innovations that could procure competitive advantage. They concluded that a strategic perspective on innovation and strategic thinking was needed to motivate the organisation to look beyond the product and process to the entire system for delivering value to the customer.

Part II of this book, therefore addresses innovation and process improvement driver topics, including strategic management, concurrent engineering, risk management, innovative procurement and knowledge management.

Chapter 7 explores the importance of strategic management on process improvement, especially how strategy can be purposefully aligned to deliver innovation opportunities. It explores the fluidity of the construction sector, and the need for organisations to continually re-visit their business models, especially cognisant of market forces, and the need to align corporate competence and capability to strategic trajectories in order to secure competitive advantage. In this respect, the concepts and application of strategy is reviewed from a business performance perspective, highlighting the importance of identifying appropriate performance metrics for subsequent review. A case study is presented for discussion, which identified the strategic challenges faced by one construction company, and the solution put in place to manage competing drivers and external forces. Research findings highlight the importance of developing strategies that have a clear focus and readily identifiable objectives and deliverables, and the need to understand how strategy (strategic positioning), skills (intellectual capital), ICT (alignment to strategy) and process (understanding) all interrelate.

Chapter 8 introduces the importance of integrating risk management at the planning stage for process improvement. A major goal of most modern organisations is to meet or exceed the demands of clients, and many attempts have been made to achieve this with various degrees of success. In this respect, it is advocated that the absence of standardised process improvement methodologies are partly attributable. This chapter critically reviews the extant literature on process improvement and risk management, and identifies failures associated with project and process improvement initiatives. It advocates the need to have clearly articulated mechanisms in place to help organisational performance, as it is posited that risk predominantly emanates from uncertainties associated with pursuing certain causes of action. The need for risk management integration when planning for process improvement is therefore seen as an important lever, as organisations need to be able to understand and differentiate their core/value-creation business processes and supportive processes. Research findings also note the importance of understanding the decisions made; particularly why improvement interventions are required, as this can help create acceptance, and also help secure other desired results such as competitiveness, improved customer satisfaction levels, enhanced profitability, etc.

Chapter 9 explores the need for the construction industry to change. It introduces Modern Method of Construction and Offsite Production approaches as exemplars for discussion that, from an innovation point of view, is seen as means for both improving and changing the construction industry's thinking and practices. The manufacturing concept and offsite production approaches are explored from a strategic as well as from an implementation perspective, in order to identify the requirements needed to help overcome the industry's inherent problems. This is also advocated as a means of promoting the construction industry and overcoming skill shortages. The need for change is presented, supported by a number of initiatives taken from other industries. A conceptual model is presented for discussion based on four core dimensions: people, product, technology and process. This is promoted as a way of evaluating 'process', 'people', 'technology', 'product', 'market' and 'risk'. Research findings identify the need to secure a common 'language' across the different stakeholder groups, along with a need to share a collective view and understanding of offsite production practices.

Chapter 10 introduces the role of knowledge management in organisations, especially how this can be used to deliver innovation and secure competitive advantage. It identifies how knowledge management impacts upon innovations in project-based environments, and the challenges faced in managing this using effective knowledge management practices. These challenges are discussed, and solutions offered, particularly the need to recognise the constraints imposed on knowledge management processes by the project environments; and to determine new means of creating, transferring, sharing, implementing and exploiting individual and project knowledge. Effective knowledge management practices are advocated to include a number of core areas, including networking, Communities of Practice, storytelling, coaching, mentoring and quality circles (to share and transfer tacit knowledge through organisational/project environments). Many factors currently confront construction organisations in the management of knowledge assets, including organisational culture and maturity, strategic decision making, existing and future capabilities, financial and technological capabilities, and the effect of internal and environment stimuli. These are all seen as being inextricably linked.

Chapter 11 presents the role of procurement to innovation, particularly in relation to the criteria needed and choice of innovative procurement methods available. Traditional approaches to procurement usually involve a chain of separate firms who add value to items purchased from other organisations through 'arms-length' one-off contracts. The use of collaborative procurement methods to deliver innovation is often employed because of the shortcomings of conventional procurement methods, and collaborative relationships have brought advantages to several companies in many industries. Consequently, there is an increasing use of collaborative working relationships, including partnering, joint ventures, strategic alliances and public private partnerships. These arrangements are evaluated and discussed, using exemplars from literature to highlight success areas. The use of integrated teams is a common feature of collaborative arrangements; and by involving the team at the earliest stage in a project, improvements are advocated in quality, productivity, health and safety, cash flow, reduced project durations, and more clearly identifiable risks. It concludes by noting that different collaborative relationships can deliver real (tangible) innovation and process improvements, but that such collaboration methods need to be carefully considered to ensure that they fit into the business plans of all contributory organisations.

Chapter 12 presents the key issues and technologies needed for the adoption of concurrent engineering in construction. It explores the concepts of concurrent engineering, and explains how this can be used to secure construction innovation and process improvement in the industry. Implementation issues are identified, emphasising the need to adopt new ways of working, as this requires a change in culture and practice with respect to integration (tools, processes, teams, etc). This also requires up-front consideration of life-cycle issues in the project development process, in order to bring about change using new methods and techniques. The critical enablers of concurrent engineering adoption within the industry are seen as being predominantly 'organisational', and 'technical', albeit acknowledged as also being influenced by many other issues, including procurement. Research findings present the importance of adopting a multi-facetted approach to concurrent engineering on order to leverage key benefits, but also mitigate potential barriers to adoption.

Chapter 13 explores complexity theory, and its relationship with the various aspects of the built environment, particularly how this can be used to leverage innovation. It overviews the development of complexity and identifies where entangled complexity interacts with construction processes. Complexity on organisations is then examined, along with toolkits and models for explication. This presents the transition of complexity to innovation and performance improvement, using worked exemplars as paradigms for exploitation. A case study covering five building phases is presented for discussion. This identifies how the different types of complexity affect building processes using an aggregate scoring matrix. It concludes by noting that whilst complexity in the built environment is still maturing, there is a greater need to understand the systems, procedures, processes, and interactions of variables, in order to learn from the past and generate solutions for the future.

1.5   Construction Innovation: Future Technologies

Han (2005) noted that the future of the industry is poised to take full advantage of the ever-increasing information and automation technologies, to advance the level of quality, efficiency, technical performance and safety. Moreover, that design, construction, as well as manufacturing and onsite application techniques, are becoming more intelligent, integrated and automated. On this theme, Boddy and Abbott (2010) identified a series of drivers, challenges and solutions including:

- ICT for construction;
- industrial research leadership and sponsorship;
- offsite manufacturing;
- material developments;
- flexibility and configurability of facilities;
- professional clients;
- virtual prototyping; and
- inspiration from nature.

Similarly, Aouad *et al.* (2010) noted that the capacity of the construction industry to innovate in response to the number of external drivers and consequent challenges could be measured by the effectiveness with which appropriate solutions were developed. Some of the solutions offered included the use of ICT; asserting that innovation platforms are needed to integrate a range of technologies to better coordinate policy and procurement, in line with a construction vision that would respond to the emerging needs of the world and construction industry in the future. Given the importance of innovation in construction, it is important to acknowledge that this can be supported by a number of collaborative networks, leveraged through methods such as open innovation, micro-innovation, open source solutions, road mapping and value mapping (CSaP, 2011).

Part III of this book explores future technologies in construction – especially, how these can be harnessed and leveraged to help procure innovation and process improvement.

Chapter 14 presents the use of tangible, immersive and interactive virtual reality interfaces as a viable solution for promoting the integration of data simulation and communication through the whole design and construction processes (to improve designers' cognition and collaboration). These interfaces are acknowledged as being able to provide intuitive interaction that supports 'free' artistic expression, and bridge the gap between artistic experimentation and accurate manufacturing-oriented modelling. This is introduced as a means of proactively fostering multidisciplinary teamwork in order to enhance outcomes in collaborative arrangements. Moreover, it is asserted that this could also contribute towards transforming the conceptual architectural design phase, thereby enabling project teams to generate and test new ideas and introduce innovation into the design and construction process. A number of design visualisation and simulation tools are evaluated, along with cognitive approaches to design. A case study is introduced that investigates designers' spatial cognition, collaboration and creativity. Core findings highlight the importance of enabling stakeholders to proactively engage in these developments as part of the project development lifecycle, especially in collaborative environments that are geographically dispersed.

Chapter 15 posits that the next generation of virtual prototyping systems will need to draw heavily upon multiple configurable knowledge sources in order to cope with the complexity that traditionally characterises construction projects (as existing construction planning methods do not adequately represent or communicate the spatial and temporal aspects of construction schedules effectively). It explores the complex nature of construction projects, and evaluates various construction planning and virtual prototyping tools available, including the impact of building information models and other emergent knowledge models. A prototype system is presented for discussion, highlighting how this can be used to support innovation in modern construction management processes. Research findings advocate the need for managers to take a wider and more strategic role, especially where their capacity to visualise and understand the implications of alternative decision choices is made clearer through the convergence of emerging digital tools. This will also help support envisioning in order to improve innovation processes. To support this, a framework is advocated that can integrate multiple applications through a project model database with knowledge-based support to handle cross-application business processes.

Chapter 16 presents the importance of e-readiness to construction firms. It highlights the current challenges facing the industry, and explores the relationship between business drivers and technological solutions. Given this, it is posited that there is an exigent need to build capability and capacity in information and communication technology (ICT) with organisational structures. This requires a thorough understanding of the link between 'business process and ICT', 'people and ICT', 'business process and implementation' and 'e-readiness'. These issues are all explored, highlighting the need to define the term 'organisational readiness' in construction. Three core themes (People, Process and Technology) are presented as a viable way forward, supported by five core enablers (Leadership & Empowerment, Change Management, Business & Information Process, Policy/Strategy/Vision, and ICT Sharability/Inter-operability). Research findings highlight the importance of securing sustained e-business initiatives. However, this is posited as needing effective measures and systems in place to design, develop, deliver and evaluate these.

Chapter 17 introduces Building Information Modelling (BIM) as a formal conduit for storing and managing building information through all stages of a project's lifecycle (from conception to demolition/disassembly). It is advocated that the implementation of the BIM paradigm can enable information exchange of several applications through agreed models (i.e. schema standards), in order to optimise these phases. The development and use of BIM is evaluated, particularly from an inter-operability, integration and data sharing perspective. Two case studies using BIM are presented for discussion. These present a number of significant findings, not least the need to establish data veracity and protocols through a formal BIM strategy. It is also advocated to create more efficient team working, enhance collaboration, secure better coordination (especially in complicated projects), and add value by automating most of the information management processes. It is noted that innovation can be secured through BIM, either through direct implementation, or through newly emerging technologies (i.e. cloud computing, sensor network, web services, etc).

Chapter 18 discusses the need for the industry to evaluate the way in which it manages projects (as these have changed significantly over the past few years), especially with advances in technology, and the increased prevalence of web-based project collaboration technologies and project extranets. This has created a fundamental need to re-visit the way in which skills and competence are designed and delivered to meet business and learners' needs. Given this, learning and training developments are explored, with particular emphasis placed on the way through which learning pedagogy has evolved; especially the current trends in learning styles and models, including the game theory approach. Developments in virtual reality systems are then evaluated, and a virtual construction site simulator is presented as a case study for discussion. This presents a development framework, along with supportive rubrics for aligning learning outcomes to actual work-based scenarios. Research findings note the importance of being able to train professionals in 'safe' and 'controlled' environments. Moreover, it is posited that future developments in simulated virtual reality environments may be able to diagnose learner styles, in order to deliver bespoke training material to individual learner types.

1.6   Conclusion

Innovation in construction is essential. The industry has continued to strive to remain competitive using a variety of approaches. It is therefore asserted that a paradigm shift in thinking is now required, which proactively engages structured initiatives that purposefully align to proven innovation concepts, techniques and applications. The higher the levels of innovation garnered, the greater the likelihood that this will in turn generate economic growth (Balyse and Manley, 2004; Gambatese and Hallowell, 2011). Continuous process improvement is also likely to play a major role in this (to achieve significant productivity improvement), along with the role of people, process and technology. These need to be linked and integrated in order to ensure that innovation enablers are cogently aligned to measurable process improvement initiatives. Finally, it is important to acknowledge that the incumbent industry stakeholders and governmental bodies are likely to influence and drive construction innovation, the remit of which will require new thinking to traditional approaches and the adoption of new workable relationships.

This book therefore emphasises the role of innovation and process improvement in construction through 18 chapters. These chapters explore the theory and practice of innovation and process improvement initiatives needed, and highlight the future technologies and formal mechanisms needed to support and deliver them.

References

Aouad, G., Ozorhon, B. & Abbott, C. (2010) Facilitating innovation in construction: Directions and implications for research and policy. *Construction Innovation: Information, Process, Management*, **10**(4), 374–394.

Banwell, H. (1964) *Report of the Committee on the Placing and Management of Contracts for Building and Civil Engineering Works*. HMSO, London.

Barlow, J. & Jashpara, A. (1998) Organisational Learning and Inter-Firm Partnering in the UK Construction Industry. *The Learning Organisation*, **5**(2), 86–98.

Blayse, A.M. & Manley, K. (2004) Key influences on construction innovation. *Construction Innovation: Information, Process, Management*, **4**(3),143–154.

Boddy, S. & Abbott, C. (2010) *Review of CIB Collected Outlook Reports, CIB Publication 334*. CIB, Rotterdam. Available from http://cibworld.xs4all.nl/dl/publications/pub334.pdf (assessed August 2011).

Bossink, B.A.G. (2004) Managing drivers of innovation in construction networks. *Journal of Construction Engineering and Management*, **130**(3), 337–345.

Construction Excellence (2009) *Never Waste a Good Crisis: A Review of Progress since 'Rethinking Construction' and Thoughts for Our Future*. Construction Excellence in Built Environment, London.

CSaP (2011) *Drivers, Challenges and Approaches to Innovation in the Construction Sector*, Professor Jeremy Watson, CONNECTIONS Lecture Series, 11 March, Centre for Science and Policy, University of Cambridge, Cambridge.

DTI (2011) *Process Understanding and Improvement*. Available from http://www.businessballs.com/dtiresources/TQM_process_management.pdf (accessed July 2011).

DTI (2003) *Innovation Report – Competing in the Global Economy: The Innovation Challenge*. HMSO, London.

Egan, J. (1998) *Rethinking Construction*. UK Department of the Environment, Transport and the Regions, HMSO, London.

Egbu, C.O., Henry, J., Kaye, G.R, Quintas, P., Schumacher, T.R. & Young, B.A. (1998) Managing organisational innovations in construction. In: *Proceedings of the 14th Annual Conference of the Association of Researchers in Construction Management*, ed. Hughes W. ARCOM, Reading, 605–614.

Fairclough, J. (2002) Rethinking construction innovation and research: a review of government R&D policies and practices. Department of Trade and Industry. Available from http://www.bis.gov.uk/files/file14364.pdf (accessed August 2011).

Gambatese, J.A. & Hallowell, M. (2011) Enabling and measuring innovation in the construction industry. *Construction Management and Economics*, **29**(6), 553–567.

Gann, D.M. & Salter, A. (2010) Innovation in project-based, service-enhanced firms: the construction of complex products and systems. *Research Policy*, **29**(7/8), 955–972.

Han, H. (2005) *Automated Construction Technologies: Analyses and Future Development Strategies*. Unpublished PhD Thesis, Massachusetts Institute of Technology, Department of Architecture, USA.

Latham, M. (1994) *Constructing the Team, Joint Review of Procurement and Contractual Arrangements in the United Kingdom, Construction Industry*. HMSO, London.

Ling, F.Y. (2003) Managing the implementation of construction innovations. *Construction Management and Economics*. **21**(6), 635–649.

Panuwatwanich, K., Stewart, R.A. & Mohamed, S. (2008) Validation of an empirical model for innovation diffusion in Australian design firms. *Construction Innovation: Information, Process, Management*, **9**(4), 449–467.

Sarshar, M., Haigh, R. & Amaratunga, D. (2004) Improving project process: Best practice case study. *Construction Innovation*, **4**, 69–92.

Sexton, M. & Barrett, P. (2003) Performance-based building and innovation: balancing client and industry Needs. *Building Research and Information*, **33**(2), 142–148.

Sidwell, A.C., Kennedy, R.J. & Chan, A.P.C. (2004) *Reengineering construction delivery process*. Report, January, Construction Industry Institute, Queensland University of Technology, Brisbane.

Slaugher, E.S. (1998) Models of construction innovation. *Journal of Construction Engineering and Management*, **124**(3), 226–232.

Stewart, I. & Fenn, P. (2006) Strategy: The motivation for innovation. *Construction Innovation*, **6**, 173–185

Van de Ven, A.H. (1986) Central problems in the management of innovation. *Management Science*. **32**(5), 590–607.

Vennstrom, A. & Eriksson, P.E. (2010) Client perceived barriers to change of the construction process. *Construction Innovation*, **10**(2), 126–137.

Widén, K. (2010) *Construction Innovation – Statsbygg, the Driving Client*. Report, Lund University, Division of Construction Management, Lund.

Construction Innovation through Change Management

Girma Zawdie

Van de Ven (1986) refers to innovation as the transformation of 'new ideas into good currency'. Innovation is also viewed as a systemic phenomenon resulting from processes in which a whole range of players interact, influencing the direction of change, and also the speed with which this is effected (Freeman, 1987; Lundvall, 1992). At the heart of these interactions underlying the innovation process are evolving systems of organisation and management at both the micro and macro levels of decision making. At the micro level, the ways in which enterprises are organised and managed have significant bearing on the extent to which the enterprises engage in knowledge exchange and its use for them to be able to realise their innovative potential and establish themselves as pace setters in emerging industrial and market trends. At the macro level, innovation possibilities are contingent on the way the complex social functions of wealth creation, knowledge production and systems of regulation and governance are organised and managed to reinforce each other to generate a culture of innovation (Leydesdorff and Zawdie, 2010). Thus, for innovation to occur on a sustainable basis, change of organisation and management cultures is essential at all levels, so that social interactions and functions that underpin creativity and innovativeness are least constrained. In other words, when systems evolve as a managed and organised process, they create the condition for innovation (Jones *et al.*, 2004; Tourish and Hargie, 2004).

Innovation is sought not as an end in itself, but to provide a sustainable basis for the achievement of industrial competitiveness that is reflected in terms of improvements in the quality, cost, delivery time, as well as the social and environmental impact of production. However, innovation does not occur in a vacuum. There is *inter-alia*, a cultural and institutional context

Construction Innovation and Process Improvement, First Edition.
Edited by Akintola Akintoye, Jack S. Goulding and Girma Zawdie.
© 2012 Blackwell Publishing Ltd. Published 2012 by Blackwell Publishing Ltd.

to it, which defines the characteristics of the institutions and organisational systems within which industrial activities take place. The occurrence of innovation would therefore presume a shift in cultural and institutional modes, which introduce the flexibility required for the generation of new ideas. This would make innovation necessarily contingent upon changes in industrial culture. In this respect, industrial cultures vary across sectors with respect to the ways in which activities are organised and managed. This difference may largely explain why some categories of activity (i.e. firms in the manufacturing industry) are more innovation-active than others (i.e. firms in the construction industry) and why some are pioneers and others followers. However, openness to change through management initiatives allows organisational learning to take place, resulting in the accretion of organisational knowledge and the development of organisational core competence (Stonehouse and Pemberton, 1999). The process of learning itself evolves over time, first reactively by emulating others – a process referred to as 'single loop' learning (Argyris and Schon, 1978) – and later proactively by exercising creativity through more complex learning processes – i.e. the 'double loop' mode (Argyris et al., 1985; Argyris, 1996) and the 'triple loop' mode (Flood and Romm, 1996; Snell and Man-Kuen Chak, 1998). Where critical and creative learning of the double loop and triple loop type takes root, those who were once followers in some areas of activity can later become leaders in other areas of activity. Indeed, with the ever increasing scope for knowledge generation, knowledge transfer and exchange, and organisational learning in contemporary society and economy, industries like construction that were traditionally considered to be 'innovation-inactive' in relation to manufacturing (Marosszeky, 1999), can no longer be seen to be so, given the nature of the dynamics in learning and the innovation process.

The case for innovation is heightened because of the growing need to enhance competitiveness of activities across the industrial spectrum, not least the construction sector. In the UK, concern about innovation in the construction industry has grown, particularly over the last couple of decades, in the wake of initiatives, including the Latham Report (1994), the Egan Report (1998), the Strategic Forum for Construction (2002) and, more recently, Construction Excellence (2009). These initiatives have been at one in their drive to stimulate innovative activities in the industry through changes in organisation and management systems, and also through their consideration of the implications of these changes for the competitiveness of industry and for the design of institutional mechanisms and policy frameworks to underpin innovation and organisational learning. However, compared with firms in the manufacturing sector, construction firms, in general, have traditionally been slow in terms of innovation performance (Marosszeky, 1999). This raises questions about the structural and cultural characteristics of the construction industry – namely, the fragmentation of the industry along the supply chain, and the adversarial relations underlying activities within the industry. It also at the same time highlights the challenge for innovation and change management in construction.

In view of these questions, this chapter explores a number of issues, including cultural context, differences in firms' with respect to the propensity to innovate, supply chain dynamics, knowledge infrastructure evolution and technological trajectories (Dosi, 1982; Leydesdorff and Zawdie, 2010). The concept of innovation is explored as a system, showing how the perspectives on innovation have evolved, followed by a discussion of the cultural context of innovation and the challenge it poses for innovation management. The chapter then looks into the experience of the construction industry in the UK in the light of recent initiatives aimed at promoting a culture of innovation, and enhancing management of change at enterprise level, and discusses management strategies that could facilitate the innovation process in construction firms. The chapter concludes by highlighting issues that are critical for change management strategies in the construction business.

2.2   The Innovation Process: Evolution as a Systemic Phenomenon

Innovation in construction, as in other areas of industrial activity, is sought as a strategy for enhancing competitiveness for firms, 'value for money' for clients, and sustainability for the economy and the environment. A first step in an attempt to influence the speed and direction of innovation would be to understand the concept in its broader context. The significance of innovation is not only in the innovated product or service, but also in the innovation process itself. The latter involves a complex set of interactions between a wide range of factors that relate to the prevailing social, economic, political and technological cultures. This view, which broadens the area of focus from the output to the process aspect of innovation, aims to capture the full extent of the dynamics in the innovation process. Management of innovation is, strictly speaking, as good as the understanding of the concept itself, which has changed significantly over the years with changes in conceptual perspectives.

2.2.1   Linear Approach to Innovation

Innovation, both as a product and a process, was first formally conceptualised in the context of the socio-economic system by Joseph Schumpeter (1934), essentially as a 'supply push' phenomenon. For Schumpeter, the innovation process starts with the entrepreneur who is endowed with the capability to generate new ideas about 'new combinations' or new ways of doing things. Supply, it is implicitly assumed, will create its own demand, much in line with the Emersonian tenet that if one made a better mousetrap, the whole world would beat a path to one's doorstep. As such, Schumpeter's conception of the innovation process would evolve linearly, starting with invention (new ideas), and leading to the translation of new ideas into innovation through the process of design, engineering and pilot production. It was then assumed that innovated products and services would enter the market in fully blown form through the diffusion mechanism, thus leaving no scope for the occurrence of incremental innovations via market-driven feedback loops. Innovation in the Schumpeterian sense is thus conceived to be a radical departure from existing 'combinations' or ways of doing things. It is an 'epoch making' event driven by the entrepreneur, occurring discontinuously through 'fits and starts' – a process Schumpeter (1934) refers to as the 'gale of creative destruction'.

The linear approach based on Schumpeter's (1934) trilogy of invention, innovation and diffusion – which Gibbons *et al.* (1994) relate to their Mode 1 paradigm of innovation – is not, however, without conceptual limitations. First, while Schumpeter (1934) acknowledges the dynamism inherent in the innovation process, the conceptualisation of the process in a trilogy of events effectively isolates innovation from the wider socio-economic and cultural milieu that is crucial for the comprehensive realisation of innovation. The linear approach conceptually fragments the innovation process and strips it of the systemic framework within which all players in the innovation process are interactively linked, as in the Mode 2 paradigm of innovation (Gibbons *et al.* 1994). This is a significant omission in as much as innovation is a product of 'a series of simultaneous activities undertaken by a number of firms, often in close co-operation with the users of the innovation and with the collaboration of other institutions, such as universities and public research bodies' (Kozul-Wright, 1995). Second, by precluding 'incremental innovation' from the definition of innovation, Schumpeter's linear approach discounts the significance of the learning process and the accumulation of knowledge, and hence the dynamism at the heart of the innovation process. Most incremental innovations are a product of 'market pull' or 'demand pull', which start from the articulation of market need in the form of ideas and, once developed, are manufactured for diffusion. Incremental innovations, which may or may not be patentable, account for the bulk of innovation observed across firms, sectors and countries. Whereas, Schumpeter fell short of recognising the significance of this category of innovation, neo-Schumpeterians such as Schmookler (1966), Freeman (1987) and Lundvall (1985), among others, have given it pride of place in contemporary innovation literature. Third, the presumption that the market remains at the receiving end, and that all that matters in the innovation process is 'supply push', is empirically untenable in view of the burden of historical evidence that necessity has almost invariably been the mother of invention (Schmookler, 1966).

The linear approach to innovation nonetheless produced the first generation of innovation studies in the form of the 'supply push' or 'technology/science push' model, and the second-generation thinking in the form of the 'demand pull' model (Figure 2.1). These early generation models dominated the innovation literature in the 1950s and 1960s. However, the 'supply push' and 'demand pull' systems, which respectively constituted the first- and second-generation innovation studies, were conceived as sequentially separable stages with no feedback loops, which made them appear as competitive approaches to innovation rather than complementary aspects of

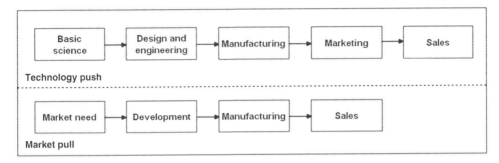

Figure 2.1   First & Second generation studies: Supply/technology push and market pull (Rothwell, 1994).

an integrated system of innovation. Lundvall (1985) viewed the two linear approaches to be no better than a 'black box', as they failed to give a full understanding of the innovation system underlying industrial activities. Moreover, the linear approach failed to capture the full extent of the complexity of the institutional context of innovation, and thus made no allowance for change management and organisational learning as the basis for innovation at the level of the firm. It is, at best, a naïve abstraction of the complex innovation process.

2.2.2   Non-Linear Approach to Innovation

A comprehensive approach to innovation is provided by what has come to be known as the innovation systems framework. This is akin to the Mode 2 paradigm of innovation proposed by Gibbons *et al.* (1994). Whereas the linear approach to innovation is based on a division of labour between 'knowledge search' and 'knowledge use', the non-linear approach is based on the understanding that knowledge cannot be independently produced in specialised research organisations and then transferred to passive users. The production and use of knowledge is a complex process, often requiring technical, social and institutional changes involving the interaction of actors across the knowledge producer-user network (Douthwaite, 2002). This approach places innovation and its producers and users in a socio-economic and cultural context and accounts for the stakeholders and partnerships, which, through their interactions, influence the innovation process. Thus, in the non-linear system of innovation, institutional and organisational factors underlying the innovation process are not assumed to be fixed or given as optimal, as in the linear system. Rather, these are expected to evolve to suit prevailing local circumstances, including stakeholders' perspectives and policy imperatives (Hall, 2002). Galbraith (1982) argues that whether it is driven by 'technology/supply push' or 'market pull', the innovation process involves knowledge of all the major elements simultaneously coupled with interactive communication paths. At an organisational level, Galbraith asserted that innovation usually occurred in groups of knowledge specialists

(a) Simultaneous coupling of knowledge by Galbraith

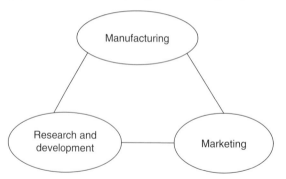

(b) The 'coupling model' of innovation by Rothwell

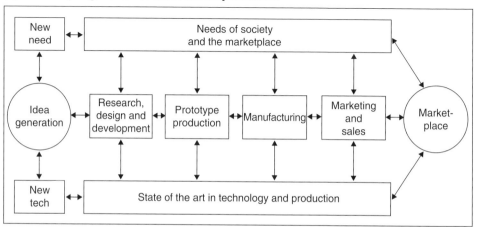

Figure 2.2   Third-generation of innovation system – the coupling model (Galbraith, 1982; Rothwell, 1994).

combined together. While the first- and second-generation innovation studies limited inputs to the innovation process from multiple knowledge sources, the third-generation studies (Galbraith, 1982) include feedback loops as communication paths generating internal inputs (e.g. idea generation, new technology, etc) and external inputs (market needs, social needs, etc) for the innovation process. This is called the 'coupling model' (Figure 2.2), in which all components connect as a complex, interactive network of technological capability, and market and social needs.

However, the coupling model does not provide information of external resources of knowledge derived from the business network and supply chain, which is particularly important, in view of the experience of large as well as small innovative firms engaging in intensive external networking activity (Rothwell, 1994). Firms would engage in external networking activities to enhance their organisational learning and knowledge sharing capability, as these are crucial factors underpinning innovation at the level of the firm. In other words, the effectiveness of external networking in terms of innovation

Figure 2.3   Integrated (fourth-generation) innovation process (Rothwell, 1994).

is contingent on the integration of activities across the organisational structure of the firm. Therefore, a fourth generation of innovation studies emerged, focusing on the parallel and integrated nature of the internal features of the innovation process at the level of the firm. This parallel and integrated system of activities within the firm (Figure 2.3) provides the basis for external interactions and strategic business alliances that are featured in the third generation of innovation system. The fourth-generation model thus adds to the third-generation model, integrating suppliers collaborating in new product design and development processes at an early stage; while at the same time integrates the activities of the different in-house departments that work on the project in parallel rather than sequentially, as in the automotive and electronic industries in Japan (Graves, 1987; Dodgson *et al.*, 2002). The integration of parallel or simultaneous activities within the firm allows intensive information and knowledge exchange among the various departments, which is crucial for organisational learning, organisational synergy and innovation.

The fifth-generation model of innovation (Rothwell, 1994) involves a 'process of system integration and networking', which, though developed based on the fourth-generation model, emphasises continuous change and improvement. A distinguishing aspect of the model is its dynamic nature. It addresses strategic elements, including time and cost management, corporate flexibility and responsibility, customer focus, electronic data processing, and quality management policy that reinforce the firm's technological capability (Galanakis, 2006). Rothwell's fifth generation of innovation, which portrays innovation as a systemic and dynamical process involving the interaction of players, mainly focuses on innovation at the level of the firm, thus making the point that innovation activities are essentially firm-led. Following Rothwell's typology, some scholars have tried to conceptualise a sixth-generation innovation model. For example, Chaminade and Roberts (2002) proposed a model that included intangible factors, such as social capital, to facilitate the sharing of tacit knowledge, interactive learning and social

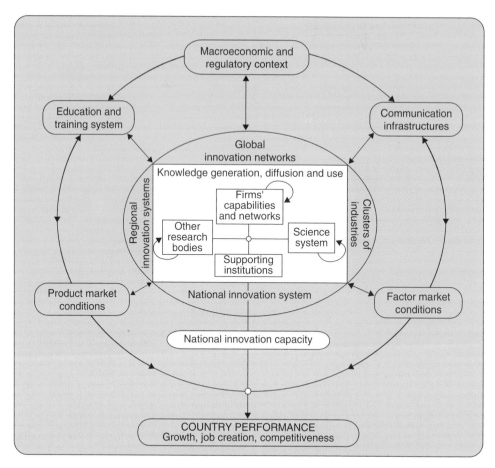

Figure 2.4   Actors and linkages in the national innovation system (OECD, 1999).

network development in an innovation system. Marinova and Phillimore (2003) also sought to extend Rothwell's typology through their contribution of the so-called 'innovative milieux' to the sixth-generation model. Their model focuses on the importance of geographical proximity and environmental conditions that facilitate knowledge generation and diffusion in certain localities. The model thus seeks to explain why innovative firms are concentrated in some locations or regions, and is similar to the concepts of innovation cluster (Porter, 1990), learning region (Florida, 1995; Morgan 1997), and regional innovation system (Cooke and Morgan, 1994; Cooke *et al.*, 1997).

The non-linear approach to innovation provided the basis for the development of the concept of 'national innovation system' (NIS) (Figure 2.4), which was first proposed by Freeman (1987) and later developed by Lundvall (1992). According to the NIS, innovation emerges from evolving systems of participants in the generation and application of knowledge. The essential elements of the system constitute interactive learning as a socially embedded process that cannot be understood without reference to its institutional and cultural context. The 'innovation system' concept thus provides a framework for exploring patterns of partnerships, revealing and managing the institutional context that governs relationships and processes, understanding research and innovation as a social process of learning, thinking about capacity development in a systems sense and linking the wide range of actors in a network with the view to promoting innovation (Hall, 2002).

The systems approach conceptualises innovation not merely in terms of output, but as a multi-dimensional, multi-directional and multi-causal process, requiring linkages and feedback mechanisms between a variety of activities both within and outside the firm (Jorde and Teece, 1990; Morroni, 1992). In the systems approach, the issue facing management of change is not whether the focus should be on the 'supply-push' or 'demand pull' aspects of innovation, but how best the complementarities between the two aspects can be exploited by matching shifts in knowledge/technology and market frontiers, since 'demand pull' and 'supply push' are, in the final analysis, part and parcel of the same dynamical innovation process (Dosi, 1982; Rothwell, 1994; Dodgson, *et al.*, 2002).

In a socio-economic system, the social functions of wealth creation, organised knowledge production and governance are fulfilled through the institution of the market integrating forces of supply and demand; the knowledge sphere, which through the provision of knowledge infrastructure in the form of R&D, skill development, etc, determine the scope for technological opportunities; and institutions of regulation and control, which, through interaction with the institution of the market, define the limits of 'selection environments' (Leydesdorff and Zawdie, 2010). These institutional actors represent the 'selection mechanisms', which, by interacting continuously and recursively, determine the scope for the management of change and technological trajectories, and act as a bridge between 'technology push' and 'demand pull' theories (Nelson and Winter, 1977, 1982; Dosi, 1982; Freeman and Perez, 1988). According to Dosi (1982), given a set of technological possibilities (paradigms) allowed by science, economic forces, together with institutional and social factors, operate as a 'selective device to choose the preferred path from a much larger set of possible ones'. Once a path (trajectory) is selected and established as a result of management of change, the trajectory evolves with 'a momentum of its own', enforcing the direction towards which "the problem solving activity" moves' (Dosi, 1982). Insofar as technological trajectories lock in selected values and systems, which could evolve into a culture of vested interests, they can pose a challenge to the management of change and, indeed, to further innovation.

2.3   Role of Culture as Challenge for Change Management and Innovation

The systems approach to innovation brings to light the importance of social processes and cultural changes as critical factors underlying the innovation process. Cultural changes affect the various aspects of social relations and modes of production. Thus, the way social and economic activities are organised and managed would be expected to reflect dominant cultures and practices that are subject to forces of change. On the other hand, innovation would occur either as a response to the needs of emergent cultures or as a reaction to a once dominant culture, which has now lost its way. Where dominant cultures prove to be resistant to change, they block opportunities for innovation. However, the focus here is on the culture of innovation. What, it may be asked, makes the culture of innovation?

2.3.1   Innovation Culture

In Schumpeter (1934), there is a clear distinction between the culture of the entrepreneurs, who lead the innovation process, and that of the imitators who follow the leaders. However, the roles of the actors in both categories are not fixed, so that those who were pioneers at one time could possibly be followers at another time in another event. Schumpeter's culture of the entrepreneur is unique and somewhat historical, insofar as it attributes the emergence of innovation to the inspiration of the occasional entrepreneurial genius, who achieves new ideas purely through the exercise of intuition and 'acts of insight' (Usher, 1954). This would make innovation the product of an entrepreneurial culture, albeit without social and historical content, so that its occurrence cannot be expected to be enhanced through policy intervention. Indeed, by this reckoning, innovation would fall outside the purview of strategic management function. Following this, Usher (1954) offered the culture of 'cumulative synthesis' as an alternative to the Schumpeterian scheme. In the Usher scheme, major 'epoch making' innovations are considered to arise from the 'cumulative synthesis' of relatively simple innovations, each of which required an individual 'act of insight' to come into being in the first place. Thus, in its entirety, the social process of innovation consists of 'acts of insight' of varying degrees of importance; and these acts converge in the course of time, culminating in a 'massive synthesis' that makes 'strategic innovation'. In comparison with the Schumpeterian view, a major advantage of the Usher scheme is that it allows conscious interventions aimed at increasing the speed or altering the direction of innovation. For example, by creating the appropriate R&D environment, the stage can be set so that only a few elements in the innovation process are left to chance. In other words, while innovation involves risk, it is not, however, essentially a purely random event. It is therefore appropriate to explain the factors that account for the making of innovation (or the absence of it) in an effort to enhance the effectiveness of management of change.

2.3.2   Organisation and Management Culture: Impact on Learning, Change and Innovation

The occurrence of change and innovation at the level of the firm is often influenced by the cultural underpinning of the organisational modes, management styles and organisational learning that define the scope or overarching environment for change within the firm. Culture influences change and innovation in proportion to the degree of resistance it poses against the counter-culture of agents of change, especially managers, project team members and consultants. Lewin (1958) explains the change process and the resistance to change envisaged thereof, as involving three steps. The first step in the process of changing behaviour associated with activities across the firm is to 'unfreeze' the existing situation. This ushers in the phase of transition, where movements take place with people having bought into the need for change. This stage examines the existing system to develop the new system through participatory approaches involving teamwork and active communication. Once the new system is in place, it would need to be embedded into the culture of the organisation in order for it to become routine. This is what Lewin (1958) refers to as the 'refreezing' stage. The task of 'refreezing' at this stage requires change agents to work actively with the people in the organisation to install the new system until the required new behaviours have replaced those that existed prior to change. Therefore, the cycle of change continues *ad infinitum* through the three steps of unfreezing, state of motion and refreezing. Following this theme, the process of change is not without incidences of conflict. It requires the organisation to be ready, not only to learn about new systems, but equally importantly not to forget some of its past (Dodgson, 1993; Prahalad and Hamel, 1994), or even obliterate all underperforming processes and structures through reengineering of business processes (Hammer, 1990; Hammer and Champy, 2003).

Figure 2.5 shows how the conflict in the crosscurrent of cultures can create opportunities for (and threats to) organisational change, thus creating

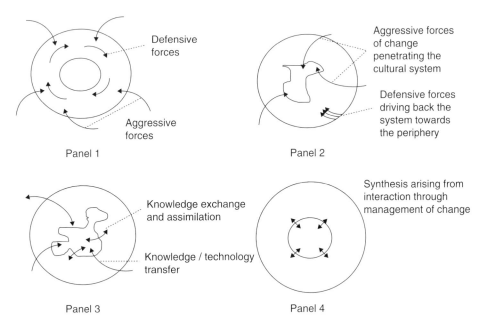

Figure 2.5 Culture of innovation evolution through change management (adapted from Zghal, 1996).

an environment for innovation. Panel 1 in Figure 2.5 is about the system of culture under attack by forces of change; Panel 2, about the disintegration of existing order under pressure of change; Panel 3, about a system in transition; and Panel 4, about a transformed state in which the round of innovation cycle is complete.

If change brings forth disequilibrium to the existing order of things, it is likely to be resisted by the culture that underpins the *status quo*. Hence, the conflict in the relationship between the aggressive forces of change (which often occur in the formation of new ideas) and the defensive forces of vested interest (who champion the moribund culture) as shown in Panel 1. The sustained pressure of change on the existing culture can force the breakdown of the system, as in Panels 2 and 3, thus giving way to the establishment of a transformed system, as in Panel 4. Therefore, at the firm level, culture can affect innovation through its influence on the modes of organisation and management. The organisational structure of firms can inhibit innovation when it is rigidly hierarchical, closed and restrictive, thus limiting the scope for information and knowledge exchange and for creativity to thrive. This would ensure that the dominant position of vested interests in the organisation is not compromised by the infiltration of new ideas. It is therefore in the interest of the 'insiders' (as in Panel 1) that the introduction of change by 'outsiders' is resisted.

The system of management at the level of the firm would either promote or inhibit innovation, depending on its commitment to change. Management styles, like organisational modes, are culture-conditioned. Basil and Cook (1974) identified three types of management mode, according to their implications for innovation and change. These include tradition-based, reform-oriented and change-oriented management types. Tradition-based management is characteristically closed, backward-looking and dependent on centralised and hierarchical approaches to decision making. It is therefore averse to reform, and *a fortiori* to radical changes. It is characteristically reactive and change resistant. Reform-oriented management is adaptive in character, so that it would be open to changes to the extent that these changes are capable of reforming and reinforcing existing structures and behavioural modes. On the other hand, 'change responsive' management is characteristically proactive and forward looking. It is capable of creating opportunities and encouraging the development of new ideas. This type of management is what Schumpeter (1934) would refer to as the harbinger or agency of 'creative destruction'. Change thus requires the removal of organisational and managerial barriers that would otherwise constrain creativity and the transmission of knowledge and information across individuals or groups. It therefore calls for a paradigm shift in the underlying culture and power structures at the level of the firm and in the wider cultural, institutional and policy environment that shapes the perspective of business behaviour at the micro level.

Change of organisational culture also requires organisational learning (Argyris and Schon, 1978; Fiol and Lyles, 1985; Huber, 1991; March, 1991; Dodgson, 1993). Organisational learning enhances the firm's adaptability to change, but it is also constrained by the prevalence of conflicts of interest within the organisation, as pressure is brought to bear on the organisation, not only to learn the new practices and the corresponding cultures, but also to unlearn or forget old ones (Prahalad and Hamel, 1994). Organisational learning, which results in the accumulation of organisational knowledge, occurs in three forms: single-loop learning, double-loop learning and deuteron-learning or triple-loop learning. Single-loop learning (Argyris and Schon, 1978) occurs reflexively as errors are detected and corrected without challenging the assumptions underlying the organisation's norms, procedures, policies and objectives. This particular mode of organisational learning is referred to as 'lower level learning' (Fiol and Lyles, 1985), 'adaptive learning' or learning by 'copying' (Senge, 1990a,b) and 'non-strategic learning' (Mason, 1993). Double-loop learning (Argyris and Schon, 1978; Argyris *et al.*, 1985; Argyris, 1990; 1992; 1994; 1996) occurs when, in addition to single-loop learning, the organisation's existing norms, procedures, policies and goals are challenged and modified. In this learning mode, the learning organisation is asking not merely if it is doing things the right way (which corresponds to single-loop learning), but more importantly, whether it is doing the right things. Double-loop learning changes the learning organisation's knowledge base or organisation-specific competences (Dodgson, 1993; Snell and Man-Kuen Chak, 1993; Stonehouse and Pemberton, 1999). Double-loop learning is also referred to as 'higher level learning' (Fiol and Lyles, 1985); 'generative learning' or learning to explain an organisation's capabilities (Senge 1990a,b); and 'strategic learning' (Mason, 1993). According to Mason (1993), strategic learning enables an organisation 'to make sense of its environment in ways that broaden the range of objectives it can pursue or the range of resources and actions available to it for pursuing the objectives'.

Argyris (1996) noted that most organisations have difficulties learning in the double-loop manner. Therefore, a third level of learning was proposed, namely 'duetero-learning', based on the ideas of Bateson (1973) or triple-loop learning (Flood and Romm, 1996; Snell and Man-Kuen Chak, 1998). Deutero-learning or triple-loop learning is about 'learning how to learn'. While single-loop learning is about rules (whether activities of the organisation are done right under the given set of assumptions, norms and beliefs), and double-loop learning about principles (whether the right things are being done), triple-loop learning is about strategies (how 'what is right' is decided). Triple-loop learning involves complexity thinking and as such, it is about 'increasing the fullness and deepness of learning about the diversity of issues and [the] dilemmas faced, by linking together all local units of learning in one overall learning infrastructure, as well as developing the competences and skills to use this infrastructure' (Flood and Romm, 1996). Triple-loop learning takes the form of 'collective mindfulness' (Romme and van Witteloostuijn, 1999) or 'awareness of ignorance or gaps' (Nevis *et al.*, 1995), which motivates members of the organisation to produce new structures and strategies for learning. If the appropriate environment, strategies and processes are not created, change through learning can be delayed or blocked for lack of good communication or feedback (Argyris, 1994). This problem of delays in feedback and communication, which retard organisational learning, can be mitigated by the introduction of a system of change management that is underpinned by information technology (IT) leveragability (Kittinger and Grover, 1995). Hammer (1990) would exploit the benefits arising from IT leveragability or of automation, say in the form of computerisation, not to prop up structures and processes that are outdated, but to 'reengineer' business processes through the promotion of organisational learning based on the deutero- or triple-loop learning mode. This reengineering of business processes is what constitutes change management as the 'handmaiden' of innovation.

2.4   General Framework for Change Management

Change management can be seen as 'reengineering business processes' by another name (Hammer, 1990; Hammer and Champy, 2003). Van de Ven (1986) found management of change and innovation as the 'most central concern' of chief executive officers (CEOs) of public and private firms in managing their enterprises. On this basis, a general management perspective on innovation would highlight four central problems CEOs have to contend with: the management of attention, the process problem of 'managing ideas into good currency', the structural problem of managing part-whole relationships and the strategic problem of institutional leadership.

2.4.1   Strategic Factors in Change Management

Management of attention is considered to be a crucial component of strategy for change insofar as people and organisations, if left to their own devices, would tend to be protective of existing practices rather than focusing their attention on the apparently risky task of developing new ideas. Indeed, it is difficult 'to trigger people's action thresholds to pay attention to new ideas, needs and opportunities' where organisations are well established facing little or no problems (Van de Ven, 1986). Under such circumstances, there is virtually no incentive for change; and if changes were desired, management would need to provide the conditions (incentives) that would motivate people to be proactive and attuned to making or accepting the changes. Thus, 'managing ideas into good currency' is, according to Van de Ven (1986), about implementing and institutionalising innovative ideas. This is where the 'selection mechanism' involving the coalition of interest groups and the associated social, economic and political dynamics come into play to determine the specific 'problem solving activity' through change and innovation.

The task of 'managing part-whole relationships' is based on the recognition that the fragmentation of efforts and responsibilities is an anathema to the innovation process, which involves multiple functions, resources and disciplines and calls for synergy through a process of integration. The systemic nature of innovation means that 'innovating within the parts while losing sight of the whole would be inherently dysfunctional' (Winch, 1998). The challenge for management, in this case, would be how to put the whole into the parts, and vice versa, to maximise the benefit of synergy. Management also has to provide institutional leadership that is capable of creating an infrastructure that is conducive to innovation. This is crucial, because 'innovations not only adapt to existing organisational and industrial arrangements (i.e. incremental innovations), but they also transform the structures and practices of these environments (i.e. radical innovations)' (Van de Ven, 1986). Given that innovation can be constrained by the state of organisational structure (Basil and Cook, 1974; Hankinson, 1999; Daft, 2001; Mullins, 2007) and organisational culture (Gagliardi, 1986; Silvester *et al.*, 1997; Line, 1999; Sardi and Lees, 2001), the strategic role of management in determining the scope for innovation at the level of the firm cannot be over-emphasised. For the culture of innovation to take root at the level of the firm, it is important for management to redesign and develop or reengineer (Hammer 1990; Hammer and Champy, 2003) organisational structures and processes, so that rigid hierarchical systems of control and outdated organisational structures are superseded by systems of operation and organisational structures with built-in flexibility. This would increase the scope for interaction between members of the organisation at all levels of operation through knowledge exchange; to promote transparency and engagement in shared decision-making systems; and encourage constructive conflict with the view to replacing the culture of conformity with a culture of change. A change-responsive management system with proactive orientation should spare no effort to redefine institutional roles and missions to encourage and provide opportunities for independent action and change. This would help re-orient individuals within the organisation to accept change and be part of the change process, through the provision of institutional support systems, such as education and training schemes geared to enabling individuals to adopt a change-responsive behaviour.

In summary, therefore, the requirement for change and innovation in the construction industry is generally influenced not only by clients' requirements to secure 'value for money', but also by the need to meet public safety standards; contractors' concern with the potential risk associated with the introduction of untried and untested methods and construction materials (Harvey and Ashworth, 1993); and the concern of policy for employment expansion, economic growth effectiveness and environmental sustainability. These can all be addressed through a dynamic framework of change management. For instance, where chronic market constraints prevail mainly as a consequence of income inelasticity of demand for products, change and innovation efforts are quickly reoriented to areas of growth (income-elastic areas facing market/demand expansion).

2.4.2   Systemic Approach to Change Management

According to Kettinger and Grover (1995), implementation of change within an organisation/enterprise would be effective when issues relating to strategic initiatives, cultural readiness, learning capacity, knowledge sharing capability, IT leveragability, and network relationship balancing are addressed in a systemic framework, in order to positively impact process efficiency and quality of work-life; quality of output and customer satisfaction, and business performance gains in terms of competitiveness and growth in market share and profit margin. This would amount to a system of management that is change-responsive and capable of refreshing itself, through the process of organisational learning upon exposure to new ideas and challenges (Argyris and Schoen, 1978; March, 1991). Thus, for example, improving organisational learning capacity and adding to organisational knowledge stock, through feedback from performance gains and/or changes in the wider business environment, would be expected to have the effect of enhancing the formulation and implementation of strategic initiatives that would transform the cultural readiness of the organisation for change.

Thus for Kettinger and Grover (1995), the reengineering of business processes and structures takes place partly at the level management, where the norms, beliefs and value systems underlying the organisational culture of business set the context for change environment; and partly at the business process level, where the impacts of changes in business process management are observed. Change invariably starts with strategic initiatives manifested in the form of visions and commitments to the transformation of organisational culture. The involvement of top management is crucial to set out strategic plans and programmes and to provide the mechanisms for achieving the targets set by these plans and programmes. The uptake of strategic initiatives for change and the effectiveness of their implementation would, however, depend on the existence of a strong coalition of interests within the organisation, while effectiveness of management in coalition-building and conflict resolution would turn on its ability to create a culture of transparency, so that the change is adopted with little or no resistance. Management would enhance the effectiveness of its commitment to change by involving the services of change agents who would ensure that the change initiative is understood and effectively implemented at all levels of activity within the organisation.

For strategic changes to take root in an organisation, the organisation must be culturally ready to be able to internalise and accept change. Change and innovation can occur within an organisation subject to the limits set by the prevailing norms and belief and value systems. These underpin the pattern of organisational behaviour that bear on the decisions to take risk, make changes, innovate, share knowledge, forge links and partnerships, etc. Where behaviours like 'risk taking, openness, shared vision, respect and trust, high expectation for action, and a focus on quality', are evident, then cultural readiness would allow the promotion of change to occur. However, at this juncture, it is also important to acknowledge that culture can act as a constraint on change where 'risk avoidance, ambivalence, group think, and excessive competition' are the dominant norms (Kettinger and Grover, 1995).

Knowledge sharing within an organisation is crucial for organisational learning and, as such, provides the basis for the generation of new ideas and the occurrence of innovation in the organisation. The knowledge-sharing capability of an organisation is a function of the organisational culture, and the ways in which individuals and groups find themselves within the organisational structure. In this context, a centralised, hierarchical and fragmented organisational structure is potentially restrictive of knowledge exchange and knowledge sharing. Knowledge sharing is best promoted under a system of organisation and management that is change-responsive and proactive, which focuses on integrative approach to problem solving, and on the building of trust and transparency as a basis for collaboration between individuals and between groups within the organisation, so that the process of learning and knowledge sharing within an organisation can be expedited by the use of IT at all levels of organisational activity. Hammer (1990) and Hammer and Champy (2003) asserted that IT should be used not to entrench outdated structures and processes, but to leverage changes in organisational culture and performance improvements through the value chain, and empower individuals through change and innovation in the organisation.

Another aspect of change management is conflict resolution and coalition building within the organisation, which brings together people with diverse skills, resources and interests – removing the boundaries around them. This calls for constructive management to balance relationships and provide suitable conditions for change and innovation to occur through the synergy arising from the interactions across the various categories of people within the organisation. Balancing relationships by proactively changing the boundaries of value chains would limit the scope for conflict and would consequently enable organisations to relax the transaction cost constraint on innovation, thus determining the range of activities to be undertaken within the organisation and those tasks that are to be contracted out to agents on the supply chain. This is particularly important for the management of change and innovation in the construction industry. The resolution of conflicts that arise in the process of change can be achieved through the reengineering of business processes and structures as part and parcel of the change management practice.

Change management is also about process management aimed at improving process quality and process efficiency; optimising the quality of employees' work-life (Cranny *et al*, 1992); and enhancing the appeal of products and services to customers. Process improvement can be achieved using systems-oriented methods of process management, which have their origin in the Japanese 'quality movement' (Kettinger and Grover, 1995). Process improvements are often derived from incremental and radical changes, which are gauged for their performance by measures, such as cycle time, defects, productivity, cost, sustainability, environmental impact, consumer appeal and marketability, etc, where incremental changes can lead to continuous process improvements. Through the incremental approach, employees can gain learning experiences that enable them to produce better quality products with little or no variation of processes over time (Yelle, 1979; Kettinger and Grover, 1995). However, radical changes, which derive from 'double-loop' and 'triple-loop' learning, and usually involve paradigm shifts, tend to occur discontinuously in the form of totally new products and processes.

In competitive market environments, the survival and growth of business organisations depends on the extent to which they appeal to consumers or clients in terms of quality, cost, delivery time, sustainability and environmental impact performance. Change management should therefore be geared to meeting customer requirements. It is therefore important to determine the orientation of the change management strategy with respect to the significance of the roles of demand-pull and supply push, and incremental changes and radical changes. This has implications for the mode of learning and hence for the development of learning capability which, according to Schumpeter (1934), has an effect on innovation. The question that has yet to be addressed here is, 'How does the conceptual framework for the analysis of change management relate to change and innovation in the construction industry?' This is discussed in the following section.

2.5   Innovation in Construction

The construction industry has traditionally been slow in the uptake of innovation. In an attempt to explain the persistence of this feature, Winch (1998) postulated that volume production, which has historically been closely associated with innovation in manufacturing, might no longer be an appropriate method for construction. However, this view begs the question about the role of prefabrication in construction and building activities. Gann *et al.* (1992) observed innovation efforts in construction were 'disproportionately orientated towards product enhancement rather than process improvement'. Yet an important factor behind the innovation-deficit in construction is the fragmentation of the industry itself as a system, and of the actors embedded in the system who broker change and innovation. Moreover, unlike many other industries, innovation in construction, which tends to occur through problem-solving exercises, is typically project-specific, constrained by client needs and circumstances pertaining to project sites. This means that construction innovation is predominantly of the incremental type; and as Winch (1998) noted, most of the problem-solving technologies and techniques adapted and applied to meet specific client needs were based on tacit knowledge that cannot be 'learned, codified and applied to future projects'. However, what has become increasingly apparent of late is that the construction industry in many countries, not least the UK, is embracing new working practices similar to those found in the manufacturing sector. Even so, the pace of construction innovation is varied across countries. For example, the dominant culture in the UK is known to have had an effect of making contractors risk-averse and reluctant to adopt new ideas (Lorenz and Smith, 1998). Gann (1997) noted that traditional construction firms in the UK tended to compete on price rather than on quality or technical competence, and that this generally accounted for the prevalence of 'an over-developed sense of price, and an underdeveloped sense of value' in the industry. Furthermore, Winch (1998) felt the British system was the victim of the so-called 'extrapolation trap', where technologies were 'continually re-invented in a circular rather than progressive manner', thus explaining why there were plenty of new ideas, but too little by way of innovation. This view is corroborated by Lorenz and Smith (1998), who observed that the 'consultancy dominated' industrial culture in the UK was prone to the adoption of 'minimalist' solutions rather than the uptake of radical and potentially risky business options. The short-term orientation of the construction business and the preference in consequence for quick pay-off opportunities has consequently limited the scope for engagement in innovation activities.

2.5.1   Reconstructing Construction Culture

In recent years, there has been increasing awareness in the UK at both government and industry levels about the significance of innovation for the competitiveness of the industry, and the need for a radical re-orientation of policy and management practices to make innovation happen in construction. This concern has been orchestrated in a range of initiatives, including the Construction Innovation Forum at the Building Research Establishment, the Construction IT Centre for Excellence, and Government task force groups and reports (Latham, 1994; Egan 1998), which led to the establishment of the Movement for Innovation (M4I). These initiatives were principally aimed at improving value for money to clients; enhancing the innovativeness and competitiveness of construction firms; making construction activities environmentally sustainable; and minimising the risks to health and safety for users of constructed facilities. Essentially, the initiatives were out to promote innovation in construction through change management, with particular focus on change in construction culture that marginalised teamwork, partnership and co-operation. However, over the last two decades, construction innovation in the UK has occurred in two major forms – namely, SCM and value engineering. Whilst supply chain fragmentation had issues concerning innovation (Dulaimi, 1995), following Latham and Egan, among other initiatives, the trend now is to move away from the pursuit of 'competitive' tendering towards partnering arrangements, involving target cost contracts; and 'traditional' construction organisations and management systems are now losing ground in the wake of new initiatives, such as partnering, supply chain management (SCM) and value engineering.

Fellows (1997) conceptualises partnering along the supply chain as a specific type of joint venture involving long-term commitment between parties, in order to achieve specific business objectives by maximising the effectiveness of resources available to each party. However, the benefits of synergy through partnering are largely contingent on the flexibility and orientation of the organisation of firms on the supply chain – i.e. whether they are traditional, hierarchical, reactive and adaptive; or change-responsive, proactive and innovative. In the context of sustainable construction (SuCo), value management is no longer about cost cutting, but about providing clients with the best value for money. Reconstructing value management means establishing a culture that recognises value in its totality as it relates to all parties along the supply chain, and encourages the planning and monitoring of value improvements. Value management means looking into objectives before providing solutions and identifying critical areas in management that influence innovative solutions to maximise value for money and achieve competitiveness and sustainability. This has brought forth the culture of 'value engineering' aimed at maximising value for money, which takes into account the whole life of projects and covers cost effectiveness, quality performance, product safety, environmental impact, competitiveness and sustainability.

2.5.2   Changes in UK Construction Culture

The Egan agenda for 'rethinking construction', which was initiated by the Government in 1998, set the scene for construction innovation to unfold. Following Egan, the Construction Industry Task Force, which was set up by the Government, initiated the M4I to provide a network for the generation and dissemination of new ideas. The implementation of the Egan agenda called for a radical overhaul of the management ethos of construction firms. Egan challenged construction firms to adopt 'lean' production techniques and to reduce costs and time by 10% and waste (in terms of reduction of defects and accidents on site) by 20% on an annual basis, by addressing the following points:

- creating an integrated project process, based on the principle of partnering the supply chain;
- using techniques for eliminating waste and increasing value for the customer, based on the principles of value management and engineering;
- designing projects that make maximum use of standard components and processes, thus enhancing the value for money objective of construction activities; and
- replacing the conventional competitive tendering practice with target cost construction contracts, based on long-term relationships arising from partnerships along the supply chain.

The Egan agenda thus sought to transform the UK construction industry through change management – making it lean in terms of sustainability performance, and competitive in terms of growth performance. However, 10 years after its launch, the Review Team at Construction Excellence (2009), found (based on a survey of over 1,000 industry professionals) that although Egan had a big impact on some parts of the industry - and the industry as a whole was moving in the right direction - the transformation expected was still incomplete, falling short of the Egan targets. The results of the survey also revealed that while the industry's performance on safety and profitability had improved, progress in other areas was found wanting. The Review Team identified the following constraining factors: the application of business models based on short-term cycles; the persistence of the fragmented nature of the industry; the poor integration of parties and activities on the supply chain; and the lack of strategic commitment at senior management and government level (CE, 2009). These issues constrained the industry from progressing along the lines set by the Egan agenda (Zawdie et al., 2003), and were partially influenced by the rigidity of the prevailing culture and lack of knowledge exchange to leverage innovation.

In a study conducted during the early phase of the implementation of the Egan agenda, 17 Scottish construction firms (including principal contractors and sub-contractors) were surveyed for the extent of cultural change impacted upon them by the Egan agenda. About 30% of these firms were aware of the main aspects of the Egan Report and had fully adopted the Egan recommendations; 35% said they were aware of the Egan agenda, having heard or read about it (but had not implemented it); and another 35% identified that they were not aware of Egan at all (Zawdie *et al.*, 2003). The results of this limited sample survey showed that the Egan agenda had a long way to go before being fully implemented in the UK. This survey highlighted some salient features about how firms respond to the challenge of innovation. Most of the firms, that were unaware of Egan, were small sub-contractors, who were generally highly risk-sensitive, and therefore reluctant to learn about the Egan agenda as the way forward. However, this did not mean that all small firms were inherently averse to innovation. Indeed, one of the small 'unaware' subcontracting firms won contracts on competitive tenders because of innovation. Furthermore, most of the firms recognised the need for cultural change in the industry, but perceived it to be an evolutionary process. They were also aware that this evolutionary and complex process could be accelerated by the development of network systems, such as links between government, universities and industry, along with supply chain partnerships including contractors and clients.

2.5.3   Change Management Initiatives for Innovation in Construction

There is growing awareness about the Egan agenda for change and innovation as the way forward for the UK construction industry. Innovation is widely understood as a factor that would, given the right circumstances, enable the industry to meet the challenges of being efficient and competitive on a global scale, as well as deliver a built environment that supports the creation of a low carbon economy. Of significance to the industry is the emergence of an environment that produces cultural readiness for change, especially by broadening the scope for organisational learning and the accumulation knowledge and experience. This would enable management to engage in strategic initiatives, resolve internal conflicts, reduce resistance to change, and provide the social capital base for innovation through the development of network partnerships that allow knowledge sharing and exchange through the supply chain.

The promotion of innovation at the firm level should therefore begin by developing strategies to make the organisation and management system forward-looking and responsive to change. A progressive approach to organisation and management would need to replace fragmented cultural systems, with flexible ones that allow firms to interact with minimum friction and minimum transaction costs. In addition, innovation-inhibiting structures, which encourage the persistence of bureaucracy and the entrenchment of vested interests, would need to make way for systems, which promote cooperation rather than conflict, and 'capacity building' rather than 'empire building'. For innovation to thrive, it is important that the *modus operandi* of firms is integrated rather than fragmented, allowing greater flexibility to respond to changes in market forces, as exemplified by the experience of car manufacturing plants in Japan (Graves, 1987). Strategies for promoting innovation would also need to provide the conditions for a progressive and proactive management system, supported by a strong management culture. The type, level and prevalence of this culture should foster open communication between management and labour, in order to envision and drive forward change. This would help establish ownership, commitment and empowerment – the rubrics of which could provide an environment that is conducive to creativity and where new ideas can be championed through an *esprit de corps*. If construction firms lacked these managerial attributes, they would not be expected to be innovative or dynamic. Nor would they be expected to be aware or capable of implementing the Egan agenda for change. However, construction innovation is more than the mere awareness of Egan. In order for it to thrive as an industrial culture, progressive management aimed at integrating activities within the firm should be complemented with the development of a wider network system, which, by exposing firms to interactive relationships of the innovation process, would enable them to realise their full innovative potential.

2.6   Conclusion

This chapter discussed the importance of innovation in the construction industry, with a particular focus on process, the role of culture, and the management of change. Innovation was identified as not being evenly distributed, with some (e.g. manufacturing) used to more frequent changes than others (e.g. construction). Notwithstanding this, there is growing evidence to suggest that this is starting to change. For example, the management of change has opened up new opportunities to re-visit skills and learning applied to business needs. This has provided the basis for the generation of new ideas and new innovation opportunities to exploit, especially through such conduits as organisational learning and knowledge management. The knowledge-sharing capability of an organisation is paramount, as a centralised, hierarchical and fragmented organisational structure can restrict knowledge exchange and knowledge sharing. Knowledge sharing is best promoted under a system of organisation and management that is change-responsive, proactive and focused upon problem solving through collaborative integration. However, short-termism can stifle entrepreneurialism and influence the prospects for change; and minimalist strategies rarely go far enough to champion major changes (Lorenz and Smith, 1998). Whilst Egan (1998) challenged construction by promoting the case for partnership and collaboration to transform the environment for decision-making and knowledge exchange, this has not fully materialised to date (CE, 2009).

For the management of change to be effective, the actors in the construction system would need to be fully integrated, so that there is a free flow of

knowledge and information exchange with a top-down adoption and implementation procedure synchronised to a bottom-up learning and problem-
solving approach. This is all the more important in view of the fact that
construction is a complex systems industry with an 'innovation superstructure' (clients, regulators and professional institutions) and an 'innovation
infrastructure' (trade contractors, specialist consultants and component
suppliers), and with 'systems integrators' (including the principal architect
and the principal contractor) (Winch, 1998). The industry therefore needs to
remove fragmentation, embrace change, and leverage innovation drivers
through new business models and strategic trajectories that streamline and
align corporate energy and competence to business goals and new market
opportunities.

References

Argyris, C. (1990) *Overcoming Organisational Defenses: Facilitating Organisational
Learning*. Allyn and Bacon, Boston.
Argyris, C. (1992) *On Organisational Learning*. Blackwell, Oxford.
Argyris, C. (1994) Good communication that blocks learning. *Harvard Business
Review*, **July–August**, 77–85.
Argyris, C. (1996) Unrecognised defenses of scholars: Impact on theory and research.
Organisation Science, 7, 79–87.
Argyris, C. & Schon, D.A. (1978) *Organisational Learning: A Theory of Action
Research*. Addison Wesley, Reading, MA.
Argyris, C., Putnam, R. & McLain Smith, D. (1985) *Action Science: Concepts,
Methods and Skills for Research and Intervention*. Jossey-Bass, San Francisco, CA.
Basil, D.C. & Cook, C.W. (1974) *The Management of Change*. McGraw Hill,
London.
Bates, G. (1973) *Steps to an Ecology of Mind*. Palladin, London.
Chaminade, C. & Roberts, H. (2002) Social capital as a mechanism connecting
knowledge within and across firms. Paper presented at the Third European
Conference on Organisational Knowledge, Learning and Capabilities, April,
Athens,.
Construction Excellence (CE) (2009) *Never Waste a Good Crisis: A Review of
Progress Since 'Rethinking Construction' and Thoughts for Our Future*.
Construction Excellence in Built Environment, London.
Cooke, P., Uranga, M.G. & Etxebarria, G. (1997) Regional innovation systems:
institutional and organisational dimensions. *Research Policy*, 26(4 & 5), 475–491.
Cooke, P. & Morgan, K. (1994) The creative milieu: a regional perspective on inno-
vation. In: ed. Dodgson, M. & Rothwell, R., *The Handbook of Industrial
Innovation*. Edward Elgar, Aldershot. 25–32.
Cranny, C.J., Smith, P.C. & Styone, E.F. (1992) *Job Satisfaction: How People Feel
About Their Jobs and How It Affects Their Performance*. Lexington Books.
New York.
Daft, R. (2001) *Organisation Theory and Design*, 7th edn. South Western College
Publishing, Cincinnati, OH.
Dodgson, M. (1993) Organisational learning: A review of some literatures.
Organisational Studies, 14(3), 375–394.
Dodgson, M., Gann, D.M. & Salter, A.J. (2002) The intensification of innovation.
International Journal of Innovation Management, 6(1), 53–83.

Dosi, G. (1982) Technological paradigms and technological trajectories. *Research Policy*, **11**(3), 147–162.

Douthwaite, B. (2002) *Establishing Innovation: A Practical Guide to Understanding and Fostering Technological Change*. Zed Books, London.

Dulaimi, M. (1995) The challenge of innovation in construction. *Building Research & Information*, **23**(2), 106–109.

Egan, J. (1998) *Rethinking Construction*. Report of the Construction Task Force to the Deputy Prime Minister. DETR, London.

Fellows, R.F. (1997) The culture of partnering. In ed. Davidson, C.H., *Proceedings of the CIB W-92 International Conference on Procurement*. Montreal: CIB.

Fiol, C.M. & Lyles, M. (1985) Organisational learning. *Academy of Management Review*, **10**(4), 803–813.

Flood, R.M. & Romm, N.R.A. (1996) *Diversity Management: Triple Loop learning*. John Wiley & Sons, Ltd, Chichester, UK.

Florida, R. (1995) Toward the learning region. *Futures*, **27**(5), 527–536.

Freeman, C. (1987) *Technology Policy and Economic Performance: Lessons from Japan*. Pinter, London.

Freeman, C. & Perez, C. (1988) Structural crises of adjustment, business cycles and investment behaviour. In: ed. Dosi, G., Freeman, C., Nelson, R.R., Silverberg, G. & Soete, L., *Technical Change and Economic Theory*. London: Pinter. 38–91.

Gagliardi, P. (1986) The creation and change of organisational cultures: a conceptual framework. *Organisation Studies*, **7**(2), 17–134.

Gann, D. (1997) *Building Innovation: Complex Contracts in a Changing World*. Thomas Telford, London.

Gann, D., Matthews, M., Patel, P. & Simmonds, P. (1992) *Construction R&D: Analysis of Private and Public Sector Funding of Research and Development in the UK Construction Sector*. Department of Environment, London.

Galanakis, K. (2006) Innovation process – make sense using systems thinking. *Technovation*, **26**(11), 1222–1232.

Galbraith, G. (1982) Designing the innovating organisation. *Organisational Dynamics*, **10**(3), 5–25.

Gibbons, M., Limoges, C., Nowotny, H., Schwartzman, S., Scott, P. & Trow, M. (eds) (1994) *The New Production of Knowledge*. Sage, London.

Graves, A. (1987) Comparative trends in automotive research and development. DRC Discussion Paper No 54. Science Policy Research Unit (SPRU), Sussex University, Brighton, UK.

Hall, A. (2002) Innovation systems and capacity development: an agenda for North-South research collaboration. *International Journal of Technology Management and Sustainable Development*, **1**(3), 146–152.

Hammer, M. (1990) Reengineering work: don't automate, obliterate. *Harvard Business Review*, **July–August**, 104–112.

Hammer, M. & Champy, J. (2003) *Reengineering the Corporation: A Manifesto for Business Revolution*. Harper Collins Publishers Inc, New York.

Hankinson, P. (1999) An empirical study which compares the organisational structures of companies managing the world's top 100 brands with those managing outsider brands. *Journal of Product & Brand Management*, **8**(5), 402–415.

Harvey, R.C. & Ashworth, A.A. (1993) *The Construction Industry of Great Britain*. Butterworth-Heinemann Ltd, London.

Huber, G.P. (1991) Organisational learning: The contributing process and the literatures. *Organisational Science*, **2**(1), 88–115.

Jones, E., Watson, B., Gardner, J. & Gallois, C. (2004) Organisational communication: challenges for the new century. *Journal of Communication*, **54**(4), 722–750.

Jorde, T. & Teece, D. (1990) Innovation and cooperation: implications for competition and anti-trust. *Journal of Economic Perspectives*, **4**(3), 75–96.

Kettinger, W.J. & Grover, V. (1995) Toward a theory of business process change management. *Journal of Management Information Systems*, **12**(1), 9–30.

Kozul-Wright, Z. (1995) *The Role of the Firm in the Innovation Process*. UNCTAD Discussion Papers, No. 98, Geneva.

Latham, M. (1994) *Constructing the Team*. HMSO, London.

Lewin, K. (1958) Group decision and social change. In: ed. Maccoby, E.E., Newcomb, T.M. & Hartley, E.L., *Readings in Social Psychology*. Holt, Rinehart & Winston, New York. 197–211.

Leydesdorff, L. & Zawdie, G. (2010) The Triple Helix perspective on innovation system. *Technology Analysis and Strategic Management*, **22**(7), 789–804.

Line, M.B. (1999) Types of organisational culture. *Library Management*, **20**(2), 73–75.

Lorenz, A. & Smith, D. (1998) Britain fails to close competitiveness gaps. *Sunday Times*, London: 11 October (cited in Akintoye, *et al.*, 1999).

Lundvall, B.A. (1985) *Product Innovation and User-Producer Interaction*. Industrial Development Research Series, vol. 31. Aalborg University Press, Aalborg.

Lundvall, B.A. (1992) *National Innovation Systems: Towards a Theory of Innovation and Interactive Learning*. Pinter, London.

March, J.G. (1991) Exploration and exploitation in organisational learning. *Organisation Science*, **2**(1), 71–87.

Marinova, D. & Phillimore, J. (2003) Models of innovation. In: ed. Shavinina, L.V., *The International Handbook of Innovation*. Elsevier Science Ltd, Oxford. 44–53.

Marosszeky, M. (1999) Technology and innovation. In: ed. Best, R. & de Valence, G., *Building in Value*. Arnold, London. 342–355.

Mason, R.M. (1993) Strategic information systems: Use of information technology in learning organisation. *Proceedings of the 26th Hawaii International Conference on System Sciences*, 5–8 January. Wailea, HI.

Morgan, K. (1997) The learning region: institutions, innovation and regional renewal. *Regional Studies*, **31**(5), 491–503.

Morroni, M. (1992) *Production Process and Technical Change*. Cambridge University Press, Cambridge.

Mullins, L.J. (2007) *Management and Organisational Behaviour*, 8th edn. Prentice Hall, Essex.

National Economic Development Office (1985) *Managing Change*. NEDO, London.

Nelson, R.R. & Winter, S.G. (1977) In search of useful theory of innovation. *Research Policy*, **6**(1), 36–76.

Nelson, R.R. & Winter, S.G. (1982) *An Evolutionary Theory of Economic Change*. Harvard University Press, Cambridge, MA.

Nevis, E.C., DiBella, A.J. & Gould, J.M. (1995) Understanding organisations as learning systems. *Sloan Management Review*, **36**(2), 75–85.

OECD (1999) *Managing National Innovation Systems*. OECD publications, Paris.

Porter, M. (1990) *The Competitive Advantage of Nations*. Free Press, New York.

Prahalad, C.K. & Hamel, G. (1994) *Competing for the Future*. Harvard University Press, Cambridge, MA.

Romme, A.G.L. & van Witteloostuijn, A. (1999) Circular organising and triple loop learning. *Journal of Organisational Change Management*, **12**(5), 439–453.

Rothwell, R. (1994) Towards the fifth generation innovation process. *International Marketing Review*, **11**(1), 7–31.

Sardi, G. & Lees, B. (2001) Development of corporate culture as a competitive advantage. *Journal of Management Development*, **20**(10), 853–859.

Schmookler, J. (1966) *Invention and Economic Growth*. Harvard University Press, Cambridge, MA.

Schumpeter, J. (1934) *The Theory of Economic Development*. Harvard University Press, Cambridge, MA.

Senge, P.M. (1990a) *The Fifth Discipline: The Art and Practice of the Learning Organisation*. Currency Doubleday, New York.

Senge, P.M. (1990b) The leader's new work: Building learning organisations. *Sloan Management Review*, 32(1), 7–23.

Silvester, J., Anderson, N.R. & Patterson, F. (1997) Organisational culture change: an inter-group attributional analysis. *Journal of Occupational and Organisational Psychology*, 72(1), 1–23.

Snell, R. & Man-Kuen Chak, A. (1993) The learning organisation: Learning and empowerment for whom? *Management Learning*, 29, 337–364.

Stonehouse, G.H. & Pemberton, J.D. (1999) Learning and knowledge management in the intelligent organisation. *Participation and Empowerment: An International Journal*, 7(5), 131–144.

Strategic Forum for Construction (2002) *Accelerating Change*. Report for the Construction Industry Council. SFC, London.

Tourish, D. & Hargie, O. (2004) The crisis in management and the role of organisational communication. In: ed. Tourish, D. & Hargie, O., *Key Issues in Organisational Communication*. Routledge, London. 1–16.

Usher, A.P. (1954) *History of Mechanical Inventions*. John Wiley & Son, Ltd, London.

Van de Ven, A.H. (1986) Central problems in the management of innovation. *Management Science*, 32(5), 590–607.

Winch, G. (1998) Zephyrs of creative destruction: understanding the management of innovation in construction. *Building Research & Information*, 26(5), 268–279.

Yelle, L. (1979) The learning curve: historical review and comprehensive survey. *Decision Sciences*, 10(2), 302–308.

Zawdie, G., Abukhder, J. & Langford, D. (2003) Organisational and managerial attributes of innovation among firms in the construction industry in the UK: why culture matters. In: ed. Botemps, F., *Systems Based Vision for Strategic and Creative Design*, vol. 3. Balkema, Amsterdam. 85–92.

Zghal, R. (1996) Science, technology and society: What makes the culture of innovation? In: ed. Zawdie, G. & Djeflat, A., *Technology and Transition: The Maghreb at the Crossroads*. Frank Cass, London. 105–113.

Construction Innovation: Theory and Practice

Martin G. Sexton and Shu-Ling Lu

3.1 Introduction

This chapter presents a broad overview of innovation in construction. It aims to equip readers with a set of key theories through which innovation can be understood and, in doing so, will be in a better position to steer and manage innovation in practice. The purpose therefore, is not to concentrate on current examples of say, innovative products or practices; rather, the purpose is to develop a conceptual treatment of the subject area, which can be mobilised across a broad spectrum of construction settings. To achieve this aim, the chapter is structured as follows. First, a brief discussion on the definition or, more correctly, the myriad of definitions of innovation is discussed. Second, a definitional position is developed through the umbrella concepts of market-based and resourced-based views of innovation. These two perspectives are then synthesised to produce a balanced innovation perspective. Finally, a case study is presented to illustrate a number of the issues raised.

3.2 Definitional Debate on Innovation

There are a wide range of, sometimes, conflicting definitions of innovation. In many respects, the development of a single definition of innovation is a fruitless and pointless exercise. The more meaningful challenge is to adopt a particular view of innovation appropriate for a specific context. For example, innovation within a high technology combined heat and power boiler manufacturer is likely to be significantly different to innovation within a low technology service provider such as a labour-only painting contractor. Furthermore, the diverse range of theoretical and methodological perspectives from which to investigate innovation demonstrates this contingent and

Construction Innovation and Process Improvement, First Edition.
Edited by Akintola Akintoye, Jack S. Goulding and Girma Zawdie.
© 2012 Blackwell Publishing Ltd. Published 2012 by Blackwell Publishing Ltd.

context-specific approach. Traditional economic approaches to innovation, for example, tend to concentrate on particular technologies and market signals that encourage or stifle uptake and diffusion. Thus, the innovation discipline then evolved to complement the micro- and macro-economic considerations with a managerial treatment that explored the company-level strategies and capabilities that influence the direction and nature of new product and service development. More recently, institutional analyses have been made of the role of a broader social system in influencing innovation trajectories, through functions such as regulations, norms and values. In order to find a productive path through these bodies of theory, this chapter concentrates on a key generic characteristic of innovation; namely, that innovation involves the development and implementation of a new idea in an applied setting. The 'newness' characteristic is found in the general literature (van de Ven et al., 1999; DTI, 2003) and in the construction literature (Barrett and Sexton, 2006).

The UK government defines innovation as 'the successful exploitation of new ideas' (DTI, 2003: 8; NAO, 2009). The 'new idea' dimension embraces a range of domains. Policy makers understand innovation as a broad, systemic concept that encompasses the 'successful introduction of new services, products, processes, business models and ways of working' (ESRC, 2008: 2), and in this respect, construction literature is generally consistent with the general literature. Sexton and Barrett (2003b: 626) define successful innovation as 'the effective generation and implementation of a new idea, which enhances overall organisational performance.' Similarly, the Civil Engineering Research Foundation (CERF, 2000: 3) defines innovation as 'the act of introducing and using new ideas, technologies, products and/or processes aimed at solving problems, viewing things differently, improving efficiency and effectiveness, or enhancing standards of living' (focusing specifically on construction professional practices). The newness characteristic needs to be further elaborated in order to distinguish between new to the world, or new to a given situation. Rogers (1983: 11), for example, defines innovation as 'a product or service that is perceived as new by the members of the social system', and that 'it matters little whether the idea is "objectively" new as measured by the lapse of time since its first use or discovery. The perceived newness of the idea for the individual determines his or her reaction to it. If the idea seems new to the individual, it is an innovation.'

Innovation literature carries the theme of distinguishing different types of innovation across a multitude of dimensions: incremental versus radical, technological versus administrative, and so on. Again, these distinctions are important, but these should not be considered as discrete, separate types. In practice, such distinctions become blurred and mutually constituted. Innovation, for example, is often classified into 'product innovation' and 'process innovation'. 'Product innovation' refers to the development and introduction of new or improved products and/or services, which create or meet a new demand, and which are successful in the market. In contrast, 'process innovation' involves the adoption of new or improved methods of manufacture, distribution or delivery of service that 'lower the real cost of producing outputs, although they may also give rise to changes in their nature' (Clarke, 1993: 143). The 'product' versus 'process' view of innovation has now evolved towards a more systemic view. Athey and Schmutzler (1995) assert that process innovation (cost reducing) and product innovation (demand enhancing) are complementary. Indeed, Imai (1992: 226) speculates that 'process improvement and product differentiation are now being fused'.

However, the key common theme across the definitional debate in the literature is that 'new ideas' are taken to be the foundation or the starting point for innovation. The central question that will now guide the discussion is 'what is the stimulus for these "new ideas"?'

3.3   Market-based, Resource-based and Balanced Perspectives on Innovation

There are two key perspectives on the principal drivers for innovation: the market-based view and the resource-based view. Each perspective will be discussed in turn, followed by a synthesis of the two.

3.3.1   Market-based Perspective on Innovation

The market-based view of innovation stresses the role of institutional and market factors in stimulating innovation within companies. Market conditions are viewed in a broad sense as encompassing both the general business environment and the interaction environment. The general business environment covers the full spectrum of social, legal, economic, political and technological forces and configurations. In contrast, the interaction or construction-specific business environment consists of industry structures, clients, suppliers, competitors, financiers, regulators, and so on. The broad argument offered is that market conditions provide the context or initial conditions that either facilitate or constrain the direction and quantity of firm innovation activity (Slater and Narver, 1994; Porter 1980, 1985).

In the general literature, a number of market-based innovation theorists have investigated market or environmental influences on innovation. For example, influences have been articulated as customer–supplier relations (von Hippel, 1988), network studies (Håkanson, 1989), market conditions (Ames and Hlavacek, 1988) and external knowledge infrastructures (Nelson, 1993). A current example of regulatory pressures can be seen in the UK, which is inducing innovation through the Code for Sustainable Homes (DCLG, 2008), which requires housing developers to radically rethink their business models, designs and production processes to comply with, amongst other criteria, the zero-carbon requirement by 2016. The emphasis of the market-based innovation position is that firms adapt or orientate themselves through innovation to exploit changing institutional and market conditions in an optimal fashion. The environment where client interaction occurs is defined as 'the task environment' (Kotler, 1980), whilst the environment where other firms compete with the firm, customer and scarce resources is termed as 'the competitive environment' (Kotler, 1980). Together, the task environment and competitive environments are labelled collectively as 'the interaction environment' (Sexton and Barrett, 2003: 36). In summary, the interaction environment is a significant market-based stimulus to innovation within the construction context.

3.3.2 Resource-based Perspective on Innovation

The resource-based view of innovation emphasis is that firms identify and nurture resources that enable them to generate innovation to 'shape' market conditions; rather than the market-based view which advocates that market conditions 'shape' the resources that firms develop and exploit to respond to opportunities and threats. In other words, the resource-based view of innovation stresses that resources available to the firm, rather than market conditions (market-based perspective), are the principal catalysts for innovation (Itami, 1987; Barney, 1991; Grant, 1995).

Resources (e.g. human capital, social capital and physical capital) in themselves are not seen as productive. However, dynamic environments often demand generation of new resources as the business environment changes (Chaharbaghi and Lynch, 1999). Therefore, the challenge for firms is to create sustainable competitive advantage in rapidly changing and competitive environments for resources to be integrated, coordinated and deployed as 'distinctive capabilities' (Teece *et al.*, 1997). Amit and Schoemaker (1993: 35) note that capabilities 'refer to firm's ability to deploy resources, usually in combination, using organisational processes, to affect a desired end. They are information-based, tangible or intangible processes that are firm specific, and are developed over time through complex interactions among the firm's resources.'

The development of 'distinctive capabilities' in dynamic environments is labelled 'dynamic capability' (Teece *et al.*, 1997), where the concept of 'dynamic capabilities' is defined as 'the firm's ability to integrate, build, and reconfigure internal and external competencies to address rapidly changing environments' (Teece *et al.*, 1997: 516). In a construction context, Green *et al.* (2008: 63) argue that dynamic capabilities 'relates to a firm's ability to reconfigure its resources in response to changing environments'. Therefore, it is important that the capability of organisations to adopt, adapt and transform existing technological applications and know-how from other environments into relevant and appropriate solutions, organisational processes and technological products/services to match the socio-cultural context of the construction industry sector, is crucial for bringing about innovation (Sexton and Barrett, 2003a,b, 2004; Harty *et al.*, 2007; Green *et al.*, 2008).

3.3.3 Balanced Innovation

The perception of a potential market-driven opportunity or imperative is a necessary condition for innovation, but not a sufficient one (Dosi, 1984). The adaptation and orientation to market conditions requires firms to choose appropriate strategies that are adequately resourced and implemented (Snow and Hrebiniak, 1980). In this context, an appreciation of the resource dimension has played a significant part in the cultivation of the resource-based view of innovation. A resource-based view focuses on firms' resources, specifically, to understand business strategies and provide direction for, amongst other issues, innovation (Prahalad and Hamel, 1990; Andreu and Ciborra, 1996; Grant, 1997). However, the market-driven orientation does not provide a secure foundation for formulating innovation strategies for markets that are dynamic and volatile; rather, firms' own resources provide a more stable basis on which to develop their innovation activities, and to shape their markets, to a limited extent, in their own image. These stocks of resources are defined as assets, capabilities, routines and knowledge that are tied semi-permanently or permanently to, or controlled by, a firm (Barney, 1991; Wernerfelt, 1984). They may be physical, human, technological or reputational (Hadjimanolis, 2000: 264). The argument here is that innovative firms are those that can sense and act upon internal 'precipitating events' to create and develop unique resources or configurations of resources that serve as the foundations for successful streams of innovation.

Maijoor and van Witteloostuijn (1996: 549) suggest that 'the resource-based view of the firm seeks to bridge the gap between theories of internal organisational capabilities on the one hand and external competitive strategy theories on the other hand.' Indeed, recent research seeking to synthesise these two perspectives suggest that 'while firms' resource endowments may determine strategy success, strategy choice is ... restricted by market structure' (Hewitt-Dunda and Roper, 2000: 1). This argument is evident in the observation that an 'innovative firm creates two kinds of products. The primary product is the innovation itself, while the secondary product is a process created by innovations, which increases the internal capacity by building up core competencies by making the *intangible capital* quicker, more flexible, more adaptable and more capable in dealing with market pressures and unexpected external shocks' (Lööf and Heshmatic, 2000: 7). In construction literature, evidence to support this balancing was reported in the observation that 'the sifting of possible [innovation] options was rigorous, with [small construction companies] being close enough to both their markets and their capabilities to instinctively know what will work, and what will not' (Sexton *et al.*, 1999: 17).

It is therefore suggested that market-based and resource-based innovation can be gainfully linked (Figure 3.1); by extending the argument that innovating firms are those that can sense and act upon 'precipitating events', both external institutional and market conditions, and internal resource conditions in an appropriately balanced and integrated fashion. This 'precipitating event' perspective is embodied in the observation that 'innovation is fostered by information gathered from new connections; from insights gained by journeys into other disciplines or places; from active, collegial networks and fluid, open boundaries. Thus, innovation arises from ongoing circles of exchange, where information is not just accumulated or stored, but created' (Wheatley, 1992: 113). However, the optimal innovation balance of market-based and resource-based innovation is contingent upon the

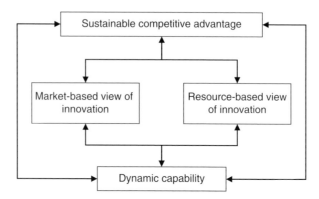

Figure 3.1   Balanced innovation.

'market pull' and/or 'resource push' implications of the prevailing precipitating events. The organisational challenge is therefore to generate the balance required to provide an appropriate innovation focus that enhances overall performance – and in so doing, dynamically links the focus and context of innovation. This view resonates with similar discussions focusing on the 'market-pull' and 'technology-push' (Coombs *et al.*, 1987) and 'research-push' and 'market-pull' (Freeman, 1982).

The market-based and resource-based views represent two stylised perspectives on how innovation can be stimulated. In practice, these two perspectives can be gainfully linked by extending the argument that there is mutual adjustment between companies 'reacting to' market opportunities and threats, and 'proactively' identifying, developing and exploiting resources and capabilities to secure a foundation for innovation in dynamic environments. The development of the optimal dynamic capabilities brings these two resources together to co-produce innovation that creates sustainable competitive advantage. This view is an extension of similar discussions focusing on the appropriate balance between market-based and resource-based views of innovation capabilities needed in small construction firms (Sexton and Barrett, 2003a).

The discussion to this point has laid out some key innovation concepts. In particular, the argument has been developed that innovation should not be seen as merely a new product or process; rather, it should be seen as a multi-layered, complex interaction that draws upon and balances market and resource-based influences through the creation of appropriate dynamic capabilities. The remainder of this chapter further develops these ideas through a case study of a small construction professional service firm.

3.4   Case Study of Innovation in a Small Construction Professional Service Firm

The aim of this case study is to demonstrate the context-specific nature of innovation in order to mobilise some of the concepts and ideas developed so far. The case study in particular, offers a definition of innovation (note, not the definition!) and identifies some key innovation management challenges for construction firms.

3.4.1   Case Study Aim and Methodology

The case study company, hereafter labelled as ArchSME (for confidentiality reasons), is a small architectural design practice based in the UK. ArchSME's principal markets are city centre and suburban residential sectors, with work varying from one-off commissions from regional clients to repeat business from national house builders.

The case study consisted of two main research phases conducted over a 22-month period. The first phase (exploratory) investigated four successful innovations and three unsuccessful innovations. Successful innovations included the development of ArchSME mission statement (innovation 1), the securing of Investors in People (innovation 2), the flow of new novel designs (innovation 3) and the company restructure (innovation 4). These were identified as being significant firm-generated innovations over the last two years. Failed innovations included the introduction and subsequent failure of in-house seminars (innovation 5), the introduction of the new materials (innovation 6) and the Learndirect project (innovation 7). These were classified as being significant innovations over the last two years that had failed. Table 3.1 identifies the summary descriptions for each of these innovations.

The second phase of this work was used to further test and develop the concept innovation model that came out of the exploratory phase. This research adopted an action research methodology, adopting the five-step process of diagnosis, action planning, action taking, action evaluation and specifying learning (Susman, 1983). The action research provided a narrative of 'real time' innovation within a company setting, and brought about a successful innovation in the case study firm. The action researcher was embedded within the case study firm full-time for a period of ten months. The action research phase began with a company workshop, the purpose of which was to discuss and evaluate the key findings from the exploratory phase and identify an action research intervention (or innovation) to be developed and implemented. The identified innovation was the design and implementation of an interim project review process innovation (innovation 8). It should be noted that an interim project review process is a procedure that consists of review activities performed by a project team to gather information on what worked well and what did not, so that current and future projects can benefit from that learning. This new process was considered as an integrated part of the ongoing preparation by the case study firm for ISO 9001 Quality Management Systems accreditation. Based on this, an interim project review process handbook (including interim project review process policy, guidelines and checklists) was jointly developed by the action researcher and the firm. This handbook was then assessed and signed off by the company senior management and integrated into the company's quality systems.

Table 3.1 Description of identified company innovations.

Types of innovation	Identified innovations	Description
Successful Innovation	Innovation 1	Mission statement is a statement that captures an organisation's purpose, customer orientation and business philosophy.
	Innovation 2	Investors in People (IiP) [1] is the national standard which sets out a level of good practice for training and development of people to achieve business goals.
	Innovation 3	New designs are novel forms of layout and structure.
	Innovation 4	Company restructure is the way in which the company of people are to coordinate work to ensure successful delivery of service to the client.
Unsuccessful Innovation	Innovation 5	Seminars are a type of meeting for an exchange ideas on a specific topic. The identified seminars included IT, project briefing, and marketing.
	Innovation 6	New materials are the building components, materials, or new products that the company has not used it before in its building designs.
	Innovation 7	Learndirect project [2] is funded by the UK government. This project aims to help the company of people to develop their IT capability in getting easy access to information about what is available.

[1] Investors in People (IiP) (http://www.investorsinpeople.co.uk/Pages/Home.aspx) is the national Standard that is widely recognised as a respected badge of quality in the UK. The standard was developed in 1990 by a partnership of leading businesses and national organisations in the UK. This standard is designed to help organisations to improve performance and realise objectives through the management and development of their people.

[2] Learndirect (http://www.learndirect.co.uk/) was launched in 2000. It has been developed by University for Industry with a remit from UK government to provide high quality learning opportunities. Its courses cover a range of subjects, including management, IT, skills for life and languages, at all levels. Most of the courses are available online, allowing people to learn wherever they have access to the internet.

3.4.2   Knowledge-based Innovation

The research findings developed a formulation of knowledge-based innovation as 'the effective generation and implementation of a new idea which enhances overall organisational performance, through appropriate exploitative and explorative knowledge capitals which develops and integrates relationship capital (RC), structure capital (SC) and human capital (HC).' This definition forms a knowledge-based innovation concept model, which is built around five variables (Figure 3.2).

1. Interaction environment is that part of the business environment that firms can interact with, and influence. The interaction environment and the firm are separated by an organisational boundary.
2. Relationship capital (RC) is the network resource of a firm. It results from interactions between individual, organisation and external supplier chain partners.

3. Human capital (HC) is defined as the capabilities and motivation of individuals within the firm and external supply chain partners to perform productive, professional work in a wide variety of situations.
4. Structure capital (SC) is made up of systems and processes (e.g. company strategies, computers, tools, work routines and administrative systems) for codifying and storing knowledge from individual, organisation and external supply chain partners.
5. Knowledge capital (KC) is the dynamic synthesis of both the 'context' and 'process' of knowledge creation and conversion within individual-organisational-individual knowledge Ba spirals, and the 'content' of RC, SC and HC.

The concept model highlights the need for senior management to strategically and systemically build, connect and energise appropriate RC, SC and HC to form KC, from which successful organisation and project innovation can flow.

Figure 3.2 Knowledge-based Innovation Concept Model for small construction professional service firms (Lu and Sexton, *Innovation in Small Professional Practices in the Built Environment*, 1st edn, Wiley Blackwell, Oxford, copyright © 2009).

3.4.3   Two Forms of Knowledge-based Innovation

The key proposition is that the market and resource-based view of innovation can be gainfully linked, by extending the argument that there is mutual adjustment between companies 'reacting to' market opportunities and threats and 'proactively' identifying, developing and exploiting resources

(a)   (b)

Mode 1: Explorative innovation   Mode 2: Exploitative innovation

[Note]
RC: Relationship capital
SC: Structure capital
HC: Human capital
KC: Knowledge capital

Figure 3.3   Two forms of knowledge-based innovation.

and capabilities to secure a foundation for innovation in these dynamic environments. The principal stimulus for innovation from the market-based view comes from knowledge workers' relationships with their clients, and the principal resource from the resource-based view of innovation is the knowledge worker. The development of optimal dynamic capabilities brings these two resources together to co-produce innovation to create sustainable competitive advantage.

Two types of knowledge-based innovation were identified: mode 1: explorative innovation and mode 2: exploitative innovation (Figure 3.3). New designs (innovation 3) and new materials (innovation 6) were classified as mode 1 explorative innovation. Mission statement (innovation 1), Investors in People (innovation 2), company restructure (innovation 4), seminars (innovation 5), Learndirect project (innovation 7) and interim project review process (innovation 8) were grouped into mode 2 exploitative innovation. It was found that the firm's short-term success was driven to a significant degree by 'explorative' innovation and long-term success by 'exploitative' innovation.

Mode 1 'explorative innovation' is made of three key attributes: RC, HC and KC. It focused on client facing, project-specific problem-solving, often in close collaboration with the client. Explorative innovation activity heavily relied on the capacity, ability and motivation of staff at an 'operational level' to solve client problems to generate short-term competitive advantage (i.e. project specific). Their outcomes focused on effective and efficient delivery of services to satisfy the prevailing fee-earning project needs; but were often not embedded in the organisational SC due to management attention and company resources being constantly focused on other current or near future project-specific demands. The use of new materials (innovation 6) in the case study firm, for example, was explorative in nature, being project-specific and individually driven.

Mode 2 'exploitative innovation' consisted of the four key attributes: RC, SC HC and KC. It focused predominantly on internal organisation and general client development activity (non-project-specific, fee-earning activity). The client had no direct involvement with the innovation activity. Exploitative innovation activity heavily relied on the capacity, ability and motivation of senior management at a 'social' level to improve organisational effectiveness and efficiency to generate sustainable competitive advantage. The securing of Investors in People (innovation 2) accreditation for the case study firm, for instance, initially came from senior management, who were aware that clients are interested in such accreditation. The distinctive feature of mode 2 'exploitative innovation' (compared to mode 1 'explorative innovation') was that new phenomena, systems or structures were securely embedded in the SC of the firm. The motivation for a new mission statement (innovation 1) for the case study firm, for example, came from senior management, who saw it as a way of instilling an integrating vision for its portfolio of activities. Key generic and distinctive variables for successful and unsuccessful explorative innovation and exploitative innovation are summarised in Table 3.2.

Table 3.2 shows that the key distinction between successful and unsuccessful innovation was the 'social' or 'operational' knowledge being applied to a specific innovation. 'Operational knowledge' was generated and created in 'operational level' interactions, where the focus was on solving project-specific issues/problems. These projects were either 'external' fee-earning projects, or 'internal', but specific client-driven projects. 'Social knowledge' was generated through 'social level' interactions, where the focus was on generating non-project-specific innovation that built up general organisational capability, and forged and replenished deeper client relationship over the medium to long term. Moreover, social knowledge was found to have a significant effect on feeding operational knowledge at a specific project level at a future date.

3.4.4   Definition of a Successful Knowledge-based Innovating Firm

The research findings revealed that successful explorative innovation did not necessarily need integrated SC. It was evident in the case study firm that there was too much emphasis on individual learning at the project level (explorative innovation) to the detriment of the organisational level learning (exploitative innovation). This emphasis of explorative KC over exploitative KC was not considered sustainable, as the limitation of SC will become increasingly evident as a significant restraining force for the effective integration of explorative and exploitative KCs. There was thus not an appropriate balance between explorative and exploitative innovation over time. The case study firm needed to create and continue a balance between explorative and exploitative KC barriers, which would allow the flow of KC between operational and social levels. The following definition of a successful

Table 3.2 Key generic and distinctive variables for successful and unsuccessful explorative and exploitative innovations (Lu and Sexton, innovation in small professional practices in the built environment, 1st Edition, Wiley Blackwell, Oxford, UK, copyright © 2009).

Type of Innovation	Variables	Generic Variables	Distinctive Variables	
			Successful Innovation	Unsuccessful Innovation
Explorative Innovation	**Human capital (HC)**	• The capacity, ability and motivation of staff	• Social or operational knowledge being applied to meet the project needs	• Social knowledge not being applied to meet the project needs
	Structure capital (SC)	• Team structure • Teamwork	• Team-based ideas • Teamwork • Senior management involvement through teamwork	• Individual-based ideas • Individual based work • Senior management not involved in teamwork • Limitation of relevant and updated information within the structure
	Relationship capital (RC)	• Operational RC: within internal, client and supplier interactions • Social RC: within internal, client and supplier interactions	• A combination of operational RC and social RC being applied to meet project needs	• Social RC not being applied to meet project needs
	Knowledge capital (KC)	• Social context[1]: company environments (office, meeting room) • Technical context[2]: e-mails, the internet	• A combination of social context and technical context	• Technical context
	Outcome	• Effective and efficient delivery of services to satisfy current and/or future project needs	• Project performance improvement	• Individual performance improvement

Exploitative Innovation			
Human capital (HC)	• The capacity, ability and motivation of senior management • Employee participation	• Top management support • Senior management implementation • Some employees buy in • Training	• Top management not supportive • Senior management not driving the implementation • Lack of time • Employees not bought in ○ Inappropriate encouragement • Not related to an individual job
Structure capital (SC)	• The administrative system • Team structure • Computer systems	• Formalised structures and documentation systems • Senior management implementation through the team structure	• No formalised structures and documentation systems • Senior management not driving the implementation through the team structure
Relationship capital (RC)	• Operational RC: within business adviser, internal, client and supplier interactions • Social RC: within internal interactions	• A combination of operational RC and social RC being applied to meet project needs	• Social RC not being applied to meet project needs
Knowledge capital (KC)	• Social context: company environments (office and open family culture) • Technical context: e-mails and the internet	• A combination of social context and technical context being applied to meet the project needs	• A combination of social context and technical context not being applied to meet the project needs
Outcome	• Organisational effectiveness and efficiency	• Organisational performance improvement	• Individual performance improvement

1 A 'social' context was used to stimulate interaction and collective 'process orientated' knowledge creation and conversion.
2 A 'technical' context was used to support the search for external knowledge and sharing of 'asset orientated' knowledge.

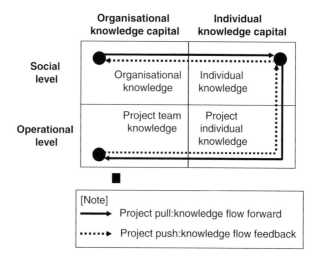

Figure 3.4   Successful innovation driven by operational focus.

knowledge-based innovating firm is therefore offered to accommodate the time dimension: 'the effective generation and implementation of a flow of new ideas, which enhance overall organisational performance over time, through appropriate exploitative and explorative knowledge capital, which develops and integrates relationship capital, structure capital and human capital.'

The time variable brings into focus the development phases of firms as they move from start-up to mature organisations. The focus and process of innovation activity will correspondingly change during the transition. It can be speculated that at the early stages of a firm's development, the emphasis is on explorative innovation, but, as the firm matures, there is an increasing need to explicitly invest in exploitative innovation to produce balanced innovation. This need was certainly evident in this case study firm.

3.4.5   Key Innovation Management Challenges

The discussion above provides insight into the nature and process of innovation for small construction professional service firms. Successful innovation in small construction professional service firms is principally characterised by 'project pull' and 'project push' individual-organisational-individual knowledge spirals, which create dynamic specific-project and/or client-driven KC. Figure 3.4 depicts specific project requirements (either external fee-producing or internal client-driven projects) 'pulling,' combining and converting, 'organisational knowledge' and 'individual knowledge' to form specific 'project individual knowledge'. Project individual knowledge is integrated and leveraged to create 'project team knowledge', which is appropriately applied to create successful innovation. The feedback individual-organisational-individual knowledge spiral is complemented by a feedback or 'project push' knowledge spiral, where new specific 'project

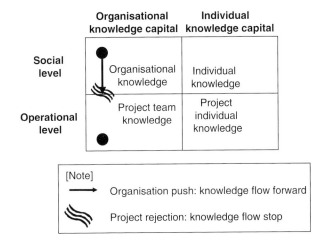

Figure 3.5 Unsuccessful innovation driven by social focus.

team knowledge' feeds back to develop 'project individual knowledge', which, in turn, further enhances 'individual knowledge' and 'organisational knowledge'. The tacit, experiential knowledge accumulation and learning is the basis for subsequent cycles of project-based innovation.

In contrast, unsuccessful innovation in small construction professional service firms is principally characterised by 'organisation push' of disjointed, unfocused 'social' non-project-specific and/or non-client-driven KC being 'rejected' by day-to-day project priorities and activities. Without a specific-project focus, innovation often fails because the individual-organisational-individual knowledge spiral does not happen. Figure 3.5 depicts that there is no specific project needs 'pulling' 'individual knowledge' and 'organisational knowledge' together. Rather, generic 'organisational knowledge' is 'pushed' into a project team setting without appropriate filtering and adaptation to meet specific project needs. Furthermore, the 'organisational knowledge' does not benefit from individual knowledge workers championing their tacit understanding. In combination, the 'organisational knowledge' is 'rejected' by day-to-day projects. Consequently, the feedback loop through individual knowledge, project knowledge and organisational knowledge does not happen.

3.5   Conclusion

This chapter presented a number of key concepts to better understand and, therefore, strategically manage innovation. A number of these ideas were mobilised and illustrated through a case study of innovation in a small construction professional service firm. From the case study, common themes can be identified that are relevant for a broad range of construction company and project settings. First, successful innovation has to balance exploitation and explorative activity. Companies have to exploit existing capabilities to produce innovation aimed at enhancing current performance. At the same time, companies have to invest in explorative innovation for the future. Second, for companies in a project-based industry such as construction, there is always the challenge to develop the necessary organisational SC to capture and diffuse innovation within and between projects. Finally, innovation is not a thing companies should engage with on a periodic basis. The pace and pervasiveness of regulatory, market and technological change is such that innovation must be embedded in all aspects of company thinking and action, all of the time.

References

Ames, B.C. & Hlavacek, J.D. (1988) *Market Driven Management: Prescription for Survival in a Turbulent World*. Irwin, Homewood, IL.

Amit, R. & Schoemaker, P.J.H. (1993) Strategic assets and organizational rent. *Strategic Management Journal*, 14, 33–46.

Andreu, R. & Ciborra, C. (1996) Organisational learning and core capabilities development: The role of IT. *Journal of Strategic Information Systems*, 5, 111–127.

Athey, S.E. & Schmutzler, A. (1995) Product and process flexibility in an innovative environment. *RAND Journal of Economics*, 26(4), 557–574.

Barney, J.B. (1991) Firm resources and sustained competitive advantage. *Journal of Management*, 17(1), 99–120.

Barrett, P.S. & Sexton, M.G. (2006) Innovation in small, project-based construction firms. *British Journal of Management*, 17, 331–346.

Chaharbaghi, K. & Lynch, R. (1999) Sustainable competitive advantage: towards a dynamic resource-based strategy. *Management Decision*, 37(1), 45–50.

Civil Engineering Research Foundation (CERF) (2000) *Guidelines for Moving Innovations into Practice*. Working Draft Guidelines for the CERF International Symposium and Innovative Technology Tradeshow, 14–17 August, CERF, Washington, DC.

Clarke, R. (1993) *Industrial Economics*. Blackwell Publishing, Oxford.

Coombs, R., Saviotti, P. & Walsh, V. (1987) *Economics and Technological Change*. MacMillan, New York.

Department for Communities and Local Government (DCLG) (2008) The Code for Sustainable Homes: setting new standards for sustainability in new homes, HMSO, London. Available from http://www.communities.gov.uk/publications/planning andbuilding/codesustainabilitystandards (accesses 03/11/2010).

Department of Trade and Industry (DTI) (2003) *Innovation Report – Competing in the Global Economy: The Innovation Challenge*, December, HMSO, London. Available from http://www.berr.gov.uk/files/file12093.pdf (accessed 1 October 2010).

Dosi, G. (1984) *Technical Change and Industrial Transformation*. MacMillan, London.

Economic and Social Research Council (ESRC) (2008) *Innovation Research Centre: Call Specification*. ESCR, Swindon.

Freeman, C. (1982) *Economics of Industrial Innovation*. Pinter, London.

Grant, R.M. (1995) *Contemporary Strategy Analysis: Concepts, Techniques, Applications*, 2nd edn. Blackwell Publishing, Oxford.

Grant, R.M. (1997) *Contemporary Strategic Analysis: Concepts, Techniques, Application*, 3rd edn. Blackwell Publishing, Oxford.

Green, S.D., Larsen, G.D. & Kao, C. (2008) Competitive strategy revisited: contested concepts and dynamic capabilities. *Construction Management and Economics*, **26**(1), 63–78.

Hadjimanolis, A. (2000) A resource-based view of innovativeness in small firms. *Technology Analysis and Strategic Management*, **12**(2), 263–281.

Håkanson, H. (1989) *Corporate Technological Behaviour: Corporation and Networks*. Printer, London.

Harty, C., Goodier, C.I., Soetanto, R., Austin, S., Dainty, A.R.J. & Price, A.D.F. (2007) The futures of construction: A critical review of construction future studies. *Construction Management and Economics*, **25**(5), 477–493.

Hewitt-Dundas, N. & Roper, S. (2000) *Strategic Reengineering – Small Firms' Tactics in a Mature Industry*. Northern Ireland Economic Research Centre Working paper Series No. 49, Northern Ireland Economic Research Centre, Belfast.

Imai, K. (1992) The Japanese Pattern of Innovation and Its Evaluation. In: ed. Rosenberg, N., Handau, R. & Mowery, D., *Technology and the Wealth of Nations*. Stanford Press, Stanford.

Itami, H. (1987) *Mobilizing Invisible Assets*. Harvard University Press, Cambridge, MA.

Kotler, P. (1980) *Marketing Management: Analysis Planning and Control*. Prentice-Hall, Englewood Cliffs, NJ.

Lööf, H. & Heshmatic, A. (2000) *Knowledge Capital and Performance Heterogeneity: A Firm Level Innovation Study*. SSE/EFI Working Paper Series in Economics and Finance No. 387, SSE/EFI: Stockholm, Sweden.

Maijoor, S. & van Witteloostuijn, A. (1996) An empirical test of the resource-based theory: Strategic regulation in the Dutch audit industry. *Strategic Management Journal*, **17**, 549–569.

National Audit Office (NAO) (2009) *Innovation Across Central Government*, March, TSO, London. Available from http://www.nao.org.uk/publications/0809/innovation_across_government.aspx (accessed 1 November 2010).

Nelson, P.R. (ed.) (1993) *National Innovation Systems: A Comparative Analysis*. Oxford University Press, Oxford.

Porter, M.E. (1980) *Competitive Strategy: Techniques for Analyzing Industries and Competitors*. The Free Press, New York.

Porter, M.E. (1985) *Competitive Advantage: Creating and Sustaining Superior Performance*. The Free Press, New York.

Rogers, E.M. (1983) *Diffusion of Innovations*, 3rd edn. The Free Press, New York.

Prahalad, C.K. & Hamel, G. (1990) The core competence of the corporation. *Harvard Business Review*, **May–June**, 71–91.

Sexton, M.G., Barrett, P. & Aouad, G. (1999) *Diffusion Mechanisms for Construction Research and Innovation into Small to Medium Sized Construction Firms*. CRISP–99/7, London.

Sexton, M.G. & Barrett, P.S. (2003a) A literature synthesis of innovation in small construction firms: Insights, ambiguities and questions. construction management and economics, **21, September**, 613–622.

Sexton, M.G. & Barrett, P.S. (2003b) Appropriate innovation in small construction firms. *Construction Management and Economics*, 21 September, 623–633.

Sexton, M.G. & Barrett, P.S. (2004) The role of technology transfer in innovation within small construction firms. *Engineering, Construction & Architecture Management*, **11**(5), 342–348.

Slater, S. & Narver, J.C. (1994) Does competitive environment moderate the market orientation-performance relationship? *Journal of Marketing*, **58**, 46–55.

Snow, C. & Hrebiniak, L.G. (1980) Strategy, distinct competence, and organizational performance. *Administrative Science Quarterly*, **25**, 317–336.

Susman, G.I. (1983) Action research: A sociotechnical systems perspective. In: ed. Morgan, G., *Beyond Method: Strategies for Social Research*. Sage, London, 95–113.

Teece, D.J., Pisano, G. & Shuen, A. (1997) Dynamic Capabilities and Strategic Management. In: ed. Foss, N.J., *Resources, Firms and Strategies*. Oxford University Press, New York, 268–287.

Van de Ven A.H., Polley, D., Garud, R. & Venkataraman, S. (1999) *The Innovation Journey*. Oxford University Press, New York.

von Hippel, E. (1988) *The Sources of Innovation*. Oxford University Press, New York.

Wernerfelt, B. (1984) A resource-based view of the firm. *Strategic Management Journal*, 5, 171–180.

Wheatley, M.J. (1992) *Leadership and the New Science*. Berrett-Koehler, San Francisco.

Culture and Innovation

Anita Liu and Richard Fellows

Why are there construction products and processes? The essential answer is that people have needs, wants and desires for buildings and infrastructure, which they strive to satisfy. In most of today's world, that satisfaction is achieved through exercising demand in a market economic system – the ability and preparedness to pay the (financial) price determines 'who gets what'. What is indisputable for construction is the centrality of 'the user' as the primary function of 'the client' stakeholder category. Complimentarily, the supply process depends on people as the 'active factor' – by making decisions and affecting the supply processes through managing and producing, both directly (e.g. an architect producing a design drawing; or a bricklayer laying bricks) and indirectly (e.g. an engineer using structural calculation software; or hiring a carpenter). However, cultural labelling has become widely used to caricature the construction industry – usually to emphasise undesirable aspects. A *macho* culture (Fielden *et al.*, 2001) conjures associations with physical strength, danger and risk taking, rather uncaring and brutal, etc; a *claims* culture (Rook *et al.*, 2003), which suggests strong pursuit of perceived rights, heightened opportunistic behaviour and self-centred individualism. Alongside such overt cultural labelling is the common criticism of fragmentation (Construction Task Force, 1998) – the separation of functions and activities, which otherwise may be described as 'division of labour' or specialisation. Of course, the key element rendering fragmentation an important detriment is the lack of the requisite integration and coordination of the components (Lawrence and Lorsch, 1967).

In construction, it is only over recent years that culture has become acknowledged as an important factor that affects performance of both products and processes; indeed, culture is a primary determinant of the

Construction Innovation and Process Improvement, First Edition.
Edited by Akintola Akintoye, Jack S. Goulding and Girma Zawdie.
© 2012 Blackwell Publishing Ltd. Published 2012 by Blackwell Publishing Ltd.

world's built environment, and how this is perceived and used. Moreover, culture underpins peoples' actions towards sustainability and so today's culture has major implications for innovation in the future.

This chapter gives an overview of culture, its relevance to construction, and examines the relationship of culture and innovation.

4.2   Culture and Construction

As construction projects and processes become ever more complicated, so the essentials of specialisation and integration grow in importance. The stakeholder perspective and agency theory have evolved to aid understanding of human behaviour in such circumstances, as multitudes of internal and external forces act on individuals. The temporary multi-organisation (TMO) (Cherns and Bryant, 1984) constitutes a useful analytic lens and incorporates the shifting, multi-goal coalition, which operates through fluid power structuring for realisation of construction projects. In this respect, construction projects, as for any good which is produced (components are produced and then assembled), these are subject to evaluative judgements of process (project management performance) and product (project performance) – not just by participants in the processes, but by a wider array of stakeholders, all of whom are likely to have differing criteria and criteria weightings. Furthermore, the realisation processes (depicted as a generic schematic in Figure 4.1) are of long duration, in which many inter-related decisions are made, which can impact on the project. In addition, performance forecasts are often required, and it is these that form the basis for many evaluations – notably by consultants advising commissioning clients. Commonly, such forecasts are 'best-guess', conglomerate estimates of input variables but treated as certain estimates with results presented in single-figure, deterministic terms (Reugg and Marshall, 1990). Given the nature of forecasts, it is only to be expected that they are unlikely to be close to the realised outcomes (Flyvbjerg, 2007) and so give rise to dissonance and dissatisfaction.

Most participants/stakeholders are business organisations for whom performance metrics can be generally categorised as financial, technical and relational. In the current world, the technical and relational criteria are usually significantly subservient to financial performance as 'Essentially, business is about appropriating value for oneself ... only by having the ability to appropriate value from relationships with others can business be sustained... [there must be conflicts of interest between vertical participants in supply chains, just as there are between those competing horizontally]... In Western culture most suppliers are basically opportunistic' (Cox, 1999). Thus, a 'business case' usually relates to a financial evaluation – the case being 'made' if the outcome indicates sufficient profit(ability).

The scenario emerges that construction projects are realised and then operate in a competitive context in which actors tend to be self-oriented and

Figure 4.1   The project realisation process (Fellows, 2009).

procurement arrangements result in projects being zero-sum 'games' in which one participant gains only at the expense of other(s). A systems approach, complimented by complexity theory, notes that a system (project, firm, industry) must respond appropriately to its environment to ensure survival, leading to the conclusion that the culture of construction is shaped by the environment (society, etc) within which it operates. The traditional analytic approach of Newtonian reductionism to understand the whole by examining the parts individually and then aggregating the results of the component analyses fails to allow for the synergistic effects of inter-relationships of the parts, and so a more holistic analytic approach is called for. In this respect, cultural investigations tend to adopt a high degree of aggregation and, essentially, give express acknowledgement to embeddedness – of behaviour in project atmosphere, in organisational climate, in organisational culture, and in national culture.

It should be noted that:
- Performance leads to satisfaction of participants and hence (perspectives of) project success;
- Performance-Satisfaction-Success also produces feed-forward in the 'cycling' of project data and information, to aid realisations of future projects through participants' perception-memory-recall filtering ('experiences'); and
- A similar model applies to projects in use (beneficial occupation), but with 'Facilities Management' and 'Maintenance and Adaptation' replacing 'Design' and 'Construction' as major functionary groups.

4.2.1   Culture

Culture is a construct that concerns people in groups, notably national, organisational and social, whereas personality relates to individuals. Kroeber and Kluckhohn (1952) carried out an extensive study of the literature and found 164 definitions of culture. They define culture as '...patterns, explicit and implicit of and for human behaviour acquired and transmitted by symbols, constituting the distinctive achievements of human groups, including their embodiment in artefacts; the essential core of culture consists of traditional (i.e. historically derived and selected) ideas and, especially, their attached values; culture systems may, on the one hand, be considered as products of action, on the other as conditioning elements of future action.'

Hofstede (1994a) defines culture as '...the collective programming of the mind which distinguishes one category of people from another.' Thus, culture is learned. Much may be learned behaviourally through perceiving, copying and responding to the behaviour of others and so much culture becomes tacit knowledge as in 'intuitively' knowing how to behave, how to interpret a message. Thus, Schein (1990) identifies the essence of culture to be a pattern of basic assumptions – constituting communal values that are taken for granted by the persons comprising the cultural group. An important aspect of the development of cultures is the formation of norms and limits of acceptable behaviour relating to critical incidents – often, as lessons learned from significant mistakes – which are communicated through stories passed on between members of the community; cultures also develop through identification with leaders and what they scrutinise, measure and control (hence, what leaders regard as important).

Models often depict culture as comprising concentric layers – physiological instincts and beliefs at the core (survival imperatives, religion, morality, etc) values as the intermediate layer (the hierarchical ordering of beliefs, perhaps with trade-offs) and cultural manifestations at the outer layer (as in behaviour, language, symbols, heroes, practices, artefacts). In this respect, Schein (2004) considers levels of culture to be artefacts, espoused beliefs and values, and underlying assumptions (as the deepest level). However, an holistic representation of these inter-relationships can be seen in Figure 4.2.

Culture may also be subject to group-based analysis and categorisation, which includes the categories of national culture, organisational culture, organisational climate, project atmosphere and behaviour of persons (Figure 4.3). The boundaries of the categories are fuzzy and permeable and so the categories 'bleed' into each other. Individuals may be of a certain nationality (e.g. Brazilian), work in a particular organisation (e.g. Skanska), belong to a 'social interest group' (e.g. Greenpeace) and exhibit certain behaviour (e.g. organisational citizenship behaviour). Furthermore, environmental and situational variables can affect behaviour which therefore can be regarded as contingent. An important consequence is confusion of the categories when 'managers' wish to effect change – in particular, what has been changed and the strength and permanence of any change – culture cannot be changed by use of a '40-hour workshop' (although behaviour modifications may result).

Behaviour, Heroes, Symbols, Artifacts, Language, etc.

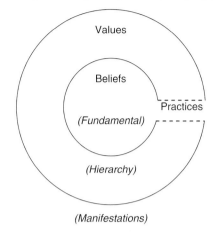

Figure 4.2 Layers of vulture (Hofstede (1980; 2001). Reproduced by permission of Geert Hofstede BV.

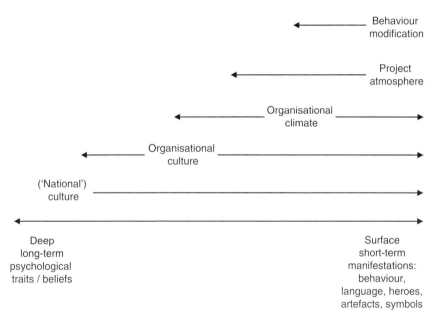

Figure 4.3 Culture spectrum (Fellows, 2006). Reproduced by permission of the Chartered Institute of Building.

Eldridge and Crombie (1974) voiced three concerns for examining culture – depth (values and commitment), breadth (coordination of the persons) and progression (coordination, development/change, over time). Often, cultures are caricatured by a small number of general perspectives, which are used to serve as simple guides to how people in those cultures behave and how visitors are expected to behave (Trompenaars and

Hampden-Turner, 1997). However, the construct, culture, contains many latent variables. To understand a culture, it is important to first determine the boundary of the culture (national, organisational, etc) and then what are the important manifest variables to examine through appropriate methods of collecting and analysing data. Such data and analyses are used to help gain insights into the deeper levels of cultural constructs – the values and beliefs (or other constructs depending on the model of culture adopted) of the members of the group(s) under study. Measurements are often comparative and so yield relative, rather than absolute, results (Hofstede, 1980).

4.2.2   National Culture

Hofstede (1980) determined the following dimensions from studying national cultures:

- *Power Distance*: 'the extent to which the less powerful members of institutions and organisations within a country expect and accept that power is distributed unequally.' (Hofstede, 1994b: 28);
- *Individualism/Collectivism*: 'individualism pertains to societies in which the ties between individuals are loose: everyone is expected to look after himself or herself and his or her immediate family. Collectivism as its opposite pertains to societies in which people from birth onwards are integrated into strong, cohesive in-groups, which throughout people's lifetimes continue to protect them in exchange for unquestioning loyalty.' (ibid: 51);
- Masculinity/Femininity: 'masculinity pertains to societies in which gender roles are clearly distinct (i.e. men are supposed to be assertive, tough, and focused on material success whereas women are supposed to be more modest, tender, and concerned with the quality of life); femininity pertains to those societies in which social gender roles overlap (i.e. both men and women are supposed to be modest, tender, and concerned with the quality of life).' (ibid: 82–83);
- *Uncertainty Avoidance*: 'the extent to which the members of a culture feel threatened by uncertain or unknown situations.' (ibid: 113); and
- *Long-Termism/Short-Termism*: 'the fostering of virtues orientated towards future rewards, in particular perseverance and thrift.' (ibid: 261)/*Short-Termism* – 'the fostering of virtues related to the past and present, in particular respect for tradition, preservation of "face", and fulfilling social obligations.' (ibid: 262–263) has been added (Hofstede, 1994b) following studies in Asia using a Chinese values survey (CVS) instrument, which detected important impacts of "Confucian Dynamism".

From this, Triandis and Gelfand (1998: 119) argue that both individualism and collectivism have horizontal (emphasising equality) and vertical (emphasising hierarchy) components – '…the most important attributes that distinguish among different kinds of individualism and collectivism are the relative emphases on horizontal and vertical social relationships.' Horizontal

Table 4.1 High context / low context (high content) cultures (Hall and Hall, 1990). Reproduced by permission of Nicholas Brealey Publishing.

Factor	High-context culture	Low-context culture
Overtness of messages	Many covert and implicit messages, with use of metaphor and reading between the lines.	Many overt and explicit messages that are simple and clear.
Locus of control and attribution for failure	Inner locus of control and personal acceptance for failure	Outer locus of control and blame of others for failure
Use of non-verbal communication	Much nonverbal communication	More focus on verbal communication than body language
Expression of reaction	Reserved, inward reactions	Visible, external, outward reaction
Cohesion and separation of groups	Strong distinction between in-group and out-group. Strong sense of family.	Flexible and open grouping patterns, changing as needed
People bonds	Strong people bonds with affiliation to family and community	Fragile bonds between people with little sense of loyalty.
Level of commitment to relationships	High commitment to long-term relationships. Relationship more important than task.	Low commitment to relationship. Task more important than relationships.
Flexibility of time	Time is open and flexible. Process is more important than product	Time is highly organized. Product is more important than process

individualists (HI) desire to be unique and distinct from groups; vertical individualists (VI) want to be distinguished, acquire status and compete with others. Horizontal collectivists (HC) emphasise common goals, interdependence and sociability; vertical collectivists (VC) emphasise the integrity of the in-group and are prepared to sacrifice their personal goals for the sake of in-group goals. Generally, collectivists belong to few in-groups, are highly loyal to in-group members, but tend to shun out-groups and their members (Gomez *et al.*, 2000); individualists can therefore be said to be loosely tied to many in-groups, and their memberships may be transitory.

Hofstede (1983) highlighted the correlation between wealth and individualism in various countries, noting '...Collectivist countries always show large Power Distances but Individualist countries do not always show small Power Distance.' Collectivist societies therefore tend to have a fairly rigid, often overt, social structure. In this respect, Hall and Hall (1990) employ high-context/low-context as the first dimension along which cultures may be analysed (Table 4.1).

In a high-context culture, many contextual elements can help people understand the meanings of messages, behaviours and other manifestations of the culture. In high context cultures, a lot is taken for granted, and so meaning

Table 4.2   Perspectives regarding time (Hall and Hall, 1990). Reproduced by permission of Nicholas Brealey Publishing.

Factor	Monochronic action	Polychronic action
Actions	Do one thing at a time	Do many things at once
Focus	Concentrate on the job at hand	Are easily distracted
Attention to time	Think about when things must be achieved	Think about what will be achieved
Priority	Put the job first	Put relationships first
Respect for property	Seldom borrow or lend things	Borrow and lend things often and easily
Timeliness	Emphasize promptness	Base promptness relationship factors

must be derived from the content of a message itself (which may appear vague, especially to a person from a high-content culture) and its interpretation in the prevailing circumstances/situation. Likewise, behaviour often tends to be indirect, and so people appear to be 'reserved'. Thus, a lot of intuition is necessary, together with a thorough understanding of both the language and the society. Conversely, in a low-context (high-content) culture, little is taken for granted. In low-context cultures, more content is needed but the resultant message is precise and explicit in its meaning, and so there is a low chance of misunderstanding; thus, people can be quite confident to interpret messages at 'face value', although such direct and obvious expression (and behaviour) can be offensive to people from high-context cultures.

Hall and Hall's second dimension of culture concerns the level of possessiveness of people over territory and objects. High territoriality includes clear and firm demarcation of (often, physical) boundaries and high needs for security to protect ownership (rights). People who are highly territorial tend to be low-context (high-content) and are likely to desire large amounts of physical space. People with low territoriality regard space, possessions and boundaries as low in importance, and so movements are easier. Low territoriality people tend to be high-context. Hall and Hall's third dimension of culture concerns how people perceive time along a continuum of monochronic/polychronic (Table 4.2). Persons who perceive time to be monochronic do one thing at a time, usually in a predetermined sequence. Such people tend to be low-context (high-content). In polychronic perceptions of time, human interaction is valued above time and material goods. That generates a low concern for 'getting things done' – things get done, 'in their own time'. Polychronic people tend to be high-context.

Trompenaars and Hampden-Turner (1997) investigated cultures' perspectives on time in sequential/synchronic terms (corresponding to monochronic/polychronic). They extended their study to examine how people of different cultures regard periods of time – past, present and future – to determine the relative importance of each period and how those periods relate to each other (overlaps or distances of separation). Their investigation yielded results that seem to correlate with Hofstede's fifth dimension of national cultures – long termism/short termism. In this respect, Trompenaars and Hampden-Turner (1997) suggested five value-oriented dimensions of culture which, they state, '...greatly influence our ways of doing business and managing as well as our responses in the face of moral dilemmas.' The dimensions are:

- *Universalism*: Particularism (rules-relationships);
- *Collectivism*: Individualism (group–individual);
- *Neutral*: Emotional (feelings expressed);
- *Diffuse*: Specific (degree of involvement); and
- *Achievement*: Ascription (method of giving status).

Although the dimensions relate to national cultures, they are of notable import for business activities, especially negotiations, and so not only blur the categorisation of national and organisational culture, but also reinforce the perspective of the embeddedness of organisational culture in national culture.

4.2.3   Organisational Culture

Denison (1996: 53) asserted that organisational culture is 'the deep structure of organisations, which is rooted in the values, beliefs and assumptions held by organisational members.' James *et al.* (2007: 21) describe organisational culture as 'the normative beliefs (i.e. system values) and shared behavioural expectations (i.e. system norms) in an organisation. However, Hofstede (1994b) defines organisational culture as '...the collective programming of the mind which distinguishes the members of one organisation from another;' presenting the following six dimensions for analysing organisational cultures:

1. *Process/Results Orientation*: technical and bureaucratic routines can be diverse – outcomes tend to be homogeneous;
2. *Job/Employee Orientation*: derives from the societal culture in which the organisation is embedded, as well as the influences of founders and managers;
3. *Professional/Parochial*: educated personnel identify with their profession(s) – people also identify with their employing organisation;
4. *Open/Closed System*: ease of admitting new people and of innovating; styles of internal and external communications;
5. *Tight/Loose Control*: degrees of formality, punctuality, etc, may depend on technology and rate of change; and
6. *Pragmatic/Normative*: how to relate to the environment, i.e. customers; pragmatism encourages flexibility.

Organisational cultures can therefore be said to be initiated by the founders of the organisation, given the culture of the society in which the organisation is embedded. Subsequently, the culture of an organisation is amended by others who have had major impact on the organisation's development (owners, major managers). Such people shape the values and behaviour of members of the organisation to develop the identity of the organisation through influence over the employment of staff and organisational practices. Organisational cultures (and climates) are self-perpetuating – persons who 'fit' are hired and they 'fit' because they are hired; errors of 'fit' are subject to resignation or dismissal. Organisational cultures develop to maintain effective and efficient working relationships amongst organisational members and stakeholders (both temporary and permanent). Thus, when organisations are brought into close operating contact, as with construction projects, their individual cultures are combined to produce the 'project atmosphere'. However, findings from amalgamations and takeovers are germane – that 'Usually the corporate culture of the most powerful or economically successful company dominates' (Furnham, 1997).

Both Denison (1997, 2009) and Cameron and Quinn (1999) employ competing values frameworks to model organisational cultures. In Denison's (1997, 2009) model, flexibility and stability are juxtaposed along one dimension with organisational focus – internal juxtaposed to external – on the other dimension. The resultant quadrants comprise mission, consistency, involvement and adaptability, each comprising three constituents (Figure 4.4). Denison employs a model comprising the same dimensions and quadrants but with different constituents to analyse leadership, thereby supporting a close relationship between leadership and organisational culture.

In Cameron and Quinn's (1999) model, 'flexibility and discretion' is juxtaposed to 'stability and control' on one dimension with 'internal

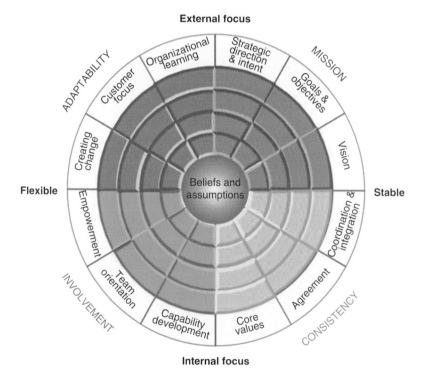

Figure 4.4   Denison's culture model. (www.denisonconsulting.com/advantage/research Model/model.aspx). Reproduced by permission of Denison Consulting.

focus and integration' and 'external focus and differentiation' juxtaposed on the other. The resultant model comprises four quadrants, each denoting a type of organisational culture – Clan, Adhocracy, Market, Hierarchy (Figure 4.5).

- *Clan:* 'Some basic assumptions in a clan culture are that the environment can be best managed through teamwork and employee development, customers are best thought of as partners, the organisation is in the business of developing a humane work environment, and the major task of management is to empower employees and facilitate their participation, commitment and loyalty' (ibid: 37).

Figure 4.5 Competing values and organisational cultures model (Fellows, 2006: 57, following Cameron and Quinn, 1999). Reproduced by permission of the Chartered Institute of Building.

- *Adhocracy:* 'A major goal of an adhocracy is to foster adaptability, flexibility and creativity where uncertainty, ambiguity and/or information-overload are typical. Effective leadership is visionary, innovative and risk-orientated. The emphasis is on being at the leading edge of new knowledge, products and/or services. Readiness for change and meeting new challenges are important' (ibid: 38–39).
- *Market:* 'The major focus of markets is to conduct transactions with other constituencies to create competitive advantage. Profitability, bottom line results, strength in market niches, stretch targets and secure customer bases are primary objectives for the organisation. Not surprisingly, the core values that dominate market type organisations are competitiveness and productivity' (ibid: 35).
- *Hierarchy:* 'The organisational culture compatible with this form is characterised by a formalised and structured place to work. Procedures govern what people do. Effective leaders are good coordinators and organisers. Maintaining a smooth-running organisation is important. The long-term concerns of the organisation are stability, predictability and efficiency. Formal rules and policy hold the organisation together' (ibid: 34).

Schein (1984) determines two main types of organisational culture, which bear strong resemblance to the organic-mechanistic organisational typology of Burns and Stalker (1961): 'free flowing' – an unbounded, egalitarian organisation with minimal formal structure, to encourage debate and internal competition; and 'structured' – a bounded, rigid organisation with clear rules, procedures and requirements. Furthermore, Handy (1985) suggests a typology of organisational cultures. Power culture is depicted as a web with the major power at the centre, emphasising control over subordinates and external agents (suppliers, etc, and nature). A role culture focuses on functions/professions that provide support to top management; emphasis is therefore on rules, hierarchy and status through legality, legitimacy and responsibility. In a task culture, jobs or projects are the major foci; an organisation is regarded as a net (as in a matrix organisation), and structures, functions and activities are evaluated in respect of their contributions to achievement of the organisation's objectives. In a person culture, people interact and cluster freely and emphasise meeting the needs of members of the organisation through consensus. Handy considers that the main factors influencing which organisational culture develops are goals and objectives, history and ownership, size, technology, environment and people. Williams *et al.*, (1989) advance categories of 'Power', 'Role', 'Task' and 'People', which correspond to Handy's (1985) typology.

4.2.4   Organisational Climate

Organisational culture is an important determinant of climate (Sarros *et al.*, 2008). Moran and Volkwein (1992) argue that climate reflects the shared knowledge and meanings embodied in an organisation's culture. Hence, organisational climate is regarded by Sarros *et al.* (2008) as the expression of underlying cultural practices that arise in response to contingencies in the organisation's internal and external environment. While organisational culture focuses on the shared behavioural expectations and normative beliefs in work units, climate describes the way individuals perceive the personal impact of their work environment on themselves (Glisson and James, 2002). 'Organisational Climate is a relatively enduring quality of the internal environment of an organisation that:

a) is experienced by its members;
b) influences their behaviour; and
c) can be described in terms of the values of a particular set of characteristics (or attributes) of the organisation.' Tagiuri and Litwin (1968: 27).

Hence, climate distinguishes an organisation from other similar organisations. Organisational climate both reflects and shapes the working experiences shared by members of the organisation and so indicates their perceptions of autonomy, trust, cohesion, fairness, recognition, support and innovation through shared knowledge and meanings. Organisational climate is an important contributor to relative homogeneity amongst members through recruitment and retention.

Organisational climate is also grounded in the practices of an organisation as experienced by its members, and so is a less deep-seated construct than culture. James *et al.* (2007) differentiate organisational climate from psychological climate - i.e. the former is an aggregation of individual perceptions of the work environment, the latter refers to the perceptions individuals have of those workplaces as they reflect personal values and psychological desires. Organisational climate can therefore measure the organisation's openness to change and its provision of resources to become innovative (Sarros *et al.*, 2008).

4.3   Culture and Innovation

The understanding of innovation has changed from scientific research and development (R&D) to include changes to services, ways of working and delivery, customer insight, etc (Roper *et al.*, 2009). The National Endowment for Science, Technology and the Arts (NESTA) (2008) argues that total innovation is integrating innovation in new technologies, products and processes with innovation in new services, business models and organisational forms. Thus, to stimulate wider innovative activities, R&D must be complemented 'with a focus on stronger and broader skills for business, using taxation, regulation and procurement to boost innovation…' (Anon. 2008: 34).

In the UK, it is acknowledged in the report on *Total Innovation* (www.nesta.org.uk) by NESTA (2008) that there are six major high technology areas with world-leading strengths and they represent the majority of R&D expenditure in the UK, comprising aerospace, pharmaceuticals, automotive telecommunications, software and electronics. However, the construction sector remains a low-level innovation sector in the UK, as measured by the Innovation Index (Roper *et al.*, 2009). UK companies often focus on a linear model of innovation enforced by the traditional innovation indicators (e.g. R&D expenditure and patent production), which obscures the potentially significant forms of 'hidden innovation' – as mostly seen in high-technology sectors. Roper *et al.* (2009) also find that there are significant levels of hidden innovation in several sectors, where levels of traditional R&D investment are low. The four types of hidden innovation (NESTA, 2008) include:

1. effective use of new materials, which involve learning on the job;
2. new organisational structures and business models;
3. novel combination of existing technologies and processes; and
4. innovative solutions to small-scale problems and challenges, which happen 'under the radar'.

Hidden innovations suggest that the traditional indicators of R&D investment and the number of patents are not sufficient to provide the full picture of innovation; whereas the focus on HC (e.g. *learning*, motivation for creativity, etc) and organisational issues (e.g. culture, climate, reward systems, leadership, empowerment, etc), which are discussed in this chapter, are essential to nurture the firms towards innovation for sustaining development.

However, construction and project management research relating to culture studies are increasing in diversity. For instance, some of the covered topics include knowledge transfer, comparative culture between sectors, role of cultural boundary spanners, organisational culture and project culture (Brochner *et al.*, 2002; Chan and Tse, 2003; Liu *et al.*, 2006; Zhang and Liu, 2006; Ajmal and Koskinen, 2008; Ankrah and Proverbs, 2009; Chen, *et al.*, 2009; Ofori and Toor, 2009; Di Marco *et al.*, 2010; Cheung *et al.*, 2011). However, to appreciate the role of culture in construction and innovation, one has to examine the concepts of various 'labels' of culture - for example, innovation culture, learning culture, trip-helix culture and project atmosphere.

4.3.1   Role of Culture in Construction

Culture represents a heritage of who we are, what we know and what we believe. Innovation systems can be seen as development of social systems in achievement of their strategy, i.e. 'Processing innovation implies rules of cooperation and social behaviour of a specific cultural setting' (Pohlmann *et al.*, 2005: 3). Thus, the structure and development of innovation depends on the cultural software of a thematic and spatial concept and the political framework, so that innovation is determined by culture in the following ways (Pohlmann *et al.*, 2005):

- affective frames of identity and difference;
- cognitive frames of knowledge; and
- normative sets of values, norms and beliefs.

While social rules of interplay are observed and analysed as development of co-operation structures (or social systems), it is noted that the cultural software defining the innovation system varies on different levels. Palazzo (2005) argues that the organisation of transnational movements of innovation are anchored on the first level, where innovation models appear as highly visible and thematic (e.g. 'Balanced Score Card', 'business reengineering', 'CIM'. However, success depends on the second level of organisation, where expressions of new innovation models are integrated into existing frames of partly thematic cognitive maps. This leaves the underground third level of culture, where communication, attitudes and values come into play in the tacit, invisible level of stabilising innovation models, untouched.

Taking the view that the innovation process encompasses the cultural intertwining of thematic, human resources and spatial/time concepts in social systems demonstrates that no single actor can be in control of all the rules and frames that dictate the development of innovation. Hence, Gebhardt (2005) argues that innovation management is more about managerial belief systems, which are acknowledged by other actors, for example, belief systems of venture capitalists differ from the inventors, hence taking this perspective, the role of culture in innovation is important.

4.3.2   Innovation Culture

Innovation culture has become the focus of recent research on innovation and technology development. It is well acknowledged that innovation is one of the drivers of a knowledge society, and researchers (Hadjimanolis, 2010) have advocated that creation, innovation and diffusion processes are embedded in culture that vary between different countries and organisations. Culture has been studied at different levels, for example, individual, team, organisational and national, and all these levels are inter-related as national culture influences individuals, thence the organisations. Hence, innovation culture of an organisation or society, can be considered as a subset of, and embedded in, the national culture.

Innovation culture reflects the societal dynamics of self- and collective aspirations. Simply, there is an innovation culture when the cultural characteristics of an organisation encourage innovation, for example, leadership that nurtures creativity (Amabile et al., 2004), communication and feedback, reward systems and innovation champions. 'Innovative culture is a way of thinking and behaving that creates, develops and establishes values and attitudes within a firm', which involves changes that 'conflict with conventional employee behaviour', but may 'in turn create highly effective cultural and managerial transformations regarding innovativeness' (Çakar and Ertürk, 2010: 345). Hadjimanolis (2010) suggests that the dimensions of innovation culture are creativity, attitude to change, attitude to risk, attitude to technology, attitude to learning, institutions, acceptance of failure and mistakes, communication and tolerance for dissenters; the continuum of the 'innovation-averse culture' and the 'ideal innovation culture' is depicted by the magnitude of each dimension. For instance, an innovation-averse culture is low on creativity, but an ideal innovation culture is high on creativity. However, innovation culture is not static and can be 'changed'; in fact, there is a constant evolutionary change in the meaning of values and norms (Inglehart and Baker, 2000) in any culture. Therefore, it is possible to change from an innovation-averse culture to a more innovation-conducive culture through encouragement of creativity, learning, communication, etc. However, changing an organisation's culture can be difficult (Johnson, 2001), if not impossible.

The tendency to focus on short-term return on investment and risk aversion can be potentially devastating to the promotion of an innovation culture and the long-term survival of the business. Little (2008, cited in Anon., 2008) advocates that during a downturn, the key to gaining value is to recognise that innovation is a significant and powerful tool for bottom line optimisation, and offers five strategies to foster innovation culture:

1. identify and understand how the organisation's unwritten rules relate to innovation behaviour;
2. proactively address risk aversion and short-termism to ensure high-return projects are maintained, even in the face of risks;
3. make sure management behaviour aligns with public declarations on the innovation agenda;
4. recognise opportunity costs and use resources creatively to pursue some riskier projects; and
5. explore open innovation partnership – past collaborators and new potential partners.

Furthermore, Hadjimanolis (2010: 97) advocated that 'innovation as an interactive process usually takes place within work groups with participation of all employees, who should receive motivation and training for creativity and innovation in a supportive work environment.' However, it should be noted that there is no single type of culture that is ideal for the development and adoption of innovation – as culture can stimulate as well as hinder innovation (van Duivenboden and Thaens, 2008). Therefore, it is crucial to 'match' the culture to the context – the organisation structure-culture fit, thereby securing continuous improvement through sustaining creativity. Finally, it is also important to acknowledge that some researchers include *learning* as one of the dimensions of innovation culture (Dobni, 2008), but others treat learning culture as a different construct. The next section examines learning culture separately.

4.3.3   Learning Culture

The role of learning is widely recognised as pivotal in innovation and the concept of organisational learning has been widely discussed (Argyris, 1992). Increasing attention has also been paid to learning organisations in human resource management and organisational development literature. Features of the learning organisation enable organisations to develop more flexible and adaptable systems that improve long-term performance (Senge, 1992; Slater and Narver, 1995). According to Kaiser and Holton (1998), the literature on learning organisations and innovation focuses on the facilitating role of the same organisational variables that enhance the adaptability and flexibility of organisations to improve long-term performance – closely related to, and influenced by, variables including culture, climate, leadership, organisational structures, systems and environment. An organisational learning culture is therefore one that values the creation, sharing and application of knowledge, and can influence specific manifestations of psychological climate in the form of a learning transfer climate (Bates and Khasawneh, 2005).

Mai (1996) suggests that learning organisations are differentiated by the degree to which they learn better or faster and they are revealed through outcomes such as creativity and innovation, which are supported by psychological climates and human resource systems that support learning. Bates and Khasawneh (2005) examined the relationship between organisational learning culture and innovation and found that the learning transfer climate is a mediating variable. More specifically, they concluded that innovation requires not only an organisational culture that allows learning and the generation of creative ideas to take place, but also a psychological climate that fosters an individual's ability to share and apply that learning. Therefore, it is suggested that organisations, which intend to pursue innovation, should analyse their culture and climate to determine what changes may be needed to facilitate learning and the transfer of creative problem solving.

4.3.4   Triple Helix Culture

The triple helix model, emphasising external linkages and collaboration, is grounded in the concept of national and regional systems of innovation, where learning (and knowledge transfer) occurs and the availability and access to knowledge is the most critical resource. It is also claimed that the triple helix model is an extension of the study of technological change advocated by Rothwell (1992), which emphasises the influence of networks, collaboration and alliances in a variety of inter-organisational relationships (Leydesdorff and Etzkwitz, 1998; Etzkowitz and Carvalho de Mello, 2004). Central to the triple helix model is the transfer and use of knowledge through networking, both intra- and inter-organisational, with the view to innovate; hence, learning and the learning transfer climate are important elements. Thus, according to Etzkowitz and Carvalho de Mello (2004), the triple helix denotes the university-industry-government in a relatively equal, yet interdependent, institutional relationship in which their roles overlap and where a triple helix culture of innovation in economic and social development is possible. Knowledge transfer is no longer considered as a linear process, but a complex set of organisational ties with overlapping boundaries (Leydesdorff and Etzkowitz, 1998), for example, universities take on entrepreneurial tasks, while firms develop an academic dimension in sharing knowledge. Saad and Zawdie (2005: 97) refer to the triple helix culture in their analysis of innovation in Algeria and assert that the 'major challenge for the development of the triple helix culture in developing countries is one of drawing a balance between the skill development objective and the knowledge accumulation objective of policy.' Learning based on actions, therefore, must be supplemented by cognition, that is, training initiatives should not be driven by short-term objectives alone. The constraints faced by developing countries concern the issues of power, bureaucracy, rigid boundaries, hierarchy, adversarial relationships and lack of trust (Saad and Zawdie, 2005). However, Pohlmann et al. (2005: 3) observed that the triple helix interaction was loaded with uncertainty and a lack of transparency, where organisations often 'try to carry out their own innovation strategy following their own rules and imply specific tools they believe in. As a consequence, belief systems differ to a great extent.'

A culture based on the triple helix model is closely associated with learning. According to Saad and Zawdie (2005), a learning strategy that supports a triple helix innovation system needs to challenge the traditional forms of learning to:

1. endorse the need for learning and change;
2. adopt a learning approach that involves both actions and cognition; and
3. develop a culture conducive to organisational learning.

However, according to Pohlmann et al. (2005), there are differences in the belief systems of the triple helix organisations; hence, if differences in their belief systems persist, it is arguable whether a triple helix culture with values and beliefs common to the participating organisations is possible.

4.3.5   Project Culture/Project Atmosphere

Organisational cultures are often initiated by the founders of the organisation, given the culture of the society in which the organisation is embedded. Consequently, the culture of an organisation is amended by others who have had major impact on the organisation's development (owners, major managers). Such people shape the values and behaviour of members of the organisation to develop the identity of the organisation through influence over the employment of staff and organisational practices.

For construction and similar project-based industries, failure to appreciate the nature of culture has spawned notions of cultural formation and change that are superficial, and so can be affected in the short term. Hence, there has arisen the concept of a 'project culture', which has been examined, even for short duration projects. Such a perspective also fosters the notion of control by management, such that a culture change can be effected rapidly and under managerial control to, usually, effect efficiency savings. While it is appropriate to consider that long-term, mega-projects are likely to develop their own cultures, the same cannot be said for smaller projects of shorter durations. On such projects, the concept of 'project culture' is essentially an amalgam of the cultures of the constituent organisations (and societies), as transmitted to the project by their more powerful agents (Liu and Fellows, 2008); and, perhaps more appropriately therefore, referred to as 'project atmosphere' (analogous to workplace atmosphere) (Hovmark and Nordqvist, 1996). In addition, acknowledging that project organisations are often of a temporary nature (Cherns and Bryant, 1984), when organisations are brought into close operating contact (as on construction projects), their individual cultures tend to combine to produce the 'project atmosphere'. Cognisant of this, Pohlmann *et al.* (2005) noted that collaborators in the triple helix innovation model of alliances could pursue their own strategy (and strategic goals), and their values and beliefs (which are fundamental elements in the construct of *culture*) may therefore differ extensively. Thus, arguably, if there are no common values or beliefs, is there still a common culture (the project culture) amongst the project organisational members?

4.3.6   Other Forms of Culture

There are other 'types' of culture associated with innovation, one of which is the cluster culture in the Kyoto Model of Innovation and Entrepreneurship (Ibata-Arens, 2008). Through this, a cluster is formed when the economic dynamism in a region has continuously produced highly profitable entrepreneurial firms leading to a self-sustaining critical mass of firms (Ibata-Arens, 2008). Hence, the term 'cluster' describes the concentration of innovative activity in certain local communities (DeBresson, 1996; OECD, 2001).

Researchers also refer to the culture of public administration (van Duivenboden and Thaens, 2008; Arnaboldi *et al.*, 2010), which has its own set of barriers and constraints to innovation. For instance, Van Duivenboden and Thaens (2008) assert that the traditional bureaucratic organisational culture within the public sector often hinders innovation, but innovations do take place within government organisations; hence, they conclude that the reciprocity iterative process of mutual influence between innovation and culture change, which co-evolve within the specific government environment. In addition, research devoted to culture change in order to achieve innovation has also gained prominence (Pitta, 2009; Hadjimanolis, 2010), along with awareness of cultural differences and characteristics attributed to Eastern societies with those in the West (note: the term 'Eastern' is used loosely in the same manner that 'Western' is), where Eastern people are often viewed as flexible/adaptive, whilst Westerners are characterised as would-be controllers. Thus, traditionally, Eastern people tend to regard themselves as subservient to natural forces and desires to be in harmony with nature (as do people from other parts of the world, e.g. Africa, Australia, etc). Change and, hence, uncertainty is accepted as inevitable, truth is determined by spiritual (religious and philosophical) principles and considerations of time are long-term oriented. Western people, in contrast, tend to regard themselves as somewhat in control of nature and so can harness many of its forces to improve human society. Following this analogy, Westwood and Low (2003) noted that it has become increasingly important to have an informed understanding of the extent to which creativity and innovation processes vary across cultures. 'The Western creativity worker is predatory: he grabs the insight for a purpose ... A process-oriented, rather than a product-oriented creative person would use insight-producing states to ... obtain 'enlightenment'" (Krippner and Arons, 1973: 121). In Eastern cultures, the role of creativity concerns providing personal fulfilment and enlightenment, or connection to an inner realm of reality (Kuo, 1996). However, 'there is insufficient evidence to enable definitive statements to be made about systematic differences across cultures in personality or cognitive style with respect to creativity' (Westwood and Low, 2003: 235).

4.4   Factors Affecting Innovation

There are various endogenous (internal to the organisational) and exogenous (external to the organisation) factors that can enhance innovative working in organisations. Whilst strategic management literature covers many of the exogenous factors (as well as endogenous ones), this chapter focuses on the variables internal to the organisations. For example, according to Patterson, *et al.* (2009), leadership capability, organisational culture and organisational values are amongst the most important factors and initiatives that enhance innovative working. However, not many working practices that promote innovation are being readily adopted by organisations. This section examines the factors of creativity, creative climate, leadership, empowerment and other related organisational variables.

4.4.1   Creativity and Creative Climate

Central to the idea of innovation is creativity: 'Creativity is the seed of all innovation', where creativity is defined as 'the production of novel and useful ideas in any domain' (Amabile *et al.*, 1996: 1155). 'Innovations are the practical application of creative ideas, and an organisation cannot innovate unless it has the capacity to generate creative ideas' (Westwood and Low, 2003: 236). In this respect, Miron *et al.* (2004) reviewed the literature on the culture of innovation, and determined that high autonomy, risk-taking, tolerance of mistakes and low bureaucracy were the most prevalent dimensions. However, despite a significant interaction effect of creativity and innovation culture, creative people are not always highly innovative. Most importantly, innovative performance depends on the organisation culture in which people operate (Miron *et al.*, 2004). Hence, a creative climate, supported by organisational culture, is essential.

The traditional psychological approach to creativity focuses on the characteristics of creative persons (MacKinnon, 1965), but the sociological approach takes the view that both the level and the frequency of creative behaviours are influenced by the social environment (Woodman *et al.*, 1993). Following this theme, it is found that while workplace atmosphere and workplace innovative activity are closely intertwined, individual employee creativity relates to these two dimensions to a lesser degree

(Wongtada and Rice, 2008), indicating that there is a need to convert creativity into innovation. In addition, Unsworth *et al.* (2005) found that support for innovation does not significantly predict creativity. Perhaps what constitutes a creative climate in the workplace therefore needs to be precisely defined? With this in mind, climate has be defined as a psychologically meaningful description of the work environment (James and Jones, 1979), which is affected by organisational characteristics such as culture, structure and managerial behaviour (Burke and Litwin, 1992). Campbell, *et al.* (1970: 390) defined climate as 'a set of attributes specific to a particular organisation that may be induced from the way the organisation deals with its members and its environment. For the individual member within an organisation, climate takes the form of a set of attitudes and expectancies which describe the organisation in terms of static characteristics … and behaviour-outcome and outcome-outcome contingencies.' In the context of innovation, Bates and Khasawneh (2005: 99) proposed that climate 'could be reflected in perceptions of task related support for creative learning and problem solving or in the cognitive (e.g. attitudes about change and innovation) and affective states (e.g. motivation to innovate) that ensue from these perceptions.'

While there are many classifications of organisational climates, the three types of climates that are more closely associated with innovation are learning climate, innovative climate and creativity climate. For instance, Bates and Khasawneh (2005) found that supportive learning transfer climates, in the form of individual efficacy beliefs, attitudes about change, and effort-outcome and performance-outcome expectancies, are consistent with organisational cultures that believe in and value learning as an adaptive strategy. An innovative climate is a climate wherein actors are willing to change (van Duivenboden and Thaens (2008), and is closely associated with innovation culture discussed earlier. In addition, based on Amabile *et al.* (1996), a creative climate is thus proposed as the psychological context of creativity representing the work environment perceptions that can influence the creative work carried out in organisations. In this respect, there are some instruments developed to assess the work environment for creativity, for instance, the Creative Climate Questionnaire (developed in Swedish) by Ekvall *et al.* (1983, cited in Amabile *et al.* 1996), where KEYS were developed by Amabile *et al.* (1996). Through KEYS, the *work environment scales* included work group supports, challenging work, organisational encouragement, supervisory encouragement, organisational impediments, freedom, workload pressure and sufficient resources; the *criterion scales* included two variables of creativity and productivity. Furthermore, Oldham and Cummings (1996) found that employees produced creative work when they had appropriate creativity-relevant characteristics (based on personality), and faced a favourable working environment in the organisational context of challenging job complexity, with supportive and non-controlling supervision. It was also found that work environment for creativity is closely associated with leader support (Amabile *et al.*, 2004). Other examples in creativity research can be found in the works of Farmer *et al.* (2003), Zhou and Shalley (2003) and Egan (2005).

4.4.2   Leadership

A creative climate is closely associated with leadership. Leader support is proposed to be a key element, which supports a work environment for creativity (Amabile *et al.*, 2004) and, more specifically, transformation leadership (Waldman and Bass, 1991) is related to organisational innovation. Specifically, Jung *et al.* (2003) assert that transformational leadership enhances innovation by engaging employees' personal value systems – encouraging employees to think creatively. Elenkov and Manev (2005) found that the socio-cultural context is important in the leadership-innovation relationship in 12 European countries, confirming that leaders positively influence innovation processes. The type of leadership required to change culture was transformational, because culture change needs enormous energy and commitment to achieve outcomes; thus, according to Sarros *et al.* (2008: 148), transformational leadership 'can help build a strong organisational culture and thereby contribute to a positive climate for organisational innovation and subsequently influence innovative behaviour.'

Ogbonna and Harris (2000) found a link between participative leadership and innovative culture; and Ostroff *et al.* (2003) identified leadership as an emergent process that acts on both organisational culture and climate. More recently, Sarros *et al.* (2008) established the link of transformational *leadership*, organisational *culture* and *climate* for innovation through structural equations, modelled from a sample of 1,158 managers. In effect, culture is the lens through which leader vision is manifested, which helps build the climate necessary for organisations to become innovative (James *et al.*, 2007).

The leader's vision is therefore strongly associated with organisational culture and innovation (Damanpour and Schneider, 2006) and visionary leaders are often associated with organisations having adequate resources, funding, personnel and rewards to innovate, as well as time for workers to pursue their creative ideas (Sarros *et al.*, 2008). More importantly, vision is mediated through organisational culture, although caution is drawn that the capacity of leaders to define a vision is one thing, and to have that vision accepted and acted upon (as anticipated) is quite another. Hence, it is suggested that 'articulating vision can achieve results only when its development involves those it is most intended to influence, the workers and clients of the organisation' (Sarros *et al.*, 2008: 154). In this respect, Amabile *et al.* (2004) also found that *vision* was important in leadership, and that the effect of the leader's behaviour on employees' perceptions and creativity are neither static nor uni-directional. Amabile *et al.* (2004) also proposed that certain behavioural traits should be reduced, if the work environment of creativity is to be protected, that is, 'giving assignments without sufficient regard to the capability or other responsibilities of the subordinate receiving them, micro-managing the details of high level subordinates' work, and dealing inadequately with difficult technical or inter-personal problems, whether due to technical incompetence, inter-personal incompetence, inattention, or sloth.'

4.4.3   Empowerment

Çakar and Ertürk (2010) defined empowerment as an energising process that expands the feelings of trust and control in one as well as in one's organisation, which leads to outcomes such as enhanced self efficacy and performance. Therefore, empowerment is constructed as participation in decision making and access to information is shared by the management; where managerial strategies and processes are derived from the organisational culture (Conger and Kanungo, 1988; Spreitzer, 1996). In Çakar and Ertürk's (2010) study of 93 small-sized and medium-sized enterprises (SMEs), with 743 respondents in Turkey, empowerment was positively related to innovation capability on both the individual and firm level analyses. Specifically, empowerment was seen to have a mediating effect on culture and innovation capability – being an antecedent of innovation capability and a consequence of organisational culture. Thus, it was deemed important to focus on managerial practices that enhanced empowerment in order to promote innovation.

From an empowerment perspective, high power distance cultures often expect supervisors to control information, make decisions and tell subordinates what to do (Newman and Nollan, 1996); which can also inhibit information sharing between supervisors and subordinates (Randolph and Sashkin, 2002). Hence, efficacy of empowerment is doubtful in high power distance cultures. Contrary to high individualist organisations, where employees prefer sharing information that directly relates to their jobs, employees in collectivistic cultures share resources and ideas, and are therefore prepared to participate in collective interests (Sagie and Aycan, 2003). Thus, it is also easier to achieve empowerment in cultures with high assertiveness focus (Randolph, 2000) and high uncertainty avoidance with low tolerance for ambiguity (Randolph and Sashkin, 2002). Therefore, organisational culture has a strong link with politics and the distribution of power within the organisation, which 'makes clear that introducing innovation in an organisation, through its cultural dimension, is shaped by, but also can have consequences for, concepts such as authority and organisational politics' (van Duivenboden and Thaens, 2008: 219). Dougherty and Hardy (1996) revealed that the inability to connect new products with organisational resources, processes and strategy often thwarted innovation in large mature organisations, where innovators lacked the power to make these connections, hence suggesting that organisations should reconfigure their systems of power to become capable of sustained innovation.

4.4.4   Other Organisational Variables Relating to Organisational Development

Dougherty and Hardy (1996: 1146) found that large mature organisations could not achieve sustained innovation, because innovators within them could not solve innovation-to-organisation problems - that is, 'availability of resources, processes and meaning was piecemeal [and] depended primarily on individuals,' rather than through the organisational system. Hence, focus on organisational development variables is essential for promoting innovation. Therefore, within business, organisational development emphasises employees' skills training and problem-solving capabilities, but another important factor is the development of a firm's structure and rewards (Pitta, 2009: 448) – where '*structure* is a group of systems by which individual creativity is harnessed by the organisation', to allow creativity to be channelled in the service of goals and objectives. For instance, in a case study of Portugal Telecom (Pitta, 2009), it was advocated that the organisation owed its success to a strategy of fostering innovation across the company by using clear metrics to guide each employee's contribution, thereby fostering individual innovation efforts – to create a climate and culture of innovation by using the company's internal *communication* system, and operating a *reward* system to build interest in the innovation effort.

Other organisational variables relating to innovativeness (Kitchell, 2001) include long-term corporate goals (in response to competitors and the environment), proactive information search (market intelligence gathering/ knowledge acquisition), international market extension (adaptability/ outreach) and flexibility (to reduce resistance to change). In particular, resistance to (organisational and culture) change is a significant barrier to innovation.

4.4.5   Culture Change

If culture is viewed as a sub-system of an organisation (where culture defines the success of the organisation), 'culture can be an important barrier for organisational change, while at the same time altering the culture of the organisation is a fundamental condition for realising a substantial change of the organisation' (van Duivenboden and Thaens, 2008: 219). However, if culture is viewed as an aspect system, it is a 'dimension of all the structures and processes within the organisation... Everything in an organisation can then have a cultural dimension, such as, for example, language, structure and technology' (van Duivenboden and Thaens, 2008: 219). In the case of innovation, it is particularly relevant where culture is a sub-system – innovation requires organisational change, and hence change in the culture of an organisation. In this respect, research findings point to the need for culture change in most cases where innovation is to be promoted (Pitta, 2009). Concepts of value shift and behaviour modifications can therefore be seen to be closely associated with culture change. Usually, motivation schemes are developed to modify the behaviour of employees to increase their output (productivity) by offering positive, systematic reinforcement through rewards that are valued by the employees (commonly financial). Securing the reward is contingent on both behavioural change and enhanced performance. The basis of the scheme, from the employer's perspective, is that intended changes in employees' behaviour should cause increased productivity output, which would be more profitable for the employer. The effectiveness of the reinforcements as motivators to change behaviour is however likely to vary between people; reinforcements can operate in the negative direction too – as 'punishments' for unwanted behaviour, as in employment dismissal.

Behaviour modification (BMod) can operate at the level of the organisation, for example, a change to be more ethical (e.g. purchasing timber from sustainable forests only, performing more corporate social responsibility, etc). However, it is common for organisational BMod to occur because the organisation's management believe that such changes are good holistically *per se*, which in turn will lead to enhanced financial performance of the organisation and, according to Williamsonian opportunism, consequently improve their personal position and rewards too. However, through any BMod scheme, there are likely to be issues of ethics relating to personal (usually employee) choice, and a significant aspect of this is that the causal chain tends to operate rapidly. Furthermore, a potential detriment of this is that (e.g. financial rewards as reinforcement) the effectiveness of this may be only temporary. However, the sustained use of legislation to affect BMod coupled with a programme of education, could lead to culture change in the long term through changes in people's beliefs and their practices. This is important for promoting personal and industrial safety, for example.

4.5   Conclusion

Traditional metrics for 'assessing' innovation have tended to focus on investment in R&D and its outputs. In this respect, various NESTA reports (www.nesta.org.uk) have emphasised the change in the understanding of *innovation*: 'where once it was understood to be largely the result of scientific R&D, it is now seen more widely to include changes to services, ways of working and delivery, customer insight and many other forms' (Roper *et al.*, 2009: 4) - that is, *hidden innovation*. Based on Hansen and Birkinshaw's (2007) conceptual framework of the three sequential phases of innovation (i.e. knowledge investment, innovation and value creation), two of the findings in Roper *et al.*'s (2009) report (comparing the Innovation Index of nine sectors in the UK) have implications for the construction sector, specifically:

1. there are significant levels of hidden innovation in traditionally low R&D investments sectors, where innovation capability also varies strongly between firms within those sectors; and
2. the construction sector is comparatively weak in all stages (i.e. accessing knowledge, building innovation, commercialisation) of the innovation process, where there are low levels of innovative activity, and firms are therefore less likely to access external knowledge or encourage employee team-working.

Hidden innovations include new business structures/models and innovative solutions to small-scale problems that happen 'under the radar'

(NESTA, 2008); where the focus on HC (e.g. learning, motivation for creativity, etc) and organisational issues (e.g. culture, climate, reward systems, leadership, empowerment, etc) are essential. This chapter examined these relationships, particularly how leaders can foster a creative climate with organisational support and rewards systems to empower and motivate employees to 'think out of the box'. In this respect, the construction sector has a number of hidden innovations, especially innovative solutions to small problems on site, etc, which have hitherto gone unnoticed and unrecorded. These creative solutions are fundamental in 'knowledge transfer' for capturing (experiential, etc) learning from project to project. The focus on construction research relating to knowledge transfer therefore needs to flourish outside the boundary of ICT *per se*, to capture some of the 'softer' issues or 'elements that foster hidden innovation'. Roper *et al.*'s (2009) message that low innovation sectors could have high hidden innovations is therefore encouraging in this sense. Furthermore, there is plenty of scope for 'creative problem solving', especially when projects have always been enveloped in many uncertainty variables.

Finally, learning (including learning from other sectors) and creativity is crucial for an innovation culture. Leaders with *vision* can therefore be considered as pivotal drivers here, especially visionary leaders with the foresight to 'plan ahead' in order to fully benefit from this.

4.6   Acknowledgements

Part of the contents of this Chapter are based on a research grant funded by the Research Grants Council of Hong Kong, China ("The influence of creative climate and learning in fostering innovation culture in construction", RGC ref.no. 715111). The support of the RGC is gratefully acknowledged.

References

Ajmal, M.M. & Koskinen, K.U. (2008) Knowledge transfer in project-based organizations: an organizational culture perspective. *Project Management Journal*, 39(1), 7–15.

Amabile, T.M., Conti, R., Coon, H., Lazenby, J. & Herron, M. (1996) Assessing the work environment for creativity. *Academy of Management Journal*. 39(5), 1154–1184.

Amabile, T.M., Schatzel, E.A., Moneta, G.B. & Karmer, S.J. (2004) Leader behaviours and the work environment for creativity: Perceived leader support. *The Leadership Quarterly*. 15, 5–32.

Arnaboldi, M., Azzone, G. & Palermo, T. (2010) Managerial innovations in central government: not wrong, but hard to explain. *The International Journal of Public Sector Management*. 23(1), 78–93.

Ankrah, N. & Proverbs, D. (2009) Factors influencing the culture of a construction project organisation. *Journal of Engineering, Construction and Architectural Management*, 16(1), 26–47.

Anon (2008) Reviewing innovation effort. *Strategic Direction*, 24(19), 32–34.

Argyris, C. (1992) *On organisational learning*. Blackwell Publishers, Cambridge, MA.

Bates, R. & Khasawneh, S. (2005) Organizational learning culture, learning transfer climate and perceived innovation in Jordanian organizations. *International Journal of Training and Development*. **9**(2), 96–109.

Bröchner, J., Josephson, P.E. & Kadefors, A. (2002) Swedish construction culture, quality management and collaborative practice. *Building Research & Information*, **30**(6), 392–400.

Burke, W. & Litwin, G. (1992) A causal model of organizational performance and change. *Journal of Management*. **18**(3), 523–545.

Burns, T. & Stalker, G.M. (1961) *The Management of Innovation*. Tavistock Publications, London.

Çakar, N.D. & Ertürk, A. (2010) Comparing innovation capability of small and medium sized enterprises: examining the effects of organizational culture and empowerment. *Journal of Small Business Management*. **48**(3), 325–359.

Cameron, K.S. & Quinn, R.E. (1999) *Diagnosing and Changing Organizational Culture*, Addison-Wesley Longman, Reading, MA.

Campbell, J.P., Dunnette, M.D., Lawler, E.E. & Weick, K.E. (1970) *Managerial Behaviour, Performance and Effectiveness*. McGraw Hill, New York.

Chan, E.H.W. & Tse, R.Y.C. (2003) Cultural considerations in international construction contracts.' *Journal of Construction Engineering and Management*, **129**(4), 375–381.

Chen, P., Josephson, P.E. & Kadefors, A. (2009) Cross-cultural understanding of construction project managers' conceptions of their work. *Journal of Construction Engineering and Management*, **135**(6), 477–487.

Cherns, A. & Bryant, D.T. (1984) Studying the client's role in construction management, *Construction Management and Economics*, **2**, 177–184.

Cheung, S.O., Wong, P.S.P. & Wu, A.W.Y. (2011) Towards an organizational culture framework in construction. *International Journal of Project Management*, **29**(1), 33–44.

Conger, J.A. & Kanungo, R.N. (1988) The empowerment process: integrating theory and practice. *Academy of Management Review*. **13**(3), 471–482.

Construction Task Force (1998) *Rethinking Construction: The Report of the Construction Task Force to the Deputy Prime Minister, John Prescott, on the scope for improving the quality and efficiency of UK Construction*. HMSO, London.

Cox, A. (1999) Power, value and supply chain management. *Supply Chain Management*, **4**(4), 167–175.

Damanpour, F. & Schneider, M. (2006) Phases of the adoption of innovation in organizations: effects of environment, organisation and top managers. *British Journal of Management*. **17**, 215–236.

DeBresson, C. (1996) Why innovative activities cluster. In: ed. DeBresson, C. *et al.*, *Economic interdependence and innovative activity: an input output analysis*. Edward Elgar, Cheltenham, UK. 149–164.

Denison, D.R. (1996) What is the difference between organizational culture and organizational climate: *Academy of Management Review*. **2**(3), 619–654.

Denison, D.R. (1997) *Corporate Culture and Organizational Effectiveness*. Denison Consulting, Ann Arbor, MI.

Denison, D.R. (2009) *Organizational Culture and Leadership Surveys: The Denison Model*, Denison Consulting, Ann Arbor, MI. Available from http://www.denison-consulting.com/advantage/researchModel/model.aspx (accessed 15 June 2011).

Di Marco, M., Taylor, J. & Alin, P. (2010) The emergence and role of cultural boundary spanners in global engineering project networks. *Journal of Management in Engineering*, **26**(3), 123–132.

Dobni, C.B. (2008) Measuring innovation culture in organizations: The development of a generalized innovation culture construct using exploratory factor analysis. *European Journal of Innovation Management*, 11(4), 539–559.

Dougherty, D. & Hardy, C. (1996) Sustained product innovation in large, mature organizations: Overcoming innovation-to-organization problems. *Academy of Management Journal*. 39(5), 1120–1153.

Egan, T.M. (2005) Factors influencing individual creativity in the workplace: an examination of quantitative empirical research. *Advances in Developing Human Resources*. 7(2), 160–181.

Ekvall, G., Arvonen, J. & Walkenstrom-Lindblad, I. (1983) *Creative Organisational Climate: Construction and Validation of a Measuring Instrument*. Report 2, Stockholm: Swedish Council for Management and Organisational Behaviour (cited in Amabile *et al.*, 1996).

Eldridge, J. & Crombie, A. (1974) *A Sociology of Organizations*. Allen and Unwin, London.

Elenkov, D.S. & Manev, I.M. (2005) Top management leadership and influence on innovation: the role of socio-cultural context. *Journal of Management*, 31(3), 381–402.

Etzkowitz, H. & Carvalho, de Mello, J.M. (2004) The rise of a triple helix culture – Innovation in Brazilian economic and social development. *International Journal of Technology Management and Sustainable Development*, 2(3), 159–171.

Farmer, S.M., Tierney, P. & Kung-McIntyre, K. (2003) Employee creativity in Taiwan: an application of role identity theory. *Academy of Management Journal*, 46, 618–630.

Fellows, R.F. (2006) Understanding approaches to culture. *Construction Information Quarterly*, 8(4), 159–166.

Fellows, R.F. (2009) Culture in supply chains. In: ed. Pryke, S., *Construction Supply Chain Management: Concepts and Case Studies*. Wiley-Blackwell, Chichester/ 42–72.

Fielden, S.L., Davidson, M.J., Gale, A.W. & Davey, C.L. (2001) Women, equality and construction, *Journal of Management Development*, 20(4), 293–304.

Flyvbjerg, B. (2007) Truth *and Lies about Megaprojects, Inaugural Speech, Faculty of Technology, Policy, and Management*. Delft University of Technology, 26 September 2007. Available from http://flyvbjerg.plan.aau.dk/Publications2007/InauguralTUD21PRINT72dpi.pdf (accessed 9 August 2010).

Furnham, A. (1997) *The Psychology of Behaviour at Work: The Individual in the Organization*. Psychology Press, Hove.

Gebhardt, C. (2005) The impact of managerial rationality in the organisational paradigm. Role models in the management of innovation. *Technology Analysis and Strategic Management*, 17(1), 21–34.

Glisson, C. & James, L.R. (2002) The cross level effects of culture and climate in human service teams. *Journal of Organizational Behavior*, 23, 767–794.

Gomez, C., Kirkman, B.L. & Shapiro, D.L. (2000) The impact of collectivism and in-group / out-group membership on the generosity of team members. *Academy of Management Journal*, 43(6), 1097–1100.

Hadjimanolis, A. (2010) Methods of political marketing in (trans) formation of innovation culture. *Journal of Political Marketing*. 9(1), 93–110.

Hall, E.T. & Hall, M.R. (1990) *Understanding Cultural Differences*. Cultural Press, Yarmount, ME.

Handy, C.B. (1985) *Understanding Organisations*, 3rd edn. Penguin, Harmondsworth.

Hansen, M. & Birkinshaw, J.M. (2007) The innovation value chain. *Harvard Business Review*. 85(6), 121–131.

Hofstede, G.H. (1980) *Culture's Consequences: International Differences in Work-Related Values*. Sage Publications, Beverley Hills, CA.

Hofstede, G.H. (1983) The cultural relativity of organizational practices and theories. *Journal of International Business Studies*, **14 (Fall)**, 75–89.

Hofstede, G.H. (1994a) The business of international business is culture. *International Business Review*, **3**(1), 1–14.

Hofstede, G.H. (1994b) *Cultures and Organizations: Software of the Mind*. Harper Collins, London.

Hofstede, G.H. (2001) *Culture's Consequences: Comparing Values, Behaviors, Institutions, and Organizations Across Nations*, 2nd edn. Sage, Thousand Oaks, CA.

Hovmark, S. & Nordqvist, S. (1996) Project organization: Change in the work atmosphere for engineers. *International Journal of Industrial Ergonomics*, **17**(5), 389–398.

Ibata-Arens, K. (2008) The Kyoto model of innovation and entrepreneurship: regional innovation systems and cluster culture. *Prometheus*. **26**, (1), 89–109.

Inglehart, R. & Baker, W. (2000) Modernization, cultural change and the persistence of traditional values. *American Sociological Review*. **65**, 19–51.

James, L.R. & Jones, A.P. (1979) Organisational structure: a review of structural dimension and their conceptual relationship with individual attitudes and behaviours. *Organisational Behavior and Human Performance*. **16**, 74–113.

James, L.R., Choi, C.C., Ko, C.M., McNeil, P.K., Minton, M.K., Wright, M.A. & Kim, K. (2007) Organisational and psychological climate: a review of theory and research. *European Journal of Work and Organisational Psychology*. **17**(1), 5–32.

Johnson, G. (2001) Mapping and re-mapping organizational culture: a local government example. In:, ed. Johnson, G. & and Scholes. K., *Exploring public sector strategy*. Pearson Education Ltd, Harlow.

Jung, D.I., Chow, C. & Wu, A. (2003) The role of transformational leadership in enhancing organizational innovation: hypotheses and some preliminary findings. *Leadership Quarterly*, **14**(4–5), 525–544.

Kaiser, S. & Holton, E. (1998) The learning organization as a performance improvement strategy. In: ed. Torraco, R., *Proceedings of the Academy of Human Resource Development Conference*. 75–82 (cited in Bates and Khasawneh, 2005).

Kitchell, S. (2001) Corporate culture, environmental adaptation, and innovation adoption: a qualitative/quantitative approach. *Journal of the Academy of Marketing Science*, **23**(3), 195–205.

Krippner, S. & Arons, M. (1973) Creativity: person, product or process. *Gifted Child Quarterly*, **17**(2), 116–123.

Kroeber, A.L. & Kluckhohn, C. (1952) Culture: a critical review of concepts and definitions. In: *Papers of the Peabody Museum of American Archaeology and Ethnology*, vol. 47. Harvard University Press, Cambridge, MA.

Kuo, Y.Y. (1996) Taoistic psychology of creativity. *Journal of Creative Behavior*, **30**(3), 197–212.

Lawrence, P.R. & Lorsch, J.W. (1967) *Organization and environment: managing differentiation and integration*. Harvard University, Boston, MA.

Leydesdorff, L. & Etzkwitz, H. (1998) The triple helix as a model for innovation studies. *Science and Public Policy*, **25**(3), 195–203.

Little, A. (2008) *Innovation Culture: maintaining a strong innovation culture during a downturn*. Available from www.adl.com/innovationculture (accessed 24 August 2010).

Liu, A.M.M. & Fellows, R. (2008) Organisational culture of joint venture projects: a case study of an international JV construction project in Hong Kong. *International of Human Resources Development and Management*, **8**(3), 259–270.

Liu, A.M.M., Zhang, S. & Leung, M.Y. (2006), A framework for assessing organizational culture of Chinese construction enterprises. *Engineering, Construction and Architectural Management*, **13**(4), 327–342.

MacKinnon, D.W. (1965) Personality and the realization of creative potential. *American Psychologist*, **20**, 273–281.

Mai, R. (1996) *Learning partnerships: how leading American companies implement organisational learning*. Irwin, Chicago, IL.

Miron, E., Erez, M. & Naveh, E. (2004) Do personal characteristics and cultural values that promote innovation, quality and efficiency compete or complement each other? *Journal of Organizational Behavior*, **25**(2), 175–199.

Moran, E.T. & Volkwein, J.R. (1992), The cultural approach to the formation of organizational climate. *Human Relations*. **45**(1), 19–48.

NESTA (2008) *Total innovation*. NESTA, National Endowment for Science, Technology and the Arts. Available from http://www.nesta.org.uk/publications/reports/assets/features/total_innovation (accessed 24 August 2010).

Newman, K.L. & Nollan, S.D. (1996) Culture and congruence: the fit between management practices and national culture. *Journal of International Business Studies*, **27**(4), 753–779.

OECD (2001) *Innovative clusters: drivers of national innovation systems*. Organisational of Economic Cooperation and Development, Paris.

Ofori, G. & Toor, S.U.R. (2009) Research on cross-cultural leadership and management in construction: a review and directions for future research. *Construction Management & Economics*, **27**(2), 119–133.

Ogbonna, E. & Harris, L.C. (2000) Leadership style, organizational culture and performance: empirical evidence from UK companies. *International Journal of Human Resource Management*, **11**(4), 766–788.

Oldham, G.R. & Cummings, A. (1996) Employee creativity: personal and contextual factors at work. *Academy of Management Journal*, **39**(3), 607–634.

Ostroff, C., Kinicki, A.J. & Tamkins, M.M. (2003) Organizational culture and climate. In: ed, Weiner, I.B., Borman, W.C., Ilgen, D.R., & Klimoski, R.J., *Handbook of Psychology: volume 12: Industrial and Organizational Psychology*. Wiley, Hoboken, NJ.

Palazzo, G. (2005) Postnational constellations of innovativeness: a cosmopolitan approach. *Technology Analysis and Strategic Management*. **17**(1), 55–72.

Patterson, F., Kerrin, M., Gatto-Roissard, G. & Coan, P. (2009) *Everyday innovation – how to enhance innovative working in employees and organisations*. NESTA, National Endowment for Science, Technology and the Arts. Available from http://www.nesta.org.uk/publications/reports/assets/features/everyday_innovation_how_to_enhance_innovative_working_in_employees_and_organisations (accessed 24 August 2010).

Pitta, D.A. (2009) Creating a culture of innovation at Portugal Telecom. *Journal of Product & Brand Management*, **18**(6), 448–451.

Pohlmann, M., Gebhardt, C. & Etzkowitz, H. (2005) The development of innovation systems and the art of innovation management – strategy, control and the culture of innovation. *Technology Analysis and Strategic Management*, **17**(1), 1–7.

Randolph, W.A. (2000) Re-thinking empowerment: why is it so hard to achieve? *Organizational Dynamics*, **29**(2), 94–107.

Randolph, W.A. & Sashkin, M. (2002) Can organizational empowerment work in multinational settings? *Academy of Management Executive*, **16** (1), 102–115.

Reugg, R.T. & Marshall, H.E. (1990) *Building Economics: Theory and Practice*. Van Nostrand Reinhold, New York.

Riley, M.J. & Brown, D.C. (2001) Comparison of cultures in construction and manufacturing industries. *Journal of Management in Engineering*, **17**(3), 149–158.

Rooke, J., Seymour, D.E. & Fellows, R.F. (2003) The claims culture: A taxonomy of attitudes in the industry. *Construction Management and Economics*, **21(2)**, 167–174.

Roper S., Hales C., Bryson, J.R. & Love, J. (2009) *Measuring sectoral innovation capability in nine areas of the UK economy*. NESTA, National Endowment for Science, Technology and the Arts. Available from (http://www.nesta.org.uk/publications/reports/assets/features/measuring_sectoral_innovation_capability_in_nine_areas_of_the_uk_economy (accessed 24 August 2010).

Rothwell, R. (1992) Successful industrial innovation: critical success factors for the 1990s. *R&D Management*, **22(30)**, 221–239.

Saad, M. & Zawdie, G. (2005) From technology transfer to the emergence of a triple helix culture: the experience of Algeria in innovation and technological capability development. *Technology Analysis and Strategic Management*, **17(1)**, 89–103.

Sagie, A. & Aycan, Z. (2003) A cross cultural analysis of participative decision-making in organisations. *Human Resources*, **56(4)**, 453–473.

Sarros, J.C., Cooper, B.K. & Santora, J.C. (2008) Building a climate for innovation through transformational leadership and organizational culture. *Journal of Leadership and Organizational Studies*, **15(2)**, 145–158.

Schein, E.H. (1984) Coming to an awareness of organisational culture, *Sloan Management Review*, **25(2)**, 3–16.

Schein, E.H. (1990) Organisational Culture. *American Psychologist*, **45**, 109–119.

Schein, E.H. (2004) *Organizational Cutlure and Leadership*. John Wiley & Sons, Inc, New Jersey.

Senge, P. (1992) Building the learning organization. *Journal for Quality and Participation*, **March**, 30–38.

Slater, S. & Narver, J. (1995) Market orientation and the learning organization. *Journal of Marketing*, **59**, 63–74.

Spreitzer, G.M. (1996) Psychological empowerment in the workplace: dimensions, measurement, and validation. *Academy of Management Journal*, **38**, 1442–1465.

Tagiuri, R. & Litwin, G.H. (eds) (1968) *Organizational Climate*. Graduate School of Business Administration, Harvard University, Boston, MA.

Triandis, H.C. & Gelfand, M.J. (1998) Converging measurement of horizontal and vertical individualism and collectivism. *Journal of Personality and Social Psychology*, **74(1)**, 118–128.

Trompenaars, F. & Hampden-Turner, C. (1997) *Riding the Waves of Culture: Understanding Cultural Diversity in Business*, 2nd edn. Nicholas Brealey Publishing, London.

Unsworth, K.L., Wall, T.D. & Carter, A. (2005) Creative requirement: a neglected construct in the study of employee creativity. *Group and Organization Management*, **30**, 541–560.

van Duivenboden, H. & Thaens, M. (2008) ICT-driven innovation and the culture of public administration: a contradiction in terms? *Information Polity*, **13**, 213–232.

Van Marrewijk, A. (2007) Managing project culture: The case of the environ megaproject. *International Journal of Project Management*, **25**, 290–299.

Waldman, D. & Bass, B.M. (1991) Transformational leadership at different phases of the innovation process. *Journal of High Technology Management Research*, **2**, 169–180.

Westwood, R. & Low, D.R. (2003) The multicultural muse: Culture, creativity and innovation. *International Journal of Cross Cultural Management*, **3(2)**, 235–259.

Williams, A., Dobson, P. & Walters, M. (1989) *Changing culture: New organizational approaches*. Institute of Personnel Management, London.

Wongtada, N. & Rice, G. (2008) Multidimensional latent traits of perceived organizational innovation: differences between Thai and Egyptian employees. *Asia Pacific Journal of Management*, **25**, 537–562.

Woodman, R.W., Sawyer, J.E. & Griffin, R.W. (1993) Toward a theory of organisational creativity. *Academy of Management Review*, **18**, 293–321.

Zhang, S.B. & Liu, A.M.M. (2006) Organisational culture profiles of state-owned construction enterprises in China. *Construction Management and Economics*. **24**(8), 817–828

Zhou, J. & Shalley, C.E. (2003) Research on employee creativity: a critical review and proposal for future research directions. In: ed. Marocchio, J.J. & Ferris, G.R., *Research in personnel and human resource management*. Elsevier, Oxford.

Innovation, Technology and Knowledge Transfer for Sustainable Construction

Emilia van Egmond

This chapter presents a series of innovation and sustainability issues facing the construction industry. In this respect, it poses the following question to set the discussion and narrative in context: 'How is innovation and international technology and knowledge transfer (TKT) related to sustainable construction performance?' In order to address this, the theoretical views on innovation, TKT and sustainable construction are presented. The chapter concludes with lessons learnt, and how the synergies from these can be leveraged in a meaningful way.

5.1.1   Construction Performance and Challenges

Construction plays an important role in national economies, contributing significantly to the Gross Domestic Product (GDP), fixed capital formation, government revenue and employment. Indeed, there is hardly any sector in the economy where the significance of construction activities and construction technologies is not felt. This explains the close relationship between the state of construction and socio-economic situations in nearly every country, not least those in the developing world (Zawdie and Langford, 2002). In terms of production output, which is still heavily concentrated (77%) in the high income countries, construction, with its many forward and backward linkages, is one of the largest industries for providing opportunities for employment (ILO, 2001). Yet, construction everywhere faces problems and challenges that are amplified by the rapid increase of

Construction Innovation and Process Improvement, First Edition.
Edited by Akintola Akintoye, Jack S. Goulding and Girma Zawdie.
© 2012 Blackwell Publishing Ltd. Published 2012 by Blackwell Publishing Ltd.

demand for construction due to population growth and the effects of industrialisation. Thus, for example, construction has been challenged to meet the enormous need for housing, particularly in rapidly urbanising areas in developing countries, where a large amount of the population still lives in deplorable conditions. Construction is resource-intensive and notorious for its contribution to greenhouse gas emissions and waste generation (Muller, 2000; Macozoma, 2002; OECD/IEA, 2009). In addition, construction firms have to face globalisation-induced international competition and pressures to meet the social, economic and environmental imperatives of sustainability. Thus, improved sustainable performance is essential if the construction industry is to move forward. This calls for a radically new *modus operandi* in construction – namely, sustainable construction (SuCo).

5.1.2   Sustainable Construction

SuCo encompasses the simultaneous pursuit of a balanced social equity, environmental quality and economic prosperity (people, planet and profit) in the built environment in such a manner as to meet the needs of the present generation without compromising the ability of future generations to respond to their demands for a sustainable built environment (WCED, 1987; Kibert, 2005). This definition, based on the Report of the Brundtland Commission of 1987, embraces two major aspects:

1. basic needs – food, clothing, shelter – and the need for an acceptable life standard above the absolute minimum; and
2. limits to the capability of construction to fulfil the needs of present and future generations.

SuCo therefore requires construction firms to deal with the *'natural limits'* of finite natural resources (energy, materials, water) and *'man-made limits'*, which are related to the development, diffusion accessibility, adoption and implementation status of technology and knowledge (T&K) in construction processes.

   Construction firms typically have to innovate in order to improve their performance to meet the increasingly complex and fast changing customer needs for a sustained quality of the built environment (Figure 5.1). Thus, SuCo requires designers, engineers, building material producers and contractors to bring about new design concepts, building elements and components as well as building processes, and integrate these into construction projects. Cognisant of this, policy makers are, for their part, expected to provide an adequate framework that facilitates improvements in construction.

   Innovation theories (Nelson and Winter, 1982) suggest a shift in the technology regime, the consequence of which would profoundly and irreversibly change the pattern of behaviour or perception underlying the current mode of construction practice.

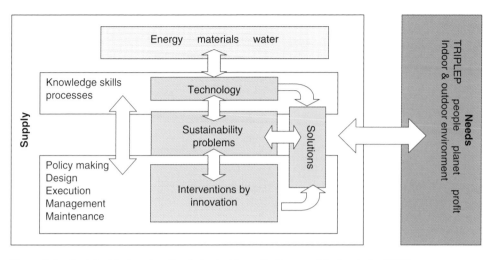

Figure 5.1   Sustainable Construction (adapted from Stofberg and Duijvesteijn, 2006).

5.2   Innovation, Technology and Knowledge Transfer Practices

Innovation and sustainability in construction needs to balance a range of important factors, from performance metrics, through to capability drivers and competence building.

5.2.1   Technology, Innovation and Production Performance

Innovation refers to the total cycle from *invention*, that is, the development of new knowledge and technologies (products and production processes) – and the *diffusion, adoption and application* of these (Rogers, 1995). The growth performance of the developed market economies over the last 150–200 years has largely been on the emergence and diffusion of fundamental technological advances, and changes of production systems in manufacturing industries linked to periods of economic expansion (Kondratiev, 1925). Innovation is therefore crucial for the production performance of industries and their competitiveness as well as for the socio-economic development of countries. Conventional mono-disciplinary economic approaches have been used to analyse and explain the role of innovation and TKT in competitiveness and economic growth. In addition, capital accumulation (in terms of advancement of technologies and innovation) has been seen as the engine for improved competitiveness of enterprises and economic growth in Western countries through traditional growth theories. The basic assumption was that a motivated *profit-maximising, cost minimising and output maximising* entrepreneur had to make choices amongst various production technologies in a perfect competition environment (Schumpeter, 1934). In this respect, product–life-cycle theories identified that the drive of firms to innovate was fostered by their need to survive and maintain their competitive position through incremental innovation (Abernathy and Utterback,

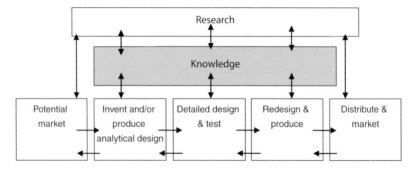

Figure 5.2 Interactions in the process of technology development and innovation (adapted from Kline and Rosenberg, 1986).

1978). Traditionally, innovation, be it incremental or radical, was conceived as a linear process. *Product innovations* were seen as successfully developed, introduced, diffused and used product technologies, and *process innovations* as successfully developed, introduced, diffused and used production process technologies (Rogers, 1995). However, Kline and Rosenberg (1986) noted innovation to be complex and not 'chain/sequential', which occurred as a process 'parallel' to or 'integrated' with upstream activities (with suppliers), and downstream linkages (with users), or in the context of alliances, with other firms with different phases overlapping (Figure 5.2).

5.2.2   Technology and Knowledge Transfer

New technologies and knowledge are not necessarily generated by in-house R&D, but can also be acquired through TKT, that is, through:

1. simple acquisition of T&K from elsewhere in the country (or from abroad); or
2. acquisition of parts of T&K components that are missing and combine these with further in-house development and production processes.

It is therefore generally more profitable and less risky for firms to acquire knowledge and technologies, for instance, through collaboration in production processes (e.g. joint-venture agreements, or licence packages) than to rely on high, often uncertain R&D investments. Moreover, due to the increasingly shorter and unpredictable life cycle of products or services, firms are increasingly expected to innovate at a faster pace. This is no longer feasible in 'traditional' production organisations. In many firms, conditions are simply not present to stimulate entrepreneurship and creativity (Chesborough, 2003), and the increased complexity of the market has brought pressure to bear on firms and organisations to be more innovate and competitive in networks (even beyond the boundaries of their own sector). In this respect, ICT can facilitate the exchange, sharing and acquisition of T&K, with increased opportunities of being able to transmit, store and manipulate large quantities of information.

The relative openness of the global economy has created opportunities for an international exchange of advanced technologies and knowledge. The essence of international TKT is that technologies, either in hardware or software forms (i.e. knowledge and information), can be transferred over spaces/borders from one source (e.g. R&D laboratories, firms, universities, state and local governments, third-party intermediaries) to other recipients in the international market (Dunning, 1981). Most technologies and knowledge flow through commercial contracts, such as:

a) *trade contracts:* the purchase and sales of, e.g. capital goods and inter-mediate goods, consultancy, turn-key projects;
b) *exchange of know-how contracts:* R&D collaboration, sales of patents, licences, trademarks, management and consultancy agreements; and
c) *private investments:* foreign direct investments, wholly owned subsidi-aries, joint ventures, other forms of collaboration between firms (Katz and Shapiro, 1985; Lall, 1987).

Knowledge also may flow *free of charge* in codified form embodied in capital goods, technical manuals, blueprints and instruction books, either as a by-product of market transactions, or through the maintenance and reverse engineering of new products. However, the imperfection of the international technology market has been blamed on the monopolistic and oligopolistic tendencies and asymmetric power relationships between technology recipi-ents and suppliers (Dunning, 1981). These theories emphasise that such ten-dencies and the resulting market imperfections are further reinforced due to government interventions (trade regulations, subsidies, and taxes) and the implementation of legal systems of protection (patents). On the other hand, where appropriately designed in the context of good governance, regulatory policy and legal mechanisms – i.e. intellectual property rights (patents, copy-rights, trade secrets, etc), then this could foster TKT and innovation activities.

T&K components are often transferred in commercial transactions as part of a contractual package deal, accompanied by particular terms and condi-tions that are built into contractual agreements, which give both the supply-ing and recipient companies the opportunity to control the TKTs. Conditions attached to TKT packages vary from limited ones, through to a full and complex set of restrictions and controls, such as: the use of the technology; markets for the end-products of the used technologies; and suppliers of nec-essary raw materials, spare parts, etc. Conditions determine whether the components – e.g. machines, equipment, documents (blueprints, designs of products, manufacturing instructions, process flow charts, equipment speci-fications, etc) or personnel in charge of specific operations/training schemes are all included in the package deal, or whether missing components have to be acquired separately from another source. For example, a licence agreement could be provided without any instructions, documentation or assistance on the use of the patented technology. Acquiring a complete ready-to-use pack-age (turn-key) means that risks can be minimal, where the quality is secured for the recipient. In this respect, conditions can be ascribed that allow the supplying firm to establish a quasi-monopoly over components of non-monopolised knowledge (Stewart, 1979; Rosenberg, 1982; Lall, 1985).

Packaging associated with discontinuities in knowledge places restraints on organisational learning and on the development of 'organisational memory' (Stiglitz, 1999). Hence the case for unpackaging (i.e. breaking down a technology into several components to purchase separately – possibly from different suppliers), as this would help to bring down costs, limit the conditions of the transactions, open opportunities for recipients to increase technological capabilities through learning by doing, maintain control over TKTs, and decrease dependence on a single supplier. However, in practice, unpacking turned out to be rather expensive, time consuming, was vulnerable to failures and involved usually 'old' technologies. Moreover, the sector did not always support unpackaged deals due to the influence of market positioning drivers.

5.2.3   Innovation System

The linear approach to conceptualising innovation does not offer a clear insight into the content and process of innovation, TKTs, or on the existence of differences in the scope of innovation across firms, sectors or countries (Rosenberg, 1976). Technology is often understood in relation to production processes as a system of interrelated know-how, skills and knowledge embodied in products and processes. Thus, a distinction is made between:

- *Product technology*: the knowledge and skills embodied in the output of a production process, which find expression in the technological attributes of products; and
- *Process technology*: the knowledge and skills embodied in the 'transformer' of inputs into the required goods and services in production processes, where the transformer is composed of four inextricable components: technoware (materials, equipment, tools); humanware (people); infoware (documented facts, blueprints, etc); and orgaware (firm, institute) (ESCAP, 1989).

Literature on innovation covers work on issues such as adoption and the diffusion of innovations, international technology transfer, and the theory of economic growth (including issues of catching-up or relative stagnation). Developments in evolutionary economics (Nelson and Winter, 1982; Lall, 1992; Metcalfe, 1995; Stiglitz, 1999; Dosi, Nelson and Winter, 2000), technological innovation studies (Nelson and Winter 1982; Teece *et al.*, 1997; Dosi, Coriat and Pavitt, 2000; Dosi, Nelson and Winter, 2000) and organisational and management studies (March and Simon 1993; March 1991; Tidd *et al.*, 2006) have coalesced to nurture the theoretical basis of empirical studies. As opposed to neo-classical thinking, evolutionary thinking assumes that innovations are not an outcome of *ex-ante* economic reasoning, but analogous to biological evolution – i.e. outcome of the evolutionary processes of social needs and competition, T&K development and government intervention, which together constitute

Table 5.1   Technology intervention and promotion agents (Egmond, 2006).

Technology Intervention & Promotion Agent	Form & Field of Technology Promotion	Resulting in
National government	Formulation and implementation of technology policies	Favourable climate by means of subsidies, incentives, tax-holidays etc. to enhance TD&I
Educational and training institutions; consultancy companies	Training and education	Human resources development (Humanware)
Documentation & information centres, libraries, statistical organizations, patent and registration offices, museums; consultancy companies	Storing and lending of documented facts Training and informing	Improved knowledge & insight (Infoware + Human ware)
Testing, certification and standardization laboratories	up-grading & standardization of technologies	Improved and standardized Technologies (Technoware)
R&D & financing organizations; design, engineering & management consultants	assistance for setting up of management and organizational structures	Improved organisational management, structure and culture (Orgaware)

the innovation system. An innovation system can therefore be said to encompass 'interconnected institutions', which form a social network of inter-related actors (individuals, organisations and enterprises) 'who share a common field of knowledge and interest regarding innovation in a certain domain' and who 'create, store and transfer the knowledge, skills and arte-facts which define new technologies' (Nelson and Winter, 1982; Metcalfe, 1995; Dosi, Coriat and Pavitt, 2000).

A number of innovation agents intervene in the processes of development, diffusion and utilisation of new technologies (Table 5.1). This is in line with the actor-centred social construction of technology theories, which suggest that an innovation process can produce different outcomes depending on the social circumstances in which it takes place (Bijker *et al.*, 1987). Similarly, Rogers (1995) postulated that innovation and TKT are accomplished through human interactions and communication between members of a community of practice, which gives rise to particular innovation trajectories that are sustained by industrial interests vested in it, along with assumptions about user needs, and the costs of making system changes (March, 1991).

5.2.4   Technological Capability, Knowledge and Learning

Capability building through knowledge accumulation and learning is central to innovation and TKT processes, since successful production and trade performance strongly depend on capability and motivation to innovate and quickly adopt new technologies. This view is supported by research that shows a high correlation between the success of countries in assimilating foreign technologies and success of the same countries in terms of the educational attainment of their population (Dosi *et al.*, 1990). Thus, *technological capabilities* encompass the total stock of resources including technologies, knowledge and skills that can be found at different levels in innovation systems – which can be categorised into three functional classes: *investment capability* (to identify, negotiate, purchase and manage suitable and feasible technologies and knowledge); *production capability*; and *innovation capability* (to create, diffuse, adopt and implement new knowledge and technological solutions) (Lall, 1992). In the absence of a strong innovation system, the development of technological capabilities is likely to be constrained, and so *a weak* endogenous *knowledge and technology base* would persist. In such circumstances, an industry (e.g. construction) may fail to use its scarce resources efficiently. This would make its performance hardly competitive in market conditions (Stewart, 1979; Rosenberg, 1982).

More recently, *knowledge* has been recognised as a key aspect of innovation capability and TKTs (Stiglitz, 1999). The argument is that individuals and organisations working in a specific innovation system create new technologies and knowledge by combining different knowledge sets, thanks to the increasing levels of knowledge and technological skills. Continuous interactive learning – i.e. the *exchange, accumulation, integration and mobilisation* of both knowledge (*know why*) and know-how (*craftsmanship, skills to carry out a job*) is expected to enhance this process (Von Hippel, 1988; Lundvall, 1992; Lundvall *et al.*, 2006). The distinction between knowledge and know-how is here emphasised by the argument that knowledge and know-how are needed in combination to effectively implement a new technology (Stiglitz, 1999). Therefore, the processes of T&K mastery – (i.e. *'learning'* or up-grading of *technological knowledge, know-how and skills formation*) – and learning processes have become the centre of analysis and debate consequent upon the recognition of the outstanding role of knowledge in the development of innovation capability (Lundvall *et al.*, 2006).

Various learning mechanisms, by which knowledge and skills flow from a source to a recipient, have been identified. These include:

a) learning by doing, using, reverse engineering, imitation, searching (formalised activities such as R&D), adoption;
b) learning by interacting with upstream or downstream sources of knowledge (suppliers or users) or in co-operation with other firms;
c) learning by absorption of new developments in science and technology; and
d) learning by querying what and how competitors and other firms in the industry are doing (inter-industry spillovers).

Therefore, it can be seen that learning mechanisms often overlap. For example, learning by searching may take place jointly with learning from advances in science and technology (Lall, 2003). Learning processes also involve personal interactions, observation and practical experience in specific contexts. The process of embodying knowledge in people (*learning*) and in products and processes (*application and integration*) is generally costly in time and resources. Various authors (e.g. Polanyi, 1967) have argued that this is because knowledge is to varying degrees *tacit*. Stiglitz (1999) considers tacit knowledge and the ways it is managed to be particularly important for a company's competitive performance; but 'translation' of tacit knowledge into fully explicit or codified statements (information) is barely possible, since it is hard to explicitly delineate or codify certain procedures and behavioural patterns. Stiglitz (1999) also highlights the importance of an extensive basis of contextual knowledge for the proper accumulation and integration of technologies and knowledge acquired through TKTs. Such knowledge might either be incomplete in the recipient enterprise to correctly apply the new materials, technologies and knowledge, or it has not yet developed sufficiently. It is not only understanding of the transferred hardware bits and pieces that might be lacking, but also the knowledge and skills to handle these, to manage the organisation around the production process with the technologies and knowledge that are acquired from elsewhere. The required pool of tacit knowledge cannot easily be transferred or just 'downloaded' from one firm to another. Indeed, it takes a certain learning period for any newly introduced technology to be correctly applied (Lall, 1992; Stiglitz, 1999).

The above indicates that the key to improved performance and competitiveness does not lie in simply the acquisition of technologies and knowledge from elsewhere. The true source of competitiveness lies in the stock of knowledge and experience, and through a deliberate investment in a complete array of knowledge regarding how, why, where and when to use technologies. These processes imply a *continuous accumulation and integration of knowledge and skills* in cyclical fashion through invention, diffusion, adoption and application of novelties. This can enable the creation of new possibilities through the combination of different sets of knowledge and skills. Currently, effective knowledge management is increasingly associated with various processes of continuous learning, which involve the acquisition and mobilisation of knowledge and technological skills of individuals and organisations to create product, process and organisational innovations (Tidd *et al.*, 2006).

5.2.5   Technological Regime and Routines

Learning, innovation and TKT practices can be considered as routine procedures or regularly followed courses of action that are mechanically and unconsciously applied (Polanyi 1967; Stiglitz 1999; Geels, 2004). These routines evolve from the *technological regime* of innovation systems. Technological regime is a social construct, a pattern made of knowledge, rules, regulations conventions, consensual expectations, collective memories, experience, assumptions or thinking shared by the stakeholders, which guide the design and further the development of innovations. It sets the achievement boundaries for innovative activities, as well as the directions (natural trajectories) along which diffusion, adoption and application of new technologies take place (Dosi *et al.*, 2000). In this respect, Malherba (2002) noted that an innovation system with strong inter-relationships between stakeholders, who share a common field of knowledge and interest (i.e. technological regime), can facilitate innovation and TKTs. Nelson and Winter (1982) note that asymmetries between industries, industrial dynamics and innovativeness can be interpreted on the grounds of *technological regimes* in *innovation systems*. New technologies are successful when they fit well in the prevailing technology regime. Technological regimes are sector specific and (to a large extent) typical for individual firms, thus making it difficult for firms to imitate one another (Patel and Pavitt, 1997; Breschi *et al.*, 2000; Marsili and Verspagen, 2002). At national and international levels, technological regime is reflected in particular through political, legal and economic settings. These are seen as important facilitating frameworks that may create a favourable climate for innovation, TKTs, competitive production and societal development (ESCAP, 1989). Technological regimes define:

1. the properties of the knowledge base;
2. technological opportunities;
3. appropriation of innovations; and
4. cumulativeness of technological advances in innovation systems (Malerba and Orsenigo, 1996; Breschi *et al.*, 2000).

The *properties of knowledge base* relate to the *nature* and *availability* of technologies and knowledge - that is, the know-how, skills, experience and perceptions. Knowledge can be seen as being partly institutionalised, which includes standards, norms, rules and regulations. *Technological opportunities* indicate the extent to which an industry can draw from the knowledge base and the technological advances of its suppliers, and major scientific advances in universities and R&D institutions. High opportunities can be found in an innovation system where collaboration, communication and knowledge exchange amongst the actors are least constrained. The existence of opportunities provides a powerful incentive for potential innovators to undertake innovative activities. A *high appropriation* indicates a high protection of innovations from imitation by means of patents, secrecy, lead times, costs and time required for duplication, learning curve effects, superior sales efforts, and differential technical efficiency due to scale economies through which firms can reap profits from innovative activities. *Cumulativeness of technical advances* reflects continuities in innovative activities and increasing returns as well as the existence of a T&K base that forms the building blocks for either subsequent incremental innovations or a completely new knowledge set that can be used as a basis for other innovations in related areas (Murray and O'Mahony, 2007). Innovation systems characterised by continuities in innovative activities and increasing returns are considered to have high levels of cumulativeness.

5.2.6   Strategic Niche Management

Kemp *et al.* (2001) noted that innovative technologies often need to be 'pampered' in the initial stage of their development, for fear of undersupply, or not even being supplied at all due to high uncertainty, high up-front costs, or because the wider social benefits arising from these technologies are not adequately valued by the market. Innovations would thus need to be managed by a 'niche manager', who could facilitate their diffusion, adoption and implementation. A novel technology can be seen as a technological niche, which forms together with other existing technologies and knowledge a *technological network* in a particular innovation system. Nodes of the technological network are technologies – each with specific embodied knowledge and skills, upon which another adjacent technology can be created. The position of a technology in the network is therefore a niche in the domain. The properties of the technology determine whether it fits the *technological regime* of the innovation system; and the expected rate of return on the investment determines its market potential. Different actors in the innovation system - for example, policy makers, regulatory agencies, local authorities, citizen groups, private companies, industrial organisations, special interest groups, etc. - may take responsibility for the *niche management* of the new technology, and promote and stimulate its diffusion.

The discussions so far have raised the importance of being able to successfully garner benefits from innovation, cognisant of both the internal and external microcosms, and embedded routines therein. Based on this, a conceptual framework was developed (Figure 5.3) to contextualise the study of innovation and TKTs underpinning SuCo performance. Thus, Figure 5.3, is based on the notion that innovation is determined by three building blocks of an innovation system:

1.   a network of interacting actors;
2.   a particular technological regime; and
3.   routines.

Technological regime defines the routines, which involve learning processes as well as the knowledge base, technological opportunities, appropriation of knowledge and technologies and cumulativeness of the

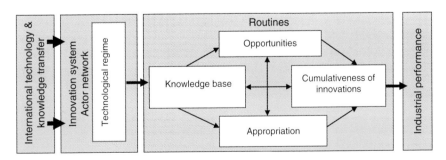

Figure 5.3   Conceptual framework for the development of innovation.

innovations. Learning occurs through collaboration, communication and knowledge exchange between the actors in the innovation system and may result in the development and supply of complementary inventions as well as in institutional, organisational and management adaptations. An innovative technology, however good technically, will only be diffused, adopted and successfully implemented if it fits well in the prevailing technological regime that characterises the professional practice (routines) of the actors in the innovation system (Douthwaite, 2002). Yet the diffusion, adoption and implementation and use of any innovative technology take a certain learning period (Stiglitz, 1999). However, this can be accelerated by a 'niche manager'.

5.3   Innovation, Technology and Knowledge Transfer in Construction

The occurrence of innovation in construction has created significant opportunities for improvements in construction performance in terms of reduction of costs, speed of construction, and construction quality and sustainability. Innovations also help to mitigate the effect of changes in weather conditions on activities at construction sites, enhance the coordination and planning of construction activities, and create new market opportunities by enhancing the competitiveness of construction firms. Innovation in construction has been stimulated largely by increasing construction resource costs and a growing lack of on-site skilled labour.

5.3.1   Construction Technologies and Innovation

Innovation in the construction sector differs from innovation in other economic sectors, as often 'old' technologies are used alongside newly developed technologies and materials, whereas, in most other industries older technologies are completely replaced by the new ones. Construction processes are nonetheless observed in many countries evolving with increasing mechanisation, rationalisation, systematisation, standardisation and automation of construction. This shows:

1. the shift of building construction activities from the site to the factory; and
2. the standardisation of industrially produced building products, components and technologies.

What seems to have happened in construction is that combinations of innovative solutions based on accumulated technological and knowledge advances were adopted in an attempt to move from craft-based construction to a systematic construction process where resources can be utilised more efficiently. In fact, what is apparent from a construction innovation perspective is the *convergence of technologies and knowledge* from different areas and disciplines. The main principles applied to increase sustainability in construction seem to have been placed on the reduction, reuse and recycling of resources, along with the elimination of toxic substances, etc (Kibert, 2003).

The majority of innovations are meant to improve construction sustainability through the introduction of new products to increase energy efficiency, by substituting traditional materials and products with innovative ones, such as eco-materials and products. Other innovations are in areas such as design and engineering, transport and equipment, ICT, robotics, and new business and procurement models. The focus to date has largely been on innovation in residential construction. In other segments, such as office building construction, only marginal improvements have been made to achieve improved SuCo performance (Rovers, 2007). Most of these construction innovations have been achieved incrementally via the traditional practice of 'innovation-by-addition' to existing technologies on component level. As such, they offer only *partial solutions* to meet the building project requirements. The total *construction process* itself has remained relatively unchanged, involving the following separate stages:

1. development and production of building materials and elements;
2. development and production of building design and engineering; and
3. construction process development and execution.

Thus, on-site construction practices take place in more or less parallel processes (Lichtenberg, 2002, 2005). On the other hand, improvement in SuCo performance requires 'innovation-by-integration' – i.e. integrated building product and process innovations. This means that new products and new forms of construction processes should be developed systemically in an integrated way. Innovation following these principles can therefore bring about:

1. improvement of the construction process in terms of reduced costs and time and improved quality;
2. flexible and lifespan-based buildings to reduce operational costs and safeguard value for the client; and
3. reduction in environmental impact (Brand *et al.*, 1999; Lichtenberg, 2005).

5.3.2   International Technology Knowledge Transfer in Construction

The dominant providers of technologies and services in the Architectural, Engineering and Construction (AEC) sector are invariably firms from high-income countries, and firms working in international markets depend on these markets for 32–50% of their incomes. Most of them offer packages composed of a wide range of services in AEC (UNCTAD, 2009). The (quasi-) monopoly position of T&K suppliers in the market often allows them to prevent local partners from becoming competitors. T&K spill-over effects in the host countries depend on the type of contract and the conditions attached to it. The bargaining position of recipients of T&K is therefore influenced by legal protection systems and capabilities to search, select and negotiate. In practice, the quality and price of T&K might be determined through crude bargaining prior to competition (Stewart, 1979; Lall, 2003; Tidd et al., 2006). Local firms in host countries are often only involved in lower value-adding segments of the respective value chains. However, countries such as China, India and Brazil have of late increased their stake in the international construction market since the turn of the century (UNCTAD, 2009). On this theme, Chinese contractors are increasingly engaged in construction technology flows, working with a relatively high level of control in their overseas operations and consequently, a low level of actual TKTs in the host country. In Africa, for example, more than 50% of the Chinese construction firms work as a subsidiary of a transnational corporation or sole venture company, and only 3% collaborate in joint ventures, whilst more than 50% of their workforce (most management staff, technicians and skilled labour) and all plant and equipment originate from China (Javernick et al., 2007).

With a growing number of companies from developing countries entering into *ad-hoc* co-operation agreements with companies of high-income countries, international TKTs have, through foreign direct investments, become the largest source of external financing. It is a crucial instrument and a powerful source of knowledge, capability building and trade expansion, which often is fully exploited in these countries that are characteristically weak in terms of bargaining position, purchasing power, investment, R&D and absorption capacity, and physical infrastructure provision. A majority of developing countries are often left disadvantaged in TKT negotiations. Technology choices are, for instance, usually led by successful advanced technology examples from high-income countries, which enhance the potential adoption of products and processes that may not always be appropriate to local conditions. However, construction has an extensive scope for TKTs from other projects, since construction operations are often transparent, easy to copy and capable of giving opportunities for job-site training (Tatum, 1986). At the same time, a major limitation in construction with respect to innovation is that activities are characteristically *sui generis*, which means that there is, at least in theory, hardly any incentive for innovation, insofar as innovation under such circumstances involves limited replication and extended usage of technologies from previous projects. The application of successful innovative solutions in other projects is even more limited due to the temporary nature of project alliances, with the involvement of a relatively large number of individual parties, and relatively low level of communication (Barlow, 2000; Tjandra and Tan, 2002). Therefore, firms face uncertainties, and their risk vulnerability reduces their willingness to share and exchange information and knowledge about their project experience and reinforces their preference for tried and tested technologies (Franco et al., 2004). This reduces the scope for organisational learning and capability building (Pries and Janszen, 1995; Barlow, 2000; Vakola and Rezgui (2000); Kumaraswamy and Shrestha, 2002; Thomassen, 2003; Bresnen et al., 2004). In this respect, small- and medium-scale enterprises generally appear to have a poor record in terms of continuous professional development, life-long learning and innovation (Davey et al., 2002).

Recent changes in the structure of construction project execution have raised barriers to formal continuous technological capability building and training. Subcontractors, who are now the real employers, tend to be small firms with limited resources and limited organisational and technical capacity. However, although most construction companies regard *training* as an important form of TKT and means of improving their existing knowledge base, they are reluctant to engage in training exercises, partly because of the perceived risk that they would lose trained workers to other firms (or other countries), and partly because of the cost of training, which (at least in the short run) can increase the price of their bids (Egbu *et al.*, 2003). Thus, workers are only persuaded to undergo training if they are paid for 'lost time' (ILO, 2001). Notwithstanding this, the importance of *debriefing* and project evaluation as a *learning mechanism*, is noted in several publications highlighting the links between learning, innovation and benefits arising from these in terms of improvement of business performance (Tjandra and Tan, 2002; Borgatti and Cross, 2003). Yet, given the marginal project profits often associated with construction projects and the time pressures due to the intensity of project activities, ex-post evaluation of the projects is rarely undertaken to document project achievements (Keegan and Turner, 2002). Therefore, knowledge gained in projects is generally neither secured nor diffused across the construction sector. This reduces the scope for learning, for the creation of organisational memory, for the diffusion of the knowledge, and for capability building.

Knowledge acquisition often takes place on the job, especially through learning from the experience of others; but many construction firms still fail to capture tacit knowledge or experience (Egbu *et al.*, 2003). The nature of knowledge, and particularly the difficulty involved in codifying knowledge, is an important constraining factor in the diffusion process. For example, in a number of developing countries, even basic construction knowledge and skills are still mainly acquired through learning-by-doing and learning-by-using, through informal traditional apprenticeship systems (although vocational training schools do exist). The informal apprenticeship system is often not well developed, with deficiencies such as:

1. restricted learning opportunity (only learning-by-doing);
2. a narrow and static range of skills, often long kept within families, clans or tribes without being passed on to 'outsiders' (Debrah and Ofori, 2001); and
3. lack of training about new technologies and techniques (ILO, 2001).

The result is that projects often show delays in delivery and weakness in the quality construction output, thus making the learning-by-doing system a rather costly and time-consuming exercise with little pay back. On this theme, Bell *et al.* (1984) assert that firms cannot rely only on learning-by-doing in order to develop the technological capabilities; they must invest in training and other knowledge creation mechanisms. This requires a deliberate allocation of resources, which is seen as an unnecessary expense rather than an investment by construction firms, workers and clients (ILO, 2001). This reflects that construction firms are working in fields of tension – trying to reconcile short-term cost efficiencies with long-term benefits. Jashpara (2003) concluded that competitive environments have a positive effect on learning and organisational performance, since learning is often focused on efficiency and proficiency to improve the competitive advantage of construction firms.

In contrast, it has been asserted that better performance can be reached in construction through engagement in long-term supply relations. This arrangement would allow knowledge creation, knowledge acquisition and sharing to be closely integrated into learning processes (Egbu *et al.*, 2003). Strategic alliances are an important means for the survival of organisations, and one of the key factors that would help improve performance and satisfy clients, whilst providing opportunities to form learning alliances which encourages mutual (and reflective) learning between partners. Co-operative alliances can create a shared vision of mutuality from which a learning organisation would be expected to evolve. This is endorsed by various authors who indicate that working in a networked context – i.e. as in Communities of Practice or Joint Ventures, which offers the opportunity to combine resources and skills beyond the capability of one single organisation (Kumaraswamy 1995; Egmond *et al* 2007). This also has the additional benefits of being able to spread financial and other risks to better capture learning and use these assets to improve the partnership's competitive advantage (Walker and Johannes, 2003). In addition, Hakansson *et al.* (1999) noted that learning that takes place in a networked context can be influenced by the nature of connections between the parties. Thus, TKTs and embedding tacit and un-codified knowledge (project experience) in firms appear to be more problematic in construction than in other sectors. Kumaraswamy and Shrestha (2002) noted that this might be partly due to conservatism along with the fragmented nature of the industry. In this respect, learning in project-based organisations (as in construction) is still in its infancy. It is therefore important to disseminate lessons learnt, as this is acknowledged to be crucial for business (Birkenbach, 2006), especially where low levels of knowledge adoption and diffusion exist (Ofori 1990; Nam and Tatum, 1997).

5.4   The Construction Innovation System

Long-term project partnering relationships are scarcely taken on board in construction (Barlow and Jashpara, 1998; Bresnen and Marshall, 2000), and linkages are mostly project bound, and are therefore temporary by nature. It is therefore important that the importance of collaboration and communication is understood from the outset.

5.4.1   Actor Network

Production chains in construction tend to be established by means of integrated tendering on the basis of functional demand specifications and a selection process based on best price-quality ratio; where construction innovation (as a system) includes a large variety of actors, which can loosely be grouped as:

- *Innovation support actors:* e.g. (inter)national/regional/local authorities and communities, standards and regulating institutions, professional associations; testing services companies, educational institutions, certification bodies;
- *Innovation supply actors:* including:
  1. researchers;
  2. construction industry participants, with designers, general contractors, specialist contractors, workforce; and
  3. materials and technologies suppliers; and
- *Innovation demand actors:* public and private investors (individuals, service providers, housing corporations, clients, owners, end-users) (Egmond, 2009).

An outline of a typical actor network can be seen in Figure 5.4. This represents the actors involved in the innovation supply and support processes, along with supply/demand continuum. Given this relationship, Winch (1998) noted that large contractors could be considered as mediators between R&D institutes to develop new technologies and knowledge.

In summary, the low and fragmented project bound levels of interaction of firms with other organisations (e.g. universities, technology service providers, governmental agencies, clients, etc) can restrict knowledge sharing; which not only impedes innovation, but also has an impact on project efficiency and efficacy (Malherba, 2002). Thus, there is a need to promote the common interests of actors in order to maximise innovation opportunities.

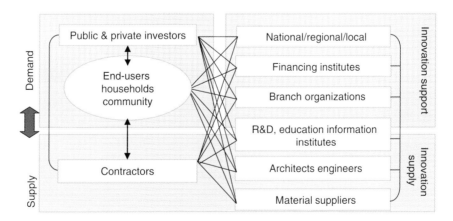

Figure 5.4   A construction innovation system actor network (Egmond, 2009).

5.4.2   Construction Collaboration and Capability

The *knowledge base* in construction is often scattered amongst distinct institutes, organisations and firms, where most of the T&K is tacit and not codified, making diffusion somewhat problematic. In contrast, the manufacturing industries relating to construction account for the majority of inventions and innovations in construction (Manley 2001; Miozzo and Dewick, 2004). This makes construction organisations rather vulnerable to market forces, which can also act as an innovation constraint – especially when under pressure to meet resource requirements in response to the social agenda for SuCo.

Construction project execution tends to follow consistent routines, with a large number of participants working side by side, with a high rate of interdependency and complexity of tasks in varying collaborations. There is also a lack of alignment between the actors in construction projects, each working with its own targets and motivations under pressure of deadlines and budget constraints. This translates into dysfunctional teams, poor levels of co-operation, miscommunication, overlaps, inefficiencies, lack of mutual respect, lost opportunities for optimum use of resources, the result of which makes it difficult for innovation and TKTs to occur (Pries and Janszen, 1995; Barlow, 2000, Lichtenberg, 2002; 2005). This is amplified by the traditional tendering system and the rather detailed specifications in tender documents, which in certain circumstances can discourage contractors from searching for innovative solutions.

The trend over the last couple of decades or so has been one in which large construction firms have moved into international markets, through mergers and acquisitions, often working mainly as service companies, concentrating on management and coordination functions, finding clients and marketing products. These changes were needed to deal with the increased complexity, size and technical sophistication of construction projects and processes as well as the increasing pressures in the international market. This stimulated firms to form consortia through such vehicles as Partnership Agreements and Strategic Alliances. However, the formation of these are often short-lived, being temporary by nature, meaning that capability building opportunities may not always be overtly evident (Wells, 2001; Bertelsen and Müller, 2003). Moreover, conditions may exist which do not support host firms' efforts to develop their capabilities (Abbott, 1985; and Carrillo, 1994). This is particularly the case in developing countries, where large projects are carried out by a handful of large foreign firms with a considerable amount of sub-contracting and other forms of collaboration between foreign and local firms, and where many of the construction technologies are imported (UNCTAD, 2000, ILO, 2001). Innovation here is therefore basically in the hands of foreign companies.

5.5   Technological Regime in Construction

Typically, the marginality of profits and the risk of unforeseen failure and damage during project execution have reinforced conservatism and the reluctance of construction firms to engage in ventures for technological change (Nam and Tatum, 1988; Ofori, 1990; Thomassen, 2003). Indeed, the experience of project implementation professionals appears to have nurtured the perception that innovations have had a negative impact on project performance, on the assumption that any alterations in a project design or implementation would involve lengthy discussions, thus involve additional time and cost (Slaughter, 1998).

The prevalence of constraints on knowledge exchange and sharing has undermined the enthusiasm for innovation. For example, clients that lack awareness and understanding of the significance of innovative solutions tend to be risk-averse and conservative in their business behaviour, and would therefore show preference for tried and tested materials and technologies. This effectively discourages manufacturers and builders from changing their practices through engagement in innovation ventures (Pries and Janszen, 1995; Miozzo and Dewick, 2004). The problem with respect to the adoption of new technologies and the willingness to share the benefits of innovation is exacerbated where construction project stakeholders are significantly dissimilar in terms of their innovation awareness, interests, objectives and motives (Ofori 1996; Malherba 2002). Building codes and regulations, and technical standards in construction can also act as barriers, which constrain innovation and international TKTs in construction along with the prevalence of a variety of contractual agreements, licensing and qualification requirements, etc (Nam and Tatum, 1997; Slaughter, 1998; Barlow, 2000; UNCTAD, 2000). Innovation and TKTs can however, be fostered through appropriate regulatory frameworks, which support predictable technology and policy regimes and good governance, with few restrictions and regulations regarding intellectual property rights (patents, copyrights, trade secrets, etc).

5.6   Opportunities, Appropriation and Cumulative Effect of Innovation

Opportunities to improve competitiveness and sustainability constitute an important driving force for building product and material manufacturers to actively develop (or look for) new ideas and technologies, given the fact that they can profit from economies of scale. Contextual factors such as the aging and shrinking construction work force and the progressively declining number of young people who enter construction have created *technological opportunities* for firms in many Western countries to innovate and apply innovatively industrialised construction processes, which require fewer specialised trades and people. Moreover, the uniqueness of each construction project and the increasingly complex and fast changing market conditions have put pressure on firms to deliver better quality goods and services, thus providing an impetus for innovation. In this respect, there are few opportunities in construction for appropriating benefits, mainly because of the interdependency in construction arising from the complementary innovations by different actors in the industry (Chesborough and Teece, 1996). Furthermore, whilst construction operations are predominantly transparent and easy to copy, they provide an extensive scope for diffusion of inventions and technological improvements from other projects and industries. However, the risk-averse nature of the industry means that innovation would rarely be adopted without the evidence of a proven track record (Hillebrandt, 1984; Tatum, 1986). This situation calls for a paradigm change, with long-term formalised collaboration between construction actors who would be willing to share innovation benefits as well as risks.

Construction technologies have developed over time by means of cumulative innovation, but this has happened at a rather slow pace compared to other economic sectors. Cumulative innovation is possible, especially where this builds on the existence of a knowledge base that is comprehensible. In this respect, tacit knowledge may be available (and comprehensible), but if it is neither accessible nor acquirable, then this will act as a barrier. This, along with the project-based characteristic of construction and the diversity of stakeholders, increases the potential for divergent interests, which can limit the scope for learning and *cumulative innovation* (Nelson, 2004).

5.7   Managing Innovation for Sustainable Construction: The Dutch Case

This section discusses the findings of a study about the factors underlying the state of SuCo in The Netherlands through the application of a network-based approach. However, it has to be noted that in The Netherlands, success in SuCo has not been as impressive as, for instance, in some of the Scandinavian countries(Hamelin, 2007).

In The Netherlands, SuCo innovation has largely focused on increasing energy efficiency and substituting traditionally used materials and building products for better ones. The main principles here are to reduce, reuse or recycle resources to protect nature in all activities, to eliminate toxic substances in construction and apply life-cycle analysis in construction decision making, using for example, innovative energy technologies. In this respect, these initiatives are seen to:

1. prevent unnecessary use of energy;
2. maximise renewables (e.g. solar boilers); and
3. deliberately use clean and high performance non-renewables (e.g. high performance boilers for central heating).

However, many of these investments are not yet completely cost-effective, and therefore not commercially appealing. Notwithstanding this, it is important to acknowledge the role that 'industrialised buildings' can play in driving up quality and value, while at the same time, saving resources and cutting down construction costs (Hendriks, 1999). The application of such building systems has been seen as a three-pronged strategy, to improve construction with the resulting benefits of:

1. flexibility for the client;
2. efficiency in industrial production with reduced material requirement, reduced costs and time, and improved output quality; and
3. demountability to decrease waste for society (www.sev.nl).

In this respect, demountability enables the separate replacement of components (with various life spans), the consequence of which not only extends the life of the building as a whole, but also decreases waste generation associated with demolition.

An elaboration of these ideas led to the development of the Slimbouwen® concept (Dutch for Smart Building and a trademark). This concept asserts that the solution for SuCo should be found in product innovations, which are integrated in the process, and through organisational innovations. Following this concept, the construction process could be transformed into a sequential process (Lichtenberg, 2005). To achieve this, the building is subdivided into four main parts, which can be prefabricated:

a) foundation, skeleton and floors;
b) building envelope;
c) services (vertical through shafts, horizontally through hollow floors); and
d) in-fill (floor finishing, partitions and ceilings).

The separation of these services package from the main structure is a basis for obtaining flexibility and adaptability, which further benefits the exploitation of this approach.

Slimbouwen® is not a building system *per se*, but can be seen as an innovation development strategy that responds to problems often encountered in traditional building construction. The Slimbouwen strategy forms a guiding framework for the development and production of innovative designs, products, building materials and construction practices in an integrated manner, whilst the functional and economic life span of the structures and recycling and deconstruction of the building components and materials are taken into account (Figure 5.5). Benefits arising out of this concept are multi-layered, from reduced construction periods, through to enhanced competitiveness. It is also possible to construct considerably lighter buildings at a much higher and predictable quality level, with increased flexibility and adaptability (to meet changing demands and market requirements). As such, the Slimbouwen innovation can reduce environmental impact, whilst achieving more sustainable and cleaner construction. For example, the materials used in a dwelling construction project in The Netherlands, weigh about 50% of comparable traditionally built houses of the same volume (Lichtenberg, 2005).

5.7.1   Technological Regime, Diffusion and Knowledge Transfer in Dutch Construction

Many innovations for SuCo in The Netherlands have been developed by organisations through relationships with universities and research centres. Some of these relationships developed through funded research projects in which innovative sustainability concepts have been applied. Knowledge and experience developed in these projects have also been used to further develop

Figure 5.5 Traditional parallel process and sequential Slimbouwen building process (Lichtenberg, 2005). Reproduced by permission of J. Lichtenberg.

and improve design tools for the use of materials, energy, buildings and the built environment (Anink and Mak, 1993; Stofberg and Duijvesteijn, 2006). In addition, it has been recognised that the application and wider diffusion of an innovative construction concept such as Slimbouwen requires an early strong cross-industrial collaboration between stakeholders, along with a multidisciplinary approach during design and production, with appropriate changes being made in some of the traditional construction roles.

For this purpose, Slimbouwen also functions as a shareware platform, providing a knowledge and information infrastructure for firms as the basis for the development of their strategies. The basic concept can be further developed and translated into integrated innovative designs, building components and materials for:

1.   services: energy, water supply, sanitation and ventilation;
2.   floor, supporting structure and built-in assembly kits;
3.   building envelope and specific façade elements; and
4.   the transformation of construction project execution.

Principal stakeholders include those involved in the production chain of buildings: knowledge institutions and universities, governmental organisations and end-users. As such, it brings coherence into the fragmented development efforts of several actors in construction; with a shared and collective purpose – to accomplish SuCo through innovative designs, building components and materials. Slimbouwen is one example of this.

Many organisations and clients mention their expectations of acquiring a 'green image' through energy saving as being an important motive. However, whilst some successful pilot projects can be evidenced, the target of complete diffusion and adoption of the new T&K, as well as of an absolute reduction in resource use within construction, has only partially been achieved (Klunder, 2002). It therefore needs to be acknowledged that successful implementation and diffusion of innovative and sustainable solutions also requires process innovation and regime shift. In this respect, whilst governmental bodies are likely to play an important role in making this happen (and Building Regulations appear to be one of the most important reasons for applying energy saving innovations in The Netherlands), further work is still needed to reinforce and encourage uptake.

5.7.2   Lessons Learned

The Dutch case identified that government support was able to influence current reluctance, beliefs, expectations and standards in order to create loyalty to SuCo and encourage innovation. Both theory and empirical evidence coalesce, acknowledging that T&K forms an important component of any innovation system. However, strategies are needed to improve the knowledge, expectations and beliefs concerning innovation for SuCo, which should involve:

a) voicing and shaping expectations about the new technologies and knowledge through, e.g. demonstration projects; and
b) stimulation of active T&K exchange amongst the actors in the innovation systems about design and engineering specifications, user characteristics and their requirements, environmental issues, industrial development options, government policies, regulatory frameworks and governmental role concerning incentives for diffusion and implementation (Kemp *et al.* 2001).

These strategies should also create an increased awareness of the potential of novel technologies in the market, thereby increasing the market needs for innovation.

SuCo innovation is a continuous learning process influenced by several drivers, not least the political, social and economic setting of a country. This notion supports the arguments for the need to differentiate policies to formulate specific policy agendas adapted to the socio-economic setting and to the particular features of the construction innovation system and the T&K

base (Aubert, 2004). However, the T&K sets in construction are not overtly exchangeable, and would to a large extent need to be developed. Moreover, learning is hampered by traditional systems, with high degrees of fragmentation, which limits transfer opportunities (Desmyter, 2007). Whilst several technological opportunities are underutilised, it is evident that promotion of the common interests of the actors in the innovation system regarding SuCo is needed. Therefore, policies should seek to remove barriers that limit interaction, communication, and knowledge exchange through formal conduits such as research, design, engineering and marketing, etc, in order to bring about a regime shift that diffuses knowledge (learning) in the actor network.

5.8   Conclusion

Innovation in construction occurs through the accumulation and convergence of technologies and knowledge from various areas and different parties (albeit at a relatively slower rate than in other economic sectors). However innovation and TKTs have been limited, and this has had a constraining effect on SuCo performance. Construction firms are therefore challenged to proactively change their practices and policies to focus on innovations for material and energy saving in buildings and waste reduction during traditional construction processes. Improving SuCo performance requires designers, building material producers and contractors to bring about innovative design concepts, building elements and components as well as adaptations in the building processes. These changes can be integrated into construction projects to achieve the optimum application of sustainability principles during all stages of a building's life cycle. Hence, SuCo necessitates innovative solutions in construction that go beyond the traditional and generally accepted way of building, – where environmental gains would be expected to be overtly matched with economic gains.

Innovation evidence from manufacturing is a good starting point for reflection, as many sustainability and innovation issues can readily be used to improve the construction sector. However, this requires a panacea approach to current thinking, which would involve creating strong relationships and long-term collaboration with supply chain partners focused on one common interest. This requires trust, transparent systems and collective thinking regarding the existing knowledge, skills and opportunities available to meet these ideals. In this respect, the Dutch experience identified one such approach leveraged by government support. However, it is also necessary to stimulate SuCo and innovation through policies that support collaborative engagement.

References

Abbott, P.G. (1985) *Technology Transfer in the Construction Industry 'Infrastructure and Industrial development*. Special Report No. 223. The Economist Intelligence Unit, The Economist Publications Ltd.

Abernathy, W.J. & Utterrback, J.M. (1978) Patterns of Industrial Innovation. *Technology Review*, **80**, 41–47.

Anink, D. & Mak, J. (eds) (1993) *Handleiding Duurzame Woningbouw. Milieubewuste materiaalkeuze bij nieuwbouw en renovatie (Rotterdam) SEV.* Stuurgroep Experimenten Volkshuisvesting, Rotterdam.

Aubert, J. (2004) *Promoting Innovation in Developing Countries: A Conceptual Framework.* World Bank Institute, Washington, DC.

Barlow, J. & Jashpara, A. (1998) Organisational learning and inter-firm partnering in the UK construction industry. *The Learning Organisation*, **5(2)**, 86–98.

Barlow, J. (2000) Innovation and learning in complex offshore construction projects. *Research Policy*, **29**, 973–989.

Bell, M. (1984) Learning and the accumulation of industrial technological capacity in developing countries. In: ed. Fransman, M. & King, K., *Technological Capability in the Third World*. Macmillan, London.

Bertelsen, P. & Müller, J. (2003) Changing the outlook: explicating the indigenous systems of innovation in Tanzania. In.Muchie M., Gammeltoft P., and Lundvall B.-Å. (eds.) (2003), Putting Africa First: The Making of African Innovation System, Aalborg, Denmark: Aalborg University Press.Bijker, W., Hughes, T. & Pinch, T. (1987) *The Social Construction of Technological Systems: New Directions in the Sociology and History of Technology*. MIT Press, Cambridge, MA.

Birkenbach, F. (2006) Innovation management in project-based firms, PhD Thesis, Erasmus University.

Borgatti, S.P. & Cross, R. (2003) A relational view of information seeking and learning in social networks. *Management Science*, **49(4)**, 432–445.

Brand, G., Van den Rutten, P. & Dekker, K. (1999) IFD Bouwen, *Principes en Uitwerkingen*.TNO. *Netherlands Organization for Applied Scientific Research*. Report 1999-BKR-R021. TNO Bouw, Delft.

Breschi, S., Malerba, F. & Orsenigo, L. (2000) Technological regimes and Schumpeterian patterns of innovation. *The Economic Journal*, **110**: 388–411.

Bresnen, M. & Marshall, N. (2000) Partnering in construction: a critical review of issues, problems and dilemmas. *Construction Management and Economics*, **18**, 229–237.

Bresnen, M., Goussevskaia, A. & Swan, J. (2004) Embedding new management knowledge in project-based organizations. *Organization Studies*, **25(9)**, 1535–1555.

Carillo, P. (1994) Technology transfer: A survey of international construction companies. *Construction Management and Economics*, **12**, 45–51.

Chesborough, H.W. & Teece, D.J. (1996) When is virtual virtuous? Organizing for innovation. *Harvard Business Review*, **January–February**, 65–73.

Chesbrough, H. (2003) *Open Innovation*. Harvard Business School Press, Boston, MA.

Davey, C.L., Powell, J.A. & Cooper, I. (2002) Action learning in a medium-sized construction company. *Building Research & Information*, **30(1)**, 5–15

Debrah, Y. & Ofori, G. (2001) The State Skills Formation and Productivity enhancement in the construction industry: the case of Singapore. *International Journal of Human Resource Management*, **12(2)**, 184–202.

Desmyter, J. (2007) *Barriers to Eco-innovation in the Construction World, Belgian Building Research Institute (BBRI)*, Belgium paper presented during the European Forum on Eco-Innovation, Markets for Sustainable Construction. Brussels, 11 June. Available from http://ec.europa.eu/environment/ecoinnovation2007/pdf/ (accessed 11 June 2007).

Dosi, G., Coriat, B. & Pavitt, K. (2000) *Competences, Capabilities and Corporate Performance*. Final Report Dynacom Project.

Dosi, G., Pavitt, K. & Soete, L. (1990) *The Economics of Technical Change and International Trade*. Harvester Wheatsheaf, Hertfordshire, UK.

Dosi, G., Nelson, R.R. & Winter, S. (2000) *The Nature And Dynamics Of Organizational Capabilities*. Oxford University Press, Oxford.

Douthwaite, B. (2002) *Enabling Innovation: A Practical Guide to Understanding and Fostering Technological Innovation*. Zed Books, London.

Dunning, J.H. (1981) *International Production And The Multinational Enterprise*. Allen & Unwin, London.

Egbu, C., Kurul, E., Quintas, P., Hutchinson, V. & Anumba, C. (2003) *Knowledge production, resources and capabilities in the construction industry*. Workpackage 1- Final Report, Knowledge Management for Sustainable Construction.

Egmond-de Wilde De Ligny, E.L.C. van (2006) *Lecture Notes International Technology Transfer*. TU Eindhoven, The Netherlands.

Egmond-de Wilde de Ligny, E.L.C. van (2009) *Industrialisation Innovation And Prefabrication In Construction*. Working paper EvE/06-2008/BCC/TUe presented to OECD, Paris.

Egmond-de Wilde De Ligny, E.L.C. van Vulink, M. & Benda, S. (2007) *Capacity Building through Joint Ventures in the Construction Industry*. Proceedings 3RD International conference on multi-national joint venture for construction works, 1–2 November, Bangkok.

ESCAP (1989) *A Framework for Technology Based Development Planning: An Overview of the Framework for Technology-based Development*, vol. I. Technology Atlas Project, United Nations ESCAP.

Franco, L.A., Cushman, M. & Rosenhead, J. (2004) Project review and learning in construction industry: Embedding a problem structuring method within a partnership context. *European Journal of Operational Research*, **152**, 586–601.

Geels, F.W. (2004) From sectoral systems of innovation to socio-technical systems Insights about dynamics and change from sociology and institutional theory. *Research Policy* **33**, 897–920.

Hakansson, H., Havila, V. & Pedersen, A. (1999) Learning in Networks. *Industrial Marketing Management*, **28**, 443–452.

Hamelin, J.P. (2007) *Vision of the Industry towards 2030 and Beyond*. European Construction Technology Platform (ECTP), France paper presented during the European Forum on Eco-Innovation. Markets for Sustainable Construction Brussels, 11 June 2007.

Hendriks, N. (1999) *Industrieel, Flexibel en Demontabe*. Bouwen IFD: Ontwerpen op veranderbaarheid, Eindhoven University of Technology.

Hillebrandt, P. (1984) *Economic Theory and the Construction Industry*, 2nd edn. Macmillan, London.

ILO (2001) *The Construction Industry in the Twenty-first Century: Its Image, Employment Prospects and Skill Requirements*. ILO Geneva.

Jashapara, A. (2003) Cognition, culture and competition: an empirical test of the learning organisation. *The Learning Organisation*, **10**(1), 31—50.

Javernick, A., Levitt, R.E. & Scott, W.R.Y. (2007) *Understanding Knowledge Acquisition, Integration and Transfer by Global Development, Engineering and Construction Firms*. Collaboratory for Research on Global Projects Working Paper #0028, 1–17. Stanford University.

Katz, M. & Shapiro. C. (1985) On the licensing of innovations. *RAND Journal of Economy*, **16**(4), 504–520.

Keegan, A. & Turner, J.R. (2002) The management of innovation in project-based firms. *Long Range Planning*, **35**(4), 367–388.

Kemp, R., Schot, J. & Rip, A. (2001) Constructing transition paths through the management of niches. In: ed. Garud, R. & Karnøe, P. *Path Dependence and Creation*, Mahwah, NJ: Lawrence Earlbaum Associates pp. 269–99.

Kibert, C.J. (2003) *Forward: Sustainable Construction at the Start of the 21st Century*. Special Issue article in: The Future of Sustainable Construction. International Electronic Journal of Construction (IeJC).

Kibert, C.J. (2005) *Sustainable Construction: Green Building Design and Delivery*. John Wiley and Son, Hoboken, NJ.

Kline, S.J. & Rosenberg, N. (1986) An overview of innovation. In: ed. Landau, R. & Rosenberg, N., *The Positive Sum Strategy: Harnessing Technology for Economic Growth*. National Academy Press, Washinton, DC. 275–305.

Klunder, G. (2002) *Hoe milieuvriendelijk is duurzaam bouwen? De milieubelasting van woningen gekwantificeerd*. Delft University Press, The Netherlands.

Kondratiev, N.D. (1925) *The Major Economic Cycles* (in Russian). Moscow. Translated and published as *The Long Wave Cycle* by Richardson & Snyder, New York, 1984.

Kumaraswamy, M.M. (1995) *Technology Exchange through Joint Ventures*. International Conference on 'Technology Innovation and Industrial Development in China and Asia Pacific towards the 21st Century', Hong Kong, November, Proceedings. 254–261.

Kumaraswamy, M.M. & Shrestha, G.B. (2002) Targeting technology exchange for faster organisational and industry development. *Building Research and Information*, 30(3), 183–195.

Lall, S. (1985) Trade in technology by a slowly industrializing country: India, In: ed. Rosenberg, N. & and Frischtak, C., *International Technology Transfer: Conc, in Concepts, Measures and Comparisons*. Praeger, New York.

Lall, S. (1987) *Learning to Industrialize*. Macmillan, London.

Lall, S. (1992) Technological capabilities and industrialization. *World Development*, 20(2), 165–186.

Lall, S. (2003) Foreign direct investment, technology development and competitiveness: issues and evidence. In: ed. Lall, S. & Urata, S., *Competitiveness, FDI and Technological Activity in East Asia*, Edward Elgar, Cheltenham. 12–56.

Lichtenberg, J.J.N. (2005) Slimbouwen [in Dutch] Boxtel: Æneas, Uitgeverij van vakinformatie voor de bouw en energie wereld, The Netherlands.

Lichtenberg, J.J.N. (2002) *Ontwikkelen van Projectongebonden Bouwproducten*. PhD thesis, Kelpen-Oler: A+.

Lundvall, B, & Gu, S. (2006) China's innovation system and the move toward harmonious growth and endogenous innovation. *Innovation: Management, Policy & Practice*, 8, 1–2.

Lundvall, B-Å. (ed.) (1992) *National Systems of Innovation: Towards a Theory of Innovation and Interactive learning*. Pinter, London.

Macozoma, D.S. (2002) *Secondary Construction Materials: An Alternative Resource Pool for Future Construction Needs*. Concrete for the 21st Century Conference. Eskom Conference Centre, Midrand, Gauteng.

Malerba F. (2002) Sectoral systems of innovation and production. *Research Policy*, 31, 247–264.

Malerba, F. & Orsenigo, L. (1996) Schumpeterian patterns of innovation are technology specific. *Research Policy*, 25, 451–478.

Manley, K. (2001) Frameworks for understanding interactive innovation processes. *The International Journal of Entrepreneurship and Innovation*, 4(1), 25–36.

March, J.G. (1991) Exploration and exploitation in organizational learning. *Organization Science*, 1(2): 71–87.

March, J.G. & Simon, H. (1993) Organizations revisited. *Industrial and Corporate Change*, 2(3): 299–316.

Marsili, O. & Verspagen, B. (2002) Technology and the dynamics of industrial structure: an empirical mapping of Dutch manufacturing. *Industrial and Corporate Change*, 11, 791–815.

Metcalfe, S. (1995) Technology systems and technology policy in an evolutionary framework. *Cambridge Journal of Economics*, 17, 25–46.

Miozzo, M. & Dewick, P. (2004) *Innovation in Construction*. Edward Elgar, Cheltenham.

Muller, R. (2000) *Green Building Basics*. US Department of energy. Available from www.sustainable.doe.gov/buildings/gbarttoc.htm

Murray, F & O'Mahony, S. (2007) exploring the foundations of cumulative innovation: Implications for organization science perspective. *Organization Science*, 18(6), 1006–1021.

Nam,C.H. and Tatum, C.B.(1997) Leaders and Champions for Construction Innovation, *Construction Management and Economics*, 15 (4), 259—270.

Nam, C.H. & Tatum, C.B. (1988). Major characteristics of constructed products and resulting limitations of construction technology. *Construction Management and Economics*, 6, 133–148.

Nelson, R. (2004) The market economy, and the scientific commons. *Research Policy*, 33(3), 455–471.

Nelson, R.R. & Winter, S.G. (1982) *An Evolutionary Theory of Economic Change*. Harvard University Press, Cambridge, MA.

OECD/IEA (2009) *World Energy Outlook 2008*. OECD, Paris. Available from http://www.worldenergyoutlook.org/docs/weo2008/WEO2008.pdf

Ofori, G. (1996) International contractors and structural changes in host-country construction industries: Case of Singapore. *Engineering, Construction and Architectural Management*, 3(4), 271–288.

Ofori, G. (1990) *The Construction Industry: Aspects of its Economics and Management*. Singapore University Press, Singapore.

Patel, P. & Pavitt, K. (1997) The technological competencies of the world's largest firms: complex and path dependent, but not much variety. *Research Policy*, 26(2): 141–156.

Polanyi, M. (1967) *The Tacit Dimension*. Doubleday & Co. Reprinted 1983, Peter Smith, Gloucester, MA.

Pries, F. & Janszen, F. (1995) Innovation in the construction industry: the dominant role of environment. *Construction Management and Economics*, 13(1), 43–51.

Rogers, E.M. (1995) *Diffusion of Innovations*, 4th edn. The Free Press, New York.

Rosenberg, N. (ed.) (1976) *Perspectives on Technology*. Cambridge University Press, Cambridge.

Rosenberg, N. (1982) *Inside the Black Box: Technology and Economics*. Cambridge University Press, Cambridge, MA.

Rovers, R. (2007) What is Sustainable building? In *Report on 2nd European Forum on Eco-Innovation Markets for Sustainable Construction EU Environmental Technologies Action Plan (ETAP)*. Brussels 11 June. Available from http://ec.europa.eu/environment/ecoinnovation2007/pdf/report_lowres.pdf

Schumpeter, J.A. (1934) *The Theory of Economic Development*. Harvard University Press, Cambridge, MA.

Slaughter, E.S. (1998) Models of construction innovation. *Journal of Construction Engineering and Management*, 124(3), 226–232.

Stewart, F. (1979) *International Technology Transfer: Issues and Policy Options*, World Bank Staff Working Paper No. 344. World Bank, USA, 22.

Stiglitz, J. (1999) *Knowledge as a Global Public Good.* World Bank. Available from www.worldbank.org/knowledge/chiefecon/articles/undpk2/

Stofberg, F. & Duijvestein, K. (2006) *Basisdocument Wat is duurzaam bouwen?SenterNovem*, 2nd edn. Ministerie van VROM.maart.

Tatum, C.B. (1986) Potential mechanisms for construction innovation. *Journal of Construction Engineering and Management*, **112**(2), 178–191.

Teece, D.J., Pisano, G. & Shuen, A. (1997) Dynamic capabilities and strategic management. In: ed. Foss, N.J., *Resources, Firms and Strategies*. Oxford University Press, New York. 268–287.

Thomassen, M.A. (2003) The economic organization of building processes., PhD thesis, BYG-DTU, Technical University of Denmark.

Tidd, J., Bessant, J. & Pavitt, K. (2006) *Managing Innovation: Integrating Technological, Market and Organizational Change*, 3rd edn. John Wiley & Sons, Hoboken, NJ.

Tjandra I. K. & Tan W. (2002) *Organisational Learning in Construction Firms: The Case Of Construction Firms Operating In Jakarta, Indonesia* – Report on research conducted at National University of Singapore. National University of Singapore, Singapore.

UNCTAD (2000) *Regulation and Liberalization in the Construction Services Sector and its Contribution to the Development of Developing Countries*. Note by the UNCTAD Secretariat. Geneva.

UNCTAD (2009) *World Investment Report 2009*. United Nations, New York.

Vakola, M. & Rezgui, Y. (2000) Organisational learning and innovation in the construction industry. *The Learning Organization*, 7(4),174–184.

Von Hippel, E. (1988) Economics of product development by users: the impact of 'sticky' local information. *Management Science*, **44**(5), 629–624.

Walker D.H.T. & Johannes D.S. (2003) Preparing for organisational learning by HK infrastructure project joint venture organisation. *The Learning Organisation*, 10(2),106–117.

Wells, J. (2001) Construction and capital formation in less developed economies: unravelling the informal sector in an African city. *Construction Management and Economics*, **19**, 267–274.

Winch, G.M. (1998) Zephyrs of creative destruction: understanding the management of innovation in construction. *Building Research and Information*, **26**(4), 268–279.

World Bank (2007) *Building Knowledge Economies: Advanced Strategies for Development; World Bank Institute, Knowledge for Development Program*. The World Bank, Washington, DC.

World Commission on Economic Development (WCED) (1987) *Our Common Future*. Oxford University Press, Oxford.

Zawdie, G. & Langford, D. (2002) Influence of construction-based infrastructure on the development process in sub-Saharan Africa. *Building Research and Information*, **30**(3): 160–170.

6

Innovation and Value Delivery through Supply Chain Management

Derek H.T. Walker

Innovation through Supply Chain Management (SCM) can take many forms and can be viewed from different perspectives. The purpose of this chapter is to provide insights into how the concept of SCM can be applied innovatively, viewed from the perspective of a value-adding process for providing the promised output to the stakeholders and the value contribution to the organisation's sustainability as an enterprise. The question of whether to settle for in-house or external sourcing of the necessary resources is a pivotal procurement decision. If the latter option is chosen, then a host of alternative strategies are open for consideration, and some of these could offer rich opportunities for innovation.

Green (1999a) warns of the dangers associated with the construction industry blindly accepting management innovations such as lean construction, SCM and associated techniques imported from the Japanese car manufacturing industry. From a critical theory perspective (Habermas and Outhwaite, 1996; Saul, 1997), workforce adopting these innovations can become disempowered, paying the price of organisational flexibility through increased employment tenure uncertainty and reduced bargaining power with their employers, as well as being increasingly subjected to an attitude of managerial prerogative at the expense of their autonomy. This chapter presents an innovative way of thinking about a supply chain to reframe concepts of value that can be delivered through projects. The Organisation for Economic Co-operation and Development's five criteria for evaluating aid projects - *efficiency, effectiveness, relevance, sustainability,* and *impact* (OECD, 2007: 37) are adopted in this chapter to conceptualise 'value'. These criteria are relevant to construction projects, although they are rarely known

Construction Innovation and Process Improvement, First Edition.
Edited by Akintola Akintoye, Jack S. Goulding and Girma Zawdie.
© 2012 Blackwell Publishing Ltd. Published 2012 by Blackwell Publishing Ltd.

or even understood by clients. The construction industry is familiar with *efficiency* values such as time, cost and fitness for purpose (quality), and these have been used to measure success for a long time (de Wit, 1988). However, more recent project management (PM) literature has focused on the need for *effectiveness* to be considered as prime importance (Cooke-Davies, 2002). *Relevance* has also become prominent as a success criterion with increasing attention now being given to responding to a broader range of stakeholders than a builder's client or even building users/tenants (Dainty *et al.*, 2003; Nogeste, 2004; Bourne and Walker, 2005). *Sustainability* has also become particularly important (Graham and Smithers, 1996; Khalfan *et al.*, 2006), as has *impact* assessment. *Impact* is a concept that is seldom considered because the focus of management has hitherto been largely on delivering a project as a product, and not on delivering service benefits through corporate expertise, competence and knowledge that enhance capabilities for delivering value in the form of constructed facilities.

An organisational sustainability perspective of value will be adopted for this chapter. Sustainability, in this context, refers to the organisation's role to deliver benefits to its core stakeholders – i.e. its clients, its employees and the society that it engages with in its business activities. Thus, a triple bottom line (3BL) approach to value becomes the operating paradigm. The 3BL approach assumes that organisations are obliged to consider not only financial returns on investment but also a social and environmental dividends (Elkington, 1997). A Latin American supra-organisation, established to radically transform SCM, provides the context of the case studies. Recourse is made to literature on the theory of the firm, outsourcing and SCM and the concept of value chains to underpin the discussion in this chapter. Therefore, the aim of this chapter is to challenge existing construction management practices through insights deriving from leading edge PM research. To this end, this chapter provides an overview of procurement trends in outsourcing that have led to concepts of SCM being more readily accepted within the construction and project management related fields. This is followed by a section on the value temporary organisations bring, and how that relates to project procurement, which in turn is followed by sections discussing seriatim outsourcing and SCM, and the emerging SCM view and what innovation it could offer as a procurement strategy. A case study from the logistics and shipping field is then presented as an illustration of SCM as a means of delivering business transformation. It concludes with a discussion of the implications of adopting the emerging SCM view for the construction industry.

6.2   Organisational Value

Construction projects are predominantly delivered by organisations. Organisations assign teams of people such as design consultants, builders, sub-contractors and materials suppliers, drawn from a wide range of companies/firms. These teams focus upon a construction project to become in many ways a single temporary organisation (Lundin and Söderholm, 1995). This organisation's value contribution extends far beyond providing design services or components, or the assembly of components. It is worth reflecting upon the fundamental value that any organisation contributes, because this lies at the heart of this chapter – providing a 'value' perspective on innovation through SCM. Even more central to individual participating firms in a project is the issue of sustainable competitive advantage that would enable them to thrive in business, moving from one project to the next, delivering real value to stakeholders. It is therefore important to consider what advantage firms perceive they would gain from being part of a managed supply chain, as this would provide a useful guide in the determination of appropriate strategies for managing this supply chain.

6.2.1   Sustainable Competitive Advantage

The concept of sustainable competitive advantage provides a suitable starting point for reflection. Porter (1985) is a widely cited authority on the theory of sustainable competitive advantage, the core tenet of which advocates:

> Competitive advantage grows fundamentally out of value a firm is able to create for its buyers that exceeds the firm's cost of creating it. Value is what buyers are willing to pay, and superior value stems from offering lower prices than competitors for equivalent benefits or providing unique benefits that more than offset a higher price… Interrelationships among business units are the principal means by which a diversified firm creates value… (Porter, 1985: 3).

Porter (1985) also advocates that firms may procure cost advantage through being able to produce at a lower cost than their competitors, or provide a highly customised product/service and therefore become the preferred supplier, or alternatively, they may offer a unique product or service that their competitors cannot deliver. This means that firms need a particular bundle of assets that they can deploy to provide what is valued by their customers. In this respect, Barney (1991) refers to the resource-based view (RBV) of the firm, noting that organisations need to develop their assets and resources in order to be competitive. These assets include tangible assets, such as money (strong balance sheet), productive resources, such as equipment and people to do the work, competence (i.e. the ability to deliver what is required) and knowledge and skill resources (systems put in place to access information and knowledge needed), that people skilled in their use can effectively deploy. The aim of companies from the RBV perspective is to try to build and deploy their resources more *efficiently* than their competitors to gain cost advantage. Alternatively, they could use their bundle of resources more *effectively* to either provide a customised or unique offering, depending upon the client's needs. However, in managing a project supply chain, there would be a cost imperative driven by cost efficiency as well as an effectiveness imperative driven by coordination, timing and relationship considerations. There may also be an unspoken or assumed expectation of relevance to the customer, supply chain partners or the organisation managing the supply chain, that the supply chain is delivering what is needed, and that the long-term impact would be positive and deliver value.

Managing a project with a supply chain may be the consequence of a desire for repeat custom that would warrant sustainable business. However, the long-term view of business would presuppose that the criteria of efficiency, effectiveness, relevance, sustainability and impact relate closely to having a sustainable competitive advantage. Efficiency and effectiveness affect the *financial* bottom line; relevance and impact affect the *social* bottom line; and sustainability should be seen not only in terms of sustainable business practice that would enable organisations to serve their stakeholders continually, but also in terms of the sustainability of the physical environment.

The RBV was later supplemented by a greater emphasis on knowledge management and the role of people bringing social capital assets to the firm through their skills, attributes and behaviours, their network connections and their potential enthusiasm and affective (want-to) commitment (Meyer and Allen, 1991), which was seen to have human resource management implications (Wright *et al.*, 2001). This wider view of a firm's competence as being strongly mediated by its management of human capital and knowledge was a natural progression of the RBV that better explained how this aspect of resources could be deployed (Sanchez, 2004). Another extension of the RBV is recognition of the dynamic nature of competition and of turbulence in the business and economic environment. This recognition led to the perceived gap in the RBV theory of the firm being addressed through the concept of dynamic capabilities (Teece *et al.*, 1997; Teece, 1998, 2001; Eisenhardt and Martin, 2000; Wang and Ahmed, 2007). This recognised that firms are subject to turbulence and shocks, and part of their ability to respond to this uncertainly is to develop the capability to be agile, reflexive and responsive. This called for a shift from being highly prescriptive in developing strategies through the adoption of a command and control strategic approach, to a position where an emergent strategic approach is adopted (Mintzberg *et al.*, 1998). This approach places emphasis upon a broad brush strategic direction being identified and planned, using milestones with shorter-term emergent crafting strategies (Mintzberg, 1987), by navigation towards milestones using a combination of detailed planning (Olsson, 2006; Olsson and Magnussen, 2007), or by creatively muddling through problems and challenges (Lindblom, 1959; Cates, 1979; Lindblom, 1979; Hällgren and Wilson, 2007).

Firms deliver value in a variety of ways. The perception of this value may be mediated by the preferred strategic stance of the client, or of the coordinating firm managing a supply chain. This can be summarised as providing:

1. *Knowledge, competence and dynamic capabilities* to engage with a client and/or coordinating manager of the supply chain to develop an efficient, effective, relevant and sustainable project design that provides positive impact towards delivering the benefits expected by the client/project owner;
2. *Resources* required to deliver the outputs to the expected five criteria – efficiency, effectiveness, relevance, sustainability and impact; and

3. *Required engagement* with, *and commitment* to the client/project owner in dynamically responding not only to 'normal' turbulence associated with uncertain ventures, such as construction projects, but also to other exigencies that may emerge as a result of a potentially changing economic and business environment over the life of the project.

The first potential value relates to knowledge, information and capabilities at the front end of the project life cycle. Williams and Samset (2010) stress the importance of project team involvement at the front end of projects, to ensure that all viable options are available for the team to be able to deliver a meaningful and realistic (i.e. sustainable and relevant) project concept (business justification and overall design). This project concept has to be developed prior to commitment to further project design development. Williams and Samset (2010) point out that often major cost/time overruns of projects from the original budget represents unrealistic initial budget estimates. They also argue that recognising this potential and requesting several viable alternatives including the zero option (do not do the project) challenges the creativity of those involved at this stage. This challenge arises out of scant information being available at the project concept stage. Also, because traditional procurement paths exclude the contractor and other supporting members at the project delivery phase, vital knowledge about practicalities and sustainable design solutions are not usually available without closer involvement of the eventual supply chain members. This leads to unwise project designs that may not be relevant or sustainable, being locked in, so that significant re-work costs may be incurred (Love *et al.*, 2000, 2009). The contractor, if involved early enough at the front-end stage of a project, can contribute significant 'buildability' knowledge (Sidwell and Mehertns, 1996; McGeorge and Palmer, 2002), which can similarly add value and reduce waste. Coordinating contractors that have this type of capacity and competence are often part of a learning alliance in construction and other manufacturing industries involved in projects (Love and Gunasekaran, 1999) to create learning chains (Maqsood *et al.*, 2007). It can be seen from the above that learning, knowledge and insights can add significant value to the front end of projects.

Firms within a supply chain deliver value through their capacity to offer specialised resources such as materials, plant and equipment or people. These may be highly specialised, in that each firm would rely, to some extent, on competitive advantage for the supply of a customised or rare service. Part of the value they offer is the 'care why' type knowledge (von Krogh, 1998; von Krogh *et al.*, 2000). This is knowledge about the relevance and significance associated with a relationship between firms, which also relates to levels of mutual commitment, so that there is a possibility to know what each partner needs to know and their being able and willing to share that knowledge. Merely having the required resources is not enough to deliver optimised value; there also needs to be commitment and social capital exchanges. Nahapiet and Ghoshal (1998) identify social capital as having a structural dimension (sharing of network links), a cognitive dimension (knowledge and insights, shared codes and language), as well as relational dimensions (trust, commitment, obligations and identification). Thus, social capital has both explicit and implicit value. The value of commitment and engagement is important because information is often scarce about what is required and what is possible, feasible or relevant at the front end of projects. Therefore, wider engagement with specialisation experts within the supply chain often contribute significant value to a project (Klakegg *et al.*, 2010). This perspective of what value is needed from SCM to effectively deliver projects or construction, clearly sees construction as a lot more complex and complicated than merely mechanistically assembling components. It involves sophisticated integration at the delivery stage where many unforeseen events throw the best-made plans into turmoil. Thus, systems integrators need access to a supply chain that not only provides the goods and services but also delivers assets that are rare and difficult to imitate – knowledge, effective commitment and intangible social capital. Without these assets being willingly deployed, projects can lapse into dysfunctional chaos as compared to the self-correcting responsiveness of well-functioning committed teams who can cope and mutually adjust (Hällgren and Maaninen-Olsson, 2005).

6.2.2   The Cost of Transacting Business

For every economic transaction involving procurement of resources for construction project work, there are usually transparent and hidden costs. These costs are explained in terms of Transaction Cost Economics (TCE). According to Coase (1937) and Williamson (1985; 1991; 1993), TCE relates to the cost of doing business, as every transaction between parties typically involves cost. This can be explicit and easily measured, such as a tendering cost involving advertising, search costs for determining where to advertise the tender, filtering or short listing, evaluation and tender award costs. There can also be a lot of implicit costs expended such as training, learning from mistakes in the award or through governance provision for oversight, assessment progress payment evaluation and a host of other costs. TCE also involves the cost of establishing relationships, trust and the like. It can be appreciated that tendering for the lowest cost can yield the lowest contract award cost, but may entail many pre-tender expenses and heavy post-tender award costs for contract administration, monitoring and evaluation and even conflict resolution related costs. Thus, the lowest cost tender award may easily result in the lowest value result, particularly if the scope of work is difficult to determine and/or the initial value to be obtained relates to knowledge and advice about potential options and solutions. This has profound implications for management of the supply chain, because the total cost, *including transaction costs*, should be considered. As suggested above, the value that organisations contribute includes what they do to lower transaction costs. SCM provides potential opportunities in this respect. Organisations therefore tend to generate value through:

▪ knowledge, skills, expertise and insights, particularly at the front end of projects;

- social capital, which includes extended networks and knowledge and linkages to provide products or services through *ad hoc* or more formal arrangements;
- products or services;
- commitment, enthusiasm and support; and
- potential savings in transaction costs based on open and mutual negotiations about the ways and means of providing trust and credibility mechanisms that are more effective and efficient than might otherwise be the case under 'normal' trading.

6.3   Value Generation and SCM

At the heart of a construction firm's procurement process lies a fundamental best value decision – a make-or-buy decision that must be taken to sell goods or services that generate more value to the organisation than it expends in terms of a variety of resources. This best value decision is a TCE value inspired decision. Traditionally, most of the literature on procurement (particularly that from the late 1980s to mid-1990s) assumes this decision is mainly a cost/time competitive advantage one (NBCC, 1989; Masterman, 1992; Australian Industry Commission, 1996; Kumaraswamy, 1996; Kelly *et al.*, 2002; Hughes, 2006). Latterly, and leading this debate during the last part of the twentieth century, this focus has shifted towards collaborative and relationship-based approaches through partnering, for example (Larson, 1995; Matthews *et al.*, 1996; Fellows, 1997; Lendrum, 1998; Thompson and Sanders, 1998). In this respect, a more recent focus has emerged based on various stakeholder's conception of what value is exchanged rather than what resources are exchanged (Kelly *et al.*, 2002; Male, 2002; Langford *et al.*, 2003). Overlapping this focus has been an interest in how this happens in construction supply chains (Dainty *et al.*, 2001; Palaneeswaran *et al.*, 2003; Pryke, 2004; Khalfan and McDermot, 2006); how e-portals or enterprise resource planning (ERP) systems (Chan and Swatman, 2000; Chan *et al.*, 2009) achieve integration; and how other means of electronic co-operation both reduce transaction costs and increase efficiency (Croom *et al.*, 2000; Akkermans *et al.*, 2003; Croom, 2005). In addition, there has been an emerging interest in value chains rather than supply chains, particularly from knowledge being a key resource being exchanged and value added (Maqsood *et al.*, 2007).

6.3.1   The Buy or Outsource Decision

Fill and Visser (2000) argue that the buy or outsource decision is triggered by a need to deliver resources from within the organisation (a make decision) or to source this requirement by using the resources from an external organisation (a buy decision). Buy decisions involve sub-contracting a service (e.g. design) or product and service (e.g. the supply and installation of air-conditioning). Apart from outsourcing services such as a consultancy, other options are in use today. This is called in-sourcing, where formally internal expertise is spun off as an external entity, but remains located in-house with project teams working as before, but in a more flexible and cost effective way to the host organisation. The spun off entity is free to take on other work, either as part of its business or on a relationship-contracted basis, usually with minimal transaction costs (McKenna and Walker, 2008). There are clearly numerous options for combining in-house and external combinations for sourcing required resources. Most construction projects require both make and buy decisions. Certainly, much procurement in the construction industry revolves around materials (e.g. ready mix concrete), equipment (e.g. crane hire) and sub-contractors (e.g. mechanical or electrical specialists). Generally these days, contractors tend to be system integrators rather than doing much of the construction work themselves (Winch, 2003). This means that the construction contractor's organisational skill set and competence rests with effectively managing a chain of goods, equipment and services.

6.3.2   Supply Chain Management

London and Kenley (2001) provide an insight into the general industrial organisation's use and development of SCM and how that has influenced the construction industry's adoption and adaptation of SCM. They show influences emerging from the automotive manufacturing industry (Womack et al., 1990), which triggered an interest in lean production (Womack and Jones, 1994, 2000) through to the construction industry where, in particular, Koskela (2000) was active in linking SCM with waste reduction and the effective transformation of construction inputs into completed built facilities. In addition, contributions from Rowlinson and McDermott (1999) and London and Kenley (2001) also trace how strategic construction procurement links to SCM and to the formation of strategic alliance forms.

SCM has been described as a process of coherently integrating all supplier inputs into product/service delivery with a general privilege of gains in competitive advantage for improved cost, time and quality efficiency measures (Sadler, 2007). An efficiency focus is centred upon the transaction; meaning, getting the lowest cost for the project, and a more reliable time delivery of project inputs in the case of construction projects. This is achieved through better capacity of negotiated price based upon bulk purchases, lower transaction costs for reducing the total numbers of suppliers and lowering storage, potential waste and handling costs by Just in Time (JIT) approaches. At the same time, efficiency gains can be achieved through JIT, lean production techniques and many of the approaches reportedly used in manufacturing, automotive and aerospace (Green, 1999b; Michaels, 1999). Part of these gains relate to reducing the number of subcontractors and the use of Keiretsu-like clusters of sub-system assembly integrators, such as those in Japan (Womack et al., 1990); and is particularly well developed in the automotive manufacturing industry (Dyer, 2000). These form an effective group to supply components involving partnered suppliers to co-operate on design and assembly in a way that minimises waste, increases smooth scheduling of

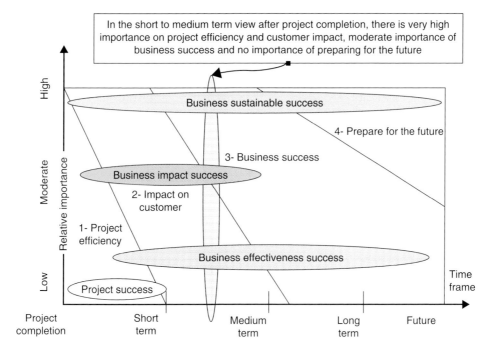

In the short to medium term view after project completion, there is very high importance on project efficiency and customer impact, moderate importance of business success and no importance of preparing for the future

Figure 6.1   Temporal views of success (adapted from Shenhar *et al.*, 2001).

assembly, and provides knowledge exchanges about potential problems or advantages of specific components' properties when combined in assemblies. These types of efficiency gain provide a strong argument for the use of SCM in construction. Effective SCM can therefore be seen to be useful in providing a positive long-term business impact rather than narrow efficiency project objectives (Shenhar *et al.*, 2001). However, this view is challenged by Green (1999a,b), as discussed earlier, and by James (2006) in an article about a range of industries using SCM ranging from supermarket retailers through to the oil and gas sector. These authors caution against unethical use of SCM as a mechanism for coercion by continually reducing costs through profit margin competition.

Figure 6.1 illustrates a series of success factors across various time perspectives. From this, efficiency is associated with project success, whereas gaining positive impact on the customer is associated with business impact success, which is a combination of efficiency and effectiveness. SCM across a business that provides outsourcing TCE benefits can therefore be seen to contribute to long-term business success. SCM can also contribute to business sustainability success by using the knowledge and social capital generated through truly relational SCM that draws firms into business transformations, and prepare them for future success. This is discussed in the next section. However, cautionary suggestions relating to the conduct of SCM (cited above) are salient in context with SCM motivation. Where an outsourcing agent's guiding principle or sole purpose is cost or time reduction, the result in the long term can be exploitation, intimidation and coercion, which could produce a dysfunctional supply chain. Outsourced entities in that chain may then be forced to cut corners or make short-term decisions that could have a detrimental impact, or prevent long-term sustainability due to 'cannibalisation' of weaker links in the chain (James, 2006).

The issue of alliances forming part of an improved and integrated supply chain in a construction context have been extensively explored. For example, research based upon the National Museum of Australia by Walker and Hampson (2003a,b,c) identified how collaboration and co-operation between the client, design team and major system integrators (a significant part of the complete supply chain) provided exceptionally successful project results (Walker and Lloyd-Walker, 2010). Alliances have also been shown to facilitate better relationships between participants (Davis, 2006), and where innovation has been enhanced through alliances (Rowlinson and Walker, 2008). This level of co-operation has been shown to be effective and sustainable in several other industries. Porter (1998), for example, discusses the concept of clusters as loose or more formal industry player groupings, which form a major part, if not all of the entire supply chain. These collaborate and cooperate not only to make business transactions but also to engage in specialised knowledge exchange that allows the chain to be efficient, effective, have a positive impact and create new products on a sustainable basis. Porter (1998) further cites examples from the Californian wine industry, the Italian leather fashion industry and German chemicals industry. The advantages posited through these clusters are similar to those claimed to be achievable through SCM. Other forms of alliance collaboration that contribute to SCM literature in construction have been discussed under the rubric of 'FAs', by which best value is agreed upon from the perspective of the purchaser and provider of goods and services, using a relationship focus based on trust and commitment. Khalfan and McDermot (2006) demonstrate through case studies how this approach can provide innovation and innovative thinking, so that previously unconsidered or poorly considered solutions to problems can be explored, evaluated and adopted. This kind of transformation of the SCM concept takes its form from a managerialist form of efficiency and effectiveness in supply chain integration and optimal management of resources (Sadler, 2007), geared to addressing relevance, sustainability and impact issues.

Fisher (1997: 109) provides some recommendations about how to devise an ideal SCM strategy. The first step is deciding whether the product/ service is functional or innovative. Functional products require an efficient process, whereas innovative products require a responsive process. In the construction context, standard mass-like products, such as estate housing, warehousing, small factory workshops – referred to in the USA as 'cooky-cutter' projects – are generally functional, although some customisation is inevitable. Innovative projects – called 'bespoke' in the UK, are highly customised, specialised and require non-routine problem solving throughout the project phases. Fisher (1997: 109) recommends mapping the characteristics of the actual supply chain, so that, if the supply chain is managed as an innovative product, which has its primary focus on responsiveness, then managing it to be primarily efficient will close out all kinds of options, reduce or inhibit knowledge transfer and create a spiral of cost/timing cutting to the detriment of long-term efficiency, long-term business impact or long-term sustainability.

Taking this idea forward, integrated information and data exchange can be viewed as an example of a functional versus responsive strategy. Chan and Swatman (2000) discuss how the use of computer systems has moved on from electronic data interchange (EDI) to e-commerce, particularly with the use of web portals. The level of e-commerce for functional products could be envisaged as being highly focused on reducing waste (particularly paperwork transactions), enhancing financial and scheduling information transfer and other product-specific technical information transfer. A high priority could be to integrate the supply chain through a common or well-linked enterprise resource planning (ERP) system. That could be contrasted with an innovation-oriented product. Here the focus would be a lower priority on mechanistic ERP e-commerce, although that would not be ignored, and a higher priority on access to external information bases, social networking software and other kinds of applications that allow and encourage people to exchange knowledge and perceptions. Jewell and Walker (2005), for example, illustrate how a community of practice social networking software application was successfully used by a UK constructor Carillion for knowledge exchange. A community of practice (CoP) can therefore be seen an informal or formal organisational structure with facilities that enables members with common interest to share knowledge and perceptions (Wenger *et al.*, 2002). Peansupap and Walker (2005) show how CoP can be facilitated by groupware software applications for personalised knowledge exchange. This brief illustration shows how SCM can be effectively sustained through the appropriately matched use of information communication technology.

6.4   Emerging Supply Chain Management Issues

This section discusses emerging conceptual SCM issues pertaining to innovation.

6.4.1   Value Chains

The conceptual shift from SCM to value chain management (VCM) has been advocated as being logical. Figure 6.1 highlighted that efficiency at the project level is a tactical issue, while preparing for or creating a future is a strategic issue. However, successful organisations move beyond merely managing supply chain intelligence, knowledge and information to actively co-create value with their array of suppliers and clients. This is particularly salient in volatile and turbulent conditions, which is highly characteristic of projects at the front end when scoping and strategic design decisions are being made. As Normann and Ramirez (1993: 66) note, 'Increasingly, successful companies do not just add value, they reinvent it. Their focus of strategic analysis is not the company or even the industry but the value-creating system itself …' In this innovation-oriented view of the need to deliver projects, importance is placed on value co-generation providing a more holistic mental model of what each supply chain member (including the client and end-users) can possibly offer. Normann and Ramirez (1993: 69) also make several salient points about the new logic of value that applies to VCM. First, where value occurs through harnessing a complex constellation rather than a linear supply chain, the business goal is to encourage and mobilise clients and customers to take advantage of creating value for them by liberating them from potential constraints for their ability to freely access value as they see it. They give examples of the multinational furniture company IKEA that mastered the innovation of pre-packaged modular furniture that customers could assemble themselves in the configuration that suits their needs. In the context of construction, this means greater involvement of the client at the briefing and front end of projects. This principle is applied in several ways, for example, by sophisticated clients engaging with visualisation tools to explore various possible options, or construction contractors involving sub-contractors and suppliers in modelling progress through a project to identify possible delivery and/or installation clashes. This approach uses 4D design modelling (Fisher et al., 1997; Fischer and Drogemuller, 2009). Significant recent advances in BIM also allows this interaction with the supply chain (Aranda-Mena et al., 2009), to promote a value chain perception of what would otherwise be referred to as the supply chain.

Following this theme, Normann and Ramirez (1993: 69) argue that as potential value contributions become more complex and involve more actors within a network, the firm's principal role becomes one of systems integrator by reconfiguring the range and types of inputs and transforming relationships between members of a value chain. From a construction context, innovative construction contractors are increasingly leading, or being within a consortium leading large-scale build-own-operate-transfer (BOOT) projects and alliance infrastructure projects. Within these contexts, the construction contractor therefore becomes a catalyst for considering the technical feasibility of options and their relationships with design teams and other consultants to be system integrators. This has evolved from innovative contractors providing 'buildability' advice (Sidwell and Mehertns, 1996; McGeorge and Palmer, 2002) to being at the heart of BOOT schemes (Hall et al., 2000; Walker and Hampson, 2003b).

Finally, if the model of co-production of value chains is accepted, then sustainable competitive advantage must be accepted as being at the core of that value chain. A construction contractor that understands how this chain may deliver sustainable value can then mobilise those value-generating entities in a coherent way to achieve the value objectives. This means that innovative contractors need to be able to map value within value chains. This has been done in other industries; in retailing for example, Kim and Mauborgne (2000: 131) produced a matrix that had on one dimension, six utility levers (including environmental friendliness, convenience characteristics) – i.e. properties of how the product/service could be perceived to be of value; with a second dimension containing six stages of a buyer experience (e.g. purchase, delivery, maintenance, etc). They explain how a product/service can be mapped on a series of cells within these coordinates in the matrix. This approach can be adapted to provide innovative solutions to novel problems. Just being able to map project features against delivery stages could expose and unearth hitherto unconsidered options. This kind of mapping needs input knowledge about the value chain to construct such maps. Walters and Lancaster (2000: 162) show a value chain model for retailing but again this can be adapted to other industries, including construction. Therefore, it is acknowledged that as a firm's core competence includes knowledge of their current and potential place within a value chain, this needs to be managed from a strategic and tactical perspective, as knowledge about competitors, collaborators, clients and environments could also be perceived as an innovative company's prime asset.

6.4.2   Knowledge Chains

Reconceptualising supply chains to value chains leads to a further re-conceptualisation – knowledge chains. Taking this view can be seen as valuable. A supplier or subcontractor, or indeed client, possesses valuable knowledge about a supply chain member's ability to be flexible, adaptable or even able to accommodate JIT delivery, or their history of getting on with others in the value chain. Supply chain members may also hold key knowledge about how their offerings could be better used by others. This knowledge then becomes critical for innovations in processes, products or relationships. For example, in a review of the knowledge management literature, Nonaka *et al.* (2006) re-visit Nonaka and Konno's (1998) concept of *ba*:

> Ba is a shared space for emerging relationships. It can be a physical, virtual or mental space, but all three have knowledge embedded in ba in common, where it is acquired through individual experiences, or reflections on others' experience. For example, members of a product development project share ideas and viewpoints on their product design in a ba that allows a common interpretation of the technical data, evolving rules of thumb, an emerging sense of product quality, effective communication of hunches or concerns, and so on. To participate in ba means to become engaged in knowledge creation, dialogue, adapt to and shape practices, and simultaneously transcend one's own limited perspective or boundaries' (Nonaka et al., 2006: 1185).

The interesting part of the above quote is that supply chains become perceived as knowledge chains in a *ba* sense. Having contractors, consultants, client representatives and those in a supply chain within a *ba* co-located either physically or virtually, can trigger enormously valuable conversations that can lead to value generation. The pre-project design office or the construction office can be seen as a *ba* rather than merely a fixed place; and perceiving this space as a *ba* may facilitate the space to be better poised for improving knowledge exchange, creativity and innovation in both decision making and production. So, what makes this way of looking at SCM provide such an advance? The answer lies in part with the way that knowledge may become sticky and flows slowly (Szulanski, 1996). Szulanski's earlier study (1995) was is based on 271 observations of 122 best-practice transfers in 8 companies, which sought to better understand the different rates of adoption and adaptation of new ideas. This work identified four characteristics of factors that affected knowledge transfer fluidity. The first of these revolved around the nature of knowledge being transferred – some types of knowledge are easier to transfer than others, and some ideas are easier to 'sell' than others. The second revolved around the characteristics of knowledge source – motivation to share knowledge and the perceived reliability and value of that knowledge source affects this. The third revolved around the recipient of knowledge – motivation to accept the knowledge and ability to absorb new knowledge (absorptive capacity). The fourth revolved around the context in which knowledge is transferred, which includes the relationship between source and recipient, and the physical and cultural environmental context.

Therefore, a *ba* that is supportive of containing actors that are committed in a fertile environmental context allows knowledge to be created, transferred and applied more easily than where conditions are less favourable. A knowledge chain view can therefore help prepare the ground for supply chains to increase their absorptive capacity and establish the mindset of actors in that network to be better positioned to exchange valuable knowledge. This can trigger efficiency, effectiveness, impact, relevance and sustainability.

6.4.3   Human Capital Chains

It is important to acknowledge the importance of human capital (HC) and its relevance to VCM. Nahapiet and Ghoshal (1998) see knowledge exchange and knowledge combination as a 'lock and key' concept, needing the opportunity for (and expectation of) parties for an exchange, their motivation to do so, and their compatibility. They present a model of how social capital, through combination and exchange of intellectual capital (knowledge in its many forms), generate new intellectual capital (innovation, knowledge, etc). They include the three dimensions of social capital in their model.

The first dimension of social capital is structural. This relates to network ties, network configuration and organisational structures to facilitate relationships on the network. In the context of construction, the entity that can do this is the supply chain, where participants in this chain can be linked together as a vital part of the vision of the value chain as stimulating intellectual capital through knowledge exchange and enacting innovation to enhance the competitive advantage of the value chain, as well as its constituent members. The second dimension is cognitive, which involves shared codes and languages. This is particularly relevant to project management, as it provides the basis for a clear vision of what the value chain sets outs to achieve in terms that are meaningful for each party (Christenson and Walker, 2004; Steinfort, 2010); and that are efficient, effective, have impact and are sustainable. The third of Nahapiet and Ghoshal's (1998) dimensions of social capital is relational. This comprises trust and commitment in terms of norms, obligations and identification. Trust and commitment are important elements of social capital. Much has been written about trust and Mayer *et al.*, (1995) offers a model of how trust works in relationships. The three principal components are the ability to deliver (as individuals or within organisational constraints), benevolence (positive intentions with no aims to harm in any way) and integrity (being open, honest and consistent in behaviour and practice as espoused and acted upon). Commitment may take several forms. Meyer and Allen (1991) identify three types of commitment: *continuance* is about cost – cost versus the benefit in a highly calculative way; *normative* is about obligation – the duty to do something perhaps as a kind of favour bank, or cultural expectation; and *affective*, which is to do with wanting to do something with aligned objectives, so that motivation is intrinsic. HC can therefore be established through an organisational structure such as a supply chain. However, structural considerations discussed by Nahapiet and Ghoshal (1998) are important here, as is the cognitive dimension; such that there should be recognition of potential contributions of knowledge and experience by members of any value chain. Finally, there is a vital human relationship component of VCM, which is about establishing common (or at least complimentary) elements of culture, norms, behavioural expectations, 'war stories', etc, to bind the chain together in some ways to common goals.

The 'stickiness' of knowledge was focused upon as being a crucial issue in getting the requisite knowledge exchange across a value chain, not only to encourage innovation, but also to make it happen. Absorptive capacity is a fundamental concept in that regard. Zahra and George (2002: 198) provide a conceptualisation of this concept by comparing numerous views of it as published by leading experts. They define absorptive capacity as 'a set of organisational routines and strategic processes by which firms acquire, assimilate, transform and exploit knowledge for purposes of value creation" This is a wider and deeper conceptualisation than previous definitions, including Cohen and Levinthal (1990) who saw absorptive capacity in less dynamic and explicitly systemic terms than Zahra and George (2002). The important additional insights that are relevant to this chapter are that Zahra and George (2002: 192) present a model in which they see experience and knowledge as an input, and competitive advantage as an output. Absorptive capacity therefore has both a potential acquisition and assimilation phase, together with a realisation transformation phase triggered by knowledge exploitation. These elements of the input/process/output model are activation triggers between the input and absorptive capacity process, with social integration mechanisms being critical to allow potential absorptive capacity to be realised by what Zahra and George (2002) call 'regimes of appropriability'. These phases facilitate flexibility of strategy, innovation and superior performance that is characteristic of competitive advantage.

It is now possible to appreciate the critical role that a VCM or SCM approach has on focusing innovation on the delivery of value in construction projects in order to establish and maintain efficiency, effectiveness, positive impact, relevance and sustainability. Readers should consider their experience within any supply chain that may have had aspirations for innovation and sustainable competitive advantage, to question how well the system integrator considered the structural, cognitive and relational dimensions of social capital that Nahapiet and Ghoshal (1998) highlighted; and means for measuring HC, perhaps through a capability maturity model (CMM)? This approach has already been used in the construction context (Manu and Walker, 2006; Maqsood *et al.*, 2007). VCM can also involve measurement, monitoring and improvement of innovation performance using CMM (or similar measurement tools), which if leveraged appropriately, could be a valuable vehicle not just for innovation but also for complete business transformation.

6.5   Case Study of Supply Chain Management Triggering Total Business Transformation

One important purpose of this chapter is to illustrate a practical example of SCM that has had a transformational impact leading to sustainable competitive advantage. A case study example has been purposefully selected that may at first appear incongruous to the construction industry context, but is highly relevant. This case study was initiated in the context of high economic turbulence, the kind of extreme triggers that force innovation and change (Nonaka, 1988; Kotter, 1995). Two main forces triggered an innovative response – the formation of the Great Southern Common Market (Mercosur) and the heightened levels and implications of globalisation for the logistics industry sector within Latin America.

The Mercosur was established during the 1990s, and like the European Union (EU), aimed to better integrate the commercial, political and cultural life of its bloc of members. These include Argentina, Bolivia, Brazil, Chile, Paraguay and Uruguay, with Peru, Venezuela and South Africa as potential future members. An initiative took place in response to the globalisation wave that hit Latin America whilst its political environment was going through drastic changes during the formation of the Mercosur (Arroyo, 2009; Arroyo and Walker, 2004; 2008; 2009). The initiative involved forming a collaborate entity called the Atlantic Corridor, which had as its aim a method of getting together a wide range of logistics supply chain participants to share problems and ideas and to promote efficiency and effectiveness through a community of practice. This turned out to be an effective business transformation vehicle that the construction industry SCM could learn from. In this respect, the research approach involved analysis of extensive documentary evidence drawn from minutes of meetings, corporate intelligence from numerous participants, semi-structured interview data and reflection on insights gained by Arroyo as an embedded actor in the Corridor. The case studies illustrate how efficiency was achieved by bringing about a change in the logistics business to make improvements resulting in cost and time savings. These also brought about effective change by bringing together logistics elements in a way that removed waste and re-work and improved service delivery. They are relevant to this chapter because this approach is similar in many ways to a supply chain delivering construction projects. They had a positive impact because the changes made and explained in these case studies not only enabled companies under threat of being eliminated by their global competitors to transform their business models; the changes made also improved the firm's integration into the global market. Sustainability was achieved by virtue of these firms not only surviving, but also prospering; and that transformation vehicle is still operating today. This case study illustrates how a SCM to VCM mindset change can lead to business transformation, and this could be the greatest innovation participating organisations could imagine.

6.5.1   The Atlantic Corridor Evolution

The globalisation wave that challenged complacency firms that were accustomed to operating in local markets within a protective context, particularly affected the Latin American continent during the late 1980s. South American regional companies had up to that time enjoyed operating within bilateral treaties under a wide array of subsidies and protective regulations that enabled them grow without having to face the competitive pressure of a free market. Foreign companies either found regional entry barriers too high, or were deterred from expanding across a new potential market. However, the creation of the Mercosur offered significant opportunities for business transformation during the early 1990s; and this resulted in Mercosur shipping and logistics firms experiencing a potential threat by global (and more resourceful) world-class shipping companies, port operators and logistic operators. The Mercosur market became strategic to these global firms that were determined to expand into Latin America to maintain their global competitive advantage. Consequently, regional firms suddenly experienced a severe and change-spurring shock to their business logic.

An innovation that emerged from this turmoil was the formation of a form of strategic community of practice (CoP) that became known as the Atlantic Corridor. The genesis of the idea came from several politicians in Brazil, who initially established 'integrating forums' in Brazil and expanded these into a CoP to include members from Argentina and neighbouring countries. The idea of the 'integrating forums' was to initially establish an on-line community at various key points in Brazil and Argentina – linking industrial hubs with consumer centres along the continent. The aim was to achieve, through an improved transportation logistics infrastructure, higher productivity, and thus make participants accomplish greater economies of scale. While this concept appears at first to relate to physical issues such as rationalisation of facilities and identifying expansion and reconfiguration potential, the problems to be solved included political, legislative, managerial and social issues. Members join the Corridor at one of a number of participation levels, ranging from involvement in forum meetings as an observer, through to gaining full access to a database of past and current problems and solutions and relevant posted documents accessible through the Corridor's intranet. This intranet was developed by linking member's own intranets; and it was only recently that this was feasible with the achievement of a critical mass of participants. The Corridor was thus initiated as a regional reaction to the global threat by an increasing number of national and regional companies (both logistic and logistic-related firms) that decided to join forces to face (by then) an uncertain and threatening business environment. These operators came from a wide array of sectors within the shipping and logistic world: ocean and river transportation companies; marine and river port operators; air-station operators; trucking and railway companies; warehousing and distribution operators; freight-forwarding firms; air-cargo freighting operators; consultancy and surveying services; law and insurance services; exporting and importing companies; ship-building and naval repair firms; traders and brokers; etc.

The Corridor provides an example of a business transformation project involving extensive knowledge transfer and trust building as core elements. Arroyo (2009) examined the Corridor's ability to first generate trust, and then to facilitate knowledge transfer among stakeholders. How the Corridor facilitated efficiency for its members, and how it facilitated effectiveness, relevance, positive impact and sustainability, is discussed in the following sub-sections through a summary of five case study results derived from Arroyo's study (2009).

6.5.2   The Atlantic Corridor Facilitating Efficiencies

This subsection provides an account of part of the Corridor's activities and is based on a paper originally presented at a New Zealand conference (Arroyo and Walker, 2004).

Corridor participants gathered fortnightly in their respective video-conference forums (e.g. in the Brazilian remote north-eastern region, or in the remote parts of the Argentine Patagonia region), where they would submit their logistic problems or business limitations for discussion to seek advice on how to quickly resolve these. The problems were wide and diverse, some of which included:

- the lack of a reliable buoying system along the Amazon River;
- the difficulty in interpreting the Buenos Aires customs legislation that affected Brazilian exports;
- the snow intensity along the Andes mountains that impeded the continuous flow of trade between Argentina and Chile;
- the lack of reliable feeder services linking Buenos Aires and Patagonian ports;
- the monopolistic barge services between Manaos and Peruvian river terminal;
- delays from changing rail gauge at the border between Argentina and Brazil;
- draft limitations to reach acceptable economies of scale to reach Bolivia by river; and
- the lack of suitable cranes at this or that port.

Members discussed their problems, proposed solutions, decided upon strategies to solve problems, recommended actions at any level in whichever country the problem lay, and did whatever was necessary to overcome these drawbacks. Member groups were connected on-line and carried out their studies and assessments, which affected their businesses from an operational, financial and commercial perspective. Participants also had a wide exposure of related activities that posed problems to trade and transport. Group membership included:

- ship owners and shipyard operators;
- operators of wide variety of transport medium, including ocean and river terminals, airports, airlines, air stations, barges, truckers, railway operators;
- support logistic groups including insurance underwriters; lawyers, chartering brokers, export and import brokers, custom brokers, bankers, members of provincial and municipal governments, consulting companies, universities; and
- law enforcement agencies, frontier police and coast guard services.

This example represents a complete paradigm shift in thinking about co-operation and collaboration. Many of these participants were loosely involved in supply chains – though early in the formation of the Corridor CoP; they did not tend to see their initiative as a supply chain, or even value chain innovation. Generally, they were reacting to a hostile and threatening environment, and trying through co-operation and collaboration to help solve problems. Sometimes, solutions were shaped by advice that pertained to an individual firm; other times the solution involved collaboration along a supply chain. The main focus of these included efficiency, removing cost and time waste, and to a large extent exposing messy situations to help them resolve systemic issues in order to focus on effectiveness. Some current similarities can be drawn with the concept of 'project alliancing' used in Australia (Walker and Hampson, 2003b; Department of Treasury and Finance Victoria, 2010) and elsewhere (Xu *et al.*, 2005), where projects are being realised in highly uncertain and complex situations.

6.5.3   The Atlantic Corridor Facilitating Business Transformation

As part of the remit of the Corridor, Arroyo was one of several facilitators whose role was to facilitate the formation of collaborative ventures. These took the form of alliances, joint ventures, mergers and formation of stand-alone business entities, with re-configured arrangements that led combining firms to form a vehicle for complete business transformation. Arroyo (2009) details five case studies. The first case study featured an ocean shipping company's joint venture (JV) linking organisations with a different combination of structure, nationality, culture, technology and vision. The JV comprised two regional firms and two extra-regional companies. Each of these firms followed different strategies in the way they got together, how they agreed on the fundamental aim of facilitating outsiders to become regional operators, and how to become more international and global in future. The overarching aim from the outset was to avoid incurring heavy investments. This case study strongly relates to issues of the role of co-operation, leadership, knowledge and corporate strategy in driving the business transformation.

The second case involved a multimodal transportation business transformation, through the way that it connected its operations in ports of the Mediterranean Sea in Europe to end destinations in South America's West Coast. More specifically, this project entailed the set-up of a land bridge between west Mediterranean ports (Spain, France and Italy) and the industrial pole of the Santiago-Valparaiso area through the port of Buenos Aires in Argentina by combining sea, road and rail transportation on a door delivery mode, that is, to the customer's 'door'. This case study demonstrated the important role of successfully combining traditional knowledge, physical assets and management to achieve differentiation and gain competitive advantage. The third case study refers to the way the longest and most strategic railways in Argentina passed on vital knowledge about how foreign companies could reengineer themselves and become a competitive asset, not only at regional level, but also in a global dimension. Without collaboration, co-operation and leadership by partners in this case study, business transformation would have not occurred. This case study illustrates the logistic complementation of knowledge and leadership between the various agents involved that was pivotal in allowing the transformation project to successfully evolve. The fourth case study embodied a Buenos Aires up-river operator that realised the urgent need to react to the globalisation process by becoming regional and gaining world-class competitive advantage to face threats posed by emerging global maritime terminal operators' structure, technology, management and investment. This case study provides a typical reactive model, where two regional players enter into a JV to face global companies that might otherwise easily outperform them individually. The case study further sheds light on aspects of leadership, co-operation and collaboration, strategy and knowledge.

Each of the four case studies refers to short-term tactical transformation project actions. The fifth case study concerned long-term business transformation, and related to the waterways supply market evolution, and the way project stakeholders had to deal with the particular business context faced (either in a purely transactional management mode or transformational style), along with the many constraints that emerged. The response by the players to the business environment, particularly radical changes in focus on SCM towards VCM, seemed to have played a more decisive role than the management styles deployed by the different actors. The specific project focus comprised the construction and operation of fully dedicated barge convoys to carry iron ore supplies from Brazil to Argentina, commencing in 2003 phased over 6 years. The first phase comprised the development and acceptance of an innovative logistics design solution and its realisation through the construction of new barges and leasing of existing barges. The project had in-built replication possibilities to roll out a series of similar projects.

Two driving forces for this joint venture form of alliance become clear from this case study: one is the global dimension of the primary stakeholder (steel manufacturing company), and the other, the complexity of the logistic operation in itself that made for the traditional knowledge of strategic relevance. One might assume that the steel company, holding a business presence in so many countries around the world, and having access to countless databases and logistic experiences to feed from (and benchmark with), would not regard the Corridor as a potentially valuable development tool. However, not only did the primary stakeholders interact during the roundtable forums, exchanging knowledge until eventually giving birth to a knowledge-based logistic design, but also the secondary stakeholders took part in the process and were interested to form part of what was about to take place. However, even though a number of functional aspects, such as financial engineering, insurance, port operations and barging services were often contracted by the steel company on diverse geographical settings, the knowledge specificity and viscosity of the logistic design, along with its unique geographic and operational particulars embodied by the waterways, seem to have found a fertile ground for these various actors to get together and become interested in one another's needs, potential and proposals.

Figure 6.2 illustrates the formation of a JV using a PM perspective of project phases based on the research findings and the role of the Corridor in establishing these JVs.

Figure 6.2   The Corridor's role in JV formation (Arroyo, 2009).

Table 6.1   Re-thinking SCM to VCM.

Moving From	To	Notes and Comments
A functional view of SCM	An innovation view of SCM with a focus on value	Other than for 'cookie-cutter' projects, most construction projects are substantially 'bespoke' and so clients welcome innovation to achieve an improved value and benefits outcome.
An efficiency agenda for SCM	Specifically an agenda of being effective, having a positive impact, focussing on value relevance and sustainability.	Clients of construction projects and member in the supply chain generally welcome ideas and expertise for improving value delivered as well as technical expertise
Focus on financial value	Broader conceptualisation of value to include improved knowledge transfer, social capital generation and potential business transformation.	As the Arroyo (2009) work demonstrates, unexpected value can be developed from collaboration in JVs, alliances or other cooperative arrangements as well as the development of new business models.

The Corridor project business transformation process first passed through an awareness gestation phase, and then through to initiation and briefing, where various forms, combinations of roles and ways of collaboration were discussed and decided upon. This was followed by the actual design of the JV. Arroyo (2009) focuses on the end of the awareness phase, as it recursively slipped into the initiation and briefing phase and then into the start of the design of JVs, and how they may be formed. Figure 6.2 also identifies how the external environment impacted upon this process, particularly, how competitive advantage helped shape the drivers for change, and how the Corridor facilitated the shaping of JVs and alliances. At the initial stage, the separate parties joined together under the facilitation and auspices of the Corridor. This entity was sanctioned by advancing the Mercosur ideals, and it was established as a safe (trustworthy) place in which representatives of member firms could meet, exchange knowledge and solve problems. This helped the engaged firms to form a CoP. Later on, more intimate groups coalesced into JV type arrangements, and so the Corridor also had a role as a business incubator and change agent. The competitive advantage achieved was reflected in terms of cost efficiency, customer focus and ability for the JV to be differentiated from potential competitors.

6.5.4   Discussion

The case studies discussed illustrate how a highly innovative concept evolved out of a SCM context in a highly volatile and turbulent economic environment, with extreme challenges of physical distribution within the supply chain. The Corridor concept is important to this chapter because it offers another way of viewing a supply chain or value chain. It reinforces the value of a facilitating vehicle to help trust, commitment and knowledge sharing, which are critical for sparking radical as well as incremental innovation. The examples in Section 6.5.2 present typical short-term efficiency-based innovation that such an entity can readily deliver, whereas Section 6.5.3 presented some longer-term innovations that were initiated through the formation of joint ventures to develop a supply chain end-to-end solution and to facilitate improved efficiency and sustainable value. These ideas relate to re-framing a supply chain regarding its primary purpose, how it can become more effective, efficient, relevant, and have a positive sustainable impact.

The example drawn from the Latin American logistics industry provides an interesting and salient model for reflection, the transition, rationality and concepts of which are summarised in Table 6.1 to illustrate this re-thinking process.

6.6   Conclusion

The chapter focused on five criteria used for evaluating aid projects that have relevance to SCM, specifically *efficiency, effectiveness, relevance, sustainability* and *impact*. The organisational contribution to value was discussed using the RBV of a firm, and what this can bring to the table in any potential SCM innovation. Furthermore, knowledge, skills, experience and social capital are all key assets that could be deployed to enhance value. Whilst this chapter concentrated on value and the value of supply chains, SCM was presented with an explanation of how this might function within a construction industry context. This led to a section on value chains, building upon and extending the seminal work of Porter (1985, 1998), Womack *et al.* (1990) and Womack and Jones (1994), but with a focus on innovation rather than functional products as outputs from such a chain. Case study examples drawn from the empirical work of Arroyo (2009) were discussed. These provided innovative approaches garnered from the Atlantic Corridor, which were considered salient, as they illustrated how an industry sector faced with enormous challenges managed to prevail through a radical transformation in the way it perceived supply chains and value.

The construction industry has been challenged by several government reports to improve its conception of value, and how it can be more innovative and sustainable (Murray and Langford, 2003). What becomes clear from this chapter is that for supply chains in the construction industry to become more efficient, effective, relevant, and have a more positive impact upon sustainability, they will need to re-frame their conception of what SCM is, and draw upon examples from other industries in order to learn from them.

6.7   Acknowledgements

Special acknowledgements are extended to Alejandro Arroyo, Southmark Logistics SA, Buenos Aires, Argentina, for edited excerpts from his Doctoral Thesis (Section 6.5).

References

Akkermans, H.A., Bogerd, P., Yucesan, E. & van Wassenhove, L.N. (2003) The impact of ERP on supply chain management: Exploratory findings from a European Delphi study. *European Journal of Operational Research*, **146**(2), 284–301.

Aranda-Mena, G., Crawford, J. & Chevez, A. (2009) Building information modelling demystified: Does it make business sense to adopt BIM? *International Journal of Managing Projects in Business*, **2**(3), 419–433.

Arroyo, A. & Walker, D.H.T. (2008) *Business transformation through an innovative alliance*. In: ed. Walker D.H.T. & Rowlinson, S., *Procurement Systems – A Cross Industry Project Management Perspective*. Taylor & Francis, Abingdon. UK. 423–444.

Arroyo, A.C. (2009) The role of the Atlantic Corridor Project as a form of strategic community of practice in facilitating business transformations in Latin America. PhD thesis, School of Property, Construction and Project Management. RMIT University, Melbourne.

Arroyo, A.C. & Walker, D.H.T. (2004) *A Latin American Strategic Community of Practice Experience*. 18th ANZAM Conference, Dunedin, New Zealand, 8–11 December, ANZAM: 11 pages on CD-Disk proceedings.

Arroyo, A.C. & Walker, D.H.T. (2009) A Latin American strategic organisational transformation project management experience: the motivation to transform business. In: ed. Bredillet, C. & Middler, C., *European Academy of Management EURAM: Renaissance & Renewal in Management Studies*, 11–14 May, Liverpool. 20.

Australian Industry Commission (1996) *Competitive Tendering and Contracting by Public Sector Agencies*. Report, Australian Government Publishing Service, Melbourne. 48.

Barney, J. (1991) Firm resources and sustained competitive advantage. *Journal of Management*, **17**(1), 99–120.

Bourne, L. & Walker, D.H.T. (2005) Visualising and mapping stakeholder influence. *Management Decision*, **43**(5), 649–660.

Cates, C. (1979) Beyond muddling: creativity. *Public Administration Review*, **39**(6), 527–532.

Chan, C. & Swatman, P.A. (2000) From EDI to internet commerce: The BHP steel experience. Internet research. *Electronic Networking Applications and Policy*, **10**(1), 72–82.

Chan, E.W.L., Walker, D.H.T. & Mills, A. (2009) Using a KM framework to evaluate an ERP system implementation. *The Journal of Knowledge Management*, **13**(2), 93–109.

Christenson, D. & Walker, D.H.T. (2004) Understanding the role of 'vision' in project success. *Project Management Journal*, **35**(3), 39–52.

Coase, R.H. (1937). The nature of the firm. *Economica.*, **4**, 386–405.

Cohen, W.M. & Levinthal, D. (1990) Absorptive capacity: A new perspective on learning and innovation. *Administrative Science Quarterly*, **35**(1), 128–152.

Cooke-Davies, T. (2002) The 'real' success factors on projects. *International Journal of Project Management*, **20**(3), 185–190.

Croom, S., Romano, P. & Giannakis, M. (2000) Supply chain management: an analytical framework for critical literature review. *European Journal of Purchasing & Supply Management*, **6**(1), 67–83.

Croom, S.R. (2005) The impact of e-business on supply chain management. *International Journal of Operations & Production Management*, **25**(1), 55–73.

Dainty, A.R.J., Briscoe, G.H. & Millett, S.J. (2001) Subcontractor perspectives on supply chain alliances. *Construction Management & Economics*, **19**(8), 841–848.

Dainty, A.R.J., Cheng, M.-I. & Moore, D.R. (2003) Redefining performance measures for construction project managers: An empirical evaluation. *Construction Management & Economics*, **21**(2), 209–218.

Davis, P.R. (2006) The application of relationship marketing to construction. PhD thesis, School of Economics, Finance and Marketing. RMIT University, Melbourne.

de Wit, A. (1988) Measurement of project success. *International Journal of Project Management*, **6**(3), 164–170.

Department of Treasury and Finance Victoria (2010) *The Practitioners' Guide to Alliance Contracting*. Department of Treasury and Finance, Melbourne. 161.

Dyer, J.H. (2000). How Chryster created an American Keiretsu. Harvard business review on managing the value chain. *Havard Business Review*, MA. **74**, 61–90.

Eisenhardt, K.M. & Martin, J.A. (2000) Dynamic capabilities: What are they? *Strategic Management Journal.*, **21**(10/11), 1105–1121.

Elkington, J. (1997) *Cannibals with Forks*. Capstone Publishing, London.

Fellows, R.F. (1997) *The Culture of Partnering*. In: ed. Davidson C.H. & Meguid, T.A., *CIB W-92 Procurement Systems* Symposium 1997, *Procurement – A Key To Innovation*, 18–22 May 1997, The University of Montreal, CIB, **1**, 193–202.

Fill, C. & Visser, E. (2000) The outsourcing dilemma: a composite approach to the make or buy. *Management Decision*, **38**(1), 43–50.

Fischer, M. & Drogemuller, R. (2009) *Virtual design and construction*. In: Newton, P., *Technology, Design and Process Innovation in the Built Environment*. Taylor & Francis, Abingdon, UK. 293–318.

Fisher, M.L. (1997) What Is the right supply chain for your product? *Harvard Business Review*, **75**(2), 105–116.

Fisher, N., Barlow, R., Garnett, N., Finch, E. & Newcombe, R. (1997) *Project Modelling in Construction: Seeing is Believing*. Thomas Telford, London.

Graham, P. & Smithers, G. (1996) Construction Waste minimisation for Australian residential development. *Asia Pacific Journal of Building & Construction Management*, **2**(1), 14–19.

Green, S. (1999a) The dark side of lean construction: exploitation and ideology. In: ed. Tommelein, I.D. & Ballard, G, *Seventh Annual Conference of the International Group for Lean Construction (IGLC-7)*, 26–28 July, Berkeley, CA. 12.

Green, S.D. (1999b) The missing arguments of lean construction. *Construction Management and Economics*, **17**(2), 133–137.

Habermas, J. & Outhwaite, W. (1996) *The Habermas Reader*. Polity Press, Cambridge.

Hall, M., Holt, R. & Graves, A. (2000) Private finance, public roads: configuring the supply chain in PFI highway construction. *European Journal of Purchasing & Supply Management*, **6**(3–4), 227–235.

Hällgren, M. & Maaninen-Olsson, E. (2005) Deviations, ambiguity and uncertainty in a project-intensive organization. *Project Management Journal*, **36**(3), 17–26.

Hällgren, M. & Wilson, T.L. (2007) Mini-muddling: learning from project plan deviations. *Journal of Workplace Learning*, **19**(2), 92–107.

Hughes, W. (2006) *Contract Management.* In: Lowe, D. & and Leiringer, R., *Commercial Management of Projects. Defining the Discipline.* Blackwell Publishing, Abingdon, UK. 344–355.

James, D. (2006) Slave to the supply chain. *Business Review Weekly,* **October,** 52–53.

Jewell, M. & Walker, D.H.T. (2005) *Community of Practice Perspective Software Management Tools: A UK Construction Company Case Study.* In: Kazi, A.S., *Knowledge Management in the Construction Industry: A Socio-Technical Perspective.* Idea Group Publishing, Hershey, PA: 111–127.

Kelly, J., Morledge, R. & Wilkinson, S. (2002) *Best Value in Construction.* Blackwell Publishing, Oxford.

Khalfan, M.M.A. & McDermot, P. (2006) Innovating for supply chain integration within construction. *Construction Innovation: Information, Process, Management,* **6**(3), 143–157.

Khalfan, M.M.A., McDermott, P. & Kyng, E. (2006) Procurement Impacts on construction supply chains: UK experiences. In: McDermott P. and Khalfan, M.M.A., *Symposium on sustainability and value through construction procurement, CIB W092 – Procurement Systems, CIB Revaluing Construction Theme,* 29 November–2 December, The Digital World Centre, Salford, UK. 449–458.

Kim, W.C. & Mauborgne, R. (2000) Knowing a winning business idea when you see one. *Harvard Business Review,* **78**(5), 129–138.

Klakegg, O.J., Williams, T., Walker, D.H.T., Andersen, B. & Magnussen, O.M. (2010) *Early Warning Signs in Complex Projects.* Project Management Institute, Newtown Square, PA.

Koskela, L. (2000) An exploration towards a production theory and its application to construction. PhD thesis, VTT Technical Research Centre of Finland. Helsinki, Finland, Helsinki University of Technology.

Kotter, J.P. (1995) Leading change: Why transformation efforts fail. *Harvard Business Review,* **73**(2), 59–67.

Kumaraswamy, H.M. (1996) *Construction Dispute Minimisation.* In: ed. Langford D.A. & Retik, A., *The Organisation and Management of Construction – Managing the construction project and project risk,* vol. 2. E&FN Spon, London. 447–457.

Langford, D.A., Martinez, V. & Bititici, U. (2003) Best value in construction: Towards an interpretation of value from the client and construction perspectives. *Construction Procurement,* **9**(1), 56–67.

Larson, E. (1995) Project Partnering: Results of Study of 280 Construction Projects. *Journal of Management in Engineering,* **11**(2), 30–35.

Lendrum, T. (1998) *The Strategic Partnering Handbook,* 2nd edn. McGraw-Hill, Sydney.

Lindblom, C.E. (1959) The science of 'muddling through. *Public Administration Review,* **19**(2), 79-88.

Lindblom, C.E. (1979) Still muddling, not yet through. *Public Administration Review,* **39**(6), 517–526.

London, K.A. & Kenley, R. (2001) An industrial organization economic supply chain approach for the construction industry: a review. *Construction Management and Economics,* **19**(8), 777–788.

Love, P.E.D. & Gunasekaran, A. (1999) Learning alliances: a customer-supplier focus for continuous improvement in manufacturing. *Industrial & Commercial Training,* **31**(3), 88–96.

Love, P.E.D., Mandal, P., Smith, J. & Li, H. (2000) Modelling the dynamics of design error induced in rework in construction. *Construction Management and Economics,* **18**(5), 567–574.

Love, P.E.D., Edwards, D.J., Irani, Z. & Walker, D.H.T. (2009) Project Pathogens: The Anatomy of Omission Errors in Construction and Resource Engineering Project. *IEEE Transactions On Engineering Management*, **56**(3), 425–435.

Lundin, R.A. & Söderholm, A. (1995) A theory of the temporary organization. *Scandinavian Journal of Management*, **11**(4), 437–455.

Male, S. (2002). Building the business value case. In: ed. Wilkinson S., Kelly, J. & Morledge, R., *Best Value In Construction*. Blackwell Science, Oxford. 12–37.

Manu, C. & Walker, D.H.T. (2006) Making sense of knowledge transfer and social capital generation for a Pacific island aid infrastructure project. *The Learning Organization*, **13**(5), 475–494.

Maqsood, T., Walker, D.H.T. & Finegan, A.D. (2007) Extending the knowledge advantage: Creating learning chains. *The Learning Organization*, **14**(2), 123–141.

Masterman, J.W.E. (1992) *An Introduction to Building Procurement Systems*, 2nd edn. E & FN SPON, London.

Matthews, J., Tyler, A. & Thorpe, A. (1996) Pre-construction project partnering: Developing the process. *Engineering, Construction and Architectural Management*, **3**(1–2), 117–131.

Mayer, R.C., Davis, J.H. & Schoorman, F.D. (1995) An integrated Model of Organizational Trust. *Academy of Management Review*, **20**(3), 709–735.

McGeorge, W.D. & Palmer, A. (2002) *Construction Management New Directions*, 2nd edn. Blackwell Science, London.

McKenna, D. & Walker, D.H.T. (2008) A study of out-sourcing versus in-sourcing tasks within a project value chain. *International Journal of Managing Projects in Business*, **1**(2), 216–232.

Meyer, J.P. & Allen, N.J. (1991) A three-component conceptualization of organizational commitment. *Human Resource Management Review*, **1**(1), 61–89.

Michaels, L.M.J. (1999) The making of a lean aerospace supply chain. *Supply Chain Management*, **4**(3), 135–145.

Mintzberg, H. (1987). Crafting strategy. *Harvard Business Review*, **65**(4), 66–75.

Mintzberg, H., Ahlstrand, B.W. & Lampel, J. (1998) *Strategy Safari: The Complete Guide Through the Wilds of Strategic Management*. Financial Times/Prentice Hall., London.

Murray, M. & Langford, D.A. (2003) *Construction Reports 1944–98*. Blackwell Science Ltd, Oxford.

Nahapiet, J. & Ghoshal, S. (1998) Social capital, intellectual capital, and the organizational advantage. *Academy of Management Review*, **23**(2), 242–266.

NBCC (1989) *Strategies for the Reduction of Claims and Disputes in the Construction Industry – No Dispute*. National Building and Construction Council, Canberra.

Nogeste, K. (2004) Increase the likelihood of project success by using a proven method to identify and define intangible project outcomes. *International Journal of Knowledge, Culture and Change Management*, **4**, 915–926.

Nonaka, I. (1988) Creating Organizational order out of chaos: Self-renewal in Japanese firms. *California Management Review*, **30**(3), 57–73.

Nonaka, I. & Konno, N. (1998) The concept of 'Ba': Building a foundation for knowledge creation. *California Management Review*, **40**(3), 40.

Nonaka, I., von Krogh, G. & Voelpel, S. (2006) Organizational knowledge creation theory: evolutionary paths and future advances. *Organization Studies*, **27**(8), 1179–1208.

Normann, R. & Ramirez, R. (1993) From value chain to value constellation: Designing interactive strategy. *Harvard Business Review*, **71**(4), 65–77.

OECD (2007) *Sourcebook for Evaluating Global and Regional Partnership Programs Indicative Principles and Standards*. Organisation for Economic Co-operation and Development, Development Assistance Committee (DAC): Washington, DC. 148.

Olsson, N.O.E. (2006) Management of flexibility in projects. *International Journal of Project Management*, 24(1), 66–74.

Olsson, N.O.E. & Magnussen, O.M. (2007) Flexibility at different stages in the life cycle of projects: An empirical illustration of the freedom to maneuver. *Project Management Journal*, 38(4), 25–32.

Palaneeswaran, E., Kumaraswamy, M. & Ng, T. (2003) Targeting optimum value in public sector projects through 'best value'-focused contractor selection. *Engineering Construction and Architectural Management*, 10(6), 418–431.

Peansupap, V. & Walker, D.H.T. (2005) Diffusion of Information and communication technology: A community of practice perspective. In: Kazi, A.S., *Knowledge Management in the Construction Industry: A Socio-Technical Perspective*. Idea Group Publishing, Hershey, PA. 89–110.

Porter, M.E. (1985) *Competitive Advantage: Creating and Sustaining Superior Performance*. The Free Press, New York.

Porter, M.E. (1998) Clusters and the new economics of competition. *Harvard Business Review*, 76(6), 77–90.

Pryke, S. (2004) Twenty-first century procurement strategies: Analysing networks of inter-firm relationships. *RICS Foundation Paper Series*, 4(27), 1–38.

Rowlinson, S. & McDermott, P. (1999) Selection Criteria. Procurement systems. In: Rowlinson S. & McDermott, P., *A Guide to Best Practice in Construction*. E&FN Spon, London. 276–299.

Rowlinson, S. & Walker, D.H.T. (2008) Case study – Innovation management in alliances. In: Walker D.H.T. & Rowlinson, S., *Procurement Systems. A Cross Industry Project Management Perspective*. Taylor & Francis, Abingdon, UK. 400–422.

Sadler, I. (2007) *Logistics and Supply Chain Integration*. Sage. Thousand Oaks, CA.

Sanchez, R. (2004) Understanding competence-based management: Identifying and managing five modes of competence. *Journal of Business Research*, 57(5): 518–532.

Saul, J.R. (1997) *The Unconscious Civilization*, 1st edn. Free Press, New York.

Shenhar, A.J., Dvir, D., Levy, O. & Maltz, A.C. (2001) Project success: A multidimensional strategic concept. *Long Range Planning*, 34(6), 699–725.

Sidwell, A.C. & Mehertns, V.M. (1996) *Case Studies in Constructability Implementation*. Construction Industry Institute Australia, Adelaide.

Steinfort, P. (2010) Understanding the antecedents of project management best practice-lessons to be learned from aid relief projects. PhD thesis, School of Property, Construction and Project Management. RMIT University, Melbourne.

Szulanski, G. (1995) *Appropriating Rents from Existing Knowledge: Intra-Firm Transfer of Best Practice*. Institut Européen d'Administration des Affaires (France), INSEAD – The European Institute of Business Administration.

Szulanski, G. (1996) Exploring internal stickiness: Impediments to the transfer of best practice within the firm. *Strategic Management Journal*, 17(Winter special Issue), 27–43.

Teece, D., Pisano, G. & Shuen, A. (1997) Dynamic capabilities and strategic management. *Strategic Management Journal*, 18(7), 509–533.

Teece, D.J. (1998) Capturing value from knowledge assets: The new economy, markets for know-how, and intangible assets. *California Management Review*, 40(3), 55–79.

Teece, D.J. (2001) Strategies for Managing Knowledge Assets: The Role of Firm Structure and Industrial Context. In: Nonaka I. & Teece, D., *Managing Industrial Knowledge - Creation, Transfer and Utilization*. Sage, London. 125–144.

Thompson, P.J. & Sanders, S.R. (1998) Partnering Continuum. *Journal of Management in Engineering*, 14(5), 73–78.

von Krogh, G. (1998) Care in knowledge creation. *California Management Review*, **40**(3), 40–54.

von Krogh, G., Ichijo, K. & Takeuchi, H. (2000) *Enabling Knowledge Creation*. Oxford University Press, Oxford.

Walker, D.H.T. & Hampson, K.D. (2003a) Enterprise Networks, Partnering and Alliancing. In: ed. Walker D.H.T. & Hampson, K.D., *Procurement Strategies: A Relationship Based Approach*, Chapter 3. Blackwell Publishing, Oxford. 30–73.

Walker, D.H.T. & Hampson, K.D. (2003b) Procurement Choices. In: ed. Walker D.H.T. & Hampson, K.D., *Procurement Strategies: A Relationship Based Approach*, Chapter 2. Blackwell Publishing, Oxford. 13–29.

Walker, D.H.T. & Hampson, K.D. (2003c) Project Alliance Member Organisation Selection. In: ed. Walker D.H.T. & Hampson, K.D., *Procurement Strategies: A Relationship Based Approach*, Chapter 4. Blackwell Publishing, Oxford. 74–102.

Walker, D.H.T. & Lloyd-Walker, B.M. (2010) *Profiling Professional Excellence in Alliance Management, Draft Report*. Alliance Association of Australasia, Sydney. 48.

Walters, D. & Lancaster, G. (2000. Implementing value strategy through the value chain. *Management Decision*, **38**(3), 160–178.

Wang, C.L. & Ahmed, P.K. (2007) Dynamic capabilities: A review and research agenda. *International Journal of Management Reviews*, **9**(1), 31–51.

Wenger, E.C., McDermott, R. & Snyder, W.M. (2002) *Cultivating Communities of Practice*. Harvard Business School Press, Boston, MA.

Williams, T. & Samset, K. (2010) Issues in front-end decision making on projects. *Project Management Journal*, **41**(2), 38–49.

Williamson, O.E. (1985) *The Economic Institutions of Capitalism: Firms, Markets, Relational Contracting*. The Free Press, New York.

Williamson, O.E. (1991) Strategizing, economizing, and economic organization. *Strategic Management Journal*, **12**(Special Issue), 75–94.

Williamson, O.E. (1993) Calculativeness, Trust, and economic organization. *Journal of Law and Economics*, **36**(April), 453–448.

Winch, G.M. (2003) *Managing Construction Projects*. Blackwell Publishing, Oxford.

Womack, J.P. & Jones, D.T. (1994) From lean production to the lean enterprise. *Harvard Business Review*, **72**(2), 93–103.

Womack, J.P. & Jones, D.T. (2000) *From Lean Production to Lean Enterprise. Harvard Business Review on Managing the Value Chain*. Review H. B. Harvard Business School Press, Boston, MA. 221–250.

Womack, J.P., Jones, D.T. & Roos, D. (1990) *The Machine that Changed the World – The Story of Lean Production*. Harper Collins, New York.

Wright, P.M., Dunford, B.B. & Snell, S.A. (2001) Human resources and the resource based view of the firm. *Journal of Management*, **27**(6). 701–721.

Xu, T., Bower, D.A. & Smith, N.J. (2005) Types of collaboration between foreign contractors and their Chinese partners. *International Journal of Project Management*, **23**(1), 45–53.

Zahra, S.A. & George, G. (2002) Absorptive capacity: A review, reconceptualisation, and extension. *Academy of Management Review*, **27**(2), 185–203.

Part II

Process Drivers

Strategic Management in Construction

Jack S. Goulding

Porter (1979) described how changes in the business environment can often require companies to reconsider their strategic options and positioning in the marketplace regarding 'traditional' economic theories of competition. In this respect, from a strategy development perspective, 'perfect' competition assumes free access to new participants and the availability of 'perfect market information'. However, the extent to which these principles are understood and applied can have a direct impact on business success, especially in periods of rapid change. Organisations are therefore increasingly concerned with providing strategic direction (Morgan, 1990), and these requirements are traditionally achieved through a structured framework often described by the term business strategy (BS). This is often used to define the pattern of decisions needed to determine organisational goals and objectives – the precise definition of which is influenced by perceptions and approaches taken by a range of authors (Ansof, 1968; Andrews, 1987; Davenport and Short, 1990; Porter, 1985). Therefore, as the business environment often involves change, the real challenge for organisations is to organise and align corporate assets to strategic capability in order to achieve corporate goals within the context of their operating market sector. This by default tends to pervade organisational systems, procedures and resources (Andrews, 1987) and consequently, requires strategic decision-makers to fully understand these needs, especially how they can be delivered in order to create strategic advantage, maximise business opportunities and improve process effectiveness (Prahalad and Hamel, 1990; Lee and Dale, 1998; Remenyi and Sherwood-Smith, 1998; Lee and Sai On Ko, 2000; Porter, 2008).

Construction Innovation and Process Improvement, First Edition.
Edited by Akintola Akintoye, Jack S. Goulding and Girma Zawdie.
© 2012 Blackwell Publishing Ltd. Published 2012 by Blackwell Publishing Ltd.

This chapter outlines the core dynamic processes and drivers associated with strategic management in construction business domains. In this respect, it identifies how strategy can be purposefully linked to business imperatives in order to leverage innovation opportunities and gain strategic advantage.

7.2   Construction Sector Dynamism and Drivers

The construction and built environment is widely acknowledged as being subject to high levels of fragmentation (Emmerson, 1962; Banwell 1964; Latham, 1994; Egan, 1998), the corollary of which has continued to adversely affect construction performance and productivity. Contemporary 'change' initiatives have tried to improve performance by focusing on time, quality or cost elements; but Kagioglou et al. (2001) noted that most of these problems were often process-related rather than product-related. This resonates with process improvement issues and opportunities cited in extant literature (Davenport, 1993; Hammer and Champy, 1993; Soares and Anderson, 1997; Chan and Land, 1999). Therefore, unprecedented levels of change (Maloney, 1997) has meant that many organisations have had to continually adapt to change by adopting new approaches to business. Typical movements have included 'quality and process management' issues (Hammer, 1990; Davenport, 1993; Al-Mashari and Zairi, 2000), through to the strategic use of ICT to generate strategic advantage (Betts, 1992; Betts and Wood-Harper, 1994; Tan, 1996; Goodman and Chinowsky, 1997; Venegas and Alarcón, 1997; Rezgui and Zarli, 2006).

The changing nature of construction activity and its operating environment is continually evolving, the dynamism and propensity of which is growing at an increasing pace. For example, the sector is influenced by internal and external social, economic, political and technological drivers, which directly affect the way construction organisations view strategy, and the way they conduct business with their stakeholders (Figure 7.1). Other factors include increasing levels of privatisation and globalisation, and a greater diversification of core construction-related business activities (Betts and Ofori, 1992). This diversification required some organisations to reaugment their business units into Architectural, Engineering and Construction (AEC) companies in order to provide a 'one-stop-shop' of bespoke client-orientated services. Other forms of diversification have included joint venturing and vertical/lateral integration, which have helped organisations to develop enhanced synergies of scale and supply to garner extended business benefits (Hillebrandt and Cannon, 1990).

Figure 7.1 identifies the relationship of strategy considerations to the construction supply chain and external governing forces. These forces include environmental, socio-political, economic and technological drivers, the nuances and importance of which are pivotally important to construction organisations, as understanding these relationships (and interplay) ostensibly governs the way strategy is developed and augmented. For example, environmental drivers have a propensity to affect the marketability of products and services, which often influences demand, and socio-political

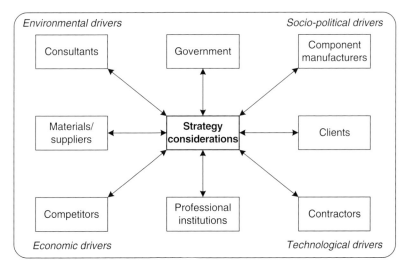

Figure 7.1   Construction supply chain environment.

drivers tend to affect clients' thinking and needs, which often causes organisations to alter their current thinking and/or working practices. However, economic drivers tends to influence the profits and pricing structure of construction organisations, and technological drivers tends to shape the way through which projects are procured and managed, which often mean that new skills are needed to meet these changes. Therefore, when organisations are considering the development of strategy, they will need to openly evaluate these variables in a cogent, robust and defendable way (so they can be defended at Board level). This approach is fundamentally important, as the development and subsequent positioning of strategy will need to not only align to these dynamic market forces and supply chain variables, but also be flexible and agile enough (using modelling options) to be one-step ahead of their competitors. Thus, the impact of stakeholder analysis on strategy should take a balanced view of outcomes and perspectives (Walker, 2000), in order to create a strategy with a clear focus and readily identifiable objectives and deliverables, along with a clear means for measuring outcomes.

7.3   Business Processes Redesign

The process approach of analysing business operations has developmental links with Systems Thinking, Industrial Engineering and the Quality Movement. Historically though, perhaps the origins of process as a discipline should be attributed to Taylor (1911), as this work focused on process improvements using the science of work-study. However, the central argument and tenet of process relates to the evolution of organisational structures and management approaches (Taylor, 1911; Mayo, 1933; Smith, 1759). More recently, the process improvement agenda has been augmented through redesign initiatives (Hammer, 1990; Davenport, 1993) in order to help organisations:

- identify core processes that directly contribute to organisational success;
- assess the current appropriateness and effectiveness of these processes;
- examine the importance and significance of these process areas;
- identify areas for change, using benchmarking and best practice approaches as appropriate;
- assess the effectiveness of process changes made to leverage innovation benefits.

The concept of Business Process Redesign (BPR) is an approach that can help organisations to fundamentally reorganise the way they operate and conduct business in order to facilitate radical improvements (Hammer and Champy, 1993). Variants of these process-based initiatives have also been termed 'Process Innovation' and 'Business Process Reengineering'. BPR therefore aims to challenge organisations to make radical improvements (Petrozzo and Stepper, 1994), along with the required changes necessary to implement change (Davenport, 1993). However, notwithstanding the nuances of nomenclature, the term 'business process' relates to the analysis of an organisation's core business activities, and the term 'redesign' focuses predominantly upon the methods and techniques associated with the business processes involved. Thus, process-related improvement initiatives are intrinsically linked to organisational strategy – the augmentation of which can help organisations optimise their processes to respond to global competition, changes in cyclical economies and changes associated with technological developments (Hammer, 1990). Therefore, organisations are increasingly focusing on processes (not tasks) in order to structure and deliver their work activities. In this context, the term 'process' can be seen as a series of linked activities that take an input activity and transform it into an output deliverable (Johansson et al., 1993). On this theme, the application of a process viewpoint tends to examine process inputs, and asks whether 'value' is being added at each step of transformation to produce these outputs; with typical questions being 'can I add more value for less effort?', 'if so, how and where?' The adoption of this approach can help organisations streamline their processes in order to deliver value-laded activities, over a shorter timescales, with more competitively priced products. However, it is important to note that organisations wishing to follow a BPR approach should attempt to focus on the inter-dependencies within and across the processes within an organisation, and not purely on functional areas alone (Hammer and Champy, 1993).

It should also be acknowledged that whilst most companies will probably have processes embedded into their current working practices, many of these processes may not have been designed or developed using a BPR approach (verbatim); the consequence of this may mean that some or all of these processes may have to be completely redesigned from first principles to fully leverage these benefits. For example, Davenport (1993) identified five key phases for applying BPR, specifically:

1. identifying processes for redesign;
2. identifying the change levers;
3. developing process visions;
4. understanding existing processes; and
5. designing and prototyping new processes.

In this respect, 'identifying processes for redesign' involves determining the aims, objectives and strategic mission of the organisation, and 'identifying the change levers' involves identifying and acknowledging that the organisational infrastructure will most probably change in order to facilitate the new process structure. This is one of the most important areas, as it includes the behavioural characteristics of employees within the organisation, who more often than not will be averse to change (Lewin, 1947). The 'developing process visions' phase includes the articulation of new process structures and metrics for evaluation in order to meet the process vision needed. This also includes the impact this may have on the supply chain, which is of particular importance in the construction industry. The 'understanding existing processes' involves the evaluation of existing processes and practices to appreciate how things work, especially the inter-connections. However, the main issue here is to determine what is wrong, and what is needed to rectify the situation, so that these issues are not repeated. Finally, the 'designing and prototyping new processes' involves detailing the knowledge within these processes, in particular, how this should operate in order to maximise business impact.

7.4   Business Strategy

The term 'business strategy' has been defined by several seminal authors, the terminology and coverage of which embraces such remits as diversification and acquisition policies (Channon, 1978), through to leveraged systems augmented to promote structure and growth (Newcombe, 1990). However, strategy can be seen to be much more than this. For example, it includes ways and methods of doing things to achieve objectives (Andrews, 1987), using controlled and managed approaches (Price and Newson, 2003), to deliver corporate objectives. Therefore, it is important that companies consider strategic development issues in line with the market forces and drivers identified in Figure 7.1, as successful companies more often than not:

1. tend to understand change;
2. often adopt a systems approach to manage and control change;
3. usually pursue competitive advantage as an investment decision;
4. understand risk well; and
5. endeavour to provide innovation to clients as an embedded solution (Perkowski, 1988).

7.4.1   Strategy Development

From an historical perspective, the School of Organisational Theory (ca. 1900) emphasised the importance of labour in business, and the Scientific Management and Classical School (1910–1920) focused on tasks and coordination. However, the concept of corporate strategy and the need to forecast future business direction was not made until the arrival of the Group Dynamics and Bureaucracy Schools of thought (ca. 1940). During this period, Fayol (1949) was one of the first main proponents of this cause, out of which long-term strategy started to develop and evolve. Advancements in strategy development from this period onwards up to the 1960s tended to converge on forecasting trends through leadership and decision making, then in the 1970s, the arrival of Systems Theory replaced the term 'long-term strategy planning' with 'strategic planning', the concept of which focused more closely on the elements of competition and the relationship of this to expanding markets. The arrival of Contingency Theory in the 1980s then led to research in organisational structures and processes, and Porter (1985) was one of the main pioneers of strategic decision making in competitive environments during this period. Therefore, developments have evolved from the strategy formulation side of the process, through to a greater focus on the implementation issues. This allowed the psychological, sociological and political domains to be better integrated into the strategic management arena, and allowed a greater amount of synthesis to occur (Robson, 1997). The current vogue in BS development is now centred on understanding the concepts and principles that govern competition. This involves 'systems thinking', 'chaos theory' and embraces issues relating to the 'learning organisation' (Huber, 1991; Senge, 2006; Stacey, 2010) and Stakeholder Perspective Management (Love and Holt, 2000).

Strategy development can therefore be seen as a core way through which organisational success can be garnered. In this respect, Porter (1979) developed a Five Forces Model to examine interrelated forces, with a particular emphasis on securing competitive advantage. These five forces included:

1. threat of New Entrants;
2. supplier Power;
3. buyer Power;
4. threat of Substitute Products; and
5. jockeying for Position.

This approach can readily be applied to strategic management within the construction domain, as it enables construction organisations to analyse product and location segments of the construction market through these five forces in order to identify areas for business performance improvement (to secure competitive advantage). From this model, the *Threat of New Entrants* force relates to the ease with which new firms can enter and compete in the market. For example, consider the position of a large construction organisation that had heavily invested in a niche area over several years to secure market dominance; a new entrant would therefore find it especially difficult to develop capability and maturity in order to compete on level terms; which, by default, would act as a barrier to entry. This category of force also includes economies of scale, product differentiation, large capital capability, and cost drivers aligned to experience curves. The *Supplier Power* force includes the proximity of supply and its relationship to the organisation, where competitive advantage can be secured from powerful supply relationships. Examples of this include situations where few enterprises dominate supply, where there is no competing product, or where the supplier holds a threat of forward integration over the buyer (vis-à-vis potential acquisition). The *Buyer Power* force includes situations where products are price sensitive but not quality sensitive, and includes positions where a threat of backward integration (securing ownership of the supply chain) over suppliers exists. For example, several large construction organisations are able to exploit their relationships with materials suppliers and specialist subcontractors in order to secure competitive advantage, which has proven to be particularly fortuitous with large construction organisations. The *Threat of Substitute Products* force is where there is potential to use other products or services in lieu of traditional ones. This is predominantly prominent when addressing the price-performance-quality trade-off, especially where new materials or products have proven benefits (cost or otherwise) against conventional solutions. This force therefore enables organisations to micro-analyse these differences with a view to securing competitive advantage. Finally, the *Jockeying for Position* force is used to analyse the marketplace of the competition. In this respect, it is argued that the greatest scope for securing competitive advantage exists where:

1. the competitors are of equal size;
2. there is slow market growth;
3. similar (undifferentiated) products or services exist; and
4. high fixed costs prevail.

This Five Forces Model therefore provides construction organisations with a mechanism for creating several strategic opportunities (Tatum, 1988).

Within a business environment, senior managers are therefore increasingly concerned with investigating the processes involved in creating strategic direction (Morgan, 1997). This direction is often channelled through a structured framework often described by the term 'Business Strategy' or 'Corporate Strategy', where this represents a formal framework that clearly defines the business goals and objectives of the organisation (Ansoff, 1968; Porter, 1985). Research on Business Strategy (BS) formulation tends to embrace a wide range of theories and perceptions, the nuances of which often invite ambiguity and misinterpretation. However, the precise definition of strategy in this remit is more difficult to determine, evidenced by perceptions and methodological approaches taken by a range of authors (Ansoff, 1968; Porter, 1985; Mintzberg and Quinn, 1991; Robson, 1997; Ward and Peppard, 1996). Therefore, from a taxonomy perspective, Business

Strategy within this chapter should be interpreted in the context defined by Porter (1985), as this viewpoint specifically identifies the link between competitive opportunities and high-level processes (Davenport, 1993). Thus, hereafter, the BS can be seen as a pattern of decisions made within a company to determine organisational goals and objectives. Therefore, the core raison d'être of developing the BS should be to establish appropriate policies and plans needed to achieve strategic direction. This includes embracing market forces, internal processes and intellectual capital (employees) and, in most cases, the consideration of shareholders, customers and the wider community. The fundamental details of the BS should consequently focus on how a company competes and positions itself in the marketplace by focusing resources and competence into strategic advantage (to deliver the corporate vision/mission). In this context, it is imperative that key drivers and enablers affecting success are fully understood, especially concerning BS formulation, implementation and subsequent evaluation.

The BS can therefore be seen as a long-term policy that expressly satisfies the needs of the core business imperatives, and not short-term operational issues. The guiding principles and focus should thus concentrate on structuring the pattern of decisions needed to perform and excel within the business environment. This requires considerable business acumen, as these decisions will often shape the way in which the business evolves (and the way it is perceived in the wider community), which can affect the character and image of the company. In essence, strategic decisions help to position the company in the operating environment, allowing it the capacity to mobilise its strengths to fulfil its corporate goals. The central functions within the company must therefore be aligned to these needs, which include systems and procedures, sales and marketing, manufacturing and production, and all organisational resources (human and physical) to support these processes. The BS should therefore be forward-looking, and wherever possible, embrace the following key attributes:

- *Include non-financial aspects* (as focusing purely on financial issues can often prevent the organisation from capturing equally important issues such as quality, corporate perception, culture, employee motivation, etc);
- *Be measurable* (as strategies that cannot be measured or quantified are relatively meaningless – goals must therefore be set, and subsequently measured and evaluated):
- *Be focused and distinctive* (as a broad or indistinct approach can often limit success);
- *Be Innovative and flexible* (as a clear strategy can help direct corporate energies more effectively, whereas flexibility enables organisations to better respond to change).

From a strategy development perspective, the process of creating a BS is normally kept confidential, as it tends to contain commercially sensitive information. Some strategists also argue that release of this information should also be withheld from employees in order to avoid internal resistance or minimise leaks to competitors (Andrews, 1987). Within the context of construction, there are many small and medium-sized enterprises (SMEs), which are currently trying to focus on continuous improvement initiatives in order to not only survive in the marketplace, but also endeavour to secure competitive advantage. Some of these initiatives have focused on the development, integration and automation of ICT, whereas others have focused on developing new products and services following the Five Forces model advocated by Porter (1979). However, business benefits can only normally be secured if the corporate strengths of the organisation are purposefully aligned to market opportunities. Therefore, BS formulation envelops many issues, not least, identifying the company's strengths and weaknesses, and the resources available to service any perceived needs. This process is often referred to as the SWOT Analysis (Strengths, Weakness, Opportunities and Threats). Consequently, strategy development has to balance processes and perceptions with aspirations, ethics, culture and organisational competence. Andrews (1987) classified these issues into four key areas, specifically Market Opportunity, Corporate Competence and Resources, Personal Values and Aspirations, and Acknowledged Obligations to Society. However, strategy formulation should also consider the company's capacity to meet the needs of the market in order to match opportunity with corporate capability (Ward and Peppard, 2002). The formulation of the BS must therefore critically examine all these factors, not least organisational strategic plans and initiatives, business processes, technology issues and corporate resources.

7.5   Business Performance Assessment

The process of assessing business performance includes a number of important areas, from the identification of the organisation's current position and standing in the marketplace, through to the identification of performance gaps with corresponding strategies and measures to address these.

7.5.1   Benchmarking and Gap Analysis

Several definitions of benchmarking are available in the extant literature. However, the fundamental philosophical approach of benchmarking is to analyse existing activities, processes or practices within the company against one or more external organisations in order to measure fundamental differences. Whilst this is typically undertaken with similarly sized companies in the same market sector, there are advantages to be secured from benchmarking against smaller (or larger) organisations in non-cognate areas. The main concept of benchmarking is to determine from the outset the precise areas that are going to be evaluated, along with the measures and metrics used. This is important, as it helps to establish the precise rubrics and purpose of this exercise, so that clarity of purpose can be objectively measured against specific performance criteria. For example, benchmarking can be directed at both micro and macro levels. The micro level may, for example, involve a detailed analysis of a small technical issue, whereas at the macro level this may include issues of a more general nature, including managerial processes, key functional areas, etc. Either way, the core raison d'être of undertaking benchmarking and gap analysis should be to purposefully identify 'best practice' and actions needed to match or exceed this in order to gain competitive advantage.

Performance analysis is a tool that can be used for applying and measuring performance targets, the procedure of which is normally undertaken on mission-critical activities. This technique is also known as Gap Analysis or Variance Analysis. Gap Analysis is widely used in the construction, manufacturing and financial sectors, and can be a valuable tool for controlling resource driven activities over time (to predict trends), the mechanics of which can often be applied to a variety of different process areas. Whilst these areas usually embrace production-related activities, it can also extend to include skills development (Van Daal *et al.*, 1998; Goulding and Alshawi, 2002); intellectual capital (Joia, 2000); gaps in ICT (Ward and Daniel, 2005); gaps in culture (Ward and Peppard, 2002), or external environment issues (Harrison and Pelletier, 2000). The application of this approach is to measure performance achievement against predetermined targets, the purpose of which is to analyse all gaps in performance. The difference between the current level of achievement and the desired target is known as the performance gap (or opportunity gap) – an example of which can be seen in Figure 7.2.

Figure 7.2 identifies three main areas for performance improvement, specifically: Area 'X', Area 'Y' and Area 'Z'. The performance target achievement levels for each of these areas is represented by the dashed line. From this, it can be seen that the greatest area for improvement rests with Area 'Y' (G2), as the opportunity gap identified is greater than G1 or G3. Therefore, if Area 'Y' was classed as a critical BS objective, then resources should be prioritised to this area, in order to address performance deficiencies and maximise performance gains.

Figure 7.2   Performance gap analysis.

7.5.2   Evaluation

Whilst it is important to understand the concepts and issues of strategy, it is equally important to understand the importance of evaluation, as this is one of the most important aspects of strategy development, and is often misunderstood and/or applied. Evaluation is not just something that needs to be completed retrospectively, it must be planned for well in advance. Things that are needed include issues such as 'What needs to be measured?', 'Why?', 'How?', 'Using what criteria?', etc. Once these decisions have been made, a set of 'measurable' indicators can then be established for subsequent analysis. However, the evaluation process should specifically target areas of particular significance, especially areas that directly contribute to the strategic objectives of the company. It should therefore be linked to the objectives and policies of the company, so that priority areas and desired outcomes can be established and appropriate measures set against predefined criteria for subsequent evaluation. This typically involves the determination of gaps between the desired levels of achievement and the current position of the company in order to appraise the type of activity undertaken, determine the level and suitability of expertise available, assess the appropriateness and effectiveness of core business processes, identify production or financial outcomes, or assess the prevailing level of organisational culture within the company (Rapert *et al,*, 1996; Warszawski, 1996; Ward and Daniel, 2005).

At this juncture is should be acknowledged that business performance issues can often be adversely influenced by a number of factors. These issues tend to embrace sociological, technological and managerial matters relating to corporate structures, and the interrelationship of people to processes. From a commercial perspective, business performance almost invariably tends to refer to fiscal performance. In this respect, financial performance measures are often used to ensure that resources are deployed appropriately and effectively, with typical measures and metrics being associated with ratio analysis, derived from company balance sheets and profit and loss accounts. However, the use of financial measures alone should be discouraged, as using these in isolation does not always create a balanced view of corporate performance (Andrews, 1987; Mintzberg and Quinn, 1991; Lee and Sai On Ko, 2000). However, when considering the term 'performance', from a definition perspective, this can be interpreted in several different ways. Therefore, in order to provide clarity, the following definitions are presented:

- *Performance Objective*: a critical success factor for achieving the mission/ vision;
- *Performance Goal*: a target level or objective;
- *Performance Measure*: a qualitative or quantitative measure of performance;
- *Performance Measurement*: the process of measuring or assessing progress/ outcomes;
- *Performance Management*: the use of performance measurement.

Figure 7.3   Business performance and improvement assessment approaches.

The areas for evaluation should form a feedback loop for reflection, so that the areas (performance objectives), measurement (performance measures), targets (performance expectations) and results (performance results) can be analysed holistically. This relationship can be seen in Figure 7.3.

When it comes to the process of evaluation, it is acknowledged that it is possible to evaluate almost anything and everything within an organisational setting. However, intrinsically, it is more important to understand what areas are needed, why these areas are important, and how much this evaluation process will cost. For example, evaluation areas within a construction organisation may include:

- functional or process areas;
- level of integration/interoperability;
- communication improvements;
- response times or time savings;
- reduced levels of data redundancy/duplication;
- fiscal savings/reductions;
- strategic advantage/market share;
- innovation/new business benefits;
- client satisfaction.

Once the areas for evaluation have been identified, it is important to decide on the criteria that is going to be used for this, for example ''What criteria can we evaluate X?', 'Will this be the same for Y?' Typical criteria includes 'success', 'efficiency' and 'effectiveness' (how well, etc). In this respect, evaluation criteria can be either quantitative, qualitative or a combination of both. The main issue to understand here is the overall rationale and thought processes behind the need to undertake this evaluation. For example, 'What do we mean by success?' Success is typically associated with something new and often embraces change or innovation. Success can also be considered subjective, as one person's view of success will often be different from another's. However, success may also be quantified, for example, X% improvement in area Y, or £X profit, or X% increase in turnover, etc. The more complex the criteria, the more involved the analysis will often be, with a corresponding increase in time and cost. Efficiency is another example: 'What do we mean by efficiency?' This tends to be used when something performs optimally, but altruistically, in certain circumstances this may not be entirely effective. Thus, evaluation can be considered as a process of asking and answering three main questions:

1. Will it meet the needs of the organisation?
2. Will it engage proven approaches (methods) to satisfy internal and external audit (if needed)? and
3. Will it provide the organisation with the 'right' results needed (e.g. reports, tables, charts, etc)?

The next section presents a construction case study for discussion. Emphasis is placed on identifying some of these strategic development issues from a practical development and implementation perspective.

7.6   Strategy Development within Construction

Many large construction organisations are often divided (and subdivided) into groups or subsidiaries for logistical or operational reasons, the majority of which tend to operate under the overall control of one parent (or holding) company. In some cases, companies are given complete autonomy from the holding company, the procedure of which enables them to set group-specific business strategies independent of the parent company's BS. This provision can allow a greater degree of flexibility to exploit niche markets, without the necessary burden of being tied into the parent company's BS and corporate infrastructure.

The following section presents a strategy development case study for one large construction organisation based in the UK.

7.6.1   Strategic Challenge

The company had an operating remit covering the AEC market sector, the work of which was predominantly undertaken in the UK (albeit with some overseas activity), with an annual turnover of over £700m, supported by 3,500 technical, managerial and operational staff. The holding company was operationally divided into discreet groups, which, for the purpose of anonymity, are hereafter labelled Group A, Group B and Group C, the representation of which can be seen in Figure 7.4.

From Figure 7.4, three separate groups (Group A, Group B, Group C) are presented, each with their corresponding business strategies. The remit and extent of each group's BS is represented by a solid-line circle, and the parent company's BS is represented by a dashed-line circle. The collective business strategies of each of these three groups can be seen to fulfil the parent company's BS through the overlap in the central core. In this area, the remits of each of the respective group's BS can be considered similar or identical to

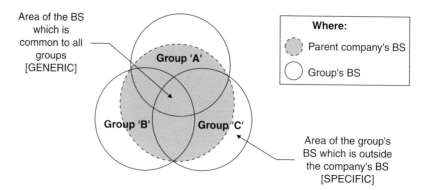

Figure 7.4   Case study business strategy structure.

each other from a needs perspective, and can be thus termed 'generic' (common to all), whereas, areas that fall outside this central core can be said to be specific to that group's needs.

The main purpose of this case study was to highlight the core drivers and barriers affecting the strategic deployment of strategy from a holding company perspective. In particular, it aimed to identify how strategic decisions were holistically managed from inception through to review. This company therefore needed a formal mechanism for assessing the effectiveness of their BS in order to purposefully leverage corporate resources and competence (Andrews, 1987; Mintzberg and Quinn, 1991). In this respect, they needed a new approach to measure their overall performance from a holding company perspective, and not just from a series of combined strategies collated at group level.

7.6.2   Proposed Solution

The first stage of this study was to assess the scale and complexity of the company organisational structure, along with the functional relationship attached to each of the three froups. This was needed to identify the scope and remit of the task, in order to conceptualise the overall scale and complexity of the main process issues involved for developing the proposed solution. Twelve interviews were conducted with all key decision makers within each of the three groups, in order to elicit key information regarding strategy formulation and core critical success factors (CSFs). From this, a case study approach (Yin, 1994) was used to develop a formal framework with actors that 'modelled' what currently happened in practice, against what should happen (best practice). The domain area for this investigation encompassed the strategic use of ICT only, specifically, the core strategic ICT process that supported group and corporate strategy. In this respect, in order to remove organisational bias, all findings were independently tested and validated with a similar-sized company and operating business remit to this company. Only findings from the first phase of this work

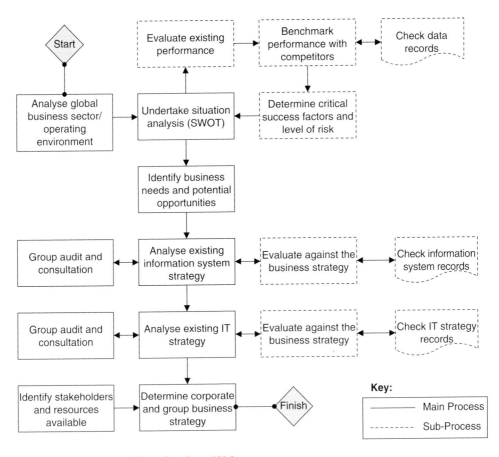

Figure 7.5   Process attributes for phase ZERO.

(Phase ZERO), together with a strategic dependency model, are presented for discussion.

Figure 7.5 represents Phase ZERO of this work, specifically a process representation highlighting the need for strategic ICT in the case study company. The starting point of Phase ZERO is commenced with the process box titled 'Analyse Global Business Sector/Operating Environment'. This allows users to identify the organisation's primary business market, the precursor of which requires a full investigation into the principal factors that can often influence outcomes. Specifically, this process box requires the identification of all current (and future) market issues and forces that could influence outcomes (directly or indirectly). This requires the process box 'Undertake Situation Analysis (SWOT)' to be commenced, as these details can help identify the position and status of the company (from a competition perspective). At this point, a detailed SWOT analysis should be undertaken to identify the key strengths, weaknesses, opportunities and threats facing the company. This is a major activity, and should be separated into readily identifiable and manageable sub-processes – the details of which are identified in 'Evaluate Existing Performance', 'Benchmark Performance with Competitors', 'Check Data Records', and 'Determine Critical Success Factors and Level of Risk' sub-process boxes. The 'Evaluate Existing Performance' sub-process box is used to collate historic key business performance measures achieved (from the previous evaluation period). Typical areas of analysis often include items that can be easily measured and quantified, for example, turnover, direct sales, return on capital employed, earnings per share, tender success percentages, etc. This information is then directed to the 'Benchmark Performance with Competitors' sub-process box, where comparisons are undertaken. At this juncture, it was acknowledged that the process of undertaking comparisons using benchmarking should only be attempted with similar sized and structured construction organisations and, if possible, using companies with a similar level of ICT process maturity. At this stage, the 'Check Data Records' sub-process box is accessed to compare the internal and external data records – the details from which are subsequently sent to the 'Determine Critical Success Factors and Level of Risk' sub-process box. Users are then able to identify all the CSFs needed to move the company forward (in terms of performance and competitiveness). At this stage 'risk' is also evaluated in terms of achieving the identified CSFs, and the corresponding effect this may have on the BS. When all sub-processes activities have been completed, the resultant data is then sent to the 'Identify Business Needs and Potential Opportunities' process box for analysis.

The 'Identify Business Needs and Potential Opportunities' process box is used to outline the business needs and remit of the strategy. Any potential opportunities identified by the benchmarking exercise are discussed at this point. Emphasis is therefore placed on focusing resources and energies effectively, particularly in areas of strength, or perhaps towards new market opportunities. However, these considerations must be tempered with company experience, the amount of risk attached and the type and level of skills available. This information forms the basis of the business need, which (as a prerequisite) requires the exact Information Systems (IS) requirements to be determined, which can be achieved through the 'Analyse Existing Information System Strategy' process box.

The activities undertaken in the 'Analyse Existing Information System Strategy' process box aims to identify the exact needs and expectations required by the BS from an Information Systems Strategy (ISS) perspective. Particular emphasis is therefore placed on assessing whether the existing ISS can deliver the BS. This requires detailed investigation into the existing organisational ISS and support mechanisms, and can be achieved using two sub-process activities, specifically 'Evaluate Against the Business Strategy' and 'Check Information System Records'. The 'Check Information System Records' sub-process box is used to identify all existing processes, procedures and systems currently deployed in the company. This information is then sent to the 'Evaluate Against the Business Strategy' sub-process box for validation and checking purposes. At this point, all IS systems and procedures are formally matched to the requirements of the BS. Group input from the 'Group Audit and Consultation' helps to shape the overall needs of the holding company regarding its overall ISS needs. Any deficiencies or identified needs are subsequently prioritised and sent to the main process box 'Analyse

Existing Information System Strategy' for final analysis. This information is later codified and directed to the 'Analyse Existing IT Strategy' process box for alignment and matching purposes. The 'Analyse Existing IT Strategy' process box is used to critically examine the current systems and procedures in place to deliver the ISS and BS. Emphasis is therefore placed on whether the ITS is able to support the demands and expectations of the ISS, contemplating the existing organisational infrastructure and level of ICT process maturity. This investigation is also supported by two sub-process areas, specifically 'Evaluate Against the Business Strategy' and 'Check IT Strategy Records'. The 'Check IT Strategy Records' sub-process box is used primarily to audit and document the ITS. Emphasis is therefore placed on how well the existing strategy supports the current business operations. However, the focus of attention will need to concentrate on the future demands determined by the 'Analyse Existing IS Strategy' process box. These findings are then sent to the 'Evaluate Against the Business Strategy' sub-process box for evaluation and alignment purposes. In this remit, the ITS is formally matched to the needs and expectations of the BS. Any deficiencies (or areas of need) in the ITS are identified at this stage, the results from which are then directed back to the main process box 'Analyse Existing IT Strategy' for further analysis. When all information has been collated and analysed in the 'Analyse Existing IT Strategy' process box, these findings are then disseminated to all groups (and subsidiaries) through the 'Group Audit and Consultation' process box. This enables consultation with the wider corporate audience, which therefore allows stakeholders to identify their current (and future) position regarding IS and ICT support measures and systems needed. From a corporate perspective, the holding company will need to gain understanding and support from stakeholders, particularly where the strategic alignment of IS and ICT resources are concerned. This undertaking therefore extends into the 'Identify Stakeholders and Resources Available' process box, where all these findings should be analysed. At this point, corporate executives should be in a position to make a formal statement of intent, conscious of the competing forces, drivers and proposed direction of the company – these details therefore naturally embrace corporate resources. The final stage of Phase ZERO is used to determine the corporate BS, which is undertaken in the 'Determine Business Strategy' process activity box. This procedure enables the key BS CSFs to be established and agreed, the findings from which are then disseminated to all groups. All decisions and requirements are formally documented at this point, in the form of a Phase Review Report. The details contained in this report then determine whether there is an intrinsic need for the strategic deployment of ICT within the company. Users are then in a position to exit this process model.

7.6.3   Discussion

Phase ZERO enables the case study company to critically analyse their core ICT business processes in line with market forces, governing conditions and immediate competitors. The next stage of this investigation required the business strategy relationships and dependencies to be determined for

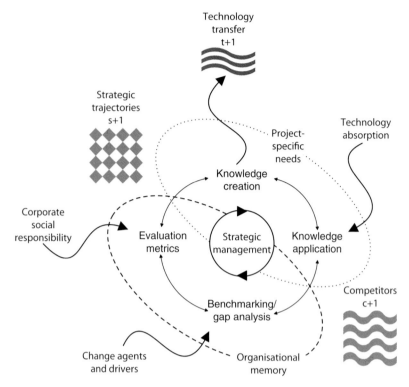

Figure 7.6   Strategic management cycles and dependencies.

the holding company and each of the three groups. This was needed in order
to understand, at Board level, how these three strategies interrelated, what
was shared and how information flowed between them. It was also important
to capture the tangential support structures and mechanisms that made
these units function, particularly from a knowledge sharing perspective.
This relationship was mapped into a dependency schema, the details of
which can be seen in Figure 7.6.

From the outset, it was considered important to understand the strategic
behaviour of construction firms (Langford and Male, 2001) and to
acknowledge that performance improvement within this sector often
extends beyond project specific measures (Smyth, 2010). Furthermore,
from a strategy perspective, it was also important to understand competition
in relation to business units (Kao *et al.*, 2009) and business/project
processes (Gann and Salter, 2000), in order to appreciate the importance of
finding the right 'fit' between the construction environment and company
specialism (Pries and Janszen, 1995). It was also acknowledged that the
implications of learning and transfer should be fully understood (Belling
et al., 2004). In this respect, Figure 7.6 identifies the Strategic Management
cycle and dependencies for this company. The central core 'Strategic
Management' is depicted as a revolving process, through which all strategic
decisions are analysed. This is supported by 'knowledge creation',

knowledge application', 'benchmarking/gap analysis' and 'evaluation metrics' activities, the hub of which controls how tacit and project specific knowledge is used. This is of particular importance to construction organisations, as it forms the main conduit for organising, embedding and actioning knowledge, especially at project and organisational levels (Senaratne and Sexton, 2011), and how knowledge-pull can deliver innovation through knowledge management (Maqsood *et al.*, 2007). The 'competitors c+1' and 'strategic trajectories s+1' activities can be considered as being symbiotically linked, as the strategic trajectories are directly linked to competitor strategies and pricing structures. In many respects, the trajectories can therefore be seen as strategic objectives, which act as signposting options, which is a useful way of predicting outcomes (Wickham and Wickham, 2007). This can be further enhanced by using probabilistic models, as these can help decision makers predict the likelihood of success of engaging option 1 (s1), option 2 (s2), etc against identified variables, for example, competitors, market niche, project mix, etc. The 'technology absorption' and 'technology transfer t+1' activities are mechanisms through which technology transfer and innovation opportunities are captured, assessed and embedded with the company. In this respect, it was deemed particularly important to understand how innovation could be implemented in construction (Slaughter, 1998; Winch, 2003; Sexton and Barrett, 2004; Ruddock and Ruddock, 2009), as this often engages organisational factors within and across organisational boundaries which, from this company's perspective, involved interaction at both group and corporate levels. Finally, the 'change agents and drivers' and 'Corporate Social Responsibility' (CSR) activities are the formal channels through which change and CSR are managed. For example, CSR embraces the organisation's corporate conscience, and the change agents and drivers include such issues as the organisation's ability to apply transformational change measures (cognisant of external perception). Thus, the extent by which this needs to be proactive or reactive needs to be carefully considered (Nadler *et al.*, 1995), as this can be used as a lever to encourage innovative transformation (Fenton and Pettigrew, 2000).

7.7   Conclusion

This chapter introduced the importance of strategy in the AEC sector in relation to business strategy theories and construction sector drivers. This highlighted the need for organisations to have a strategy with a clear focus and readily identifiable objectives and deliverables. This is especially important where the effects of competition, market positioning and strategy are overtly prominent. In this respect, it was noted that strategy formulation should therefore consider a company's capacity to meet the needs of the market, by matching opportunity with corporate capability. This process should critically examine the issues most likely to affect outcomes – specifically strategic plans and initiatives, business processes, technology, organisational culture and the prevailing level (and type) of corporate resources. On this theme, BPR was introduced as an approach that can often help organisations fundamentally reorganise the way they conduct business operations from a process perspective in order to garner improvements. This was followed by a discussion on performance analysis, especially how this can be used to set and measure performance targets using appropriate measures and metrics. Strategy formulation issues were then presented for discussion through a construction case study exemplar. Particular emphasis was placed on determining this company's capacity to meet the needs of the market, by aligning group corporate capability and resources to strategic plans. This emphasised the strategic challenges facing one company in relation to the strategic deployment of strategy from a holding company perspective, and noted the need to identify functional and organisational areas matched to deliverables with predefined critical success factors. Research findings presented a Phase ZERO process attribute map for the case study company, together with a strategic management dependency schema. The process attribute map identified high-level process activities associated with matching business decisions to corporate strategy, and presented the governing dependencies and interrelationships, and how these can be effectively managed in order to procure defendable business solutions. The strategic management dependency schema highlighted the internal and external dynamics of strategic management from a holistic perspective. In particular, it also identified the importance of embracing project specific needs with organisational needs, especially cognisant of governing forces, competition and strategic trajectory positioning.

In summary, it is particularly important to acknowledge that the construction industry can benefit from understanding how strategy (strategic positioning), skills (intellectual capital), ICT (alignment to strategy) and process (understanding) all interrelate. Understanding these relationships can help companies focus on their particular areas of strength and, if appropriately augmented, could be used to garner strategic advantage.

References

Al-Mashari, M. & Zairi, M. (2000) Revisiting BPR: A holistic review of practice and development. *Business Process Management Journal*, 6(1), 10–42.

Andrews, K.R. (1987) *The Concept of Corporate Strategy*. Irwin Inc, Illinois.

Ansoff, H.I. (1968) *Corporate Strategy: An Analytic Approach to Business Policy for Growth and Expansion*. Penguin Publishers, Harmondsworth.

Banwell, H (1964) *Report of the Committee on the Placing and Management of Contracts for Building and Civil Engineering Works*. HMSO, London.

Belling, R., James, K. & Ladkin, D. (2004) Back to the workplace: How organisations can improve their support of management learning and development. *Journal of Management development*, 23(3), 234–255.

Betts, M. (1992) How strategic is our use of information technology in the construction sector. *International Journal of Construction Information Technology*, 1(1), 79–97.

Betts, M. & Wood-Harper, T (1994) Reengineering construction: A new management research agenda. *Journal of Construction Economics and Management*, 12, 551–556.

Betts, M. & Ofori, G. (1992) Strategic planning for competitive advantage in construction. *Construction Management and Economics*, **10**(6), 511–532.

Chan, P.S. & Land, C. (1999) Implementing reengineering using information Technology. *Business Process Management Journal*, **5**(4), 311–324.

Channon, D.F. (1978) *The Service Industries: Strategy, Structure & Financial Performance*. MacMillan, London.

Davenport, T.H, (1993) *Process Innovation: Reengineering Work through Information Technology*. Harvard Business School Press, Boston, MA.

Davenport, T.H. & Short, J.E. (1990) The new industrial engineering: Information technology and business process redesign. *Sloan Management Review*, **31**(4), 11–27.

Egan, Sir J. (1998) *Rethinking Construction: The Report of the Construction Task Force*. Blackwell Science Ltd, Oxford.

Elton, M. (1933) *The Human Problems of an Industrial Civilisation*. MacMillan, New York.

Emmerson, H. (1962) *Survey of Problems before the Construction Industries*. HMSO, London.

Fayol, H. (1949) *General and Industrial Management*. Pitman Publishing, London.

Fenton, E.M. & Pettigrew, A.M. (2000) *The Innovating Organization*. Sage Publications Ltd, London.

Gann, D.M. & Salter, A.J. (2000) Innovation in project-based, service enhanced firms: The construction of complex products and systems. *Policy Research*, **29**(7-8), 955–972.

Goodman, R. & Chinowsky, P. (1997) Preparing construction professionals for executive decision making. *Journal of Management in Engineering*, **13**(6), 55–61.

Goulding, J.S. & Alshawi, M. (2002) Generic and specific IT training: A process protocol model for construction. *Journal of Construction Management and Economics*, **20**(6), 493–505.

Hammer, M. (1990) Reengineering work: don't automate, obliterate. *Harvard Business Review*, **July–August**, 104–112.

Hammer, M. & Champy, J. (1993) *Reengineering the Corporation: A Manifesto for Business Revolution*. Harper Business, New York.

Harrison, E.F. & Pelletier, M.A. (2000) Levels of Strategic Decision Success. *Management Decision Journal*, **38**(2), 107–117.

Hillebrandt, P.M. & Cannon, J. (1990) *The Modern Construction Firm*. Macmillan, London.

Huber, G.P. (1991) Organizational learning: The contributing processes and the literatures. *Journal of Organization Science*, **2**(1), 88–115.

Johansson, H.J., McHugh, P., Pendlebury, A.J. & Wheeler, W.A. (1993) *Business Process Reengineering: Breakpoint Strategies for Market Dominance*. John Wiley and Sons, Chichester, UK.

Joia, L.A. (2000) Measuring intangible corporate assets – Linking business strategy with intellectual capital. *Journal of Intellectual Capital*, **1**(1), 68–84.

Kagioglou, M., Aouad, G. & Cooper, R. (2001) Performance management in construction: A conceptual framework. *Journal of Construction Management and Economics*, **19**(1), 85–95.

Kao, C., Green, S.D. & Larsen, G.D. (2009) Emergent discourses of construction competitiveness: localized learning and embeddedness. *Construction Management and Economics*, **27**, 1005–1017.

Latham, M. (1994) *Constructing the Team*. HMSO, London.

Langford, D. & Male, S. (2001) *Strategic Management in Construction*, 2nd edn. Wiley-Blackwell, London.

Lee, R.G. and Dale, B.G. (1998) Business process management: a review and evaluation. *Business Process Management Journal*, **4**(3), 214–225.

Lee, S.F. & Sai On Ko, A. (2000) Building Balanced Scorecard with SWOT Analysis, and implementing 'Sun Tzu's The Art of Business Management Strategies' on QFD methodology. *Managerial Auditing Journal*, **15**(1/2), 68–76.

Lewin, K. (1947) Frontiers of group dynamics. *Journal of Human Relations*, **1**(1), 5-41.

Love, P.E.D. & Holt, G.D. (2000) Construction business performance measurement: The SPM alternative. *Journal of Business Process Management*, **6**(5), 408–416.

Maloney, W.F. (1997) Strategic planning for human resource management in construction. *Journal of Management in Engineering*, (**13**)3, 49–56.

Mayo, E. (1933) *The Human Problems of an Industrial Civilization*. Macmillan, New York.

Maqsood, T., Walker, D.H.T. & Finegan, A.D. (2007) Facilitating knowledge pull to deliver innovation through knowledge management: A case study. *Journal of Engineering, Construction and Architectural Management*, **14**(1), 94–109.

Mintzberg, H. & Quinn, J.B. (1991) *The Strategy Process: Concepts, Contexts, Cases*. Prentice Hall International (UK) Ltd, London.

Morgan, G. (1997) *Images of Organization*, 2nd edn, Sage Publishers, London.

Morgan, G (1990), Organizations in Society, Macmillan, London, UK

Nadler, D., Shaw, R.B., Walton, A.E., *et al.* (1995) *Discontinuous Change: Leading Organizational Transformation*. Jossey-Bass, San Francisco, CA.

Newcombe, R. (1990) The evolution and structure of the construction firm. *Proceedings, CIB 90, Joint Symposium on Building Economics and Construction Management*, Sydney, 6 March, 358–369.

Perkowski, J.C. (1988) Technical trends in the E&C business: The next 10 years. *Journal of Construction Management and Engineering*, **114**(4), 565–576.

Petrozzo, D.P. & Stepper, J.C. (1994) *Successful Reengineering*. Van Norstrand Reinhold, New York.

Porter, M.E. (1979) How competitive forces shape strategy. *Harvard Business Review*, **March-April**, 137–145.

Porter, M.E. (1985) *Competitive Advantage: Creating and Sustaining Superior Performance*. Free Press, New York.

Porter, M.E. (2008) *On Competition*, updated and expanded edn. Harvard Business School Press, Boston, MA.

Prahalad, C.K. & Hamel, G. (1990) The core competence of the corporation. *Harvard Business Review*, **68**(May–June), 79–91.

Price., A.D.F. & Newson, E. (2003) Strategic management: consideration of paradoxes, processes, and associated concepts as applied to construction. *Journal of Management in Engineering*, **19**(4),183–192.

Pries, F. & Janszen, F. (1995) Innovation in the construction industry: the dominant role of the environment. *Construction Management and Economics*, **13**, 43–51.

Rapert, M., Lynch, D. & Suter, T. (1996) Enhancing functional and organisational performance via strategic consensus and commitment. *Journal of Strategic Marketing*, **4**(4), 193–205.

Remenyi, D. & Sherwood-Smith, M. (1998) Business benefits from information systems through an active benefits realisation programme. *International Journal of Project Management*, **16**(2), 81–98.

Rezgui, Y. & Zarli, A. (2006) Paving the way to the vision of digital construction: A strategic roadmap. *Journal of Construction Engineering and Management*, **132**(7), 767–776.

Robson, W. (1997) *Strategic Management & Information Systems*. Pitman Publishing, London.

Ruddock, L. & Ruddock. S. (2009) Reassessing productivity in the construction sector to reflect hidden innovation and the knowledge economy. *Construction Management and Economics*, **27**, 871–879.

Senaratne, S. & Sexton, M. (2011) *Managing Change in Construction Projects: A Knowledge-Based Approach*. Wiley-Blackwell, London.

Senge, P.M. (2006) *The Fifth Discipline: The Art and Practice of the Learning Organization*, 2nd edn. Random House Business, New York.

Sexton, M. & Barrett, P. (2004) The role of technology transfer in innovation within small construction firms. *Journal of Engineering, Construction and Architectural Management*, **11**(5), 342–348.

Slaughter, E.S. (1998) *Models of construction innovation. ASCE Journal of Construction Engineering and Management*, **124**(3), 226–231.

Smith, A. (1759) *The Theory of Moral Sentiments*. Adam Smith Institute, London.

Smyth, H. (2010) Construction industry performance improvement programmes: the UK case of demonstration projects in the 'Continuous Improvement' programme. *Construction Management and Economics*, **28**, 255–270.

Soares, J. & Anderson, S. (1997) Modelling process management in construction. *Journal of Management in Engineering*, **13**(5), 45–53.

Stacey, R.D. (2010) *Strategic Management and Organisational Dynamics: The Challenge of Complexity (to Ways of Thinking About Organisations)*, 6th edn. Financial Times/ Prentice Hall, London.

Tan, R. (1996) Information technology and perceived competitive advantage: An empirical study of engineering consulting firms in Taiwan. *Construction Management and Economics Journal*, **14**(3), 227–240.

Tatum, C.B. (1988) Technology and competitive advantage in civil engineering. *Journal of Professional Issues in Engineering, American Society of Civil Engineers*, **114**(3), 256–264.

Taylor, F.W. (1911) *The Principles of Scientific Management*. Harper Bros., New York.

Van Daal, B., De Haas, M. & Weggeman, M. (1998) The knowledge matrix: A participatory method for individual knowledge gap determination. *Knowledge and Process Management Journal*, **5**(4), 255–263.

Venegas, P. & Alarcón, L. (1997) Selecting long-term strategies for construction firms. *Journal of Construction Engineering and Management*, **123**(4), 388–398.

Walker, D.H.T. (2000) Client/customer or stakeholder focus? ISO 14000 EMS as a construction industry case study. *The TQM Magazine*, **12**(1), 18–25.

Ward, J. & Daniel, E. (2005) *Benefits Management: Delivering Value from IS & IT Investments*. John Wiley and Sons, Ltd, Chichester, UK.

Ward, J.L. & Peppard, J. (2002) *Strategic Planning for Information Systems*, 3rd edn. John Wiley and Sons, Chichester, UK.

Ward, J and Peppard, J (1996), Reconciling the IT/Business Relationship: A Troubled Marriage in Need of Guidance, Journal of Strategic Information Systems, Vol. 5, No. 1, pp 37-65

Warszawski, A. (1996) Strategic planning in construction companies. *Journal of Construction Engineering and Management*, **122**(2), 133–140.

Wickham., P.A. & Wickham, L. (2007) *Management Consulting: Delivering an Effective Project*, 3rd edn. Financial Times/Prentice Hall, London.

Winch, G. (2003) How innovative is construction? Comparing aggregated data on construction innovation and other sectors – a case of apples and pears. *Journal of Construction Management and Economics*, **21**(6), 651–654.

Yin, R.K. (1994) *Case Study Research: Design and Methods*. Sage Publications, London.

Risk Management in Planning for Process Improvement

Oluwaseyi Awodele, Stephen Ogunlana and Graeme Bowles

8.1   Introduction

The concept of continuous improvement as a means of improving processes, services and products in a competitive marketplace has long been established in business (Blick *et al.*, 2000; Momoh and Ruhe, 2006). To this end, many guidelines and models for process improvement within individual organisations have been produced. This chapter contends that conventional process improvement models are predominantly too rigid for organisations and their projects within the construction industry given its dynamic and volatile nature. A review of literature relating to business process and improvement models is presented and the need to incorporate risk management to make these more meaningful to the needs of construction organisations is argued. For example, organisations can benefit in a number of ways from investing in process improvement, including improvements in product quality, reduction in the time-to-market of the product, improvements to productivity and increased organisational flexibility and stakeholder satisfaction (Florac *et al.*, 1997; Zahran, 1998). Couple this with the reality of ever challenging and competitive markets; organisations must strive to increase productivity, improve relationships with customers and reduce the time to launch new products. In this respect, Kagioglou, *et al.* (1999) acknowledged the need for improvement to the conventional design and construction process was well reported in the literature, and that the construction sector in the UK has, since the 1930s, voiced a desire to change the way it performs its primary activity – the construction of building and civil engineering works. They reported that a succession of government and institutional reports have examined this activity, particularly the practice of construction management, and noted the need for improvement and change.

Construction Innovation and Process Improvement, First Edition.
Edited by Akintola Akintoye, Jack S. Goulding and Girma Zawdie.
© 2012 Blackwell Publishing Ltd. Published 2012 by Blackwell Publishing Ltd.

In a UK Government investigation, Latham (1994) re-affirmed the conclusions of all other previous studies, such as Banwell (1964) and British Property Federation (1983) among others. The report noted the need for effective processes throughout the construction life cycle, starting from the management of the client brief to the selection of the supply chain participants and eventual construction and decommissioning. The main outcome and recommendation of the Latham report was that it called for significant cost savings by the utilisation and formation of effective construction processes, which could lead to increased performance (Kagioglou et al., 1999). It is imperative therefore, for the construction industry to embrace this concept of process improvement, to improve productivity and efficiency of the sector in those areas that have long been the focus of criticism. Furthermore, Egan (1998) recommended an annual reduction of 10% in construction cost and construction time, and a reduction of 20% per annum of defects in projects. This performance improvement requires significant improvements in the way the construction process is enacted, which implies significant reengineering of the construction process and sub-processes. However, ever since these findings, businesses within the construction sector have been applying new methods of working and technologies to improve productivity and attain quality gains (Amaratunga et al., 2002). Furthermore, efficient implementation of different process improvement efforts is problematic, as much of the process research has concentrated on the development of methodologies for understanding process initiatives. Edwards et al. (2000) opined that these methodologies tend to be prescriptive and formulaic, consisting of a series of steps that lead to redesigned processes and hence theoretically significant performance improvements. In their opinion, the variety of organisational elements affected, when combined with the breadth of definition of process orientation, made it difficult to imagine any single process development methodologies being appropriate. The construction industry has therefore few recognised methodologies or frameworks on which to base process improvement initiatives. This lack of clear guidelines has meant that improvements are isolated and benefits are difficult to co-ordinate or repeat. Even when there are methodologies, Pritchard and Armistead (1999) assert that the same methods are unlikely to be equally successful in all cases.

The foregoing implies that the construction industry is limited in its ability to assess construction processes, prioritise process improvements and direct resources appropriately. In an attempt to address this problem, Sarshar et al. (1998) developed a process improvement framework for the construction industry called Structured Process Improvement for Construction Environments (SPICE). SPICE is based on the Capability Maturity Model (CMM), developed by the US Department of Defense, and widely used in the software industry. Evidence from other sectors show that continuous process improvement is based on many small evolutionary steps, rather than revolutionary measures (Paulk et al., 1993; Saiedan and Kuzara, 1995; Sarshar et al., 1998, 1999). Moreover, these steps do not take the possibilities of surprises in the course of improving a given process into cognisance, thus there is lack of integration of risk management in process improvement effort. This lack of integrated implementation approach to exploiting process improvement has been described as one of the important reasons responsible for failure of Process Improvement (Rohleder and Silver, 1997). Hammer and Champy (1993) estimated that 70% of process improvements and reengineering projects are less than successful. It is imperative therefore to raise the success rate of process improvement exercises by integrating risk management throughout the life cycle of a process improvement effort.

An effective process improvement framework begins with the formulation of one or more detailed process improvement plan(s), with the aim of achieving optimum balance of demands with available resources. The planning process in a business context therefore involves:

- identifying the goals or objectives to be achieved;
- formulating strategies to achieve them;
- arranging the means required; and
- implementing, directing and monitoring all steps in their proper sequence.

In planning for process improvement, there are possibilities that certain predictable events might occur, whose exact likelihood and outcomes are uncertain but could potentially affect the objectives in some way, either positively or negatively. The predictable events whose exact likelihood and outcome are uncertain are what manager's term risk (Grimsey and Lewis, 2002). Their capacities for affecting objectives explain the need for adequate risk management exercises in planning for process improvement. In this chapter, it is argued that business process improvement is a complex, risk-prone, collaborative process that requires a set of coordinated risk management processes. Risk management is presented as a proactive rather than a reactive, positive rather than negative effort, which seeks to increase the probability of process improvement. Process improvement is introduced and the integration of risk management at the planning stage for process improvement is also explained.

8.2   Process Improvement

There are many processes common to most, if not all, construction projects: preparation of a brief, establishing project scope, estimating probable cost, procurement of suitable contractors and suppliers, information management, measuring and analysing performance, training employees, closing out the project, etc. Most important business processes span several functional areas. For example, in construction there are many functional areas that tend to operate as separate units, for example, the estimating department is different from the design department. Improvements in this sector therefore are difficult to achieve, due to the cross-functional processes involved. Rohleder and Silver (1997) remarked that, to truly embrace the process improvement philosophy in this type of organisation, the organisation must make firm commitments to both a change in its thinking, and associated modification to the existing, vertical organisational structure, to a horizontal, process-oriented one. They further asserted that management must provide adequate time and resources for the improvement teams and that almost all the people in the organisation, not just a few at the top, should be actively involved in solving problems, reducing costs and eliminating waste.

Since improvement projects tend to ostensibly be managed through regular portfolio management in many organisations, an improvement project must have a sound business case in order to get firm commitment to the process improvement. The business case used in justifying the process improvement project needs to identify measurable impacts on a variety of performance measures for project organisation and the enterprise as a whole. Moreover, there may be measures of value to the process users, often exemplified in adoption or compliance measures that show the new processes are both used and useful. Both impact and adoption measures will be used to provide motivation for change, compare results of alternative approaches, ensure ongoing value of the ongoing investment and meet a variety of other organisation specific needs. Furthermore, people should not perceive identification of problems or the need for improvement as an indication of negative performance, rather it should be seen as the need to overcome complacency, switching to an attitude of preventing instead of reacting to problems. In addition, because process improvements can often naturally lead to higher productivity, fewer workers may then be needed to accomplish the same output. One may tend to feel that process improvements could then lead to layoffs from work. Robinson (1991) asserts that no layoffs should be made because of process improvements, but where possible, reductions should be achieved through attrition, where excess staff could be used to meet increased levels of demand. Care must be taken during the fact gathering exercise for process improvement. This is because fact gathering for process improvement tends to create fears about job changes and job losses. The skills and the integrity of the professional can go a long way towards reducing these anxieties and gaining cooperation. Skills enable the professional to collect critical, relevant data easily and assure that once collected it will not be lost. However, integrity is more important. It includes making sure that the focus of improvement treats people as a resource to be utilised and not an expense to be cut.

8.2.1   Definitions of Business Process

One source of ongoing confusion is the imprecise use of terminology. Process is a word that means different things to different people. Even for practitioners who are extremely familiar with the concepts of process management, there is still confusion across disciplines (Gulledge and Sommer, 2002). For instance, when software engineers document processes, they are often interested in the relationships amongst static activities. When industrial engineers discuss process, they most often focus on the dynamic linking of activities; for example, process flows. For this reason, the following are some definitions of process in general and in construction.

Johansson *et al.* (1993) defined a process as a set of linked activities that takes an input and transforms it to create an output, and it should add value to the input and create an output that is more useful and effective to the recipient. Davenport (1993) describes a process as a specific ordering of work activities across time and place, and which has a beginning and an end, and clearly identified inputs and outputs. Hammer and Champy (1993) remarked that a business process is a set of activities with one or more types of input that creates a valuable output for a customer. A process according to Earl and Khan (1994) is a lateral or horizontal organisational form that encapsulates the inter-dependence of tasks, roles, people, department and functions required to provide a customer with a product or service. In the same vein, Ahmed and Simintras (1996) defined a process as a system, which interlocks cross-functional flows of resources and deals with tasks that were previously considered as isolated in an integrated way. Evans and Lindsay (2008) define a process as how work creates value for customers. Kagioglou, *et al.* (1999) opined that lack of an established definition of a process in the construction industry has led the industry into using procurement systems rather than looking at the overall process as a whole entity. They asserted that a number of lessons could be learned from the manufacturing sector about the implementation and practical use of a 'process view' within the construction industry.

Whilst there are obvious similarities in the definitions, there seems general agreement that process involves a sequence of inter-dependent and linked procedures which, at every stage, utilise one or more resources (time, energy, money) to convert inputs (labour, material, equipments, etc) into outputs. These outputs then serve as inputs for the next stage, until a known goal or *objective* is achieved. In this respect, several authors on process improvement have argued that the change towards a business process approach is directly linked to a company's strategy, and that it would be impossible to create business processes to support a company's objectives if these were not known beforehand. The business objectives need to be linked directly to business strategic planning. Thus, processes are also, directly or indirectly, related to business strategic planning (Sommerville, 2007). Processes without connection to strategic planning have no reason to exist, because they are consumers of resources that add no value. For an effective management of construction project processes, project managers need to understand, control and improve them. In order to understand a process, Kloppenborg (2009) assert that the process boundaries need to be defined, as this will help prevent occurrence of future scope creep.

Another fundamental characteristic of business processes is that the quality of the process can often directly affect the quality of delivered products. In the manufacturing industry, there is a clear link between process and product quality, because the process is relatively easy to standardise and monitor. Once manufacturing systems are calibrated, they can be run repeatedly to output high-quality products. However, construction activities tend to be more bespoke in nature than manufacturing processes, so the influence of individual skills and experience is significant. In addition, construction is prone to many external factors that can influence the achievement of project objectives, namely adherence to the budget and schedule. There is therefore a need for a holistic improvement methodology to provide the means for generalising and describing the knowledge and experience in a structured way, that is, to some extent, transferable to other situations in terms of roles, tasks and the required skills. This can be achieved through a framework that integrates risk management at the planning stage for process improvement.

8.2.2   Classification of Business Processes

It is important to recognise that not every process in an organisation requires the same effort for improvement. For example, Evans and Lindsay (2008) classified business processes under value-creation and support categories. They argue that organisations need to understand their processes well and should differentiate between value-creation and support categories. This will differ across organisations, depending on the nature of the business. Since value-creation processes add, as the term suggests, value to end products and services, they warrant a higher level of attention than the support processes. Value creation processes are often termed core processes (Evans and Lindsay, 2008), since they are fundamental to businesses in maintaining and achieving sustainable competitive advantage. They drive the creation of products and services, and are critical to customer satisfaction. They can be said to have a major impact on the strategic goals of an organisation. Leading companies identify those value-creating processes that affect customer satisfaction throughout the value chain. On the other hand, support processes are those that are most important in supporting an organisation's core processes, employees and daily operations. They provide infrastructure for value-creation processes but, generally, do not add value directly to the product or service. Having now established an understanding of process, it is also important to reflect on process improvement. Process improvement concerns understanding existing processes and making them better in order to increase product quality and/or reduce costs and development time. According to Sommerville (2007), most of the literature on process improvement has focused on perfecting processes to improve product quality and, in particular, to reduce the number of defects in delivered product.

8.2.3   Process Improvement

According to Rohleder and Silver (1997), a survey of the business landscape shows widespread initiatives in process improvements and reengineering. Process improvement helps an organisation meet long-term goals and objectives. One key goal for all organisations is to meet the demands of customers – both internal and external. Customers needs change over time – whether due to economic factors, new product developments, mergers or acquisitions, expansion or contraction. Continuously reviewing processes for potential improvements and efficiencies enables companies to adapt effectively to their clients' changing needs. However, when engaging in true process improvement, organisations should seek to learn what causes things to happen in a process and to use this knowledge to reduce variation, remove activities that contribute no value to the product or service produced, and improve customer satisfaction. A team examines all of the factors affecting the process: the materials used in the process, the methods and machines used to transform the materials into a product or service, and the people who perform the work. Process improvement does not simply mean adopting or 'bolting on' a particular tool or model of a process that has been used elsewhere. Similar organisations that do similar things will have processes in common, however, there will always be some contextual factors, such as procedures and standards that influence the process. It is important that an organisation should always look on process improvement as being specific to itself, or a part of the larger organisation. Furthermore, process improvement initiatives are continuous and as organisations grow, they need to continuously analyse and refine their processes to ensure they are operating as effectively and efficiently as possible to gain competitive advantage. Kagioglou *et al.* (1999) concluded that construction process improvement/reengineering is an area where the construction industry in the UK needs to consider and adopt so that significant improvements in performance could be achieved.

8.2.4   Project and Process Improvement Failures

The aim of process improvement is to meet and often exceed customer expectation in products and services. Organisations through process improvement seek to improve their efficiency, reduce costs or increase revenues. However, with these good intents, too few of these efforts are completed or even partially successful. Many process improvement efforts have ended in failure. This leads one to question: 'Why do companies ever make such efforts in the first place?' A major reason for this is that when process improvements do succeed, they can have significant economic benefit. For example, Gilbert (1993) cited in Rohleder and Silver (1997), gave examples of huge cost savings resulting when the Electric Boat Division of General Dynamics Corporation improved its contracting process, which resulted in a 50% reduction in the number of process steps, eventually saving the company over $3 million annually. However, many factors can prevent the effective implementation of process improvement and hence restrict innovation and continuous improvement. Irani *et al.* (2000) identified some of these issues as:

- loss of nerve, focus and stamina;
- senior management who are comfortable in their ivory towers;
- lack of holistic focus and settling for minor improvement gains;
- human and organisational issues;
- organisation culture, attitude and skills;
- resources restriction; and
- fear of IT.

Bashein and Markus (1994) asserted that senior management commitment and sponsorship, realistic expectation, empowered and collaborative

Figure 8.1   Process improvement cycle.

workers, strategic context, shared vision, sound management practices and sufficient human and financial resources are positive preconditions for efficient business process improvement. According to Paper (1998), successful process improvement hinges on top management support, customer satisfaction, cross-functional teamwork and a systematic means of solving problems. The greatest obstacles faced by process improvement efforts are:

1. lack of sustained management commitment and leadership;
2. unrealistic scope and expectation; and
3. resistance to change.

8.2.5   Steps in a Process Improvement Model

Sommerville (2007) asserts that process improvement is a cyclical activity that involves three principal stages: process measurement, process analysis and process change (Figure 8.1).

Sommerville (2007) described process measurement as a stage where the attributes of the current project or the product is measured with the aim of improving the measures according to the goals of the organisation involved. Process analysis is a stage in process improvement where the current process is assessed to reveal process weaknesses and bottlenecks. Process models that describe the process, are usually developed during this stage, while process change is the stage where changes to the process that have been identified during analysis are introduced. In this context, processes can be improved in either a continuous or a breakthrough fashion. It is important for all project core team members and experts in a particular process to be thinking of ways they can improve at any time. Kloppenborg (2009) asserts that slow and steady improvement is a good foundation, but that sometimes substantial improvement may be what is needed.

Whichever one, or regardless of the size of improvement desired, many models exist to guide the effort, such as Six Sigma, that uses the define, measure, analyse, improve and control (DMAIC) methodology. In Kloppenborg (2009), the DMAIC methodology is seen as a 15-step process

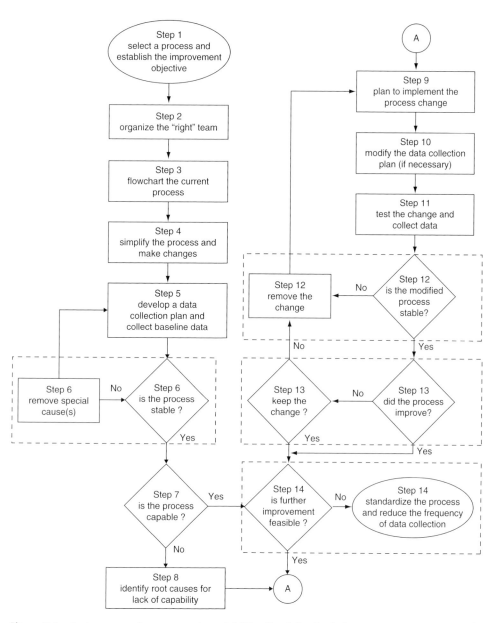

Figure 8.2 Basic process improvement model (*Handbook for Basic Process Improvement*, 1996). Reproduced by permission of the Balance Scorecard Institute.

comprising 5 project phases: define, measure, analyse, improve and control. However, most improvement models are based on the plan-do-check-act (PDCA) cycle, as contained in *Basic Process Improvement Handbook* (1996). This handbook presented a process improvement model, which has two parts:

1. a process simplification segment; and
2. a Plan-Do-Check-Act (PDCA) cycle (Figures 8.2 and 8.3).

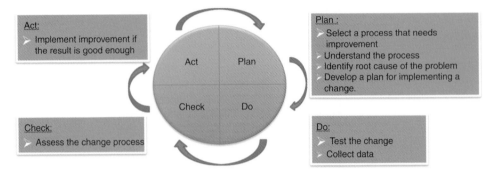

Figure 8.3 Plan-do-check-act cycle for process improvement. From Kloppenborg. *Aise-Contemp Proj Mgmt*, 1E. © 2009 South-Western, a part of Cengage Learning, Inc. Reproduced by permission. (www.cengage.com/permissions).

Table 8.1 Steps and actions in the process simplification segment (handbook for basic process improvement, 1996). Reproduced by permission of the Balance Scorecard Institute.

Steps	Description of actions
1	Select the process to be improved and establish a well-defined process improvement objective. The objective may be established by the team or come from outside.
2	Organize a team to improve the process. This involves selecting the "right" people to serve on the team; identifying the resources available for the improvement effort, such as people, time, money, and materials; setting reporting requirements; and determining the team's level of authority. These elements may be formalized in a written charter.
3	Define the current process using a flowchart. This tool is used to generate a step-by-step map of the activities, actions, and decisions which occur between the starting and stopping points of the process.
4	Simplify the process by removing redundant or unnecessary activities. People may have seen the process on paper in its entirety for the first time in Step 3. This can be a real eye-opener which prepares them to take these first steps in improving the process.
5	Develop a plan for collecting data and collect baseline data. The data will be used as the yardstick for comparison later in the model. This begins the evaluation of the process against the process improvement objective established in Step 1. The flowchart in Step 3 helps the team determine who should collect data and where in the process data should be collected.
6	Assess whether the process is stable. The team creates a control chart or run chart out of the data collected in Step 5 to gain better understanding of what is happening in the process. The follow-on actions of the team are dictated by whether special cause of variation is found in the process.
7	Assess whether the process is capable. The team plots a histogram to compare the data collected in Step 5 against the process improvement objective established in Step 1. Usually the process simplification actions in Step 4 are not enough to make the process capable of meeting the objective and the team will have to continue on to Step 8 in search of root causes.

The process simplification cycle consists of seven steps, and the process improvement is expected to start process improvement with these steps. Depending on the stability and capability of the process, the team may continue on to Step 8 or go directly to Step 14. The PDCA cycle, which is the second part of the improvement model, consists of seven steps (Steps 8 through 14) flowing from the process simplification segment. In the handbook, it is stated that using all 14 steps of the model should increase the team's process knowledge, broaden decision-making options and enhance the likelihood of satisfactory long-term results.

The PDCA cycle is similar to what was presented as plan, do, study and act in Deming's cycle (PDSA) – a tool that was developed and promoted by Edward Deming who worked with Japanese industry after World War II to improve quality. The cycle was named the 'Deming Cycle' by the Japanese sponsors of the work in 1950 (Evans and Lindsay, 2008).

From Table 8.1 it is evident that Step 7 marks the ends of the process simplification cycle. It should be emphasised that even if the data indicates that the process is meeting the objective, the team should consider whether it is feasible to improve the process further before going on to Step 14. In Step 8, which is the beginning of PDCA Cycle, the team should start by identifying what causes the product or service to be unsatisfactory. As the team plans a change, they normally conduct a test and collect data, evaluate test results to find out whether the process has improved, and decide whether to standardise or continue to improve the process.

8.3   Planning for Process Improvement

Companies often redesign business processes to achieve improvements in their performance, such as better service and quality (Lee and Ahn, 2008). Process improvement is a long-term approach to improving organisational performance, with substantially less risks of destroying value when compared to short-term approaches. Planning, according to the *Cambridge Advance Learner Dictionary Online* is the act of deciding how to do something. Kerzner (2009) defines planning as '… the function of selecting the enterprise objectives and establishing the policies, procedures and programs necessary for achieving them… by establishing a predetermined course of action within a forecasted environment.' This assertion advocates that without proper planning, programmes and projects can start-off 'behind the eight ball' and identifies consequences of poor planning to include:

1. project initiation without defined requirements;
2. wild enthusiasm;
3. disillusionment;
4. chaos;
5. search for the guilty;
6. punishment of innocent; and
7. promotion of the non-participants.

Table 8.2 Steps and actions in the plan-do-check-act cycle (handbook for basic process improvement, 1996). Reproduced by permission of the Balance Scorecard Institute.

Steps	Description of actions
8	Identify the root causes which prevent the process from meeting the objective. The team begins the Plan-Do-Check-Act Cycle here, using the cause-and-effect diagram or brainstorming tools to generate possible reasons why the process fails to meet the desired objective.
9	Develop a plan for implementing a change based on the possible reasons for the process's inability to meet the objective set for it. These root causes were identified in Step 8. The planned improvement involves revising the steps in the simplified flowchart created after changes were made in Step 4.
10	Modify the data collection plan developed in Step 5, if necessary
11	Test the changed process and collect data.
12	Assess whether the changed process is stable. As in Step 6, the team uses a control chart or run chart to determine process stability. If the process is stable, the team can move on to Step 13; if not, the team must return the process to its former state and plan another change.
13	Assess whether the change improved the process. Using the data collected in Step 11 and a histogram, the team determines whether the process is closer to meeting the process improvement objective established in Step 1. If the objective is met, the team can progress to Step 14; if not, the team must decide whether to keep or discard the change.
14	Determine whether additional process improvements are feasible. The team is faced with this decision following process simplification in Step 7 and again after initiating an improvement in Steps 8 through 13. In Step 14, the team has the choice of embarking on continuous process improvement by re-entering the model at Step 9, or simply monitoring the performance of the process until further improvement is feasible.

With these possible consequences of poor planning, it is evident that in every endeavour, it is important to prepare a road map as to what needs to be done, who is responsible for it and when it should be delivered. Thus, planning for project improvement can be described as all effort geared towards determining what needs to be done, by whom and by when, that is, in order to achieve desired process improvement, it is also necessary to ascertain which process needs improvement, how these are going to be improved, who will carry out the improvement and when this is expected. Similar to general project planning, where a project management plan is developed, the outcome of process improvement planning is the production of process improvement plan, which forms part of the overall process management plan.

The planning for process improvement stage involves prioritising the key areas for improvement, and identifying the process whose improvement in the project will make the greatest difference. The improvement plan should contain a small number of 'breakthrough' process (i.e. those value-creation process within the organisation) rather than many minor process or support processes relating to parts of the organisation. This justifies the need for adequate knowledge of the processes in the organisation and the need to be able to classify them as either value-creation (core processes) or support processes. Kloppenborg (2009) opines that to manage project processes effectively, project managers need to understand, control and improve them. Similar to the project manager's need to produce a comprehensive project management plan (PMP) for effective management of a project, managing project processes requires detailed planning to establish how the improvement process will progress.

A cursory review of the actions involved in the planning stage for process improvement in the model in Figure 8.3 and supported by Tables 8.1 and 8.2, shows that actions in Step 1 through to Step 10 can be regarded as planning for process improvement stage. Where possible, improvement projects should be allocated to improvement teams who are given complete responsibility to plan and implement improvement actions. Ideally, these teams should comprise staff involved in the particular process at all levels. The improvement plan is reported on a periodical basis to senior management. Thus, for improvements to be worthwhile, they should aspire to achieve sustainable change. This may be through focusing the exercise on identifying and tackling the root causes of the problem, changing the organisation's management system in line with the proposed improvement, embedding changes into process documentation, and incorporating training and development plans where necessary.

8.4   Risk and its Management

The main objective of Project Management is to maintain a healthy balance between the three conventional objectives of any construction project (i.e. cost, time and quality), which is often referred to as the 'iron triangle'. Anything that can threaten the achievement of these objectives is considered as a risk to the project, which can prevent the project manager from meeting cost, time, quality and any other objectives predefined for the project. Risk can affect productivity, performance, quality and budget of a construction project (Kangari, 1995). Risk is therefore a permanent element in every decision-making process, including design and planning decisions and is inherent in every human endeavour, which can prove difficult to deal with. As such, it is important to develop a proper risk management framework, both in theoretical and in practical terms (Wang *et al.*, 2004). Many researchers have defined risk based on their perceptions and the needs or outcomes of their studies. For example, Wideman (1986) and Akintoye and Macleod (1997) defined risk as the likelihood of unforeseen factors occurring, which would adversely affect the successful completion of the project in terms of cost, time and quality. Cooper and Chapman (1987) defined risk as 'the exposure to the possibility of economic or financial loss or gain, physical damage or injury, or delay as a consequence of uncertainty associated with pursuing a particular course of action.' In this respect, Skorupka (2008) noted that the term 'risk' was derived from an Italian verb 'riscare', which means 'to have the cheek to do something'. Risk to the economist focuses on the financial aspects, engineers relate risk to process disruption and cost, the military consider the risk of completing a task, police officers treat risk as threat to the citizens, and employees may see risk as being dismissed from work. It is therefore an imperative to clearly specify the meaning of risk in this respect. The definition given in the Project Management Body of Knowledge Guide (PMBOK, 2004) is therefore adopted in this chapter.

PMBOK Guide (2004) defines project risk as an uncertain event or condition that, if it occurs, has a positive or a negative effect on at least one project objective, such as time cost, scope or quality. Two things are important in this definition. The first is the possibility of loss or gain in any risk situation. Risk is about deviation from a desired target, and loss and gain are possibilities at all times. It is possible to have cost over-run or cost under-run, and it is also possible to have time over-run or under-run. However, when there is positive gain, most people are not concerned, but when adverse effects are experienced (i.e. when the project manager fails to meet the set objectives), people get angry or are unhappy with the outcome. It is now commonly realised that risk and opportunity should therefore go together.

Kloppenborg (2009) suggested two tactics that project managers and teams can adopt in addressing risks. First, any risk that may inhibit success-ful project completion (to the satisfaction of stakeholders, on time, and on budget) needs to be identified, and a plan must be developed to overcome it. Second, a risk that can create a positive effect on a project can be considered as an opportunity to complete the project better, faster and or at lower cost, and a plan should be developed to capitalise upon it. The implication is that risk has the potential for causing loss, often called the downside risk. According to Smith *et al.* (2002), the loss can be financial, time, corporate image, poor quality, etc. There is also the possibility of the event leading to favourable outcomes, whereby things turn out better than what was planned; this is referred to as the upside of risk.

The focus in this chapter is on the downside of risk, that is, the unfavour-able impacts those events can cause on the project objectives when they occur, since the overriding intention of most risk management actions is to minimise potential losses. Given this, risk emanates from the uncertainty associated with pursuing a particular cause of action. Uncertainty derives from the absence of sufficient information about the action and/or the possible out-comes. From an information perspective, it is possible to identify two levels of uncertainty. The first level of uncertainty is experienced when decision makers have sufficient information to make probability judgement about a particular event, even though information may be incomplete (i.e. it is pos-sible to say this event is more probable than not). This is the region of risk management. Risk then is concerned with being able to make probability judgement. A second level of uncertainty is experienced when the informa-tion available to decision makers is so bad or insufficient that it is not possi-ble to make probability judgement. Such a situation is called pure uncertainty. There are procedures for dealing with pure uncertainty in economic analysis, but managing pure uncertainty is outside the scope of this chapter. In the context of process improvement, risks are those factors that can jeopardise the successful implementation of process improvement effort or the realisation of the expected benefits (i.e. efficiency, reduction in cost or increase in revenues). This therefore underscores the need for their management.

8.4.1   The Risk Management Process

Kezsbom and Edward (2001) stated that risk management is an important and integral element of project management. All managers manage risk either consciously or unconsciously, but rarely systematically. Managing risk is a forward thinking act, where individuals or groups take a look at the future of a particular process or endeavour to identify, in a responsible manner, the downsides or upsides of actions or inactions. With this, balanced thinking is achieved, which provides a framework to facilitate more effective decision making. Risk Management is therefore all about maximising opportunity, that is, increasing the probability and impact of positive events, and decreasing the probability and impact of events adverse to the project. While corporate governance can be said to be the 'glue' that holds the organisation together in pursuit of its objectives, risk management provides the resilience. Risk management can therefore be said to be a formal and orderly process of systematically identifying, analysing and responding to risks throughout the life cycle of a project, to obtain the optimum degree of risk elimination, mitigation and/or control. Smith and Merritt (2002) posit that project risk management has become a popular management topic because many organisations now recognise the high cost of dealing with project problems that could have been anticipated. Risk management continues to be a major feature of project management and is becoming increasingly important globally. The popularity of risk management in the management arena can be seen as a product of the following factors:

- global economic problem/budgetary constraints;
- recognition of true cost of underperformance;
- legislations;
- competitiveness of global markets; and
- true payback of risk management.

The PMBOK Guide (2004) defines risk management as the processes concerned with identifying, analysing and responding to uncertainty throughout the project life cycle. It includes maximising the result of positive events and minimising the consequences of adverse events. The body of knowledge asserts 'to be successful, the organisation should be committed to addressing the management of risk proactively and consistently throughout the project.' Dey (1999) suggested that project risk management processes are threefold:

1. identifying risk factors;
2. analysing their effect; and
3. responding to risk.

Winegard and Warhoe (2003) prescribed that the risk management process should follow five consecutive steps:

1. identification of risk;
2. risk assessment and analysis;
3. risk mitigation, i.e. development of risk reduction and reaction to threats;
4. implementation of risk management plan; and
5. review and correction of risk assessment.

PMBOK (2004) provides the project risk management processes through six stages as:

1. *Risk Management Planning*: deciding how to approach, plan and execute the risk management activities for a project;
2. *Risk Identification*: determining which risks might affect the project and documenting their characteristics;
3. *Qualitative Risk Analysis*: prioritising risks for subsequent further analysis or action by assessing and combining their probability of occurrence and impact;
4. *Quantitative Risk Analysis*: numerically analysing the effect on overall project objectives of identified risks;
5. *Risk Response Planning*: developing options and actions to enhance opportunities, and to reduce threats to project objectives, and
6. *Risk Monitoring and Control*: tracking identified risks, monitoring residual risks, identifying new risks, executing risk response plans, and evaluating their effectiveness throughout the project life cycle.

It should be noted that risk management is not just a one-way process but rather an iterative process, as these processes often interact with each other, and also with processes in other knowledge areas of project management. Each process can involve effort from one or more persons (or groups) based on the needs of the project. Each process occurs at least once in every project and occurs in one or more project phases, if the project is divided into phases. It is evident then that risk management needs to be integrated at the planning phase of process improvement, which is the stage at which process improvement areas are identified in order to understand process issues, issues to be dealt with and plans for improvement. Before moving on to how risk management can be integrated into planning for process improvement, it is important to understand the different stages involved in the risk management planning process.

8.4.2   Risk Management Planning

Winning is the science of being totally prepared; and to fail to plan, is planning to fail. These two popular sayings highlight the importance of planning to most enterprises and most often such planning is taken for granted. Kerzner (2009) asserts that the primary benefit of not planning is that failure will then come as a complete surprise rather than being preceded by periods of worry and depression. Risk Management Planning is therefore a crucial part of the risk management process, and in fact determines the success of all the other five processes. To be totally prepared means to be ready to deal with any situation. It therefore can be described as all efforts geared towards deciding how best to approach and conduct risk management activities for a particular project or process. Just as in general project planning where a project management plan is developed, the outcome of Risk Management Planning is the production of a risk management plan (RMP) that forms part of the overall project management plan (PMP). Depending on the size and the complexity of the project, for example, in small projects, risk management may be informal, whereas for large, complex projects, management needs to develop and prepare a written RMP.

When preparing the RMP, managers rely greatly on a good historic database that details and records the attitudes and tolerance of their organisations and the people they have worked with towards risk. Moreover, it is possible that their organisations have pre-defined approaches to risk management. For instance, the organisation may have developed standard templates for risk planning. Then it will be easy for the manager to make use of the template, but with some level of care. This is so because, though it is possible to generalise or adopt a given risk template for all projects in an organisation, some projects may have specific or unique risk elements inherent in them. Therefore, having considered the attitude towards risk as well as the risk tolerance of the organisation, managers need to evaluate project risks through the statement of work (SOW) and examine the work breakdown structure (WBS) for the project to be able to understand the sources of risks.

The roles and responsibilities of the people that will be involved in risk planning could also be assessed using the SOW and WBS. This allows thorough evaluation of the risks associated with sub-tasks separately (Dey et al., 1994). In this respect, a good RMP gives a brief summary of the approach, tools and data sources that are to be used to perform risk management on the project. It should also define the roles of the risk management team members, for every activity in the risk management process, along with their responsibilities. The plan also assigns resources, and contains estimates of costs needed for risk management, and also defines when and how often the risk management process will be performed throughout the project life cycle. Finally, the RMP provides a structure that ensures a comprehensive process of systematic identification of risk to a consistent level of detail and contributes to the effectiveness and quality of risk identification, which is the next process in risk management. To be able to develop the RMP, there is a need for project team members to hold a planning meeting. This meeting is usually attended by the project manager and some selected project team members, depending on the complexity of the project, and by other stakeholders, that is, anyone in the organisation with responsibility to manage the risk planning and execution. In the context of process improvement, this meeting can also involve process team leaders within an organisation.

In summary, if the organisation has pre-defined approaches to risk management, for instance, standard templates for risk categories and definitions of terms, such as levels of risk, probability by type of risk, impact by type of objectives and the probability and impact matrix can then be tailored to a specific project. In the absence of such predefined templates for planning, the project manger will need to create new templates, and discuss these with others who are working or have worked on similar projects. This helps to establish the standard for use on subsequent projects. Risk planning therefore helps managers to know the feasibility of risk management activities in order to decide whether the effort is worthwhile when compared to the resources/time expended against the risk exposure.

8.4.3   Risk Identification

Risk identification is essentially a process for uncovering any risks that could potentially afflict a process. This step is of considerable importance because other processes such as risk analysis and response can only be performed on the identified potential risks. In this context, the process must involve an investigation into all the potential sources of process risks and their consequences. Risk identification must be done iteratively as new risks may be identified as the process of improvement progresses throughout its life cycle. The risk identification process is beneficial to process improvement as it focuses the attention of process managers on strategies for the control and detection of potential risks. This highlights those areas where further efforts are needed. Risk identification is a simple but difficult task, because there are no absolute procedures that may be used to identify risks in a process. Often, managers rely heavily on their experience and on the insight of other key personnel involved in the process. Depending on the process documentation available and the nature of the process, a variety of thought starters can prompt risk discovery. Regarding risk, Smith and Merritt (2002) noted that managers need to focus on the interface between the consultant and the client, between departments of the client organisation, between phases or tasks of a client process, or between geographic areas. They further suggest that the project schedule should clearly show dependencies between tasks, to help pinpoint risk-prone areas. Alternatively, managers may use process maps that show interfaces between processes or tasks. Flanagan and Norman (1993) compared attempts of risk identification in projects with multiple layers of planning, complex vertical and horizontal interactions.

Organisations that keep good records of their past projects or project managers that conduct reviews of their projects at closure, can use this experience of tacit knowledge and lessons learned to garner insights on potential risks. Furthermore, a good project scope statement will detail all assumptions in the project; it is then easier to evaluate uncertainty and determine project assumptions. The outcome of the risk identification exercise is a document called the 'risk register'. This document includes *inter alia*, a list of identified risks, including their root causes and uncertain project assumptions. Often at the risk identification stage, the potential responses to a risk may be identified. These potential responses will also be recorded in the risk register, which becomes a useful input to the risk response planning process.

Thus, in order to choose the right technique for identifying risk, practitioners should consider several factors, such as the organisation's objectives, the nature of the project in terms of sizes, duration and the company's strategies for risk management.

The following are some of the tools and techniques suggested by the PMBOK guide (2004):

- documentation review;
- information gathering techniques;
- checklist analysis;
- assumptions analysis; and
- diagramming techniques.

These can be supported by information gathering techniques for risk identification, which include:

- brainstorming;
- Delphi technique;
- interviewing;
- root cause identification, and
- strengths, weakness, opportunities and threats (SWOT) analysis.

8.4.4   Qualitative Risk Analysis

In the risk analysis stage, managers try to estimate the overall magnitude of the risk and the expected losses. Typically, the risk event drivers and their impact drivers are determined at this stage. Any risk event that cannot be justified through probability of occurrence and impact are automatically dropped from the risk register. Broadly, risks can be analysed either qualitatively or quantitatively, depending on the purpose, required degrees of detail, and data and resources available for analysis. In qualitative analysis, risks are subjectively estimated and ranked in a descriptive manner. Jiang *et al.* (2002) described qualitative risk analysis as the process of prioritising risks for subsequent further analysis or action by assessing and combining their probability and impact. Qualitative estimation can be used for the following purposes:

- as an initial screening activity to identify risks that require more detailed estimation, when it provides sufficient information for decision making; or
- where available data or resources are insufficient for a quantitative estimation.

Because of such analysis, risks can be rated, for example, as high, moderate or low. Usually qualitative risk analysis is a rapid and cost-effective means of establishing priorities for risk response planning, and lays the foundation for quantitative risk analysis. As in risk identification, review of process documentation of past experiences or lessons learned from previous projects can be good sources of information to prioritise the identified risks. With this, an update is made to the risk register. Risks are listed in terms of their probability and impact in matrix form, which the project manager can use to focus attention on those risks with high significance to the project, where responses can lead to better project outcomes. In the risk register, risks may also be grouped by categories showing the root causes of risks or areas of the project that require particular attention or urgent attention and those that can be handled later. From this, some risk items will go straight to the response stage, while some may require further analysis, for example, quantitative risk analysis.

8.4.5   Quantitative Risk Analysis

Quantitative risk analyses are performed on risks that have been prioritised through the qualitative risk analysis process as potentially and substantially influencing the project's competing demands (PMBOK, 2004). Quantitative risk analysis is the process of numerically analysing the effect on overall project objectives (Kloppenborg and Deborah, 2004). The evaluation of both consequences and probability are based on data from a variety of sources, for example, past project records, collected field data, experimental data (including prototype testing), etc. Quantitative risk analysis is often used when the need to predict with confidence the probability of completing a project on time, on budget, at the agreed-upon scope, and/or the agree-upon quality is critical (Kloppenborg, 2009). Dey and Ogunlana (2004) identified some of the quantitative risk analysis tools and techniques currently in use as:

- Statistical Probability Distribution;
- Simple Multi-Attribute Rating Technique;
- Expected Value Technique;
- Sensitivity Analysis;
- Decision Trees;
- Bayes' Theorem;
- Simulation;
- Utility Theory;
- Analytic Hierarchy Process;
- Fuzzy-set Theory;
- Neuro-Fuzzy Networks, and
- Financial Methods.

After the identified risk have been analysed quantitatively, the risk register initiated in the risk identification stage is then updated accordingly, where risks are prioritised according to the level or threat posed, or opportunity offered.

8.4.6   Risk Response Planning

After the risk is estimated, it should be determined whether the risk level is acceptable or not by comparing it with the acceptance criteria determined at the risk management planning stage. Risk response planning therefore involves determining in advance how to respond to each major risk. Minor risks are handled by simply being aware of their potential and dealing with them if and when they occur. Kloppenborg (2009) identify six types of risk response strategies that can be applied to major risks as:

1. avoid
2. transfer
3. mitigate
4. accept
5. research, and
6. exploit.

PMBOK (2004) categorised risk response under four main headings:

- strategies for threats (i.e. those risks that have negative impacts) are avoid, transfer and mitigate;
- strategies for positive risks (i.e. opportunities) are exploit, share and enhance;
- strategies for both threats and opportunities is acceptance; and
- contingent response strategies, which are strategies, put in place for use only if certain events occur.

It must be stated that the approaches are not mutually exclusive, and in most cases, their combination will provide the most efficient solution. It is also important to note that risk response measures should be addressed as part of the initial risk assessment during the planning stage, as many risk response measures may be impossible or costly to implement once the structure has been commissioned. After proper consideration of alternatives for risk response, the most appropriate ones should be selected and implemented. Since new risks could be introduced by the risk treatment, they should also be identified, assessed, treated and monitored. For action plans to work, they must be taken seriously. This means they become another task in the project and require budget, schedule and labour resources, which is no different from other project tasks (Smith and Merrit, 2002). Communication and consultation are important considerations at each step of the risk management process. Effective communication can help ensure that those responsible for implementing risk management on the process under improvement and those with stakes, understand the basis on which decisions are made and why particular actions are required. Since stakeholders have significant impacts on the decisions made, it is important that their perceptions of risk, as well as their perceptions of benefits, are identified and documented, and that the underlying reasons for them are understood and addressed appropriately.

8.4.7   Risk Monitoring and Control

Risk monitoring and control is the process of identifying, analysing and planning for newly arising risks, keeping track of the identified risks and those on the watch list, reanalysing existing risks, monitoring trigger conditions for contingency plans, monitoring residual risks, and reviewing the execution of risk responses, while evaluating their effectiveness (PMBOK, 2004). It is therefore evident that under risk monitoring and control, managers try to focus on the proposed processes and responses proffered for the identified risks. The outputs of the other five stages must be kept under review as things evolve. Changes in the environment, or simply the discovery of better information, may render the original assessment out of date, thereby triggering the need for reassessment. There should be periodic reassessment of risks (i.e. re-measurement) and risk audits. Risk audits examine and document the effectiveness of risk responses in dealing with identified risks and their root causes, as well as the effectiveness of the risk management process. Thus, Kerzner (2009) commented that risk monitoring and control is not a problem-solving technique but, rather, a proactive technique to obtain objective information on the progress to date of reducing risks to acceptable levels. Earned Value Analysis or other methods of project variance and trend analysis (e.g. programme metrics, schedule performance monitoring and technical performance measurement) could be used to monitor overall performance; and deviation from the baseline plan may indicate the potential impact of new threats. It is not generally necessary to begin the whole process over again when this happens, unless the change or deviation is particularly profound, but those parts that are directly affected by changing circumstances must be brought up to date.

8.5   Integrating Risk Management into Planning for Process Improvement

Having understood what the actions are, in terms of risk management and planning for process improvement, and where planning for improvement should be situated, it is important to highlight the need for integration of risk management into planning for process improvement. When management sets a goal, these may sometimes be missed because of foreseeable and unforeseeable circumstances. Risk is predominantly inherent in most human endeavours, including planning for process improvement. It is also important to acknowledge that improving one process may have unintended knock-on effects on other processes. For example, if a property development company makes an improvement in its sales order processing, once that process is improved, the improvement will affect order fulfilment process – the delivery of the product to customers. The improvement in sales order processing may apparently create a backlog in order fulfilment in the production department. Implementing a proper project management approach – effective project risk management – would have addressed such issues as part of the risk planning, and the order fulfilment processes should have been reviewed as an extension of the sales order process. In other words, the initial process (i.e. sales order processing) would have been assessed to determine if making changes to it would be beneficial to the company as a whole, given investments needed in other parts of the company.

Chrissis *et al.* (2003) stated that there is a need for risk management integration into day-to-day decision making, and that by employing a collective set of activities for identifying, assessing, handling, monitoring and communicating risk information, this could uncover potential issues before they can disrupt normal operations. They explain that two areas were targeted for proactive risk management:

1. change as a major source for introducing new risks into a system or process – risk assessment will be performed whenever change to the baseline is proposed; and
2. communication and monthly reviews of significant risks as proactive measures – the presentation of risk information from one programme element may help identify collateral risks in other areas.

Therefore, since planning for process improvement can be conceptualised as a stage, managers seek to propose a plan for change to a system or process, by understanding that the process may need improvement, cognisant of threats and opportunities along the paths to achieving this change. This is also true when the change is finally introduced. It is important, therefore, that risk management is integrated into planning for process improvement. In addition, it is known that risk can affect productivity, performance, quality and budget of a construction project (Kangari, 1995). It implies therefore that at the planning for process improvement stage, where decisions as to 'whether to improve', 'what processes need to be improved', 'when to improve them', 'how they should be improved' and 'alternative plans on the steps to follow in their improvement' are taken, require adequate risk management. This is because organisations need to be able to make informed decisions to help achieve goals or objectives, improve efficiency and procure competitive advantage.

Considering the activities or the types of questions planning seeks to answer, it is evident that after actions have been completed in a process simplification segment (Table 8.1, Steps 1–7), it is at that point (i.e. starting from Step 8) that risk management needs to be incorporated (Table 8.2, Steps 9 and 10). It is the point where questions such as 'Are there any risks associated with the proposed change?' 'What will the change cost?' and 'What are the costs aside from money?' It includes time, number of people, materials used and other factors. 'Which employees will be affected by the change?' 'How will they be affected (positively or adversely)?' 'Who should be responsible for implementing the change?' 'What has to be done to implement the change?' 'Where will the change be implemented?' 'How will the implementation be controlled?' 'At what steps in the process will measurements be taken?' 'How will data be collected?' 'Is a pilot (small-scale) test necessary prior to full implementation of the change?' 'How long will the test last?' 'What is the probability of success?' 'Is there a downside to the proposed change?' Risk management offers answers to all of these and many other questions. Moreover, as the team picks one of the processes to work on, after considering the possible root causes identified in Step 8, they can then develop a plan to implement a change in the process to reduce or eliminate the root cause. The change action developed for implementation can be a source of another potential risk to the organisation in achieving desired objectives (Pipattanapiwong *et al.*, 2003). It is only through deploying project management techniques such as risk management that this potential risk can be exposed and adequately mitigated against '*ab initio*'. Although risk management process can be introduced at any time into process improvement, at a particular point – planning for process improvement – it has the potential to yield the most significant organisational, operational or external benefits to the organisation. It is proposed therefore that risk management processes should be installed at the planning stage for process improvement (Figure 8.4).

8.6   Conclusion

This chapter described process improvement initiatives, along with the need to have clearly articulated mechanisms in place to help organisational performance. In this respect, business process was seen as a series of steps, both at the process simplification stage and at the plan-do-study-act stage. It was argued that risk predominantly emanates from uncertainties associated with pursuing certain causes of action. Therefore, it is important when planning an improvement exercise, to acknowledge that unforeseen events may (and often do) occur, which can adversely affect outcomes in terms of cost, time and quality. The need for risk management integration when planning for process improvement was therefore stressed in this chapter. In addition, organisations need to understand (and should be able to differentiate) their core/value-creation business processes and supportive processes; and greater effort should be given to improving value-creation processes, rather than wasting resources on improving supportive processes that add little or no value to the entire system. There is also a need for effective communication and adequate consultation at every stage in risk management process. This is urgent, as improvement teams, and those affected by the improvement, should understand what decisions are made, and why improvement interventions are required, as this can help create acceptance (i.e. facilitate buy-in) for changes.

Project risk management was also presented, and risk management integration into the planning stage of process improvement was advocated, particularly as an iterative exercise, rather than a single point intervention. It is through this holistic approach that practitioners can critically appraise how work is being performed, to help understand unforeseen events that may impinge on process improvement outcomes. By way of conclusion therefore, practitioners in the construction industry need to be aware that when developing and implementing a plan for process improvement, it is essential to integrate risk treatment strategies in order to be effective. Achievement of goals and objectives of any proposed plan depends on proper integration of

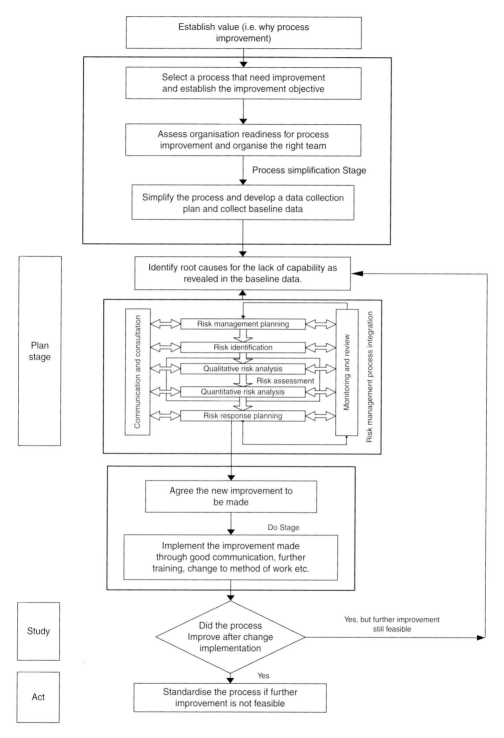

Figure 8.4   Risk management integration in planning for process improvement.

risk management at the planning stage. Only then, can the capital invested by the organisation in process improvement produce the desired results, for example, increased market share, improved customer satisfaction levels, enhanced profitability through cost, time and quality performance, etc.

References

Ahmed, P.K. and Simintras, A.C. (1996) Conceptualizing business process reengineering. *Business Process Management Journal*, 2(2), 73–92.

Akintoye, A.S. & MacLeod, M.J. (1997) Risk analysis and management in construction. *International Journal of Project Management*, 15(1), 31–38.

Amaratunga, D., Sarshar, M. & Baldry, D. (2002) Process improvement in facilities management: the SPICE approach. *Business Process Management Journal*, 8(4), 318–337.

Banwell, H. (1964) *Report of the Committee on the Placing and Management of Contracts for Building and Civil Engineering Works*. HMSO, London.

Bashein, M.L & Marcus, M.L. (1994). Preconditions for BPR success. *Information Systems Management*, 11(2), 7–13.

Blick, G., Gulledge, T. & Sommer, R. (2000) Defining business process requirements for large-scale public sector ERP implementations: a case study. *Proceedings of the European Conference on Information Systems*, Wirtschafts Universitat, Wien.

British Property Federation (BPF) (1983) Manual of the BPF system for building design and construction. In: ed. Kagioglou, M, Cooper, R. & Aouad (1999), *Reengineering the UK Construction Industry: The Process Protocol*. British Property Federation, London. Available from http://www.processprotocol.com/pdf/cpr99.pdf (accessed 7 March 2011).

Cambridge Advance Learner Dictionary. Available from http://dictionary.cambridge.org/ (accessed 7 March 2011).

Chrissis, M.B., Konrad, M. & Shrum, S. (2003) *CMMI Guidelines for Process Integration and Product Improvement*, Software Engineering Institute (SEI) Series. Addison Wesley Publishing Co, London.

Cooper, D.F. & Chapman, C.B. (1987). *Risk Analysis for Large Projects – Models, Methods and Cases*. John Wiley & Sons, Inc, New York.

Davenport, T.H. (1993), *Process Innovation – Reengineering Work through Information Technology*, Harvard Business School Press, Boston, MA.

Dey, P. (1999), Process reengineering for effective implementation of projects. *International Journal of Project Management*, 17(3), 147–159.

Dey, P., Tabucanon, M.T. & Ogunlana, S.O. (1994) Planning for project control through risk analysis: The case of a pipeline project in India. *International Journal of Project Management*, 12(1), February, 23–33.

Dey, P.K. & Ogunlana, S.O. (2004) Selection and application of risk management tools and techniques for build-operate-transfer projects. *Industrial Management & Data Systems*, 104(4), 334–346.

Earl, M. & Khan, B. (1994) How new is business process redesign? *European Management* Journal, 12(1), 20–30.

Edwards, C., Braganza, A. & Lambert, R. (2000) Understanding and managing process initiatives: A framework for developing consensus. *Knowledge and Process Management*, 7(1), 29–36.

Egan, J. (1998) *Rethinking Construction*. Department of the Environment, Transport and the regions, HMSO, London.

Evans, J.R. & Lindsay, W.M. (2008) *The Management and Control of Quality*, 7th edn. South-Western Learning, Canada.

Flanagan, R. & Norman, G. (1993) *Risk Management and Construction*. Blackwell Scientific Publications, London.

Florac, W.A., Park, R.E. & Carleton, A.D. (1997) *Practical Software Measurement: Measuring for Process Management and Improvement*. CMU/SEI-97-HB-003. The Software Engineering Institution, Pittsburgh. PA.

Gilbert, P.A. (1993) The road to business process improvement – can we get there from here? *Production and Inventory Management Journal*. **34**, 80–86.

Grimsey, D. & Lewis, M.K. (2002) Evaluating the risks of public private partnerships for infrastructure projects. *International Journal of Project Management*, **20**, 107–118.

Gulledge, T.R. & Sommer, R.A. (2002) Business process management: public sector implications. *Business Process Management Journal*, **8**(**4**), 364–376.

Handbook for Basic Process Improvement (1996) Available from http://www.balancedscorecard.org/portals/0/pdf/bpihndbk.pdf (accessed 10 September 2010).

Hammer, M. & Champy, J. (1993) *Reengineering the Corporation: A Manifesto for Business Revolution*. Harper Business, New York.

Irani, Z., Hlupic, V., Baldwin, L.P. & Love, P.E.D. (2000) Reengineering manufacturing processes through simulation modelling. *Journal of Logistics and Information Management*, **13**(**1**), 7–13.

Jiang, J.J., Chen, E. & Klein, G. (2002) The importance of building a foundation for user involvement in information system projects. *Project Management Journal*, **22** (**1**), 20–26.

Johansson, H.J., McHugh, B., Pendlebury, A.J. & Wheeler, W.A. (1993) *Business Process Reengineering, Breakpoint Strategies for Market Dominance*. John Wiley & Sons, Ltd, Chichester, UK.

Kagioglou, M., Cooper, R. & Aouad, G. (1999) *Reengineering the UK Construction Industry: The Process Protocol*. Available from at http://www.processprotocol.com/pdf/cpr99.pdf (accessed 7 March 2011).

Kangari, R. (1995) Risk management perceptions and trends of US: Construction. *ASCE Journal of Construction Engineering and Management*, **121**(**4**), 422–429.

Kerzner, H. (2009) *Project Management A Systems Approach to Planning, scheduling, and Controlling*, 10th edn. John Wiley & Sons, Inc, Hoboken, NJ.

Kezsbom, D.S. & Edward, K.A. (2001) *The New Dynamic Project Management*. John Wiley & Sons, Inc, New York.

Kloppenborg, T.J. (2009) *Project Management A Contemporary Approach*, International student edn. South-Western Cengage Learning. Canada.

Kloppenborg, T.J. & Deborah, T. (2004) Using a project leadership framework to avoid and mitigate information technology project risks. In: ed. Slevin, D.P., Cleland, D.I. & Pinto, J.K., *Innovations: Project Management Research*. Project Management Institute, Newton Square, PA.

Latham, M. (1994) *Constructing the Team*. HMSO, London.

Lee, S. & Ahn, H. (2008) Assessment of process improvement from organisational change. *Information and Management*, **45**, 270–280.

Momoh, J. & Ruhe, G. (2006) Release planning process improvement – An industrial case study. *Software Process Improvement and Practice*, **11**, 295–307.

Paper, D. (1998) Business process reengineering: Creating the conditions for success. *Long Range Planning*, **31**(**3**), 426–435.

Paulk, M.C., Curtis, B., Chrissis, B. & Weber, C.V. (1993) *Capability Maturity Model for Software*, Version 1.1 Tech Report, CMU/SEI-93-TR-24. Carnegie Mellon University, Pittsburgh, PA.

Pipattanapiwong, J., Ogunlana, S.O. & Watanabe, T. (2003) Multi-party risk management process for a construction project. In: ed. Akintoye, A., Beck, M. & Hardcastle, C., *Public Private Partnership: Managing Risks and Opportunities*, Chapter 16. Blackwell Science, Oxford. 351–367.

PMBOK Guide (2004) *A Guide to the Project Management Body of Knowledge*, 3rd edn. Project Management Institute, Newtown Square, PA.

Pritchard, J. & Armistead, C. (1999) Business process management – Lessons from European business. *Business Process Management Journal*, **5**(1), 10–35.

Robinson, G.D. (1991) *Continuous Process Improvement*. Free Press, New York.

Rohleder, T.R. & Silver, E.A. (1997) A tutorial on business process improvement. *Journal of Operation Management*, **15**, 139–154.

Saiedan, H. & Kuzara, N. (1995) SEI capability maturity model's impact on contractors. *IEEE Computer*, **28, January**, 16–26.

Sarshar, M., Hutchinson, A., Aouad, G., Barrett, P., Minnikin, J. & Shelley, C. (1998) *Standardised Process Improvement for Construction Enterprises (SPICE)*. Proceedings of 2nd European Conference on Product and Process Modelling, Watford.

Sarshar, M., Finnemore, M. & Haigh, R. (1999) SPICE: Is the capability maturity model applicable in the construction industry. *Proceedings of 8th International Conference on durability of Building Materials and Components (CIB W78)*, 30 May–3 June, Vancouver, BC.

Skorupka, D. (2008) Identification and initial risk assessment of construction projects in Poland. *Journal of Management in Engineering*, **24**(3), 120–127.

Smith, C.M.C. & Merritt, G.M. (2002) Managing consulting project risk. *Consulting to Management*, **13**(3), 7–13.

Sommerville, I. (2007) *Software Engineering*, 8th edn. Addison-Wesley Publishing Co, London.

Wang, S.Q., Dulaimi, M.F. & Aguria, M.Y (2004) Risk management framework for construction projects in developing countries. *Construction Management and Economics*, **22**, 237–252.

Wideman, R.M. (1986) Risk Management. *Project Management Journal*, **17**(4), 20–62.

Winegard, A. & Warhoe, S.P. (2003) Understanding risk to mitigate changes and avoid disputes. AACE *International Transactions*. The Association for the Advancement of Cost Engineering, Orlando, FL.

Zahran, S. (1998) *Software Process Improvement: Practical Guidelines for Business Success*. Addison Wesley Publishing Co., Reading, MA.

Modern Methods of Construction

Wafaa Nadim

9.1 Introduction

The construction industry is widely acknowledged for its vital economic role and contribution to countries' GDP. In addition to this economic importance, the construction industry also accounts for a high political, environmental and social profile, which is attributed to its key role in providing housing, its impact on the environment, as well as being a major employer (EC, 2006). Over time, construction practices, methods and materials have continuously evolved to fulfil nations' needs (Ngowi *et al.*, 2005). The amount of raw material and natural resources used in construction for creating and operating the built environment is estimated to exceed those consumed in any other sector (EC, 2006).

From a scope perspective, the construction industry is subjected to two definitions, namely a 'narrow' definition and a 'broad' definition. The 'narrow' definition mainly concerns 'on-site' construction activities, whereas the 'broad' definition encapsulates the whole supply chain from quarrying raw material to demolition of the product and the associated professional services (Pearce, 2003). The construction output by value is mainly concentrated in the developed countries (ILO, 2006), with Europe accounting for 30% of global output, followed by the USA (21%) and Japan (20%). However, construction employment is almost the exact reverse of the distribution of output. This is explained by the differences in technology use that substitutes expensive labour in the developed countries (ILO, 2006). Given the scale and impact of construction, from an application perspective, the construction industry is still fraught with problems and challenges, which includes, among others, failure to meet market demands, skills shortages and poor quality of products (Morton, 2002; CIOB, 2006, 2008).

Construction Innovation and Process Improvement, First Edition.
Edited by Akintola Akintoye, Jack S. Goulding and Girma Zawdie.
© 2012 Blackwell Publishing Ltd. Published 2012 by Blackwell Publishing Ltd.

Thus, many initiatives have been launched worldwide to improve the construction industry practices, one of which is through Modern Methods of Construction (MMC).

This chapter explores the need for the construction industry to change, introduces MMC, and exemplifies the different systems therein, with particular emphasis on Offsite Production (OSP). Hence, OSP is explored from a strategic as well as from an implementation perspective, in order to identify the requirements needed to help overcome the industry's inherent problems. The chapter further reports on a study carried out in the UK (2008) to identify and quantify the main OSP knowledge gaps amongst construction professionals. Finally, the chapter concludes by introducing a flexible training and education model based on the quality function deployment (QFD) concept, the remit of which can help quantify and prioritise the construction industry's OSP training, education and business needs.

9.2   The Need for Change

The criticism of the construction industry has been mainly attributed to its underperformance, resulting in poor quality of products, and poor health and safety record in comparison to other industries (Emmerson, 1962; Banwell, 1964; Latham, 1994; Egan, 1998; Koskela, 2000; Morton, 2002; Lambert, 2003; Woudhuysen and Abley, 2004; EMCC, 2005). This is largely due to the peculiar needs of the end product (predominantly a building of some kind), which often necessitate production to take place on site, and therefore tends to be a one-of-a-kind product. Vrijhoef and Koskela (2005) identified and disaggregated the peculiarities of the construction industry at three different levels, namely the product, project/production and industry levels. This peculiarity is further perplexed by the fragmented nature of the industry, which has been identified as a major contributor to the complex nature of construction industry practices, often leading to the so-called 'over the brick-wall/silo approach' (Palotz, 2006). Fragmentation often refers to the increase in the number of firms accompanied with the decrease in their average size. This fragmentation in structure consequently results in low investment in research and development (R&D) and a fragmented delivery process (Gonsález, 1999). The ramifications of this are manifested in the disparate and uncoordinated procedures that create an environment for 'risk dumping' and hence, lead to a 'fully-fledged' blame culture (Saffin, 2007), which is a fundamental barrier to improvement (NAO, 2001). This is also evidenced by the inadequate capture of client requirements, lack of integration of information, lack of life-cycle analysis, and poor communication flow amongst project stakeholders (Evbuomwan and Anumba, 1998; Anumba *et al.*, 2008).

Given the challenging nature of the construction industry, many initiatives have been instigated worldwide to effect change, in order for the construction industry to overcome and mitigate the inherent problems, be able to compete globally, and hence maintain its strategic importance (Egan, 1998; NAO, 2001). A summary of these initiatives can be seen in Table 9.1.

Table **9.1** International initiatives to promote change in the construction industry (Nadim, 2009).

Report/Initiative	Year	Context
Australia	1999	Building for growth
Finland	2002	Reengineering the construction process using Information Technology
Ireland	1997	Building our future together
Japan	1998	Future Directions of the construction industry, coping with structural changes of the market
Singapore	1999	Construction 21, Reinventing Construction
South Africa	1997	Creating an enabling environment for reconstruction growth and development in the construction industry
USA	1994	National Construction Goals
UK	1962	Greater integration of the design and construction process
UK	1994	Constructing the Team (Latham report), to review contractual and procurement arrangements
UK	1998	Construction Task Force (Rethinking Construction), Committed leadership, focus on customer, integrated process and teams, quality driven agenda, commitment to people
UK	2004	Construction Client Group CCG, To support private and public clients

The common trend noted amongst the international initiatives to promote the construction industry was the emphasis on meeting client needs, integrating design and construction, and benchmarking performance. These achievements were mainly sought through process improvement (NAO, 2001). However, the future driving forces for change were anticipated to extend beyond merely 'process improvement', to further embrace 'sustainable communities' concepts and emphasising the 'social needs' (RIBA, 2005). In this context, the future driving forces for change are envisioned to encompass:

- climate change and the depletion of natural resources;
- 'building information object modelling and larger industrialisation and standardisation of buildings;
- increasingly demanding and powerful consumers;
- growing global competition to deliver high-quality buildings more effectively and
- demand for intelligent buildings to minimise the increasing energy costs.

However, change can only take place and be successful when governed by a set of ingredients such as change in culture, the introduction of enabling technologies, promotion of new contractual arrangements, and risk management (Adamson and Pollington, 2006; Saffin, 2007).

9.3   Modern Methods of Construction

The idea of improving performance in the construction industry, by learning from other industries such as 'manufacturing', is not a new phenomenon (Womack *et al.*, 1990; Gann, 1996; Egan, 1998; Höök and Stehn, 2008). This was particularly evidenced in the 1960s, when the 'future' dream for improving the construction industry was:

> ... a group of white coated, well paid workers, slotting and clipping standard components into place in rhythmic sequence on an orderly, networked and mechanised site to a faultless programme without mud, mess, sweat, or swearing...' (Carter, 1967).

This 'dream' has apparently driven the call to improve the construction industry through the take up of the production concept, which is governing the manufacturing industry (Leabue and Viñals, 2003). This call for change is multifaceted, incorporating: the people involved, the technology used and the processes employed. In other words, it was a call for 'innovation', the mode of which largely depended on the 'degree' of change required from current practices (Van de Ven, 1986; Laborde and Sanvido, 1994; Seaden *et al.*, 2003). Slaughter (1998) distinguished five modes for innovation, which encompassed:

1. *Incremental innovation*: requiring small change to occur;
2. *Modular innovation*: requiring change in concept;
3. *Architectural innovation*: i.e. change in concept which requires change in the link of units;
4. *System innovation*: requiring multiple innovations to occur that are linked together and require major change in components; and finally
5. *Radical innovation*: that requires an entirely new approach, resulting in major change.

From an innovation point of view, MMC is one of the means sought to improve and change the construction industry practices through emphasising the manufacturing concept and the introduction of different levels of mechanisations, hence catering for the different modes of innovation (Slaughter, 1998). In this context, MMC is closely intertwined with the concept of industrialising the construction industry (Tatum *et al.*, 1986; Warszawski, 1999; O'Brien *et al.*, 2000; Gibb, 2001; Morton, 2002). Intrinsically, industrialisation can be seen as a business strategy that transforms the traditional construction process into a manufacturing and assembly process by engaging people, embracing (new) technologies and translating clients' needs into building requirements (Nadim, 2009). Hence, industrialisation aims to improve business efficiency, quality of product, customer satisfaction, environmental performance, sustainability, and predictability of timescales. This makes industrialisation broad-based, rather than merely confined to a particular product and therefore requires engaging people and processes in order to improve the delivery and performance of construction (CABE, 2004; MBS, 2004; Taylor *et al.*, 2004; NAO, 2005; Plus Group and Riverside, 2005; Barker 33 Cross-Industry Group, 2006; Gibb and Pendlebury, 2006).

9.3.1   MMC Classification

MMC is subject to numerous classifications, which range from those defining the type of product produced to those specifying the location of production. The type of products include panelised, volumetric units, hybrid (which combines panelised and volumetric approaches) subassemblies, and components such as floor or roof cassettes, pre-cast concrete foundation assemblies, pre-formed wiring looms and engineering composites (NAO, 2005). Other classifications distinguished location of production such as site-based systems, for example, tunnel from, slip form, jump form, etc (Homein, 2006; NHBC, 2006) (Figure 9.1). Another classification suggested by Gibb and Pendlebury (2006) represents four distinctive levels, which may overlap, namely components sub-assembly, non-volumetric sub-assembly, volumetric preassembly and complete buildings.

MMC may also be regarded as an overarching umbrella, which embraces a variety of building approaches such as Offsite Manufacturing (OSM) and onsite work. Hence, MMC and OSM should not be considered as synonyms (Goodier and Gibb, 2005; Homein, 2006). OSM is a process that incorporates prefabrication and pre-assembly, and involves the design and manufacture of units often remote from the work site and their installation. These units are then transported and assembled at the work site, thus referred to as 'offsite fabrication/production'. From a terminology perspective, Offsite Manufacturing, Offsite Construction (OSC), Offsite Production (OSP), Offsite Fabrication (OSF), factory built assembly, industrialised construction, prefabrication, modular construction, and system building have often been used interchangeably (Gibb and Pendlebury, 2006; NHBC, 2006; BRE, 2007).

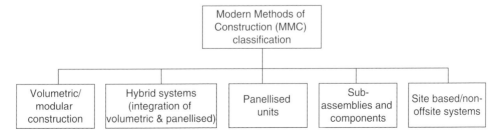

Figure 9.1   MMC classifications.

9.3.2   Offsite Production Evolution and Application

Gibb (1999) and Leabue and Viñals (2003) attributed the development of OSP as a response to sporadic demands for buildings and facilities. These encompassed colonisation in the nineteenth century, commercial developments in the late 1980s, natural disasters, industrial revolution and advances in technology. Further drivers, which called for the wider use of OSP, included the decrease of available skilled labour and the consequent increase in labour costs, change in client demands and expectations, development of digitally controlled manufacturing, and the increased concern about the health and safety of workers. In addition, clients have become more pragmatic with respect to their expectations, requiring better quality products that are delivered faster at a reasonable cost (Gibb, 1999).

OSP has been employed in several construction projects worldwide, predominately in the commercial sector, where the high cost of projects often justifies the associated initial capital investments (Leabue and Viñals, 2003). However, residential projects to a large extent lagged behind with respect to OSP implementation. The most iconic residential buildings featuring OSP are Kisho Kurokawa's 1972 Capsule Tower in Japan and Moshe Safdie's Habitat 67 in Montreal Canada (Sebestyen and Pollington, 2003). The mode of production and delivery of OSP buildings, as well as the mode of intervention and support of the State/Government, is largely governed by historical, geographical and social elements (O'Brien *et al.*, 2000; Leabue and Viñals, 2003, ManuBuild, 2009). While a number of failures were recorded internationally, successful OSP examples were often underpinned by R&D and through collaboration with the industry, as was the case in Sweden and Japan (O'Brien *et al.*, 2000). Therefore, OSP arguably provides a safe, efficient and productive work environment when compared to traditional construction practices (Figure 9.2), which are fraught with problems and challenges (Gibb, 1999). From a sustainability point of view, OSP allow reduced levels of defects, thus resulting in a better quality, less waste, improved health and safety, improved environmental performance of the final product, social benefits (from improved working conditions), less deliveries to site, in addition to greater efficiency in the use of resources – both materials and labour (Gorgolewski, 2003). While

Figure 9.2   Hard and labour intensive work environment (Nadim, 2001).

it is argued that OSP may help reduce the amount of labour needed on the job; Gibb (1999) negated this notion, suggesting that OSP should be seen as part of an effective use of labour rather than a reduction in labour.

Initiatives and calls have been launched worldwide to promote the wider use of OSP in order to reap the benefits (Egan, 1998; Barker, 2003; Leabue and Viñals, 2003; CIDB, 2009). These benefits include meeting market demands, overcoming skill shortages and improving the quality of final product. In response to these initiatives, the UK and Australia, for example, have incorporated OSP in their construction industry vision for 2020 (Hampson and Brandon, 2004; ConstructionSkills, 2008). However, when employing OSP working practices, there is a need to distinguish between an 'offsite produced product' and 'processes of OSP'. A 'house' may be entirely prefabricated in a factory using the traditional procedures and then trans-ported to the site. In this case, the factory would only allow a better work environment by simply moving work from a site to a factory. This does not acknowledge the benefits derived from the production technology, such as using machines, robots and new methods for management (Leabue and Viñals, 2003). Notwithstanding this, the degree of industrialisation used in OSP can differ depending on the enterprise, the region, and type of com-ponent/product produced, where Leabue and Viñals (2003) identified five levels of industrialisation, these being:

1. *Use of simple machinery*: components of the building is produced in a factory and assembled using traditional methods;
2. *Mechanisation*: using specialised tools in order to reduce the depend-ence on labour;
3. *Automation*: replacing labours with machines;
4. *Robotisation*: using sophisticated programmable machines that accom-plish complex and diversified work to allow replacing more labour;
5. *Reproduction*: replacing the rest of the traditional work with new procedures, in order to reduce the number of operations required for producing complex objects so as to bring gains that far exceed mecha-nisation and robotisation.

In order to capitalise on the benefit from employing OSP systems, a 'project-wide' strategy should be developed at an early stage in the project to allow measuring of the effects. This strategy requires that key decisions are made during the concept design and detail design phase prior to the start of the production phase. The earlier the OSP decision is made, the more likely the benefits are to be maximised. The key decisions required encom-pass agreeing on the strategy for employing OSP, OSP applications, logistics for unit installation, and OSP details (Gibb, 1999). However, to allow these decisions to take place, special procurement methods are suggested such as 'strategic partnering', 'two-stage tendering', 'nominated suppliers', 'manage-ment forms of contract', 'design and build', and 'design and manage'. In addition, a number of issues need to be agreed upon and determined to help realise and maximise the benefits of OSP application (Homein, 2006; build-offsite and BAA, 2008), which include:

- a date for design freeze/phased freeze;
- a timetable for delivery of the units;
- notice required by the manufacturer to check that tolerances on site are within the agreed limits;
- penalties for late delivery;
- penalties for delays if the site is behind schedule and unable to accept delivery at the agreed time;
- tolerances and standards that the units will be manufactured to;
- formal procedures for checking the units prior to accepting handover;
- latent defects liability period;
- manufacturers' responsibilities on site during the erection/installation of their units, and their requirements/conditions during that period.

In contrast to the traditional construction process, the amount of work required prior to going to site in OSP projects often increases, as the super-structure and fitting-out can take place in the factory, thereby decreasing the amount of work carried out on site (NHBC, 2006). The amount of work carried out in the factory depends largely on the type of the system employed, which in the case of volumetric systems is larger than the work required for panellised systems for example. Consequently, the amount of work required on site is reduced compared to all other systems. At a strategic level, OSP as a technology differs from other technologies, as it is not realistically feasible to be solely acquired by one single organisation or across a single supply chain. Therefore, in order for OSP to justify the capital investment and hence, be cost effective, it needs to be taken up widely by the construction industry to provide market continuity and stability. This requires the industry to move beyond the notion of a 'learning organisation' (Senge, 1992; Andrew and Ciborra, 1996) to the notion of a 'learning industry' (Eurich, 1990; Rezgui et al., 2004).

9.3.3   Offsite Production Strategies

Industrialisation is a notion that transcends the use of offsite-produced elements and the assembly of buildings to a rather 'visionary' system. This, in addition to the technical aspects, tends to include economic, management and market exploitation aspects. In this respect, the industrialisation process is envisioned to start with market analysis, management and design, followed by marketing of the finished product, which is then distributed, installed and finally maintained (Leabue and Viñals, 2003). This often requires exten-sive communication channels throughout the different stages of the process and so necessitates that different stakeholders are 'on the same side of the fence' and share a common 'language' to accommodate the new work conditions (Carter, 1967).

There are five main distinguished manufacturing strategy models that may be applied in the industrialised construction industry, namely buy-to-order, make-to-order, assemble-to-order, make-to-stock and ship-to-stock. These strategies are governed by a 'decoupling' point that defines the extent to which the process allow capturing customer's requirements, and whether these are real or speculative requirements (Barlow *et al.*, 2003); thus, are dependent on the extent of standardisation/customisation allowed. In the context of standardisation, this typically involves the 'extensive' use of components, methods or processes, in which there is regularity and repetition (Gibb, 1999). This is predominately governed through the design on a modular basis to coordinate the size of factory-made components with the design of buildings, that is, through 'dimensional coordination' (Gann, 1996) and jointing conventions (Carter 1967; Jones, 1967; Tindale, 1967). In order to avoid 'identical standardisation' of products, which does not consider customer preferences (Gibb, 1999), 'high-powered' computer-aided design and digitally controlled manufacturing machinery is often sought to facilitate the provision of mass customisation. This requires flexible production lines to allow produce a wide range of alternative assemblies and final products. Thus, the call is for more emphasis to be placed on the standardisation of interfaces between components – for example, smart components (ManuBuild, 2009) rather than through the standardisation of products. These interfaces are not necessarily physical, but may to be extended to encapsulate managerial/contractual and/or organisational interfaces (Gibb, 1999). However, the level of standardisation/customisation is often dependent on the number of stages that allow customisation along the different stages of the supply chain, such as design, fabrication, assembly and distribution (Barlow *et al.*, 2003), which can affect time and cost of delivery. In this context, pure standardisation does not conventionally allow customisation at any stage of the supply chain. In contrast, pure customisation does allow configuration to meet customer requirements across all stages of the supply chain, but consequently has a relatively high impact on cost and lead-times. Nevertheless, the Japanese construction industry managed to balance production cost reduction and mass customisation through the rationalisation of the manufacturing processes (Toffler, 1970; Noguchi, 2005).

9.4   Open Building Manufacturing – ManuBuild Project

ManuBuild was a European Framework Six Integrated Research Project (2005–2009), partly funded by the European Commission (EC). In an attempt to measure the perception of the construction industry stakeholders in Europe, semi-structured interviews were conducted to capture views with regard to the shift towards OSP and the introduction of 'openness' to the system. The interviews addressed the business models, the information platforms, the level of automation and production systems, the involvement of end users in the construction process, maintenance and refurbishment, the market and the risk involved (Hervàs and Ruiz, 2007). Transcripts from 54 open-ended interviews (carried out in 4 European countries) were analysed to help inform and effect change, and thus help improve the construction industry. The analysis suggested the need to balance the people involved, the technology used and the process underpinning the business. Whilst there is

Figure 9.3   OSP Conceptual Model (adapted from Nadim and Goulding, 2011).

an already acknowledged model to balance people, process and technology (Wysocki, 2004), two extra dimensions were suggested to this relationship, namely the 'product' dimension and the 'market' dimension (Nadim and Goulding, 2011). This relationship was consolidated in a conceptual model to help identify and create a focal point concerning the OSP knowledge needed and the subsequent implementation thereof (Figure 9.3).

Figure 9.3 presents a conceptual model based on four core dimensions (people, product, technology and process) and relationship with risk and the market; and vice versa, i.e. how process, technology and people involved affect and govern the selection of the OSP product in question (Nadim and Goulding, 2011):

9.4.1   The 'Process' Dimension

The process dimension represents the backbone of the OSP business. It therefore requires an appropriate infrastructure and means to allow the OSP business to grow and prosper. This mandate requires processes to be less complicated, with the removal of non value-adding activities – and should clearly demonstrate value for money. In addition, the roles of the different stakeholders need to be well defined and integrated throughout the different phases, from conception to maintenance and demolition. This necessitates improving the organisational structure and awareness of the awarding authorities regarding the new processes and contractual models.

9.4.2   The 'People' Dimension

OSP, like any (new) technology, often involves change, which can attract resistance associated with protectionism and conservatism inherent within the construction industry (Gibb, 1999; Mtech Group, 2008). This makes the people dimension one of the most important drivers, and at the same time, an inhibitor to the wider uptake of OSP. This may be related to a number of factors, not least culture, change required and skill shortages. Hence, multi-skilling could be seen as a possible solution (Cather *et al.*, 2001).

9.4.3   The 'Technology' Dimension

The technology dimension entails the product, the process (Gibb, 1999; Goodier and Gibb, 2005; NAO, 2005), as well as ICT needed to underpin the business vis-à-vis integration of information. This requires information and communication processes be simplified, particularly the process to move from 'made-for-stock' to cater for 'made-to-order'; and the product technology automation to extend beyond the successful implementation evidenced in kitchen and bathroom pods (Pan *et al.*, 2005) to include building material.

9.4.4   The 'Product' Dimension

Whilst a wide range of products/systems are available (Gibb, 1999; Gibb and Pendlebury, 2006; Homein, 2006), the selection tends to depend on several parameters such as cost, quality, design, sustainability and flexibility (NAO, 2005). However, the cost parameter seems to represent the determinant factor for accepting and employing OSP (Gibb, 1999; Warszawski, 1999; Barlow *et al.*, 2003; Leabue and Viñals, 2003; Goodier and Gibb, 2005). However, for successful OSP implementation, the cost element needs to be counterbalanced by 'adaptability', 'customisability', 'flexibility', quality of interfaces, and most importantly how these coalesce with needs, cognisant of the 'multi-generation house' concept (ASID, 2001).

9.4.5   The 'Market' and 'Risk' Dimension

There is an element of risk associated with the process, technology, people and product relationship, the level of which largely determines the market characteristics and market availability for the OSP system in question. The wider uptake of OSP is therefore dependent on the market, and the amount of investment behind it (Gorgolewski, 2003; Venables *et al.*, 2004; Goodier and Gibb, 2005; NAO, 2005; Bill, 2008). In contrast to the traditional construction practice, where is predominantly low capital intensive and tends to use clients' money, the OSP approach often requires intensive capital investment in order to set up and help provide continuity. This capital investment can only be made if there is a consistent and predictable market driven by demand (Barlow *et al.*, 2003; Bill, 2008). Furthermore, this should also take into consideration the trend to build in an existing building environment (i.e. reconstruction, refurbishment, extension), the trend of individualisation, and also the decreasing population evident in most EU countries. This confines OSP risk, as unstable/unpredictable market demand, along with the perceived uniformity of this approach, which is perceived to restrict architectural creativity, especially where alternative (traditional) products of similar qualities are available.

9.5   Offsite Production in the UK Construction Industry

Meeting market demands is one of the major drivers, which instigated the call for the wider use of MMC in the UK. The amount of dwellings needed over a period of 16–25 years starting in 2002/03 was estimated to range from 160,000–225,000 units/year (Barlow *et al.*, 2002; Gorgolewski, 2003). This led to the Office of Deputy Prime Minister setting targets of 25% of all new social housing schemes in the Registered Social Landlords sector to use OSP/MMC in anticipation of reducing the shortfall in housing production by increasing the speed at which industry could build to meet this demand. However, whilst MMC in general and OSP in particular has been the focus of much attention in the UK (Barker, 2003; Venables and Courtney, 2004; NAO, 2005; BRE, 2007), the actual value of the MMC market in the UK in 2004 was £2.2 billion, representing only 2.1% of the total value of the UK construction sector, 3.6% of new build (Goodier and Gibb, 2005). In addition, the UK OSP market accommodates a wide range of OSP products, including foundation, superstructure, envelope, mechanical and electrical services, etc (Ogden, 2007; Buildoffsite, 2008); where the greatest area for potential OSP exploitation is estimated to include kitchen and bathroom pods, external walls, timber frame, and roofs (Pan *et al.*, 2005). Other drivers cited for using OSP in the industry were overcoming skills shortages, ensuring time and cost certainty, achieving high-quality products and minimising on-site activities (Goodier and Gibb, 2005). Whilst the OSP concept is not new (Gibb, 1999), the advancement in technologies together with the increasing complexity of current construction projects introduces a challenging proposition to the wider uptake of OSP.

9.5.1   The UK Construction Industry Skill Problem

Approximately 70–80% of the UK construction workforce have been estimated to have no formal qualifications, with 35% being classified as labourers; compared to 5% in Denmark, 7% in the Netherlands and 17% in Germany (Venables *et al.*, 2004; Clarke and Winch, 2006). This phenomenon suggests that the UK construction industry is largely dependent on the 'lower level skills'. This is further compounded by the claim that 80% of firms within the built environment experience skills problems with their existing workforce (CIC, 2004), along with a failure to attract younger generations to the construction industry (McNair and Flynn, 2006; Stephen and Flynn, 2006). Therefore, without appropriate skills, there is a real risk of decline in competitiveness and reduction in economic growth (Leitch, 2005, 2006).

The introduction of new technologies often requires new ways of working and thinking along with new skills and/or the enhancement of existing skills (Eurich, 1990; Construction Skills, 2008). The term 'skill' was initially used to refer to the capabilities of an individual to undertake a particular task (Taylor, 2005). This interpretation has evolved over time to be used interchangeably with the term 'competence', thus implying attributes that encompass adaptability and flexibility to change within the workplace, in addition to the possession of 'transferable behavioural characteristics (Prahalad and Hamel, 1990). This is particularly important, as the development of competence within organisations often provides access to a variety of markets, and can significantly enhance the customer experience. Therefore, from a skills perspective, new skills are important, especially where new material, equipment, systems, processes and practices are constantly maturing and evolving (Eurich, 1990). However, whilst acknowledging that improving the construction industry cannot solely be dependent upon the provision of new skills *per se*, improvement is unlikely to occur or be effective without the appropriation of skills matching. In this respect, future technological developments in the construction industry suggest that skills are needed to move the workforce away from blue-collar labourers towards white-collar employees (Hauck and Rockwell, 1997; Leitch, 2005; Gurjao, 2006). In this context, future skill requirements are anticipated to be largely 'generic', encompassing soft skills (e.g. problem solving, communication, and the ability to work in teams) as opposed to job specific skills (Nateriello, 1989; Hauck and Rockwell, 1997; Hager *et al.*, 2001; Stasz, 2001; Leitch, 2006).

Skill shortages often occur in businesses operating with less skilled workers, leading to increase in operating costs, and consequently losing business to competitors (DFEE, 2000; Construction Skills, 2006). While serious shortfalls in manual skills are evidenced in the UK construction industry, professionals and managerial skill shortages are argued to be just as acute (Dainty *et al.*, 2005). These shortages are linked to a number of issues, not least failure to modernise recruitment and training, the changing nature of construction markets, the introduction of new technologies, the growth of self-employment, the fragmentation of the industry and associated decline in construction training (Gann and Senker, 1998; Mackenzie *et al.*, 2000). It is further anticipated that an increase in construction demand would be affected by skill gaps in middle and senior management (CIOB, 2008; Bill, 2008). In this context, skills gaps are perceived as being 'holes' in the knowledge and competence of existing staff; leading to lower profitability and productivity, reduced quality output and an 'under par' health and safety record (Construction Skills, 2006), where skilled craft workers are likely to lack technical and practical skills, while managers, administrators and professionals are most likely to lack management and team working skills (DFEE, 2000). Nevertheless, skill gaps seem to be more evident within the 'lower level' occupations rather than within management or professional positions (LSC, 2005).

9.5.2   Multidisciplinary Training and Education

Technological advancements and increased competition often require transforming the skill profile of construction personnel from highly trained individual 'specialists' to broadly trained 'generalists', who are able to work in groups across multi-disciplinary projects making 'cradle-to-grave' decisions, including finance, design, construction, operation and maintenance (Eraut, 1994; Farr and Sullivan, 1996). In addition to the soft skills required, future skills will also need to be aligned with the increased use of ICT in construction processes, along with new products, new materials, etc (Gann and Senker, 1998). In light of the type of skills required, managers and professionals are expected to account for an increased share of employment, whereas skilled crafts are expected to form a declining share (DFEE, 2000). Furthermore, there is likely to be a growing need for customer-focused staff and possible increase in 'less-skilled manual workers when prefabrication techniques become more widespread' (Clarke and Wall, 1998). This notion was also emphasised by Williamson and Bilbo (1999), with respect to administrating construction technologies and the design/construct/manage interface, rather than performing them. Accordingly, change in the construction industry is suggested to take place on two levels, namely on the process and the technology level where the bulk of work is transferred offsite, hence initiating the need for 'offsite' as well as 'onsite' skills (Gurja, 2006). Therefore, due to the continuously changing environment, and the increased amount and complexity of information exchanged amongst construction stakeholders (Jaraiedi and Ritz, 1994), training and education should be seen as a continuous rather than a 'one-off' process, in line with the pace of change (Eurich, 1990).

From a training perspective, inter-disciplinary/multi-disciplinarily training and education allows greater collaboration amongst the different professions, thereby enabling shared understanding, minimising the chance of friction amongst professions, and facilitating a seamless workflow (Gann and Salter, 1999; Wood, 1999; Campbell, 2001; Chan et al., 2002; Slotte and Tynjälä, 2003; Anumba et al., 2008). However, this requires the industry to establish the capabilities needed by (potential) employees (Tener, 1996) and requires commitment through appropriate channels supported by two-way communication between industry and academia (Trauth et al., 1993; Slotte and Tynjälä, 2003).

Numerous benefits can be established through industry–academia collaboration (Lamancusa et al., 1995; Tener, 1996). Slotte and Tynjälä (2003) identified benefits on three different levels, namely at industry, academia and student levels. Industrial benefits can be manifested in the access granted to the broad theoretical knowledge, inquiry and reflection, as well as in the skilled and knowledgeable workforce attained. Academia, on the other hand, would benefit from coming in contact with work practices, thereby improving business awareness, and access to work-based case studies. Finally, students would gain access to lifelong learning opportunities, which would help with their career development through the exposure to real-world factors and interaction with industrial personnel (Lambert, 2003). In other words, industry–academia collaboration could help encapsulate theory, practice and problem solving, which is often referred to as 'theorising practice' and 'particularising theory' (Eraut, 1994; Slotte and Tynjälä, 2003).

9.5.3   An OSP-QFD Collaborative Training and Education Model

The UK construction industry and academia collaboration has long been sought to improve the industry practices through skill development (Tener, 1996; NWDA, 2004; ACBEE, 2007). However, in order to measure the extent to which the UK's industry-academia collaboration considered OSP professional skill requirements, a study was carried out in the UK in 2008 to explore the construction industry and academia OSP perception and future requirements (Nadim and Goulding, 2009). This study suggested that academia is often unaware of the specific and disparate training needs of the industry in general (Alter and Koontz, 1996; Wang, 2003; Kunstler, 2005), and recognised that there was a mismatch between industry and academia with respect to industry skill requirements (and the delivery thereof). This study further noted that uncertainty prevailed within both the construction industry and academia with respect to OSP requirements, and the future of OSP in the UK.

Drawing on the argument that professional and managerial skill shortages represent a major challenge for the wider uptake of OSP, Nadim and Goulding (2010) investigated the UK construction industry professionals' perception with regard to OSP implementation. Whilst there is general agreement that the UK construction industry is ready to embrace OSP practices, findings suggested a number of problems, concerns and uncertainties. These were not merely discipline-specific, rather multidisciplinary, which need to be addressed to fully appreciate and understand OSP practices. The study concluded that major factors contributing to OSP perceived problems in the UK were mainly associated with culture and resistance to change, as well as inadequate current construction processes. The initial increased cost, manifested by the capital investment and alteration of cash flow, and the perceived design inflexibility further compounded the problem. These assertions associated with OSP implementation, necessitates the provision of adequate OSP training and education programmes to enlighten industry stakeholders of the specifics of OSP practices.

In the context of training and education, Sahney et al. (2003) argued that 'education' was a service industry and would thus need to learn from other industries with respect to measuring the quality of its services to the satisfaction of their customers. In this context, 'education' would need to be broken down into 'system components', reflecting the 'manufacturing process' (Jaraiedi and Ritz, 1994; Hwarng and Teo, 2001; Ahmed, 2006; Gonzalez *et al.*, 2008). Therefore, current educational programmes need to be built upon a product platform concept to satisfy customer needs and allow the desired outcomes to be measured. It was suggested that the supply chain management concept be applied to the relationships between industry, university and associations to rapidly provide and continuously update knowledge and competence needed to run businesses in a timely and cost-efficient manner (Shunk, 2002). This requires knowledge to be seen as a transferable commodity, changing the knowledge supply process from 'push' to 'pull', and including academia as an integral partner. In this context, industry needs to define their requirements to help set the exit capabilities for training and education, in order to enable academia to satisfy those needs (Shunk, 2002).

Quality Function Deployment (QFD) is one of the various tools of 'Total Quality Management' (TQM) that supports product/system design through considering and incorporating customer requirements. It was first developed in Japan during the 1960s by Yoji Akao in the ship-building industry vis-à-vis incorporating customer demands/needs into the product development process (Akao, 1990; Cohen, 1995; Brackin and Rogers, 1999; Akao and Mazur, 2003). This is achieved by capturing the voice of customer (VOC) and working 'backwards' towards defining the design specifications (Abdul-Rahman *et al.*, 1999). The main goal of QFD is to translate subjective quality criteria into objective ones that are quantifiable and measurable, which are then used to design and manufacture a product that satisfies the customer (Hauser and Clausing, 1988; CIRI, 2007). QFD therefore supports interdisciplinary work for effective communication and coordination beyond the borders of organisational units and disciplines, and hence integrate the views of the disparate stakeholders (Cohen, 1995; Chan and Wu, 2002; Pietsch, 2002). QFD also allows prioritisation and benchmarking competitiveness to take place. Drawing on Jaraiedi and Ritz (1994), and in the context of OSP training and education, the QFD tool was seen as an approach to help answer the question: 'How to deliver quality training and education programmes and services based on the needs of customers/industry?' (Figure 9.4).

Figure 9.4 represents an OSP-QFD development concept model for scrutinising and synchronising industry and training/education institutions' polarised views and expectations. It was designed specifically to provoke OSP multidisciplinary dialogue, where Nadim (2009) identified, quantified and prioritised the major OSP knowledge gaps within the UK construction industry. The VOC (the 'What'], was extrapolated from the knowledge gaps captured from the construction industry stakeholders perceptions and sorted according to their importance from a training and education perspective. The areas suggesting 'larger' knowledge gaps (with higher means) would consequently take priority from a training and education perspective. The service elements (SE) (the 'How'], were then identified as the measurable means by which the VOC could be addressed from a training and education perception. In this context, the 'How' represents the voice of the training/education organisations (Han *et al.*, 2001), as the specific courses that

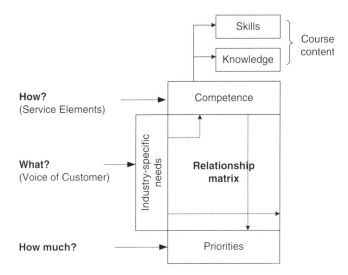

Figure 9.4 OSP-QFD development concept (adapted from Nadim, 2009).

contain topics/knowledge areas that would satisfy customers' expectations/
requirements (Gonzalez *et al.*, 2008). The SEs were derived from qualitative
data analysis and literature, and were categorised under the four main OSP
dimensions of: process, product, people and technology.

From an OSP-QFD implementation perspective, the VOC is located in the
first column on the left-hand side of the matrix, followed by the importance
of each VOC in the adjacent column to the right (Figure 9.5). The SE (the
competence needed) is placed at the top of the matrix. The strength of
relationship between each VOC and SE is determined in the relationship
matrix using three modes of strengths, strong relationship (r = 9), medium
relationship (r = 3) and weak relationship (r = 1), whereas an empty 'blank'
cell suggests no relationship exists between VOC and SE. The SE priorities
('how much'), identify the SEs that fulfil most of the VOC, and should
therefore be considered for further deployment and development. These
priorities are determined based on the weights for each SE using the following formula: *weight* $(w_j = \Sigma_{i=1} d(i) * (ij)$, where d_i is the degree of importance
of the VOC and r_{ij} represents the strength of relationship between VOC *(i)*
and SE *(j)*. The number of SE priorities considered for further deployment,
ultimately depend on the training/education institutions capacity and availability of resources to develop and deliver those training/education priority
programmes.

The first three resultant priorities of the OSP-QFD training and education
model are customer/end user oriented, mainly concerned with the final
product with respect to affordability, life-cycle costing (LLC) and customer
satisfaction. These are then followed by the management side of OSP practices with regard to the supply chain involved and design to manufacture
concept, taking into consideration logistics and assembly, building technology

Mean (scale 1-5) (*industry* perception)	Voice of Customer VOC vis-à-vis OSP	Importance (5-Mean+1)
2.31	OSP need to allow design flexibility	3.69
2.33	OSP need to satisfy the refurbishment market	3.67
2.57	OSP need to cater for good aesthetic	3.43
2.64	OSP need to allow easy maintenance/ maintenance planning	3.36
2.72	OSP need to be cost effective along the life cycle of building	3.28
2.77	OSP need to demonstrate high residual value for future investment	3.23
2.94	OSP require effective on-site management	3.06
3.22	OSP need to comply with transportation regulations	2.78
3.28	There is a need to generate adequate OSP market demand	2.72
3.29	OSP require effective procurement methods	2.71
3.53	OSP need to reduce accidents	2.47
3.81	OSP require coordination among project team/ participants	2.19
3.83	OSP success require a clear OSP strategy	2.17

VOC (i)   Degree of Importance (d)

Product

People   Technology   Risk   Market

Business Process

SE (How) (j)

defined qualitatively

Industry-Specific Needs

Training and Education Topics

Relationship Matrix

Strength of relationship between eachVOC and SE

r = 9 = strong relationship
r = 3 = medium relationship
r = 1 = weak relationship
Blank = no relationship

Topics Priorities

VOC (What)

defined quantitatively

How much

SE weighting

Weight $(w_j) = \Sigma_i = 1^{d(i) * r(ij)}$

Figure 9.5 The development scheme of the OSP-QFD training and education model.

used, environmental performance and energy efficiency. Other priorities included issues such as regulation, customisation, standardisation and risk management.

The OSP-QFD model is particularly flexible, as it allows the development of OSP training and education programmes based on industry needs and priorities in response to the changing environment. This can be used to define and develop OSP training and education programmes in accordance with organisational expertise, capacity and resources. This can also be used to help shape programmes with training/education providers, in order to enhance overall competitiveness through bespoke alignment with industry drivers.

9.6   Conclusion

The major reasons for construction industry problems and challenges relate predominantly to the nature of the one-of-kind product, with unique project characteristics and fragmented industry. These challenges have prompted the need for change, which was initially driven by process improvement. However, future drivers for change will mostly be driven by political agendas, such as climate change and the depletion of natural resources. Despite global technological advances, the construction industry still lags behind regarding the uptake of these advances to improve industry practice. This has largely contributed to the industry's failure to attract young professionals, resulting in skills shortages – a barrier for meeting future demands.

Offsite Production, under the overarching umbrella of Modern Methods of Construction, has been sought as one means of promoting the construction industry to overcome skill shortages and meet market demands. However, the invocation of this will require extensive communication channels across the supply chain, along with a common 'language' and a shared understanding of OSP practices amongst the different stakeholders. In order to achieve such multidisciplinary understanding, an OSP consolidated conceptual model was proposed as a viable solution to help inform, scrutinise and synchronise industry and training/education institutions' polarised views and expectations. It is envisaged that this could help create and secure a shared and collective congruence of understanding amongst construction industry stakeholders with regard to OSP training and education priorities.

References

Abdul-Rahman, K.C.L. & Woods, P.C. (1999) Quality function deployment in construction design: Application in low-cost housing design. *International Journal of Quality & Reliability Management*, **16**(6), 591–605.

ACBEE (2007) *Accelerating Change in the Built Environment Education*. Available from http://www.cebe.ltsn.ac.uk/ (accessed 7 April 2011).

Adamson, D.M. & Pollington, T. (2006) *Change in the Construction Industry*. Routledge. Oxford.

Ahmed, S. (2006) QFD application to improve management education at KIMEP. *Issues in Information Systems*, **7**(1), 193–198.

Akao, Y. (1990) *Quality Function Deployment: Integrating Customer Requirements Into Product Design*. Productivity Press, Cambridge.

Akao, Y. & Mazur, G.H. (2003) The leading edge in QFD: past, present and future. *International Journal of Quality & Reliability Management*, **20**(1), 20–35.

Alter, K. & R. Koontz, J. (1996) Curriculum development and continuing education in project management for the speciality subcontracting industry. *Journal of Construction Education*, **1**(2), 66–78.

Andrew, R. & Ciborra, C. (1996) Organisational learning and core capabilities development: the role of IT. *Journal of Strategic Information Systems*, 5, 111–127.

Anumba, C.J., Issa, R.R.A., Pan, J. & Mutis, I. (2008) Ontology-based information and knowledge management in construction. *Construction Innovation*, 8(3), 218–239.

ASID (American Society of Interior Designers) (2001) *Aging in Place: Aging and the Impact of Interior Design*. Available from http://www.asid.org/NR/rdonlyres/837A82C3-48C1-4C92-BFC9-2E37E9C8E1C7/0/aging_in_place1.pdf

Banwell, H. (1964) *Report of the Committee on the Placing and Management of Contracts for Building and Civil Engineering Works*. HMSO, London.

Barker 33 Cross-Industry Group (2006) *Modern Methods of Construction – Executive Summary of Final Report*. Available from http://www.hbf.co.uk/fileadmin/documents/barker/MMC_Final_Draft.pdf

Barker, K. (2003) *Barker Review of Housing Supply – Final Report – Recommendations*. HM Treasury. Available from http://www.hm-treasury.gov.uk/consultations_and_legislation/barker/consult_barker_index.cfm

Barlow, J., Childerhouse, P., Gann, D., Hong-Minh, S., Naim, M. & Ozaki, R. (2003) Choice and delivery in housebuilding: Lessons from Japan for UK housebuilders. *Building Research & Information*, 31(2), 134–145.

Bill, T. (2008) *Caledonian says Crunch will Boost OffSite Sector Building*. Available from http://www.building.co.uk/story.asp?sectioncode=30&storycode=3123901&c=2 (accessed 22 October 2008).

Brackin, P. & Rogers, G.M. (1999) *Assessment and Quality Improvement Process in Engineering and Engineering Education*. 29th ASEE/IEEE Frontiers in Education Conference, 10–13 November. San Juan, Puerto Rico.

BRE. (2007) *Modern Methods of Construction*. Available from http://www.bre.co.uk/housing/section.jsp?sid=377 (accessed April 2007).

Buildoffsite (2008) *Year Book*.

CABE (2004) *Design And Modern Methods of Construction Review*.

Campbell, M. (2001) *Skills in England 2001: The Key Messages*. Policy Research Institute, Leeds Metropolitan University, Leeds.

Carter, J. (1967) Components and architect. *RIBA Journal*, **November**, 476–477.

Cather, H., Morris, R. & Wilkinson, J. (2001) *Business Skills for Engineers and Technologists*. Butterworth-Heinemann. Oxford.

Chan, E.H.W., Chan, M.W., Scott, D. & Chan, A.T.S. (2002). Educating the 21st century construction professionals. *Journal of Professional issues in Engineering Education and Practice*, 128(1), 44–51.

Chan, L.-K. & Wu, M.-L. (2002) Quality function deployment: a literature review. *European Journal of Operational Research* 143(3), 463–497.

CIC (Construction Industry Council) (2004) *Built Environment Professional Services Skills Survey 2003/2004*. London.

CIDB (2009) *Malaysia International IBS Centre*. Available from www.cidb.gov.my

CIOB (2006) *Skills Shortages in the UK Construction Industry: Survey 2006*. The Chartered Institute of Building, Berkshire.

CIOB. (2008) *Skills Shortage in the UK Construction Industry Survey*.

CIRI (2007) Quality Function Deployment. *Product Brief Development Tools*, AUT University. Available from http://www.ciri.org.nz/resources.html. (accessed 2 August 2008).

Clarke, L. & Wall, C. (1998) UK construction skills in the context of European developments. *Construction Management and Economic*, 16(5), 553–567.

Clarke, L. & Winch, C. (2006) European skills framework? – but what are skills? Anglo-Saxon versus German concepts. *Journal of Education and Work*, 19(3), 255–269.

Cohen, L. (1995) *Quality Function Deployment: How to Make QFD Work for You*. Addison Wesley Publishing, Ltd, Reading, MA.

Construction Skills. (2006) Sector Skills Agreement. Available from http://www.constructionskills.net

ConstructionSkills (2008) *2020 Vision – The Future of* UK. A scenario based report.

Dainty, A.R.J., Ison, S.G. & Briscoe, G.H. (2005) The construction labour market skills crisis: the perspective of small-medium-sized firms. *Construction Management and Economic*, **23**(4), 387–398.

DFEE (2000) *An Assessment of Skills Needs in Construction and related Industries. Skills Dialogue: A comprehensive summary from employers of skills required in Construction and related Industries*. The Institute for Employment Studies.

Egan, J. (1998) *Rethinking Construction: The Report of the Construction Task Force to the Deputy Prime Minister*. DTI. London.

Eichert, J. & Kazi, A.S. (2007) Vision and Strategy of ManuBuild – Open Building Manufacturing. In: ed. Kazi, A.S., Hannus, M., Boudjabeur, S. & Malone, A. *Open Building Manufacturing: Core Concepts and Industrial Requirements*. Espoo, Finland, Manubuild in collaboration with VTT – Technical Research Centre of Finland.

EMCC (2005) *EMCC dossier on the European Construction Sector*. Available from http://www.emcc.eurofound.eu.int/content/source/eu05017a.html (accessed 6 November 2005).

Emmerson, H. (1962) *Survey of Problems before the Construction Industries*. HSMO, London.

Eraut, M. (1994) *Developing Professional Knowledge and Competence*. Routledge Falmer. London.

Eurich, N.P. (1990) *The Learning Industry. Education for Adult Workers*. ED330812. Carnegie Foundation for the Advancement of Teaching. Princeton, NJ.

European Commission (2006) *Construction Overview. Enterprise and Industry*. Available from http://ec.europa.eu/enterprise/construction/index_en.htm (accessed 29 December 2006).

Evbuomwan, N.F.O. & Anumba, C.J. (1998) An integrated framework for concurrent lifecycle design and construction. *Advances in Engineering Software*, **29**(7–9), 587–579.

Farr, J.V. & Sullivan, J.F. (1996) Rethinking training in the 1990s. *Journal of Management in Engineering*, **12**(3), 29–33.

Gann, D. & Salter, A. (1999) *Research Interdisciplinary Skills for the Built Environment Professionals: A Scoping Study*. Sussex University Science and technology Policy Research Unit (The Ove Arup Foundation).

Gann, D. & Senker, P. (1998) Construction skills training for the next millennium. *Construction Management and Economics*, **16**(5), 569.

Gann, D.M. (1996) Construction as a manufacturing process? Similarities and differences between industrialized housing and car production in Japan. *Construction Management and Economics*, **14**, 437–450.

Gibb, A. & Pendlebury, M. (2006) *Glossary of Terms*. Buildoffsite: Promoting Construction Offsite.

Gibb, A.G.F. (1999) *Offsite Fabrication*. Whittles Publishing Services, Scotland.

Gibb, A.G.F. (2001) Standardisation and pre-assembly – distinguishing myth from reality using case study research. *Construction Management and Economic*, **19**(3), 307–315.

Gonzalez, M.E. (1999) Regulation as a cause of firm fragmentation: The case of the Spanish construction industry. *International Review of Law and Economics*, **18**, 433–450.

Gonzalez, M.E., Quesada, G., Gourdin, H. & Hartley, M. (2008) Designing a supply chain management academic curriculum using QFD and benchmarking. *Quality Assurance in Education*, **16**(1), 36–60.

Goodier, C. & Gibb, A. (2005) *buildoffsite: The value of the UK market for offsite*. Loughborough University, Loughborough. Available from http://www.buildoff site.org

Gorgolewski, M. (2003) Offsite Construction, SIPs. Building for a future, the independent journal for 'green building' professionals and enthusiasts. *Offsite Fabrication: from Building for a Future Spring*. Available from www.buildingforafuture.co.uk/spring03/offsite_fabrication_SIPs.php

Gurjao, S. (2006) *Inclusivity: The Changing Role of Women in the Construction Workforce*. CIOB, University of Reading, Reading.

Hager, P., Crowley, S. & Melville, B. (2001) *Changing Conceptions of Training Ffr Evolving Workplaces: The Case of the Australian Building and Construction Industry. RCVET working paper 01–03*. Research Centre for Vocational Education and Training. TD/TNC 68.177. University of Technology, Sydney. Research Centre for Vocational Education and Training (RCVET), Sydney.

Hampson, K. & Brandon, P. (2004) *Construction 2020: A Vision for Australia's Property and Construction Industry*. Cooperative Research Centre for Construction Innovation, Brisbane.

Han, S.B., Chen, S.K., Ebrahimpour, M. & Sodhi, M.S. (2001) A conceptual QFD planning model. *International Journal of Quality & Reliability Management*, **18**(8), 796–812.

Hauck, A.J. & Rockwell, Q.T. (1997) Desirable characteristics of the professional constructor: The results of the Constructor Certification Skills and Knowledge survey. *Journal of Construction Education*, **2**(1), 24–36.

Hauser, J.R. & Clausing, D. (1988) The House of Quality. *Harvard Business Review*, **66**(3), 63–73.

Hervàs, F.C. & Ruiz, M.I.V. (2007) Stakeholder requirements for open building manufacturing. In: ed. Kazi, A.S., Hannus, M., Boudjabeur, S. and Malon, A., *Open Building Manufacturing: Core Concepts and Industrial Requirements*. Espoo, ManuBuild in collaboration with VTT.

Homein (2006) *Modern Methods of Construction*. Available from http://www. homein.org/searchresults.jsp?category=7&q=mmc (accessed April 2007).

Höök, M. & Stehn, L. (2008) Applicability of lean principles and practices in industrialised housing production. *Construction Management and Economics*, **26**, October, 1091–1100.

Hwarng, H.B. & Teo, C. (2001) Translating customers' voices into operations requirements: a QFD application in higher education. *International Journal of Quality & Reliability Management*, **18**(2), 195–225.

ILO International Labour organisation. (2006) *Global Distribution of Construction Output and Employment. Construction*. Available from http://www.ilo.org/public/english/dialogue/sector/sectors/constr/global.htm (accessed December 2006).

Jaraiedi, M. & Ritz, D. (1994) Total quality management applied to engineering education. *Quality Assurance in Education*, **2**(1), 32–40.

Jones, A. (1967) Components and the Builder. *RIBA Journal, November*, 485–488.

Kazi, A.S., Hannus, M., Boudjabeur, S. & Malon, A. (2007) *Open Building Manufacturing: Core Concepts and Industrial Requirements*. ManuBuild in collaboration with VTT – Technical Research Centre of Finland. Finland.

Koskela, L. (2000) An exploration Towards a production theory and its application to construction. PhD thesis 296. Espoo. Technical Research Centre of Finland, VTT Publications, Finland.

Kunstler, B. (2005) The hothouse effect: a model for change in higher education. *On the Horizon*, **13**(3), 173–181.

Laborde, M. & Sanvido, V. (1994) Introducing new process technologies into construction companies. *Journal of Construction Engineering and Management*, **120**(3), 488–508.

Lamancusa, J.S., Jorensen, J.E., Zayas-Castro, J.L. & Ratner, J. (1995) *The Learning Factory – A New Approach to Integrating Design and Manufacturing into Engineering Curricula*. ASEE, 25–28 June, Anaheim, CA.

Lambert, R. (2003) *Lambert Review of Business-University Collaboration*. Final report. HMSO, London.

Latham, M. (1994) *Constructing the Team*. HSMO, London

Leabue, D. & Viñals, J. (2003) *Avis Bâtir et innover: Tendances et défis dans le secteur du bâtiment*. Conseil de la science et de la technologie. Gouvernement du Québec.

Leitch, S. (2005) *Skills in the UK: A Long-term Challenge*. Interim report. HSMO, London.

Leitch, S. (2006) Leitch Review of Skills: Prosperity for All in the Global Economy – World Class Skills. Final report. HMSO. TSO, London.

LSC (Learning and Skills Council) (2005) *National Employers Skills Survey 2004: Key Findings*. LSC, UK.

Mackenzie, S., Kilpatricik, A.R. & Akintoye, A. (2000) UK construction skills shortage response strategies and an analysis of industry perceptions. *Construction Management and Economics*, **18**(7), 853–862.

Manubuild. (2009) *Open Building Manufacturing*. Available from http://www.manubuild.net

MBS (2004) *Modern Building Services: Enjoying the Benefits of Prefabrication*. Available from http://www.modbs.co.uk/news/printpage.php/aid/285/Enjoying_the_benefits_of_prefabrication

McNair, S. & Flynn, M. (2006) *Managing an Ageing Workforce in Construction: A Report for Employers*. Department for Work and Pension (DWP).

Mtech Group (2008) What disigners think. In: *Offsite Director 08*. Building Magazine.

Morton, R. (2002) *Construction UK: Introduction to the Industry*. Blackwell Science Ltd, Oxford.

Nadim, W. (2001) *The Work Environment in the Construction Industry: Hard and Labour Intensive*, Mubarak TV Studio Complex Project Image. Cairo, Egypt.

Nadim, W. (2009) Industrialising the construction industry: A collaborative training and education model. PhD thesis. School of the Built and Human Environment. University of Salford, Salford.

Nadim, W. & Goulding, J.S. (2009) Offsite production in the UK: The construction Industry and academia. *Architectural Engineering and Design Management (AEDM)*, **5**(3), 136–152.

Nadim, W. & Goulding, J.S. (2010) Offsite production in the UK: The way forward? A UK construction industry perspective. *Construction Innovation*, **10**(2), 181–202.

Nadim, W. & Goulding, J.S. (2011) Offsite Production: a model for building down barriers - A European construction industry perspective. *Engineering, Construction and Architectural Management*, **18**(1), 82–101.

NAO (National Audit Office) (2001) *Modernising Construction*. Comptroller and Auditor General.

NAO (National Audit Office) (2005) *Using Modern Methods of Construction to Build Home More Quickly and Efficiently*. National Audit Office.

Nateriello, G. (1989) *What do Employers Want in Entry-Level Workers? An Assessment of Evidence*. Trends and Issues No. 12.OERI-RI88062013. Columbia University, New York.

Ngowi, A.B., Pienaar, E., Talukhaba, A. & Mbachu, J. (2005) The globalisation of the construction industry – a review. *Building and Environment*, **40**, 135–141.

NHBC (2006) *A Guide to Modern Methods of Construction*, NF1. NHBC Foundation. Housing Research and Development in partnership with BRE Trust.

Noguchi, M. (2005) *Japanese Manufacturers' 'Cost-Performance' Marketing Strategy for the Delivery of Solar Photovoltaic Homes*. Solar World Congress, Orlando, FL.

NWDA (2004) *North West Development Agency – Construction Sector: Mapping, Strategy and Action Plan*. NWDA.

O'Brien, M., Wakefield, R. & Beliveau, Y. (2000) *Industrializing the Residential Construction Site. Center for Housing Research*. Virginia Polytechnic Institute and State University. Virginia.

Ogden, R. (2007) *Discovering Offsite. Buildoffsite Promoting Construction Offsite PowerPoint Presentation*. Available from buildoffsite. www.buildoffsite.com

Palotz, T.R. (2006) *Eine neue Ökonomie für den Wohnungsbau: Konzepte des Kosten- und Flächensparenden Bauens und Ansätze der Übertragbarkeit*. Books on Demand, Norderstedt, Germany.

Pan, W., Gibb, A. & Dainty, A. (2005) *Offsite Modern Methods of Construction in Housebuilding: Perspectives and Practices of Leading UK Housebuilders*. Loughborough University, Loughborough.

Pearce, D. (2003) *The Social and Economic Value of Construction*. Davis Langdon Consultancy.nCRISP New Construction Research and Innovation Strategy Panel, London.

Pietsch, W. (2002) QFD dissemination – principles and practice. *1st international Symposium on Quality Function Deployment (KFG)*, Dokyuz Eylül Üniversitesi, Faculty of Business, Izmir.

Plus Group and Riverside (2005) *Modern Methods of Construction in the North West: Breaking the Barriers*. MMCNW Steering Group.

Prahalad, C K. & Hamel, G. (1990) The core competence of the corporation. *Harvard Business Review*, **68**(May–June), 79–91.

Rezgui, Y., Wilson, I.E., Damodaran, L., Olphert, W. & Shelbourn, M. (2004) *ICT Adoption in the Construction Sector: Education and Training Issues*. ICCCBE-X: the Xth International Conference on Computing in Civil and Building Engineering, Bauhaus-Universität, Weimer, Germany, 2–4 June 2004. Professur Informatik in Bauwesen.http://e-pub.uni-weimar.de/frontdoor.php?source_opus=207&la=de

RIBA (2005) *RIBA Constructive Change: A Strategic Industry Study into the Future of the Architects' Profession*. RIBA. Available from http://www.architecture.com/go/Architecture/Debate/Change_2096.html

Saffin, D. (2007) Breaking down barriers to collaboration. *Insite Magazine*. The IT Construction Forum.

Sahney, S., Banwet, D.K. & Karunes, S. (2003) Enhancing quality in education: application of quality function deployment – an industry perspective. *Work Study*, **52**(6), 297–309.

Seaden, G., Guolla, M., Doutriaux, J. & Nash, J. (2003) Strategic decisions and innovation in construction firms. *Construction Management and Economics*, **21**(6), 603–612.

Sebestyen, G. & Pollington, C. (2003) *New Architecture and Technology*. Architectural Press, Oxford.

Senge, P.M. (1992) *The Fifth Discipline: The Art and Practice of the Learning Organisation*. Century Business, London.

Shunk, D. (2002) *Competency-based, Anytime-Any place System*. e-Business and e-Work Conference, 16–18 October. Corinthia Towers Hotel. Prague, Czech Republic.

Slaughter, S.E. (1998) Models of construction innovation. *Journal of Construction Engineering and Management*, **124**(3), 226–231.

Slotte, V. & Tynjälä, P. (2003) Industry-University Collaboration for Continuing Professional Development. *Journal of Education and Work*, **16**(4), 445–464.

Stasz, C. (2001) Assessing Skills for work: two perspectives. *Oxford Economic Papers*, **53**(3), 385–405.

Stephen, M. & Flynn, M. (2006) *Managing and Ageing Workforce in Construction: A Report for Employers*. Centre for Research into the older Workforce. Department for Work and Pensions.

Tatum, C.B., Vanegas, J.A. & Williams, J.M. (1986) *Constructability Improvement Using Prefabrication, Preassembly, and Modularisation*. Stanford University. Department of Civil Engineering. Technical Report No. 297. Construction Industry Institute. Constructability Task Force.

Taylor, A. (2005) What employers look for: the skill debate and the fit with youth perceptions. *Journal of Education and Work*, **18**(2), 201–218.

Taylor, P.L., Morrison, S., Ainger, C. & Ogden, R. (2004) *Design and Modern Methods of Construction Review*. The Commission for Architecture and the Built Environment (CABE).

Tener, R.K. (1996) Industry-University Partnership for Construction Engineering Education. *Journal of Professional issues in Engineering Education and Practice*, **122**(4), 156–162.

Tindale, P. (1967) Components and the nation. *RIBA Journal*, **November**, 478–481.

Toffler, A. (1970) *Future Shock*. Bantam Books. New York.

Trauth, E.M., Farwell, D.W. & Lee, D. (1993) The IS Expectation Gap: Industry versus Academic Preparations. *MIS Quarterly*, **17**(3), 293–307.

Van de Ven, A.H. (1986) Central problems in the management of innovation. *Management Science*, **32**(5), 590–607.

Venables, T., Barlow, H. & Gann, D. (2004) *The Housing Forum: Manufacturing Excellence*. UK capacity in offsite manufacturing. Innovation Studies Centre, Tanaka Business School, Imperial College.

Venables, T. & Courtney, R. (2004) *Modern Methods of Construction in Germany: Playing the Offsite Rule*. Global Watch Mission Report, DTI.

Vrijhoef, R. & Koskela, L. (2005) *Revisiting the Three Peculiarities of Production in Construction*. IGLC-13 Lean Construction Theory, Sydney.

Wang, J.T.J. (2003) Curricular planning of upgrading the practical and professional competence of students in Technological Colleges. *International Conference on Workforce Education and Development*, 17–19 November. Taipei, Taiwan.

Warszawski, A. (1999) *Industrialized and Automated Building Systems*. 2nd edn. E&FN Spon, London.

Williamson, K.C. & Bilbo, D. (1999) A Road Map to an effective Graduate Construction Program. *Journal of Construction Education*, **4**(3), 260–277.

Womack, J.P., Jones, D.T. & Ross, D. (1990) *The Machine that Changes the World*. Rawson Associates, Maxwell Macmillan, New York.

Wood, G. (1999) Interdisciplinary working in the built environment education. *Education + Training*, **41**(8), 373–380.

Woudhuysen, J. & Abley, I. (2004) *Why is Construction so Backward?* Wiley-Academy, Chichester, UK.

Wysocki, R.K. (2004) *Project Management Process Improvement*. Artech House Inc, Boston, MA.

Construction Innovation through Knowledge Management

Charles Egbu

10.1 Introduction

The business environment of today is uncertain, unpredictable and competitive. Organisations conduct businesses in this second decade of the twenty-first century facing fiercer economic and market conditions than ever before. To survive, remain in business and profit-maximise, organisations need to be competitive and draw on organisational assets that distinguish them from others. More than ever before, there is a growing recognition and acceptance, in competitive business environments and project-based industries, that knowledge is a vital organisational and project resource that gives market leverage and contributes to organisational innovations and project success. Barney (1991) noted that sustained competitive advantage is obtained through capabilities and resources that are valuable, rare, non-imitable and non-substitutable. Such capabilities can be seen in the knowledge and experiences of individuals who are the workforce of organisations. Two decades later in 2011, after Barney (1991), the role of knowledge (individual and organisational knowledge) in contributing to organisational competitiveness and innovation is even greater. However, today, many organisations are at a crossroads. They are having to shed their workforce to remain in business. By so doing, they run the risk of depleting their valuable knowledge base, which is so important for organisational innovations and competitiveness. It is therefore important that organisations are able to manage their knowledge assets in an environment of uncertainty and economic turbulence. If they do not do so effectively, they may end up having organisational memory loss and serious depletion of knowledge assets, which would be detrimental to competitiveness and organisational innovations and renewal.

Construction Innovation and Process Improvement, First Edition.
Edited by Akintola Akintoye, Jack S. Goulding and Girma Zawdie.
© 2012 Blackwell Publishing Ltd. Published 2012 by Blackwell Publishing Ltd.

Knowledge management (KM) has truly emerged as a vital activity for organisations to preserve valuable knowledge and exploit the creativity of individuals that generates innovation. Egbu (2005) argued (in Anumba *et al.* (2005) that knowledge management is important for a number of reasons. First, it is important because the rise of time-based competition as a marketing weapon requires organisations to learn quickly. Second, it is important because of the globalisation of operations and because of the growth in number of mergers and takeovers where multiple organisations share knowledge in a collaborative forum. In project-based industries, such as the construction industry, the situation is even more complex. The activities of construction organisations are often characterised by short-term working contracts and diverse working patterns. Knowledge management is important in this context, because it brings together diverse knowledge sources from different sections of the demand and supply chains achieving cross-functional integration. Given this, an understanding of how organisations manage knowledge assets for improved innovation is important.

This chapter presents the role of KM in the acquisition, storage and use of tacit and explicit knowledge in an organisation. It also discusses how knowledge management impacts upon innovations in project based environments, along with the challenges facing project based organisations in managing knowledge through effective knowledge management practices, particularly in turbulent economic and market conditions.

10.2   Knowledge and Knowledge Management – Context and Definition

Few would contest the fact that people conceptualise knowledge according to their subjective interpretations. The debate about the meaning of knowledge is a pastiche of abstract ideas, which is too substantial to approach in this chapter. However, it is useful to explore the epistemological ideas of some authors briefly to establish a better conceptual understanding of knowledge in different contexts. Egbu and Botterill (2001) postulate that there is a complex dialectic between those who define knowledge as a scientific truth that exists independently of human action, and those who argue that knowledge is socially constructed. Knowledge has been traditionally thought of as a static concept, something that exists independently of human beings. Western philosophical preoccupations with the idea of knowledge as truth failed to account for essential dimensions in epistemology. Positivism took this view further by asserting that scientific truths exist objectively in the world, and that knowledge is a random combination of these truths. Epistemologists of this perspective have repeatedly neglected the human element of knowledge. In contrast, there are those who assert that knowledge is socially constructed and is completely determined by social structures. In this respect, knowledge can be seen as a process that is context-specific. This social constructionist perspective has Marxist undertones, and has been further revised by a view that human action determines knowledge (Habermas, 1984). Thus, social interaction is the principal motor of knowledge and human beings are responsible for conditioning their own environment (Nonaka and Takeuchi, 1995). Davenport and Prusak (1998) define knowledge as consisting of truths, beliefs, perspectives, concepts, judgements, expectations, methodologies and know-how, and originates in the minds of 'knower's'.

Defining knowledge management precisely can therefore be somewhat problematic. Nowhere in the literature on knowledge management is there a single unified meaning of the concept. Alvesson (1993) (cited in Despres and Chauvel, 1999: 110) argue that knowledge management is clearly on the slippery slope of being intuitively important but intellectually elusive. Many authors have attempted to explain certain elements of KM, specific to their own academic domains. Much of the ambiguity associated with KM is rooted in these authors' epistemological beliefs. Knowledge management could arguably be viewed as any process or practice of creating, acquiring, capturing, sharing and using knowledge wherever it resides, in order to meet existing and emerging needs, to identify and exploit existing and acquired assets and to develop new opportunities. For example, Nonaka and Takeuchi (1995) classified knowledge into two main types, and have adopted this distinction and applied it to the organisation. Explicit knowledge describes the type of knowledge that is documented and public, structured, fixed-content, externalised and conscious. Tacit knowledge can be generally understood as the form of knowledge that exists within an individual, and is intuitive and unarticulated. Tacit knowledge has been conceptualised by a myriad of academics from differing perspectives. Collins (1995) sees three types of tacit knowledge that present challenges to epistemological concerns of management. Embodied knowledge describes a type of knowledge that is a function of the physical environment. It cannot be easily transferred from one brain to another, as it is specific to the unique 'hardware' that accompanies an individual's brain; it is an integral part of the unique make-up of the human body. For example, a boxer's knowledge of fighting may be transferred to a professor, but the latter may not be physically able to use that knowledge in practice. Second, 'embrained knowledge' describes a type of knowledge that is specified by the exclusive physicality of an individual brain. Finally, 'encultured knowledge' describes a type of knowledge that is embedded within a social context, and cannot exist apart from it.

A thorough review of literature in the area of knowledge management suggests that it is diverse in perspective, approach and focus, yet there is a common bond that knowledge is a valuable asset in organisations throughout the industrial world. From an economic perspective, Drucker in the 1990s (as cited in McAdam and McCreedy, 1999: 93) noted 'we are entering the knowledge society in which the basic economic resource is no longer capita… but is and will be knowledge.' In a similar vein, Edvinsson (2000) claimed that there has been a shift in focus from local and physical to global and intangible. Knowledge is celebrated as a resource that is as important for organisations to understand and manage as labour and capital was in the 'old economy'. Similarly, O'Regan and O'Donnell (2000) also noted 'we are living in an era where the intangible is rapidly assuming economic, social and psychological supremacy over the tangible.'

10.3   Knowledge Management and Innovations in Project Based Environments

It is now generally accepted that the ability to innovate depends partly on the way in which an organisation uses and exploits the resources available to it, and a vital organisational resource, at the heart of innovation, is knowledge. Innovation can be viewed as the successful introduction and exploitation of an idea (product, service, technology and market). Knowledge management is highly associated with innovation because of its ability to convert tacit knowledge of people into explicit knowledge. This is grounded in the notion that unique tacit knowledge of individuals is of immense value to the organisation as a whole, and is the 'wellspring of innovation'. Given the close connection between knowledge possessed by personnel in an organisation, and the products and services obtainable from the organisation, it is uncontroversial that an organisation's ability to produce new products and other aspects of performance are inextricably linked to how it organises its human resources. It is tacit rather than explicit knowledge, which will typically be of more value to innovation processes. Yet, tacit knowledge is knowledge, which cannot be easily communicated, understood or used without the 'knowing subject'. The implication of the above discourse is that knowledge management that focuses on creating network structures to transfer only explicit knowledge will be severely limited in terms of its contribution to innovation and organisational and project success.

Construction organisations will therefore have to meet the needs and expectations of their clients, by drawing on the knowledge and expertise of project teams. Deploying experts into project teams is a mechanism by which professional service organisations coordinate and apply the diverse expertise and experience embedded within individuals, creating a knowledge network within the team, although sharing knowledge between team members may also create some tensions concerning competitive positions of the team members. The ability to match expertise with client needs and expectations is key to improving the competitive advantage of project-based professional or technical service organisations, where collaborative knowledge gained through successive projects is captured by organisations to continually enhance their market position. From a knowledge-based strategic management perspective, the creation of an optimal mix of a project team (i.e. having expertise in its membership drawn from across organisations) that has requisite skills and competence matched to the client's project requirements, will more often than not lead to client satisfaction and the project objectives being met. In addition, it provides opportunity for innovations through the maximisation of knowledge and expertise within a team.

Many innovation processes in the management and procurement of construction activities are becoming increasingly interactive, requiring simultaneous networking across multiple 'communities of practice', such as professional groups, functional groups and business units. This networking involves communication and negotiation amongst different social communities with distinctive norms, cultural values and interest in the innovation process. This therefore means that knowledge needed for innovation is distributed within organisations and across organisational boundaries through different supply chains. In the UK construction industry, there is a steady increase in collaborative working practices, such as partnering, alliances, Public Private Partnerships and Joint Ventures. In addition, projects are growing in complexity and cost, and clients' demands and expectations are also increasing more than ever before. This presents a situation where organisations have to collaborate and share knowledge, skills and expertise, in order to meet the needs of the clients. However, in sharing knowledge, organisations need to be both mindful of the communicative behaviours and practices associated with knowledge exchange as well as the 'knowledge paradox'. Organisations will have to be open to formal and informal information and knowledge flows from both networks and markets. At the same time, they must protect and preserve their intellectual capital and knowledge base, because it is upon this latter point that survival depends.

10.4   Managing Knowledge in Construction: Challenges Facing Project Based Organisations

Understanding how organisations manage knowledge assets involves due cognisance of a number of factors. It involves understanding the strategies that underpin KM practices within organisations, the structure and culture that sustains KM, the tools and technologies that support KM and how organisations measure the effects of KM. All these raise real challenges to managers in organisations and in projects. The construction industry is a project-based industry, and it remains the case that the UK construction industry contains a small number of relatively large firms and a large number of small firms. About 95% of construction firms employ fewer than eight people. The characteristics of the UK construction industry are well rehearsed and documented; however, it is important to see this from a knowledge management perspective.

The fragmentation of the construction industry reflects the economics of production, encouraging small firms organised by trade or craft. Construction firms typically involve relatively low capital investment. There are also relatively low barriers to entry and exit of firms within the construction industry. There are also characteristics of small firms, which affect their ability to access and transfer knowledge. First, this is related to their perceived technological weakness, such as a specialised range of technological competencies, inability to develop and manage complex systems, inability to fund long-term and risky knowledge management programmes. Similarly, investment in formal and informal training and education in the acquisition and sharing of requisite knowledge could be said to be more challenging for smaller than for larger organisations. Other perceived disadvantages of small organisations include little management experience, power imbalance when collaborating with large firms, difficulty in coping with complex regulations and associated cost of compliance. However, small size organisations could be said to have organisational strengths, which could stand them in good stead for managing knowledge assets. In the main, small firms often do not need the formal strategies used in large firms to ensure communication and coordination. These less-formal strategies in small firms, it could be argued, ease the communication of knowledge, improve informal networks, increase speed of decision-making, and improve the degree of employee commitment and receptiveness of novelty. Smaller organisations also tend to react faster to changing market requirements.

The construction industry is also characterised by projects, by short-term employment and by temporary coalitions of contractors and subcontractors. It is also perceived to have an adversarial culture. It could be argued that the nature of projects does not lend itself to knowledge management practices. For a start, projects tend to be temporary events; whereas, knowledge management programmes are usually seen as long-term investments. Projects can also be seen as temporary coalitions of individuals and teams who come together for the duration of the project, and are then disbanded after the end of the project. This latter characteristic of a project poses some challenges in terms of knowledge management. These include the difficulty of building trust amongst project team members, and motivating project staff and operatives during the project period. These are important issues for knowledge management.

Project culture is also likely to be different from an organisational culture. The project manager also has the project objectives (e.g. cost, time, quality, safety and environmental issues) as the overriding project concerns, as it is on the fulfilment of these objectives that they are normally judged. There is also the added complication in project environment, which is the fact that there may be members of the wider project team (i.e. those involved in the project supply chains) who, for many reasons, may not have the interest, drive and commitment towards knowledge management. There are also those who are committed to the project for a short period (e.g. a week or two, or even less) and who are bound to ask the question: 'What is there for me (WITFM) in knowledge management anyway?' However, it is important to point out that project knowledge is not just made up of the explicit type that is easily documented and archived. There is also the tacit knowledge. There is a need to be reminded that projects are made up of people, many of whom have requisite skills, knowledge, competence and wisdom. Some will also bring with them knowledge dimensions from previous jobs, which could be of use in solving problems and for providing innovative solutions to their new projects. In essence, knowledge management from a project perspective is about harnessing individual and project knowledge to the benefit of the project. The challenges therefore, for project managers and leaders of projects, are firstly to recognise the particular constraints imposed on knowledge management processes by the project environments, and secondly to find the means of creating, transferring, sharing, implementing and exploiting individual and project knowledge in such a way that they lead to project success and provide benefits to project clients.

Addressing the challenges of knowledge management calls for effective leadership and an understanding of the fundamental roles that people play in knowledge capture and knowledge sharing. If construction leaders are interested in knowledge capture, sharing and exploitation, then it is necessary to consider that knowledge workers (project staff and team members) should be included in a dynamic knowledge management process. This process is one that demands the support of motivation, creativity and the ability to improve an intellectual and comprehensive vision of the relationship between the project and the project team members. In other words, individual and project knowledge should be seen as a project's intellectual capital, and an important factor in project success. Targeted education and training geared towards construction personnel is important to improve cultural awareness in these important areas.

10.5   Knowledge Management Strategy – Issues and Contexts

It is important to stress at the outset, that there is no one KM strategy that best addresses knowledge management issues in all organisations. Organisations are different. Their needs are different and their capacity and capabilities to address issues are also different. Similarly, the wider contexts in which they operate are different, and so these are likely to impact on whatever strategy they decide to adopt and implement. However, whatever knowledge management strategy is being considered, sufficient attention should be given to both informal knowledge processes and formalised knowledge management initiatives. Attention should also be given to the complexities of *knowledge*, rather than any proxies, such as information. It is the case that many accounts of 'Knowledge Management' default to a focus on information management. Such a view underestimates the richness of the subject of knowledge, and the opportunities a knowledge focus offers for re-thinking business processes. It is argued elsewhere (Egbu *et al.*, 2003a) that whereas certain types of knowledge can be codified and treated as information, much knowledge is personal, being based on experience and reflection, and remains tacit.

Knowledge also has a social dimension, being created and shared in social groupings, within which tacit knowledge sharing may often occur (Brown and Duguid, 1991). Related to its social nature, knowledge is also created in specific contexts, and is to varying degrees 'situated' (Lave and Wenger 1991) or context specific, and may be 'sticky' and difficult to transfer or share (von Hippel, 1994). This reduces the potential for the simple and costless transfer of lessons learned between contexts, such as companies or industries. Thus, there are different approaches to knowledge management, and many of these emphasise the capture and processing of knowledge resources or assets (or intellectual capital) that the organisation already possesses. There is also an approach that focuses on knowledge processes and dynamic capabilities, as well as knowledge resources. An emphasis on organisational processes, such as knowledge creation and sharing, provides a greater indication of dynamic capabilities. Another approach is one that emphasises on practitioner knowledge (Gibbons *et al.*, 1994). In *The New Production of Knowledge*, they identify a shift in modes of knowledge creation from Mode 1 to Mode 2. Mode 1 knowledge is produced in institutions, is disciplinary, with a hierarchical control system through peer review, and an emphasis on generating codified knowledge that is transferable. Mode 1 knowledge grows cumulatively, is stored in libraries and forms the content of university syllabuses and professional qualifications. In contrast, Mode 2 knowledge is created in the context of application – it results from practice, is transient and often unrecorded. It is trans-disciplinary, and the capability to produce it is widely diffused. Gibbons *et al.* (1994) argue that Mode 2 has hitherto been undervalued, and also that it is increasing in importance.

A further approach focuses on cross-boundary knowledge processes, and particularly the need for organisations to acquire knowledge from external sources. Arguably, no firm has ever been independent in knowledge terms and today all organisations are likely to be increasingly dependent on external sources of knowledge. The capability to track, make sense of, understand and assimilate externally sourced knowledge is known as *absorptive capacity* (Cohen and Levinthal 1990). The skills required to absorb knowledge include techniques of sourcing, sense-making and learning.

So, it is important for a knowledge management strategy to give due consideration to organisational knowledge capabilities or processes as well as resources, to take account of informal knowledge processes as well as formal knowledge management and values practitioner (or Mode 2) knowledge, and consider context and address the issue of absorptive capacity. It should also acknowledge the richness and complexity of the subject of knowledge, whilst recognising that firms need to address practical issues. Thus, there is need for the following knowledge processes occurring within and between firms:

- creating/generating/producing knowledge;
- communicating, sharing knowledge;
- searching/sourcing knowledge;
- synthesising/transforming/combining knowledge;
- capturing/codifying/storing/classifying knowledge;
- mapping knowledge or knowledge proxies; and
- applying and re-using knowledge.

10.6   Knowledge Management Techniques and Technologies

For knowledge management, the term 'tools' is used loosely. Too often, knowledge management 'tools' is used to mean only IT tools. There is a need for a better understanding of Information Technology (IT) and non-IT tools, their differences and characteristics. A host of technologies (IT-based) and techniques (non-IT based) exist for knowledge management in organisations. In the main, the selection of appropriate technologies appears to follow a more structured approach than the selection of techniques for knowledge management. In industrial settings, there are two main approaches for selecting appropriate knowledge management technologies. The first approach is based on knowledge management 'sub-processes'. The second approach is based on 'technology families'. The former appears more popular, as it allows the 'users' to identify sub-processes that they need to manage and then select the most appropriate technologies geared for the need of the identified sub-processes. In construction organisations, the potential benefits of technologies and techniques for KM are not fully understood. There is a need for some guidance in the approaches employed by organisations for selecting appropriate technologies and techniques for knowledge management.

In this respect, knowledge management techniques do not depend on IT, although it provides support in some cases. Examples include brainstorming, communities of practice, face-to-face interactions, recruitment, training, story-telling, coaching, job-rotation, shadowing and quality circles. KM techniques, arguably, require strategies for learning, more involvement of people, and are more focused on tacit knowledge. They are relatively more affordable to most organisations. This is because no sophisticated infrastructure is required, although some techniques require more resources than others (e.g. training requires more resources than face-to-face interactions). KM techniques are relatively easy to implement and maintain due to their simple and straightforward nature. They focus on retaining and increasing the organisational tacit knowledge, a key asset to organisations. Furthermore, KM techniques are not new, as organisations have been implementing them for a long time, where their use has been under the umbrella of several management approaches (e.g. organisational learning and learning organisations). Using these tools for the management of organisational knowledge requires their use to be enhanced so that benefits from them, in terms of knowledge gain/increase, are properly managed.

Communities of Practice (CoPs) consist of a group of people of different skill sets, development histories and experience backgrounds, who work together to achieve commonly shared goals. These groups are different from teams and task forces. People in CoPs can perform the same job, collaborate on a shared task (software developers), or work together on a product. They are peers in the execution of 'real work.' What holds them together is a common sense of purpose and a real need to know what each other knows. Usually, there are many communities of practice within a single company and most people normally belong to more than one.

Post-Project Reviews are an important KM technique. They are debriefing sessions used to highlight lessons learnt during the course of a project. These reviews are important to capture knowledge about, causes of failures, how they were addressed, and the best practices identified in a project. This increases the effectiveness of learning, as knowledge can be transferred to subsequent projects. However, if this technique is to be effectively utilised, adequate time should be allocated for those who were involved in a project to participate. It is also crucial for post-project review meetings to take place immediately after a project is completed, as project participants may move or be transferred to other projects or organisations. Whilst project reviews are important, their limitations need to be acknowledged. There is also increasing importance for live-capture of knowledge as projects progress.

Apprenticeship as an important KM technique is a form of training in a particular trade carried out mainly by practical experience or learning by doing (not through formal instruction). Apprentices often work with their masters and learn craftsmanship through observation, imitation and practice. The masters focus on improving the skills of the individuals so that they can later perform tasks on their own. This process of skill building requires continuous practice by the apprentices until they reach the required level. For example, mentoring is a process whereby a trainee or a junior staff member is attached or assigned to a senior member of an organisation for advice relating to career development. The mentor provides a coaching role to facilitate the development of the trainee (mentee) by identifying training needs and other development aspirations. This type of training usually consists of career objectives given to the trainee, whereby the mentor checks if the objectives are achieved and provides feedback.

There are many KM tools and techniques used in construction (Egbu *et al.*, 2003b), to capture knowledge through knowledge mapping tools, knowledge bases, Case-based Reasoning, etc. KM technologies consist of a combination of hardware and software technologies. In this respect, hardware technologies and components are important for a KM system as they form the platform for the software technologies to perform and the medium for the storage and transfer of knowledge. Some of the hardware requirements for a KM system are:

- the personal computer or workstation to facilitate access to the required knowledge;
- highly powerful servers to allow the organisation to be networked;
- open architecture to ensure inter-operability in distributed environments;
- media-rich applications requiring Integrated Services Digital Network (ISDN) and fibre optics to provide high speed;
- Asynchronous Transfer Mode (ATM) as a multi-media switching technology for handling the combination of voice, video and data traffic simultaneously; and
- use of the public network (e.g. Internet) and private networks (e.g. Intranet, Extranet) to facilitate access to and sharing of knowledge.

Software technologies also play an important part in facilitating the implementation of KM. The number of software applications has increased considerably in the last few years. Solutions provided by software vendors take many forms and perform different tasks. The large number of vendors that provide KM solutions makes it extremely difficult to identify the most appropriate solutions. This has resulted in organisations adopting different models for establishing KM systems. KM software technologies have seen many improvements in the last decade due to many alliances, and mergers and acquisitions between KM and Portal tool vendors. Data and text mining is a technology for extracting knowledge from masses of data or text. The process of data/text mining enables meaningful patterns and associations of data (words and phrases) to be identified from one or more large databases or 'knowledge-bases'.

The more commonly used technologies for knowledge capture and sharing in the construction industry include groupware, Intranet, Internet, Extranet and knowledge bases. Groupware, as a software product, helps people to communicate, share knowledge and information, perform their work efficiently and effectively, and helps in decision-making. It supports distributed and virtual project teams, where team members are from multiple organisations and in geographically dispersed locations. Groupware tools usually contain email communications, instant messaging, discussion areas, file area or document repository, information management tools (e.g. calendar, contact lists, meeting agendas and minutes) and search facilities. An Intranet is an internal organisational Internet that is guarded against outside access by special security tools called firewalls, and an Extranet is an Intranet with limited access to outsiders – often making it possible for them to collect and deliver certain knowledge over the Intranet. This technology is useful for making organisational knowledge available to geographically dispersed staff members, and is therefore used by many organisations. Knowledge bases are repositories that store knowledge about a topic in a concise and organised manner. They present facts that can be found in a book, a collection of books, websites or even human knowledge. This is different from the knowledge bases of expert systems, which incorporate rules as part of the inference engine that searches the knowledge base to make decisions.

10.7   Effective Knowledge Management Practices in Turbulent Economic and Market Conditions

Effective knowledge management practices depend on a host of factors. There is no one strategy or theory that explains successful knowledge management in all organisational or project contexts. It depends on an appropriate balance of such issues a:

- organisational strategy, choices and path dependency;
- people in organisations, organisational culture and structure;
- technological and financial resources; organisational processes and routines; and
- a thorough consideration of internal and external stimuli – the context in which knowledge this is to be managed.

However, leaders of organisations and projects need to see knowledge management as important, and an integral part of strategic decision making, which can influence profitability and competitiveness of the organisation, as well as project success. Leaders of organisations should therefore endeavour to establish at all levels of the organisation a strategic intent of knowledge acquisition, creation, accumulation, protection and exploitation of knowledge. In the same vein, the linkages between strategic management and human values need to be examined carefully, along with the role of a KM orientation in an effort to support adequately successful strategies. Leaders of organisations should not pay 'lip service' or just be interested in knowledge development, but should proactively support it.

As part of effective knowledge management, it is important that leaders consider employees as a fundamental part of the dynamic knowledge process; this will not only help support motivation and enhance creativity, but also help provide a comprehensive vision of the relationship between the organisation, people, the project and its environment. Leaders should also endeavour to determine and put in place an effective communication infrastructure for the effective capture, transfer and leveraging of knowledge. Above all, leaders would have to create an appropriate culture for effective knowledge management. Such culture should encourage workers' autonomy, so that they may express and share the knowledge they possess in a 'free environment'. An effective knowledge management should also be able to determine methods for mapping knowledge, determining who has what knowledge, needs what knowledge, and where this knowledge resides, and measuring the extent of KM effectiveness. Auditing the knowledge present at, or accessible to, the organisation, and managing adequately the inventory of 'knowledge repositories', is vital for continuing improvement and organisational renewal.

The role that leaders play in effective knowledge management is therefore vital, and should provide opportunities for:

- sharing culture where there is openness and willingness to share information, experience and knowledge across organisation and project teams. This should allow 'flexibility' in the lines of communications allowing top-down, bottom-up and lateral communications within project and organisational structures;
- creating a risk tolerant climate, where it is accepted that lessons could be learned through mistakes;
- developing knowledge teams, i.e. staff from all disciplines to develop or improve methods and processes;
- introducing knowledge webs (networks of experts/communities of practice who collaborate across project teams) and the provisions of collaborative technologies, such as Intranets or GroupWare for rapid information access;
- defining and communicating knowledge performance behaviours, and identifying key knowledge workers and knowledge performance positions;
- make knowledge performance part and parcel of organisation and project performance;
- rewarding knowledge-sharing behaviours and incentivise key knowledge management actions.

As part of effective knowledge management practices, networking, CoPs, storytelling, coaching, mentoring and quality circles are important mechanisms for sharing and transferring tacit knowledge in organisation and project environments. These should be considered, encouraged and promoted more by project leaders. Communities of practice are needed to encourage individuals to think of themselves as members of 'professional families' with a strong sense of reciprocity.

Human networking processes can encourage sharing and the use of knowledge for project and organisational innovations are important. Leaders of projects should also espouse 'the law of increasing returns of knowledge' as a positive way of encouraging knowledge sharing – shared knowledge stays with the giver, while enriching the receiver. Intuitive knowledge is managed by individuals being valued and not by being heavy-handed through project 'controlled processes'. It is folly to believe that any project or organisational environment can make people have ideas and force them to reveal intuitive messages or share their knowledge in any sustained manner. An individual's intuitive knowledge cannot be manipulated in any meaningful way nor controlled without the individual being willing and privy to it. The process of trying to manipulate or control intuitive knowledge in fact creates their destruction. The issues of trust, respect and reciprocity are vital elements of a conducive environment for managing tacit knowledge. It is through these that individual members of the project or organisation can be motivated to share their experiences and exploit their creativity. Leaders would need to recognise, provide incentives and reward knowledge performance and sharing behaviour patterns. They should also take action on poor knowledge performance. The regular communication of the benefits of knowledge management is important in sustaining the co-operation of project team members. A variety of ways exist for doing this, including regular meetings, project summaries, project memos and through project GroupWare/Intranet facilities where they exist. Every organisation and project strategy for KM should consider training, recruitment and selection of project team members (e.g. subcontractors and suppliers). It should also pay due cognisance to the team members' competencies, requisite knowledge and their willingness and effectiveness in sharing knowledge for the benefit of the project and the organisation.

10.8   Conclusion

Knowledge management continues to have a significant role to play in organisational competitiveness and innovation. People are at the heart of knowledge management and organisations need to view their people as their greatest asset. It is understandable that for many organisations the current economic climate provides added challenges for managing organisational assets. However, through effective leadership and a clear strategic vision, organisations are able to manage their knowledge assets effectively in the current turbulent economic environments. In this respect, hardware technologies and components are important for a KM system, as they form the platform for the software technologies to perform, and the medium for the storage and transfer of knowledge. Software technologies also play an important part in facilitating the implementation of KM. The number of software applications has increased considerably in the last few years. Solutions provided by software vendors take many forms and perform different tasks. The more commonly used technologies for knowledge capture and sharing in the construction industry include groupware, Intranet, Internet, extranet and knowledge bases.

Many factors confront organisations in the management of knowledge assets. These include organisational culture, motivation and incentivising their workforce. Their strategic choices, knowledge assets and capabilities, and financial and technological capabilities, and also the effect of internal and environment stimuli are all inextricably linked.

References

Alvesson, M. (1993) Organisation as rhetoric: knowledge intensive firms and the struggle for ambiguity. *Journal of Management Studies*, 30(6), 997–1020.

Anumba, C., Egbu, C., & Carrillo, P. (2005) *Knowledge Management in Construction*. Blackwell Publishing, Oxford.

Barney, J.B. (1991) Firm resources and sustained competitive advantage. *Journal of Management*, 17(1), 99–120.

Brown, J.S. & Duguid, P. (1991) Organizational learning and communities of practice: towards a unified view of working, learning and organization. *Organization Science*, 2(1), 40–57.

Cohen, W.M. & Levinthal, D.A. (1990) Absorptive capacity: a new perspective on learning and innovation. *Administrative Science Quarterly*, 35, 128–152.

Collins, H.M. (1995) Humans, machines, and the structure of knowledge. In: ed. Ruggles, R.L., *Knowledge Management Tools*. Butterworth-Heinnemann, Newton, MA. 145–165.

Davenport, T.H. & Prusak, L. (1998) *Working Knowledge*. Harvard Business School Press, Boston, MA.

Despres, C. & Chauvel, D. (1999) Knowledge management(s). *Journal of Knowledge Management*, 3(2), 110–120.

Edvinsson, L. (2000) Some perspectives on intangibles and intellectual capital 2000. *Journal of Intellectual Capital*, 1(1), 12–16.

Egbu, C.O. (2005) Knowledge Management as a Driver for Innovation. In: Anumba, C., Egbu, C.O. & Camillo, P. *Knowledge Management in Construction*. Blackwell Publishing, Oxford. 121–131.

Egbu, C.O., Kurul, E., Quintas, P., Hutchinson, V., Anumba, C., Al-Ghassani, A. & Kuitar, R. (2003a) *A Systematic Analysis of Knowledge Practices in Other Sectors: Lessons for Construction*. September, Report: Work Package 2; Department of Trade and Industry (DTI) – Partners in Innovation project: CI 39/3/709.

Egbu, C.O., Kurul, E., Quintas, P., Hutchinson, V., Anumba, C., Al-Ghassani, A. & Kuitar, R. (2003b) *Techniques and Technologies for Knowledge Management*. September, Report: Work Package 3; Department of Trade and Industry (DTI) – Partners in Innovation project: CI 39/3/709.

Egbu, C.O. & Botterill, K. (2001) Knowledge management and intellectual capital: Benefits for project based industries. *Proceedings of the RICS Foundation – Construction and Building Research Conference (COBRA)*, vol. 2. Glasgow Caledonian University, 3–5 September, ed. Kelly, J. & Hunter, K. 414–422.

Gibbons, M., Limoges, C., Nowotny, H., Schartzman, H., Scott, P. & Trow, M. (1994) *The New Production of Knowledge: the Dynamics of Science and Research*. Sage, London.

Habermas, J. (1984) *The Theory of Communicative Action: The Rationality of Action and the Rationalization of Society*, vol. 1. Polity Press, Cambridge.

Hippel, E. von (1994) 'Sticky information' and the locus of problem solving: implications for innovation. *Management Science*, 40(4), 429–439.

Lave, J. & Wenger, E. (1991) *Situated Learning: Legitimate Peripheral Participation*. Cambridge University Press, Cambridge.

McAdam, R. & McCreedy, S. (1999) A critical review of knowledge management. *The Learning Organisation*, 6(3), 91–100.

Nonaka, I. & Takeuchi, H. (1995) *The Knowledge-Creating Company*. Oxford University Press, Oxford.

O'Regan, P. & O'Donnell, D. (2000) Mapping intellectual resources: Insights from critical modernism. *Journal of European Industrial Training*, 24(2/3/4), 118–127.

Innovation through Collaborative Procurement Strategy and Practices

Akintola Akintoye and Jamie Main

In recent times, the way in which construction activities are managed and procured to achieve clients' requirements is receiving greater attention. There is an increasing concern over the 'ineffectiveness' of existing procurement systems. In some ways, this has been attributable to the fragmented nature of the construction industry, mainly because of a large number of relatively small firms, combined with a large number of relatively small construction projects and low barriers to entry, particularly in the (small) contracting sub-sector. In this respect, the 'industry is fragmented because of the many disciplines involved – designers, constructors, professional consultants and engineers, and specialist contractors. It is fragmented because of long and complex supply chains, bringing together the different specialists. Low profit margins combined with traditional procurement in construction led to adversarial relationships and poor service to clients (Fairclough, 2002). These issues have not been limited to a particular system of procurement, although the management forms appear to have taken the main criticism. This is not to say that any one system is better or worse than its contemporaries, merely that the industry is concerned that, at present, there is no universal solution for solving the problems associated with procurement systems.

Procurement on a project-by-project basis has been regarded as stifling innovation, ostensibly through the lack of security, continuity and critical mass of projects to encourage longer-term work programmes that help to develop in-depth research skills and development (Fairclough, 2002). Another contention is that the problem is not about procurement *per se*, but rather the process of tendering that is stifling innovation. Sidwell and

Construction Innovation and Process Improvement, First Edition.
Edited by Akintola Akintoye, Jack S. Goulding and Girma Zawdie.
© 2012 Blackwell Publishing Ltd. Published 2012 by Blackwell Publishing Ltd.

Budiawan (2001) highlight problems with the competitive tendering process in relation to contractor-led innovation, and explore ways in which owners can develop procurement procedures that allow and encourage innovation from contractors. In addition, Khalfan and McDermont (2006) demonstrated that innovation procurements with integrated supply chain participants within the construction industry often requires innovative thinking, supported by trust and transparency.

This chapter presents procurement in relation to the criteria needed for the choice of procurement methods available, the problems associated with conventional procurement approaches, and how innovative procurement methods can be used to address some of the inherent problems facing the industry.

11.2   Construction Procurement and the Procurement Cycle

Procurement can be described in several ways: as 'the act of obtaining by care or effort, acquiring or bring about' (*Oxford English Dictionary*). Mohsini and Davidson (1989) describe this as 'the acquisition of new buildings, or space within buildings, either by directly buying, renting or leasing from the open market, or by designing and building the facility to meet a specific need.' Lenard and Moshsini, (1998) define this as a strategy to satisfy client's development and/or operational needs with respect to the provision of constructed facilities for a discrete life cycle. Notwithstanding these differences, typically, the procurement involves:

1. identification of requirements;
2. market sourcing;
3. selection of tenders;
4. evaluation of tenders;
5. contract award; and
6. managing and evaluation of delivery.

The CIB W92 Procurement Systems Working Group (CIB, 2011) identified that construction procurement as a framework within which construction is brought about, acquired or obtained. In essence, building or construction procurement is the organisational structure adopted by the client for the management of the design and construction of a building project (Masterman, 1992). In this respect, Rowlinson and McDermott (1999) noted that elements such as contract strategy and the client are functional parts of the procurement system, and that the effectiveness of the client organisation or the contract strategy is modified by other procurement system variables such as culture, sustainability, economic and political environment and more practical concepts such as partnering. Similarly, the Byatt Report (2001) regards procurement as 'the whole process of acquisition of goods, services and construction projects spanning the whole life cycle from the initial concept and definition of business needs through to the end of the useful life of an asset, services contract or need for the activity.'

NEDO (1985) 'Think about Building' lists seven steps to successful construction procurement, specifically:

1. selection of an in-house project executive;
2. appointment of a 'Principal Advisor' if required;
3. careful definition of the requirements of the project;
4. realistic determination of project timing;
5. selection of an appropriate procurement path;
6. considered choice of organisation to be employed; and
7. commitment to a building or site held back until it has been professionally appraised.

In addition, they identified eight criteria for the selection of procurement path as follows:

1. timing
2. controllable variation;
3. complexity;
4. quality level;
5. price certainty;
6. completion;
7. division of responsibility, and
8. risk.

Notwithstanding these nuances, the procurement process often leads to a contract between the parties in order to deliver goods and services. One of the fundamental reasons for entering into a contract is to allocate the risk inherent in a project. In this respect, a construction contract, for example, typically specifies the roles of the client and the contractor, along with the dates by which tasks must be completed, and the formal mechanisms for payment. These issues are particularly important, as all too often contract documents contain uncertainties, and organisations then enter into contracts with conflicting assumptions. This is compounded where the complexity of the activities involved in the procurement cycle involves many professions and practitioners that are expected to work together to deliver a project. Consequently, OGC (2010) views procurement as a cyclical activity rather than a linear project, which is expected to engage with informing and supporting strategic management of organisational deliverables.

11.3   Procurement Strategies

It is possible to divide procurement methods into two broad categories: conventional procurement methods, and innovative or collaborative procurement methods – the details of which can be seen in Table 11.1. The procedure for the selection of the contract and the building team is predominantly influenced by the procurement method. However, fundamental to the categorisation of procurement methods and contract

Table 11.1   Procurement: categories, types and strategies.

Procurement	Type	Strategies
Conventional	Designer-led competitive tendering Designer-led construction managed for a fee Package Deal	Traditional Lump Sum approach Management contracting Construction Management Turnkey Design and Build (Construct) British Property Federation
Innovative/ Collaborative	Package Deal Framework agreements Partnering	Public Private Partnership Design, Build, Finance and Operate Prime contracting Partnering: strategic and project Joint Venture Supply Chain Management

selection is the apportionment of risk between the parties to a construction contract, which naturally include the client and contractor. In this respect, risk apportionment can be influenced by various factors, including:

1. the complexity and uniqueness of the project;
2. the employer's involvement with the design process;
3. the client's involvement with the construction process;
4. the required speed from inception to completion;
5. the required degree of price certainty; and
6. the amount of risk to be transferred to the construction team, etc.

Recently, clients (particularly public sector clients) have moved from traditional or conventional methods to more innovative procurement methods in order to tap into private sector finance, transfer more risk to contractors, and/or achieve better efficiency in the management of construction development to garner value for money for the taxpayers.

11.4   Conventional Procurement Methods

The last 30 years have seen the development of three main procurement systems in the construction industry. The systems that generally reflect the position of the design team in relation to the contractor can be seen as:

- *Traditional*: Designer Lead;
- *Design and Build*: Contractor Lead;
- *Management*: Design Team (including Contractor) Lead.

There are further subdivisions of each of the procurement systems, each system having its own unique characteristics, advantages and drawbacks.

11.4.1   Traditional Procurement System

The traditional procurement system is often referred to as being designer-lead, and has the unique characteristic of the separation of the responsibility for the design of the project from that of its construction. Most architects regard this approach as the 'normal' way to build, and therefore continue to support it (Pain, 1993). This system was widely used on construction projects, although the popularity of this method is now decreasing. The main features of this approach include:

- the contractor not being involved at all during the pre-construction stage;
- long gestation period until commencement on site;
- construction period agreed at tender stage;
- full contractual and commercial risks/opportunities accepted by contractor;
- complete competition on price;
- lump sum contract and agreed construction period;
- adversarial roles between contractor and design team likely;
- changes and variations lead to claims and extensions of time; and
- lack of contractor advice available to client/design team.

11.4.2   Design and Build Procurement System

The Design and Build (D&B) procurement system tends to bring together the responsibilities for design and construction within one organisation, that is, a single point of responsibility for design and construction with one party, the contractor. This direct set up often improves lines of communication. Thus, the level of integration of design and construction in D&B depends on the level of organisation of the contractor. It is recognised that the nature of this integration improves 'buildability', which has a significant effect on cost, time and quality. The major attractions of this method to the client are a 'one-stop-shop' technique of building production, along with the cost security associated with the guaranteed maximum price and the transfer of risk to the contractor. The term design and build now encompasses a multitude of hybrids, including develop and construct, innovation design and build, traditional, turnkey and package deal (Akintoye, 1994; Akintoye and Fitzgerald 1995). In general, some of these hybrids have been introduced by clients to bring more competition into the process, and by contractors to relieve them of some of the project risks.

11.4.3   Management Procurement System

The management procurement system is industry's attempt to reduce the 'them and us' feeling, often embedded in procurement systems. This is an entwined design and construction processes. Management forms include

Table 11.2 Employer's objectives in relation to procurement methods.

Employer's Objective	Procurement methods		Management	
	Traditional	Design and Build	Management Contract	Construction Management
Complex and unique project			X	X
Employer's involvement with the design	X		X	X
Employer's involvement with the construction				X
Employer's requirement for early completion		X	X	X
Price certainty prior to construction start	X	X		
Requirement to transfer majority of risk		X		

management contracting, construction management, fee management, fast track construction, and design and manage. The most popular of the management forms is management contracting. A management contractor is appointed as a professional to the design team to offer expertise, which is usually reimbursed on a fee basis. The actual construction work is carried out solely by works contractors appointed by the management contractor. The management contractor is therefore responsible for setting out, managing, organising and supervising the project. This system ensures early appointment of the management contractor, allows buildability to be increased, and because design often runs in parallel to construction, it provides a high degree of flexibility for changes to building costs. However, because of this flexibility there tends to be a greater number of variations in the management contracting process. This coordinated approach, and potential flexibility results in greater operational speed and efficiency, but this idea is only apparent on larger, more complex and innovative projects. This system apportions large amounts of risk to the client and a low, but not a no-risk option to the contractor.

11.4.4   Comparison of Conventional Procurement Methods

Table 11.2 presents a comparison of employer's objectives and apportionment of risk between the employer (client) and contractor for the four main conventional contract procurement methods. This identifies that Design and Build apportions the least risk to the employers, while construction management allocates the greatest risk to the employer.

This is also demonstrated through a case study relating to a Heath Service project in the UK. The project had two main significant requirements, which were:

1. the critical programming requirements dictated by the occupation by a specified date; and
2. the absolute requirement for effective cost planning, tender documentation and cost control/monitoring activities to be carried out in accordance with the procedures laid down by the Health Board.

Table 11.3 shows the various features of contract routes used in conventional procurement methods. This compares the routes, and allows an evaluation to be made of each method relative to the requirements of the particular project. It was considered based on the evaluation that the most appropriate contract route in terms of the prime objectives of the project (i.e. time scale and control) was management contracting and two stage tendering (fast track). For this reason, the management contract was selected for the procurement of this project.

11.4.5   Problems with Conventional Procurement Methods

Typical problems often involved in conventional procurement methods have been articulated in Black (1998). Traditional approaches to procurement usually involve a chain of separate firms who add value to items purchased from other organisations via arms-length one-off contracts. In this respect, according to Lewis (1995), buyers source the market for the best price trading suppliers off against each other. Typically, buyers focus on transaction exchange relationships with suppliers, and source requirements from two or more organisations to avoid becoming dependent on any one source. Buying organisations usually stipulate their requirements via the specification, and the supplier is required to meet the specification at the most competitive price and within an acceptable delivery period to secure the contract. This focus on short-term advantage therefore results in a significant degree of uncertainty and volatility for suppliers (Chadwick and Rajagopal, 1995). MacBeth and Ferguson (1994) provide a framework to describe traditional procurement relationships as follows:

11.4.5.1 *Time Span*

The interaction between client and supplier is regarded as a discrete occurrence, although negotiating parties make use of their experience of each other. It is relatively inexpensive to change suppliers, therefore contracts only cover a few months at most, and suppliers must recover all their costs on each transaction. In addition, competitive tendering exercises are commonly used to keep prices low and play suppliers off against each other. This forces suppliers to tender for more work than their resources can meet, in anticipation that only a proportion of tenders will be successful.

Table 11.3 Comparison of conventional procurement methods for a health project.

Type of contract	Early involvement of contractor	Time scale	Level of competition/ Accountability	Degree of cost control	Early agreement of final account	Degree of Risk	Total	Comments
Traditional – Single stage	0	0	10	10	6	10	36	Unsuitable due to pre-contract time scale required
Traditional – Two stage	8	0	6	8	6	8	36	Unsuitable due to pre-contract time scale required
Fast track: Two stage	8	8	5	6	8	7	42	Considered appropriate for this project
Management Contract	9	8	8	8	10	8	51	Considered appropriate for this project
Prime cost	8	6	0	0	10	0	24	Unsuitable due to lack of accountability and cost control
Negotiated contract	7	6	2	6	6	6	33	Unsuitable due to lack of accountability and cost control
Design and Build	10	0	3	2	6	6	27	Not considered appropriate for this project
Target cost	8	8	2	2	8	4	32	Unsuitable due to lack of accountability and cost control

* Individual features are rated on a scale of 1 to 10.

11.4.5.2 Personal Attitudes

Organisations are fiercely protective of their expertise, and will only usually part with this in return for financial reward. Therefore, negotiators are constantly wary of giving too much away, and try to reveal as little information as possible. There is thus a tendency for buyers to use their purchasing power as a threat against poor pricing or service, while suppliers rely on threatening to withdraw their services. The buying organisation's specification is rigid, and suppliers learn not to make suggestions (as these are usually ignored), and often the head office design team is blamed for the inflexibility of the specification. In addition, contact between the buyer and supplier tends to occur at the contract negotiation stage, and it is typically thereafter when problems are encountered.

11.4.5.3 Behaviour

Parties tend to concentrate on personal gain, even at the expense of the other party. This results in a short-term view, whereby individuals are apathetic about problems that will be faced by those that follow them. Individuals can therefore be perceived to be aggressive in their interactions, often with both colleagues and with external organisations.

11.4.5.4 Organisational Processes

Personal interactions are often avoided where possible, and individuals are not kept informed of the big picture. Procedures are neither questioned nor changed over time.

11.4.5.5 Measurements

Clients measure only price, quality and delivery, while suppliers only consider the ability of the customer to pay, and the likelihood of winning a tender as a basis for selecting tender lists or deciding to bid respectively. Feedback is rarely provided and is used only as 'ammunition' when conducting future negotiations. Organisations concentrate on efficiency as the best way in which to make savings, and often carry out multiple inspections, for example, regarding the quality of goods received, without seeking to identify and eliminate root causes of problems encountered.

11.5   Collaborative Procurement or Innovation Procurement Methods

Innovation procurement methods are often devised as a result of the shortcomings of conventional procurement methods, and therefore attest to achieve best value for the parties involved in project development. In support of collaborative procurement approaches and innovation, Egan (1998) encouraged long-term procurement relations to improve construction development quality and efficiency. This was followed by Egan (2003), who argued for integrated supply chains for construction procurement. Khafan and McDermott (2006) noted how innovative procurement methods could bring about improvements in existing processes, resulting in the development of innovative solutions by different supply chain partners to different problems through an integrated approach.

Collaborative relationships or procurements are now used in many industries, including manufacturing, retailing, construction and service sectors. In the construction industry, this has been encouraged by two major reports produced by Latham (1994) and Egan (1998). These reports have a recurring theme in that they suggest the industry would be improved through greater teamwork, not only at site level and organisational level, but also with clients and suppliers. Recommendations within these reports have led to some construction clients and companies using collaborative arrangements, such as long-term/strategic arrangements, project and strategic partnering, joint venture, partnership, prime contracting and SCM in order to improve the construction development process. This usage has brought many advantages to companies, where balanced collaborative relationships are achieved. Despite these benefits, the intensity of these relationships and the central philosophy of commitment embedded in such relationships can lead to a high level of pressure to perform, whereby partners under pressure may be encouraged to take unnecessary risks to prove their worth. Lorange and Roos (1991) commented that it was an overstatement to say that all collaborative relationships were successful.

Typically, the conventional procurement process is comprised of six stages, specifically:

1. identify the requirement
2. source the market
3. seek tenders
4. evaluation of tenders
5. contract award, and
6. managing and evaluation of delivery.

This is mainly limited to pre-contract and contract award stage activities and less on what happens at the post-contract stages. This is a particular shortcoming that collaborative procurement has attempted to address.

11.5.1   An Overview of Collaborative Procurement Methods

Collaboration procurement relies on cooperation and teamwork, openness and honesty, trust, equity and equality, if it is to succeed (Bennett and Jayes, 1998). Collaboration can provide a framework for the establishment of mutual objectives amongst the building team as well as encouraging the principle of continuous improvement. This framework encourages trust, co-operation and teamwork into a fragmented process, which enables the combined effort of the participants of the industry to focus upon project objectives (Naoum, 2003). Some authors advocate that collaboration is a long way from returning tangible benefits to the contractor, mainly because clients still have a deep-rooted cost-driven agenda (Green, 1999; Taylor, 1999). Consequently, they expect to reduce costs, or to pass costs and risks down the supply chain, and thereby do not genuinely adopt a win-win attitude (Wood and Ellis, 2005).

One of the key elements and common feature of collaborative procurement is a high level of commitment between parties at management level. This was found in a study by Black *et al.* (2000), where organisations with experience of partnering rated management commitment more highly than those without. Communication between stakeholders is essential whenever an organisation is dealing with change, and it is equally true when introducing or managing a partnership, as communication between parties is vital for understanding each party's expectations, attitudes and limitations. This was considered crucial for success (Black *et al.*, 2000).

Continuous evaluation of collaborative procurement is needed in order to ensure that it is developed according to the expectations of the parties involved, as Bennett and Jayes (1995) highlighted that continual performance improvement was necessary in order to deliver the benefits of collaboration. Furthermore, as advocated by Egan (1998), the use of integrated teams is a common feature of collaborative arrangements, and by involving the team at the earliest stage in a project, improvement can be made in quality, productivity, health and safety and cash flow, along with reduced project durations and risks (Egan, 2003).

Additional exemplars include a study by Burnes and New (1996), which revealed many examples of the ways in which different industries and organisations have sought to use collaborative relationships. Examples of the benefits realised include the minimisation of waste, improvements in operational efficiency and productivity, and improved supply chain coordination (Hamza and Hibberd, 1999). On this theme, collaboration through innovative procurement methods can encourage openness and communication as 'neither side benefits from exploitation of the other, innovation is also encouraged and each partner is aware of the others needs, concerns and objectives and is interested in helping their partner achieve such' (Cook and Hancher, 1990). This can therefore lead to better mutual understanding of each other needs. Therefore, the working process becomes more efficient, which in turn can reduce wastage (McGeorge and Palmer, 1997) and promote organisational flexibility, which is beginning to be seen as a means for developing an environment supportive of innovation and learning (Bennett and Jayes, 1995).

Litigation is also a major problem in many construction projects, which does not help realise potential saving. However, in collaborative arrangements, dispute problems, claims and litigation can be greatly reduced through open communication and improved working relationships (Cook and Hancher, 1990). Similarly, Bennett and Jayes (1995) noted the financial benefits of collaboration, highlighting that collaborative workshops and other related collaborative efforts could achieve savings of around 10% of total costs. Furthermore, collaboration has the potential to improve cost performance, as it can reduce the risk of budget overruns through improved cost control by alleviating rework and reducing schedule time through improved communication and clearer project goals (Albanese, 1994). Thus, by improving communication on projects, parties are less likely to be 'surprised' by schedule delays and additional costs, which often lead to disputes and litigation (Moore *et al.*, 1992). This was reinforced by Arntzen *et al.* (1995), noting that collaboration could improve project quality by building an atmosphere that fosters a team approach along with improved communication. This enables potential problems and quality issues to be recognised earlier (Albenese, 1994), and can also enhance customer satisfaction as the customer is closer to the construction process and better informed (Nielsen, 1996). There is therefore general consensus that collaboration has the potential to bring consistently better results than the more traditional approach. Typical benefits from partnering would be:

- reduced exposure to litigation;
- improved project outcomes in terms of cost, time and quality;
- lower administrative and legal costs;
- increased opportunity for innovation and value engineering; and
- increased chances of financial success (CIIA, 1996).

In summary, collaborative relationships have brought many advantages to companies where a balanced collaborative relationship is achieved, which include:

- ability to leverage internal investments;
- ability to focus on core competencies;
- leverage core competencies of other organisations;
- reduce capital needs, broaden products offerings;
- gain access or faster entry to new markets;
- share scarce resources;
- spread risk and opportunity;
- improve quality and productivity;
- having access to alternative technologies;
- provide competition to in-house developers;
- use a larger talent pool and satisfy the customer (Crouse, 1991).

However, Lamming (1993) noted that despite these benefits, the intensity of the relationship and the central philosophy of commitment embedded in such relationships could lead to a high level of pressure to perform, especially taking unnecessary risks. Notwithstanding this, it is also important to acknowledge that several success factors can be espoused, especially through benchmarking and continuous improvement studies. These collaboration issues (risk, success factors, etc) are well acknowledged (Akintoye and Main 2006b).

11.5.2   Comparison of Collaborative Procurement Methods

There are various types of collaborative procurement approaches in use in the construction industry (McDermott *et al.* 2004), the main issues of which can be seen as follows:

11.5.2.1 Joint Ventures

The IPPR (2002) stated that 'Joint ventures benefit from not relying on arms length relationships between the public and private sectors – the organisational form of joint ventures gives tangible expression to the commitment to work in partnership. However, they can prove unstable in the face of changing circumstances and also raise difficult issues concerning accountability and risk transfer.' In addition, Cheatham (2004) noted that more often than not, joint ventures form because of a mutual interest by two contracting parties in sharing and spreading the risk associated with large, complex or long-term contracts, which could have dire consequences if not all goes as planned. Other reasons for entering into joint ventures can be as simple (or as varied) as:

- to leverage unique skills and/or assets (equipment, personnel, etc);
- to gain complimentary skills (or pool resources);
- to take advantage of local geographic and/or sub-trade knowledge (or expand market penetration);
- for political connections and/or owner relationships;
- to maximise surety capacity and/or influence surety underwriting;
- to meet set aside requirements;
- to obtain pricing security (i.e. second opinion);
- to strengthen financial structure and/or pre-qualification validation; or
- to meet pre-qualification requirements (experience, capacity, licensing, etc).

11.5.2.2 Partnering

Partnering has been defined as 'a long-term commitment between two or more organisations for the purpose of achieving specific business objectives by maximising the effectiveness of each participant's resources' (NEDO, 1991: 5). Therefore, partnering can be seen as a structured management approach for facilitating team working across contractual boundaries. The fundamental components of this are formalised mutual objectives, agreed problem resolution methods, and an active search for continuous measurable improvements (CBP, 2003). Cognisant of this, in recent years, influential reports (Latham Report, 1994; Egan Report, 1998) have garnered an increased awareness amongst clients, that the lowest priced bids do not always present the best value for money. These reports have also highlighted the importance of partnering arrangements to improve team working across contractual boundaries. Thus, 'partnering and integration strategies attempt to address a fundamental characteristic of the industry that it is fragmented, as individuals from different organisations which are geographically and temporally dispersed are involved in the construction process' (Luck, 1996:.1). Therefore, particular attention has focused upon improving relations between the project team and client, as well as encouraging feedback and adjustment between design and construction processes (Banwell, 1964; Higgin and Jessop, 1965; Harvey and Ashworth, 1993). In this respect, the partnering concept represents the latest in this series of initiatives (NEDO, 1991; Latham, 1994), such that 'the confrontational culture which is endemic in the sector has resulted in the development of inefficient business processes, which feed through, as overheads, to total project costs' (ACTIVE, 1996: 7). Partnering as a concept is intended to reduce the adversarial nature of the construction industry, and central to the ethos of partnering, is a move away from adversarialism and litigation, towards ways of resolving problems jointly and informally through more effective forms of collaboration. In this respect, Khalfan and McDermott (2006) highlighted two partnering cases studies, with 'the potential benefits at the start of the framework approach which motivated the client to introduce the innovative procurement route, and also the other parties involved especially the main contractors.' These benefits included savings on tendering/procurement costs, time savings on programme, lesson learned and rolled forward within the delivery team, benefits of performance management systems, fewer delays and added value.

11.5.2.3 Alliances

In the manufacturing industry, there are several methods of long-term buyer-supplier relationships. However, unlike the construction industry, these methods are used in controlled production environments where the supply of goods is a repeating process. This is generally not applied to the construction industry, as repetition is rare, and works are procured typically on a one-off project-by-project basis. Furthermore, the design, construction and supply chain parties tend to work together in constantly changing coalitions on different building projects, and these temporary coalitions disappear on the completion of these projects (O'Brien et al., 1995). In the traditional method of construction, the contractor wins a building project by tendering, and the client often chooses the contractor who offers the lowest price. However, due to the cost-driven nature of the industry, the contractor who wins the project in turn tries to get the lowest price from its suppliers and subcontractors. The project therefore consists of several contracts for which each firm involved allocates resources accordingly (Winch, 1989). Thus, members of the project team are only responsible for their specific project input – the corollary of which creates professional and organisational boundaries that are rarely crossed. Therefore, problems tend to occur, as the design, construction and supply firms often differ from each other in size and culture. This can be exacerbated, where firms have their own methods of construction and organisational approach to construction, which consequently give rise to conflicts between parties during the building process (Pries and Janszen, 1995).

In the construction industry, there are few clients that are able to offer repeat orders for work over a long time periods, as works are typically procured on a one-off project-by-project basis, therefore suppliers tend not to work with each other on a regular basis. In addition, projects tend to attract unique uncertainties, which require new design and production solutions. This, combined with time pressures and project complexity, can often result in insufficient information supply and poor planning, which in turn can lead to conflicts between project parties (Winch, 1989). Cognisant of this, part-nering/alliances have become prevalent in today's construction industry. Altruistically, the core essence of alliances is the quest for mutual benefit, that is, working together to address a market need – acknowledging that the combined alliance would be more valuable/successful than the contributors could deliver by themselves. Thus, alliances are a specific type of partnering arrangement, where organisations come together to form a new joint organ-isation to target a particular market or category of end customer. Consequently, by their nature, they can often be more complex to achieve than normal partnering arrangements. This increased complexity arises from greatly enlarging the scope and scale of projects; conversely, however, this can also lead to greater rewards than more conventional contractual arrangements. Therefore, a key component of an alliance is to agree up front all expectations of each partner in that alliance. This agreement is impor-tant, so that any gaps uncovered at a later stage do not hold up progress. Thus, by forming an alliance, organisations are able to change the nature and the scope of what they do; and in some instances, upsizing organisa-tions can enter a more intensive and competitive market where the competi-tion is more intense. Therefore, all aspects of business need to be taken into consideration, as it often influences the choice of organisation a company chooses to go into partnership with.

In summary therefore, the risks and rewards of an alliance/partnering arrangement can be shared and allocated purposefully and appropriately, in accordance with the key business drivers of each particular instance, such that all parties share fully in the planning and organisation of the operation, along with an appreciation of the risks and responsibilities are allocated therein. This requires trust as an essential ingredient (Bresnen and Marshall, 2000), particularly to resolve areas of possible contention. Therefore, organ-isations in the alliance need to rely implicitly on each other to act in full accord with the aims and objectives of the alliance arrangement, and not for individual or vested interests.

11.5.2.4 Strategic Alliances

The migration away from the traditional approach towards collaborative long-term relationships often involves the formation of partnerships or stra-tegic alliance, particularly with manufacturer-supplier relationships (Kalwani and Narayandas, 1995). However, Macneil (1981) recognised that this departure from the traditional approach required the establishment of relationships with an orientation focus and 'closeness' aligned to relation-specific goals. This is particularly important, as expectations of continuity (in relationships) require understanding the unique behaviours of firms (Noordewier et al., 1990).

Strategic alliances are inter-firm co-operative arrangements aimed at achieving the strategic objectives of the partners (Das and Teng, 2001). They therefore provide a way for organisations to pool their resources to create value that each partner could not achieve if they acted alone (Inkpen and Ross, 2001). In this respect, Agapiou *et al.* (1998) emphasised the importance of active participation of senior management in the formation of strategic alliances, as this is a continuous development process, which requires inter-relationships and confidence between parties to be established. These voluntary organisational relationships therefore often involve the exchange, sharing or co-development of new knowledge, products, services or technologies (de Rond, 2003: 90). This is especially true, as strategic alliances tend to come in many forms, including horizontal alliances between competitors, vertical alliances between buyers and suppliers, and diagonal alliances between firms in different industries (Nooteboom, 1999: 1). They can also take the form of outsourcing, franchises, joint ventures, joint product development, joint R&D and joint marketing arrangements. Strategic alliances can therefore be said to be a source of competitive advantage (Das and Teng, 2000; Ireland *et al.*, 2002). However, there is also a growing body of evidence intimating a high failure rate exists in such arrangements (de Rond, 2003; Gerwin, 2004), one cause of which relates to the high level of risk associated with alliances, compared to 'in-house' activities (Das and Teng, 2001). This risk may be caused by the difficulties inherent in gaining co-operation with partners who have different objectives and orientations, and the potential for partners to opportunistically exploit the dependence relationship (Dekker, 2003).

11.5.2.5 Prime Contracting

Holti *et al.* (1999) noted that 'prime contracting replaces short-term, contractually driven single project adversarial inter-company relationships with long-term, multiple project relationships based on trust and cooperation.' The 'prime contracting' arrangement to which government procurement guidance refers is essentially similar to management contracting, an arrangement with which construction professionals are largely familiar. In this respect, the prime contractor needs to be an organisation with an ability to bring together all of the parties (consultants, contractors and suppliers) necessary to meet the client's requirements effectively (Scottish Executive, 2004).

A Prime Contract incorporates certain fundamental principles, such as whole service procurement, economies of scale and collaborative working. All parties to the contract must therefore have a common interest and willingness to co-operate in order to achieve mutual goals to the highest degree. Thus, under Prime Contracting (PC), one organisation acts as a single point of responsibility (the Prime Contractor) between the client and the supply chain. The prime contractor is normally an organisation with an ability to bring together all of the parties (the supply chain) necessary to meet the clients requirements effectively, such that there is nothing to prevent a designer, facilities manager, financier or any other organisation from acting as the prime contractor. A key part of the PC route is the development of a whole life cost model before construction commences. Clients therefore need prime contractors to provide details of all the parties in their supply chain when tendering. However, it may not be possible to appropriately assess the technical capacity of a prime contractor under the EC procurement rules unless a significant number of the other organisations that make up the supply chain are known and taken into account during the assessment (Scottish Executive, 2004). Notwithstanding this, PC is traditionally best suited to large, complex projects, particularly where there are many variables, but where an early start to work is required, thus allowing work to start whilst other sections are still being designed. Furthermore, as PC does not have price certainty, this by default only makes it financially viable on larger projects.

Target pricing (i.e. set a target cost and design the product to achieve that cost) is employed in PC. This 'design to cost' approach enhances innovation in the achievement of clients' (owners and users) expected outputs. The essence of PC is to achieve superior underlying values rather than lower margins. Therefore, the prime contractor engages 'lead' specialist-contractors (cluster leaders) to design and construct various aspects of the project, such as building structure, building envelope, mechanical services, electrical services, etc. These various subcontracts are then often let on a competitive basis. Cluster leaders thus prepare, submit and unite their method statements in accordance with the structured activities. The prime contractor must therefore have project management capabilities that can coordinate the activities of all the cluster leaders to derive value. However, value gains in PC can only be sustained by a structured programme of continuous innovation, where 'tried and tested' ways of doing things are continually challenged (and if possible) changed, to develop better alternatives.

11.5.2.6 Public Private Partnerships

Public Private Partnerships (PPP), particularly Private Finance Initiative (PFI) projects, were created for the provision of services and not specifically for the exclusive provision of capital assets such as buildings. However, PPPs are not a single model, they need to be tailored to individual circumstances, but the breadth of these include a full range of partnerships from PFI, joint ventures and concessions, to the sale of equity stakes in state-owned businesses (HM Treasury, 2000). Under PPP arrangements, private sector contractors become long-term providers of services, rather than simply up-front asset builders, combining the responsibilities of designing, building and operating (and possibly financing) assets, in order to deliver the services needed by the public sector. The overall aim of PPP is to increase the flow of capital projects against a background of restraint on public expenditure, and with a particular remit of transferring risk from the public to the private sector. Thus, through PPP, the contractor has an incentive to design a facility that will have a low operating cost, or provide an incentive to generate the lowest operational cost over the long term. This may result in the delivery of a higher specification facility than might otherwise have been expected, which is particularly effective where there are limitations on capital spend under traditional procurement routes. Under this form of procurement, authorities can also make significant savings in operational costs, which may also involve the transfer of existing employees to the contractor. One of the main advantages of PPP is that the entire construction risk rests with the contractor. Therefore, in the event of a cost or time overrun, this will (depending upon the terms of the principal agreement) be the contractor's responsibility (HM Treasury, 2003).

From a PFI perspective, this normally involves a complex collection of agreements, including a principal agreement (between authority and contractor), a construction contract (between contractor and subcontractors) and a Facilities Management agreement (for maintenance of the completed facilities), together with loan agreements with banks and a range of collateral agreements and warranties. Due to the long-term commitment involved, the contracts are often drafted on a bespoke basis, which tends to involve many months of negotiation with contractors, bankers, lawyers, insurers, operators and their respective advisors. However, as far as the transfer of financial risk is concerned, Akintoye et al. (1999) noted that many bodies involved in PFI viewed financial risk (e.g. debt risk, banker's risks) as less important than many other risks (i.e. design risk, construction cost risk, performance risk, etc).

Another advantage of PPPs is the provision of an improved quality of service, which is often better than that achieved by traditional procurement (EC, 2003). This may reflect the better integration of services with supporting assets, improved economies of scale, the introduction of innovation in service delivery, or the performance incentives and penalties typically included within a PPP contract. However, one disadvantage of PPP is the long lead-time for completion of the project compared to capital project work. For example, it normally take many months to negotiate a completed contract with a contractor, which often involves complex drafting in order to incorporate specifications both for the facility and its maintenance, revenue and payment arrangements and compatibility of construction contract, facilities management agreement, Project Agreement and credit agreements. However, although there are financial and construction risks associated with the construction of the PPP project, risks remain with the management of the project throughout the concession period. This requires careful monitoring to ensure continuity of desired service, and often requires the use of risk management skills to identify any potential threats. Good risk management is also an effective way of developing innovative solutions to service delivery challenges, and coping with adverse consequences in order to maximise value for money (National Audit Office, 2002). It is generally recognised that this form of public sector contracting is already changing the climate within which decisions about procurement are made and managed, the operationalisation of which encourages a longer-term perspective to be taken throughout the whole life of a built asset.

11.5.2.7 Framework Agreements

Framework Agreements (FA) are agreements undertaken with suppliers, to establish the terms governing contracts to be awarded during a given period, with particular regard to price and quantity. In other words, an FA can be seen as a general term for agreements with suppliers, which set out terms and conditions under which specific purchases (call-offs) can be made throughout the term of the agreement. Therefore, FAs (including call-off contracts) with a single supplier or a limited number of suppliers can result in significant savings to both parties. The resource implications for the client of managing more than one FA for each type of work should however be borne in mind when deciding whether to award more than one FA (Scottish Executive, 2004).

FAs are generally inappropriate for clients that only occasionally procure buildings. In this respect, these agreements often cover procurement routes such as prime contracting and design and construct. They can be particularly appropriate for maintenance projects, or where a stream of similar projects are planned. These agreements have several advantages, as this approach tends to provide contractors with a continuous workflow; the familiarity and continuity of which can help improvements to be secured by transferring the learning from one project to another. In addition, FAs enable the contractor to make potential savings in respect of bidding costs, as there is no requirement for re-bidding for each individual project. Cost savings from FAs tend to come from:

- no requirements for re-bidding of each individual project;
- continuous improvement through the transference of learning from one project to another;
- reduced confrontation (conflicts and disputes); and
- workflow continuity.

FAs do not normally have a standard form of contract, therefore considerable time and effort may have to be invested to secure the FA required. In addition, the time taken to enter into a framework can be considerable, particularly regarding EC procurement compliance and time taken to pre-qualify contractors. Details of a typical FA can be seen in Table 11.4.

11.5.2.8 Supply Chain Management

SCM is not a procurement route in itself; however, it is used in many forms of construction procurement such as PPP and prime contracting. SCM deals with the management of materials and information resources across a network of organisations that are involved in the design and production process. It therefore recognises the inter-connectivity between materials and information resources within (and across) organisational boundaries, and seeks systematic improvements in the way these resources are structured and controlled. Applications of the SCM techniques in

Table 11.4 Example framework agreement. Reproduced by permission of Place North West (www.placenorthwest.co.uk).

PLACE North West (2010) http://www.placenorthwest.co.uk/homepage.html [accessed 3 June, 2011]

(PLACE North West - For property and regeneration professionals

Contractors share £1bn public sector framework

27 Jul 2010, 17:29

Fourteen construction companies have been appointed to the North West Construction Hub Medium Value Framework established by councils across the region.

The panel covers 13 lots broken down by sub-region and type of work. The contracts that will be handed out according to the contract range from £500,000 to £10m, for duration of four years. The four-year framework will be used by local authorities and other public sector organisations in the North West.

Manchester City Council, supported by the Centre for Construction Innovation, led the framework development with financial support from the North West Improvement and Efficiency Partnership.

The contractors appointed are: Bramall Construction; Cruden Group Limited; Eric Wright Construction; FMP Construction; GB Building Solutions; Herbert T. Forrest; ISG Regions; Kier Regional; Laing O'Rourke; Mansell Construction Services; Morgan Ashurst; Seddon Group; Wates Group; Willmott Dixon Construction.

This is the second of three regional frameworks to be delivered by the North West Construction Hub aimed at creating a better deal for public sector authorities in the region. The larger panel for contracts over £10m was decided in April. The smallest of the three frameworks, for works under £500,000, will be published later this year.

The framework will enable public sector organisations and the construction companies to work in partnership to deliver projects more efficiently, on time and cost, with an enhanced focus on quality and added value / sustainability outcomes.

John Lorimer, NWCH Lead said: "I am pleased with the outcome of the tendering process and look forward to working with our new partners over the coming years. The Medium Value Framework will eliminate costly procurement exercise for individual projects whilst providing benefits including cost savings for authorities, reductions in contract time, improved quality of work and the ability to deliver added value objectives that are not obtainable through traditional procurement methods."

Andrew Thomas, chief executive of the Centre for Construction Innovation North West, said of the framework: "We would like to commend the local authorities' efforts in its creation. The basis of integrated supply chain working and adoption of fair payment practices are more important than ever in these challenging times. Innovative and collaborative initiatives can provide solutions to some of the challenges, especially when delivered in a stable framework environment. CCI will continue to provide ongoing support of the Hub's work and deliver the benefits this framework will bring in providing a stable workload for local contractors and better value solutions to clients in the North West."

manufacturing environments have saved hundreds of millions of pounds while improving customer service (Arntzen et. al., 1995); where, as subcontractors and the supplier production comprise the largest value of project cost, supply-chain approaches may have similar benefits. However, in contrast to manufacturing, construction projects are usually unique and temporary. This implies a temporary organisation of production for each project, again characterised by a short-term coalition of participants with frequent changes of membership, often called 'temporary multi-organisation' (Cherns and Bryant, 1984; Burbridge et al., 1993). This fragmentation has been cited as a contributor to low productivity, cost and time overruns, conflicts and disputes, additional claims, and time-consuming litigation. Other issues include:

- inadequate capture, structuring, prioritisation and implementation of client needs;
- fragmentation of design, fabrication and construction data, with data being generated in isolation not being readily re-used downstream;
- development of pseudo-optimal design solutions;
- lack of integration, coordination and collaboration between the various functional disciplines involved in the life-cycle aspects of the project;
- poor communication of design intent and rationale, which leads to unwarranted design changes, inadequate design specifications, unnecessary liability claims, and increase in project time and cost.

There is therefore a need to integrate the supply chain to achieve mutual benefits, develop organisational learning, promote efficiency, improve quality, and leverage full value and profitability opportunities (Akintoye and Main, 2007). The key to SCM is the information flows associated with inter-organisational communications. As a result, a core issue is the effective management of information, in the form of information flows that permit rapid inter-organisational transactions between supply chain partners.

In summary, the relationship between construction project participants is often multifarious, complex and intertwined. Thus, attention and focus must be given to the intensive collaboration amongst project participants to synchronise both the input and output of the supply chain. A key enabler to successful collaboration is the ability to communicate, and share and exchange project information in a timely and accurate manner.

11.6   Conclusion

The need for innovation through procurement strategies is now more important than ever before. The industry is faced with the need to deliver enhanced value for money, with increasingly complex projects, enhanced competition, and additional pressures to comply with legislative demands and requirements, for example, sustainable development. Innovative construction procurement methods have developed out of these new demands, which have helped to improve risk management, value for money, etc. These new methods are now transforming the industry.

This chapter presented an overview of new procurement methods and how these can be used to leverage innovation, from the construction supply chain, through to collaborative relationship between the demand and supply sides of the industry. Acknowledging that some collaborative relationships might involve a limited number of construction industry players working with a single client group in an FA to garner benefits, innovation procurement can provide avenues for integrated teams to explore in order to secure similar benefits. This is in line with the four main areas identified in 2002 through the Strategic Forum's 'Accelerating Change' (cited in BERR, 2008); where:

1. *Client leadership*: clients procure projects in a way that allows all in the integrated team to maximise the added value their expertise can deliver;
2. *Integrated teams and supply side integration*: created at the optimal time in the process to release fully the contribution each can make and share risk and reward in a non-adversarial way;
3. *Culture change in people issues*: a positive image, an emphasis on education and training and behaviour based on mutual respect) and
4. *a focus on the end product.*

Integrated procurement in the form of construction joint ventures, partnering, alliances (including project and strategic), prime contracting, public private partnerships, and all the associated FAs and SCM opportunities have been identified as being able to deliver construction innovation and process improvement (as opposed to the conventional adversary procurement method types). These integrated methods provide a framework for establishing mutual objectives amongst the building team, as well as encouraging and engaging the principles of continuous improvement. These methods also provide an enabling environment to engender trust, co-operation and teamwork (within these fragmented processes), which thereby enables the combined efforts of the project participants to focus upon the actual project objectives. Having said that, the principal success factors for innovative procurement methods would be commitment of adequate resources from the partners, equity of relationship, recognition of the importance of non-financial benefits, and clarity of objectives, while the principal failure factors are lack of trust and consolation, and lack of experience and business fit (Akintoye and Main, 2007). However, if augmented and managed appropriately, these relationships can deliver real (tangible) innovation and process improvements, but such collaboration methods need to be carefully considered to ensure that they fit into the business plans of all contributory organisations.

References

ACTIVE (1996) ACTIVE Engineering Construction Initiative, The Action Plan, ACTIVE, London.

Agapiou, A., Flanagan, R., Norman, G. & Notman, D. (1998) The changing role of builders merchants in the construction supply chain. *Construction Management and Economics*, **16**, 351–361.

Akintoye, A. (1994) Design and build: A survey of construction contractors' views. *Construction Management and Economics*, **12**, 155–163.

Akintoye, A. & Fitzgerald, E. (1995) Design and build: A survey of UK architects. *Engineering, Construction and Architectural Management*, **2**(1), 27–44.

Akintoye, A. & Main, J. (2006a) Collaborative advantages in construction development. In: ed. Baldwin, A., Hui, E. & Francis Wong, F., *Construction Sustainability and Innovation*. Proceedings of CIB W89 International Conference on Building Education and Research (BEAR), 10–13 April, Hong Kong Polytechnic University, Hong Kong.

Akintoye, A. & Main, J. (2006b) Perception on success and failure factors for construction collaborative relationships. In: ed. Dulami, M., *Sustainable Development through Culture and Innovation*. Proceedings of the Joint International Conference of Construction Culture, Innovation and Management, 26–29 November, The British University of Dubai, Dubai. 143.

Akintoye, A. & Main, J. (2007) Collaborative relationships in construction: The UK contractors perception. *Engineering, Construction and Architectural Management*, **14**(6), 597–617.

Albanese, R. (1994) Team-building process: key to better project results. *Journal of Management in Engineering, ASCE*, **10**(6), 36–44.

Arntzen, B.C., Brown, G.G., Harrison, T.P. & Trafton, L.L. (1995) Global supply chain management at digital equipment corporation. *Interfaces*, **25**(1), 69–93.

Banwell, H. (1964) *Report of the Committee on the Placing and Management of Contracts for Building and Civil Engineering Works*. HMSO, London.

Bennett, J. & Jayes, S. (1995) *Trusting the Team: the Best Practice Guide to Partnering in Construction*. Centre for Strategic Studies in Construction/Reading Construction Forum, Reading.

Bennett, J. & Jayes, S. (1998) *The Seven Pillars of Partnering*. Reading Construction Forum, Reading.

BERR (Department of Business Enterprise and Regulatory Reform (2008) *Innovation in Construction Services*. BERR.

Black, C., Akintoye, A. & Fitzgerald, E. (2000) An analysis of the success factors and benefits of partnering in construction. *International Journal Project Management*, **18**(6), 423–434.

Black, C. (1998) *Partnering in Construction: Opportunities and Reward*. MSc thesis, Construction Management dissertation, Glasgow Caledonian University, Glasgow.

Bresnen, M. & Marshall, N. (2000) Partnering in construction: a critical review of issues, problems and dilemmas. *Construction Management and Economics*, **18**, 229–237.

Burbridge, J. L & Falster, P. (1993) Reducing delivery times for OKP products. Production Planning and Control, **4**(1), 77–83.

Byatt, I. (2001) *Delivering Better Services for Citizens, A review of local government procurement in England*. Department for Transport, Local Government and the Regions, June.

Burnes, B. & New, S. (1996) *Strategic Advantage and Supply Chain Collaboration*. Manchester School of Management, UMIST, Manchester.

Chadwick, T. & Rajagopal, S. (1995) *Strategic Supply Management*. Butterworth-Heinemann Ltd, London. 92–117.

Cheatham, W. (2004) *Surety Bonding Joint Ventures*. Construction Executive Surety Bonding, November.

Cherns, A.B. & Bryant, D. (1984) Studying the client's role in construction management. *Construction Management and Economics*, **2**(2), 177–184.

CIB (2011) International Council for Research and Innovation in Building and Construction. Available from http://www.cibworld.nl/site/home/index.html (accessed June 2011).

Construction Industry Institute Australia (CIIA) (1996) *Partnering: Models for Success*. Research Report No. 8., Sydney.

Construction Best Practice (2003) *Partnering Fact Sheet*. Available from http://www. constructingexcellence.org.uk/ (accessed June 2011).

Cook, E.L. & Hancher, D.E. (1990) Partnering: contracting for the future. *Journal of Management in Engineering, ASCE*, 6(4), 431–447.

Crouse, H.J. (1991) The power of partnerships. *The Journal of Business Strategy*, **November/December**, 4–8.

Das, T. & Teng, B. (2000) A resource-based theory of strategic alliances. *Journal of Management*, 26(1), 31–61.

Das, T. & Teng, B. (2001) Trust, control and risk in strategic alliances: an integrated framework. *Organisation Studies*, 22(2), 251–283.

de Rond, M. (2003) *Strategic Alliances as Social Fact*. Cambridge University Press, Cambridge.

Dekker, H.C. (2003) Value chain analysis in inter-firm relationships: a field study. *Management Accounting Research*, 14, 1–23.

Egan, J. (1998) *Rethinking Construction*. Department of the Environment, Transport and the Regions, London.

Egan, J. (2003) *Accelerating Change*. A report of Strategic Forum for Construction for Rethinking Construction, London.

Fairclough, J. (2002) *Rethinking Construction Innovation and Research*. A Review of Government R&D Policies and Practices, UK Department of Trade and Industry/February.

Gerwin, D. (2004) Coordinating new product development in strategic alliances. *Academy of Management Review*, 29(2), 241–257.

Green, S.D. (1999) Partnering: the propaganda of corporatism? In: ed. Ogunlana, S.O., *Profitable Partnering in Construction Procurement, CIB W92 and CIB TG23 Joint Symposium*. E&FN Spon, London, 3–14.

Hamza, A., Djebarnu, R. & Hibberd, P. (1999) The implications of partnership success within the UK construction industry supply chain. In: ed. Ogunlana, S.O., *Profitable Partnering in Construction Procurement, CIB W92 and CIB TG23 Joint Symposium*, 39–46.

Harvey, R.C. & Ashworth, A.A. (1993) *The Construction Industry of Great Britain*. Butterworth-Heinemann Ltd, London.

Higgin, G. & Jessop, N. (1965) Communications in the Building Industry. Tavistock Publications, Tavistock Institute of Human Relations, London.

HM Treasury (2003) *PFI: Meeting the investment challenge*. HMSO, London.

HM Treasury (2000) *Public Private Partnerships: The Government's Approach*. HMSO, London.

Holti, R., Nicolini, D. & Smalley, M. (1999) *Prime Contractor Handbook of Supply Chain Management*. Sections 1 & 2. Crown, London.

Inkpen, A.C. & Ross, J. (2001) Why do some strategic alliances persist beyond their useful life? *California Management Review*, 44(1), 132–148.

Institute of Public Policy Research (IPPR) (2002) *Building Better Partnerships*, IPPR, London. 41.

Ireland, R.D., Hitt, M.A., & Vaidyanath, D., 2002. Alliance management as a source of competitive advantage. *Journal of Management*, 28, 413–446.

Kalwani, M.U. & Narayandas, N. (1995) Long-term manufacturer-supplier relationships: Do they pay off for supplier firms? *Journal of Marketing*, 59(1), 1–16.

Khalfan, M.M.A. & McDermott, P. (2006) Innovating for supply chain integration within construction. *Construction Innovation*, 6, 143–157.

Lamming (1993) *Beyond Partnership: Strategies for Innovation and Lean Supply*. Prentice Hall International (UK) Ltd, London. 168–175.

Lenard, D. & Mohsini, R. (1998) Recommendations from the organisational workshop. *Procurement – The Way Forward, Proceedings of CIB W92 Conference*, University of Montreal, CIB Publication 203.

Lewis, J.D. (1995) *The Connected Corporation*. Free Press, New York. 1–13.

Latham, M. (1994) *Constructing the Team: Joint Review of Procurement and Contractual Arrangements in the United Kingdom Construction Industry*. HMSO, London.

Lorange, P. & Roos, J. (1991) Why some strategic alliances succeed and others fail. *The Journal of Business Strategy*. **January/February**, 25–30.

Luck, R.A.C. & Newcombe, R. (1996) The case for the integration of the project participants' activities within a construction project environment. In: ed. Langford, D.A. & Retik, A., *The Organisation and Management of Construction: Shaping Theory and Practice*, vol. 2. E & FN Spon, London. 458–470.

MacBeth, D.K. & Ferguson, N. (1994) *Partnership Sourcing*. Pitman Publishing, London. 96–140.

Macneil (1981) Economic analysis of contractual relationship: Its shortfall and the need for a rich classificatory apparatus. *Northwestern University Law Review*, 77, 1022.

Masterman, J.W.E. (1992) *An Introduction to Building Procurement Systems*, 1st edn. E & FN SPON, London.

McDermott, P., Khalfan, M.M.A. & Swan, W. (2004) An exploration of the relationship between trust and collaborative working in the construction sector. *Construction Information Quarterly*, 6, 140–146.

McGeorge, D. & Palmer, A. (1997) *Construction Management: New Directions*. Blackwell Science Ltd, Oxford.

Mohsini, R. & Davidson, C.H. (1989) Building procurement – key to improved performance. In: ed. Cheetham, D., Carter, D., Lewis, T. & Jagger, D.M., *Contractual procedures for building: proceedings of the international workshop*, 6–7 April, University of Liverpool, Liverpool.

Moore, C., Mosley, D. & Slagle, M. (1992) Partnering guidelines for win–win project management. *Project Management Journal*, **22(1)**, 18–21.

Naoum, S. (2003) An overview into the concept of partnering. *International Journal of Project Management*, **21**, 71–76.

National Audit Office (2002) Managing the relationship to secure a successful partnership in PFI projects. Report by the Controller and Auditor General, HC 375 Session 2001–2002.

NEDO (1985) *Thinking about Building – A Successful Business Consumer's Guide to Using the Construction Industry*. Building Economic Development Committee, London.

NEDO (1991) *Partnering: Contracting without Conflict*. HMSO, London.

Nielson, C. C. (1996). An empirical examination of switching cost investments in business-to-business marketing relationships. *The Journal of Business and Industrial Marketing*, 11, 38–60.

Noordewier, G.N., John, G. & Nevin, J.R. (1990) Performance Outcomes of Purchasing Arrangements in Industrial Buyer-vendor Relationships. *Journal of Marketing*, 54(October), 80–93.

Nooteboom, B. (1999) *Inter-firm Alliances – Analysis and Design*. Routledge, London.

OGC (2010) *Faster Procurement, Procurement Process Study Report*. Available from http://www.ogc.gov.uk/documents/Faster_Procurement_Process_Study_Report.pdf (accessed 15 August 2010).

O'Brien, M.J., Fischer, M.A. & Jucker, J.V. (1995) An economic view on project. *Construction Management and Economics*, **13**(5), 93–400.

Pain. J. (1993) Design and Build compared with traditional contracts. *Architects' Journal*, **November**, 34–35.

Pries, F. & Janszen, F. (1995) Innovation in the construction industry: the dominant role of construction. *Construction Management and Economics*, **13**(1), 43–51.

Rowlinson, S. & McDermott, P. (1999) *Procurement Systems: A Guide to Best Practice in Construction*. E&FN Spon, London.

Scottish Executive (2004) *Construction Works Procurement Guidance*. Client Pack.

Sidwell, A.C. & Budiawan, D. (2001) The significance of the tendering contract on the opportunities for clients to encourage contractor-led innovation. *Construction Innovation*, **1**, 107–116.

Taylor, S. (1999) Can partnering work for you? *Contract Journal*, **January**, 18–19.

Winch, G. (1989) The construction firm and the construction project: a transaction cost. *Construction Management and Economics*, **7**, 331–345.

Wood, G. & Ellis, R. (2005) Main contractor experiences of partnering relationships on UK construction projects. *Construction Management and Economics*, **23**, 317–325.

Concurrent Engineering in Construction

Chimay J. Anumba and John M. Kamara

Chimay J. Anumba and John M. Kamara

12.1 Introduction

This chapter focuses on the concept of Concurrent Engineering (CE) and its contribution to construction innovation and process improvement. CE has been widely implemented in the manufacturing industry with notable benefits in reducing product development times, and improvements in product quality through the early consideration of life-cycle issues and the systematic incorporation of customer requirements in the product development process. The benefits arising from the implementation of CE in manufacturing, and the realisation that construction can be considered as a manufacturing process, led to calls for the adoption of CE in construction. The goal was to exploit the benefits of CE to bring about innovation and process improvements in the construction industry, the problems of which relate ostensibly with fragmentation in the design and construction process.

The main aim of this chapter is to provide an overview of the key issues and technologies needed for the adoption of CE in construction, and the implications for construction innovation and process improvement in the industry. It begins with an overview of the concept of CE, highlighting the benefits garnered in the manufacturing sector, and describes the applicability and implementation considerations of this along with organisational and technological enablers for the adoption of CE in Construction (CEC). The chapter concludes with a discussion on the contribution of CEC to construction innovation and process improvement.

12.2   The Concept of Concurrent Engineering

Concurrent Engineering was coined in the late 1980s to explain the systematic method of concurrently designing both the product and its downstream production and support processes (Evbuomwan and Anumba, 1995; Huovila et al., 1997). CE was proposed as a means to minimise product development time (Prasad, 1996). This was necessitated by changes in: manufacturing techniques and methods, management of quality, market structure, increasing complexity of products, and demands for high quality and accelerated deliveries at reduced costs. These changes resulted in a shift in corporate emphasis with the result that the ability to rapidly react to changing market needs and time-to-market became critical measures of business performance (Constable, 1994: Thamhain, 1994). The earliest definition of CE by Winner et al. (1988) refers to 'integrated, concurrent design of products and their related processes, including manufacture and support'; with the ultimate goal of customer satisfaction through the reduction of cost and time-to-market, and the improvement of product quality. CE embodies two key principles: integration and concurrency. Integration here relates to the process and content of information and knowledge, between and within project stages, and of all technologies and tools used in the product development process. Integrated concurrent design also involves up-front requirements analysis by multidisciplinary teams and the early consideration of all life-cycle issues affecting a product. Concurrency relates to the way that tasks are scheduled, and the interactions between different actors (people and tools) in the product development process. Table 12.1 identifies a concurrency matrix that can be used to assess the level of 'concurrency' within a project team (Prasad et al., 1993).

The rows represent modes of operation and the columns represent the possible work-group configurations. A co-operating user is 'a person who completes the work left unfinished by previous users' (Prasad et al., 1993).

Table 12.1   Matrix of concurrency (Prasad et al. 1993).

No.	Modes of interactions	Single user	Work-Group configurations		
			Cooperating users	Simultaneous users	
				Different versions	Same version
1	Access own products' interaction tools or applications (PITA)	Sequential Engineering (SE)	SE	SE	SE
2	Run against their own data	SE	SE	SE	SE/CE
3	Access PITA belonging to other work-groups	SE/CE	CE	CE	CE
4	Access data belonging to other work-groups	CE	CE	CE	CE
5	Access both PITA and data from other work-groups	CE	CE	CE	CE

Simultaneous users refer to other members of the project team who may access 'the same design, tool or application concurrently, or ...different versions of product information tools or applications (PITA) at the same time' (Prasad *et al.*, 1993). The level of concurrency depends on the type of interactions, and this increases as one moves from top to bottom and from left to right. It is observed that some situations are described as both sequential and concurrent, when simultaneous users run their own data, and when a single user accesses the Product Interaction Tools and Applications (PITA) belonging to other work groups (Table 12.1). The interaction is sequential if two or more users cannot edit and save changes to a document until another user has finished with it, even though they may be working in parallel.

The key features of CE can therefore be summarised to include:

- concurrent and parallel scheduling of all activities and tasks as much as possible;
- integration of product, process and commercial information over the life cycle of a project;
- integration of life-cycle issues during project definition (design);
- integration of the supply chain involved in delivering the project through effective collaboration, communication and coordination;
- integration of all technologies and tools utilised in the project development process (e.g. through inter-operability).

12.3   Implementation of CE

CE is a philosophy that contains (or is implemented by) several methodologies. The attainment of 'integrated, concurrent design' requires a variety of enablers, which include tools (software applications), techniques, technologies and support structures. These enablers can be generic and can be used to support other concepts. The extent to which these principles are implemented determines the level to which the objectives of CE (e.g. shorter lead times) are realised. Figure 12.1 shows a framework for the implementation of CE with respect to the inter-relationships between the goals, objectives, strategies and tactics (tools and technologies) for CE.

The goal of fully satisfying the customer and operating a competitive business is made possible by shorter lead times (time-to-market), lower costs and high-quality products. These in turn, are achieved through rigorous requirements analysis, early consideration of all life-cycle issues affecting a product, integrated and concurrent product development, and the use of multi-disciplinary teams and other strategies. The overall CE framework is facilitated by various tools and techniques, which include quality function deployment (QFD), agent and knowledge based tools, computer aided design (CAD) and computer aided manufacturing (CAM) tools, and other relevant tools (Evbuomwan and Sivaloganathan, 1994; Prasad, 1998). These CE enablers (tools and techniques) can be grouped into two broad categories, which are inter-related: organisational and technological. Organisational enablers provide the framework for people and machines to work

Figure 12.1   Framework for understanding CE (Kamara *et al.*, 2000).

Table 12.2   Support requirement matrix for concurrent engineering (Harding and Popplewell, 1996).

	Levels		
Dimensions	Organizational	Team	Individual
Distribution	Move information between multiple sites.	Reduce remoteness and promote exchange of information between team members at different physical locations.	Make information available to individuals.
Heterogeneity	Support organizations to achieve different missions.	Support Project Teams to achieve different goals.	Support Individuals to perform different jobs.
Autonomy	Discourage multiple individual stores of information.	Support team members to work as individuals, or as a group, and transitions between these two types of working.	Support individual's preferred manner of working.

'concurrently'. This includes facilitating the work of multi-disciplinary teams, involving all relevant parties in the product development process, and managerial/technological support for organisational, team and individual levels of working. Technological enablers facilitate concurrent working within organisations. They include all the information and communications technology (ICT) and computer-based applications required for integration, concurrent working, communication and collaboration. Table 12.2 summarises the kind of support required for CE at the organisational, team and individual levels with respect to distribution, heterogeneity and autonomy.

Table 12.3   Savings in product development time using concurrent engineering (Prasad, 1996).

| Company | Product | Best development time (months) | | | Major contributing factors* |
		Before CE	After CE	Reduction	
ABB	Switching Systems	48	10	79%	CMS
AT & T	Phones	24	12	50%	ACM
British Aerospace	Aeroplanes	36	18	50%	MS
Digital Equipment	Personal Computers	30	12	60%	ACMS
Ford	Cars	60	42	30%	—
General Motors	Engines	84	48	43%	MS
GM/Buick	Cars	60	41	32%	MS
Goldstar	Telephone Systems	18	9	50%	CM
Honeywell	Thermostats	48	12	75%	MS
Honda	Cars	60	36	40%	—
Hewlett-Packard	Printers	54	22	59%	ACMS
IBM	–	48-50	12-15	70-75%	ACM
Motorola	Mobile Phones	36	7	81%	ACM
Navister	Trucks	60	30	50%	MS
Warner Electric	Clutch Brakes	36	9	75%	M
Xerox	Copiers	60	24	60%	ACM
Xerox	–	53	36	32%	ACM

Legend:
*M: Multi-functional Teams
*A: Analytical Methods and Tools'
*C: Computer Integration
*S: Suppliers in the Project Team

12.4   Benefits of Concurrent Engineering

The benefits of CE derive from the fact that it is predominantly focused on the design phase (Koskela, 1992), which determines and largely influences the overall cost of a product; as much as 80% of the production cost of a product can be committed at the design stage (Dowlatshasi, 1994). Therefore, addressing all life-cycle issues up front at the design stage to ensure that the design is 'right-first-time' should lead to cost savings, products that precisely match customers' needs, and those which are of a high quality. The adoption of CE can also result in reductions in product development time of up to 70% (Madan, 1993; Carter, 1994; Constable, 1994; Dowlatshahi, 1994; Evbuomwan *et al.*, 1994; Frank, 1994; Nicholas, 1994; Thamhain, 1994; Smith *et al.*, 1995; Prasad, 1996). Table 12.3 provides a summary of documented savings in product development time through the adoption of CE by particular companies in the manufacturing sector.

12.5   CE in Construction

The construction industry has largely depended on collaborative working between a number of professional teams brought together, often in an *ad hoc* manner, for the translation of its clients' requirements into physical

Figure 12.2   The Over the Wall Approach (Evbuomwan and Anumba, 1998).

constructed facilities. Whilst this has entrenched the practice of collaborative working, it has also reinforced traditional disciplines to the extent that, on many projects, an adversarial environment prevails and the fundamental ethos of collaboration is not fully evident. This has resulted in numerous problems for the construction industry, with the result that the industry is now highly inefficient compared to other sectors (Anumba *et al.*, 1995) and is characterised by serial processes, as illustrated in the Figure 12.2, which depicts the 'over the wall' syndrome (Evbuomwan and Anumba, 1998). Competitive pressures from within the industry as well as external political, economic and other considerations are now forcing the industry to re-examine and improve its *modus operandi*. Therefore, CE within the construction sector seeks to optimise the design of a facility and its construction process in order to achieve reduced lead times, improve quality and cost by the integration of design, fabrication, construction and erection activities, and maximise concurrency and collaboration in working practices (Evbuomwan and Anumba, 1995, 1996).

The success of CE in manufacturing is one of the main motivators for adopting this in construction (de la Garza *et al.*, 1994; Anumba and Evbuomwan, 1995; Huovila and Serén, 1995; Evbuomwan and Anumba, 1995, 1996; Hannus *et al.*, 1997; Kamara *et al.*, 1997; Love and Gunasekaran, 1997; Anumba *et al.*, 1999). It is based on the assumption that because construction can be considered as a manufacturing process, concepts which have been successful in the manufacturing industry could bring about similar improvements in the construction industry. Furthermore, the goals and objectives of CE directly address the challenges that currently face the construction industry.

12.5.1   Construction as a Manufacturing Process

The interest in modelling construction as a manufacturing process is primarily based on the similarities between the two industries, and the assumption that aligning business processes of the construction industry to those of the manufacturing industry will significantly improve its competitiveness (Sanvido and Medeiros, 1990; Anumba *et al.*, 1995; Anumba and

Table 12.4 Rationale for adopting concurrent engineering in construction (Anumba et al, 2007).

Need for change in construction	Goals and principles of CE
The need for change in construction is brought about by the uncompetitive nature of the industry, and the inability to fully satisfy its clients with respect to costs, time and value.	The goals and objectives of CE (Figure 12.1) include: customer satisfaction, competitive business, reduction of product development time and cost, improvement of quality and value.
Integration of the construction process is seen as one of most important strategies to improve the notoriously fragmented construction industry.	The use of CE facilitates the integration of the members of the product development team, and the manufacturing process, thereby improving the product development process
Emerging strategies for improving the construction process are inadequate; they only address one aspect of the problem, resulting in 'islands of automation' as in the case of computer-integrated construction strategies.	As an amalgam of other methodologies, tools and techniques, CE provides a framework for not only integrating the construction process, but also the various tools and technologies that are used in the process.

Evbuomwan, 1995; Crowley, 1996; Egan, 1998). Both the manufacturing and construction industries:

- produce engineered products that provide a service to the user;
- are involved in the processing of raw materials and the assembly of many diverse pre-manufactured components in the final products;
- utilise repeated processes in the design and production of their products;
- experience similar problems, e.g. the high cost of correcting design errors due to late changes, poor resource utilisation and inadequate information management.

The differences between manufacturing and construction with regard to the location of production activities, and the production of 'one-off' facilities in construction, as opposed to mass production in manufacturing, have led to suggestions that the two industries are profoundly different (Sanvido and Medeiros, 1990; Crowley, 1996; Egan, 1998). However, the parallel between construction and manufacturing is not with respect to repeated (or mass-produced) *products*, but rather to the repeated *processes* that are involved in the design and production of products in both industries. The implication of this is that developments in manufacturing, such as CE which have led to improvements in productivity (as a result of *process* reengineering), can be used in construction.

12.5.2   Relevance of CE Principles to Construction

Another justification for the adoption of CEC is because the goals and strategies (principles) of this directly address the problems facing the construction industry. Table 12.4 provides a summary of how the needs in construction (previously discussed) could be addressed by CE. This pairing of needs versus capabilities in support of CEC is further reinforced by the

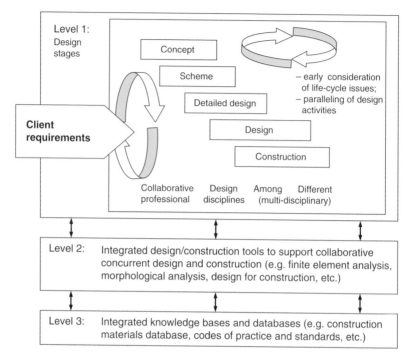

Figure 12.3   Simplified CLDC framework (Kamara *et al.*, 2000).

fact that existing practices in the construction industry, which are similar to CE, could readily facilitate its successful implementation in construction.

Given these espoused benefits, CE has considerable potential in construction. In this respect, its capacity to provide an effective framework for integrating and improving the construction process is now also widely acknowledged in the industry (Anumba and Evbuomwan, 1997; Egan, 1998). From both the context in which it evolved (manufacturing) and its inherent features, CE can be matched to the construction process. Evbuomwan and Anumba (1998) developed a Concurrent Lifecycle Design and Construction (CLDC) framework as a basis for the implementation of CE in the construction industry. A simplified version of the CLDC framework is presented in Figure 12.3. However, CE implementation in construction needs to be tailored to the particular needs of the construction industry; this is discussed in the next section.

12.5.3   Implementation of CEC

The construction industry, otherwise referred to as the Architecture, Engineering and Construction (AEC) industry, is typically organised around projects that are paid for by clients who are technically not part of the industry. Construction projects are also delivered by many firms, unlike the manufacturing industry, where a greater proportion of the skills required are often held within one organisation. Achieving 'true concurrency' in AEC (Table 12.2) for example, might require users from one firm (e.g. structural engineering consultants) to access both PITA (product interaction tools and applications – e.g. CAD workstations) and data from other work groups that might be located in other firms.

Because of the project-based nature of the AEC industry, CE implementation in construction should be considered at both the project and organisational levels (i.e. individual consulting/contracting firm). At the organisational level, it is relatively easy to devise strategies that reflect the requirements set out in Tables 12.1 and 12.2, which are ostensibly based on a single-organisation model. At the project level, 'concurrency' and 'integration' should focus only on issues pertaining to the project. The matrix of concurrency in Table 12.1 is also applicable at this level, but rather more difficult to implement; some aspects of Table 12.2 (e.g. organisational, team and individual support for heterogeneity) may not be applicable, since a specific project can be considered as a homogenous entity.

Other challenges for CE in AEC include the linkages between organisational (i.e. firm level) support structures and project-level support requirements. For example, someone operating at the organisational level may store data on different projects in their PITA; therefore, access to information relating to a specific project by someone outside the organisation could become problematic. Another challenge relates to the role of clients who govern the nature and form of the project organisation, through procurement and contractual strategies adopted, and in some cases, even the range of technologies that can be used. The fact that the project and organisational levels are influenced by different (and sometimes) opposing forces (i.e. client and industry), poses challenges for the linkages between the two.

Construction organisations intending to adopt CE therefore need to address a number of key issues in order to ensure that they maximise the potential benefits. It is particularly important that organisations undertake a readiness assessment exercise, to ensure that CE implementation is tailored to its specific objectives and business strategy. Some of the main considerations in CE implementation include the following (Anumba *et al.*, 2007):

- the availability of a robust project development process, which is documented, adaptable, periodically evaluated, and facilitates concurrency;
- the existence of an organisational framework and policies that support both individuals and teams, and enables the project development process to be controlled;
- the need for a clear business strategy that outlines an organisation's objectives with regard to interaction with clients and other project team members;
- the agility of an organisation and its capacity to respond quickly to changes in its operating environment;
- the appropriateness of strategies for team formation and operation, including the need to ensure that team members understand their roles and work towards a common purpose;
- appropriate selection and delegation of authority to team leaders;

- the need for appropriate guidelines for maintaining team discipline;
- the provision of training to enable team members to fulfil their roles and the institution of reward structures that recognise both individual and team achievements;
- maintaining focus on the client's requirements and having the capacity to respond to any changes that might occur;
- the institution of appropriate procedures and policies for quality assurance;
- the development of designs that are flexible, robust and informed by the client's requirements;
- the availability of appropriate technologies to facilitate information exchange and knowledge sharing;
- the use of an integrated project model and systems that facilitate integration between members of a project team;
- use of common hardware and software platforms to ensure the seamless exchange of information on projects;
- use of standard and proven information and communications technologies.

The above list is not exhaustive, but includes the majority of issues that need to be considered.

12.6   Critical Enablers of CE Adoption in the Construction Industry

There are several developments in the construction industry that could enable the adoption of CE. For simplicity, these can be broadly categorised into organisational enablers and technological enablers.

12.6.1   Organisational Enablers

The term 'organisational enablers' is used here to describe those elements that relate either to an individual organisation or project organisation, and which have an influence on CE with respect to processes, procurement, client and organisational readiness for CE.

In this respect, Khalfan *et al.* (2007) identified readiness assessment approaches for CE implementation within the construction industry. Following a detailed study of existing readiness assessment tools, they developed a new tool – BEACON (Benchmarking and Readiness Assessment for CEC) – specifically for the construction industry. Based on a synthesis of existing tools, the model enables construction sector organisations to assess themselves on a range of critical success factors grouped under four key elements, Process, People, Project and Technology. The BEACON model was subsequently used to assess different sectors of the construction supply chain (Khalfan *et al.*, 2007) and demonstrated its utility in facilitating a targeted and effective implementation of CE at the level of individual organisations as well as within project organisations.

Another important enabler for CE implementation in the construction industry is the availability of tools for capturing and incorporating the 'voice of the client' in construction projects. Such tools can facilitate both a CE approach and a focus on the needs of the client, which is critical to delivering and exceeding customer/client expectations – a key aspect of CE. Kamara and Anumba (2007) describe a model (the Client Requirements Processing Model) and an associated software tool, ClientPro, which facilitates the capture and translation of client requirements into actionable design attributes. The growth in the number of so-called 'expert clients' who procure construction services on a routine basis also augurs well for the implementation of CE, as these clients are well placed to understand and implement CE, as well as reap the attendant benefits. In addition, the effective implementation of CE in the construction industry is dependent on a move away from adversarial procurement and contractual arrangements that often reinforce the fragmentation within the industry. Thus, the move towards more collaborative and integrated procurement and contractual methods, such as Design and Build and Integrated Project Delivery (AIA, 2007), is a positive one from a CE perspective. Bowron (2002) went further and developed a tailor-made procurement process for CEC. Walker (2007) also sees opportunities for the adoption of CE in practices such as partnering and framework agreements (FA's), which enable both clients and industry practitioners to adopt a more long-term collaborative perspective in projects.

The increasing focus within the industry on process modelling, process mapping, and the standardisation of processes is seen as a key enabler for CE adoption. Kagioglou *et al.* (2007) view process management as crucial to the adoption of CEC. They outline the key principles of an improved holistic process for CEC that allows for continuous learning through feedback mechanisms. This approach is encapsulated in Process Protocol (Kagioglou *et al.*, 2000) and offers an appropriate industrial platform for the adoption of CEC projects. Other organisational enablers include the Integration Toolkit, which was developed by the Strategic Forum for Construction in the UK. The toolkit provides guidance in setting up integrated project teams and supply chains. This is based on the principles of committed leadership, a change in culture and values and the adoption of appropriate processes, tools and commercial arrangements (SFC, 2003).

12.6.2   Technological Enablers

Numerous technological developments have the capacity to facilitate CE implementation in construction. These include ontologies and standards-based approaches to inter-operability, integrated product and process modelling, document management systems, 4D CAD, telepresence and end-user support tools. In this respect, ontologies provide a means of describing common concepts within a given domain. They are now increasingly being developed for use in the construction industry and, along with emerging inter-operability standards such as IFCs, XML, BIM standards, etc, provide a solid basis for the integration of tools and technologies within a CE framework. Pouchard and Cutting-Decelle (2007) provide a discussion on the role of interoperability standards in supporting the exchange of information and the collaborative teamwork that are integral components of CE. Given this, many modelling systems now enable the integration of product and process information. This is also an important enabler for CEC, as the co-evolution of the process information in line with the product representation is vital for the integration of design and construction. Kimmance (2002) developed an integrated product and process model that provided dynamic linkages between product representations and the associated production process; while Anumba et al. (2007a) presented a practical example within the context of the ProMICE project.

The primary medium for communication and exchange of project information in the construction industry remains predominantly through formal documentation. As such, advanced electronic document management systems have a key role to play in the implementation of CEC. In addition to geometric information, which is now increasingly being exchanged or communicated through 3D/4D models, construction projects involve many other documents. Amor and Clift (2007) show that the proper management of documents not only provides information about all aspects of a project, but also facilitates the effective coordination of project activities and processes within a CE framework. Furthermore, developments in CAD and BIM also serve as important enablers for CE implementation in construction. For example, BIM facilitates the digital generation of a computer model of a building, which contains, 'precise geometry and relevant data needed to support the construction, fabrication and procurement activities needed to realise the building' (Eastman et al., 2008). The ability to visualise designs in 3D, 4D and nD provides project teams with the capacity to purposefully evaluate the potential downstream implications of early decisions. This makes it easier to 'get it right first time', thereby reducing expensive late changes, minimising rework and improving the quality of the end product. Staub-French and Fischer (2007) discussed the use of 4D models for effective coordination and project planning during the pre-construction phase of a project, and illustrated this with a case study. Integrated computing environments have been demonstrated in, for example, the Heathrow Terminal 5 project, where a Single Model Environment was created to facilitate collaborative working on the project (Lion, 2004).

An important tenet of CE is collaborative teamwork. While this can be easily achieved when team members are collocated, it becomes problematic when they are geographically dispersed – sometimes across time zones, continents and cultures. The emergence of distributed collaboration tools and telepresence systems has made this aspect of CE implementation more readily implementable. Telepresence provides the means whereby collaborating team members can be virtually collocated within a given 3D environment in which they are able to interact with one another or with virtual objects that are also present in the environment (Anumba and Duke, 1997). Specific areas in which Telepresence could support CE implementation in construction include facilitating multi-disciplinary teams, integrating communication facilities with design tools and supporting project team communications with the use of collaborative virtual environments (Anumba and Duke, 2007). Scherer and Turk (2007) see support for teamwork as a vital enabler for CEC. They developed an open, human-centred web-based collaboration environment (otherwise known as 'project extranets'), maintained by a service provider, which supports CE while working on multiple projects simultaneously and offers easy access to specialised engineering services distributed over the web on a rental basis.

12.6.3   Other Core Enablers

In addition to organisational and technological enablers, there are also several other developments that make CE implementation far more feasible in many construction project settings. However, only a few examples will be provided here. The recognition that 'Best Value' is a more appropriate basis for tender decisions than 'Least Cost' is one specific example. This has enabled government agencies and other public bodies to dispense with the outmoded compulsory competitive tendering practices that usually insisted on least cost bidders. The move towards public-private partnerships (PPPs) and novel project financing models all support the formation of the entire project team early in the project life cycle, and often require collaborative working at those early stages to ensure the best possible outcome for the team and the client. The most prevalent form of PPP is the Private Finance Initiative (PFI), where the private sector funds, builds and owns public assets and the public sector purchases the flow of services from the assets through a long-term commitment (Group, 1997; Li *et al.*, 2005). While the key motivation behind PFI projects is to minimise the Public Sector Borrowing Requirements of governments (Dixon *et al.*, 2005), the consideration of life-cycle issues early on in the project development process reflects a key principle of CE.

12.7   Overcoming Barriers to CE Adoption

There are still many barriers to the uptake of CEC and consideration needs to be given to overcome these to ensure successful CE implementation (Anumba *et al.*, 2007b). In this regard, some of the main barriers that need to be overcome include:

- fragmentation and traditional adversarial relationships between team members;
- lack of trust between team members;
- lack of a recognised stakeholder for overall process improvements;
- traditional adherence (usually by government bodies) to a 'lowest bidder' model of tendering rather than best value;
- conservative nature of the construction industry;
- low levels of awareness and understanding of the principles and benefits of CE.

These barriers can be addressed in a variety of ways, but by far the most promising approaches include the following (Anumba *et al.*, 2007b):

- adoption of collaborative procurement and contractual arrangements that promote collaborative working and knowledge sharing;
- improvements in education and training for both new entrants and established practitioners in the construction industry;
- provision of incentives for collaborative working;
- use of demonstration projects with innovative clients to showcase the benefits of the CE approach;
- changes in government regulations, particularly with regard to compulsory competitive bidding (which is no longer required by many public bodies);
- adoption of established information and communications technologies (e.g. groupware, 3D modelling, Web-based project collaboration systems, etc) that facilitate collaborative working; and
- establishment of strategic alliances and partnerships.

Current industry interest in the adoption of integrated project delivery methods and the enabling technologies (such as BIM) is strong evidence that the basic principles of collaborative and CE principles are being surreptitiously embedded in industry practice. This bodes well for the future of the AEC sector, but more needs to be done to ensure the long-term sustainability of CEC.

12.8   Benefits of CE to the Construction Industry

The benefits of CE to the AEC sector derive from similar benefits achieved in other industry sectors, while others are based on the anecdotal evidence from construction organisations and project teams that have implemented aspects of CE. Nevertheless, it is useful here to reiterate these benefits (Anumba *et al.*, 2007b):

- improved quality of facilities relative to cost;
- reduced duration of capital projects;
- enhanced efficiency and productivity due to reduction in rework;
- better coordination and management of the construction process;
- better informed decision making and coordination, with decisions taken at the right time and by the right person(s);
- improved competitiveness of the construction industry relative to other industry sectors;
- better project definition due to more time provision at the early project stages;
- improved integration of life-cycle considerations;
- enhanced collaboration and teamwork between members of the project team;
- more robust information exchange between team members and across the stages in the project delivery process;
- improved quality of the end product – the constructed facility;
- greater client satisfaction, given the improved focus on the client's requirements and the delivery of greater value;

- waste reduction;
- reduced scope for conflicts and litigation;
- greater profits for construction companies due to the ability to control more aspects of the project, reducing overall construction time, and improved interaction with designers and other team members;
- improved safety and 'uptime' for existing operations.

Realisation of the above potential benefits therefore depends largely on the effectiveness of CE implementation within the whole construction supply chain, rather than in individual firms. However, it is important to note that there is scope for all participants in the construction process to benefit from this.

12.9   Conclusion

This chapter presented the key principles of CE and its applicability to the construction industry. It argues that, while the fundamental principles have much to offer the sector, there is a need for the construction industry, which is primarily project-based, to adopt these in a way that maximises their potential benefits. The main considerations for the implementation of CEC were outlined, along with the importance of adopting a multi-facetted approach, in order to leverage enablers and mitigate barriers to CE adoption. The implementation of CEC represents a new way of working, as it promotes a change in culture and practice with respect to integration (of tools, processes, teams, etc) and the upfront consideration of life-cycle issues in the project development process. This in essence represents innovation in the construction process with respect to bringing about change through the introduction of new methods and techniques in the development and implementation of construction projects. Innovation is not only restricted to the introduction of new methods and working practices. It is also '...aimed at improving efficiency in some way – whether the goal is shortened construction time, improved quality of product, reduced rework or rectification work during construction or any of a number of other possible outcomes' (Marosszeky, 1999). The goal and benefits of CE are in keeping with the general aims of innovation in construction. Indeed, the key motivation for the adoption of CEC was fuelled by the need for change in the industry due in part to its uncompetitive nature and its inability to satisfy its clients with respect to costs, time and value (Table 12.4).

Finally, it should be pointed out that while there are several enablers for the adoption of CEC, these tools and techniques may not necessarily be marketed (or explicitly described) as 'Concurrent Engineering' tools. However, these enablers can facilitate the realisation of the core CE strategies (e.g. integrated and concurrent processes). Notwithstanding this, there is currently no single tool that supports every aspect of CE at every level, and a precise measurement (or assessment) of its level of uptake in the industry is therefore unrealistic. However, the concept of CE embodies (in a comprehensive and holistic way) the aspirations for an integrated and efficient construction process – which are key ingredients of the quest for innovation and process improvement in the industry.

12.10   Acknowledgement

Much of the content of this chapter is reproduced, with permission, from Chapter 1 – 'Introduction to Concurrent Engineering' (and other sections) *Concurrent Engineering in Construction Projects*, edited by Anumba, C.J., Kamara, J.M. and Cutting-Decelle, A-F., © 2007 Taylor and Francis, Abingdon (ISBN: 978-0-415-39488-8).

References

AIA (2007) *Integrated Project Delivery: a Guide*. American Institute of Architects, California.

Amor, R. & Clift, M. (2007) Document management in concurrent life cycle design and construction. In: ed. Anumba C.J., Kamara J.M. and Cutting-Decelle A.F., *Concurrent Engineering in Construction Projects*. Taylor and Francis Books Ltd, London. 183–200.

Anumba, C.J., Evbuomwan, N.F.O. & Sarkodie-Gyan, T. (1995) an approach to modelling construction as a competitive manufacturing process. *12th Conference of the Irish Manufacturing Committee*, Cork. 1069–1076.

Anumba, C.J. & Evbuomwan, N.F.O. (1995) The Manufacture of Constructed Facilities. *Proceedings, ICAM '95*, A.9.1–A.9.8.

Anumba, C.J. & Duke, A.K. (1997) Telepresence in Virtual Project Team Communications. *Proceedings ECCE Symposium on Computers in the Practice of Building and Civil Engineering*, 3–5 September, Lahti, Finland. 80–84.

Anumba, C.J. & Evbuomwan, N.F.O. (1997) Concurrent Engineering in Design-Build Projects. *Construction Management and Economics*, **15**(3), 271–281.

Anumba, C.J., Baldwin, A.N., Bouchlaghem, N.M., Prasad, B., Cutting-Decelle, A.F., Dufau, J. & Mommessin, M. (1999) Methodology for integrating concurrent engineering concepts in a steelwork construction project. *Advances in Concurrent Engineering, Proceedings of the CE99 Conference*, Bath, September, Technomic Publishing Company.

Anumba, C.J. & Duke, A.K. (2007) Telepresence environment for concurrent lifecycle design and construction. In: ed. Anumba C.J., Kamara J.M. & Cutting-Decelle A.F., *Concurrent Engineering in Construction Projects*. Taylor and Francis Books Ltd, London, 218–249.

Anumba, C.J., Kamara, J.M. & Cutting-Decelle, A.F. (2007b) *Concurrent Engineering in Construction Projects*. Taylor and Francis Books Ltd, London. 290 pp.

Anumba, C.J., Bouchlaghem, N.M., Baldwin, A.N. & Cutting-Decelle, A.F. (2007a) Integrated product and process modelling for concurrent engineering. In: Anumba C.J., Kamara J.M. & Cutting-Decelle A.F., *Concurrent Engineering in Construction Projects*, Taylor and Francis Books Ltd, London. 161–182.

Bowron J. (2002) *Reengineering the Project Procurement Process through Concurrent Engineering*, PhD Thesis, Loughborough University, Loughborough.

Carter, D.E. (1994) Concurrent engineering. *Proceedings of the 2nd. International Conference on Concurrent Engineering and Electronic Design Automation (CEEDA '94)*, 7–8 April. 5–7.

Constable, G. (1994) Concurrent engineering – Its procedures and pitfalls. *Measurement and Control*, **27**(8), 245–247.

Crowley, A. (1996) Construction as a manufacturing process. In: ed. Kumar, B. & Retik, A., *Information Representation and Delivery in Civil and Structural Engineering Design*. Civil-Comp Press, Edinburgh. 85–91.

de la Garza, J.M., Alcantara, P., Kapoor, M. & Ramesh, P.S. (1994) Value of concurrent engineering for A/E/C Industry. *Journal of Management in Engineering*, **10**(3), 46–55.

Dixon, T., Pottinger, G. & Jordan, A. (2005) Lessons from the private finance initiative in the UK: Benefits, problems and critical success factors. *Journal of Property Investment and Finance*, **3**(5), 412–423.

Dowlatshahi, S. (1994) A comparison of approaches to concurrent engineering. *International Journal of Advanced Manufacturing Technology*, **9**, 106–113.

Eastman, C., Teicholz, P., Sacks, R. & Liston, K. (2008) *BIM handbook – A Guide to Building Information Modelling for Owners, Managers, Designers, Engineers and Contractors*. John Wiley and Sons, Inc, Chichester, UK.

Egan, J. (1998) Rethinking construction. *Report of the Construction Task Force on the Scope for Improving the Quality and Efficiency of UK Construction*. Department of the Environment, Transport and the Regions, London.

Evbuomwan, N.F.O., Sivaloganathan, S. & Jebb, A. (1994) A state of the art report on concurrent engineering. In: ed. Paul, A.J. and Sobolewski, M., *Proceedings of: Concurrent Engineering: Research and Applications, 1994 Conference*, August 29–31, Pittsburg, Pennsylvania. 35–44.

Evbuomwan, N.F.O. & Sivaloganathan, S. (1994) The nature, classification and management of tools and resources for concurrent engineering. In: ed. Paul, A.J. & Sobolewski, M., *Proceedings of: Concurrent Engineering: Research and Applications, 1994 Conference*, August 29–31, Pittsburgh, Pennsylvania. 119–128.

Evbuomwan, N.F.O. & Anumba, C.J. (1995) Concurrent life-cycle design and construction. In: ed. Topping, B.H.V., *Developments in Computer Aided Design and Modelling for Civil Engineering*, Civil-Comp Press, Edinburgh. 93–102.

Evbuomwan, N.F.O. & Anumba, C.J. (1996) Towards a concurrent engineering model for design-and-build projects. *The Structural Engineer*, **74**(5), 73–78.

Evbuomwan, N.F.O. & Anumba, C.J. (1998) An integrated framework for concurrent lifecycle design and construction. *Advances in Engineering Software*, **5**(7–9), 587–597.

Frank, D.N. (1994) Concurrent engineering: A building block for TQM. *Annual International Conference Proceedings – American Production and Inventory Control Society (APICS)*, Falls Church, VA, 132–134.

Hannus, M., Huovila, P., Lahdenpera, P., Laurikka, P. & Serén, K-J. (1997) Methodologies for systematic improving of construction processes. In: ed. Anumba, C.J. & Evbuomwan, N.F.O., *Concurrent Engineering in Construction: Proceedings of the First International Conference*, Institution of Structural Engineers, London. 55–64.

Group, P.A. (1997) The economics of the Private Finance Initiative. *Oxford Review of Economic Policy*, **13**(4), 53–66.

Harding, J.A. & Popplewell, K. (1996) Driving concurrency in a distributed concurrent engineering project team: a specification for an engineering moderator. *International Journal of Production Research*, **36**(3), 841–861.

Huovila, P. & Serén, K-J. (1995) customer-oriented design methods for construction projects. *International Conference on Engineering Design, ICED 95*, Praha, August 22–24, 444–449.

Huovila, P., Koskela, L. & Lautanala, M. (1997) Fast or concurrent: The art of getting construction improved. In: ed. Alarcon, L., *Lean Construction*. A. A. Balkema, Rotterdam. 143–159.

Kagioglou M., Cooper R., Aouad G. & Sexton M. (2000) Rethinking construction: The generic design and construction process protocol. *Engineering, Construction and Architectural Management*, 7(2), 141–154.

Kagioglou, M., Aouad, G., Wu, S., Lee A., Fleming, A. & Cooper, R. (2007) Process management for concurrent life cycle design and construction. In: ed. Anumba C.J., Kamara J.M. & Cutting-Decelle A.F., *Concurrent Engineering in Construction Projects*. Taylor and Francis Books Ltd, London, 98–117.

Kamara, J.M., Anumba, C.J & Evbuomwan, N.F.O. (1997) Considerations for the Effective Implementation of Concurrent Engineering in Construction. In: Anumba, C.J. & Evbuomwan, N.F.O., *Concurrent Engineering in Construction: Proceedings of the First International Conference*. Institution of Structural Engineers, London. 33–44.

Kamara, J.M., Anumba, C.J. & Evbuomwan, N.F.O. (2000) Developments in the implementation of concurrent engineering in construction. *International Journal of Computer-Integrated Design and Construction*, 2(1): 68–78.

Kamara, J.M. & Anumba, C.J. (2007) The 'Voice of the Client' within a concurrent engineering design context. In: *Concurrent Engineering in Construction Projects*. Taylor and Francis Books Ltd, London. 57–79.

Khalfan, M.M.A., Anumba, C.J. & Carrillo, P.M. (2007) Readiness Assessment for Concurrent Engineering in Construction. In: Anumba C.J., Kamara J.M. & Cutting-Decelle A.F., *Concurrent Engineering in Construction Projects*. Taylor and Francis Books Ltd, London. 30–56.

Kimmance, A. (2002) An integrated product and process information modelling system for construction, PhD Thesis, Loughborough University, Loughborough.

Koskela, L. (1992) Application of the new production philosophy to construction. *Technical Report No. 72*, Centre for Integrated Facility Engineering (CIFE), Stanford University.

Li, B., Akintoye, A., Edwards, P.J. & Hardcastle, C. (2005) Critical success factors for PPP/PFI projects in the UK construction industry. *Construction Management and Economics*, 23(5), 459–471.

Lion, R. (2004) Terminal 5 single model environment – vision, reality and results. *Design Productivity Journal*, 3(3), 53–58. Available from: http://www.excitech.co.uk/DPJ/library.asp

Love, P.E.D. & Gunasekaran, A. (1997) Concurrent engineering in the construction industry. *Concurrent Engineering: Research and Applications*, 5(2), 155–162.

Madan, P. (1993) Concurrent engineering and its application in turnkey projects management. *IEEE International Management Conference*. 7–17.

Marosszeky, M. (1999) Technology and innovation. In: ed. Best, R. & de Valence, G., *Building In Value: Pre-Design Issues*. Arnold, London. 342–355.

Nicholas, J.M. (1994) Concurrent engineering: overcoming obstacles to teamwork. *Production and Inventory Management*, 35(3), 18–22.

Prasad, B., Morenc, R.S. & Rangan, R.M. (1993) Information management for concurrent engineering: research issues. *Concurrent Engineering: Research and Applications*, 1(1), 3–20.

Prasad, B. (1996) *Concurrent Engineering Fundamentals*, vol. 1: *Integrated Products and Process Organization*. Prentice Hall PTR, NJ.

Prasad, B. (1998) Editorial: How tools and techniques in concurrent engineering contribute towards easing co-operation, creativity and uncertainty. *Concurrent Engineering: Research and Applications*, 6(1), 2–6.

Pouchard, L. & Cutting-Decelle, A.F. (2007) Ontologies and standards based approaches to inter-operability for concurrent engineering. In: Anumba, C.J., Kamara, J.M. & Cutting-Decelle, A.F., *Concurrent Engineering in Construction Projects*. Taylor and Francis Books Ltd, London. 118–160.

Sanvido, V.E. & Medeiros, D.J. (1990) Applying computer-integrated manufacturing concepts to construction. *Journal of Construction Engineering and Management*, **116**(2), 365–379.

Scherer, R.J. & Turk, Z. (2007) Support for users within a concurrent engineering environment. In: Anumba, C.J., Kamara, J.M. & Cutting-Decelle, A.F., *Concurrent Engineering in Construction Projects*. Taylor and Francis Books Ltd, London. 250–277.

Strategic Forum for Construction (SFC) (2003). Integration Toolkit. Available from http://www.constructingexcellence.org.uk/tools/sfctoolkit/ipt_workbooks/00.html (accessed June 2011).

Smith, J., Tomasek, R., Jin, M.G. & Wang, P.K.U. (1995) Integrated system simulation. *Printed Circuit Design*, **12**(2), 22,63.

Staub-French, S. & Fischer, M. (2007) Enabling concurrent engineering through 4D CAD. In: Anumba C.J., Kamara J.M. & Cutting-Decelle A.F., *Concurrent Engineering in Construction Projects*. Taylor and Francis Books Ltd, London. 201–217.

Thamhain, H.J. (1994) Concurrent engineering: Criteria for effective implementation. *Industrial Management*, **36**(6), 29–32.

Walker, P. (2007) Procurement, contracts and conditions of engagement within a concurrent engineering context. In: Anumba C.J., Kamara J.M. & Cutting-Decelle A.F., *Concurrent Engineering in Construction Projects*. Taylor and Francis Books Ltd, London. 80–97.

Winner, R.I., Pennell, J.P., Bertrend, H.E. & Slusarczuk, M.M.G. (1988) The role of concurrent engineering in weapons system acquisition. *IDA Report R-338*, Institute for Defence Analyses, Alexandria, VA.

Complexity Theory: Implications for the Built Environment

Mark D. Sharp

13.1 Introduction

This chapter introduces 'entangled complexity' and its relationship with the various aspects of the built environment. Particular emphasis is placed on its interaction in process, as this may be used to leverage innovation. The first section of this chapter presents the formal foundations of complexity, its evolution, and relevance to current thinking. This is followed by an analysis of the extant literature and key determinants of complex procedures, and how entangled complexity interacts with the built environment. The final section presents the transition of complexity to innovation and performance improvement, using worked exemplars as paradigms for exploitation.

Thus, the core aim of this chapter is to present readers with a cogent message of just how entangled and complex the built environment is – from inception through to use, demolition and reuse, across several longitudinal continuums.

13.2 Complexity Overview

Complexity is probably one of the most commonly used terms without being recognised in its truest sense. It is often used to describe something that is either not easily understood, or has many components (variables) that go to make up a larger situation. The difficult part of complexity is how to define this as a tool for analysis. What is clear is that complexity (*per se*) is not particularly easy to define. There are numerous definitions that have appropriated themselves to complexity, with varying degrees of understanding, from vague meaningless labels through to descriptive definitions that also become

Construction Innovation and Process Improvement, First Edition.
Edited by Akintola Akintoye, Jack S. Goulding and Girma Zawdie.
© 2012 Blackwell Publishing Ltd. Published 2012 by Blackwell Publishing Ltd.

meaningless in their description (Edmunds, 1996). However, there are two main descriptions that can be used to define the meaning of complexity; first, the origins of the word followed by the historic beginnings of complexity. Thus, the Latin word '*complexus*' indicates 'entwined', or 'twisted together'; and the appropriateness of using Latin was validated by Aristotle, who wrote about the need for balance in *Metaphysics*, Vol. II (Aristotle, 1045, a10).

The discovery of complexity is drawn from Oscar II (Swedish nineteenth-century king) who offered a prize if someone could solve the problem collectively known as the three celestial bodies. He identified that when two bodies were in motion, Newton's Laws of motion were sufficiently accurate to calculate the path. However, when a third body is added, so one orbits around a central body and the third body orbits around the second body; like the moon, earth and sun, predicting where the path is going to be becomes far more complicated (Sharp, 2007a). Much in the same way that the discovery of the electron being more than 2D model by Sommerfield in 1919, which was the final clue to Bohr's model and led to the splitting of the atom. In the later nineteenth century, Jules Henri Poincaré concluded that the celestial problem could never be solved, and identified that infinitely complicated behaviours could arise in simple non-linear systems. Therefore, if it was not possible to calculate the motions of three celestial bodies, then there was no way to predict the outcome of systems we see about us every day with millions, trillions, or more, intensely interacting parts.

Complexity has often been confused with the misnomer of chaos (Yorke, 1975), which relates to a 'simple lack of order', whereas Poincare's Deterministic chaos (Poincaré, 1957) is founded on mathematical measurement principles. Thus, complexity finds itself building the bridge between unpredictability and determinism (Geyer, 2005). However, complexity cannot exist without its own paradigm criteria, i.e.:

- The system must have *causality*.
- *Reductionism* should be kept to a minimum, although it is accepted that some reductionism must exist.
- The system will probably be *predictive* and *determinism* is likely to be within the system.
- The system is also likely to be *probabilistic*.
- *Interpretation* is likely by the users and *emergence* will most likely be present.

The term used to describe the above is 'entangled complexity'. The built environment holds all of the terms described above in *causality*. The original intention of the built environment from its inception is to be a shelter from the earth's elements (Neolithic man was essentially the last of the cave dwellers). Ancient Greeks (7000 BC) became some of the first known house builders, building 'megaron' houses, which formed the basis of the types of structures recognised in today's residential accommodation. Thus, the determination of the above is that none of these elements can operate in isolation; it is only when they are conjoined can they operate as a process. These relationships therefore entwine to make a process.

Innovation is found in the Innovation (from the Latin *innovatus*, 'to renew or change', from *in* – 'into' + *novus* 'new') of these processes. From this, processes are therefore the fuel that makes other disassociated elements operate (acting as the enabler). The entanglement of these elements is determined by its operational efficiency. For example, inducted elements such as aggregate, cement and water on their own do not make concrete. It is the chemical reaction that occurs when these elements are brought together, when the process becomes more complex, which also relates to the strength of the concrete (by means of prior calculation). However, due to the number of variables in the process (weather conditions, slump of concrete, type of cement, etc), each batch of concrete is measured to determine the mix and quality of mix, which is particularly important with its consideration of load bearing components of a building. Thus, the use of reductionism in the built environment is evidenced by the means of desire to only build what is needed (Seeley, 1976). On this theme, although they did not know it at the time, early construction methods utilised a range of inter-related processes, the primary purpose of which was to withstand the elements (e.g. to ensure that the roof kept the water out). The use of innovation in these processes has now evolved to ensure raw materials are optimised, along with time, cost and efficiency measures.

Predictiveness within the built environment is clear; it is known that when buildings are built, they are somewhat predictable; for example, they have a predictability of being able to withstand certain loads on the foundations, the floors, roof, etc. It is also predictable on how buildings will look, how an estate will look (through plans and now visualisation software), or how an urban environment will behave. Other aspects of the built environment can be *determined*, for example, the amount of water and electricity consumed, as well as the amount of carbon to be produced from the built environment. The same applies to the performance of the internal activities within the building (Clements-Croome and Baizhan, 2000). For validity and reliability of statistics and validation of scientific reasoning, see Büttner (1997) and Kendall (2003). However, in terms of causality on process and innovation, predictiveness is not always present, especially where untried and untested methods are being used for the first time. An example is when Terminal 5 at Heathrow was being planned; a new type of scaffold was to be used to aid the optimisation and specification of construction as well as to improve safety. This new type of scaffold was also used in the construction process (note: there was a specific requirement to construct offsite for joining elements together); therefore, replica scaffolding was constructed on a test site to ensure that the new scaffolding system would work (in order that the construction process would continue at optimum loads of efficiency). Thus, predictiveness can be seen as a viable option, especially in complex systems where untried and untested methods have not been used before.

Probability also exists in the built environment. For example, it is *probable* (in some countries) that in the winter, some form of heating will be required (but *probably* not in the summer). In an urban environment, it is also probable that more consumables will be needed, such as energy for street lighting, which would probably not be needed in a rural environment. See also Bayesians (Stigler, 1986; Aldrich, 2008; Lucien Le Cam, 1986; Fienberg,

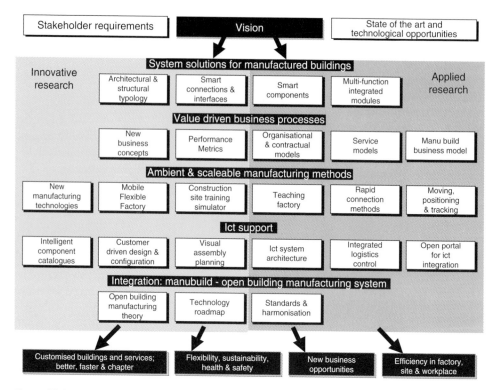

Figure 13.1   ManuBuild vision (ManuBuild, 2009). Reproduced by permission of Samir Boudjabeur, ManuBuild (www.manubuild.org).

2006), on how probability can be interpreted from a mathematical perspective of its use in the built environment. These types of predictable connotations and permutations have both a direct and indirect causality on innovation and process, as there is often uncertainty when calculations are too large to show immediate impact, and an example of this would be climate change. Thus, complex calculations can be used, but the question is, are the outcomes predictable?

Interpretation by users is likely to be present in this context by taking the form of the users interpreting different styles (fashion) to personalise both the external and internal environments. This is best exemplified by the innovative interpretation of quantum mechanics that plays such a vital role in the built environment (Carnap, 1939; Reichenbach, 1944; Popper, 1963; Bub and Clifton, 1996; Omnès, 1999). For example, even Modern Methods of Construction can be used to keep the external façade of a building aesthetically near to (mock) Georgian or Victorian, in order to entertain a certain sense of establishment and security (which is deemed important by building purchasers, and indeed mortgage vendors). However, the end user is often given little consideration of individual interpretation, as the designer has already interpreted this in the design (load variation and material limitations accepted).

This leads to the final part of determinations of entangled complexity, which is emergence. Goldstein (1999) noted that emergence was 'the arising of novel and coherent structures, patterns and properties during the process of self-organisation in complex systems' (Corning, 2002). This can also be perceived as a definition of innovation. Thus, in the context of the innovative built environment, there have been numerous attempts to use emergence to improve processes. This is exemplified by the recent hive of activity directed towards the use of production methodologies used by manufacturing industries in the built environment. A recent European initiative – ManuBuild (Figure 13.1) was the first of these that attempted to join the numerous variables of the building process in a form of open building manufacture to using the numerous components available at the time (Sharp, 2007b; ManuBuild, 2009).

This can be seen as an example of emergence, as it presents a good case study of how the built environment uses innovation to move the body of knowledge forward.

13.3   Complexity in the Built Environment

This section identifies the boundaries of complexity in the built environment, especially where entangled complexity interacts with construction processes in general. However, due to the diversity and range of variables offered, it may be difficult to ascribe sufficient value to this as an holistic tool kit of understanding. The key here is in the scalability of entangled complexity. For example, Havel (1995) identified 'scale-thin', where if its distinguishable structure extends only over one or a few scales, for example, a building seen from the outside may have a distinguishable structure on two or three scales: the building as a whole, the windows and doors, and perhaps the individual bricks. Reverse scalability of reverse differentiation (linearity), therefore extending outwards from the brick to the house, to the estate, to the county, to the world etc., shows how scalability can be used throughout the built environment and so forms part of the entangled complexity body of knowledge. This relates to only the physical components of the building, but does not take into consideration the least known variable, human beings.

Complexity has been traditionally associated with the physical sciences and human biology (Heylighen, 1990; Solè and Goodwin, 2000; Mazzocchi, 2008). Furthermore, both Kraugman (1996) and Stacey (1996) report on the macro and local simulations of behaviour, from the flocking migration of birds to the trail laying of ants. This is further complicated by complexity within the social domain, as Mitteleton-Kelly (1997) recognised that behaviour in the former can be 'assumed' to be governed by laws, whereas the latter claimed law may itself generate changed behaviour. In this respect, social systems (including organisations and their management) are fundamentally different from all other complex systems. This is important, as complex relations have an effect on both innovation and process, not in one specific area but throughout the whole process. For example, the UK construction industry accounts for approximately 1.5 million people (DTI,

Figure 13.2   Building life total costs (Sharp, 2007a). Reproduced by permission of the CIB World Congress.

2010), with an incredibly complex infrastructure that embraces socio–political and economic subsystems. It is therefore advocated that in order to be able to predict future needs, then complex models could be a viable option. For example, predictions are still used predominantly for new build construction, which consider refurbishment as a type of exogenous constant (Kohler, 2002); and several existing models are available in extant literature (Briggs, 1992; Bezelga, 1991; Johnstone, 1995; Schwaiger 1997). This naturally leads to the market orientated cost dimension, combined with life-cycle models (Figure 13.2).

13.4   Complexity in Organisations

Having looked at the entangled complexity issues that impinge upon macro factors of residential markets, the following section looks at the way that organisations in the built environment approach the market.

Generally, organisational management has focused on how to maintain and promote a common culture within an organisation. The need for 'more of the same, but with larger profit margins', does not promote divergence (Cohendet and Llerena, 1997). However, the need to think about 'how' to promote a divergent 'thriving' business is a prerequisite for the promotion of staff within organisational culture (Darvas *et al.*, 2005); and political stamina and general risk adversity of individuals to business continuity is also a prerequisite – which leads to lack of ideas and innovation within business culture (Coombs and Tomlinson, 1998). Generally, a construction organisation is structured on a cohesive management structure reliant on hierarchical precedence, based on strategic planning and supported by common culture. The organisation likes to stick to the things that the business was built on (core business), with its focus firmly on the bottom line (Yin, 2008; Hui *et al.*, 2009). The emphasis for the organisation is not on survival but growth. Why? Because that is the way business, given the constraints of the 'market', exists; except in times of recession where there is a complete revision of this core business value, and where there is a knee jerk reaction that organisations prefer to adopt in the contracting of the business (Druker, 1954). Thus, in dynamic markets, the role of creative disorder shows that organisations need to be aware of market change and diversification. Stacey (1993) summarises these issues, noting:

- Analysis loses its primacy.
- Contingency (cause and effect) loses its meaning.
- Long-term planning becomes impossible.
- Visions become illusions.
- Consensus and strong cultures become dangerous.
- Statistical relationships become dubious.

Organisations therefore need to look and learn from other perspectives. If the future is unknowable, you cannot predict a long-term future, thus making any forward planning irrelevant. Whilst it is not easy for an organisation to adjust to these models of divergence, they will surely not survive if they do not adapt to the complex markets in which they operate. Successful organisations will be those who do not just set organisational objectives, but mobilise the organisation around these objectives for the sake of conformity. In a similar guise, sustainability in the market will be attained by those who recognise that the organisation has to adapt to complex and continued interactions, both from within the organisation and those outside it. Thus, innovation must show adaptability and service offering to end-users, as emergence often evolves from diversity which, as Wheatley (1992) notes, requires an 'act of faith'. Thus, the difficulty for entangled complexity is not in the evidence within specific fields, as the acceptance that these findings can be substantiated outside their fields; if they are substantiated, can they then be 'generalised' to all systems outside that field? The following section looks at the methods available to substantiate this, by relating this to theory and practice examples.

13.5   Toolkits

It is clear from the above that old approaches to complex issues in the built environment will no longer be valid once the full realisation of entangled complexity is explored. Whilst research into complexity continues to advance, it is in the application of the tacit knowledge of applied theory to the built environment, especially where entangled complexity links to innovation. In this respect, innovation has been acknowledged as being a means of successfully applying ideas into a meaningful application in practice (Schumpeter, 1934). Innovation is also frequently associated with creativity (Amabile, 1996; Keegan, 1996; Luecke and Katz, 2003) but this is more than just creativity, as it requires the means of being applied to a situation. This section looks at complexity, not just from a value to innovation practice *per se*, but using a whole life value approach applied to the built environment. This in turn highlights the benefits to organisations and industry, in order to identify which complex hierarchical factors to use (along with their priorities).

There have been various attempts to model the whole life cycle of a building, ranging from transactions that take place over the construction project life cycle (Winch, 2001), through to the incorporation of maintenance and refurbishment (Clements-Croome *et al.*, 2003). In this respect, the factors that affect the prioritisation have been identified both diagrammatically and mathematically. For example, Spedding *et al.* (1995) identified these factors diagrammatically, as shown in Figure 13.3.

Whilst these factors are important to the prioritisation, Holmes and Shen (1995) also identified five criteria used to set up maintenance, which can be used in complex systems such as the built environment:

1. *Building Status* – the relative importance compared to others in terms of function;
2. *Physical Condition* : physical condition of the defective element, and possibility of its breakdown;
3. *Importance of Usage* : the effects of breakdown to the occupants and users of the building;
4. *Effects on Fabrics* : the cost implication of defective element; and
5. *Effects on Service Provision* : the cost implication of the breakdown or failure.

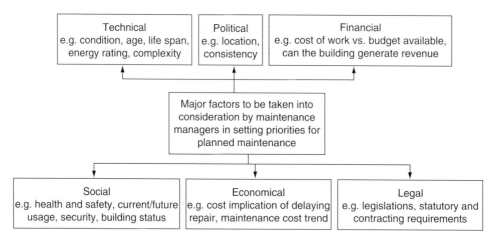

Figure 13.3   Factors of prioritisation for planned maintenance (Spedding *et al.*, 1995).

These factors can then be delineated into levels, depending on the number of situations.

Thus, probabilistic models have concentrated on Whole Life-Cycle Costing (WLCC) issues of how to design out problems, with general emphasis being placed on the designer to design out complex processes. This gives a true cost value over the buildings life, rather than simply building as cheaply as possible. Furthermore, Aarseth and Hovde (1999) and Moser (1999) proposed a methodology for dealing with uncertainty in the factor method, by treating the individual factors as stochastic inputs; thus, providing a probability distribution of the service life prediction, with an associated confidence interval. In this respect, the EuroLifeForm Model (ELF) (Kirkham *et al.*, 2004) is an integrative attempt to respond to some of the problems identified in normal WLCC methods. The ELF model consists of three distinct elements, a probabilistic life-cycle cost model, a probabilistic deterioration model and a decision support application (The Logbook). In addition, a simple environmental impact analysis is supported that can be accessed through the decision support application and maintained throughout the design process. These elements work in synergy to enable the user to produce stochastic WLCCP results, based on accurate predictions of life-cycle replacement and maintenance costs, in a logical and iterative manner, as represented in the ELF model.

The logbook acts as the gateway to the WLCC and performance modelling process, and is designed to work as a repository of information for the project, from design through to eventual disposal. It not only stores this information, but also provides a framework in which to carry out the logical and iterative application of WLCC techniques to a particular design scenario. The logbook is therefore not just confined to the design process and construction phase of the project. The logbook also facilitates Post Occupancy Analysis, the idea being that the building owner utilises this logbook to record up-to-date operational cost data, thereby providing the necessary information to update the WLCC model forecasts if required.

In the ELF application, a deterioration model is provided that uses a combination of deterministic methods, for example, the Factorial Approach (Bird, 1987) and stochastic models including the Weibull Distribution (Weibull, 1951) to provide this information at the detailed design stage of the WLCC process. It also includes a semi-quantitative risk analysis, which can be used to assign a likelihood and consequence score to the failure of any element under consideration, to allow users to prioritise complex actions. One highlighted problem with this method is the reliance on deterministic values, and then applying cost once the process is identified; this, combined with the need to derive data from the two models, clearly makes this the best of the probabilistic models.

There have been numerous attempts at quantifying complexity process issues through numerical methods (Ostwald and Tucker, 2007). Numerical methods are often divided into elementary ones, such as finding the root of an equation, integrating a function, or solving a linear system of equations to intensive ones like the finite element method. Intensive methods are often needed for the solution of practical problems, which often require the systematic application of a range of elementary methods, often thousands or millions of times over. In the development of numerical methods, simplifications need to be made to progress towards a solution; as 'numerical methods do not usually give the exact answer' to a given problem, they can only tend towards a solution, getting closer and closer with each iteration, which lends itself to be a bridge towards determinism (Salinaros, 1999).

Maintenance policies are often based on a perfect monitoring assumption, and the status of each unit (running, failed, level of degradation, etc) is supposed to be continuously and perfectly known (Cho and Parlar, 1991). However, in many realistic situations, it is impossible or too expensive to verify this assumption, as the state of a unit can be totally unknown or submitted to many diagnosis errors: measurement errors, false alarm, non-detection, detection delay, etc (Basseville and Nikifirov, 1993). On this theme, developed by Thomas Saaty (1977), the Analytical Hierarchical Approach (AHP) provides a proven, effective means to deal with complex decision-making. It can also assist with identifying and weighting selection criteria, analysing the data collected and expediting the decision-making process. AHP can help capture both subjective and objective evaluation measures, thereby providing a useful mechanism for checking the consistency of the evaluation measures, whilst also using alternatives to reduce bias in decision-making.

The first step is to decompose the goal into its constituent parts, progressing from the general to the specific. In its simplest form, this structure comprises a goal, criteria and alternative levels. Each set of alternatives are then further divided into an appropriate level of detail, recognising that the more criteria included, the less important each individual criterion may become. Next, a relative weight is assigned to each, where criterion has a local (immediate) and global priority. The sum of all the criteria beneath a given parent criterion in each tier of the model must therefore equal one; and the global priority shows its relative importance within the overall model. Finally, after the criteria are weighted and the information is collected, the information is uploaded to the model. Scoring is made on a relative basis, not an absolute basis, comparing one choice to another. Relative scores for each choice are then computed within each leaf of the hierarchy, and synthesised to yield a composite score for each choice at every tier, as well as an overall score. A worked example of AHP can be seen in Figure 13.4.

Thus, assume that a set of objectives have been established along with a normalised set of weighting for comparing alternatives. For simplicity, assume four objectives exist: O1, O2, O3 and O4. From a pair-wise comparison matrix A, where the number in the i_{th} row and j_{th} column gives the relative importance of O_i as compared with O_j.

Using a Likert Scale (1–9), where:

a_{ij} = 1 if the two objectives are equal in importance;
a_{ij} = 3 if O_i is weakly more important than O_j
a_{ij} = 5 if O_i is strongly more important than O_j
a_{ij} = 7 if O_i is strongly more important than O_j
a_{ij} = 9 if Oi is absolutely more important than O_j
a_{ij} = 1/3 if Oj is weakly more important than O_j

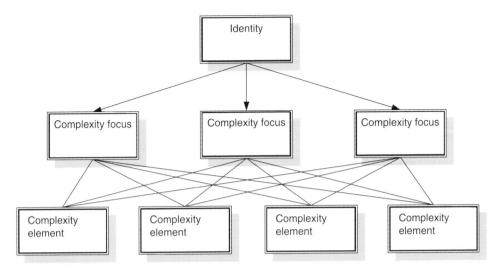

Figure 13.4 Worked example of Saaty's hierarchy applied to complexity.

the following matrix can then be formulated:

$$A = \begin{bmatrix} 1 & 1/5 & 1/3 & 1/7 \\ 5 & 1 & 3 & 5 \\ 3 & 1/3 & 1 & 3 \\ 7 & 1/5 & 1/3 & 1 \end{bmatrix} = \begin{bmatrix} 1.000 & 0.200 & 0.333 & 0.143 \\ 5.000 & 1.000 & 3.000 & 5.000 \\ 3.000 & 0.333 & 1.000 & 3.000 \\ 7.000 & 0.200 & 0.333 & 1.000 \end{bmatrix}$$

To normalise the weightings, the sum of each column are computed, then each column is divided by the corresponding sum. Using an over-bar to denote normalisation:

$$A = \begin{bmatrix} 0.063 & 0.115 & 0.071 & 0.016 \\ 0.313 & 0.577 & 0.643 & 0.547 \\ 0.188 & 0.192 & 0.214 & 0.328 \\ 0.438 & 0.115 & 0.071 & 0.109 \end{bmatrix}$$

Because the numbers in the second row are generally larger than the rest of the matrix (except for those in column 1), this would indicate there was some inconsistency in comparisons used in the original matrix. Ideally, the four normalised columns would all be identical if the pair-wise comparisons were consistent. In practice, the consistency measure would normally be measured using Eigenvalues of the normalised comparison matrix. Eigenvalues are a special set of scalars associated with a linear system of equations (i.e. a matrix equation) that are sometimes also known as characteristic roots, characteristic values (Hoffman and Kunze, 1971), proper values or latent roots (Marcus and Minc, 1988: 144). The determination of the Eigenvalues and Eigenvectors of a system is extremely important, where it is equivalent to matrix diagonalisation. Each Eigenvalue is paired with a corresponding so-called Eigenvector (or, in general, a corresponding right Eigenvector and a corresponding left Eigenvector; there is no analogous distinction between left and right for Eigenvalues).

The decomposition of a square matrix λ into Eigenvalues and Eigenvectors is known as Eigen decomposition, and the fact that this decomposition is always possible as long as the matrix consisting of the Eigenvectors of λ is square, is known as the Eigen decomposition theorem. It is on this theory that Saaty (1980) based the principles of AHP and like many theories, came under scrutiny. For example, Spedding et al. (1995) reviewed the AHP methodology and identified that the system was inherently flawed for use in manufacturing systems. The reason for this was because the AHP approach is based on deriving ratio scale measurements. However, it is a valuable tool to identify entangled complexity evaluation, as it has the flexibility and characteristics to evaluate either individual buildings, projects or multiple connotations of projects, or indeed project versus project evaluation.

13.6   Complex Innovation in Organisations

Processes within organisations must constantly be dynamic to improve the quality of both the company's internal and external services. This calls for 'appropriate' measurement of the process, thereby requiring diligence in monitoring, controlling and assessment in both the technical and non-technical (or socio-cultural) approaches (Stewart, 1995); and technical and instrumental tools, rather than socio-cultural (or non-technical) aspects (Low, 1993). In addition, Spekknink (1995) argued that to maintain a Quality Management System effectively in construction, a balance of the technical requirements and theoretical approach was necessary.

Spekknink's (1995) concept can be seen in Figure 13.5, highlighting a theoretical approach for effective maintenance of a complex system, using

Figure 13.5   Technical and non-technical approaches for improving service quality (Spekknink, 1995).

the application of an integrative approach in an organisation rather than a segmentalist approach. While the integrative approach has a structure and culture that advances towards an egalitarian and meritocratic ideal, the segmentalist approach, on the other hand, has a structure that insists on traditional bureaucracy, isolating labour from management, and focusing on uncrossable boundaries between functions for effective management. It appears that segmentalism is currently prevalent in many construction companies because of their conservative attitude towards change and innovation. The management of change and innovation should therefore be an integral part of the building process (Tan and Low, 1991).

Rather than analyse these reasons from a historical perspective, it is important to understand organisational excellence, which potentially leads to the success of businesses (Kanji, 2001), especially in terms of entangled complexity, where it is not always obvious what these success factors may be. Again, the AHP approach can be applied to organisational needs. Other indicators of business performance (i.e. quality, customer satisfaction, innovation and market share) also reflect an organisation's economic condition and growth prospects better than reported earnings (Eccles and Pyburn, 1992). Therefore, performance measures must go beyond the presentation of financial figures to serve as the driver for fostering performance, not purely in financial terms, but also in non-financial aspects such as quality, customer satisfaction, innovation and market share. These performance measures must also be prioritised so that appropriate decisions can be made. Thus, the assessment of process performance using complexity can be used, as, according to Baird (1989), this refers to the relative liking on the part of an evaluator for particular outcomes. Furthermore, assuming a predefined set of performance measures exist, a mathematical function between all possible outcomes of each individual measure and their corresponding relative importance may be developed. Such function is commonly referred to in the literature as the 'utility function', where a multiple attribute utility function integrates these individual utility functions into a single platform, thus providing a collective assessment of engineering performance on a project.

The integration of various measures of process performance in the form of a multiple attribute utility function requires identifying a preference structure that depicts the relative importance of each measure to the others. Clemen (1991) reported on various techniques for developing the preference structure, including pricing out technique, the lottery weight technique, etc. Amongst all of the possibilities, this study uses the Eigenvector prioritisation method commonly employed in the AHP developed by Saaty (1980). This method is a popular alternative for deriving the preference structure in various practical applications of Multi Criteria Decision Making (Zeleny 1982; Mollaghasemi and Pet-Edwards 1997). The major strengths this method brings are its systematic procedure, and its ability to examine the consistency of the evaluator's judgments. However, the evaluation of process performance during the operation and maintenance phase requires several years of full production of the industrial facility (Tucker and Scarlett, 1986). Given this, it is often difficult to collect data measures of process performance pertinent to the operation (within a reasonable timeframe). This is an

Table 13.1 Level of complexity in building processes.

| Type of Complexity | Process | | | | | | | | | |
| | Building Phases | | | | | | | | | |
	Identifying need	Score	Design	Score	Contract	Score	Construction	Score	Payment	Score
Causality	✓	0	✓	2	✓	27	✓	24	✓	26
	✓✓	2	✓✓	26	✓✓	2	✓✓	5	✓✓	4
	✓✓✓	28	✓✓✓	2	✓✓✓	1	✓✓✓	1	✓✓✓	0
Reductionism	✓	0	✓	2	✓	18	✓	1	✓	3
	✓✓	1	✓✓	0	✓✓	0	✓✓	1	✓✓	0
	✓✓✓	29	✓✓✓	0	✓✓✓	0	✓✓✓	0	✓✓✓	0
Predictive	✓	6	✓	9	✓	3	✓	2	✓	27
	✓✓	20	✓✓	21	✓✓	1	✓✓	0	✓✓	2
	✓✓✓	4	✓✓✓	0	✓✓✓	27	✓✓✓	27	✓✓✓	1
Determinative	✓	6	✓	5	✓	1	✓	3	✓	1
	✓✓	22	✓✓	19	✓✓	2	✓✓	5	✓✓	26
	✓✓✓	2	✓✓✓	6	✓✓✓	27	✓✓✓	23	✓✓✓	3
Probabilistic	✓	19	✓	0	✓	3	✓	1	✓	2
	✓✓	7	✓✓	3	✓✓	1	✓✓	0	✓✓	0
	✓✓✓	4	✓✓✓	27	✓✓✓	0	✓✓✓	29	✓✓✓	0
Interpretive	✓	8	✓	25	✓	23	✓	21	✓	4
	✓✓	19	✓✓	5	✓✓	7	✓✓	9	✓✓	0
	✓✓✓	3	✓✓✓	0	✓✓✓	0	✓✓✓	0	✓✓✓	0
Emergence	✓	0	✓	2	✓	5	✓	27	✓	3
	✓✓	30	✓✓	21	✓✓	25	✓✓	3	✓✓	1
	✓✓✓	0	✓✓✓	7	✓✓✓	0	✓✓✓	0	✓✓✓	0

important part in the utilisation of Building Information Modelling and IT in order to identify, collect, analyse and use decisions. These issues were used in a case study of a commercial international lending organisation to determine the complex nature of the organisations built asset relationship with its business performance. This included undertaking pre- and post-occupational evaluation, as well determinative criteria specific to this organisation. In order to determine whether the same complex issues could be correlated with data outside of the specific requirements of the organisation, a further electronic survey was undertaken to identify how complex the built environment was in terms of processes and innovation. Specific groups involved in the various stages of the construction process were identified, in order to give a holistic approach to the issues of complexity, and how integrated complexity arose in the built environment. Five areas were identified, taking a broad spectrum of activities across the construction processes.

13.6.1   Case Study Findings

The following matrices (Table 13.1 and Table 13.2) were developed as a means of identifying where respondents felt that complexity existed in built environment processes. Scores were derived from the survey regarding whether respondents either did not register an opinion, or where the data was too low to register a score, so this was shown as a nil score, so not considered as wasteful. These results represent an aggregated mix from both the case study organisation and survey respondents. The following discussion presents the results of opinions and views expressed in the telephone survey follow-up.

13.6.2   Discussion

An *ad-hoc* sample of 30 respondents (~10%) was undertaken using telephone follow-up interviews to substantiate the survey in order to both ground and validate findings. In this respect, there are a number of issues that are worthy of comment. Causality in the process identified that there were complex issues in construction. This was not particularly surprising, given the socio-economic and cultural issues already identified at the start of this chapter. The impact of the design process is significant, in that most people thought that it was a moderately complex issue. The steps of the process would impact on the next stage of the process, although this was not

Table 13.2   Aggregated scoring matrix.

Score	<16	17 – 32	33 – 48	>49
Type of Waste	Not complex	Low amount of complexity	Medium amount of complexity	High amount of complexity

the same as the construction phase; most people considered that this followed a logical procedure. The same can be said for payment, as the cause and effect is if you do the work, you are paid, and this was not perceived as a particularly complex issue. The reductionism issues can be explained in the context as epiphenomena (a secondary phenomenon occurring along-side or in parallel to the primary phenomenon), as respondents considered that there was a high level of complexity in identifying need, but not in any other part of this process. Upon further investigation, it was perceived that reductionism was taken as a metonymy, and thus an unsuspecting aspect of construction's physicality.

Most respondents felt that there was a moderate amount of determinative complexity in the first two phases of identifying need and design. However, most respondents determined that the next two phases were highly determi-native in complexity of process. Further indication of this was that of uncer-tainty for bidding for contract, and once on site that issues arose; that meant that what they thought would happen generally did. Some respondents thought that generally you had to determine to expect the unexpected. In terms of probabilistic complexity in the building phases, the majority of respondents felt that it was not a particularly complex process, as the prob-ability of identifying need was either there or not. However, in the design, almost all respondents felt that the design was probabilistic. Upon further investigation, most respondents thought that architects only knew how to design buildings in a certain way. Some respondents also felt that architects were too far removed from the actual building process to see the probability of design flaws and the effect they had on the rest of the project. In addition, the majority of respondents determined that the construction phase was highly complex, and further investigation identified that there was a com-plete lack of understanding of what goes on in the construction phase. Thus, time, resource management and a huge array of products and services were under a continuous flux of change, which made the construction phase even more complicated and prone to miscommunication.

Interpretive complexity in the process is quite complex for identifying need and it is likely that this result is because of the degree of interpretation needed for identifying demand. It was acknowledged that there was little interpretive complexity in the design stage, as the architect had a brief to work from, and it was only one stage that an insignificant (architects) part of the process interprets the brief to a design. The rest of the process appears not to be too interpretive due to the logical nature of the process. Interestingly, the emergence of processes appears to be at the front end of the process rather than the construction and payment phase. Emergence was determined to mean the constant state of flux felt in identifying needs as a companion in trying to determine how designs were changing to incorporate these changes. This was identified as being partly down to the perception of public opinion, what was acceptable or what was needed, for example, design needed to incorporate possible changes in dwellings to take advantage of technological developments for WiFi or 4G technology. Furthermore, whilst there has been little change in contracts, respondents considered that there was significant amount of complexity in the contract with the amount and different clauses used for the different types of contracts. The rest of the process was deemed determinative rather than emergent.

Complexity in innovation was also identified at this stage due to two factors:

1. how complexity is a way of doing something in a different way; and
2. how to measure it, is also different.

Thus, the traditional 'S' curve of identifying innovation can be used to identify two things for complexity:

1. where you currently are in terms of processes; and
2. where you want to be (even if this is two complete 'S' cycles away).

Therefore, this study identified that this was a way of identifying complexity in process, and also responsive to perception of what complexity is and how this can be measured. The key here is to be able to identify where you are on the initial 'S' curve to start with. It is this identification of the joining of complexity to both known processes, and understanding how this interacts with innovation to determine new entangled complex processes, such that, it is now time for entangled complexity to be able to make a substantial impact on the built environment processes and innovation.

To go beyond this concept, a case study was undertaken to either prove or disprove the results and discussion thus far. The scenario for this was a major commercial organisation that had followed the progress of the primary study. In this respect, a building due for refurbishment was allocated for testing as it had already pre-qualified for the complex nature of the project to be undertaken. The processes for a traditional approach identified that certain processes would mean that the property would not be in use for 32 months. However, by using an innovative approach to the design, and through using different dimensions of resources, it was ensured that this project could be completed in 27 months. This was because a different emphasis was placed on both the use of the building and the change in design to complement its end use. This generality aligns with the discussion to date, and innovative processes were then sought to determine whether the double 'S' curve would enable the building to become more productive (Figure 13.6).

Using a model to decompose the goal into its constituent parts, progressing from the general processes into their elements, each set of alternatives were divided into an appropriate level elemental detail. The resulting condition and performance based model was then developed. New innovative complex entangled processes were found to be at least one and a half 'S' curves (life cycles) in front of the traditional processes. The result of this case study was that not only were new processes used, but also the building presented additional benefits (not just an increased bottom line). The success of this project also enabled the organisation to review other built asset portfolios.

Figure 13.6   Enhanced performance of entangled complexity.

13.7   Conclusion

This chapter presented an holistic approach to 'entangled complexity' and its relationship with the various aspects of the built environment in an attempt to present a cogent picture of conjoined events. It reviewed the theory of complexity, and how contextual information can describe how entangled the process of building our living environment can be. It presented how complexity plays an important part in both innovation and its impact on processes. Thus, through theory and worked examples, entangled complexity in the built environment provides several fruitful avenues to explore. Whilst the issues themselves are often complex, it is also important to acknowledge that complexity can also be used to solve both theoretical and actual problems. This unique quality gives it distinct advantages over other approaches.

Finally, whilst complexity in the built environment is still in its infancy (as far as deterministic and applied research is concerned), it is clear that more research is needed in order to understand the systems, procedures, processes and interactions of variables. Entangled complexity is a pivotal tool that can help identify all of the above (and provide holistic meaning), so that lessons from the past can help shape and generate solutions for the future.

References

Aarseth, L.I. & Hovde, P.J. (1999) A stochastic approach to the factor method for estimating service life. *Proceedings of the 8th International Conference on the Durability of Building Materials and Components*. National Research Council Canada, Vancouver. BC, Canada.

Aldrich, A. (2008) R A. Fisher on Bayes and Bayes' Theorem. *Bayesian Analysis*, 3(1), 161–170.

Amabile, T. (1996) *Creativity in Context*. Westview Press, Boulder, CO.

Aristotle (1045a) Metaphysics. In: Ross, W. (1924) *Aristotle's Metaphysics*, 2 vols. Clarendon Press, Oxford.

Baird, B.F. (1989) *Managerial Decisions Under Uncertainty: An Introduction to the Analysis of Decision Making*. John Wiley & Co. In c, New York.

Basseville, M. & Nikifirov, I. (1993) *Detection Of Abrupt Changes: Theory And Application*. PTR Prentice Hall, Englewood Cliffs, NJ.

Bezelga, A. (1991) *Management Quality & Economics in Building*: CIB Congress in Lisboa. E&FN Spon, London.

Bird, B. (1987) Costs-in-use: principles in the context of building procurement. *Construction Management and Economics*, 5, Special Issue.

Bub, J. & Clifton, R. (1996) A uniqueness theorem for interpretations of quantum mechanics. *Studies in History and Philosophy of Modern Physics*, **27B**, 181–219.

Büttner, J. (1997) Diagnostic validity as a theoretical concept and as a measurable quantity. *Clinical Chim. Acta*, **260**(2),131–143.

Carnap, R. (1939) The interpretation of physics. In: *Foundations of Logic and Mathematics of the International Encyclopedia of Unified Science*. University of Chicago Press, Chicago, IL.

Cho, D. & Parlar, M. (1991) A survey of maintenance model for multi-unit systems. *European Journal of Operation Research*, **51**, 1–23.

Clemen, R. (1991) *Making Hard Decisions: An Introduction to Decision Analysis*. Duxbury Press, Belmont, CA.

Clements-Croome, D. & Baizhan, L (2000) *Productivity and Indoor Environment: Proceedings of Healthy Buildings*, vol. 1. Helsinki.

Clements-Croome, D., Godfaurd, J., Loy, H. & Jones, K. (2003) Through-life environmental business modelling for sustainable architecture. *CIBSE/ASHRAE International Conference on Building Sustainability Value and Profit*, 24–26 September, ASHREA, Edinburgh.

Cohendet, P. & Llerena, P. (1997) Learning, technical change and public policy: How to create and exploit diversity. In: ed. Edquist, C., *Systems of Innovation: Technologies, Institutions and Organizations*. Pinter Publishers, London.

Coombs, R. & Tomlinson, M. (1998) Patterns of UK company innovation styles: new evidence from the CBI innovation trends survey. *Technological Analysis and Strategic Management*, **10**, 3.

Corning, P. (2002) The re-emergence of 'eergence': a venerable concept in search of a theory. *Complexity* 7(6), 18–30. Available from http://www.complexsystems.org/publications/pdf/emergence3.pdf

Darvas, Z., Rose, A. & Szapary, G. (2005) *Fiscal Divergence and Business Cycle Synchronisation: Irresponsibility is Idiosyncratic*. Berkely edu.

Drucker, P. (1954) The Practice of Management: Harper-Collins.

DTI (2010) *Department of Trade and Industry, Constructing the Future*. HMSO, London.

Eccles, R. & Pyburn, P.J. (1992) Creating a comprehensive system to measure performance. *Management Accounting*, **October**, 41–44.

Edmonds, B. (1996) What is Complexity? In: ed. Heylighen. F. & Aerts, D., *The Evolution of Complexity*. Kluwer, Dordrecht.

Fienberg, S. (2006) When did Bayesian inference become 'Bayesian'? *Bayesian Analysis*, **1**(1), 1–40.

Geyer, R. (2005) *Keynote: Centre for Complexity Research*, 13 September. University of Liverpool, Liverpool.

Goldstein, J. (1999) Emergence as a construct: history and issues. *Emergence: Complexity and Organization*, **1**(1), 49–72.

Havel, I. (1995) Scale dimensions in nature. *International Journal of General Systems*, **23**(2), 303–332.

Heylighen, F. (1990) Relational closure: a mathematical concept for distinction-making and complexity analysis. In: ed. Trappl, R., *Cybernetics and Systems '90*. World Science Publishers, 335–342.

Hicks (1999) *Social Democracy and Welfare Capitalism*. Cornell Press, Ithaca, NY.

Holmes, A. & Shen, Q. (1995) A comparative study of priority setting methods for planning maintenance of public buildings. *Facilities* **15**(12/13), 331–339.

Hui, K., Matsunaga, S. & Morse, D. (2009) The impact of conservatism on management forecasts. *Journal of Accounting and Economics*, **47**, 3.

Johnstone, I. (1995) The mortality of New Zealand housing stock. *Arch Science Review*, **37**, 181–188.

Kanji, G.K. (2001). *An Integrated Approach of Organisational Excellence*. Available from http://www.gopal-kanji.com (accessed December 2001).

Keegan, R.T. (1996) Creativity from childhood to adulthood: a difference of degree and not of kind. In: ed. Runco, M.A., *New Directions for Child Development*, No. 72. Jossey-Bass, San Francisco, CA. 57–66.

Kendell R., Jablensky A. (2003) Distinguishing Between the Validity and Utility of Psychiatric Diagnoses: Am J Psychiatry. January; 160(1):4–12.

Kirkham, R.J., Alisa, M., Pimenta da Silva, A., Grindley, T. & Brondsted, J. (2004) Eurolifeform: an integrated probabilistic whole life cycle cost and performance model for building and civil engineering. *Proceedings of COBRA 2004*.

Kohler, N. (1999), The relevance of Green Building Challenge: an observer's perspective, Building Research & Information , Volume, 27, Issue: 4-5, pp 309–320

Krugman, P. (1996) The self organising economy: Blackwell, USA.

Low, S.P. (1993) The rationalisation of quality in the construction industry: some empirical findings. *Construction Management and Economics*, **11**(4), 247–259.

Lucien Le Cam (1986) *Asymptotic Methods in Statistical Decision Theory*, Springer Series in Statistics, Springer-Verlag.

Luecke, R. & Katz, R. (2003) *Managing Creativity and Innovation*. Harvard Business School Press, Boston, MA.

ManuBuild. (2009) *Open Building Manufacturing*. Available from http://www.manubuild.net (accessed June 2011).

Marcus, M. & Minc, H. (1998) Introduction to Linear Algebra. Dover Publications Inc, New York.

Mazzocchi, F. (2008) Complexity in biology. Exceeding the limits of reductionism and determinism using complexity theory EMBO reports. *EMBO*, **9**(1), 10–14.

Mitteleton-Kelly, E. (1997), 'Organisation as Co-Evolving Complex Adaptive Systems', British Academy of Management Conference, London 8–10 September 1997.

Mollaghasemi, M., Pet-Edwards, J (1997) Making Multi-Objective Decisions: IEEE Computer Society Press. Los Alamitos 1997.

Moser, K. (1999) Towards the practical evaluation of service life – illustrative application of the probabilistic approach, *Durability of Building Materials and Components 8: Service Life and Asset Management*, vol. 2, *Service Life Prediction and Sustainable Materials*. National Research Council Canada Press, Ottawa.

Omnès, R. (1999) *Understanding Quantum Mechanics*. Princeton University Press, Princeton, NJ.

Ostwald, M. & Tucker, C. (2007) Calculating characteristic visual complexity in the built environment: an analysis of Bovill's Method. *Symposium: Building Across*

Borders Built Environment Procurement CIB WO92 Procurement Systems, 23–26 September, Hunter Valley, NSW. 305–314.

Poincaré, H. (1957) *Les Méthodes Nouvelles de la Mécanique Céleste,* vol. III. Dover Publications Inc, New York.

Popper, K. (1963) *Conjectures and Refutations.* Routledge, London.

Reichenbach, H. (1944) *Philosophic Foundations of Quantum Mechanics.* University of California Press.

Saaty, T. (1977) A scaling method for priorities in hierarchical structures. *Journal of Mathematical Psychology,* **15**, 234–281.

Saaty, T. (1980) *The Analytic Hierarchy Process.* McGraw Hill, New York.

Salinaros, N. (1999) Architecture, patterns and mathematics. *US Network Journal,* **1**, 75–85.

Schumpeter, J. (1934) *The Theory of Economic Development.* Harvard University Press, Cambridge, MA.

Seeley, I. (1976) *Building Maintenance*: Macmillan, New York.

Sharp, M. (2007a) *Complexity Theory and the Maintenance Paradigm* (Becon, 2007), CIB World Congress, Cape Town, SA.

Sharp, M. (2007b) *Proceedings of the 1st International Conference, The Transformation of the Industry: Open Building Manufacturing.* The Netherlands.

Sommerfield, A. (1919) *Atombau und Spektrallinie.* Friedrich Vieweg und Sohn, Braunschweig.

Spedding, A., Holmes, R. & Shen, Q. (1995) Prioritising planned maintenance in county authorities. In: *International Conference on Planned Maintenance, Reliability and Quality Assurance.* Cambridge University, Cambridge. 72–78.

Spekknink, D. (1995) Architect's and consultant's quality management system. *Building Research and Information,* **23**(2), 97–105.

Stacey (1993) *Strategic Management and Organisational Dynamics.* Pitman Publishing, London.

Stewart (1995) Does God Play Dice? The mathematics of chaos: Blackwell.

Stigler, S. (1986) *History of Statistics,* Chapter 3. Harvard University Press, Cambridge, MA.

Solè, R. & Goodwin, B. (2000) *Signs of Life: How Complexity Pervades Biology*: Basic Books.

Stacey, R. (1996) *Complexity Creativity in Organizations.* Berrett-Koehler, USA.

Schwaiger, K. (1997) Mass flow, energy flow and cost of the German building stock. *CIB 2nd International Conference Buildings and the Environment.*

Tan, O.B. & Low, S.P. (1991) Kanter's strategic approach to managing innovation and change in the construction industry. *The Professional Builder,* **6**(1), 26–31.

Tucker, R. & Scarlett, B. (1986) Evaluation of design effectiveness. *Research Rep. No. SD-16,* Construction Industry Institute, Austin, TX.

Weibull, W. (1951) A statistical distribution function of wide applicability. *Journal of Applied. Mech.-Trans. ASME,* **18**(3), 293–297.

Wheatley, M. (1992) *Leadership In The New Science: Learning About Organization From An Orderly Universe.* Berrett-Koehler, USA.

Winch, G. (2001) Governing the project process: a conceptual framework. *Construction Management and Economics,* **19**, 799–808.

Yin, Y. (2008) *Business and Financial Service: New engine of Economic Growth.* Available from www. Herts.ac.uk

Yorke, J. & Li, T. (1975) Period three implies chaos. *American Mathematical Monthly,* **82**, 985.

Zeleny, M. (1982) *Multiple Criteria Decision Making.* McGraw-Hill, New York.

Part III

Future Technologies

Design Innovation: Advanced Visualisation Futures

Farzad Pour Rahimian

14.1   Introduction

The quality of design can often strongly affect the quality of buildings that we live in (Moum, 2006). Design is an exclusive human activity and a critical aspect of many modern industries, where for example Lawson (1997) acknowledged design as being a multi-aspect, iterative and complicated process. In this context, amongst all the design stages, the early phases of design process tend to be drastically affected by the quality of the communications amongst team members. This chapter categorises design communications into two groups, as follows:

1. the 'design reasoning', which is the interaction between a designer and the design situation; and
2. the 'design collaboration', which is the communication amongst different designers.

Over the last two decades, the communication culture within the design process has changed drastically, influenced predominantly by advances in Information and Communications Technology (ICT) along with increased globalisation.

Lawson (1997) posited that communication culture within every society depends on the tools that people use for their transactions. Today, we are witnessing the revolutions made by globalisation in many societies. In this regard, the culture and the way people interact are often affected by their needs and the emerging communication tools. Cera et al. (2002) asserted that ICT has revolutionised product design in the Architecture Engineering-Construction (AEC) industries, as well as any other area where geometric computation and visualisation have proven essential. Friedman (2005) also

Construction Innovation and Process Improvement, First Edition.
Edited by Akintola Akintoye, Jack S. Goulding and Girma Zawdie.
© 2012 Blackwell Publishing Ltd. Published 2012 by Blackwell Publishing Ltd.

recognised the ICT as the most effective phenomenon, which affected the world's interaction culture in the twentieth-first century. From a similar perspective, Moum (2006) argued that participants within the AEC design process have recently faced ICT related benefits and challenges at several levels. Therefore, with progressive globalisation and specialisation trends within the AEC industry, collaboration amongst design stakeholders at distant locations became crucial (Wojtowicz, 1994; Seng et al., 2005). Today, Computer Supported Collaborative Works (CSCWs) (Wojtowicz, 1994) are no longer mere facilities, but an integral part of comprehensive AEC firms in developed countries. An example of this is the design of the Boeing 777 (Dietrich et al., 2007), which comprised over 10,000 designers in 238 teams organised across 17 time zones.

Moum (2006) proposed the high-level use of the advanced visualisation media to address the emerging issues within the AEC industry; whereas, Fruchter (1998) ascertained that integration of design and construction process could better support collaboration within the global AEC teams, hence significantly decrease labour and material costs. This was further reinforced by Goulding et al. (2007), concerning the increased tendency of using ICT tools within design and construction, with the acknowledgement that design engineers are able to experiment and experience decisions in a 'cyber-safe' environment in order to mitigate or reduce risks prior to construction. This was also aligned with Petric et al.'s (2002) idea regarding capability of such applications in predicting the cost and performance of optimal design proposals to search for good solutions, and the implementation of such applications as they enable design engineers to compare the quality of any one tentative solution against the quality of all previous solutions. Notwithstanding these potential benefits, the use of such applications is not quite evident within the early stages of the building design process, due to the inherent characteristics of existing Computer Aided Design (CAD) tools, which did not fit into the conceptual architectural design process (Lawson, 1997; Suwa et al., 1998; Craft and Cairns, 2006; Levet et al., 2006; Kwon et al., 2005). This chapter therefore highlights the potential differences between the latter technical architectural and the engineering documentations versus the intuitive conceptual design ideation during the early stages of the design process. The resultant heterogeneity in the utilised design tools during different phases of the whole building design process therefore hinders the integration of the whole process, hence leading to the potential tacit knowledge loss through the transitions of the interrupted procedure (Fruchter, 1998). It also provides theoretical foundations for facilitating the digitalisation of the conceptual architectural design process. It proposes the use of tangible, immersive and interactive Virtual Reality (VR) interfaces as a viable solution, particularly for promoting the integration of data simulation and communication through the whole design and construction processes as well as improving the designers' cognition and collaboration. It also discusses how the aforementioned interfaces could provide supreme intuitive interactions to support 'free' artistic expression, and bridge the gap between artistic experimentation and accurate manufacturing-oriented modelling. It is therefore argued that this approach could proactively foster multidisciplinary teamwork synergies and provide enhanced outcomes for respective collaborative participants in the AEC industries.

This chapter firstly provides a comprehensive literature review to justify the background issues and challenges within the design representation field. Afterwards, it reports the theoretical highlights of the conducted sequential mixed method research methodology, including the qualitative case study and the cognitive-based quantitative protocol analysis experiment. It then presents the tangible VR design interfaces as a viable solution, particularly for promoting the integration of data simulation and communication throughout the whole design and construction processes.

14.2   Design Innovation and Existing Visualisation Tools

Moum (2006) asserted that a good design process is a fundamental mainstay for a successful building project. Design is an exclusive human activity and a critical aspect of many modern societies. Like most of the other design processes, building design often starts with emergence of the particular needs and ends when the users start using the final product (building). In this vision, the building design process consists of five major phases: Originate, FocusDesign, Build and Occupy (AIA, 1993). Through all five stages, a good project requires a comprehensive teamwork and a good degree of communication and collaboration amongst all stakeholders. However, this communication and collaboration is more crucial during the early phases of problem finding, analysis and conceptual design, which contribute to the determination of 70–80% of production cost of the project (Schütze et al., 2003). The following subsections discuss and elaborate the characteristics of the early stages of building design process and the quality of communications within these phases.

14.2.1   The Conceptual Architectural Design Process

Since the early 1960s, many endeavours have been undertaken to explain or clarify the architectural design process and the genesis of design solutions (Lundequist, 1992). So far, diverse research agendas have been evident in the design thinking area (Akin and Lin, 1995). Some of these agendas dealt with the internal and external representations of designed objects (Akin, 1978); others with the issues of design generation (Cuomo, 1988), for example, the knowledge basis of the design thinking (Waldron and Waldron, 1988), the formulation of design problems (Akin et al., 1992) and the thought processes that apply to the learning (Schön, 1983). Yet, most others deal with refining the general descriptions of the design process offered by the initial group of studies (Akin and Lin, 1995). The first generation of the design methodologies dealing with design process as something chronological and linear are no longer taken into account (Moum, 2006). New generations of design studies generally acknowledge design as a learning domain in which experiences and basic techniques play a large role. However, Suwa *et al.* (1998) argued that the obtained skill in design process is rarely explicit so that even the experienced designers have difficulties in understanding their own design proficiency. As a remarkable effort in explaining the design process, Lawson (1997) critically emphasised that there was no obvious difference between problem and solution, analysis, syntheses or assessment in this procedure. Moum (2006) defined the architectural design as a concurrent learning process about the nature of the problem and the variety of the achievable solutions. Moum's taxonomy for all the activities of the whole design process comprises of four categories: generation of design solutions, communication, evaluation of design solutions and decision making. However, Lawson (1997) argued that the design problem is not easy to define or expose, as it is multi-aspect and iterative. According to Lawson (1997), design process starts with a basic idea in the designer's mind and proceeds as a complex and iterative process between problem and solution. In this manner, while the design team members are fulfilling the different requirements of the project, the primary idea 'materialises' into something to be considered as the conceptual base of the building project.

From a cognitive perspective, Schön (1983) asserted that every designer operates in a mental virtual world as an imitated simulation of the real world in practice; that is, during the conceptual design process, designers generate and develop design solutions by conducting diverse intellectual and physical tasks. However, the human mind is not strong enough to handle such a complicated task without any external aid. In this regard, Fish and Scrivener (1990) argued that the graphic forms provided by the external representations could facilitate the development of the useful ideas and concepts. Lawson (1997) further developed this discussion and asserted that the abstract external design representation could provide the designers with great manipulative and instantaneously analytical autonomy without wasting their time and resources. Lawson indicated that this wasting could be inevitable if the ideas had to be tested directly at the building site. Finally, Moum (2006) acknowledged this idea mentioning that the external design representation tools could significantly help the designers organise the design process and design ideas in a rational and logical way. Moum (2006) therefore asserted that studying the design communication culture and the new external design representation tools could still have great significance.

14.2.2   Communication Culture within the Architectural Design Process

Moum (2006) asserted that decisions made during the early conceptual building design stages were significantly affected by the transactions amongst different stakeholders. Every transaction comprises of the senders, the receivers, and the communication media. In essence, during the architectural design process, a transaction could comprise of an architect as the sender, who sends the design solution to the engineers as receivers. In this example, the design solution is encoded in a drawing as a form of symbolic language (transaction medium) to be understood by all design team members. In practice, even a client also might need to receive a copy of the design solution and decode the message to understand the solution. However, the success in decoding and encoding usually depends on both senders' and receivers' background knowledge (Kalay, 2004). Donath *et al.* (2004) therefore asserted that the success of interaction between designers and clients is dependent upon designers' competence in using some design media that is understandable by the clients.

Although conventional design tools and the symbolic design languages utilised in design disciplines are often compatible with its members' knowledge, the nuances of these are usually misunderstood by the clients and the designers from the other disciplines. Griffith *et al.* (2003) linked this misunderstanding to the tacit nature of the design knowledge. They asserted that a new generation of external representation media are needed to translate design knowledge into an explicit form, in order to be attained by all team members.

14.2.3   External Design Representation Tools

The early conceptual phases of the design process are characterised by fuzziness, coarse structures and elements, and the trial-and-error processes. Craft and Cairns (2006) asserted that searching for form and shape are the designers' principal goal during the early conceptual design stages. Here, the needs of correcting errors are the highest, so that the use of low-expenditure and sketch-like media is crucial. Cross (1999) asserted that during the conceptual design process, the designers' cognitions hinge around the relationship between internal mental processes and their expressions or the external representations through design media.

Cross (2007) argued that the famous architect, Santiago Calatrava, used sketching not only as a communication tool, but also as a means to orchestrate the mental thinking process and to develop the design ability. According to Cross (2007), acknowledging the dialogue or the 'conversation' that goes on between internal and external representations is a part of the recognition that design is reflective. Cross (2007) finally asserted that the designers have to have a medium to enable ill-defined ideas to be articulated, represented, reconsidered, revised and deployed. This supports an earlier claim by Frankenberger (1997) that since the design process is strongly influenced by feedback and dialogue, the communicative function of external representation tools is of great importance within the design profession. Finally, through a cognitive study, Schütze *et al.* (2003) ascertained that the external representations could serve designers as an aid for analysis, solution generation, evaluation, communication and external storage. They asserted that self-made sketch-like external representations could compensate for the shortcomings of the limited human memory regarding processing the complex design problems often encountered in global projects.

14.2.4   Conventional Computer Aided Design Tools

CAD tools are currently being more frequently used in drafting and modelling rather than early conceptual design stages. However, Kalay (2004) argued that a new generation of CAD tools should change the traditional entity of the conceptual design tasks as well. Moum (2006) asserted that such tool could have potential benefits for the conceptual designers, by helping them to generate a huge amount of highly realistic and professional representations of the design solution within a restricted time, hence transferring tacit design knowledge into an explicit form (Griffith *et al.*, 2003) in order to be attained by all other partners. However, according to Lawson (1997) – who ironically used the term 'Computer Aided Drafting' that such tools are yet to attain capabilities to support designing and intuitive thinking of humankind. In this regard, both Lawson (1997) and Griffith *et al.* (2003) argued that a new generation of more flexible digital media is needed, in order to provide the spontaneous reflections required during the conceptual design phases.

14.2.5   ICT and Virtual Reality

Cross (2007) asserted that design support systems should not just be designed to emulate or replace designers, acknowledging that design is also a pleasant and easy task for humankind. Cross (2007) argued that machines should only perform the tasks that are arduous and difficult for human beings. Kalay (2004) proposed the development of some expert Artificial Intelligence (AI) systems (as design agents) that can handle design operations on behalf of the designers. According to Kalay (2004), a design agent is a system, which can make a designer aware of inconstancy in construction checklists. However, in this approach the computers are merely design support tools, not designers. In this respect, VR is an example of emerging design support tools. VR has been defined as a 3D computer-generated alternative environment to be immersed in, for navigating around and interacting with (Briggs, 1996), or as a component of communication taking place in a 'synthetic' space, which embeds humans as its integral part (Regenbrecht and Donath, 1996). The justifications of VR systems usually includes a computer capable of real-time animation, controlled by a set of wired gloves and a position tracker, and use of a head-mounted stereoscopic display for visual output. For instance, Regenbrecht and Donath (1996) defined the tangible components of VR as a congruent set of hardware and software, with actors within a 3D or multi-dimensional input/output space, where actors can interact with other autonomous objects, in real time. Some other studies (Greenbaum, 1992; Yoh, 2001) defined VR as a simulated world, which comprises of some computer-generated images conceived via head-mounted eye goggles and wired clothing – thereby enabling the end users to interact in a realistic 3D situation.

Early studies that incorporated VR into the design profession used it as an advanced visualisation medium. Since as early as 1990, VR has been widely used in the AEC industry, as it forms a natural medium for building design by providing 3D models, which can be manipulated in real time and used collaboratively to explore different stages of the construction process (Whyte *et al.*, 2000). It has also been used as a design application to provide collaborative visualisation for improving construction processes (Bouchlaghem, 1996). However, expectations of VR have changed during the current decade. According to Sampaio *et al.* (2008), it is increasingly important to incorporate VR 3D visualisation and decision support systems with interactive interfaces, in order to perform real-time interactive visual exploration tasks. This thinking supports the position that a collaborative virtual environment is a 3D immersive space, in which 3D models are linked to databases, which carry characteristics. This premise has also been followed through other lines of thought, especially in construction planning and management by relating 3D models to time parameters in order to design 4D models (Fischer and Kunz, 2004), which are controlled through an interactive and multi-access database. In similar studies, 4D VR models have been used to improve many aspects and phases of construction projects by:

1. developing and implementing applications for providing better communication amongst partners (Leinonen *et al.*, 2003);
2. supporting conception design (Petzold *et al.*, 2007);
3. introducing the construction plan to stakeholders (Khanzade *et al.*, 2007); and
4. following the progress of construction (Fischer, 2000).

14.3   Cognitive Approach to Design

Kan (2008) defined design as a series of decisions that expose the relationship of geometries, materials and performance. Kan clustered some of design activities as thinking and knowing (Cross, 2007), free-hand sketching and interactions (Lawson, 1997), social construction of design solutions (Minneman, 1991) and designing-by-making (Jones, 1970). Goldschmidt and Porter (2004) defined designing as a cognitive activity, which entails the production of sequential representations of a mental and physical artefact. Goldschmidt and Porter (2004) defined designing as a cognitive activity, which entails the production of sequential representations of a mental and physical artefact, and Tversky (2005) noted that when constructing the external or internal representations, designers are engaged in spatial cognition process in which the representations serve as cognitive aids to memory and information processing. Schön (1992) asserted that with the execution of action and reflection, each level of representation makes designers evolve in their interpretations and ideas for design solutions. Such cognitive approach to designing considers design media as something beyond a mere presentation tool. In this approach, reflections, which are caused by design media, are expected to either stimulate or hamper designers' creativity during design reasoning.

Visser (2004) discussed two main paradigms in the cognitive approach to designing: the *'symbolic information-processing'* (SIP) approach represented by Simon (1979), and the *'situativity'* (SIT) approach represented by Schön (1983). Visser described SIP as an approach, which deals with the designers, and the design problems emphasising the designers' rational problem solving process, and SIT as the one that depends on the designers' situational environment and context. Visser (2004) asserted that SIT approach defines designing as a reflective communication with the materials, which belong to design situation. Thus, Visser (2004) adopted a cognitive approach to design by focusing on individuals' activities, which are implemented in professional design projects. In the mentioned study, Visser is particularly concerned with dynamic aspects of designing focusing on the implemented activities by designers and the cognitive processes that they use. In this report, Visser criticised both SIT and SIP approaches, then integrated them into one comprehensive cognitive approach. Here Visser defined design process as an 'opportunistically organised' activity. Visser (2004) defined design as a process to define an artefact and to describe the characteristics, which can satisfy that artefact. Visser's asserted that design is the evolution of representations and there is no permanent hierarchy amongst representations of differing levels of idea abstraction. According to Visser, non-concrete problems cause interruptions, which do not hinder design quality, but can make some opportunities for reflection and improvement of practice. Visser argued that this reflection occurs by a mutual discovery process between the external representation and the designer's cognitive reasoning model.

In cognitive design studies, the other term for discussion is the role of visuo-spatial representations. According to Bruner (1973), external visuo-spatial representations monitor static and dynamic visuo-spatial characteristics of the design ideas. Burner (1973) asserted that deductive reasoning is the basis of the abstract cognition, which is something beyond mere recall from visual literature. In this regard, there are two steps for obtaining a clear understanding of *'design ideas'* and to enhance the *'design creativity'*: to transform tacit design ideas into visuo-spatial representations and to make deduction from the external representations (Tversky, 2005). Whereas, from a design creativity perspective, the term 'creative' is used as a value for design artefacts (Kim and Maher, 2008). Yet, according to Visser (2004), in cognitive psychology discussions, creativity is often linked to a design activity, which also comprises particular procedures that have the potential to produce creative artefacts. Cross and Dorst (1999) defined a creative design procedure as a kind of non-routine designing activities that usually are differentiated from the others by the emergence of some considerable events or unanticipated novel artefacts. Kan (2008) asserted that the design process should be evaluated with the level of its creativeness, and that generating ideas and creativity should make common sense. On the other hand, Finke *et al.* (1992) acknowledged that creativity is a result of various mental processes, which totally lead design process towards the phase of creative insight and discovery. They posited that creativity should include initiative stages through which mental representations of *'pre-inventive structures'* are formed.

The 'Unexpected discoveries' model by Suwa et al. (2000) is a more developed tool for measuring design creativity. They introduced unexpected discoveries as some perceptual activities of articulating tacit design semantics into visuo-spatial forms through unanticipated findings by the later inspections. Goldschmidt and Porter (2004) argued that unexpected discoveries (which happen when a designer perceives the depicted items) are some results of external representations that are more important than the representations per se. Suwa et al. (2000) considered unexpected discoveries as the stimuli that force design process to develop and evolve the 'solution-space'. They argued that there is an iterative interaction between development of the 'solution-space' and sparking new ideas about the 'problem-space'. 'Situative-invention' is another key factor for improving design process. According to Suwa et al. (2000), situative inventions refer to the actions in which a designer goes beyond the initial definitions of the problem space. In their explanation, by the situative-inventions, designers form new goals for the solution space to grab the significant parts of the design problem and go beyond a synthesis of solutions that suits the given requirements. On the other hand, Cross and Dorst (1999) posited the modelling of the design creativity as a co-evolution for both problem and solution spaces. Co-evolutionary design is an approach to 'problem solving' defined by Maher et al. (1996). In this approach, the design requirements and design artefacts are formed disjointedly while mutually affecting each other. Kim and Maher (2008) asserted that in this approach the changes of the problem could have an effect on the designer's insight into the solutions.

14.4   Virtual Reality Interfaces within Conceptual Architectural Design

The first generation of the design literature highlighted manual sketching using pencils and papers as the main abstract representation method for conceptual design phase. By the year 2000, its effectiveness was frequently appreciated by the scholars (Fish and Scrivener, 1990; Goldschmidt, 1994; Lawson, 1997; Kavakli et al., 1998; McGown et al., 1998; Purcell and Gero, 1998; Cross and Dorst, 1999; Rodgers et al., 2000; Scrivener et al., 2000). This advocacy was at the highest level when Schön and Wiggins (1992) highlighted the importance of freehand sketches as the indispensable media for designers to make reflective dialogue with their own ideas. However, the predisposition to manual sketching methodologies started to diminish with improvements in CAD tools, and their increasing use in the new complex global projects. The reviewed literature noted the increasing tendency for using CAD tools during the early conceptual architectural design process commencing after the year 2000. Scholars were impressed with its excellent capabilities, especially in advanced photorealistic visualisation of the projects (Madrazo, 1999; Marx, 2000). However, doubts about the effectiveness of CAD tools in handling early conceptual design stages started almost concurrently with the appreciations. For instance, Lawson (1997) ironically called such tools 'Computer Aided Drafting' rather than design. Other researches (Suwa et al., 1998; Bilda and

Demirkan, 2003) doubted the usability of such tools, stating that although the CAD media have had a huge impact on the effectiveness of design groups, there are still some characteristics of designing that are exclusively related to freehand sketches. A study by Kwon et al. (2005) attributed this inadequacy to the limitation in the intuitive ideation capabilities of the current CAD media. Therefore, they posited that conventional CAD tools might not be desired during the conceptual design phases. Yet, due to the changes caused by the globalisation trends, conventional design representation media are no longer sufficient for handling engineering parts of the design process; the design of Boeing 777 (Dietrich et al., 2007) supports this idea. The difference in the needs for supporting both ill-defined and well-defined aspects of the emerging global design projects highlights the potential stark differences between the engineering documentation versus the intuitive conceptual design ideation by the architects. Currently, this difference makes designers use different design tools when dealing with the different phases of the design process. This transitional utilisation of different media could lead to potential loss of tacit design knowledge (Fruchter, 1998) within transitions of the interrupted process.

To address the aforementioned issues, a new generation of external design representation tools to compensate the shortcomings of both the conventional manual sketching tools and current CAD media, are needed. To fill this theoretical gap, VR as an emerging technology was considered appropriate. With a cognitive approach to the designing, the advanced features of tangible user interfaces (TUIs) and haptic devices, which could help designers to 'feel' the virtual objects and include the touch sense in the design reasoning, are introduced. TUIs are an expression used to represent a technology, including digital information and physical objects to mimic an actual environment. Kim and Maher (2008) defined the characteristics of TUIs as similar to what is defined earlier for the graspable user interfaces by Fitzmaurice et al. (1995). Both studies defined five fundamental properties for such systems as space-multiplex for input and output systems, simultaneous control and manipulation of all components in the interface, high technology tools, spatially responsive digital tools and 3D re-configurability of the tools. According to Kim and Maher (2008), as opposed to a simple time-multiplexed technology that is used in ordinary input devices (e.g. a mouse), the main advantages of TUIs is the space multiplexing input technology that is able to control various functions at different times. One instance of such machinery is haptic technology. In computer science discussions, the term 'haptic' relates to the sense of touch. In other words, this is a technology that unites the user to a digital system, by simulating the sense of touch and applying force-feedback, vibrations and motions to the user (Basque Research, 2007). This physical interaction with the real world is the quality that Stricker et al. (2001) described as the technology that reinforces human's cognition by interaction with the physical world. Considering the aforementioned capabilities, this author believes that haptic technology can provide an advanced TUI for designers.

In haptic technology, the sense of touch is not limited to a feeling and it facilitates a real-time interactivity with virtual objects. According to Brewster

(2001), haptic technology is a space in the VR area, since it allows users to use their touch sense to feel virtual objects. Brewster argues that although touch is an extremely powerful sense, it has so far been abandoned in the digital world. Therefore, this study focused on the role of force-feedback facilitated by SensAble Technology TUIs in forming designers' spatial cognition and the effects of the proposed tangible VR 3D sketching interface on designers' collective cognitive and collaborative design activities.

Figure 14.1 illustrates the preceding theories for supporting VR TUIs as a solution for supporting the emerging global design processes. This presents the development of the conceptual architectural design process in order to enhance the integration of the whole building process besides developing and enhancing the current state of the design interfaces (Ibrahim and Pour Rahimian, 2010). This was expected to improve designers' cognition and collaboration during the conceptual architectural design process. This aim is intended to be achieved by developing a new design methodology based on Schön's (1983) 'reflective practitioner' theory and Fitts' (1964) 'motor learning' theory, then verifying its effectiveness based on the collected empirical data. The reflective practitioner theory argued that designers are in a mutual relationship with the external representations and getting reflections from them, whereas, the motor learning theory stated that the tangible interfaces could improve designers' cognitive actions. In this theory, the focus was on the integration of the designers' other senses (e.g. the sense of touch) with their visual sense.

The development of the conceptual architectural design process investigated the current state of the utilised conceptual design interfaces and the existing communication culture amongst the conceptual designers. According to Shuttleworth (2008), a qualitative case study research methodology is an appropriate research methodology for this kind of research that tests theoretical models by using them in 'real-world' situations. The quality of the designers' cognitive and collaborative actions in using VR 3D sketching as an instance of tangible VR design interfaces is also examined.

Design protocol analysis as a quantitative research methodology is predominantly used in the development of conceptual design process as the most prevailing research methodology for studying design processes (Cross et al., 1996). A qualitative case study research approach was undertaken at Universiti Putra Malaysia (Ibrahim and Pour Rahimian, 2010) based on ethnography for data collection and artefact analysis for data analysis was employed. The units of analyses that informed the development of the conceptual framework were design artefacts of the selected second-year architectural design studio, comprising 37 students and 4 studio mentors (Figure 14.2). The gatekeeper during the data collection was the Studio Master of the subject. The case study identified the characteristics of the current design media and the collaborative design culture within the conceptual architectural design process. Consequently, the recommendations of the case study helped to develop theoretical foundations of the study.

The purpose of the quantitative element of the study was to provide empirical evidence for the subjective view that proposed a VR-based 3D sketching interface could improve the designers' spatial cognition and

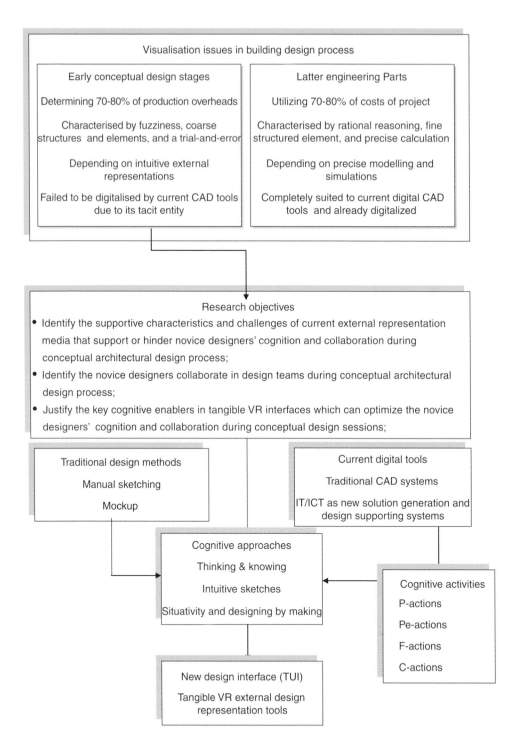

Figure 14.1   Theoretical framework for VR interfaces to support global design processes.

Figure 14.2   Traditional sketching (left) and 3D sketching (right) design settings.

collaboration. In conducting the experiment, a traditional sketching toolkit was developed as a baseline to be compared with the proposed 3D sketching design interface (Figure 14.2). The purpose was to reveal the cognitive and collaborative impacts of the proposed design system. Three pairs of fifth-year architecture students with relevant experience of traditional design and CAD systems were selected as participants for this experiment. During the experiment, protocol analysis methodology (Schön, 1983; Ericsson and Simon, 1993, Dorst and Dijkhuis, 1995, Lloyd *et al.*, 1995, Foreman and Gillett, 1997) was employed for data acquisition. The adapted methodology evaluated the designers' spatial cognition at four different cognitive levels, 'physical-actions', 'perceptual-actions', 'functional-actions' and 'conceptual-actions'. In addition, the designers' spatial cognition in two different collaborative levels, 'cognitive synchronisations' and 'gestures', were evaluated.

14.4.1   Conceptual Architecture Design Experiment: Results

The case study listed three dominant types of sketching (i.e. fully manual, mixed and fully digital) used by the students and their studio mentors. The study also employed four dependent variables and three independent variables in order to identify the supportive characteristics and challenges of the current external representation media. The dependent variables were solution quality, certainty of the correctness of the solution, total solution time and the experienced difficulty in design problem solving while the independent variables were fully manual (FM), mixed method (MM) and fully digital (FD) external design representation modes.

Based on the results from the selected sample, the variance analysis (ANOVA) revealed that the design solutions by the subjects using mixed traditional sketching and CAD modelling tools (MM) produced significantly higher solution quality compared to the other two groups. On the other hand, the fully manual sketching subjects had significantly higher solution quality compared to those subjects who solved the design problems completely in CAD environment. This study therefore posited that using the conventional CAD tools hindered the designers' creativity in the early conceptual design stages.

The analysis of the second dependent variable revealed a significant decrease in the certainties of the correctness of the solutions of FM subjects compared to the other two groups. The results also showed no significant difference amongst the three groups regarding the total time spent for creating their respective solutions. The aforementioned analysis therefore triggers doubts on the competence of the conventional manual sketching media in handling the complicated design stages. It implied that while the MM and FD groups used 3D prototyping techniques to ensure that various design parts fitted together, the FM group was unsuccessful in convincing designers in this regard.

The study applied subjective protocol to enable the difficulty experienced in the design problem solving to be evaluated. Based on the subjective protocol evaluation using the narrative stories transcribed from the recorded videotapes, results indicated that the subjects who had utilised mixed design media were able to pace their design processes with considerable lesser difficultly compared to the subjects from the other two groups. The observations also noted that the same subjects were able to manipulate free-hand sketches to solve design problems faster and easier. They were also able to use digital capabilities for solving the communicational problems, either within the design situations or with other designers. The results of the artefact analysis can be seen in Table 14.1.

From Table 14.1, the study found that amongst the three evaluated external design representation methods, the best tool comprises of both manual and digital tools. The observations and analytical results illustrated that neither manual sketching tools nor conventional CAD software applications are the better media for the conceptual design communications. This study posited that design semantic gets lost when the manual design tools fail in visualising complicated design ideas and design creativity diminishes when the arduous CAD software tools interrupt the designers' intuitive reasoning. The results supported the proposal for development of a tangible VR interface for filling the existing gap between the creative experimentation and the precise manufacturing-oriented modelling.

The experimental protocol analysis research identified key enablers in the VR 3D sketching interface that can optimise novice designers' cognition and collaboration during conceptual design sessions (Pour Rahimian and Ibrahim, 2011). This study employed a cognitive approach to design process to articulate all aspects of the utilised medium during the conceptual architectural design process. The traditional sketching method was selected as the baseline system to be compared with the proposed 3D sketching design methodology and to reveal the cognitive and collaborative impacts of the proposed design system. The experiment comprised of five main steps (van Someren et al., 1994):

1. to conduct the experiment;
2. to transcribe the protocols;
3. to parse process into the segments;

Table 14.1 Quality of the solution, total solution time, and certainty regarding the correctness of the solution (adapted from Ibrahim and Pour Rahimian, 2010).

Dependent variable			Solution quality				Certainty of the correctness of the solution				Total solution time			
(I) Type of sketching		N	Mean Std. Dev	(J) Type of sketching	D = J − I	Sig.	Mean Std. Dev	(J) Type of sketching	D = J − I	Sig	Mean Std. Dev	(J) Type of sketching	D = J − I	Sig
Fully manual mode (FM)		14	3.38 0.47	MM	−.43564*	.03	2.38 0.40	MM	− 1.42***	.00	466.6 229.8	MM	170.07	.13
				FD	.47*	.03		FD	− 1.54***	.00		FD	88.49	.60
Mixed mode (MM)		13	3.81 0.34	FM	.43*	.03	3.80 0.37	FM	1.42***	.00	296.5 168.7	FM	− 170.07	.13
				FD	.91***	.00		FD	− 0.12	.74		FD	− 81.57	.66
Fully digital mode(FD)		10	2.90 0.44	FM	−.47*	.03	3.92 0.38	FM	1.54***	.00	378.1 262.7	FM	− 8.49	.60
				MM	−.91***	.00		MM	0.12	.74		MM	81.57	.60
Total		37	3.40 0.54	Total	f = 13.3***	.00	3.29 0.81	Total	f = 64.5***	.00	382.9 226.3	Total	f = 2.012	.15

* p < 0.05 (significant difference), ** p < 0.01 (very significant difference), *** p < 0.001 (absolutely significant difference).

4. to encode the segments based on the developed coding scheme; and
5. to analyse and interpret the encoded protocols.

In encoding the data collected and developing the hypotheses, the study categorised the designers' cognitive actions into five major action categories as physical, perceptual, functional, conceptual and collaborative. In interpreting the findings, the study relied on the observations of the designers' behaviours during the experiment and on the statistical analysis of the encoded design protocols. The encoded protocol data included the pairs' verbal accounts concurrently per experiment, hence providing adequate data for an empirical exploratory study. Therefore, the conclusion of this study relied more on the encoded protocol data rather the behavioural observations.

14.4.2   Conceptual Architecture Design Experiment: Discussion

The ethnography study (Pour Rahimian et al., 2008) and the artefact and protocol analyses on the ethnography findings (Ibrahim and Pour Rahimian, 2010) show that there is no better winner for the choice of the current media for external design representations. Both studies affirmed the inflexibility of the traditional geometric modelling tools in intuitive ideations. Moreover, both equally noted the shortcomings of the conventional manual sketching tools for further articulating design ideas, whereby it had difficulties in turning tacit knowledge into explicit knowledge (Griffith et al., 2003) for collaboration purposes. In other words, the results showed that neither manual sketching tools nor current CAD interfaces were the perfect media for emerging conceptual design communications. The study proposed that an alternative tool was needed to support the intuitive ideation, the precise manufacturing oriented modelling and the effortless design walkthroughs.

The results of the artefact and protocol analyses showed major barriers with conventional manual external design representation tools when designing complex design artefacts. This was due to their shortcomings in advanced visualisation as the design became further complicated. The current geometrical CAD modelling applications could not directly replace the aforementioned manual external design representation tools, given that the existing CAD software applications are unable to support certain intuitive design requirements of the conceptual design process. In short, the inflexibility of the ordinary arithmetical modelling software on one hand, and the restricted visualisation capabilities of the manual sketching tools on the other hand, increase the tendency for proposing a new generation of design representation media. In using the sketching metaphor, Levet et al. (2006) proposed the use of some design interfaces in which designers can swiftly produce a 3D prototype to exemplify the 3D object they have in mind. Kwon et al. (2005) considered this factor in order to improve computing performance for integrating the progress of the conceptual phase with the remaining design stages. There is an urgent need therefore to develop tangible VR interfaces that have some particular characteristics, as proposed by Levet et al. (2006) and Kwon et al. (2005).

The aim of the conducted experiment therefore was to provide objective and empirical evidence for the subjective view that the proposed sample tangible

Figure 14.3   Sample 3D sketching design outcome (Pour Rahimian and Ibrahim, 2009).

VR interface, the 3D sketching interface, could improve the designers' spatial cognition and collaboration during the conceptual architectural design phase. The focus was on the designers' cognitive and collaborative actions that were developed. This provided an evidence to support that in 3D sketching sessions the increased integration between the physical actions and the mental perceptions could lead to occurrence of the epistemic actions to improve the designers' spatial cognition. In this regard, Kirsh and Maglio (1994) posited that the epistemic actions could offload the designers' mental cognition partly into the physical world, thus letting them have freer minds to create more design ideas. The tangible VR interface that is proposed has the potential to improve the designers' perception of visuo-spatial features, particularly in terms of unexpectedly discoveries of the spatial features and relationships. This has shown how association between mental cognition and the perception of the physical attributes can offload the mental load and stimulate creativity. According to Suwa et al. (2000), the occurrence of unexpected discoveries could lead to the occurrence of more situative inventions and consequently to more creativity.

In terms of functional-conceptual actions of the design process and utilisation of tangible VR design interface improved the participating three pairs of designers' problem finding behaviours as well as improving their co-evolutionary conceptions of perceptions. An example of this improvement is demonstrated by a sample 3D sketching design complied within three hours, as shown in Figure 14.3. Lastly, in terms of the collaborative activities, the tangible VR design interface is capable of motivating the participating three groups of designers to share more ideas together. Moreover, the study explained how the proposed tangible VR design interface was capable to change the type of conversations from ordinary clarifications to new proposals and arguments, which is evidence of more development of both problem and solutions spaces (Kim and Maher, 2008).

Emerging VR technologies (if developed and deployed appropriately) are capable of facilitating some senses beyond the visual aspects of the design artefact, by offering a new generation of 'promising' CAD tools, which embrace designers' cognition and collaboration during the conceptual architectural design process. This provides a theoretical basis for the development of cutting-edge collaborative virtual environments (Maher et al., 2006) in architectural education and associated professional remits.

14.5   Technical Implications for Developing Tangible Virtual Reality Design Interfaces

Existing VR interfaces have ostensibly been formed, based on a single idea: creating 3D models and incorporating them with some pieces of information, so that both 3D models and information are editable through an interactive real-time interface (Pour Rahimian and Goulding, 2010). However, they differ from each other based on their architecture and the utilised methods for data creation and retrieval. Data creation and retrieval methods in VR interfaces can be investigated from two different perspectives, namely creating 3D bodies of constructional elements *per se* and defining characteristics of the elements.

Although creating 3D objects directly in VR environments is not impossible, this is usually created in CAD applications, since doing so in VR is often cumbersome and time-consuming. Consequently, current VR interfaces can be categorised considering how they convert CAD models into VR elements. In terms of transforming design elements from CAD into VR, there are three *de facto* approaches used by different practitioners. Whyte *et al.* (2000) noted three approaches for this translation as:

1. straightforward translation approach and importing the whole environment from CAD to VR;
2. library-based approach and putting the elements of construction in the library of VR environment, then calling them up when and where necessary; and
3. database-oriented approach with a central database for controlling the module characteristics.

Here the database uses both CAD and VR environments as graphical interfaces. Therefore, the third approach can be characterised as a combination of computer graphics and web programming.

Due to the ease of creating the environments by direct translation, most of the current VR systems in AEC projects use the straightforward translation method. Nevertheless, the new generation of interfaces have to migrate to the third paradigm in order to allow designers to see their artefacts throughout the design representation process. Moreover, this is the only way that can help participants share ideas from distance locations. VR interfaces in the AEC industry also vary based on the method of manipulating the objects within the environment and the adapted programming method in the VR interface. There are three major kinds of programming applications currently used by VR programmers:

1. 3D Application Programming Interfaces (APIs);
2. Virtual Reality Modelling Language (VRML) and 3D web technologies; and
3. recent commercialised object oriented VR programming packages.

In this respect, 3D Application Programming Interfaces (APIs) (e.g. Open GL and Direct 3D) are principal environments for VR programming in C++ and Visual Basic. Falling in the category of computer graphics, they are capable of either creating all models directly inside the space or/and importing them from CAD applications. They are perfect environments for advanced programmers for creating Win32 console applications, which are used in developing computer games; however, integration of such interfaces with web programming is difficult and often leads to failures in cases of complicated works.

Virtual Reality Modelling Language (VRML) and 3D web technologies in their first version were made as a division of Open Inventor, thereafter, having become the international standard for 3D web modelling. These applications provide a variety of facilities for manipulating immersive library-based web interfaces; however, they lack the capability of integration with inter-related databases, as they are not essentially database-oriented applications.

Recent commercialised object oriented VR programming packages contain built-in modelling environments for creating VR spaces directly or importing them from CAD applications. Such VR programming applications also contain logical libraries for defining behavioural links amongst the objects and simulating physical phenomena. Although the architecture of such applications is made based on APIs of C++, in some aspects they can offer a higher-level abstraction for programmers. Nowadays, there are three frontier commercial VR programming applications, namely Quest3D™, EON Reality™ and Virtools™. The outcomes of these applications are directly deployable into C++ and Visual Basic's web programming platforms (EON Reality, Inc, 2008). This makes them extremely flexible in terms of integrating VR programming (which is a part of computer graphics) with web programming and data mining. They also come with full Software Development Kits (SDKs) in order to help advanced programmers add some building blocks and prototypes to create rationales or behaviours that were not originally provided by the application. Besides, the SDKs let programmers integrate their interfaces with particular VR I/O devices, for example, Head-Mounted-Displays (HMDs) and data gloves. In this respect, it is now possible to employ tangible VR design interfaces as a new paradigm for simulating truly immersive AEC design collaboration – this technology could easily embrace a database-driven approach using structured modelling phases and API based programming for the development stages. By linking 3D objects to datasets through a web environment, such systems would therefore be able to optimise performance during detailed design stages, which contain collaboration among multiple designers.

14.6   Conclusion

A sequential case study and protocol analysis studies (Pour Rahimian, 2009) was reported in this chapter to present theoretical foundations for improving designers' cognition and collaboration during conceptual design process.

This has become necessary to improve and optimise the operational behaviour of design project teams. The purpose of the protocol analysis was to empirically evaluate and verify the role of 3D sketching using VR interface in facilitating integration between conceptual and engineering parts of building design process. This chapter identified:

1. issues and challenges of the multidisciplinary AEC teams in the emerging global project collaborations;
2. inherent characteristics of the conceptual design process and its external representation tools; and
3. the theoretical and technical requirements of the proposed tangible VR design interfaces as the future external design representation tools.

It is posited that by adopting a cognitive approach to design, the supportive characteristics of tangible VR interfaces to enhance design cognition and collaboration within the AEC practice and profession need further investigation. The introduced advanced digital interfaces could expedite knowledge transfer and stimulate 'creativity' and 'learning through experience' (Suwa et al., 1998) within the AEC education and the associated professional remits. It could also contribute towards transforming conceptual architectural design phase from analogue to digital format, hence linking it to the remaining digital engineering parts of the building design process. This process integration and digitisation could become the leading edge of the AEC enterprises through revolutionising their essential systems, for example, design representations within the interdisciplinary communications, tacit knowledge reuse via organisational memory, documenting and addressing the clients' needs, etc. Such improvements in dynamicity and flexibility of the communicational systems will therefore enable the AEC professionals to share and amplify design semantics throughout the project development life cycle and secure competitiveness of global projects via working collaboratively in geographically dispersed locations.

This chapter presented how innovation and process improvement in the design process could be achieved by adapting existing VR technologies to enhance the conceptual architectural designers' cognition and collaboration. However, further research is recommended to reveal more technical and theoretical aspects of employing tangible VR design interfaces for multidisciplinary teamwork and utilising ICT in delivering of projects within time and budget. In order to progress the development of the conceptual and theoretical tangible VR design interface, there is a need for extensive research into various aspects of the protocol. Consequently, the of the recommended fields for future studies are development of tangible VR design interfaces in non-collocated collaborative design projects, investigation of the effects of the fully immersive interfaces on the designers' cognition and collaboration, and exploration of higher capabilities of VR interface tools in architectural design by developing customised interfaces based on open source programming applications, etc.

References

AIA (1993). Standard Form of Agreement Between Owner and Architect for Designated Services, AIA (No. B163): The American Institute of Architects (AIA).

Akin, Ö. (1978) *How do Architects Design? Artificial Intelligence and Pattern Recognition in Computer-Aided Design*. North Holland, NY. 65–104.

Akin, Ö. & Lin, C. (1995) Design protocol data and novel design decisions. *Design Studies*, **16**, 211–236.

Akin, Ö., Dave, B. & Pithavadian, S. (1992). Heuristic generation of layouts (HeGeL): based on a paradigm for problem structuring. *Environment and Planning B: Planning and Design*, **19**, 33–59.

Basque Research (2007). Using Computerized Sense Of Touch Over Long Distances: Haptics For Industrial Applications: ScienceDaily.

Bilda, Z. & Demirkan, H. (2003) An insight on designers' sketching activities in traditional versus digital media. *Design Studies*, **24**(1), 27–50.

Bouchlaghem, N., Thorpe, A. & Liyange, I.G. (1996) Virtual reality applications in the UK's construction industry. *CIB W78 Construction on the Information Highway, Bled*, 10–12 June.

Brewster, S. (2001). The Impact of Haptic 'Touching' Technology on Cultural Applications. Glasgow: Glasgow Interactive Systems Group, Department of Computing Science, University of Glasgow.

Briggs, J.C. (1996, 09-01-1996). The Promise of Virtual Reality. *The Futurist Magazine*, 30–31.

Bruner, J. S. (1973). Beyond the information given: studies in the psychology of knowing. Oxford, UK: W.W. Norton.

Cera, C.D., Reagali, W.C., Braude, I., Shapirstein, Y. & Foster, C. (2002) A collaborative 3D environment for authoring design semantics. *Graphics in Advanced Computer-Aided Design*, **22**(3), 43–55.

Craft, B. & Cairns, P. (2006). *Work Interaction Design: Designing gor Human Work*. Paper presented at the IFIP TC 13.6 WG conference: Designing for human work. Madeira.

Cross, N. & Dorst, K. (1999) Natural intelligence in design. *Design Studies*, **20**(1), 25–39.

Cross, N. (2007) *Designerly Ways of Knowing*. Birkhäuser, Basel.

Cross, N., Christiaans, H. & Dorst, K. (1996) *Analysing Design Activity*. John Wiley & Sons, Inc, New York.

Cuomo, N.L. (1988) *A Study of Human Performance in Computer Aided Architectural Design*. PhD thesis, University of New York at Buffalo, New York.

Dietrich, A., Stephans, A. & Wald, I. (2007) *Exploring a Boeing 777: Ray Tracing Large-Scale CAD Data*. Paper presented at the Real-Time Interaction with Complex Models.

Donath, D., Loemker, T.M. & Richter, K. (2004) Plausibility in the planning process– reason and confidence in the computer-aided design and planning of buildings. *Automation in Construction*, **13**(2), 159–166.

Dorst, K. & Dijkhuis, J. (1995) Comparing paradigms for describing design activity. *Design Studies*, **16**(2), 261–274.

EON Reality, Inc., (2008) *Introduction to Working in EON Studio*. Available from http://www.eonreality.com

Ericsson, K.A. & Simon, H.A. (1993) *Protocol Analysis: Verbal Reports as Data*. Cambridge MIT Press, Cambridge, MA.

Finke, R. A., Ward, T. B., & Smith, S. M. (1992). Creative Cognition: Theory, Research, and Applications. Cambridge, MA: MIT Press.

Fischer, M. (2000) 4D CAD–3D models incorporated with time schedule, CIFE Centre for Integrated Facility Engineering in Finland. *VTT-TEKES, CIFE Technical Report*. Stanford University, Helsinki.

Fischer, M. & Kunz, J. (2004) The scope and role of information technology in construction. *CIFE Centre for Integrated Facility Engineering in Finland, Technical Report #156*. Stanford University, Helsinki.

Fish, J. & Scrivener, S. (1990) Amplifying the mind's eye: Sketching and visual cognition. *Leonardo*, 4, 117–226.

Fitts, P.M. (1964) Perceptual–motor skill learning. In: ed. Melton, A.W., *Categories of Human Learning*. Academic Press, New York.

Fitzmaurice, G. W., Ishii, H., & Buxton, W. (1995). Bricks: laying the foundations for graspable user interfaces. Paper presented at the Proceedings of the CHI'95 Conference on Human Factors in Computing Systems New York.

Foreman, N. & Gillett, R. (1997) *Handbook of Spatial Research Paradigms and Methodologies*. Psychology Press, Hove, UK.

Frankenberger, E. (1997) *Arbeitsteilige Produktentwicklung:empirische Untersuchung und Empfehlungen zur Gruppenarbeit in der Konstruktion*. VDI, Düsseldorf.

Friedman, T.L. (2005) *The World is Flat: A Brief History of the 21st Century*. Farrar, Straus and Giroux, New York.

Fruchter, R. (1998) Internet-based web mediated collaborative design and learning environment. In: *Artificial Intelligence in Structural Engineering Lecture Notes in Artificial Intelligence*. Springer-Verlag, Berlin. 133–145.

Goldschmidt, G., & Porter, W. L. (2004). Design representation. New York: Springer.

Goldschmidt, G. (1994) On visual design thinking: the vis kids of architecture. *Design Studies*, 15(2), 158–174.

Goulding, J., Sexton, M., Zhang, X., Kagioglou, M., Aouad, Ghassan, F. & Barrett, P. (2007) Technology adoption: breaking down barriers using a virtual reality design support tool for hybrid concrete. *Construction Management and Economics*, 25(12), 1239–1250.

Greenbaum, P. (1992). The lawnmower man. Film and video, 9(3), 58–62.

Griffith, T.L., Sawyer, J.E. & Neale, M.A. (2003) Virtualness and knowledge in teams: Managing the love triangle of organizations, individuals and information technology. *MIS Quarterly*, 27(2), 265–287.

Ibrahim, R. & Pour Rahimian, F. (2010) Comparison of CAD and manual sketching tools for teaching architectural design. *Automation in Construction*, 19(8), 978–987.

Jones, C.J. (1970) *Design Methods: Seeds of Human Futures*. Wiley, London.

Kalay, Y.E. (2004) *Architecture's New Media–Principles, Theories and Methods of Computer-Aided Design*. The MIT Press, MA.

Kan, W.T. (2008) *Quantitative Methods for Studying Design Protocols*. The University of Sydney, Australia.

Kavakli, M., Scrivener, S.A.R. & Ball, L.J. (1998). Structure in idea sketching behaviour. *Design Studies*, 19(4), 485–517.

Khanzade, A., Fisher, M. & Reed, D. (2007) Challenges and benefits of implementing virtual design and construction technologies for coordination of mechanical, electrical, and plumbing systems on large healthcare project. *CIB 24th W78 Conference*, Maribor, Slovenia, 205–212.

Kim, M.J. & Maher, M.L. (2008) The impact of tangible user interfaces on spatial cognition during collaborative design. *Design Studies*, 29(3), 222–253.

Kirsh, D. & Maglio, P. (1994) On distinguishing epistemic from pragmatic action. *Cognitive Science*, 18(4), 513–549.

Kwon, J., Choi, H., Lee, J. & Chai, Y. (2005) *Free-Hand Stroke Based NURBS Surface for Sketching and Deforming 3D Contents*. Paper presented at the PCM 2005, Part I, LNCS 3767.

Lawson, B. (1997) *How Designers Think – The Design Process Demystified*. Architectural Press, Oxford.

Leinonen, J., Kähkönen, K., Retik, A. Raja., Flood, R.A., William, I. & O'Brien, J. (2003) new construction management practice based on the virtual reality technology. *In: 4D CAD and Visualization in Construction: Developments and Applications*. A.A. Balkema Publishers, Amsterdam. 75–100.

Levet, F., Granier, X. & Schlick, C. (2006) 3D Sketching with Profile Curves. *LNCS*, **4073**, 114–125.

Lloyd, P., Lawson, B. & Scott, P. (1995). Can concurrent verbalization reveal design cognition? *Design Studies*, **16(2)**, 237–259.

Lundequist, J. (1992) *Prosjekteringsmetodikens teoretiska bakgrund*. KTH Reprocentral, Stockholm.

Madrazo, L. (1999) Types and Instances: A paradigm for teaching design with computers. *Design Studies*, **20(2)**, 177–193.

Maher, M. L., Poon, J., & Boulanger, S. (1996). Formalising design exploration as co-evolution: a combined gene approach. In J. S. Gero & F. Sudweeks (Eds.), Advances in formal design methods for CAD (pp. 1–28). Sydney: Key Centre of Design Computing, University of Sydney.

Marx, J. (2000) A proposal for alternative methods for teaching digital design. *Automation in Construction*, **9(1)**, 19–35.

McGown, A., Green, G. & Rodgers, P.A. (1998) Visible ideas: information patterns of conceptual sketch activity. *Design Studies*, **19(4)**, 431–453.

Minneman, S.L. (1991) *The Social Construction of a Technical Reality: Empirical Studies of the Social Activity of Engineering Design Practice*. Stanford University, Greater Manchester, UK.

Moum, A. (2006). A framework for exploring the ICT impact on the architectural design process. *ITCon, 11 Special Issue: The Effects of CAD on Building Form and Design Quality*. 409–425.

Petric, J., Maver, T., Conti, G. & Ucelli, G. (2002) *Virtual Reality in the Service of User Participation in Architecture*. Paper presented at the CIB W78 Conference, Aarhus School of Architecture, 12–14 June.

Petzold, F., Bimber, O. & Tonn, O. (2007) CAVE without CAVE: on-site visualization and design support in and within existing building, eCAADe 07. *25th Conference of Education and Research in Computer Aided Architectural Design in Europe*, Frankfurt. 161–168.

Pour Rahimian, F. (2009) *Cognitive Transformation Mediated by Digital 3D Sketching during Conceptual Architectural Design Process*. Universiti Putra Malaysia (UPM), Serdang.

Pour Rahimian, F., Ibrahim, R. & Jaafar, F.Z. (2008) Feasibility study on developing 3D sketching in virtual reality environment. ALAM CIPTA. *International Journal on Sustainable Tropical Design Research and Practice*, **3(1)**, 60–78.

Pour Rahimian, F. & Ibrahim, R. (2009) *Protocol Analysis Experiment Report for Developing VR Supportive Environment FRSB/EDI/TR2* (No. 2). Environmental Design Integration Group, Faculty of Design and Architecture, Universiti Putra Malaysia, Serdang.

Pour Rahimian, F. & Ibrahim, R. (2011) Impacts of VR 3D sketching on novice designers' spatial cognition in collaborative conceptual architectural design. *Design Studies*, **32(3)**, 255–291.

Pour Rahimian, F. & Goulding, J.S (2010) Game-Like Virtual Reality Interfaces in Construction Management Simulation: A New Paradigm of Opportunities. *9th International Detail Design in Architecture Conference 2010.* The Central University of Lancashire, Preston, UK.

Purcell, A.T. & Gero, J.S. (1998) Drawings and the design process: A review of protocol studies in design and other disciplines and related research in cognitive psychology. *Design Studies,* **19**(4), 389–430.

Regenbrecht, H. & Donath, D. (1996) *Architectural Education and Virtual Reality Aided Design (Vrad).* uni-weimar.

Rodgers, P.A., Green, G. & McGown, A. (2000) Using concept sketches to track design progress. *Design Studies,* **21**(5), 451–464.

Sampaio, A.Z. & Henriques, P.G. (2008) Visual simulation of civil engineering activities: didactic virtual models, WSCG 2008. *16th International Conference in Central Europe on Computer Graphics, Visualization and Computer Vision.* Plzen, Czech Republic. 143–149.

Schön, D. A., & Wiggins, G. (1992). Kinds of seeing and their functions in designing. Design Studies, 13(2), 135–156.

Schön, D. (1983) *The Reflective Practitioner: How Professionals Think in Action.* Temple Smith, London.

Schütze, M., Sachse, P. & Römer, A. (2003) Support value of sketching in the design process. *Research in Engineering Design,* **14**, 89–97.

Scrivener, S.A.R., Ball, L.J. & Tseng, W. (2000). Uncertainty and sketching behaviour. *Design Studies,* **21**(5), 465–481.

Seng, W.K., Palaniappan, S. & Yahaya, N.A. (2005) *A Framework for Collaborative Graphical Based Design Environments.* Paper presented at the 16th International Workshop on Database and Expert Systems Applications.

Shuttleworth, M. (2008) *Case Study Research Design.* Podcast, available from http://www.experiment-resources.com/case-study-research-design.html (accessed 5 January 2009).

Simon, H. A. (1979). Models of thought (Vol. 1). New Haven, CT: Yale University Press.

Stricker, D., Klinker, G., & Reiners, D. (2001). Augmented reality for exterior construction applications. In W. Barfield & T. Caudell (Eds.), Augmented reality and wearable computers (pp. 53): Lawrence Erlbaum Press.

Suwa, M., Gero, J.S. & Purcell, A.T. (2000) Unexpected discoveries and S-inventions of design requirements: important vehicles for a design process. *Design Studies,* **21**(6), 539–567.

Suwa, M., Purcell, T. & Gero, J. (1998) Macroscopic analysis of design processes based on a scheme for coding designers' cognitive actions. *Design Studies,* **19**(4), 455–483.

Tversky, B. (2005) Functional significance of visuospatial representations. In: ed. Shah, P. & Miyake, A., *Handbook of Higher-Level Visuospatial Thinking.* Cambridge University Press, Cambridge. 1–34.

van Someren, M.W., Barnard, Y.F. & Sandberg, J.A.C. (1994) *The Think Aloud Method: A Practical Guide to Modelling Cognitive Processes.* Academic Press, London.

Visser, W. (2004) *Dynamic Aspects of Design Cognition: Elements for a Cognitive Model of Design.* France: Theme 3A-Databases, Knowledge Bases and Cognitive Systems, Project EIFFEL.

Waldron, M.B. & Waldron, K.J. (1988) A time sequence study of a complex mechanical system design. *Design Studies,* **9**, 95–106.

Whyte, J., Bouchlaghem, N., Thorpe, A. & McCaffer, R. (2000) From CAD to virtual reality: modelling approaches, data exchange and interactive 3D building design tools. *Automation in Construction*, **10**(1), 43–55.

Wojtowicz, J. (1994) *Virtual Design Studio*. Hong Kong University Press, Hong Kong.

Yoh, M. (2001) The reality of virtual reality. In: *Seventh International Conference on Virtual Systems and Multimedia (VSMM'01), Organized by Center for Design Visualization*. University of California Berkley, Berkley CA.

Virtual Planning and Knowledge-based Decision Support

Joseph H.M. Tah

15.1 Introduction

The construction industry is experiencing unprecedented change and dynamic conditions resulting from societal demands for low impact buildings and infrastructural assets with ever-increasing standards of performance, constantly diminishing environmental impacts, and steadily reducing costs of construction, operation and decommissioning challenges. This has fuelled the development of an increasing number of new methods, materials, technologies, processes and innovative practices aimed to improve buildings and communities, with respect to a multitude of sustainability performance considerations and indicators. In this respect, as the number of methods and technological options increases, so does the complexity and associated cost of choosing alternative combinations for any given situation. Therefore, informed decisions require the management of vast amounts of information and knowledge about the combinations of available options and the assessment of their performance. Given this, it is almost impossible to apply manual methods and physical prototypes to address these issues. Furthermore, it has been recognised that the use of computer-based virtual prototyping could offer some solutions to these challenges, and significant Research and Development (R&D) efforts have been made to develop various generations of virtual prototyping systems. These have evolved from early 3D CAD modelling software, through computer integrated environments ranging from 4D modelling, and more recently, to nD Modelling (Lee *et al.*, 2006), including the use of advanced virtual and augmented reality techniques with varying degrees of success.

Although significant progress has been made, further advances are needed as the current generation of virtual prototyping systems are still not 'smart'

Construction Innovation and Process Improvement, First Edition.
Edited by Akintola Akintoye, Jack S. Goulding and Girma Zawdie.
© 2012 Blackwell Publishing Ltd. Published 2012 by Blackwell Publishing Ltd.

enough to cope with the increasingly complex and dynamic nature of construction projects and problems facing the construction industry. This chapter posits that the next generation of virtual prototyping systems will need to draw heavily on multiple configurable knowledge sources in order to cope with the complexity that characterises construction projects. A brief examination of the complexity inherent in construction projects is therefore presented for discussion. An overview of research work related to virtual prototyping that has been undertaken to address these challenges and complexities is discussed, along with a selection of emerging technologies being developed to address this situation. On this theme, emerging developments in Building Information Modelling (BIM) (Eastman *et al.*, 2008) and Industry Foundation Classes (IAI, 2010) that facilitate inter-operability between disparate systems that support virtual prototyping are also examined. The case for the development and use of configurable knowledge bases to provide autonomous real-time decision support for virtual prototyping is introduced, along with a prototype system developed to support this. It is concluded that the current interest in BIM presents an opportunity to develop the next generation of virtual prototyping systems that include configurable knowledge bases. This would facilitate autonomous decision making, thereby rendering such systems more easy to use, and so encouraging wider adoption and use, particularly to support innovation processes in practice.

15.2   The Complex Nature of Construction Projects

It is widely acknowledged that by addressing the contemporary problems facing society, it is not just sufficient to be concerned with the physical built assets, but also the interplay between assets and the social, economic and environmental consequences that arise out of human activity. However, this presents significant challenges due to inherent complexities within and between the elements that constitute the physical built assets and the organisational systems used in their procurement, delivery, use and disposal. Construction projects are characterised by complexity, from their inception, through design, construction and operational life, to their disposal and recycling. For example in buildings, there are multiple interacting subsystems such as building materials and components, the structure, building fabric, building services, utilities, communication networks and the external environment. The procurement of these assets often involves complex interactions between multiple stakeholders and organisations operating in complex value and supply networks, often with conflicting perspectives on their creation, configuration and use. These organisational networks are characterised by social, economic, legal, regulatory and cultural interactions that strongly influence the management of the planning, design and production processes, which involves varying degrees of cooperation, competition and conflict. Thus, construction is a complex multi-disciplinary field that requires integrating expertise and input from various constituencies, with many people processing and exchanging complex heterogeneous information over complex human and communication networks with varying challenges and ever-changing constraints. The host of contemporary problems, together with the inherent complexities in the construction process when taken together, presents considerable challenges to decision makers. Existing conventional problem-solving methods are not always able to deal with this complexity adequately, given that the industry needs to constantly evolve and adapt in response to rapidly changing societal demands. It is for these reasons that there is a lot of interest in virtual prototyping, BIM, inter-operability using open semantic standards and knowledge-based decision support are discussed in the following sections.

15.3   Construction Planning and Virtual Prototyping

Construction planning plays a fundamental role in the process of construction management, and a good construction plan can often be used as a basis for developing the budget and schedule of work. Furthermore, it can also facilitate the formulation of correct strategies for guiding construction activities, and coordinating different construction processes. Therefore, developing a construction plan, (especially a robust one), is a critical task in construction management, given the complex nature of projects. A construction plan is normally represented using a bar chart or Gantt chart, which illustrates the relationship between construction activities and corresponding times, as well as logical constraints amongst the activities. Traditional off-the-shelf construction planning tools, such as Microsoft Project and Primavera Project Planner (P3), bring the convenience of specifying the plan tasks and generating static bar charts and network diagrams. However, they do not represent and communicate the spatial and temporal aspects of construction schedules effectively. Consequently, they do not allow project managers to create robust construction plans. The need for alternative approaches to creating construction plans have long been recognised, and virtual prototyping has emerged as one such approach. Virtual prototyping evolved in response to the requirement for designers and others involved in product development to have a better 'feel' for the end product at the earliest possible opportunity, without the expense of building a physical prototype or making the product itself. This is increasingly seen as necessary within the construction industry, and various technologies are emerging to support this. One such technology that is receiving wider acceptance in the construction industry is 4D CAD (3D CAD with the added dimension of time). This supports a kind of simulation approach to creating a construction plan. In 4D CAD, a construction plan is created and tasks are associated with the 3D building model. This essentially links the work breakdown structure (WBS) to the product breakdown structure (PBS). It allows users to generate a 3D dynamic construction sequence along the time dimension. Through this, a PBS-plus-WBS approach, potential conflicts in the construction plan can be visually identified and updated to formulate a feasible plan. The term '4D CAD technology' in construction was coined at the Centre for Integrated Facility Engineering (CIFE) at Stanford University (Collier and Fischer, 1996). This has been an area of active research due to its potential to facilitate the analysis of the multitude of factors and relationships amongst the logical, temporal, spatial and other dimensional information in construction.

In recent years, the possibilities offered by 4D CAD have spurred researchers into the exploration of the potential of virtual reality (VR) techniques in construction planning. Several prototypes of VR-based construction planning tools have been proposed by researchers. For example, Jaafari *et al.* (2001) developed a prototype application for the evaluation, visualisation and optimisation of construction schedules in a virtual reality environment and Waly and Thabet (2002) developed a Virtual Construction Environment (VCE), which allowed project teams to undertake rehearsals of major construction processes to examine various execution strategies before the start of the actual construction work. Similarly, Yerrapathruni *et al.* (2003) developed an immersive virtual environment (IVE) for generating and reviewing construction plans in a virtual environment and Kunz and Fischer (2005) developed a Virtual Design and Construction method for the simulation of the process of design and construction of buildings. Dawood *et al.* (2005) developed the VIRCON system to allow planners to rehearse and better understand project schedules through 4D visualisation and simulation. Other studies (McKinney-Liston, 1998; Kim *et al.*, 2001; Dawood *et al.*, 2002; Heesom and Mahdjoubi, 2004; Chau *et al.*, 2005; de Vries and Harink, 2007) have demonstrated related advancements adopting this notion. In addition, Li *et al.* (2008) presented cases of how virtual prototyping has been successfully adopted on a number of construction projects where it has integrated both in the design and construction processes, and a number of state-of-the-art virtual prototyping opportunities in construction are now emerging (Brandon and Kocatürk, 2008).

Commercial software for virtual prototyping has matured significantly in recent years. Current 4D modelling products and vendors include:

- ConstructSim™ from Common Point;
- fourDscape™ from Balfour Technologies;
- Innovaya Visual 4D Simulation from Innovaya;
- Navigator™ from Bentley Systems;
- PM-Vision™ from Construction System Associates
- the SmartPlant™ series from Intergraph; and
- Synchro from Synchro, Ltd.

Recognising the benefits of 4D-CAD, more and more construction projects used this technology during the construction process. However, although 4D modelling presents significant advantages over traditional planning tools, 4D models are often time-consuming to generate. Ostensibly, existing 4D systems rely on a plan to be pre-constructed and tasks individually associated with the PBS. This can be time-consuming, which limits the number of simulations and what-if scenarios that can be explored. Existing 4D models also tend to lack configurable data and knowledge bases of construction methods, procedures and resources, which can provide the context for rapidly generating alternative plans for different project scenarios. Although the experience and knowledge of construction managers cannot be wholly replicated in computer systems *per se*, the potential of computers to provide some decision support in automating or semi-automating the process of generating plans is not fully exploited in existing systems. However, the difficulty and cost of creating and using such models is currently limiting the widespread adoption of 4D systems in construction; but the evolution in Building Information Systems and semantic standards for interoperability could allow configurable knowledge bases to be developed to provide decision support for innovation.

15.4   Building Information Modelling

Building Information Modelling is one of the most promising developments in the construction industry. It allows an accurate virtual model of a building to be constructed digitally. When completed, the computer-generated model contains precise geometry and relevant data needed to support the construction, fabrication and procurement activities needed to realise the building. Autodesk (2010) claims to have coined the phrase BIM in 2002, and defined it as 'the creation and use of coordinated, consistent, computable information about a building project in design – information used for design decision making, production of high-quality construction documents, predicting performance, cost-estimating and construction planning, and, eventually, for managing and operating the facility.' Underpinning this is a BIM that has been defined as 'a digital representation of physical and functional characteristics of a facility'. As such, it serves as a shared knowledge resource for information about a facility forming a reliable basis for decisions during its life cycle from inception onwards. The basic premise of BIM is collaboration by different stakeholders at different phases of the life cycle of a facility to insert, extract, update or modify information in the BIM process to support and reflect the roles of those stakeholders. BIM is therefore a shared digital representation founded on open standards for interoperability (NIBS, 2010), which can facilitate information sharing amongst multiple project stakeholders (Figure 15.1). Further examples of BIM data sharing with multidisciplinary stakeholders can be seen in Figure 15.2.

In recent years, there has been a growing interest in the construction industry in the use of BIM tools. This has been brought about by the vendors of 3D CAD software that have re-positioned their software to exploit the BIM concept. Examples of these are:

- Revit and Architectural Desktop from Autodesk (Autodesk, 2010);
- ArchiCAD from Graphisoft (Graphisoft, 2010);
- MicroStation from Bentley (Bentley, 2010); and
- Tekla Structures by Tekla (Tekla, 2010).

However, these tools have their own internal models. These models are different from the information models implemented in applications used downstream in the construction process, for example, applications for

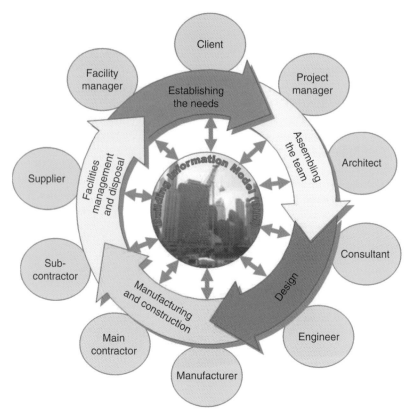

Figure 15.1 Stakeholder information sharing through BIM.

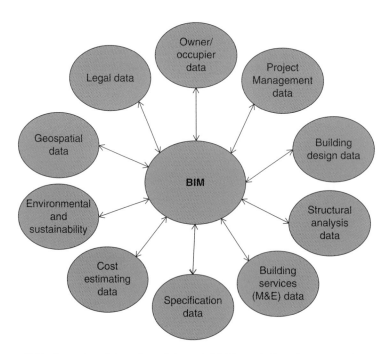

Figure 15.2 Examples of data shared through BIM by multidisciplinary stakeholders.

quantity take-off, cost estimation, construction planning, structural or environmental analyses, etc. This is an unfortunate consequence of the multidisciplinary nature of the construction industry, where historically the development of software has mirrored the specific requirements of individual disciplines, instead of taking a holistic view to facilitate integration and data sharing between project participants. This has led to the reproduction of data for different purposes, which is non-value adding and often error-prone. A study by NIST (Gallaher *et al.*, 2004) identified approximately $15.8 billion in annual interoperability costs in the US capital facilities industry, representing 1–2% of industry revenue. Gallaher *et al.* (2004) also acknowledged that this is likely to be only a portion of the total cost of poor interoperability, as the study did not cover all related costs. It has therefore long been recognised that the solution to this problem is the use on an open and neutral data format to ensure data compatibility across the different applications.

15.5   Interoperability and Industry Foundation Classes

The International Alliance for Interoperability (IAI) has been developing a specification for an international BIM standard, called the Industry Foundation Classes (IFC) since 1994 (IAI, 2010) to address the interoperability problem. The IAI has produced several versions of the specifications for IFC. For example, the IFC2x Platform was officially accepted as the ISO/PAS 16739:2005 in October 2005 (ISO, 2010). IFC is a comprehensive data representation of the building model; it is also a set of rules and protocols of how to define the data describing the building. In this respect, IFCs have been defined by the construction industry, which provides a foundation for the shared project model or BIM. This works through the specification of classes of components in an agreed manner that enables the development of a common language for construction. IFC-based objects allow construction professionals to share a project model, yet also allow each profession to define its own view of the objects contained in that model. IFC also enables interoperability amongst construction software applications, and software developers can use IFC to create applications that use universal construction objects based on the IFC specification. Applications that support IFC can allow members of a project team to share project data in an electronic format. This ensures that the data is consistent and coordinated. Furthermore, this shared data can continue to evolve after the design phase and throughout the construction and occupation of the building. The information generated by the project design team is therefore available to the building construction team and building facilities managers in an intelligent, electronic format through their IFC-compliant software. Numerous IFC-compliant tools have emerged in recent years, and some projects have already started to implement IFC-based applications in the design and construction process. In addition, some countries have adopted IFC specification as the basis of their national ICT strategy for the construction industry (BSA, 2010; Corenet, 2010; Vera, 2010). This has strengthened the status of IFC specifications as a *de-facto* standard and now it appears to be the only significant standard for inter-operable BIM. The CAD vendors previously mentioned now provide IFC-compliant import/exchange interfaces to their software, to facilitate information exchange between the various BIM systems. Therefore, developments in BIM models and IFCs present a basis on which to explore the development of configurable knowledge bases to provide autonomous decision support for virtual prototyping and testing of innovative solutions for construction projects.

15.6   Knowledge-based Decision Support for Virtual Prototyping

Whilst advocating the development of configurable knowledge bases to support virtual prototyping, it has to be acknowledged that previous attempts at utilising knowledge-based systems techniques for decision support in project management are yet to make an impact in the construction industry. This can be attributed to the slow pace of technology adoption in the industry, and to some extent the lack of semantic data standards or ontologies on which to base this development. However, it is now timely to revisit the use of such techniques as part of BIM systems implementation that are now being widely adopted. The ensuing section presents a prototype system that was developed by the author to demonstrate the integration of 3D-CAD and project management for real-time 4D modelling (Tah *et al.*, 1997). The work centred on creating an information and knowledge continuum across the 3D CAD and Project Management interface. Initially, the goal was to establish the basis for information and knowledge continuum thinking by exploring the application of a combination of emerging techniques such as object-oriented modelling, knowledge-based systems, integrated project-model databases and integrated environments. A brief description of the work undertaken is presented as follows.

15.6.1   Semantically Enhanced Object Models

A comprehensive integrated project object model was developed to represent the data, behaviour and interrelationships between project information. It consisted of the following sub-system object models:

- a project object model;
- a structural system object model;
- a project task system object model;
- a resource system object model; and
- a productivity object model.

The project object model represented the top-level object classes, which provides associations to the other sub-system models. The structural system object model represented information about a building's structural system, extending abstract structural element concepts into specialised concepts such as columns, beams, slabs with their associated material specifications. The structural elements are associated with the project task system object model via the task class, as they are constructed by tasks. This provides the link to project management. A construction project plan is often centred on the task class. The task class is sufficient for traditional planning systems, as is typical of current packaged project management software. However, the task class is predominantly too abstract for knowledge-level inferencing. Thus, the task class was specialised into classes that are more concrete. A task can be a 'work packet' or a 'unit of work' (UoW). The UoW class acts as a base class to specialised units of work, which for example in the case of work involving *in-situ* concreting could be 'fix reinforcement', 'erect form-work', 'place concrete', 'strike formwork', etc. A work packet consists of many units of work. The unit of work is significant for the purposes of knowledge representation and intelligent decision support. Through these methods, several knowledge bases are triggered to provide information and advice on the selection of methods of concreting, the selection of appropri-ate resources, and the retrieval and adjustment of productivity rates for task duration estimation. The resource system object model represents detailed information about construction resources, including labour, plant, materi-als, sub-contractors and resource group build-ups. The productivity object model represents different construction methods and their corresponding production rates for the individual units of work. The semantically enhanced object models provided the basis for developing a common language for representing information and an ontology for developing the knowledge models for knowledge-based development.

15.6.2   Knowledge Models

The following rules sets were produced from a knowledge elicitation exercise:

a) setting of the structural component material specifications;
b) elaboration of activities or tasks for each structural component type into units of work and work packets;
c) determining the amount of work in tasks;
d) selecting appropriate concreting methods;
e) selecting resources for concrete placement;
f) selecting resources for fixing bar reinforcement;
g) selecting resources for fixing mesh reinforcement; and
h) selecting resources for erecting formwork.

A plain English-like syntax was used to represent production rules conceptually. The names of classes and attributes in the object models were used in the syntax, where object instances participated in rules. The object models provided a basis and a common language for representing knowledge in the form of rules consistent with the information models. This helped form an information and knowledge continuum to facilitate the prototype development process.

15.6.3   The Prototype System

The object and knowledge models were used as the basis for developing a prototype system (Tah *et al.*, 1997). The MicroStation CAD and Microsoft Project packages were selected to provide CAD and project management services, as they both support Microsoft's Object Linking and Embedding (OLE) Automation capability. This allows systems to be developed inter-operably in real time. The object models were used to build an integrated database server that handled all the data required to be shared by all applications when inter-operating in real time. Two further software components (connectors/adapters), described in the following sections, were then built to provide the link between MicroStation and Microsoft Project.

A software component was built to map building object instances in MicroStation CAD and their interrelationships to the database server and vice versa. This component allows CAD and the database server to inter-operate in real time. It was developed to semantically enhance building objects in CAD to meet the object model's specification. In building this component, it was decided that the full drawing production facilities in MicroStation should be used for producing a drawing. This meant that this software component should be able to scan a MicroStation database to identify individual objects and create instances of objects and their inter-relationships in the integrated database server. A simple computation of the sizes of structural elements in terms of length, width, height and volume was also performed as part of the process of creating instances of objects in the database server. This software component was developed to allow bi-directional communication between MicroStation and the database server. In this respect, a software component was built to access and use the building design objects in the database server to generate construction project programmes using the KBS techniques based on the Units of Work concept presented earlier within MS Project. The KBSs were developed to retrieve instances of structural objects from the database server, and to automatically generate the units of work or work items and the work breakdown structure in Microsoft project. The full facilities of the Microsoft project were used to manually fine-tune the program, and the resulting program information was used to automatically update the database server. The intention was to use the fully populated database server to produce a simulation of the construction sequence in MicroStation using the start and finish times of activities.

The prototype was developed as an open software environment that allowed all applications to inter-operate through the integrated database server in real time. Figure 15.3 shows a working session with MicroStation running in the top left, and Microsoft project running in the bottom, and the software component that allows bi-directional communication between MicroStation and the database server on the top right-hand side. It depicts an object explorer to display the instances of the building objects in the database server. The database server and the software component linking Microsoft Project to the database runs in the background, and is therefore not shown.

Figure 15.3   A screenshot of a working session.

This prototype demonstrated how complex behaviour could be handled through interactions amongst independent software components. The object classes presented here provide a powerful means for representing data and their interrelationships, to integrate disparate information and knowledge sources from the fragmented construction disciplines. The sharing of information through distributed processing amongst disparate disciplines provides the much needed coordination and communication of information, thereby minimising waste and errors and so resulting in significant reduction in costs. The functionality of the prototype was limited to the creation of construction programmes for the structural system of a building. In this respect, considerable effort concentrated on establishing the approach, as a significant amount of model development, knowledge acquisition and programming effort was required to produce a fully functioning system. This work contributed to the advancement of our understanding of how the next generation of virtual prototyping systems might be developed.

15.7   The Promotion of Innovation through Virtual Planning in Practice

Whilst significant work is still necessary to develop smarter knowledge-based virtual prototyping systems, virtual planning is already supporting innovation in modern construction management processes in practice. Recent improvements in technologies have significantly enhanced the ability to represent and visualise computer-generated information graphically, enabling professionals and practitioners to recognise patterns quickly and accurately. Visualisation enables experts and non-experts to understand the outputs resulting from often highly complex computations and information held in large-scale project and enterprise databases. It provides new ways of communicating options and choices across the multiple and diverse stakeholders involved in a construction project. Computer-graphics and visualisation is usually far better than text-based information for communicating with decision makers and involving them in innovation processes. This allows innovators to look for, and experiment with, new ideas in ways that were not previously possible.

Virtual planning is already influencing contemporary design and construction management practice, by allowing project teams to generate and test new ideas and introduce innovations in the design and construction process. In the UK, for example, construction firms such as Laing O'Rourke, Mace and VINCI, are already using virtual planning systems to explore alternative strategies to help pre-plan large-scale construction processes ahead of the commencement of on-site activities. These firms make extensive use of visualisation technologies to explore design options, cutting costs and reducing the time taken to deliver projects. Laing O'Rourke, for example, has established a Collaboration Centre with two digital prototyping theatres dedicated to virtual planning. This facilitates 4D modelling, simulation and visualisation of complex development and construction projects, from master-planning and regeneration schemes through to detailed structural, mechanical and electrical engineering, including construction sequencing and cost planning. This has enabled better decisions to be made when exploring alternative options for different designs and construction methods. The use of the facility was instrumental in the CLM team from three separate companies (Laing O'Rourke, CH2MHill and Mace) mounting a successful bid to become program managers for the construction work for the 2012 Olympics (Gann and Dodgson, 2008). The ability to produce fly-through simulations has proven invaluable for demonstrating virtual prototypes projects to clients.

Virtual planning can enhance the coordination of innovation processes and changes the traditional design and construction practice. This allows managers to take a wider and more strategic role in their capacity to visualise and understand the implications of alternative decision choices, which continues to improve with the convergence of emerging digital tools that support envisioning and innovation processes. Virtual planning has the potential to improve communication across professional, functional and organisational boundaries, thereby allowing professionals to search for better solutions to complex problems. This requires new management practices and organisational structures to enable collaboration across disciplines and between firms, and skills to broker, interpret, translate and recombine knowledge in multidisciplinary teams. It has been widely acknowledged that the benefits of any technological innovation accrue only when technological possibilities are aligned with clear management objectives, aligned to supportive organisational structures and skills. For example, the emergence of BIM has led large firms to establish new BIM management roles within their organisational structures, where for example, the BIM Manager oversees the successful exploitation of BIM (including virtual planning) and the coordination of input from the multi-disciplinary teams that contribute information to the BIM model. Therefore, the BIM Manager's role is pivotal, as it acts as a conduit to leverage strategy, especially how these parties should work together in the BIM environment.

15.8   Conclusion

The use of the object-oriented methodology provided the basis of a common language or an ontology for the representation of information for the development of the project-model database, the knowledge base and the connectors/adapters ensuring consistency across all applications and facilitating the development and integration process. The development of such systems is necessarily evolutionary and the availability of a widely accepted standards-based common language should inspire confidence in investing the enormous time and resources necessary to achieve real-world practical applications. Thus, the evolution and maturity of the IFCs as such a standard is viewed with a lot of interest. The potential of knowledge-based systems techniques to handle cross-application knowledge representation, data interpretation and transformation to support cross-application business processes and decision support to facilitate virtual prototyping is yet to be fully exploited. What is required is a framework within which to integrate multiple applications through a project model database with knowledge-based support to handle cross-application business processes. Preliminary work has provided a strong indication that multi-agent systems techniques could provide such a framework underpinned by Web Services technologies, but further work is still required (Tah, 2008). This, together with the current burgeoning interests in emerging developments in BIM models and IFCs, provides a strong basis for developing the next generation of virtual prototyping systems with configurable knowledge bases, in order to provide near real-time autonomous decision support. This would allow the modelling and simulation of complex construction projects in ways that are currently not possible. Furthermore, it would also provide multi-disciplinary project teams with easy-to-use collaborative virtual planning tools to support them in exploring alternative innovations in projects, and allow decision makers to select the best options for implementation.

References

Autodesk (2010) *Architectural Desktop and Revit by Autodesk*. Design software. Available from http://www.autodesk.com/ (accessed August 2010).

Bentley (2010) *MicroStation by Bentley*. Design software. Available from http://www.bentley.com/ (accessed August 2010).

Brandon, P. & Kocatürk, T. (2008) *Virtual Futures for Design, Construction and Procurement*. Blackwell Science, Oxford.

BSA (2010) *buildingSMARTalliance – National Institute of Building Sciences*. Available from http://www.buildingsmartalliance.org/index.php/about (accessed August 2010).

Chau, K.W., Anson, M. & Zhang, J.P. (2005) 4D dynamic construction management and visualization software: 1. Development. *Automation in Construction*, **14(4)**, 512–524.

Collier, E. & Fischer, M. (1996) Visual-based scheduling: 4D modelling on the San Mateo County Health Centre. *Proceedings of the 3rd ASCE Congress on Computing in Civil Engineering*. Anaheim, CA.

Corenet (2010) *Construction and Real Estate Network*. Available from http://www. corenet.gov.sg (accessed August 2010).

Dawood, N., Sriprasert, E., Mallasi, Z. & Hobbs, B. (2002) Development of an integrated information resource base for 4D/VR construction processes simulation. *Automation in Construction*, **12**, 123–131.

Dawood, N., Scott, D., Sriprasert, E. & Mallasi, Z. (2005) The *Virtual Construction Site (VIRCON) Tools: An Industrial Evaluation*, Itcon, vol. 10, Special Issue from 3D to nD modelling. 43–54. Available from http://www.itcon.org/ (accessed August 2010).

de Vries, B. & Harink, M.J. (2007) Generation of a construction planning from a 3D CAD model. *Automation in Construction*, **16(2007)**, 13–18.

Eastman, C., Teicholz, P., Sacks, R. & Liston, K. (2008) *BIM handbook – A Guide to Buildong Information Modelling for Owners, Managers, Designers, Engineers and Contractors*. John Wiley and Sons, Ltd, Chichester, UK.

Gallaher, M.P., O'Connor, A.C., Dettbarn, J.L & Gilday, L.T. (2004) *Cost Analysis of Inadequate Inter-operability in the US Capital Facilities Industry*. NIST GCR 04-867. Available from http://www.fire.nist.gov/bfrlpubs/build04/art022.html (accessed August 2010).

Gann, D. & Dodgson, M. (2008) Innovate with vision. *Ingenia*, 45–48.

Graphisoft (2010) *ArchiCAD by Graphisoft*. Design software. Available from http:// www.graphisoft.com/ (accessed August 2010).

Heesom, D. & Mahdjoubi, L. (2004) Trends of 4D CAD applications for construction planning. *Construction Management & Economics*, **22**, 171–182.

IAI (2010) *International Alliance for Inter-operability*. Available from http://www. buildingsmart.com (accessed August 2010).

ISO (2010) *International Organization for Standardization ISO, Publicly Available Standards*. Available from http://www.iso.org/iso/en/CatalogueDetailPage. CatalogueDetail?CSNUMBER=38056 (accessed August 2010).

Jaafari, A., Manivong, K.K. & Chaaya, M. (2001) VIRCON: Interactive System for Teaching Construction Management. *Journal of Construction Engineering and Management*, **127**, 66–75.

Kim, W., Lee, H., Lim, H.C., Kim, O. & Choi, Y.K., (2001) visualized construction process on virtual reality. *Fifth International Conference on Information Visualisation (IV'01)*, **July**, 684.

Kunz, J. & Fischer, M. (2005) *Virtual Design and Construction: Themes, Case Studies and Implementation Suggestions*, CIFE Working Paper #097. Available from http://www.stanford.edu/group/CIFE/online.publications/WP097.pdf (accessed August 2010).

Lee, A., Wu, S., Marshall-Ponting, A., Aouad, G., Tah, J.H.M. & Cooper, R. (2006) nD modelling – A driver or enabler for construction improvement? *RICS Research Paper Series*, **5(6)**, 45.

Li, H., Huang, T., Kong, C.W., Guo, H.J., Baldwin, A., Chan, N. & Wong, J. (2008) Integration design and construction through virtual prototyping. *Automation in Construction*, **17(8)**, 915–922.

McKinney-Liston, K., Fischer, M. & Kunz, J. (1998) 4D annotator: a visual decision support tool for construction planners. In: ed. Wang, K.C.P., *Computing in Civil*

Engineering, Proceedings of International Computing Congress, Boston, 18–21 October, ASCE, 330–341.

NIBS (2010) *National BIM Standards*. Available from http://www. buildingsmartalliance.org/index.php/nbims/about (accessed August 2010).

Tah, J.H.M., Howes, R. & Wong, H.W. (1997) Towards a concurrent engineering environment for integration of design and construction (CEE-IDAC). In: ed. Anumba, C.J. & Evbuomwan, N.F.O., *First International Conference on Concurrent Engineering in Construction*, The Institution of Structural Engineers, London. 206–215.

Tah, J.H.M. (2008) Future agent-driven virtual prototyping environments in construction. In: ed. Brandon, P. & Kocatürk, T., *Virtual Futures for Design, Construction & Procurement*. Blackwell Science, Oxford.

Tekla (2010) *Tekla Structure*.Design, software. Available from http://www.tekla.com (accessed August 2010).

Vera (2010) *Vera – Information Networking in the Construction Process 1997–2002*. Available from http://vera.vtt.fi (accessed August 2010).

Waly, A.F. & Thabet, W.Y. (2002) A Virtual Construction Environment for preconstruction planning. *Automation in Construction*, **12**, 139–154.

Yerrapathruni, S., Messner, J.I., Baratta, A. & Horman, M.J., (2003) Using 4D CAD and immersive virtual environments to improve construction planning. *Proceedings of CONVR 2003, Conference on Construction Applications of Virtual Reality*, Blacksburg, VA, 179–192.

16

E-readiness in Construction

Eric Lou, Mustafa Alshawi and Jack S. Goulding

16.1 Challenges Facing the Construction Industry

The construction industry is often hailed as the gauge of the global economy. From a value perspective, the industry contributes an estimated 9.8% towards the Gross Domestic Product (GDP) of the EU economy (Business Watch, 2005), and around 8% of GDP in the USA (Researchandmarkets, 2011). In this respect, the European Commission's Information and Communication Technology (ICT) Uptake Working Group report highlighted the importance of ICT-based innovation in bringing productivity improvements and competitive advantage to the industry (EC, 2006). This task force also reported a constant decline in labour productivity, which was mainly attributed to the lack of ICT-related investment since the mid-1990s. This evidence also highlights that higher productivity growth rates were observed in the USA and other world trade partners of Europe through the greater use/integration of ICT by all segments of the economy. However, industries have not been in a position to capitalise on the investment in terms of productivity growth (OECD, 2003). In this context, sustainability, competitiveness and growth of this vital sector of the economy can only be sustained through the pursuit of knowledge and innovation, the latter of which has historically been driven by rapid developments of ICT systems, specifically the ability to capture, store, analyse/manage and exchange data. Therefore, in an increasingly knowledge-based industry such as construction, it is vital to have early access to knowledge-based tools, together with an ICT infrastructure that can handle media-rich services; and in order to remain competitive, construction firms will have to fully embrace this technology (BERR, 2008).

Concerning ICT and the construction industry, whilst several success stories can be highlighted over the past decade, these have mainly focused

Construction Innovation and Process Improvement, First Edition.
Edited by Akintola Akintoye, Jack S. Goulding and Girma Zawdie.
© 2012 Blackwell Publishing Ltd. Published 2012 by Blackwell Publishing Ltd.

on technical operations such design, planning, estimating, etc. In addition, there has been continued growth in the uptake of collaborative environments. These applications are designed to manage and control project documents amongst partners, whilst also providing up-to-date information on their progress. However, although these applications can provide 'value' to projects, their actual role in achieving competitive advantage is not overtly documented in seminal literature. In addition, whilst a 'technology push' approach may bring about 'first comer' advantages to organisations, implementing ICT applications to create competitive advantage can only be leveraged by improving businesses processes in line with management objectives, and using ICT as the core enabler (Alshawi, 2007). Therefore, in today's economic climate, competitive advantage can be achieved by focusing on issues such as providing high-quality services and products with minimal cost, having the flexibility to predict and respond to market needs, or through the efficient management of resources. These can be realised by embracing ICT to enable streamlined business processes, which not only make organisations operate efficiently but also allow them to build their knowledge base in order to gain competitive advantage. Notwithstanding this, investment in IT-based business systems such as Building Information Modelling (BIM) collaborative environments (extranets), enterprise resource planning (ERP) and intelligent systems have not realised their full potential (Alshawi and Goulding, 2008). Furthermore, it is estimated that the worldwide cost of IT failure could account to US$6.2 trillion per year, or an estimated US$500 billion per month (Krigsman, 2009; Sessions, 2009) and similar failure stories are reported elsewhere (Alshawi, 2007; Burns, 2008; Business Wire, 2008; Krigsman, 2010). This situation also pervades the construction industry, for example, Salah (2003) identified that 75% of ICT investment in business-oriented systems did not meet there intended business objectives. Furthermore, some of these projects were abandoned, significantly redirected or 'kept alive' despite business integration failures. On reflection, the main attributes of these failures were rarely purely technical by origin, but more often than not related to organisational 'soft issues', which underpin the capability of organisations to successfully absorb ICT into their work practices. In this respect, Basu and Jarnagin (2008) noted that business executives did not fully recognise the full functionality and value of technology to the business, nor did ICT personnel possess an understanding of the business and its strategic objectives. This was reinforced through a survey of Chief Executives and Directors of construction organisations in the UK, where the results demonstrated a high level of awareness regarding the strategic benefits of ICT to achieve innovation and competitive advantage, but a lack of direction on how best to achieve these benefits in their organisations (Construct IT, 2008). This resonates with the findings by Goulding et al. (2007) regarding the importance of understanding technology adoption and diffusion issues, and with findings by Mata et al. (1995) concerning investment uncertainty.

16.2   Business Dynamics and Technology

Today's global business competition is forcing organisations to start using ICT, not just for performance improvement and cost reduction, but also to open up new markets and/or gain a niche advantage over their competitors (Coyne *et al.*, 2000; Davis and Walker, 2009; Toften and Hammervoll, 2009). In this respect, executives who hold a better understanding of ICT are more able to align ICT strategies to their business strategies in order to exploit and leverage innovative business processes. This alignment requires a careful and balanced approach between the level and complexity of the enabling technology, and the required level of process change (expected) within the organisation. However, achieving this balance can often be difficult, as it requires highly skilled professionals who fully appreciate the strategic needs of the business and the benefits and functionalities that advances in ICT could offer in order to leverage the business strategy (Alshawi, 2007). Therefore, the interrelationship between the dynamic nature of business and the supporting IT infrastructure can best be described in five layers, where:

- Layer 1 covers the business environment;
- Layer 2 identifies the ICT and business processes;
- Layer 3 identifies the package solutions;
- Layer 4 presents the enabling software; and
- Layer 5 identifies the hardware and communication technology infrastructure.

Whilst this five-layer approach can be used to influence the effective selection, development and implementation of ICT within organisations, it is also important to highlight the congruence and interrelationship of the four core elements (people and skills, business processes, IT infrastructure and work environment) on the successful implementation of ICT within organisations (Goulding and Alshawi, 2004). From a construction sector perspective, business dynamics embraces a wide range of disparate types and sizes of organisations, with a corresponding range of project scale and complexity. In this respect, the skills and resources needed range from highly skilled designers to non-skilled site workers. This skill set is used to deliver a project, which often includes teams from a range of different organisations and the complexity of each party's arrangements often causes communication problems (Cheng *et al.*, 2001, 2003). It is therefore important that organisations appreciate the importance of building ICT capability with this in mind, especially cognisant of internal and external communication and transfer protocols.

16.3   Building ICT Capability

Organisational capability requires the careful development and deployment of specific organisational competence to achieve business imperatives. In the context of ICT, organisational capability embraces many facets, not least highly flexible skills sets, an acute awareness of change, flexible management structures, well-articulated process improvement schemes, clear business goals and an advanced ICT infrastructure, which is aligned to deliver corporate goals (Brewer and Runeson, 2009; Ahuja *et al.*, 2010). For example, the competence of an organisation needs to develop in order to acquire the capability to strategically benefit from IT falls under four main elements, people, process, work environment and ICT infrastructure. These elements are highly interrelated, that is, developing competence in one element must be accompanied by improvement in the others. In this respect, these interrelationships need people with the necessary skills (and power) to implement process improvements. However, improvements often require management consent and approval, which requires organisations to instil an environment, which can facilitate the proposed change through activities such as motivation, empowerment and management of change. Therefore, the high level of integration between these elements can be enabled by a flexible and advanced ICT infrastructure. The first two elements (people and process) are the key to change and improvements (Lou and Alshawi, 2009), while the other two elements (IT infrastructure and work environment) can be seen as enablers, without which the first two elements could not materialise. Therefore, environments should be created where people are motivated, empowered and made aware of the expected change. They need to be ready to innovative, absorb new ideas and develop and implement them effectively. However, this requires business goals and improvement targets to be clearly articulated and communicated to employees, underpinned by strong support from senior management. In this respect, the time required for an organisation to build up ICT capability is therefore dependent on the level of maturity of the organisation in each of these elements. The following sections explain the relationship between these four elements in terms of achieving ICT capability in order to leverage business needs and secure competitive advantage.

16.4   Business Process and ICT

Business process and the ICT infrastructure within companies are ostensibly governed and augmented by the organisational culture and work practices. The more streamlined and effective these processes are, the more efficient the organisation is likely to be. Given this, careful alignment of ICT can help reshape business processes and facilitate the flow of information between processes (Coltman *et al.*, 2005; Siha and Saad, 2008; Yen, 2009). However, while ICT may be used to automate existing business processes, it is also important to note that automating inefficiently designed business processes will often end in failure (Dickinson, 1997). This is widely categorised as helping to 'do the wrong things faster'. Either way, the required process change is predominantly dependent upon how ICT is deployed, that is, implementing through a third-party product or developing and implementing a bespoke system. In the case of opting to engage a third-party product, business functions will often be 'challenged' by the functionalities of the

Maturity of IT in the Organisation

		Low	High
Process Management	High	Missed opportunity	Optimum solution
	Low	Third party dependent (high risk)	Mechanising the "Old horse"

Figure 16.1   Relationship between process and IT maturity (Alshawi, 2007).

proposed system. Therefore, the implementation process will require the organisation to change its business processes from its current practice to the one required by the ICT system. In the case of developing a bespoke ICT system, it is likely that the new system will mimic existing practices followed by the core business processes, with a slight change to the supporting business functions to accommodate the new technology. The following section examines the organisational capability needed to maximise the benefits of ICT investment (Figure 16.1). The nature of this process/maturity relationship can be separated into four quadrants. These quadrants link the level of maturity of organisations to manage process improvement with their maturity to utilise and manage ICT (Alshawi, 2007).

From an improvement perspective, innovation and improvement drivers are often initiated and led from within organisations by people (Wells, 2000; Dahlgaard-Park and Dahlgaard, 2010), but this can only be realised when employees are fully aware of the holistic processes involved in achieving sustainable business improvement leading to competitive advantage. Thus, this requires a shared congruence of organisational maturity, where people's readiness is aligned with organisation readiness, that is, they have the capability to change, and the mechanisms available to drive forward the strategic benefits; in essence, creating new core business functions that are enabled by ICT. However, this state of readiness requires investment in the ICT infrastructure, along with investment in people, and is often achieved over a considerable period of time, where systematic iterations of investment (technology/skills) evolve to reach the required a state of readiness. In this respect, there is an inverse correlation between investment and skills/benefits (Figure 16.2).

16.5   People and ICT

Organisational change often cites the paradigms of change in several layers, be it at individual, team, group or at corporate level. Ultimately, organisations need to be able to successfully adapt themselves to new situations and this cannot normally be accomplished without the influence and support of its constituent members (Gardner and Ash, 2003; Vakola *et al.*, 2004;

Figure 16.2   Relationship between IT investments, organisational benefits and time (Alshawi, 2007).

Brook, 2009). Thus, wherever the need for change is recognised within an organisation, and wherever the precise nature of such change is formulated, eventually it will be up to the 'people managers' to create the right environment for change to occur. This means that they will have a key role to play in the management of change in organisations. In this situation, organisations therefore need to find out how to release the 'creative energy', intelligence and initiative of people at every level, as resistance to change can be somewhat counterproductive. Consequently, in order for any business improvement to be successful, new behavioural patterns consistent within that of the business improvement initiative must be developed, or business performance will not improve. In this respect, effective change in organisational culture and structure is considered an essential ingredient of ICT augmentation, such that the role of people and organisational culture in delivering successful IT systems is paramount (Kennedy, 1994; Arendt, 2008). For example, Towers (1996) explained that managing change and people together is a major contributing factor to the success of process and IT, and Cooper and Markus (1995) stated that the inadequate treatment of the human aspect is the major cause of reengineering failure. Similarly, Kennedy (1994) highlighted that elements of human change management was 'the most difficult challenge', as employees often felt threatened by new processes and IT systems, which was supported by Arendt (2008), noting that the problem was predominantly down to a lack of proper knowledge, education and skilled owner-managers and employees within the enterprise.

Leadership of the ICT department can therefore be said to be paramount for the success of ICT planning, development, implementation and operation within an organisation. However, the precise role and remit of operations can vary considerably, due primarily to changes in both the technology and business challenges that currently face organisations. In this respect, Computer Sciences Corporation (CSC, 1996) identified six core IT leadership roles needed to execute an ICT initiative, these being: the Chief Architect, Change Leader, Product Developer, Technology Provocateur,

Coach, and the Chief Operating Strategist. Notwithstanding the importance of these, it is also important to acknowledge that the director of the ICT department may also be influenced by a range of issues, not least previous experience, technology predilection/aversion, level of incumbent support and rank/position within the organisation.

16.6   Business Process and Implementation

The work environment is often considered the main enabler of the process and people elements, and is often described as the *esprit de corps* of the organisation. This can be influenced by several factors, the most notable of which are committed leadership, empowerment of employees, communication, process vision development, project management and process-based team formation (Al-Mashari and Zairi, 2000; Damij, 2007). For example, leadership can play a vital role in directing change efforts towards success. The importance of leadership stems from its role in providing a clear vision of the future, communicating this vision and being able to involve people in all aspects of any transition. This includes the ability to motivate people and a holistic perspective and understanding of change. From an employee empowerment perspective, this can be an effective factor for influencing the success of ICT implementation, particularly where it promotes self-management and collaborative teamwork principles (Mumford, 1995; Keatin *et al.*, 2001). Furthermore, employees can become empowered when they are involved in deciding how work (change) should be approached, which technologies to use, and are given the chance to participate in the change and implementation process (Arendt *et al.*, 1995; Bovey and Hede, 2001). Another important facet is that of communication. Communication of change is a vital component of the implementation process, yet this is considered one of the most difficult aspects to achieve (CSC, 1994). The work environment also embodies process vision, as this embraces not only customers and competitors, but also the strategic direction of the company, and the integral links between strategy and process (Davenport, 1993). However, it is important not to lose sight of the importance of project management in the ICT implementation process, particularly concerning piloting (Hammer and Stanton, 1995). Piloting can help to identify potential risks and failures, the nuances of which embrace such issues as politics, through to investment decision making (Dekkers, 2008). The final ingredient within the work environment is that of teamwork. Teamwork has long been acknowledged as an important aspect in the implementation of change, the remit of which encapsulates managing work by making group decisions and coordinating activities, managing relationships by promoting trust, openness, and resolving conflicts, and finally, managing relationships with customers, suppliers and market partners. Thus, teamwork can leverage many advantages, such as facilitating interactions between functions, and speeding up the redesign process (Koufteros *et al.*, 2007; Loukis *et al.*, 2009) through to creating a learning environment in which team members are encouraged to share knowledge and expertise.

16.7   E-readiness

From an e-readiness perspective, it is imperative to implement the 'right' ICT solutions for the right processes, to the right degree, with the right timing. In this respect, organisations and employees need to be prepared and ready for the changes to come – the mantra of which is echoed in a myriad of Change Management literature. Therefore, striking the right balance is the main goal, and all organisations should be striving to achieve this concordance. Industry chiefs and leaders will therefore need to continuously assess and re-evaluate their business models and drivers. On this theme, successful e-business and e-commerce initiatives only take place if, and only if, emergent initiatives are built on robust foundations of readiness (Ruikar *et al.*, 2006; Waseda University, 2007; UN, 2008). Thus, the notion of e-readiness means different things to different people, in different contexts, and for different purposes. As a result, a large gap exists between ideas and concepts on one hand, and practical applications and implications, on the other (bridges.org, 2005; UN, 2008).

There is no single definitive definition for e-readiness, as different people describe and practice it differently. Therefore, the precise definition and meaning of e-readiness is still evolving. To provide a holistic overview, a few thoughts are outlined here to help this discussion. For example, The World Information Technology and Services Alliance (WITSA) stated that an e-ready country required consumer trust in e-commerce security and privacy along with better security technology, more trained workers and lower training costs, less restrictive public policy, new business practices adapted to the information age and lower costs for e-commerce technology (WISTA, 2004). However, the United Nations (UN) perceive e-readiness as the public sector e-Government initiatives of member states according to a weighted average composite index of e-readiness, based on website assessment; telecommunication infrastructure and human resource endowment (UN, 2008). The community assessment of e-readiness by the Center for International Development, Harvard University (CID, 2007) describes an e-ready society as one that has the necessary physical infrastructure (high bandwidth, reliability and affordable prices), has integrated current IT throughout businesses (e-commerce, local IT sector), along with communities (local content, many organisations online, IT used in everyday life, IT taught in schools), has Government (e-Government), has strong telecommunications competition, has independent regulation with a commitment to universal access and has no limits on trade or foreign investment. Furthermore, the Technology CEO Council (2005) views an e-ready community as being equipped with high-speed access in a competitive market, with constant access and application of IT in schools, Government offices, businesses, healthcare facilities and homes, user privacy and online security, and Government policies that are favourable to promoting connectedness and use of the network.

Following these themes, e-readiness can also be defined as the ability of an organisation or economy to deploy Internet-based computers and information technologies to transform traditional businesses into a new economy – an economy that is characterised by the ability to perform business transactions in real time – in any form, anywhere, anytime, and at any price (Bui *et al.*, 2002). Table 16.1 presents an overview of the worldwide

Table 16.1 E-readiness definitions.

Report	Definition of e-readiness
United Nations (UN) (2008)	This UN report assesses e-government readiness of Member States, according to a quantitative composite readiness of e-readiness based on website assessment; telecommunication infrastructure and human resource endowment.
Economist Intelligence Unit (EIU) (2009)	E-readiness is the "state of play" of a country's ICT infrastructure and the ability of its consumers, businesses and governments to use ICT to their benefit. The ranking allows governments to gauge the success of technology initiatives against other countries. It also provides companies that wish to invest in online operations with an overview of the world's most promising investment locations.
Center for International Development (CID), Harvard University (2007)	Readiness is the degree to which a community is prepared to participate in the Networked World. It is gauged by assessing a community's relative advancement in the areas that are most critical for ICT adoption and the most important applications of ICT. When considered together in the context of a strategic planning dialogue, an assessment based on these elements provides a robust portrayal of a community's readiness. The value to a community of assessing its readiness lies in evaluating its unique opportunities and challenges.
The World Information Technology and Services Alliance (WITSA) (2004)	The survey states that an 'e-ready' country requires consumer trust in e-commerce security and privacy; better security technology; more trained workers and lower training costs; less restrictive public policy; new business practices adapted to the information age; and lower costs for e-commerce technology.
McConnell International (2000)	E-readiness measures the capacity of nations to participate in the digital economy. E-readiness is the source of national economic growth in the networked century and the prerequisite for successful e-business.
Asian Pacific Economic Cooperation (APEC) (2000)	Readiness is the degree to which an economy or community is prepared to participate in the digital economy. Every economy, regardless of its level of development, presents a readiness profile on the global stage, composed of its national policies, level of technology integration, and regulatory practices. Readiness is assessed by determining the relative standing of the economy in the areas that are most critical for e-commerce participation. Six broad indicators of readiness for e-commerce are developed into a series of questions that provide direction as to desirable policies that could promote e-commerce and remove barriers to electronic trade.

definitions of e-readiness by leading international groupings, research groups and non-profit organisations. From this, it can be seen that the myriad of differences in e-readiness definitions raises the question: 'What is the most accurate definition for e-readiness?' The answer to this question is an ongoing debate, reflecting that there is no complete literature definition for e-readiness. In spite of all the differences in definitions and opinions, this chapter defines e-readiness as 'the degree to which an organisation may be ready, prepared, or willing to obtain benefits, which arises from the digital economy'. This definition reflects the importance of organisational soft issues such as business processes, management structures, change management initiatives, people and culture. Now it is important to note that e-readiness is increasingly being considered as part of organisational plans and business trajectories.

16.8   Organisational E-readiness in Construction

The construction sector is predominantly project-oriented, where teams of companies get together to design and construct a project, and the team is then disbanded after the project has been completed. Whilst it can be argued that the industry's main functions and processes are still relatively unchanged, there has been a challenge to improve performance and reduce costs using ICT as a lever of change (Marsh and Flanagan, 2000). However, although the potential to improve performance still exists, efforts have been hampered by:

1. the industry's structure;
2. the fragmented supply chain;
3. lack of investment in ICT;
4. limited ICT 'champions' who are able to understand innovation opportunities; and
5. limited support and empowerment of senior decision makers (Lou and Alshawi, 2009).

In this respect, two critical elements can significantly influence the level of ICT project integration, specifically:

1. *Process alignment*: the ability to align organisational processes with the proposed system's functionalities; and
2. *People*: the ability of employees to accept and adapt to the system.

Thus, the relationship between people, process and technology are common themes and enablers of e-readiness. These elements are highly interrelated, as developing competence in one element must be accompanied by improvement in the others. For example, process improvement is a competence that an organisation needs to develop in order to achieve the sought technology capability. By default, this element therefore needs people with the necessary skills and position power to implement process improvements – the mandate of which also embodies the creation of an environment that is conducive to, and can facilitate these proposed changes. This organisational context also embraces such levers as motivation, empowerment and the management of change. Thus, it is important to encourage and support the integration between people and process through a flexible and advanced technology infrastructure. Contextually therefore, the key elements of organisational e-readiness should consider the findings of e-readiness reports, rankings, assessments and measuring tools as 'building blocks for change'.

16.8.1   People

People are the pivotal drivers of a business, and the intellectual capital through which an organisation operates. As a collective force, the people element can be considered the most important asset for e-readiness success. However, people need leadership and a clear vision of the e-readiness future. Therefore, communicating this vision is exceptionally important (Hammer and Stanton, 1995), as they need to understand organisational processes and implement change where necessary. Leadership, empowerment and organisational culture are also important drivers of success in this respect (Lee-Kelley, 2002). One concept that has been particularly effective here is that of Organisational Learning, as this can be used to avoid repeating common mistakes (Oliver, 2009). Culture and society can also be seen as core levers of success, as this embodies organisational behaviour, which in turn contributes to organisational communication (Diefenbach, 2007). Consequently, it is important for organisations to align people (skills) to the right jobs, in order improve innovation and creativity (de Jong and Den Hartog, 2007). Therefore, the promotion of learning through people is fundamental to creating a sustainable ICT workforce that supports, underpins and integrates ICT into the organisation (MacPherson *et al.*, 2005).

16.8.2   Process

Business process can be perceived as a core indicator of how an organisation functions. As a rule, the more effective business processes are, the more efficient the organisation tends to work. As Mulcahy (1990) observes, to be successful, construction organisations need to have clear objectives, and recognise the markets they wish to address, services they wish to provide, risk they may undertake, structures they will use, the environment they will operate within, the controls they will put in place and the returns they wish to achieve. These are core processes, therefore, capturing and disseminating knowledge provides a central organising theme for business change, which can be seen as a continuous process of adaptation and innovation – aligning external requirements with internal capabilities, and linking the two together (Nanoka and Takeuchi, 1995). However, it is important to acknowledge that processes are not typically isolated, as they more often than not are infused with people and technology elements. For example, processes involving project collaboration tend to embody the people involved in the project, and work processes associated with technology employed.

16.8.3   Technology

Within the construction sector, issues surrounding e-commerce, electronic transactions and collaborative environments are increasingly becoming more prevalent (4projects, 2011; BIW Technologies, 2011). Therefore, technology is a major factor of organisational e-readiness, especially as it embraces several core areas, from management and operation, through to standardisation, maintenance, forecasting and investment (APEC, 2000). Thus, ICT needs to be managed in order to ensure that new and emergent technologies are aligned with organisational strategic plans to leverage identifiable benefits. In this respect, this alignment can also help secure competitive advantage, using ICT as a core competency enabler (Construct IT, 2008). A key aspect of this is an organisation's ability to encourage users to engage in this process to procure the information infrastructure and develop management readiness (Boomer, 2006). These issues were reinforced by a strategic study into the thinking of UK AEC executives and IT/innovation directors, on their perception of investment for ICT-based innovation linked to competitive advantage (Construct IT, 2008). Research findings highlighted a series of 'missed opportunities', including people, process and the work environment – to develop core capabilities and be in a state of e-readiness (organisational) to effectively absorb technology into their work practices (to achieve innovation and competitive advantage). In this respect, the key enablers and subcategories can be seen in Table 16.2.

This work was supported by research findings from two scoping studies (Lou and Goulding, 2010) involving 40 domain experts, which identified that the People, Process and Technology issues also had core enablers – the ranking of which can be seen in Table 16.3. These findings identified that the industry did not perceive the solution to becoming e-ready as being predominantly technology-driven, but more through the engagement of leadership, to align change management issues to business processes and the strategic vision.

16.8.4   Means of Achieving E-readiness

Measures for assessing the performance and impact of ICT have predominantly focused upon post-investment/project appraisal decisions. This feedback helped executives learn from their ICT investment decisions. However, extant literature on ICT project failures indicates that many issues still need addressing. In this respect, it is advocated that organisational e-readiness models may be able to help here. The closest approach to this so

Table 16.2   People, process and technology (adapted from Lou and Goulding, 2010).

People	Process	Technology
Leadership & Empowerment	Business & Information Process	Connectivity & Reach
Culture & Society	Information Access & Connectivity	IT & Communication Infrastructure (Technology)
Human Capital & Skills	Security & Integrity	IT & Communication Infrastructure (Reliability)
Learning & Further Education	Policy & Vision	New Technologies
Promotion & Facilitation	Knowledge Sharing & Capture	New Investments
Change Management	Services & Support	Information Infrastructure & Management
Communication	Networked Economy	Interconnectability & Interoperability
Capacity Building	Web Measure & Services	Technology Transfer

Table 16.3   Ranking of the top five e-readiness core enablers (adapted from Lou and Goulding, 2010).

Rank	Enabler	Factor
1	Leadership & Empowerment	People
2	Change Management	People
3	Business & Information Process	Process
4	Policy / Strategy / Vision	Process
5	ICT Sharability / Interoperability	Technology

far is the VERDICT model (Ruikar, 2006), which presents e-readiness points/scores for organisations; but does not specifically address 'how' these organisation might improve their current situation, for example, through maturity level steps, etc. Other attempts include the General Practitioner IS Consultant Tool (Salah, 2003), which provides a generic e-readiness 'snapshot' of organisations. Notwithstanding this, the main objective of self-assessment is to produce an all-inclusive and quantifiable overview of organisational e-readiness that encapsulates the people-process-technology factors, as a well-planned and executed self-assessment (and follow-up action), can deliver significant benefits and help reinforce direction (Hillman, 1994). On this theme, self-assessment techniques are increasingly being used (Benavent *et al.*, 2005), reflecting the importance of these for self-positioning in the market.

In terms of providing a 'quantifiable' overview, maturity level rankings and benchmarking approaches can be used to provide a yardstick for executives to know 'where they are', and 'where they wish to be' in the future (Zairi, 1998), as best practice measures can often create breakthrough improvements (Andersen and Camp, 1995). However, in order to measure the current and expected organisational e-readiness capabilities, maturity-level techniques can be used (Galliers and Sutherland, 2003). For example, the Capability Maturity Model approach has been used successfully by many organisations in a variety of sectors to assess the relative maturity of practices (Rogers, 2009; Zwikael, 2009).

16.8.5   Case Study: E-readiness Construction Framework

Research findings from initial scoping studies identified that the main support mechanisms needed from a priority perspective was for e-readiness assessment tools to gauge organisational e-readiness maturity. Given this, an E-Readiness in Construction (ERiC) framework was developed for organisations to achieve e-readiness. ERiC is a self-assessment framework based on the concepts of maturity modelling. It provides a step-by-step guide for executives to evaluate their business holistically in order to secure e-readiness best practice. This can also be used to undertake benchmarking exercises in order to position themselves in the marketplace. A sample self-evaluation ranking questionnaire from ERiC covering Leadership and Empowerment can be seen in Figure 16.3.

This e-readiness framework presents a solution for construction industry executives to evaluate their state of e-readiness. From an operational perspective, one of the fundamental parameters needed from the outset is that of transparency. Executives therefore need to undertake an organisation-wide audit through this model. This includes strategic and operational issues, from executives and senior management, through to middle management and functional levels. The framework questionnaire consists of five factors, specifically Leadership and Empowerment, Organisational Change Management, Business and Information Process, Organisational Policy and ICT Interoperability. Each factor is evaluated through five separate questions with five maturity-modelled statements. The framework can also include additional weightings to create additional flexibility.

The results from this framework are displayed in a 'web' diagram, which identify the maturity of the five framework factors (Figure 16.4). Each level is characterised by conditional requirements for an organisation to achieve. The maturity levels show a sequential development, from an initial level with basic requirements (Level 1), through to a maximum maturity level (Level 5), categorised as the optimum performance level. The operationali-sation of this approach follows the principles of Sarshar et al. (2004), where progression from one level to the next represents a step change in maturity. In this respect, organisations in Level 5 are classified as 'Comprehensively Ready'. at Level 4 'Advanced', Level 3 'Intermediate', Level 2 'Restrictive' and at Level 1 'Obsolete'. The questionnaire results are analysed and presented based on the average score of each sub-factor. Organisations are then provided with factors for improvement, along with corresponding action plans.

Factor

Maturity level

Leadership & empowerment

Involvement	Hands-on	Open-door	Filtered	Restrictive	Non-existent
High-involvement leaders view employees at all levels as true partners – such practices allow the organisation to tap into the creativity and energy of their employees to an extent that is not possible with traditional forms of management.	Top management is involved in developing, participating, delivering and collaborating in new IT ideas/projects from its beginning; and providing an equal platform for communication/debate between all levels in the organisation.	Top management shares initial IT ideas and projects, and employees are free to participate and comment, only then the final decisions are made.	View of employees for new IT ideas/projects is sought through internal IT teams. Team leader will filter the ideas and discussions before passing to top management.	Top management establishes new IT ideas/projects – employees' feedback are welcomed.	An autocratic regime is practised – top management provide the idea/strategy, and the operational people executes – there is a clear divide between the management and operational levels in the organisation.
	Example (Collaborative Environments/Extranets implementation)				
	Top management and employees participate in open forum discussions of the possibility extranets implementation – tapping into the experiences and knowledge of employees before decision is taken by top management to implement extranets in the organisation.	Top management and employees participate in open forum discussions of the possibility extranets implementation – tapping into the experiences and knowledge of employees before decision is taken by top management to implement extranets in the organisation.	Top management and employees participate in open forum discussions of the possibility extranets implementation – tapping into the experiences and knowledge of employees before decision is taken by top management to implement extranets in the organisation.	Top management and employees participate in open forum discussions of the possibility extranets implementation – tapping into the experiences and knowledge of employees before decision is taken by top management to implement extranets in the organisation.	Top management and employees participate in open forum discussions of the possibility extranets implementation – tapping into the experiences and knowledge of employees before decision is taken by top management to implement extranets in the organisation.
Notes					*Score*

Figure 16.3 Questionnaire sample.

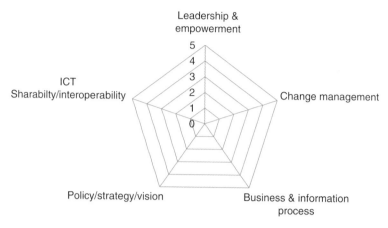

Figure 16.4   ERiC framework: five core factors.

16.9   Conclusion

Whilst globalisation has fundamentally changed businesses, the construction industry has not readily absorbed the integration and implementation of ICT into its business to improve innovation and productivity. It has invested heavily in ICT, and several success stories can be cited, including design, planning, costing, etc. However, there is little evidence to support success in areas such as generating competitive advantage, opening up new market leverage opportunities, applying high levels of innovation, etc. One of the principal reasons behind this is an open acknowledgement that the industry needs executives with a strategic understanding of ICT in order to align and exploit strategies to leverage innovation and secure competitive advantage. This requires organisations to build ICT competence, with agile and flexible skill sets that are aligned to business deliverables – the precursor of which requires flexible management structures, well-articulated process improvement schemes, clear business goals and leaders fully conversant in Change Management. However, it is also important to recognise at this juncture that the prevailing level of organisational culture can work as both a lever and a barrier to success. In this respect, the role and importance of people and organisational culture should not be underestimated.

Sustained successful e-business initiatives traditionally only occur if they are based upon robust foundations. This requires companies to have effective measures and systems in place to design, develop, deliver and evaluate these. For example, e-readiness initiatives embrace a myriad of factors, from business processes, through to management, people and culture. These elements are all interrelated, and more often than not, improving one area in isolation will not ordinarily procure success without improvements in other areas being made at the same time. On this theme, research findings identified three pivotal areas existed, specifically People, Process and Technology. These were recognised as the main underpinning factors, with leadership and empowerment, managing business and information processes, and change management seen as the main enablers. In this respect, an e-readiness framework was presented for discussion. This framework enables construction executives to critically evaluate their organisation and position against five levels of maturity: Leadership and Empowerment, Organisational Change Management, Business and Information Process, Organisational Policy and ICT Interoperability. Approaches of this nature are posited as being increasingly important in the construction industry, as organisational e-readiness can be seen as a conduit for leveraging business excellence. However, for this to happen, organisations will have to radically re-think their People, Process and Technology relationships (internally and externally), as these symbiotic relationships will govern the success or otherwise of any approach adopted.

References

4projects (2011), Available from *http://www.4projects.com/OurProduct/Integration. aspx* (Date accessed 20/12/2011)

Ahuja, V., Yang, J. & Shankar, R. (2010) IT-enhanced communication protocols for building project management. *Engineering, Construction and Architectural Management*, **17**(2), 159–179.

Al-Mashari, M. & Zairi, M. (2000) Revisiting BPR: A holistic review of practices and development. *Business Process Management Journal*, **6**(1), 10–30.

Alshawi, M. (2007) *Rethinking IT in Construction and Engineering: Organisational Readiness*. Taylor and Francis, Oxford.

Alshawi, M. & Goulding, J. (2008) Organisational e-readiness: Embracing IT for sustainable competitive advantage. *Construction Innovation: Information, Process Management*, **8**(1),

Andersen, B. & Camp, R.C. (1995) Current position and future development of benchmarking. *The TQM Magazine*, **7**(5), 21–25.

APEC (2000) *E-Commerce Readiness Assessment Guide*. Asia-Pacific Economic Co-operation (APEC) Readiness Initiative, Electronic Commerce Steering Group.

Arendt, C.H., Landis, R.M. & Meister, T.B. (1995) *The Human Side of Change*, Part 4. IIE Solutions, 22–27.

Arendt, L. (2008) Barriers to ICT adoption in SMEs: how to bridge the digital divide? *Journal of Systems and Information Technology*, **10**(2), 93–108.

Basu, A. & Jarnagin, C. (2008) How to tap it's hidden potential. *Wall Street Journal* Available from http://online.wsj.com/article/SB120467900166211989. html (accessed 6 January 2011).

Benavent, F.B., Ros, S.C. & Moreno-Luzon, M. (2005) A model of quality management self-assessment: an exploratory research. *International Journal of Quality & Reliability Management*, **22**(5), 432–451.

BERR (2008) *Supporting Innovation in Services, Department for Business*. Enterprise and Regulatory Reform, Crown copyright, URN 08/1126, London.

BIW Technologies (2011), Available from *http://www.biwtech.com/cp_root/h/ Applications/Performance/201/?lang=* (Date accessed 20/12/2011)

Boomer, L.G. (2006) The 10 rules of technology management. *Accounting Today*, **20**(3), 20–23.

Bovey, W.H. & Hede, A. (2001) Resistance to organizational change: the role of cognitive and affective processes. *Leadership and Organization Development Journal*, **22**(8), 372–382.

Brewer, G. & Runeson, G. (2009) Innovation and attitude: Mapping the profile of ICT decision-makers in architectural, engineering and construction firms. *International Journal of Managing Projects in Business*, **2**(4), 599–610.

Bridges.org (2005) *E-readiness assessment: Who is Doing What and Where?* Cape Town. Available from http://www.bridges.org/files/active/0/ereadiness_ whowhatwhere_bridges.pdf (accessed 28 February 2008).

Brook, I. (2009) *Organisational Behaviour: Individuals, Groups and Organisation*, 4th edn. Financial Times/Prentice Hall, Essex, UK.

Bui, T.X., Sebastian, I.M., Jones, W. & Naklada, S. (2002) *E-Commerce Readiness in East Asian APEC Economies – A Precursor to Determine HRD Requirements and Capacity Building*. Asia Pacific Economic Co-operation (APEC), Telecommunication and Information Working Group.

Burns, M. (2008) Enterprise software survey 2008. *CA Magazine*, **September**, 14–15.

Business Watch (2005) *The European e-Business Market Watch, Sector Report No. 08-II, ICT and Electronic Business in the Construction Industry*, IT adoption and e-business activity in 2005, European Commission, Enterprise and Industry Directorate General.

Business Wire (2008) *Survey Cites Dissatisfaction with Incumbent ERP Vendors.* Available from www.sys-con.com/node/594952 (accessed 11 January 2009).

Chan, A.P.C., Chan, D.W.M. & Ho, K.S.K. (2003) Partnering in construction: Critical study of problems for implementation. *Journal of Management in Engineering. (ASCE)*, **19**(3), 126–135.

Cheng, E.W.L., Li, H., Love, P.E.D. & Irani, Z. (2001) Network communication in the construction industry. *Corporate Communications: An International Journal*, **6**(2), 61–70.

CID (2007) *Readiness for the Networked World. A Guide for Developing Countries, Information Technologies Group*. Center for International Development (CID), Harvard University.

Coltman, T.R., Devinney, T.M. & Midgley, D.F. (2005) Strategy content and process in the context of e-business performance. In: ed. Baum, B., *Strategy Process (Advances in Strategic Management)*. Emerald Group Publishing Ltd, UK. 349–386.

Construct IT (2008) *Strategic Positioning of IT in Construction: An Industry Leaders' Perspective*. Construct IT for Business, Salford, Greater Manchester, UK.

Cooper, R. & Markus, M. (1995) Human Reengineering. *Sloan Management Review*, 36 (Summer), 39–50.

Coyne, K.P., Buaron, R., Foster, R.N. & Bhide, A. (2000) Gaining advantage over competitors. *McKinsey Quarterly*, June. Available from http://mkqpreview1. qdweb.net/PDFDownload.aspx?ar=1057 (accessed 20 August 2010).

CSC (1994) *State of Reengineering Report, Computer Sciences Corporation*. CSC Index Research, London.

CSC (1996) *New IS leaders*. Computer Sciences Corporation, CSC Index Research, London.

Dahlgaard-Park, S.M. & Dahlgaard, J.J. (2010) Organizational learnability and innovability: A system for assessing, diagnosing and improving innovations. *International Journal of Quality and Service Sciences*, **2**(2), 153–174.

Damij, N. (2007) Business process modelling using diagrammatic and tabular techniques. *Business Process Management Journal*, **13**(1), 70–90.

Davenport, T. (1993) *Process Innovation: Reengineering Work through Information Technology*. Harvard Business School Press, Boston, MA.

Davis, P.R. & Walker, D.H.T. (2009) Building capability in construction projects: a relationship-based approach: Engineering. *Construction and Architectural Management*, **16**(5), 475–489.

de Jong, J.P.J & Hartog, D.N. (2007) How leaders influence employees' innovative behaviour. *European Journal of Innovation Management*, **10**(1), 41–64.

Dekkers, R. (2008) Adapting organizations: the instance of business process reengineering. *Systems Research and Behavioral Science*, **25**, 45–66.

Dickinson, B. (1997) Knowing that the project clothes have no emperor. *Knowledge and Process Management*, **4**(4), 261–267.

Diefenbach, T. (2007) The managerialistic ideology of organisational change management. *Journal of Organizational Change Management*, **20**(1), 126–144.

EIU (2009) The 2009 e-readiness rankings. The Usage Imperative. *Economist Intelligence Unit (EIU) Research Reports*. Available from http://graphics.eiu.com/pdf/E-readiness%20rankings.pdf (accessed 7 September 2009).

European Commission (2006) *ICT Uptake, Working Group 1, ICT Uptake Working Group draft Outline Report*, October 2006. Brussels.

Galliers, R.D. & Sutherland, A.R. (2003) The evolving information systems strategy. In ed. Galliers, R.D. & Leidner, D.E., *Strategic Information Management*, 3rd edn. Butterworth Heinemann, Oxford.

Gardner, S. & Ash, C.G. (2003) ICT-enabled organisations: a model for change management. *Logistics Information Management*, **16**(1), 18–24.

Goulding J.S., Sexton, M.G., Zhang, X., Kagioglou, M., Aouad, G. & Barrett, P. (2007) Technology Adoption: Breaking Down Barriers Using a Virtual Reality Design Support Tool for Hybrid Concrete. *Journal of Construction Management and Economics*, **25**(12), 1239–1250.

Goulding, J.S. & Alshawi, M. (2004) A Process-Driven IT Training Model for Construction: Core Development Issues. *Journal of Construction Innovation*, **4**(4), 243–254.

Hammer, M. & Stanton, S. (1995) *The Reengineering Revolution*. Harper Collins, New York.

Hillman, G.P. (1994) Making Self-assessment Successful. *The TQM Magazine*, **6**(3), 29–31.

Keating, C.B., Fernandez, A.A., Jacobs, D.A. & Kauffmann, P. (2001) A methodology for analysis of complex socio-technical processes. *Business Process Management Journal*, **7**(1), 33–50.

Kennedy, C. (1994) Reengineering: the human costs and benefits. *Long Range Planning*, **27**(5), 64–72.

Koufteros, X.A., Nahm, A.Y., Cheng, E.T.C. & Lai, K-H. (2007) An empirical assessment of a nomological network of organizational design constructs: From culture to structure to pull production to performance. *International Journal of Production Economics*, **106**(2), 468–492.

Krigsman, M. (2009) *IT Project Failure. Worldwide cost of IT failure: $6.2 Trillion*. Available from http://blogs.zdnet.com/projectfailures/?p=7627&tag=col1;post-7695 (assessed 6 January 2011).

Krigsman, M. (2010) *Understanding Marin County's $30 million ERP failure. ZDNet*. Available from http://www.zdnet.com/blog/projectfailures/understanding-marin-countys-30-million-erp-failure/10678?tag=nl.e539 (assessed 13 September 2010).

Lee-Kelley, L. (2002) Situational leadership. Managing the virtual project team. *Journal of Management Development*, **21**(6), 461–476.

Lou, E.C.W. & Alshawi, M. (2009) Critical success factors for e-tendering implementation in construction collaborative environments: people and process issues. *Journal of Information Technology in Construction (ITcon)*, **14**, 98–109.

Lou, E.C.W. & Goulding, J.S. (2010) The pervasiveness of e-readiness in the global built environment arena. *Journal of Systems and Information Technology*, **12**(3), 180–195.

Loukis, E., Pazalos, K. & Georgiou, S. (2009) An empirical investigation of the moderating effects of BPR and TQM on ICT business value. *Journal of Enterprise Information Management*, **22**(5), 564–586.

MacPherson, A., Homan, G. & Wilkinson, K. (2005) The implementation and use of e-learning in the corporate university. *Journal of Workplace Learning*, **17**(1/2), 33–48.

Marsh, L. & Flanagan, R. (2000) Measuring the costs and benefits of information technology in construction. *Engineering and Architectural Management*, 7(4), 423–435.

Mata, F.J., Fuerst, W.L. & Barney, J.B. (1995) Information technology and sustained competitive Advantage: A resource-based Analysis. *MIS Quarterly*, **19**(4), 487–505.

McConnell International (2000) *Risk E-Business: Seizing the Opportunity of Global E-Readiness*. McConnell International and WISTA publishing.

Mulcahy, J.F. (1990) Management of the Building Firm. *Proceedings CIB 90, Joint Symposium on Building Economics and Construction Management*, Sydney. 11–21.

Mumford, E. (1995) Creative chaos or constructive change: business process reengineering versus socio-technical design. In: ed. Burke, G. & Peppard, J., *Examining Business Process Reengineering: Current Perspective and Research Directions*. Kogan, New York, 192–216.

Nanoka, I. & Takeuchi, H. (1995) *The Knowledge Creating Company – How Japanese Companies Create the Dynamics of Innovations*. Oxford University Press, Oxford.

OECD (2003) *Comparing Labour Productivity Growth in the OECD Area: The Role of Measurement*. OECD Statistics Working Paper 2003/5. OECD Statistics Directorate, Paris.

Oliver, J. (2009) Continuous improvement: role of organisational learning mechanisms. *International Journal of Quality and Reliability Management*, **26**(6), 546–563.

Researchandmarkets (2010) US Construction Sector: An Analysis. Available from http://www.researchandmarkets.com/reports/335700/us_construction_sector_an_analysis (assessed 6 January 2011).

Rogers, G.P. (2009) The role of maturity models in it governance: a comparison of the major models and their potential benefits to the enterprise. In: ed. Cater-Steel, E., *Information Technology Governance and Service Management: Frameworks and Adaptations*. IGI Global, New York. 254–265.

Ruikar, K., Anumba, C.J. & Carrillo, P.M. (2006) VERDICT-An e-readiness assessment application for construction companies. *Automation in Construction*, **15**, 98–110.

Salah, Y. (2003) IT *Success and Evaluation: A General Practitioner Model*, PhD Thesis, Research Institute for the Built Environment (BuHu), University of Salford, Greater Manchester, UK.

Sarshar, M., Haigh, R. & Amaratunga, D. (2004) Improving project processes: best practice case study. *Construction Innovation: Information, Process, Management*, **4**(2), 69–82.

Sessions, R. (2009) *The IT Complexity Crisis: Danger and Opportunity*. ObjectWatch, Inc, Houston, TX.

Siha, S.M. & Saad, G.H. (2008) Business process improvement: empirical assessment and extensions. *Business Process Management Journal*, **14**(6), 778–802.

Technology CEO Council (2005) *Freeing Our Unused Spectrum*. CEO, Washington, DC.

Toften, K. & Hammervoll, H. (2009) Niche firms and marketing strategy: An exploratory study of internationally oriented niche firms. *European Journal of Marketing*, **43(11/12)**, 1378–1391.

Towers, S. (1996) Reengineering: middle managers are the key asset. *Management Services*, 40(12), 17–18.

United Nations (2008) *UN E-Government Survey 2008. From E-Government to Connected Governance*. Department of Economic and Social Affairs, Division for Public Administration and Development Management, United Nations Online Network in Public Administration and Finance (UNPAN), United Nations Publications, New York.

Vakola, M., Tsaousis, I. & Nikolaou, I. (2004) The role of emotional intelligence and personality variables on attitudes toward organisational change. *Journal of Managerial Psychology*, **19(2)**, 88–110.

Waseda University (2007) *e-Government Ranking 2007, Waseda University Institute of E-Government*. Graduate School of Global Information and Telecommunications Studies, Japan.

Wells, M.G. (2000) Business process reengineering implementations using Internet technology. *Business Process Management Journal*, **6(2)**, 164–184.

WITSA (2004) *The WITSA Public Policy Report 2004*. World Information Technology and Services Alliance (WISTA), Geneva.

Yen, V.C. (2009) An integrated model for business process measurement. *Business Process Management Journal*, **15(6)**, 865–875.

Zairi, M. (1998) *Effective Management of Benchmarking Projects. Practical Guidelines and Examples of Best Practice*. Butterworth-Heinemann, Oxford.

Zwikael, O. (2009) Critical planning processes in construction projects. *Construction Innovation: Information, Process, Management*, **9(4)**, 372–387.

Building Information Modelling

Umit Isikdag, Jason Underwood and Murat Kuruoglu

Building Information Modelling (BIM) has become a key research area for addressing problems relating to the sharing of information and collaboration throughout the life cycle of a building. The importance of BIM stems from having an open interchange of information across platforms and a transferable record of building information throughout a life cycle of a building. BIM is a general term used for defining the information management process throughout the life cycle of a building, which mainly focuses on enabling and facilitating the integrated way of project flow and delivery, through the collaborative use of semantically rich 3D digital building models in all stages of the project and building life cycle. BIMs are semantically rich shared 3D digital building models that form the backbone of the BIM process.

The traditional nature of the Architecture Engineering and Construction (AEC) industry involves bringing together multi-disciplines/practitioners in a one-of-a-kind project, which requires a high amount of collaboration and coordination. The AEC industry is therefore an information intensive industry, the work practices of which are 'document-centric' with construction project information being captured predominately in documents, such as CAD drawings, specifications, blueprints and so on. Therefore, information is ostensibly distributed amongst the various multi-disciplinary teams involved in the project as disparate documents. This document-oriented nature of the industry combined with the lack of interoperability between applications has resulted in significant barriers to communication and collaboration between the stakeholders; which in turn, has significantly affected the efficiency and performance of the industry (Latham, 1994; Egan, 1998, 2002). The software applications used in the

Construction Innovation and Process Improvement, First Edition.
Edited by Akintola Akintoye, Jack S. Goulding and Girma Zawdie.
© 2012 Blackwell Publishing Ltd. Published 2012 by Blackwell Publishing Ltd.

AEC design processes have until the last 15 years been focused on automating 2D drawing board techniques, structural analysis and time/cost management activities, while model-based information management and interoperability was mostly disregarded. Gallaher *et al.* (2004) indicated that US$15.8 billion was lost annually in the USA Capital Facilities Industry due to the lack of interoperability. In order to tackle the problems related to information integration and interoperability, recent Research and Development (R&D) has focused on:

1. facilitating collaboration of teams over the Internet. for supporting virtual AEC enterprises;
2. developing tools for generating semantically rich 3D digital building models; and
3. utilising distributed platforms and databases for managing building information.

Having evolved from the term Building Product Modelling (i.e. the realisation of the Product Modelling paradigm for the AEC industry), BIM has now become a key research area in addressing the problems related to the sharing of information and collaboration in AEC industry. For example, Underwood and Isikdag (2010) noted that in the late 1990s BIM was prescribed as a remedy for overcoming the illness of 'Data Interoperability' between applications in the AEC industry. However, today it apparent that this 'magic remedy' has evolved to cure many more issues than it was originally prescribed for, where BIM is now promising to be the new facilitator of integration, interoperability and collaboration towards reshaping the traditional AEC industry. BIM is now also widely accepted as a new and promising information management process and strategy for integrating the processes and stakeholders of an AEC project. BIMs are intelligent digital building models that can either reflect the 'to-be' or 'as-is' situation of a project/building, and resides at the centre of the BIM strategy.

This chapter focuses on BIM as a process and strategy of information management based on using BIMs to store and manage building information in all stages of an AEC project (from conception to demolition/disassembly). Currently, the implementation of the BIM paradigm is achieved by enabling information exchange of several applications supporting BIMs by the use of agreed models (i.e. schema standards), such as Industry Foundation Class (IFC) and CIS/2. In this context, BIM can be realised in many different areas and on different levels, including facilitating the design phase of the project life cycle, and depending on the environment in which they are used, they can have different functions such as linking macro (outdoor) and micro urban spaces (i.e. buildings) to facilitate information sharing between software applications. They can also store building information throughout the life cycle of a building, including procurement related tasks in the building life cycle, whilst supporting the simulation of construction processes (i.e. in nD). In addition, BIM can help facilitate the integration of information systems, provide real-time and on-demand building information over the Internet, and enable advanced analysis, whilst supporting the design and construction of environment friendly/energy efficient buildings, including facilitating emergency response operations.

Recent research demonstrates many examples on the different uses and applications of BIMs for fulfilling a variety of requirements in the building life cycle. A few key examples are explained in Rebolj *et al.* (2010) and Spearpoint (2010), who identified how 4D to nD simulation applications can be facilitated using BIMs and countries such as Singapore have used BIM in earnest. BIM can also facilitate the design of energy-efficient buildings towards addressing sustainability and reduction in CO_2 emissions issues (Hua, 2010; Solis and Mutis, 2010). In fact, the use and functions of BIMs as intelligent digital models is not limited to these few areas – BIM is firmly developing as the solid information management strategy for the AEC industry. This chapter focuses on introducing BIM as an innovative approach to information management for AEC processes. It develops the different viewpoints on BIM, from sharing and exchange, through to implementation planning. Latter sections of this chapter present case studies on different BIM implementations/practices, in Turkey and UK, for discussion and reflection.

17.2   Background

BIM has emerged as an evolution from *de-facto* standards of drawing exchange formats, for example, Drawing Exchange Format (DXF) through to Building Product Models (BPM), which in the main are based on ISO 10303 technologies. Most of the BPMs adopted product-modelling concepts by being enablers of communication, exchange, sharing, interpretation and processing of information. In parallel with the wider recognition of IFC and CIS/2 models in the AEC industry, BPMs have more recently been referred to as BIMs, as most of the BPMs (including IFC and CIS/2) are defined using the ISO 10303 standard, which uses the term information modelling in its model definition language EXPRESS. The term BIM is highly recognised with distinguished efforts of valuable R&D groups in academia and industry, and with wide support of buildingSMART (formerly the International Alliance for Interoperability). Today, IFC and CIS/2 are the key schema standardisation efforts in the area of BIM, and IFC is the effort of IAI/buildingSMART whose goal is to specify a common language for technology to improve the communication, productivity, delivery time, cost and quality throughout the design, construction and maintenance life cycle of buildings. For example, in 2005, IFC became an ISO Publicly Available Specification (as ISO 16739). In addition, CIS/2 is a widely adopted open standard for the digital exchange and sharing of the engineering information relating to a structural steel framework.

17.2.1   Overview on Building Information Modelling

BIM has been defined as a new way of creating, sharing, exchanging and managing the information throughout the entire building life cycle (NBIMS, 2007). The NBIMS initiative categorised BIM in three ways:

1. a product (an intelligent digital representation of a building);
2. a collaborative process which covers business drivers, automated process capabilities and open information standards use for information sustainability and fidelity; and
3. a facility of well-understood information exchange, workflows and procedures, which teams use as a repeatable, verifiable, transparent and sustainable information-based environment used throughout the building life cycle.

The US General Services Administration BIM Guide (2006) indicated that the information in a BIM catalogues the physical and functional characteristics of the design, construction and operational status of the building. This information spans a number of disciplines and application types. BIM therefore integrates this information into one database in a consistent, structured and accessible way. The importance of BIMs stems from having an open interchange of information across platforms and a transferable record of building information throughout a building life cycle. Isikdag *et al.* (2007) identified the definitive characteristics of BIMs as being object-oriented, data rich/comprehensive, in 3D, spatially-related and rich in semantics. Cerovsek (2010) underlined five standpoints for BIM analysis, which can be interpreted as viewpoints to BIM. From these standpoints, BIM can be viewed as:

1. a Model
2. a Modelling Tool
3. Communicative Intent
4. Individual Project Work, or
5. Collaborative Project Work.

From this perspective, Cerovsek (2010) describes a 'BIM' as a digital representation of an actual building for project communication over the whole building-project life cycle. This includes the physical, tangible appearance of a building from a time standpoint, which can be represented by three model categories, 'as-it was', 'as-it-is' or 'as-to-be'. Furthermore, a 'Building Information Model Schema' can be defined as a non-linguistic data structure that describes abstractions of generalised properties of a collection of states of information about buildings to be used in project communication. Underwood and Isikdag (2010) defined BIM as the information management process throughout the life cycle of a building, from conception to demolition, which mainly focuses on enabling and facilitating the integrated way of project flow and delivery, through the collaborative use of semantically rich 3D digital building models in all stages of the project and building life cycle. The authors interpreted BIMs as the set of semantically rich shared 3D digital building models that form the backbone of the BIM process.

17.2.2   BIMs, Interoperability, Integration

In Information Systems, interoperability is the ability for two systems to understand one another and to use the functionality of one another. The word 'interoperable' indicates that one system can perform an operation of the other system as if it is the other system. The case of interoperability equates to loose system integration. As mentioned by Panetto and Molina (2008), integration goes beyond interoperability as it involves functional dependence. While interoperable systems can also function independently, an integrated system loses significant functionality if one of the systems is interrupted. Two integrated systems are inevitably interoperable, but two interoperable systems are not necessarily integrated. The literature review in the area of software integration highlights two main levels of integration/interoperability as Data/Information Level and Application/Service Level (Hohpe and Woolf, 2003; Linthicum, 2003; Erl, 2004; Imhoff, 2005; Ruggiero, 2005). Data/Information Level Interoperability refers to the situation where software can perform functions using the data produced by other software that is interoperable with the first one. In fact, if two systems are considered as integrated in the data level, then one must use the data produced by the other system to function properly. From the perspective of software integration and interoperability, BIMs can be categorised as standard data/information models, which act as enablers of Data Level Interoperability. In other words, software applications exchange BIMs or interact with a shared BIM residing in a database to perform operations over the building information that is generated, processed or stored by another application.

17.2.3   Sharing and Exchange of BIMs

From an ISO 10303 viewpoint, in the information exchange scenario one software system maintains the master copy of the data internally and exports a 'snapshot' of the data for others to use. In information sharing, there is a known master copy of the data, and Create/Read/Update/Delete (CRUD) operations can be performed over the data by multi-user interactions. A BIM schema represents the logical data structure (or data model) containing all entities, attributes and relationships in the model. The model is then created by software and stored in physical files or databases. It is therefore possible to exchange physical files representing the entire set of model classes or a model subset between different applications. BIMs can be stored in a shared database where CRUD operations can be performed by multiple applications. This type of shared data stores are referred to as Shared Databases or Building Information Model Servers (e.g. Express Data Manager, 2010). BIMs can be accessed over the web for querying and visualisation purposes, where applications automating web-based querying and visualisation of BIMs are known as Building Information Model Servers (BIMServer, 2010). The information stored in BIMs can be accessed by using web-services (web interfaces to data and applications). Two definitive characteristics of web services are Loose Coupling and Network Transparency (Pulier and Taylor, 2006). Web services are *loosely coupled*, that is, when a piece of software has been exposed as a web service, it is simple to move it to another computer as the service functions are independent of the client application that is using the service. On the other hand, as web services' consumers and providers send messages to each other using open Internet protocols, web services offer total *network transparency* (i.e. the location of the web service does not have an impact on its function). Stateless Web Services (i.e. Representational State Transfer – REST) are built upon resources (i.e. anything that is available digitally over the web), their names (identified by uniform indicators, i.e. URIs), representations (i.e. metadata/data on the current state of the resource) and links between the representations. In Stateless Web Services, each client request is treated as an independent transaction, and the service does not store information regarding the client that makes the request. From the perspective of BIMs, services can be used to query the models.

17.2.4   Implementation Planning

Implementation planning often has to be performed prior to any BIM implementation, the nuances of which involve the development of an implementation/execution plan in order to make full use of the exchange and sharing of building information based on the developed implementation/execution plan. A valuable information resource of this area is the *BIM Execution Planning Guide* (2010) developed by Pennsylvania State University. This guide can be viewed as a tool that provides process maps on accomplishing several design, analysis and construction processes for using BIMs. A BIM Project Execution Plan is therefore developed in the early stages of a project, and updated as additional participants are added to the project. It is also monitored, updated and revised (as needed) throughout the implementation phase of the project. The plan defines the scope of BIM implementation on the project, identifies the process flow for BIM tasks, defines the information exchanges between parties and describes the required project and company infrastructure needed to support the implementation. The guide provides a four-step procedure to develop a detailed BIM Execution Plan. These steps are:

1. identifying the appropriate BIM goals and use on the project;
2. designing the BIM execution process;
3. defining the BIM deliverables; and
4. identifying the supporting infrastructure needed to successfully implement the plan.

Each organisation or project can follow its own route of BIM implementation, as each individual AEC project tends to have its own unique characteristics. Thus, the BIM implementation effort can be seen as being distinct. However, in order to understand how BIMs can be implemented, it is useful to investigate previous real-life experiences. Following this, the implementation of BIM real-life case studies from two different countries, specifically Turkey and the UK, are presented for discussion.

17.3   A Case Study on the Implementation of BIM

Various case studies on the implementation of 4D modelling for visual representation of construction processes (with or without BIM) have been reported in literature (Collier and Fischer, 1995; Haymaker and Fischer, 2001; Kam and Fischer, 2002; Yerrapathruni, 2003; Heesom and Mahdjoubi, 2004; Gao et al., 2005; Faddoul et al., 2006; Gao and Fischer, 2008; Hsieh, 2009; Mahalingam et al., 2010). This case study explains the use of BIM in the process of visualisation (i.e. 4D modelling) for a real-life large-scale AEC project completed in Turkey. This case study used BIM to generate a 4D model of a football stadium. The Galatasaray Türk Telekom Stadium project is based in Istanbul (Turkey), the project of which consisted of a stadium, an indoor sports hall and shopping centres, and areas assigned for concerts, meetings and congress. The project encompassed a structure that included technical characteristics that were different from other stadiums in Turkey, in terms of architecture and technology. The groundwork of the construction commenced in December 2007. The stadium spans a horizontal axis of 190 m and a longitudinal axis of 228 m, with a ground area of approximately 43,000 m^2. Cast concrete and pre-cast concrete construction technology was used in the construction of the main parts of the structure. The stadium can accommodate 52,647 people and it was formally opened in January 2011. The work schedule for the stadium construction was prepared by the contractor's planning group using Primavera Project Planner (P3) software. When the work schedule was being prepared, the project was considered in six main phases covering the construction of six blocks of the stadium. Each construction block was named A, B, C, D, E and F, and each main phase (block) was divided into three sub-phases within itself (to simplify the scheduling process). The main purpose of this segmentation was to define an efficient production planning strategy by dividing the work schedule into phases and sub-phases. The BIM for this stadium was generated using BIM applications (i.e. AutoCAD and Revit) and transferred into Synchro 4D Modelling software. Synchro was then used to link the work schedule and 3D geometric representation of the building provided by the BIM (Figure 17.1).

In the object linking process, Synchro considers the building elements available in the BIM as material resources, which can be linked with the tasks in the work schedule. In the linking process, any incorrect resource assignment can be deleted from the resources based on the warnings issued by the software or by user perception. In every stage of the linking process, new tasks may be assigned to resources. Following the object linking procedure, the software prepares the visualisation and simulation of the construction process (i.e. the 4D model of the construction). In the 4D visualisation of the construction processes, the state of the construction can be observed for any given date and from various angles. Figure 17.2 presents four different states of the construction starting from early dates through to completion.

Figure 17.1 Linking work schedule with 3D geometric representation.

Figure 17.2 Synchro showing different phases of the project.

The strategic analysis conducted with the contractor organisation indicated that the IT knowledge level of users, their BIM related experience and technical support from software vendors could play a critical role in the successful implementation of BIMs for 4D visualisation. Problems encountered during the BIM-based 4D visualisation process have often been acknowledged as being related to the time spent on establishing the 4D model, along with reporting difficulties. This study revealed that BIM-based 4D visualisation was not well recognised in Turkey, due mainly to the lack of focus in Turkish AEC industry regarding BIM technologies and process visualisation of AEC projects. The next section explores how well BIM technologies were received and recognised in the UK AEC industry.

17.4   Building Information Modelling in the UK

BIMs can be seen as interoperability enablers. In this respect, the interoperability requirements of construction include the drawings, procurement details, environmental conditions, submittal processes and other specifications necessary for building quality. Proponents advocate that BIM can be utilised to bridge the information loss associated with handing a project from the design team, to the construction team and the building owner/operator, by allowing each group to add to and reference back to all information they acquire during their period of contribution to the BIM. This interoperable element is vital for a number of reasons. First, there is little evidence to indicate that any single tool can contain all the data relating to the entire building for its entire life. This was reinforced by Smith and Tardif (2009), who stated that:

- The entire building life cycle of business process and workflows is too complex to be modelled effectively in one system.
- Business processes vary too much across the industry.
- A single project model would involve too much change to existing information management infrastructure and business processes to support viable migration paths from existing workflows to new ones.
- The cost and technical challenges of such a system would be prohibitive.

Therefore, an open non-proprietary exchange method for data and processes is an essential element of any BIM system. Observations of all of the BIM definitions seem to lead to significant consistency, but all of these fall short of a clear, concise definition that could be placed before a client or chief executive. This has proved to be the biggest downfall in the UK market, as the industry has failed to recognise the importance of this. However, the BIM market is still gaining momentum.

17.4.1   The Evolutionary Adoption of BIM

The industry is now faced with a new economic situation that both threatens and offers real opportunities for exploitation. For example, it is important to observe how the industry has evolved to this point since moving from

Figure 17.3 BIM Evolutionary Ramp – construction perspective (adapted from Bew *et al.*, 2008). Reproduced by permission of Mark Bew & Marilyn Richards.

drawing boards in the 1970s and 1980s, towards facilitating industry-wide adoption, where the BIM vision can be seen in a strategic way. This can be observed as a pseudo-Darwinian evolution (Bew *et al.*, 2008; Bew and Underwood, 2010). The 'evolutionary ramp' model (Figure 17.3) recognises that all forms of asset data managed in a collaborative way form part of what could loosely be called a BIM, and in the context of the model outlined, this would indicate anything beyond Level 1.

An important theme in the development of any implementation and adoption strategy is the separation of the management of data and process (Figure 17.3). The BIM levels presented within the 'evolutionary ramp' have been identified to enable a simple identification for the level of BIM a business or project is using. Tangible savings have been identified at each level, as progress is made along the evolutionary ramp. The level definitions can be seen as:

- *Level 0:* Unmanaged CAD, probably 2D with paper as the most likely data exchange mechanism.
- *Level 1:* Managed CAD in either 2D or 3D format using BS1192:2007, with a collaboration tool providing a common data environment and possibly some standard data structures and formats. Commercial data is managed by standalone finance and cost management packages with no integration.
- *Level 2:* Managed 3D environment held in separate discipline 'BIM' tools with attached data. Commercial data is managed using Enterprise Resource Planning (ERP), while integration is based on proprietary interfaces or bespoke middleware that could be regarded as 'pBIM'. The approach may also utilise 4D program data and 5D cost elements.

Figure 17.4 BIM evolutionary ramp – commercial systems (adapted from Bew *et al.*, 2008). Reproduced by permission of Mark Bew & Marilyn Richards.

- *Level 3:* Fully open process and data integration enabled through IFC/ IFD. This is managed by a collaborative model server that could be regarded as iBIM or integrated BIM, potentially employing concurrent engineering processes.

Later stages where there are fully interoperable models will need new technologies to deliver the concept, possibly using Atomic or Federated BIM, to enable effective large data model sharing. This may need advanced Identity Lifecycle Management systems to control access and security. As can be seen from these definitions, 3D CAD data or model data alone is only a small part of the story, and tools that create data and enable processes to act on that data are the vital differentiator in the world of true BIM. Clearly, all of these tools have a similar evolution to create, save and transact processes over asset data. In this respect, leading players in ERP and environmental markets have been active in enabling their products with features to enable BIM-like operation. The model in Figure 17.4 shows the parallel route the 'commercial systems' (ERP) market is taking, developing more functionality that could support moving BIM into the core ERP toolset. This is also evident in the consolidation at the top end of the market, with large players such as Oracle acquiring businesses such as Symmetry and Primavera to give object viewing, planning/project control and life-cycle management capabilities.

While there are common characteristics in definitions with respect to the people, process and technology aspects, the wide variety of definitions that exist have emanated from the perspectives and vested interests of individual industry stakeholders. However, it is important to note that none of these definitions are from the practising UK industry itself. Consequently, this has significantly contributed to what appears to be a distinct lack of understanding and awareness of BIM across the UK industry, with BIM currently meaning different things to different stakeholders. The implications could potentially stall progress towards a significant uptake and critical mass of industry-wide adoption. Therefore, to drive industry-wide BIM adoption, there needs to be a concerted effort towards agreeing and establishing a universal, industry-wide definition, along with benefits statements to facilitate greater awareness and increased coherency across the sector. This also requires the different dimensions of People, Processes and Technology to be considered as part of the holistic solution.

17.4.2   Selected Cases on Evolutionary Ramp

BIM evolution can be seen as a journey of building data and process sets, which improve as the organisation progresses. The benefits that can be accrued at each evolutionary step can be seen through a number of case studies, towards incremental improvement, and it is anticipated that the step to stage three will yield even more significant returns. The examples described below have been selected as representative of each of the various stages of evolutionary development described by the 'ramp'. The case studies presented below have been selected to demonstrate the characteristics of how the various projects have approached key issues of technology, contracts, training, etc, to deliver significant improvements in performance over their traditionally run projects at different stages of BIM evolution.

17.4.2.1 Level 'o' BIM Adoption

In terms of BIM adoption and potential benefits, the focus is towards the top of the evolutionary ramp and level of BIM adoption, therefore no case studies at level 0 are presented. However, it worth reflecting on the figures quoted by the research into the US market by the National Institute of Standards and Technology (NIST) in 2004 in relation to the UK market. NIST conservatively estimated the cost of poor interoperability to be $15.8M, which represents around 2% of the industry's revenue. By extrapolating this to the UK market, which employs 2.1 million people in 250,000 companies, and is responsible for 8.2% of Gross Value Added, this demonstrates a proportionally larger number based on a more complex, bespoke market.

17.4.2.2 Level '1' BIM Adoption

The vast majority of businesses are currently focused on seriously attempting to move towards the Managed CAD Environment level of the model. Leading businesses such as Laing achieved good results in early production pilots during the early 1990s using these techniques, and the work they pioneered subsequently resulted in the development of BS1192:2007 and Avanti Processes. This section provides a case study to demonstrate a BIM implementation at BIM Level '1'.

17.4.2.3 Basingstoke Festival Place

The Festival Place Shopping Centre in Basingstoke was a £110 M redevelopment involving a complex jigsaw of rebuilding parts of the old shopping centre without disturbing any remaining shops in Festival Place. The project was a client-led design team project with the contractor (Laing) employed on a traditional JCT Design and Build contract. Laing decided to build a full 3D model from the design team's drawings/documentation. The project also made use of a bespoke in-house collaboration system for the model, including document and project information control; although no model-based data management was attempted. All errors and clashes were identified in the model using Navisworks software, from which RFIs (Request for Information) were raised in the project as a result. The RFI procedure is used to confirm the interpretation of a detail, specification or note on the construction drawings or to secure a documented directive or clarification from the architect or client that is needed to continue work. For example, an RFI raised by the general contractor that has been answered by the client or architect and distributed to all stakeholders is generally accepted as a change to the scope of work, unless further approval is required for costs associated with the change. It is therefore common and accepted practice for a subcontractor or supplier to use an RFI to state concerns related to the omission or misapplication of a product, in order to seek further clarification of the building owner's intended use or the building official acceptance of the specified product. It is also acceptable for the subcontractor to use an RFI to call attention to an inferior product that may not meet the building owner's needs, with discretion to recommend a better/more correct product (Blanker, 2011).

As the RFIs raised in this project were not fully dealt with, the budget increased by approximately 25%. Some of this growth was due to client changes, but some £10 M was attributed to design ambiguity, which represented 9% of the final construction cost, that could have been avoided. It was concluded that a more appropriate way would be for the design supply chain, rather than the contractor, to collaborate and develop the 3D models as part of the normal design development and data management activity. It was further opined that models, built as a secondary activity on projects where the design teams do not have the required skills, are also effective in reducing cost and risk. Therefore, it was acknowledged that investment in building the model was likely to be approximately 0.5–1.5% of the project cost, with a reduction of 50% of the normal package growth of 25%. equating to 10% of the final construction cost for material cost only.

17.4.2.4 BIM Level '2' BIM Adoption

Level '2' is the managed 3D environment, where commercial data is managed by ERP. This section introduces a case study on the BIM implementation at Level '2'.

17.4.2.5 Enfield Town Centre Project, London

One of the first projects to employ the standards supported by Avanti was a multi-use development in Enfield, North London, designed by Reid Architecture and funded by the client ING Real Estate. The £25 M scheme of largely retail/restaurant/health club users also included a civic facility incorporating council offices, a library and a public theatre. The main contractor, Costain, took the decision to adopt the Avanti Standards and operate in a shared model environment, that is, Costain's bespoke extranet iCosnet, while the collaborative model was built using active (.dwg) files. The team therefore exchanged and built live model files, the orientation, origin point and scaling of which were completely aligned, which avoided the necessity of swapping fragments of digital information. The process of restructuring the previously completed CAD work to achieve this alignment required considerable concentration and effort, but the benefits far outweighed the initial reticence. Subsequent coordination of the work of the subcontractors, all of whom were obliged to participate in using the system, was vastly simplified. Bourne Steel also used the model data, together with Revit software, as the basis for its own detailed modelling. The 3D expression of the shared model was facilitated, managed and updated by a third-party company employed by Costain. They assisted the team with the coordination activity, focusing on 3D clash detection along with also providing construction process simulations (4D), which were used by Costain to improve the efficiency of construction programming. The models were also used as the basis for photo-realistic renderings for marketing, which were built using 3D object tools including Autodesk Architectural Desktop, Tekla, Multisuite and BS Link, and brought together for coordination in Navisworks. Considerable cost savings were noted by adopting this BIM approach. In addition, appreciable benefits were experienced by the entire team associated to the clarity, simplicity and efficiency of use of the model for everyday processing of information, design creation and data exchange. For example, the team claimed that at least 20 weeks were saved in the time needed to prepare information for issue to others.

17.4.2.6 BIM Level '3'

Currently, there are no true end-to-end implementations of 'iBIM', as no commercial environments are available to implement the IFC data exchange, in addition to the Information Delivery Manual (IDM) process models still being developed. However, this does not mean that great things have not yet been achieved with the technology in the specific line of business, including the environmental market. Developments in this area are progressing rapidly and efforts are in place to bring this approach to market.

17.5   Innovation through BIM

The philosophy that lies behind BIM stems from four dimensions in relation to the management of building information, and these have been articulated and agreed by the industry over the last two decades. These dimensions can be summarised as enabling i) model-based management of ii) shared building information, which provides iii) meaningful data about a building/facility in a iv) standardised way. Four newly emerging dimensions in the management of building information towards transforming from BIM to BIM 2.0 focuses on enabling an i) integrated environment of ii) distributed information, which is always iii) up-to-date and open for iv) derivation of new information. In this respect, innovation through BIM can be investigated in two dimensions, specifically innovation through the implementation of BIM and innovation through the use of BIM together with newly emerging technologies, such as cloud computing, sensor network, web services, etc).

17.5.1   Innovation through the Implementation of BIM

Innovation through BIM can be achieved by:

1. increasing the organisational and industrial adoption rate of BIM;
2. focusing on BIM maturity;
3. moving towards lean and green construction;
4. benefiting more from process simulation and monitoring by use of BIMs; and
5. facilitating processes in urban management and disaster response fields, by bridging the gap between building and geoinformation.

17.5.1.1 Adoption

The implementation of product modelling approaches and BIMs has been the subject of research for nearly 30 years in the AEC industry. In fact, the low interest and investment in ICT and the lack of strategic perspective on the use and implementation of this have prevented the successful adoption of collaborative systems and interoperable information models within the industry. In addition, the move from CAD-based thinking to the vision of BIM is more difficult, as it involves a shift in fundamental data management philosophy. In a similar manner to the move from old accounting packages to ERP systems, this transformation includes the formal management of processes on a consistent, repeatable basis (Bew and Underwood, 2010). It also has to be acknowledged that implementation can often be difficult to achieve, and the lack of mature process management tools and methodologies for projects have made this transition more confusing. In addition, the industry's approach to contracts, training and education will need greater attention if it is to deliver this operating model and approach. In this respect, as BIM adoption is most likely to occur in phases, considerable effort will need to take place in order to move from one phase into another. For example, in the evolutionary approach to implementing BIM, organisations must be realistic about their current capability and maturity to undertake this evolution. Industry-wide adoption should therefore consider the bigger picture when contemplating BIM adoption. The focus of studies on industry-wide adoption is towards the positioning of BIM adoption across disciplines in relation to their status and future expectations, based on such factors as tools, people and processes, and Gerrard *et al.* (2010) provides a bird's eye view of this. In addition, efforts to measure the extent to which BIM has been implemented nationwide provides an indication of the industrial uptake of BIM, which can be used to position the BIM maturity of organisations in the context of national BIM adoption levels. This positioning is important, as the adoption levels are affected by the environment and the incumbent barriers facing organisations (Underwood and Isikdag, 2010).

17.5.1.2 Maturity

A key area in successful BIM adoption is developing the necessary capabilities and core competence concerning organisational readiness, as this can play a significant role in the absorption and diffusion of ICT within enterprises. The level of absorption and diffusion can also affect the rate of success in ICT implementation and subsequent uptake. If BIM is considered as a set of new technology and methodologies supporting information management in the AEC industry, then maturity in terms of implementing and using BIM (technology and methodologies) is critical to the success of a BIM implementation. Frameworks for measuring BIM maturity can greatly facilitate organisations in positioning themselves against their competitors in terms of technological, methodological and process maturity. Such a maturity framework is explained in Succar (2010), where a five-level BIM-specific maturity index is developed to measure the BIM maturity of organisations.

17.5.1.3 Lean and Green

In recent years, the AEC industry has begun to adopt lean production principles that have been successfully applied in manufacturing – the approach of which is known as Lean Construction. The aim of Lean Construction is to enable continuous improvement of all construction processes in the building life cycle, starting from design through the demolition of the building (Solis and Muits, 2010). Process improvement is carried out to maximise 'value' in construction (i.e. building production) and minimise the cost of production. On the other hand, the industry is also embracing initiatives to build more 'environment-friendly' buildings, along with reducing its own carbon footprint to address global concerns on environmental issues. The use of shared building models, together with collaborative environments (i.e. BIM methods), can contribute to leaner and greener construction. For example, this would minimise the need for travelling to project meetings, and the intelligent BIMs for design optimisation (i.e. in CO_2 emission analysis, etc) could play an important role in the design and operation of environmentally friendly buildings. Finally, in terms of leaner construction, the Integrated Project Delivery (IPD) approach (a US perspective on the future of project life-cycle management and project delivery) covers a lot of process changes/improvements and information management over shared digital models, which in turn could help in the process changes required by IPD (IPD, 2007).

17.5.1.4 Process Simulation and Monitoring

Construction process simulation has been facilitated through visualisation for over 10 years. This approach involves the visual simulation of construction processes is known as 4D CAD/4D Modelling. The efforts in this area are making more use of 3D CAD models, and in recent years, BIMs have superseded 3D CAD models in the visual simulation of construction processes. In this respect, analysis such as clash detection, can now be completed using BIM software. BIMs are also used in monitoring the construction progress, where activity progress can be monitored directly using a combination of data collection methods based on the BIM, especially on the 4D model of the building (Rebolj et al., 2010).

17.5.1.5 Building and Geo-information Integration

There is significant value in integrating BIMs and GeoInformation Systems into a single system (Peters, 2010). The differences between CAD applications and GeoInformation Systems have generated barriers of integration of different representations of buildings in AEC and urban models. For example, the need to integrate geometric models and harmonise semantics between the two domains could tackle interoperability issues (Van Oosterom et al., 2006; Isikdag and Zlatanova, 2008). In addition, Song et al. (2010) reviewed the benefits of integrating BIM with urban-scale contextual data, and indicated that a range of stakeholders such as building contractors, estate agents, city management and the public sector, etc could benefit from the integration of BIMs and (3D) GIS. Wang and Hamilton (2010) also provided information on the design and development of an integration framework for BIM and geospatial information using the Building Feature Service (BFS) – a service defined to retrieve building information similar to OGC web services, used for retrieving geospatial information. Support for semantic queries in BIMs can also enable users to extract partial spatial models from a full building model (Borrmann and Rank, 2010). Connectivity relationships in BIMs also have significant importance in terms of correct mathematical representation of the building (Paul, 2010). If these relations are structured correctly, the transformation of geometric information between BIMs to GeoInformation models can easily be validated.

17.5.1.6 Emergency Response

Emergency response operations indoors require a high amount of geometric, semantic and state information related to the building elements. Until recently, Egress Models used in building evacuation have mainly been based on 2D floor plans. This situation is now about to change, as the required level and amount of information can now be transferred from BIMs. In addition, BIMs are now used in fire simulations. For example, Spearpoint (2010) identified how the IFC building information model could be used to transfer building geometry and property data to fire simulation models, and suggests improvements to the IFC model with respect to the needs of fire engineering.

17.5.2   Innovation through BIM and Emerging Technologies

Innovation through BIM can be achieved through several newly emerging technologies, namely: i) Web Services, ii) Cloud Computing and iii) Sensor Networks.

17.5.2.1 Web Services

A current trend in the software industry is towards enabling interoperability over web services. In fact, the AEC industry has yet to benefit from the service-oriented approaches as the focus is still data integration-oriented. As indicated in the recent Construction Informatics roadmaps (ROADCON, 2003; Strat-CON, 2007), BIM-based web services are likely to be the catalysts of information integration and interoperability in the near future. The use of BIM servers is now increasing with open-source implementations such as BIMServer (BIMServer, 2010). London *et al.* (2010) explained a framework developed to facilitate multi-disciplinary collaborative BIM adoption through the informed selection of a project specific BIM approach and model servers. The framework consisted of four interrelated key elements, including a strategic purpose and scoping matrix, work process mapping, technical requirements for BIM tools and model servers, and a framework implementation guide. The authors concluded that the future BIM approaches would require shared models in model servers to be linked with external systems in a heterogeneous environment.

17.5.2.2 Cloud Computing

The term 'cloud computing' involves the use of the Internet (i.e. the cloud) for managing highly scalable and customisable virtual hardware and software resources, which are provided as services. Cloud computing can be disaggregated into three segments, specifically 'Software as a Service (SaaS)', 'Platform as a Service (PaaS)' and 'Infrastructure as a Service (IaaS)'. Cloud computing also involves the virtualisation of storage environments to form a virtual data centre, available over the Internet. The AEC industry will benefit from cloud computing, mostly by making use of the SaaS approach and data centre virtualisation. Applications used in various stages of the building's life cycle can work within a distributed environment (i.e. offered as software services), where the information backbone of the construction project or building (i.e. the BIMs) would reside in a virtual data centre (and offered as a data service).

17.5.2.3 Sensor Networks

Recent developments in the field of BIM have shown that they can be successful in presenting semantic information about building elements along with their geometric representation. In essence, by querying a BIM, one can understand that a rectangular prism visualised in CAD is not just a simple rectangular box, but a column made up of concrete, residing in the second floor of a residential building; specifically, the information contained in a BIM is meaningful. Although information within BIMs can be meaningful, this becomes 'stateless' after the construction of the building is completed. In this situation, up-to-date building information should be provided by sensors, or by a network of sensors, which monitor the building. In the context of BIM, distributed sensors and Wireless Sensor Networks are increasingly likely to be used to monitor conditions such as temperature, gas levels, pollutants, humidity, state of doors and windows (e.g. being open/closed and so on), room occupancy, etc. The information provided by the sensors, when integrated with the building information infrastructures, therefore would become valuable for transforming building information into meaningful full-state information.

17.6   Conclusion

Since the advent of the personal computer, the last 40 years has witnessed an 'information/digital' revolution. This is comparable with that of the industrial revolution, which has shaped our world and becoming embedded in our culture at a personal, business and global level. This has facilitated considerable change and improvements to the AEC industry. For example, the historic approach to document management and lack of interoperability between software applications created significant barriers to communication and collaboration between the various stakeholders, which in turn adversely affected efficiency and performance. BIM is a key area that could offer important opportunities to revolutionise the sector by enabling seamless processes that support the complete life cycle of the facility. BIM is an emerging information management strategy that could also resolve problems relating to information sharing and collaboration, from enabling and facilitating integrated project flow and delivery, through the collaborative use of semantically rich 3D digital building models in all stages of the project and building life cycle. BIM is currently being employed across the globe on a variety of projects, from housing through to high prestige projects, and clients are increasingly aware of the potential of BIM to deliver real value beyond the conventional design and construction phases.

The BIM momentum is now changing the AEC industry in a way that is likely to cause a paradigm shift in the overall construction process towards intelligent construction and intelligent buildings. However, this paradigm shift in the overall construction process can only be achieved by a combination of:

1. more efficient information management;
2. further automation of processes;
3. better collaboration between stakeholders; and
4. enabling leaner and greener construction for producing eco-sensible buildings.

The requirement for consistency and accuracy can be realised using BIM strategy, which makes it *sine-qua-non* for enabling the paradigm shift towards intelligent construction and intelligent and eco-sensible buildings. BIM strategy is therefore likely to play a key role in enabling efficient team working, better collaboration and better coordination (especially in complicated projects), along with adding value by automating most of the information management processes. The next paradigm shift is likely to occur when offsite and rapid manufacturing become more common, and production processes become leaner and more value-oriented. In this respect, as offsite manufacturing and design processes become leaner and value-oriented (with the support of BIM), this will provide inertia to move the industry and associated industries from design-produce/build, to produce-design-assemble types of construction.

References

Bew, M. & Underwood, J. (2010) Delivering BIM to the UK Market. In: ed. Underwood, J. & and Isikdag, U., *Handbook of Research on Building Information Modelling and Construction Informatics: Concepts and Technologies*. IGI Global.

Bew, M., Underwood. J., Wix, J. & Storer, G. (2008) *Going BIM in a Commercial World*. 7th European Conference on Product and Process Modelling (ECPPM),. Sophia Antipolis, France, 10–12 September.

BIM Execution Planning Guide (2010) *BIM Project Execution Planning Guide*. Available from http://www.engr.psu.edu/bim/download/ (accessed 11 Jan 2011).

BIM Server (2010) *Open Source BIM Server*. Available from http://www.bimserver.org (accessed 5 January 2010).

Blanker (2011) *Definition of RFI*. Available from http://blanker.org/request-information

Borrmann, A. & Rank, E. (2010) Query support for BIMs using semantic and spatial conditions. In: Underwood, J. & Isikdag, U., *Handbook of Research on Building Information Modelling and Construction Informatics: Concepts and Technologies*. IGI Global.

Cerovsek, T. (2010) A review and outlook for a 'Building Information Model' (BIM): A multi-standpoint framework for technological development. *Automation in Construction*, article in press doi:10.1016/j.aei.2010.06.003

Collier, E. & Fischer, M. (1995) *Four-dimension Modelling in Design and Construction*. CIFE Technical Report No. 101, CIFE Stanford University, CA.

Egan, J. (1998) *Rethinking Construction*. Department of Environment, Transport and Regions (DETR), UK.

Egan, J. (2002) *Accelerating Change: a report by the Strategic Forum for Construction* (Chaired by Sir John Egan). Strategic Forum for Construction, London.

Erl, T. (2004) *Service-Oriented Architecture: A Field Guide to Integrating XML and Web Services*. Prentice Hall, London.

Express Data Manager (2010) *Object Database Server*. Available from http://www.jotne.com/products.41332.en.html

Faddoul, M., Messner, J., Hagan, S. & Morrell, J. (2006) *Revolutionary Scheduling: The Practical Application of 4D Technology from a CM Perspective*. CMAA 2006 Spring Leadership Forum, Philadelphia.

Gallaher, M.P., O'Connor, A.C., Dettbarn, J.L. & Gilday, L.T. (2004) *Cost Analysis of Inadequate Interoperability in the US Capital Facilities Industry*. NIST Publication GCR 04-867. Available from http://www.bfrl.nist.gov/oae/publications/ gcrs/04867.pdf)

Gao, J. & Fischer, M. (2008) *Framework & Case Studies Comparing Implementations & Impacts of 3D/4D Modelling Across Projects*. CIFE Technical Report #TR172. Stanford University, Stanford.

Gao, J., Fischer, M., Tollefsen, T. & Haugen, T. (2005) *Experiences with 3D and 4D CAD on Building Construction Projects: Benefits for Project Success and Controllable Implementation Factors*. Available from http://itc.scix.net/data/works/att/w78-2005-D3-1-Gao.pdf (accessed 5 September 2010).

Gerrard, A., Zuo, J. Zillante, G. & Skitmore, M. (2010) Building Information modelling in the Australian architecture engineering and AEC industry. In: ed. Underwood, J. And Isikdag, U., *Handbook of Research on Building Information Modelling and Construction Informatics: Concepts and Technologies*. IGI Global.

Panetto, H. & Molina, A. (2008) Enterprise integration and interoperability in manufacturing systems: Trends and issues. *Computers in Industry*, 59(7), 641–646.

Haymaker, J. & Fischer, M. (2001) *Challenges and Benefits of 4D Modelling on the Walt Disney Concert Hall Project*. CIFE Working Paper No. 64. CIFE, Stanford, CA.

Heesom, D. & Mahdjoubi, L. (2004) Trends of 4D CAD applications for construction planning. *Construction Management and Economics*, 22, 171–182.

Hophe, G. & Woolf, B. (2003) *Enterprise Integration Patterns: Designing, Building, and Deploying Messaging Solutions*. Addison Wesley, Reading, MA.

Hsieh, C. (2009) Four-Dimensional Computer-Aided Drafting – Current Status and Potential Business Applications. In: ed. Rao, M., *Proceedings of University of*

Southern Mississippi, Decision Science Institute Conference 2009, 344–351. Available from http://www.swdsi.org/swdsi2009/Papers/9K03.pdf

Hua, G.B. (2010) A BIM based application to support Cost Feasible 'Green Building' concept decision. In: ed. Underwood, J. & Isikdag, U., *Handbook of Research on Building Information Modelling and Construction Informatics: Concepts and Technologies.* IGI Global.

Imhoff, C. (2005) Understanding the Three E's of Integration EAI, EII and ETL. *DM Review Magazine* 1023893-1.

IPD Working Definition (2007) *A Working Definition: Integrated Project Delivery.* Available from http://www.ipd-ca.net/images/Integrated Project Delivery Definition. pdf (accessed 5 January 2010).

Isikdag, U. and Zlatanova, S. (2008) Towards defining a framework for automatic generation of buildings in CityGML using building information models. In: ed. Lee, J. & Zlatanova, S., *3D Geo-Information Sciences.* Springer LNG&C, Berlin.

Isikdag, U., Aouad, G., Underwood, J. & Wu, S. (2007) Building Information Models: A review on storage and exchange mechanisms. In: ed. Rebolj, D., *Proceedings of 24th W78 Conference :Bringing ITC Knowledge to Work.* Maribor, 135–144.

Kam, C. & Fischer, M. (2002) PM4D final report. *CIFE Technical Report No. 143.* CIFE, Stanford, CA.

Latham, M. (1994) *Constructing the Team. Joint Review of the Procurement and Contractual Arrangements in the UK Construction Industry, Final Report.* HMSO, London.

Linthicum, D.S. (2003) *Next Generation Application Integration: From Simple Information to Web Services.* Addison Wesley, Reading, MA.

London, K., Singh, V., Gu, N., Taylor, C. & Brankovic, L. (2010) Towards the development of a project decision support framework for adoption of an integrated building information model using a model server. In: ed. Underwood, J. & Isikdag, U., *Handbook of Research on Building Information Modelling and Construction Informatics: Concepts and Technologies.* IGI Global.

Mahalingam, A., Kashyap, R. & Mahajan, C. (2010) An evaluation of the applicability of 4D CAD on construction projects. *Automation in Construction,* **19**(2), 148–159.

NBIMS (2007) *National Building Information Modelling Standard Part-1: Overview, Principles and Methodologies.* US National Institute of Building Sciences Facilities Information Council, BIM Committee. Available from www.wbdg.org/pdfs/ NBIMSv1_p1.pdf

Paul, N. (2010) Basic topological notions and their relation to BIM. In: ed. Underwood, J. & Isikdag, U., *Handbook of Research on Building Information Modelling and Construction Informatics: Concepts and Technologies.* IGI Global.

Peters, E. (2010) BIM and geospatial information systems. In: Underwood, J. & Isikdag, U., *Handbook of Research on Building Information Modelling and Construction Informatics: Concepts and Technologies.* IGI Global.

Pulier, E., Taylor,H. (2006) Understanding Enterprise SOA, Manning Publications, Greenwich, USA.

Rebolj, D., Babic, N.C. & PodBreznik, P. (2010) Automated building process monitoring. In: ed. Underwood, J. & Isikdag, U., *Handbook of Research on Building Information Modelling and Construction Informatics: Concepts and Technologies.* IGI Global.

ROADCON (2003*) ROADCON Final Report.* Available from http://cic.vtt.fi/projects/roadcon/docs /roadcon_finalreport.pdf (accessed: 22 September 2007).

Ruggiero, R. (2005). Integration Theory, Part 1. Infomanagement Direct, Online at http://www.information-management.com/infodirect/20050812/1034584-1. html?pg=1 (accessed November, 2011)

Smith, D. & Tardif, M. (2009) *Building Information Modelling: A Strategic Implementation Guide*. John Wiley & Sons, Inc, New York.

Solis, J.L.F. & Mutis, I. (2010) The idealization of an integrated BIM, lean, and green model (BLG). In: ed. Underwood, J. & Isikdag, U., *Handbook of Research on Building Information Modelling and Construction Informatics: Concepts and Technologies*. IGI Global.

Song, Y., Boghdan, J., Hamilton, A. & Wang, H. (2010) Integrating BIM with urban spatial applications: A VEPS perspective. In: ed. Underwood, J. & Isikdag, U., *Handbook of Research on Building Information Modelling and Construction Informatics: Concepts and Technologies*. IGI Global.

Spearpoint, M. (2010) Extracting fire engineering simulation data from the IFC. In: ed. Underwood, J. & Isikdag, U., *Handbook of Research on Building Information Modelling and Construction Informatics: Concepts and Technologies*. IGI Global.

Strat-CON (2007) *Strat-CON Final Report*. Available from http://cic.vtt.fi/projects/stratcon/stratcon_ final_report.pdf (accessed 16 March 2008).

Succar, B. (2010) Building information modelling maturity matrix. In: ed. Underwood, J. & Isikdag, U., *Handbook of Research on Building Information Modelling and Construction Informatics: Concepts and Technologies*. IGI Global.

Underwood, J. & Isikdag, U. (2010) *Handbook of Research on Building Information Modelling and Construction Informatics: Concepts and Technologies*. IGI Global.

US General Services Administration BIM Guide (2006) *GSA BIM Guide Series 01 3D-4D-BIM Overview*. Available from http://www.gsa.gov/bim

Van Oosterom, P., Stotter, van, J. & Janssen, E. (2006) Bridging the worlds of CAD and GIS. In: ed. Zlatanova, S. & Prosperi, U, *Large-scale 3D data integration – Challenges and Opportunities*. Taylor & Francis, Abingdon, UK. 9–36.

Wang, H. & Hamilton, A. (2010) BIM integration with geospatial information within the urban built environment. In: ed. Underwood, J. & Isikdag, U., *Handbook of Research on Building Information Modelling and Construction Informatics: Concepts and Technologies*. IGI Global.

Yerrapathruni, S. (2003) *Using 4 D CAD and Immersive Virtual Environments to Improve Construction Planning*. Pennsylvania State University.

Industry Preparedness: Advanced Learning Paradigms for Exploitation

Jack S. Goulding and Farzad Pour Rahimian

The European Union (EU) Architecture, Engineering and Construction (AEC) sector is one of the largest industrial employers, encompassing more than 2 million enterprises and approximately 12 million employees. This represents 9.8% of the EU's Gross Domestic Product (GDP) as it employs over 7.1% of the workforce (Business Watch, 2005). However, well-documented problems relating ostensibly to failures in communication and information processing still exist (Latham, 1994; Egan, 1998). These failures have contributed to an increased proliferation of adversarial relationships between the different parties involved in a project (Forcade et al., 2007), which has also affected the veracity of design information (Fruchter, 1998; Cera et al., 2002) within the project life cycle. In essence, the nature and complexity of communication within AEC projects has changed significantly over the last ten years, especially with advances in technology and the increased prevalence of web-based project collaboration technologies and project extranets. Within the AEC sector, Information and Communications Technology (ICT) has revolutionised production and design (Cera et al., 2002), which has led to dramatic changes in terms of labour and skills (Fruchter, 1998). However, it is also important to acknowledge that the capabilities of such applications (and implementation thereof) can be used to predict the cost and performance of optimal design proposals (Petric et al., 2002) or mitigate/reduce risks prior to construction (Goulding, 2007). Consequently, the success of AEC projects is highly dependent upon the type, level and quality of the innovative communication exchange between various disciplines involved in the design and implementation phases.

Construction Innovation and Process Improvement, First Edition.
Edited by Akintola Akintoye, Jack S. Goulding and Girma Zawdie.
© 2012 Blackwell Publishing Ltd. Published 2012 by Blackwell Publishing Ltd.

Acknowledging these issues, project teams are also continuing to face real and signification problems and challenges regarding heterogeneous project extranet systems (Alshawi and Ingirige, 2003; Ibrahim and Pour Rahimian, 2010). The problem here is that the industry is experiencing confusion as to how to manage project information in order to meaningfully support the decision-making processes. This is the point where Fruchter (2004) suggested the need for digital integration (creation, retrieval and management) in order to prevent tacit knowledge loss and miscommunication amongst various parties from different disciplines. In this respect, recent innovation in Virtual Reality (VR) technologies and AEC decision-support tools have matured sufficiently to enable tele-presence engagement to occur in collaborative environments. In this respect, several opportunities are now available, including improved immersive interactivity with haptic support that can enhance users' engagement and interaction (Rahimian and Ibrahim, 2011). These advanced interfaces are also expected to leverage new training systems within the AEC sector (Fruchter, 1998), to address the shortcomings of 'typical' learning models that often provide trainees with only general instructions (Laird, 2003), which is especially important when considering the different approaches available (Clarke and Wall, 1998). This is even more apparent with VR, as learning environments are now able to provide enhanced interactivity that incorporate innovative experiential learning approaches (Alshawi et al., 2007, Goulding et al., 2012).

This chapter extends the findings of previous studies in this area, with specific emphasis on learning and learning styles. Moreover, it explains how learning support tools can be used to assist the decision-making process in construction, the potential of applying Game Theory in training environments to non-collocated design teams, approaches for mitigating the problem of 'compartmentation' of knowledge (Mole, 2003) and new ways for enhancing actor engagement. A VR interactive learning environment prototype, based on offsite production (OSP) and Open Building Manufacturing (OBM), is presented for discussion within the AEC sector.

18.2   Learning and Training Developments and Opportunities

The AEC sector has witnessed unprecedented levels of technological change over the last 20 years. This has enabled decision makers to fundamentally re-think and reflect on the ways that they have historically done business in the past, especially in light of the new challenges and opportunities ahead. Examples of this can been seen through the increased use, proliferation and maturity of ICT, in such areas as Enterprise Resource Planning, Building Information Modelling (BIM) and Computer Integrated Construction. These developments are now enabling organisations to capture, store and reuse knowledge from organisational settings in a structured, strategic and more coherent way. Moreover, e-readiness initiatives are now starting to become a focal point for discussion (Lou and Goulding, 2010), along with the enhanced effectiveness of ICT, especially across multidisciplinary collaborative teams (Lam et al., 2010). However, whilst it is acknowledged that ICT has revolutionised and transformed business operations within the sector, it is increasingly important to acknowledge that there is also a need to engage appropriately trained and skill personnel to leverage these developments, through new business models. This requires the appropriation of 'appropriate' training and education programmes that are designed specifically to meet these needs. In this respect, the way in which training and education is delivered, managed and assessed has also changed significantly over the last 20 years. For example, pedagogical solutions can now be matched to learning outcomes, and the delivery of online learning has matured to such an extent that interoperability, scalability, adaptability and mass-customisation are now becoming mainstream solutions. However, whilst advocates of virtual learning environments, and advanced learning management systems often extol the virtues of e-learning *per se*, they often fail to articulate the limitations of such systems, especially concerning the 'personalisation' of the learning process and incompatibility with current pedagogic needs (Alshawi *et al.*, 2006). Learning therefore needs to be carefully managed in order to maximise the effectiveness of Organisational Learning (Argyris and Schon, 1978; Senge, 1990; Huber, 1991), and through the development of organisational intellectual capital (Nonaka and Takeuchi, 1995; Edvinsson and Malone, 1997; Sullivan, 1999; Ward and Daniel, 2005).

18.2.1 Learning Pedagogy

Current e-learning literature encompasses several pedagogical theories, from Constructivism, through to Systems theory and Behaviourism. These are ostensibly based on the underlying principles of pedagogical and andragogical learning (Knowles, 1980), where andragogy relates to *'man'* and pedagogy relates to *'child'* (Davenport, 1993). This also includes experiential issues (Kolb, 1984) through to reflection and learning (Jarvis *et al.*, 2003). Each of these theories have their relative strengths and weaknesses, for example, Bloom's Taxonomy identified classification levels of intellectual behaviour associated in the learning process (Bloom, 1956), whereas Piaget (1952) identified four stages of logical and conceptual learning growth and Gagne (1965) determined the 'Conditions of Learning'. It is therefore important to appreciate the subtle nuances of these, especially the context through which these are to be applied, and the learner profiles involved.

From an e-learning perspective, Conole *et al.* (2004) noted that there was little evidence to link new learning models to pedagogical effectiveness, especially regarding mapping pedagogical approaches to specific characteristics of learning. However, emergent technological developments and innovation approaches are now creating new opportunities through increased understanding on learning styles and learner preferences (Weber and Brusilovsky, 2001; Dimitrova, 2003). Similarly, the effectiveness of virtual learning is a promising avenue that is still unfolding (Stonebraker and Hazeltine, 2004; Davis and Wong, 2007) and meta-cognitive techniques are now starting to facilitate individual preferences concerning inquiry learning and reflective thinking (Wen *et al.*, 2004). These developments are likely to present instructors with powerful knowledge-based learning environments that can be tailored to suit individual learner needs (to blend learning content with learner styles).

18.2.2   Learning Styles and Models

Technology-enhanced learning is often associated with improving the efficiency and cost-effectiveness of learning practice in order to meet learners' needs (Wang and Hannafin, 2005; Bouzeghoub *et al.*, 2006). This is area is still evolving, especially in e-Learning (Sampson *et al.*, 2002; Clark and Meyer, 2011), with several definitions and terminologies being offered (often interchangeably), which adds to this confusion (Syed-Khuzzan *et al.*, 2008). However, from a learning styles perspective, much of what is described can more easily be explained in terms of informative and behaviourist approaches to learning (Conole *et al.*, 2004), underpinned by pedagogical techniques aligned to domain-specific knowledge (Govindasamy, 2002). Pedagogical principles can be seen as backbone theories that govern content and delivery approaches. It is therefore important to acknowledge the role of technology as a key enabler of existing and new pedagogical concepts (Pahl, 2003).

Given these issues, there are a variety of different models that can characterise learning styles (Coffield *et al.*, 2004; Karagiannidis and Sampson, 2004). Whilst some of these have attracted conceptual and empirical problems (De Bello, 1990; Pashler *et al.*, 2008), the philosophical foundations of these are still considered to enhance learning, particularly when the instructional process accommodates the various learning styles of learners (Kim and Chris, 2001). However, it also has to be acknowledged that learners often come from a variety of different backgrounds (especially in the AEC sector), which by default has a wide variety stakeholders, with differing profiles, learning styles, preferences, etc. Thus, when considering the type and level of skill sets needed, it is particularly useful to try and accommodate learners' learning experiences, in order to make learning as personalised as possible (Vincent and Ross, 2001). This is especially important, as the adoption of a 'one-size-fits-all' approach to learning has generally been considered as being ineffective (Watson and Hardaker, 2005). Cognisant of this, 'There needs to be a deliberate and documented choice of model, which reflects a broad awareness of the field and which will allow for results and outcomes to be dealt with within a clear a clear conceptual framework' (Cassidy, 2004).

18.2.3   Learning through Game Theory

Game theory was first introduced as an alternative solution to conventional approaches to learning. Turocy *et al.* (2003) defined Game theory as a method of studying 'conflict and cooperation' of multiple participants, especially where their actions are co-dependent. Turocy *et al.* (2003) proposed this theory as a common protocol for formulating, structuring, analysing and understanding strategic scenarios. Based on this protocol, a game was described as a 'formal strategic situation' encompassing interactions of various agents. More intrinsically, Nisan *et al.* (2007) identified that Game theory could be used to model complex situations with multiple parties and outcomes using algorithms. However, Goulding *et al.* (2007) noted that educational training tools needed to 'engage' learners by putting them in the role of decision makers in order to 'push' them through challenges, hence enable different ways of learning and thinking through frequent interaction and feedback (to engender and create real-world context). Similarly, Wellings and Levine (2010) suggested redesigning existing text-based lessons into problem-based learning processes, noting that this was possible using immersive visualisation and simulation environments, which embedded games and interactive interfaces (to increase engagement), and Thai *et al.* (2009) asserted that educational digital games offered opportunities to empower trainees' engagement, to help transform teaching and learning into a new stage. However, within the milieu of game-based learning environments, it is equally important to acknowledge the formal transference of learning and the context of this learning (Gross, 2007). There is also a need to distinguish between playing and learning – especially a need '...to appreciate how content, skills and attitudes are not just transferable, and neither merely a question of interaction between player and computer game' (Egenfeldt-Nielsen, 2007).

18.3   Virtual Reality Systems

Virtual Reality (VR) has been defined as a 3D computer-generated alternative environment, which facilitates high degrees of immersion, navigation and interaction (Briggs, 1996; Yoh, 2001; Pour Rahimian *et al.*, 2008), or a component of communication that takes place in a 'synthetic' space (Regenbrecht and Donath, 1996, Sampaio *et al.*, 2010). The various components of VR systems usually include a computer capable of real-time animation, controlled by a set of wired gloves and a position tracker, along with a head-mounted stereoscopic display as visual output. For instance, Regenbrecht and Donath (1996) defined the tangible components of VR as a congruent set of hardware and software, with actors engaged in a 3D or multi-dimensional input/output space; where the actors interact with autonomous objects in real time.

18.3.1   Virtual Reality in Architecture, Engineering and Construction

Over the last 30 years, ICT systems have matured sufficiently to enable construction organisations to fundamentally restructure and enhance their core business functions. Sampaio and Henriques (2008) asserted that the main objective of using ICT in the construction field was to support the management of digital data; specifically to convert, store, protect, process, transmit and securely retrieve datasets. They acknowledged VR as an important stepping stone for data integration in construction design and management, as this was seen as being able to present holistic information about buildings (e.g. size, material, spatial relationships, mechanical and electrical utilities, etc) through one single conduit. Similarly, Zheng *et al.* (2006) proposed the use of VR to reduce time and costs in product development, and also to enhance the quality and flexibility of providing continuous support during the development life cycle. In this respect, early studies incorporating VR into the design stage used this predominantly as an advanced visualisation medium. However, since as early as 1990, VR has been widely used in the AEC industry for creating 3D design visualisation models that can be manipulated in real time and used to explore different stages of the construction process (Whyte *et al.*, 1998), especially for improving construction processes in collaborative environments (Bouchlaghem *et al.*, 2005). However, the expectations of VR have changed significantly over the last decade. For example, Sampaio and Henriques (2008) noted that it was increasingly important to incorporate VR 3D visualisation and decision support systems with interactive interfaces, in order to perform real-time interactive visual exploration tasks. This resonates with thinking that supports the increased use of collaborative virtual environments in which 3D models are linked to databases, which carry enhanced characteristics and metadata (knowledge on data). For example, construction planning and management can now link to 3D models along with time parameters (known as 4D), in order to design 4D models (Fischer and Kunz, 2004), which are controlled through interactive and multi-access databases. VR models can therefore be used to improve many aspects and phases of construction projects by:

1. providing better communication amongst partners (Leinonen *et al.*, 2003);
2. enhancing design creativity (Rahimian and Ibrahim, 2011);
3. improving coordination (Khanzade *et al.*, 2007);
4. aligning directly with construction processes (Fischer, 2000); and
5. integrating with BIMs to enhance data integration (Xie *et al.*, 2011).

18.3.2   Virtual Reality as a Training Medium

VR applications are increasingly being used as a part of the teaching and learning process, as this can contribute to the trainees' professional future by developing learning activities beyond what is available through conventional training systems (Zudilova-Seinstra *et al.*, 2009). With respect to educational issues in the AEC industry, Sampaio *et al.* (2010) asserted that interaction with 3D geometric models could lead to active learner thoughts (which seldom appear in conventional pedagogical conditions). Moreover, Juárez-Ramírez *et al.* (2009) noted that when learning is augmented to 3D modelling, VR could lead to better communication in the process of AEC training. Moreover, Gomes and Caldeira (2004) identified new opportunities for enabling trainees and trainers to exchange information about specific domains, in order to enhance interaction and learn collaboratively. However, VR training environments are still evolving and presently are not capable of delivering some learning outcomes. This is primarily down to the ways in which technology is aligned to systems, processes, learning outcomes and pedagogical delivery mechanisms. It is therefore argued that educational training tools need to 'engage' learners by putting them in the role of decision makers and 'pushing' them through challenges, hence enabling different ways of learning and thinking through frequent interaction and feedback, and connections to the real-world context (Goulding *et al.*, 2007). In this regard, Wellings and Levine (2010) suggested focussing on problem-based learning processes, where training is matched to real-world problems. They asserted that this was possible using immersive visualisation and simulation environments, which increased the engagement of trainees and trainers. Similarly, Thai *et al.*, (2009) noted that educational digital games offered opportunities for empowering trainees' engagement, to help transform teaching and learning into a new stage. In this respect, ACS (2009) summarised the benefits of interactive game-like immersive training environments as:

1. exploring knowledge by clicking on objects with linked information;
2. strengthening education by providing a repository of aids, tools, etc, associated with 3D objects;
3. offering collaborative workspaces, e.g. 3D informal discussion forums;
4. providing traditional instructor-based education via a distance delivery method; and
5. creating simulated learning by modelling a process or interaction that closely imitates the real world in terms of outcomes.

It is therefore argued that paring instructional content with game features is more likely to engage users in the learning process (to help achieve the desired instructional goals). This follows similar thinking where instructional programmes that incorporate certain features or characteristics from gaming technology are used to trigger a cycle of user judgment or reaction (often based on enjoyment or interest), to maximise persistence or time on task, in order to achieve the desired learning outcomes (Garris *et al.*, 2002).

18.4   Case Study

This section presents the rationale and rubrics for the development of a VR construction site simulator. This simulator was designed to help learners appreciate the subtle nuances and differences facing construction professionals that wished to adopt offsite manufacturing concepts into traditional work practices. The development aim of this simulator was to capture and present 'real life' OSP issues facing construction professionals in an innovative way that proactively stimulated actor engagement, to provide meaningful solutions. In this respect, a real-life construction project was used to govern the authenticity of the learning environment. The simulator was therefore purposefully designed to allow 'things to go wrong', thereby allowing 'learning through experimentation' or 'learning by doing'. The 'scenes' within the simulator take place on a virtual construction site, and the target audience is aligned to construction professionals (e.g. project managers, construction managers, architects, designers, suppliers, etc). Thus, the construction site (within the simulator) was used as a domain through which unforeseen issues and problems (caused through upstream decisions, faulty work, etc) could be enacted, so that real implications could be better appreciated in respect of time, cost, resources, etc. The simulator was developed not purely to solve OSP problems *per se*, but rather to allow things to 'go wrong' in order to demonstrate the implications of decisions taken by learners. In this context, the simulator was designed to:

- *Maximise learner autonomy*: allowing learners to make all decisions (independently);
- *Stimulate engagement*: where interactivity is promoted, supported by feedback on decisions taken, and their implications, e.g. cost, time, resources, health and safety, etc;
- *Engender personal reflection*: where users can defend their decisions, especially on means for mitigating future problems in areas, such as:

1. OSP strategies, e.g. Design for Manufacture Logistics and Assembly (DFMLA);
2. new business processes, procurement/contractual arrangements, project management, quality assurance, etc;
3. impact on Health and Safety procedures;
4. supply chain integration;
5. new manufacturing technologies, etc.

The simulator was created using scenarios with predefined learning objectives. In this respect, learning was driven by problems, encountered in the VR environment, and aligned to the following design contextual constraints:

- All scenarios/scenes had to occur within the virtual construction site simulator;
- Learners would adopt the sole role of a construction manager;
- Training would engage instructional signposting techniques (e.g. interactive messaging, multi-decision criteria, time-dependent options, etc); and
- Learning outcomes would be aligned to OSP working practices only.

18.4.1   Simulator Development Framework

The simulator development framework encompasses four main activities, specifically: Training Objectives; Development Scenario; VR Environment; and Validation (Figure 18.1). This framework required extensive input from domain experts selected from the construction industry in order to help secure relevance and govern authenticity of these stages.

The training objectives underpinning the simulator were gathered from a synthesis of seminal literature covering the potential risks and threats facing OSP in general, and Open Building Manufacturing in particular. This knowledge was seen as fundamental, as learners would need to understand how different stakeholders deal with the implications of problems; and consequently, help them to appreciate how these could be mitigated for future practice. In this context, the following seven core risks were identified:

1. late design changes;
2. loss of factory production, or production capacity;
3. unpredictable planning decisions and designs that are not suited to offsite manufacturing;
4. issues associated with tolerances;
5. suppliers' failure to deliver on time;
6. manufacturer bankruptcy; and
7. issues associated with alternative manufacturer selection.

The scenarios were developed to expose learners to new working conditions and issues that they were likely to face on real construction projects employing OSP concepts. It was therefore deemed important to challenge learners to think about the underlying causes of these problems, rather than just reacting to the problems themselves. This philosophy was used to 'provoke' learners to think proactively about future OSP projects. In this context, the main scenario was based on identifying possible problems and issues that could be faced – colloquially referred to as problem 1, problem 2, etc (Figure 18.2). For each of these problems, there were a

Figure 18.1   VR environment development framework.

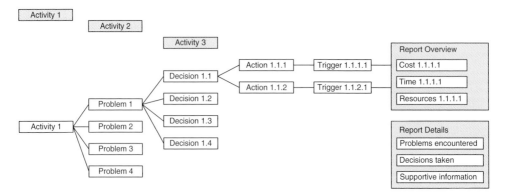

Figure 18.2 Scenario implementation concept.

number of possible decisions with associated actions. Depending on the action chosen, the programme schedule, along with corresponding costs, time and resources are affected.

These scenarios were used to simulate how OSP operates in real life; which allowed learners to think 'how' and 'why' things go wrong, and consequently why OSP may end up being more expensive than traditional ways of working and thinking. The rationale here was to stimulate learners to think about the holistic process and implications regarding the decisions they take (rather than just the immediacy of the options available). In this respect, a debriefing session was identified as a conduit for questioning learners further on the decisions they took in the learning environment. This approach was seen as a way to help distinguish between 'being immersed' within the environment and the process of critical reflection that often takes place outside the VR environment (De Freitas and Oliver, 2006).

To run a scenario, various information and data has to be input into the system in order to help populate the scenario. This data includes:

a) construction site type, location, constraints and layout;
b) project type and primary use of the building (e.g. commercial or residential), budget allocated, type of structure, special layout and planning, etc;
c) manufacturer type, in terms of scope, capacity, location, costs associated and maintenance;
d) equipment hire, in terms of size, capacity, assembly rate, required labour, hire rate, etc; and
e) work plan and associated possible interruptions/problems, including manufacturing options.

This information was 'mirrored' from the case study project and mapped into a relational database within the simulator. A schematic representation of this workflow approach can be seen in Figure 18.3.

The first stage of the prototype development established the requirements and priorities in an ontological structure. The generic structure and content for the knowledge objects were then assigned wrappers using metadata.

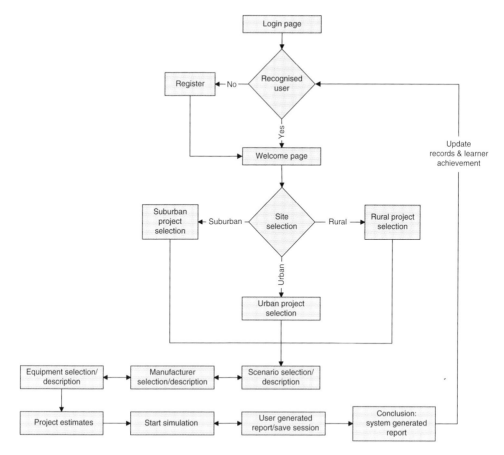

Figure 18.3   Simulator workflow.

The next stage established object classes and their hierarchy to satisfy multiple abstractions, and compliance with extranet metadata. The final stage developed the user interface to comply with Human-Computer Interaction protocols and accessibility guidelines, etc, in order to provide the system with a robust and reliable structure. The developed system included simulated scheduling of the project; association of the 3D models and building blocks with project life cycle; supply chain analysis monitoring for each building block or activity; management of delays in material delivery and a final breakdown for project costs and labour.

18.4.2   System Architecture

Existing VR interfaces have ostensibly been formed based on one single idea-creating 3D models and incorporating them with some pieces of information so that both 3D models and information are editable through an interactive real-time interface (Pour Rahimian and Goulding, 2010).

Consequently, data creation and retrieval methods in VR interfaces can be investigated from two different perspectives, namely, creating 3D bodies of constructional elements, and then defining the characteristics of these elements. However, whilst creating 3D objects directly in VR environments is not impossible, these are normally created in CAD applications; since doing so in VR is often cumbersome and time-consuming. In terms of transforming design elements from CAD into VR, there are three *de facto* approaches used by different practitioners. Whyte *et al.* (2000) noted three approaches for this translation as being:

1. *Straightforward translation approach*: importing the whole environment from CAD to VR;
2. *Library-based approach*: putting the elements of construction in the library of the VR environment, then 'calling' them as necessary; and
3. *Database-oriented approach*: using a central database for controlling the module characteristics.

In this study, the database-oriented approach was selected, as this enables learners to gain access to the system from multiple remote locations.

From an environment development perspective, there are three major kinds of programming applications currently used:

1. 3D Application Programming Interfaces (APIs);
2. Virtual Reality Modelling Language (VRML) and 3D web technologies; and
3. Commercialised object oriented VR programming packages.

From the above, 3D Application Programming Interfaces (e.g. Open GL and Direct 3D) are the principal environments for VR programming in C++ and Visual Basic. Falling into the category of computer graphics, they are capable of either creating the models directly inside the space, and/or importing them directly from CAD applications. Anecdotally, VRML and 3D web technologies in their first iteration were made as a division of Open Inventor; thereafter have become the international standard for 3D web modelling. These applications provide a variety of facilities for manipulating immersive library-based web interfaces, but lack the capability of integrating with interrelated databases, as these are ostensibly not database-oriented applications. On this theme, recent commercial object oriented VR programming packages contain built-in modelling environments for creating VR spaces directly, or importing them from CAD applications. Such VR programming applications also contain logical libraries for defining behavioural links amongst the objects and simulating physical phenomena. Although the architecture of such applications is made based on APIs of C++, in some aspects they can offer a higher-level abstraction for programmers. Nowadays, there are three frontier commercial VR programming applications, namely: Quest3D™, EON Reality™ and Virtools™. These applications are directly deployable into Visual C++ and Visual Basic web programming platforms (EON Reality Inc, 2008). This

Figure 18.4 Simulator architecture.

makes them extremely flexible in terms of integrating VR programming with web programming and data mining. They also come with full Software Development Kits (SDKs) in order to help programmers add building blocks and prototypes to create rules and behaviours that were not originally provided by the host application.

This study implemented a database-driven approach, using structured modelling phases and API-based programming for the development stages. This was adopted primarily because 3D objects can be linked to datasets through the web environment along with schedules of activities (4D visualisation) – the product of which can be used to visualise changes in real time, which can be used to enhance learning outcomes. In this respect, all elements and components of the construction site were modelled in either AutoCAD™ or 3D Studio Max™, two of most the popular modelling software applications used today, and the scenarios were scheduled in MS Project™. All VR programming tasks were performed in Quest3D™ environment, whilst the Active Server Pages (ASP.Net™) web development tool using C#™ programming language was employed for developing the user interface. Finally, a MySQL™ database that was compatible with both programming environments was installed on a server in order to track, manage and transmit user data. The adapted Unified Software Development Process (Jacobson et al., 1999) was used to iteratively test, diagnose and troubleshoot the prototype regarding functionality, compliance, grouping, integration, maintenance, version control and validation. The simulator architecture arrangements can be seen in Figure 18.4.

18.4.3   3D Modelling in AutoCAD and 3D Studio Max

AutoCAD and 3D Studio Max were employed as the main geometrical modelling platforms. Different construction site elements including both permanent (e.g. structural/architectural element and building blocks) and temporary (e.g. scaffolds and site barriers) constructional objects were created in these environments. Models for construction machinery and equipment (e.g. tower cranes and trucks) were downloaded from CAD forums and websites. In order to optimise system performance, the project created the models at a primitive level (e.g. beams, columns, walls, building blocks) and left the final assembly for Quest 3D as the 4D simulation tool to regenerate and replicate single models, as geometrical arrays do not place as much demand on physical storage space or require as much graphical memory. For the same reason, the project used bitmap graphics to give the illusion of secondary details, rather than creating them in 3D models. The bitmaps also helped the simulation look more realistic by visualising texture of different materials (e.g. concrete, wood, etc). Ultimately, the models were converted into the 3DS file format, in order to be readable by Quest3D.

18.4.4   Project Scheduling Environment

MS Project™ was used for scheduling project activities based on the developed scenarios. For each scenario, the temporal relationships amongst different assembly tasks were planned from the commencement of the project to the day of completion. This approach also included the inclusion of random occurrences relating to 'unexpected' problems and interruptions during the project life cycle for learners to solve (to minimise repetition). These schedules formed the essential basis for data regarding sequence amongst different assembly activities, duration of different constructional tasks and their commencement time and finishing time. Finally, the schedules were converted to MySQL databases, which are accessible for both C# and Quest3D programming tools. Figure 18.5 shows a sample project array within Quest3D that is imported from MySQL, which identifies the details of assembly of various building blocks in terms of the 3D position of the building block, sequence of assembly, exact delivery time, and the machinery involved in transportation and assembly of it. Since this data is stored in

Figure 18.5   Sample project array within Quest3D, imported from MySQL database.

a relational database, the pieces of information regarding costs and labour for both building blocks and equipment were also automatically associated to the tasks. This made it possible for learners to modify or update scheduling data through the ASP.Net interfaces.

18.4.5   Data Warehouse Environment

MySQL™ was selected as the platform to host the databases of this simulator, as it is the only application that provides Quest3D with a SDK. This is also accessible the in MS Visual Studio environment through Devart DotConnect™ and ADO.Net™. A relational database comprising of 44 different tables was created in MySQL to manage information regarding manufacturers, equipment, labour and costs associated with different tasks, schedules for different scenarios, etc. This enhanced flexibility provides learners with full control of project data, both through web forms, and through the project simulation environment.

18.4.6   Main Human Computer Interaction Interface

The simulator provides ASP.Net web forms as the initial Graphical User Interface to transfer messages from users to the system, in order to gather data regarding specifications of the desired construction process. Using these web forms, learners are able to control the type and sequence of construction tasks and make appropriate decisions; for example, on the type and level of machinery involved in the project. The system also provides learners with estimates of project costs and time, then proceeds to the simulation of the project. The simulation is generated in the ASP.Net environment as an embedded object by 'calling' an external object exported by Quest3D. Based on the collective decisions made by the learner, the system calculates the total costs of the project and provides comparison between the results obtained, compared with optimal solutions. The system then generates a detailed report on the performance of learners. Figure 18.6 presents a sample screenshot of this report, together with the supportive C# code derived from the project database.

18.4.7   Programming Environment

The geometrical 3D models of the constructional elements were imported by Quest3D™ in order to provide the basic entities and building blocks of VR programming. Quest3D is an Object Oriented programming platform in which the programming logic is formed through interconnection of Logical Building Blocks. The structure of the program is comprised of four main components, specifically:

1. static 3D models of construction site, including tower cranes, trucks, land, surroundings and supporting elements (which do not change from one learner to another, e.g. scaffolding);

Figure 18.6   Design interface (Left) and C# code-behind (right).

2. building blocks as the dynamic 3D models of project;
3. project schedules for controlling all events of assembly and delivery process; and
4. monitoring tools for controlling project time and resources.

Static elements were directly generated using 3DS and bitmap files, which appear at particular locations. However, tower cranes and trucks were programmed to perform the desired animations at certain points of time. The modules of all static objects were directly connected to the project interface, except additional tower cranes and trucks that may (or may not) have been hired by the learners. In these two cases, the modules were connected to the interface through an IF Toggle Channel, in order to 'call' the entities based on the preferences of the learner. In terms of assembling dynamic objects, the system relies on project schedule imported from MySQL database (Figure 18.5), for the assembly sequence and project time. Based on the given sequence, the system checks for assembly permission for each module, and if the project time coincides with the time allocated to any module, the program runs the related animations in order to deliver and assemble that module. However, at certain intervals, some random interruptions are programmed to occur in the project sequence, so the implementation process can only continue after the learner has responded to the prompt, and sent the right email to the appropriate recipient. In this case, a Trigger Channel reinitiates the performance of system, subject to the delivery of these emails to the database. Delays in making the right decisions therefore result in an increased project cost and completion time. Finally, with respect to project scheduling and monitoring tools, the system relies on system arrays formed and updated based on MySQL databases and particular algorithms, which control project time and retrieve and visualise project cost in real time. In essence, the simulator interface provides learners with a 4D simulated environment and an IPod-type interface for showing project statistics in real time (Figure 18.7).

Figure 18.7   Project interface in channel and design view.

18.4.8   Case Study Discussion

This construction site simulator was designed as an interactive learning environment for learners to appreciate the subtle differences required with offsite production, as opposed to the more traditional approach to construction. It was developed as a web-based simulation tool using both non-immersive and immersive pages, in order to allow learners to experience new OSP challenges based on real-life AEC projects using simulated scenarios. The Graphical User Interface was designed to be as simple and straightforward as possible with respect to data input, and was developed to be accessible through any standard web browser (to provide users with login account details and other criteria, e.g. selection of available construction sites, projects, contractors, equipment, scenarios, etc). All choices made by the learners, as well as their registration data, are automatically recorded in a MySQL database, which is also accessible through the immersive application for project simulation. After completing the initial decision-making process through the interactive ASP.Net Web Forms, learners are able to commence the training session, starting with a 'walkthrough' to experience and appreciate the complexity of the project. At this stage, the application provides users with a summary of the project and contract, and runs the simulation of the project within an immersive and interactive environment developed in Quest3D™ VR programming Application Programming Interface.

Within the simulated Quest3D environment, learners are able to experience the outcomes of all decisions made. They are also challenged by unexpected random events, designed specifically to invite them to make decisions for dealing with these issues. The simulation runs in a fully immersive 3D environment, where learners are able to navigate the whole interior and exterior spaces of the project site. At various points in the scenario, they are also able to interact with the different elements of the simulator in order to retrieve further information, for example, technical specifications, videos on selected OSP construction systems/details, project data, etc. In order to keep them on track, the simulator also provides them with monitoring tools, which reveals issues such as the project time, latest assembled module, accumulative costs of the project, team communication, etc. The monitoring and communication tools are embedded in different parts of the main interface as well as the facilitated standard embedded virtual IPod-type interface, which appears when required. The simulator ultimately records and tracks learners in the database and navigates to the conclusion page to reveal project outcomes.

On commencement of the simulator, learners are required to read the instructions and enter their login information (or create a new user account). This feature keeps a record of accomplishment to date, and allows learners to save or review their previous activities in order learn from previous decisions. After the logon process, learners are required to select the location of the project, for example, rural, suburban or urban. The location of a project has implications on access, equipment, storage, etc – thereby affecting the triggered scenarios. Afterwards, learners are then requested to select the type of system/structure to explore, from a repository of stored systems as different systems have different requirements – some suitable for some locations and not for others. Based on the selected site, learners are then requested to select the type of scenario for the current 'Game'. In the next step, they are provided with brief descriptions of each scenario, details of the selected site, details of the selected OSP system and associated contract. In terms of learning outcomes, different scenarios have different learning outcomes based on the events embedded in them; this allows learners to experience different types of constructional project issues within each scenario. When the scenario has been selected, users are required to select the manufacturer as the provider of building blocks and select the site set-up arrangements with respect to the equipment required. There are various issues associated with manufacturer selection, from product differences, through to the costs of materials, completion and delivery dates, labour costs, fluctuating assembly costs, transportation costs, etc. Logistics solutions are also affected by the type of equipment and site set-up chosen, in addition to equipment requirements and constraints. At the next stage, learners are provided with a summary of all decisions made at this stage, and some figures about the anticipated project costs, duration, etc are presented for review. Learners can then compare the effects of all selected type of project site, OSP type, manufacturer and equipment selection, and scenarios with those from previous attempts. After these initial selections, users are then able to run the VR simulation to experience how the project progresses based on their selections. Different scenarios are then triggered at various times in order to exert 'pressure' on learners, particularly to make them think about options and consequences of their choices, as these will affect the overall project cost, time, resources, etc. A sample screenshot of the simulator in progress can be seen in Figure 18.8. A formal report is then generated at the end of the simulation exercise. This report is used in conjunction with a debriefing session with a nominated instructor to discuss these findings and the thought processes behind them.

Day: 10
Time: 17 : 50 : 0
Module: H01_801_H_2B

Camera 1
Camera 2
Camera 3
Camera 4
Camera 5

Figure 18.8   Simulator screenshot.

18.5   Conclusion

This chapter reviewed the seminal literature on learning and the development of VR tools used in the AEC sector. It also presented a series of challenges facing construction personnel regarding the need for up-skilling in light of changes in the operating environment. New approaches for learning using game-like immersive educational interfaces were then discussed in order to highlight the potential benefits these can offer, especially being able to help learners experience real-world problems in a risk free virtual environment. The implementation of such approaches are now able to leverage significant benefits (ACS, 2009; Thai *et al.*, 2009; Wellings and Levine, 2010), not least improve users' engagement in the process. Whilst several systems are now being promoted in the marketplace (Autodesk, 2011; Bentley, 2011; Cisco, 2011), the use and propensity of these have not yet reached maturity. However, further development (with an AEC focus) could lead to the emergence of truly immersive environments. Moreover, the concatenation of a Game-like VR interface could offer the AEC sector further enhanced opportunities. An example was then presented to explain the theoretical and technical challenges involved. This case study identified the formal development rubrics adopted for a VR Construction Site Simulator. It also showed how learning can take place in a risk free environment, where learners (AEC professionals) are able to evaluate their decisions, and see how these affect project and business outcomes.

Construction projects are increasingly becoming more complex, often engaging new business processes and technological solutions in line with the clients' requirements. This is likely to continue. Moreover, it is advocated that the AEC sector in particular is likely to require a myriad of increasingly new skilled professionals, operatives, and interdisciplinary teams in order to meet these new challenges. It is therefore important that the industry as a whole engages the right type (and level) of skill sets and competence to meet these project requirements and business imperatives. Acknowledging this, the causal drivers and influences associated with successful decision-making in non-collocated design teams need to be fully understood, as this is an important stepping-stone for developing new insight and understanding into collaborative environments, particularly though new social interactions (and decision-making criteria) generated through Game Theory techniques. It is also important to be able to 'measure' and gauge actor involvement and positioning (cognisant of learner domain expertise), so that project teams can anticipate any issues that are likely to cause problems beforehand. Advanced VR training and simulation tools are likely to be pivotal drivers in this respect, as they are increasingly well poised to deliver focused learning outcomes. Future research in this area is also likely to acknowledge the importance of learner styles, thereby delivering bespoke training material to individual learner types.

18.6   Acknowledgements

Part of the work presented in this chapter was funded by the EU IP Framework 6 Programme: ManuBuild – 'Open Building Manufacturing. Special thanks are extended to Vinci (David Leonard and Jeff Stephens); Corus (David Shaw and Samir Boudjabeur); the Technical Research Centre of Finland (Kalle Kähkönen); Technische Universität München (Ron Unser), CIRIA (Mark Sharp), the University of Salford, UK (Mustafa Alshawi, Jack S. Goulding, Wafaa Nadim and Panos Petridis) and all ManuBuild partners for their feedback and support throughout.

References

ACS (2009) *3D Learning and Virtual Worlds*: An ACS: Expertise in Action™ White Paper. Available from http://www.trainingindustry.com/media/2043910/acs%20 3d%20worlds%20and%20virtual%20learning_whitepaper%20april%202009. pdf (accessed August 2011).

Alshawi, M., Goulding, J.S. & Faraj, I. (2006) Knowledge-based learning environments: a conceptual model. *International Journal of Education in the Built Environment*, 1(1), 51–72.

Alshawi, M., Goulding, J.S. & Nadim, W. (2007) Training and education for open building manufacturing: Closing the skills gap. In: ed. Kazi, A.S., Hannus, M., Boudjabeur, S. & Malone, A., *Open Building Manufacturing: Core Concepts and Industrial Requirements*. Helsinki. ManuBuild in collaboration with VTT – Technical Research Centre of Finland.

Alshawi, M, Ingirige., B, (2003) Web-enabled Project Management: An Emerging Paradigm in Construction, Automation in Construction, Vol. 12, Iss 5, pp. 349–364.

Argyris, C. & Schon, D.A. (1978) *Organizational Learning: A Theory of Action Perspective*. Addison-Wesley, MA.

Autodesk (2011) Available from http://usa.autodesk.com/ (accessed December 2011).

Bentley (2011) Available from http://www.bentley.com/en-GB (accessed December 2011).

Bloom, B.S. (Ed.), Engelhart, M.D., Furst, E.J., Hill, W.H., & Krathwohl, D.R. (1956). Taxonomy of Educational Objectives: The Classification of Educational Goals. Handbook 1: Cognitive Domain, Longman, New York.

Bouchlaghem, D., Shang, H., Whyte, J. & Ganah, A. (2005) Visualisation in architecture, engineering and construction (AEC). *Automation in Construction*, **14**(3), 287–295.

Bouzeghoub, A., Defude, B., Duitama, J.F. & Lecocq, C. (2006) A knowledge-based approach to describe and adapt learning objects. *International Journal on E-Learning*, **5**, 95–98.

Briggs, J.C. (1996, 09-01-1996) The promise of virtual reality. *The Futurist Magazine*, **30–31**.

Business Watch (2005) *ICT and Electronic Business in the construction Industry, IT adoption and e-business activity in 2005. The European e-Business Market Watch*. European Commission, Enterprise and Industry Directorate General.

Cassidy, S. (2004) Learning styles: An overview of theories, models, and measures. *Journal of Educational Psychology*, **24**(4), 419–444.

Cera, C.D., Reagali, W.C., Braude, I., Shapirstein, Y. & Foster, C. (2002) *A Collaborative 3D Environment for Authoring Design Semantics*. Graphics in Advanced Computer-Aided Design, 43–55.

Cisco (2011) Available from http://www.cisco.com/en/US/netsol/ns1007/products.html (accessed December 2011).

Clark, R.C. & Meyer, R.E. (2011) *E-Learning and the Science of Instruction: Proven Guidelines for Consumers and Designers of Multimedia Learning*, 3rd edn. John Wiley and Sons, Ltd, Chichester, UK.

Clarke, L. & Wall, C. (1998) UK construction skills in the context of European developments. *Construction Management and Economics* **16**(5), 553–567.

Coffield, F., Moseley, D., Hall, E. & Ecclestone, K. (2004) *Learning Styles And Pedagogy In Post-16 Learning: A Systematic And Critical Review*. Learning and Skills Research Centre, Cromwell Press Ltd, Trowbridge, UK.

Conole, G., Dyke, M., Oliver, M. & Seale, J. (2004) Mapping pedagogy and tools for effective learning design. *Journal of Computers and Education*, **43**(1–2), 17–33.

Davenport, J. (1993) Is there any way out of the andragogy morass? In: ed. Thorpe, M., Edwards, R. & Hanson, A., *Culture and Processes of Adult Learning*. Routledge, London.

Davis, R. & Wong, D. (2007) Conceptualizing and measuring the optimal experience of the elearning environment, decision sciences. *Journal of Innovative Education*, **5**(1), 97–126.

De Bello, T.C. (1990) comparison of eleven major learning styles models: variables, appropriate populations, validity of instrumentation, and the research behind them. *Journal of Reading, Writing, and Learning Disabilities International*, **6**(3), 203–222.

De Freitas, S. & Oliver, M. (2006) how can exploratory learning with games and simulations within the curriculum be most effectively evaluated? *Computers and Education*, **46**(3), 249–264.

Dimitrova, V. (2003) STyLE-OLM: Interactive open learner modelling. *International Journal of Artificial Intelligence in Education*, **13**, 35–78.

Edvinsson, L. & Malone, M.S. (1997) *Intellectual Capital: Realising Your Company's True Value by Finding Its Hidden Roots*. Harper Business, New York.

Egan, J. (1998) *The Egan Report – Rethinking Construction*. Report of the Construction Industry Taskforce to the Deputy Prime Minister. HMSO, London.

Egenfeldt-Nielsen, S. (2007) Third generation educational use of computer games. *Journal of Educational Multimedia and Hypermedia*, **16**(3), 263–281.

EON Reality Inc (2008) *Introduction to Working in EON Studio*. Available from http://www.eonreality.com (accessed August 2011).

Fischer, M. (2000) *4D CAD-3D models incorporated with time schedule*. CIFE Centre for Integrated Facility Engineering in Finland, VTT-TEKES, CIFE Technical Report, Stanford University, USA

Fischer, M. & Kunz, J. (2004) *The Scope and Role of Information Technology in Construction*. Technical Report, No. 156 February 2004), San Francisco. Center for Integrated Facility Engineering, Stanford University, USA.

Forcade, N., Casals, M., Roca, X. & Gangolells, M. (2007) Adoption of web databases for document management in SMEs of the construction sector in Spain. *Automation in Construction*, **16**, 411–424.

Friedman, T.L. (2005) *The World is Flat: A Brief History of the 21st Century*. Farrar, Straus and Giroux, New York.

Fruchter, R. (1998) Internet-based web mediated collaborative design and learning environment. In: *Artificial Intelligence in Structural Engineering Lecture Notes in Artificial Intelligence*. Springer-Verlag, Berlin. 133–145.

Fruchter, R. (2004). Degrees of Engagement in Interactive Workspaces. International Journal of AI & Society, 19(1), 8–21.

Gagne, R.M., (1965), The Conditions of Learning, Holt, Rinehart and Winston, New York, USA.

Garris, R., Ahlers, R. & Driskell, J.E. (2002) Games, motivation, and learning: A research and practice model. *Simulation Gaming*, **33**(4), 441–467.

Gomes, C. & Caldeira, H. (2004) *Virtual Learning Communities in Teacher Training, International Conference on Education, Innovation, Technology and Research in Education*. IADAT, International Association for the Development of Advances in Technology. Paper presented at the Bilbao, Spain.

Goulding, J., Sexton, M., Zhang, X., Kagioglou, M., Aouad, G.F. & Barrett, P. (2007) Technology adoption: Beaking down barriers using a virtual reality design support tool for hybrid concrete. *Construction Management and Economics*, **25**(12), 1239–1250.

Goulding, J., Nadim, W., Petridis, P., Alshawi, M., (2012) Construction Industry Offsite Production: A Virtual Reality Interactive Training Environment Prototype, *Advanced Engineering Informatics*, **26**(1), 103–116.

Govindasamy, T. (2002) Successful Implementation of e-Learning Pedagogical Considerations. *Internet and Higher Education*, **4**, 287–299.

Gross, B. (2007) Digital games in education: the design of games-based learning environments. *Journal of Research on Technology in Education*, **40**(1), 23–38.

Huber, G.P. (1991) Organizational learning: The contributing processes and the literatures. *Journal of Organization Science*, **2**(1), 88–115.

Ibrahim, R. & Pour Rahimian, F. (2010) Comparison of CAD and manual sketching tools for teaching architectural design. *Automation in Construction*, **19**(8), 978–987.

Jacobson, I., Booch, G. & Rumbaugh, J. (1999) *The Unified Software Development Process*, Object Technology Series. Addison-Wesley Professional, MA.

Jarvis, P., Holford, J. & Griffin, C. (2003) *The Theory and Practice of Learning*. Kogan Page Ltd, London.

Juárez-Ramírez, R., Sandoval, G.L., Cabrera Gonzállez, C. & Inzunza-Soberanes, S. (2009) *Educational Strategy Based on IT and the Collaboration Between Academy and Industry for Software Engineering Education and Training.* Paper presented at the m-ICTE 2009, V International Conference on Multimedia and ICT's in Education.

Karagiannidis, C. & Sampson, D. (2004) Adaptation rules relating learning style research and learning objects meta-data. In: ed. Magoulas, G.D. & Chen, S.Y., *Proceedings of International Conference on Adaptive Hypermedia and Adaptive Web-based Systems*, 23–26 August, The Netherlands.

Khanzade, A., Fisher, M. & Reed, D. (2007) *Challenges and Benefits of Implementing Virtual Design and Construction Technologies for Coordination of Mechanical, Electrical, and Plumbing Systems on Large Healthcare Project.* Paper presented at the CIB 24th W78 Conference.

Kim, B. & Chris, S. (2001) Accommodating diverse learning style in the design and delivery of on-line learning experiences. *International Journal of Engineering Education*, **17**, 93–98.

Knowles, M. (1980) *The Modern Practice of Adult Education: From Pedagogy to Androgogy*, 2nd edn. Cambridge Books, New York.

Kolb, D.A. (1984) *Experiential Learning: Experience as the Source of Learning and Development.* Prentice-Hall Inc, NJ.

Laird, D. (2003) *New Perspectives in Organisational Learning, Performance, and Change: Approaches to Training and Development*, 3rd edn. Preseus Books Group, USA.

Lam, P.T.I., Wong, F.W.H. & Tse, K.T.C. (2010) Effectiveness of ICT for construction information exchange among multidisciplinary project teams. *Journal of Computing in Civil Engineering*, **24**(4), 365–376.

Latham, M. (1994) *Constructing the Team, Joint Review of the Procurement and Contractual Arrangements in the UK Construction Industry, Final Report.* HSMO, London.

Leinonen, J., Kähkönen, K., Retik, A R., Flood, R.A., William, I. & O'Brien, J. (2003) New construction management practice based on the virtual reality technology. In ed. Balkema, A.A., *4D CAD And Visualization In Construction: Developments and Applications.* 75–100).

Lou, E.C.W. & Goulding, J.S. (2010) The pervasiveness of e-readiness in the global built environment arena. *Journal of Systems and Information Technology*, **12**(3), 180–195.

Mole, T. (2003) Mind your manners. In: ed. Newton, R., Bowden, A. & Betts, M., *Proceedings of CIB W89 International Conference on Building and Research Bear 2003.* School of Construction and Property Management, University of Salford, Salford, UK.

Nisan, N., Roughgarden, T., Tardos, É. & Vazirani, V.V. (2007) *Algorithmic Game Theory.* Cambridge University Press, Cambridge.

Nonaka, I. & Takeuchi, H. (1995) *The Knowledge Creating Company – How Japanese Companies Create the Dynamics of Innovation.* Oxford University Press, Oxford.

Pahl, C. (2003) Managing evolution and change in web-based teaching and learning environments. *Computer and Educations*, **40**(2), 99–114.

Pashler, H., McDaniel, M., Rohrer, D. & Bjork, R. (2008) Learning styles: concepts and evidence. *Psychological Science in the Public Interest*, **9**(3), 105–119.

Petric, J., Maver, T., Conti, G. & Ucelli, G. (2002) *Virtual Reality in the Service of User Participation in Architecture.* CIB W78 Conference, Aarhus School of Architecture.

Piaget, J, (1952), The Origins of Intelligence in Children, International University Press, New York, USA

Pour Rahimian, F., Ibrahim, R. & Baharudin, M.N. (2008) Using IT/ICT as a new medium toward implementation of interactive architectural communication cultures. *Proceedings of the International Symposium on Information Technology 2008*, ITSim.

Pour Rahimian, F. & Goulding, J.S (2010) game-like virtual reality interfaces in construction management simulation: A new paradigm of opportunities. *9th International Detail Design in Architecture Conference 2010*. The Central University of Lancashire, Preston, UK.

Pour Rahimian, F. & Ibrahim, R. (2011) Impacts of VR 3D sketching on novice designers' spatial cognition in collaborative conceptual architectural design. *Design Studies*, **32**(3), 255–291.

Regenbrecht, H. & Donath, D. (1996) Architectural education and virtual reality aided design (VRAD). InL ed. Bertol. D., *Designing Digital Space – An Architect's Guide to Virtual Reality*. John Wiley and Sons, Inc, New York. 155–176.

Sampaio, A.Z. & Henriques, P.G. (2008) Visual simulation of previous term civil engineering next term activities: Didactic virtual previous term models. *WSCG 2008, 16th International Conference in Central Europe on Computer Graphics, Visualization and Computer Vision*. Plzen, Czech Republic.

Sampaio, A.Z., Ferreira, M.M., Rosário, D.P. & Martins, O.P. (2010) 3D and VR models in civil engineering education: Construction, rehabilitation and maintenance. *Automation in Construction*, **19**(7), 819–828.

Sampson, D., Karagiannidis, C. & Kinshuk. (2002) personalised learning: educational, technological and standardisation perspective. *Interactive Educational Multimedia*, **4**, 24–39.

Senge, P.M. (1990) *The Fifth Discipline: The Art and Practice of the Learning Organization*. Currency Doubleday, New York.

Stonebraker, P.W. & Hazeltine, J.E. (2004) Virtual learning effectiveness: An examination of the process. *The Learning Organization Journal*, **11**(3), 209–225.

Sullivan, P. (1999) Profiting from intellectual capital. *Journal of Knowledge Management*, **3**(2), 132–143.

Syed-Khuzzan, S.M., Goulding, J.S. & Underwood, J. (2008) Personalised learning environments, Part 1: Core development issues for construction. *Industrial and Commercial Training*, **40**(6), 310–319.

Thai, A.M., Lowenstein, D., Ching, D. & Rejeski, D. (2009) *Game Changer: Investing in Digital Play to Advance Children's Learning and Health*: The Joan Ganz Cooney Center. Available from http://www.healthgamesresearch.org/our-publications/research-briefs/Game-Changer (accessed 22 July 2011).

Turocy, T.L., Stengel, B.V. & Hossein, B., (2003) *Game Theory Encyclopedia of Information Systems*. Elsevier, New York. 403–420.

Vincent, A. & Ross, D. (2001) Personalise training: Determine learning style, personality types and multiple intelligence. *The Learning Organisation*, **8**, 36–43.

Wang, F. & Hannafin, M.J. (2005) Design-based research and technology-enhanced learning environments. *Journal of Educational Technology Research and Development*, **53**(4), 5–23.

Ward, J. & Daniel, E. (2005) *Benefits Management: Delivering Value from IS & IT Investments*. John Wiley and Sons, Inc, New York.

Watson, J. & Hardaker, G. (2005) Steps towards personalised Learner Management System (LMS): SCORM implementation. *Campus-Wide Information Systems*, **22**, 56–70.

Weber, G. & Brusilovsky, P. (2001) ELM-ART: An adaptive versatile system for web-based instruction. *International Journal of Artificial Intelligence in Education*, **12**, 351–384.

Wellings, J. & Levine, M.H. (2010) *The Digital Promise: Transforming Learning with Innovative Uses of Technology*: A white paper on literacy and learning in a new media age, Joan Ganz Cooney Center at Sesame Workshop Available from http://www.digitalpromise.org/Files/Apple.pdf (accessed 22 July 2011).

Wen, M.L., Tsai, C., Lin, H. & Chuang, S. (2004) Cognitive-metacognitive and content-technical aspects of constructivist internet-based learning environments: A LISREL analysis. *Journal of Computers and Education*, **43**(**3**), 237–248.

Whyte, J., Bouchlaghem, N. & Thorpe, A. (1998) *The Promise and Problems of Implementing Virtual Reality In Construction Practice. Paper presented at The Life-cycle of Construction IT Innovations.* Technology Transfer from Research to Practice (CIB W78), Stockholm.

Whyte, J., Bouchlaghem, N., Thorpe, A. & McCaffer, R. (2000) From CAD to Virtual reality: Modelling approaches, data exchange and interactive 3d building design tools. *Automation in Construction*, **10**(**1**), 43–55.

Xie, H, Shi, W. & Issa R.R.A. (2011) *Using Rfid and Real-Time Virtual Reality Simulation For Optimization in Steel Construction*. ITcon vol. 16, 291–308. Available from http://www.itcon.org

Yoh, M. (2001) *The Reality of Virtual Reality*. Paper presented at the Seventh International Conference on Virtual Systems and Multimedia (VSMM'01), Organized by Center for Design Visualization, University of California Berkley, Berkley, CA.

Zheng, X., Sun, G., & Wang, S. W. (2006). An Approach of Virtual Prototyping Modeling in Collaborative Product Design. Paper presented at the CSCW 2005, LNCS 3865.

Zudilova-Seinstra, E., Adriaansen, T. & van Liere, R. (2009) *Trends in Interactive Visualization: State-of-the-Art Survey*. Springer-Verlag, London.

Index

Construction Innovation and Process Improvement, First Edition.
Edited by Akintola Akintoye, Jack S. Goulding and Girma Zawdie.
© 2012 Blackwell Publishing Ltd. Published 2012 by Blackwell Publishing Ltd.